U.S. Navy Codebreakers, Linguists, and Intelligence Officers against Japan, 1910–1941

U.S. Navy Codebreakers, Linguists, and Intelligence Officers against Japan, 1910–1941

A Biographical Dictionary

Captain Steven E. Maffeo,
U.S. Naval Reserve, Retired

ROWMAN & LITTLEFIELD
Lanham • Boulder • New York • London

Published by Rowman & Littlefield
A wholly owned subsidary of The Rowman & Littlefield Publishing Group, Inc.
4501 Forbes Boulevard, Suite 200, Lanham, Maryland 20706
www.rowman.com

Unit A, Whitacre Mews, 26-34 Stannary Street, London SE11 4AB

British Library Cataloguing in Publication Information Available

Library of Congress Cataloging-in-Publication Data

Maffeo, Steven E.
  U.S. Navy codebreakers, linguists, and intelligence officers against Japan, 1910–1941 : a biographical dictionary / Capt. Steven E. Maffeo.
    pages cm
  Includes bibliographical references and index.
  ISBN 978-1-4422-5563-0 (cloth : alk. paper) — ISBN 978-1-4422-5564-7 (e-book).
  1. United States. Office of Naval Intelligence—Biography—Dictionaries.
  2. Cryptographers—United States—Biography—Dictionaries. 3. Linguists—United States—Biography—Dictionaries. 4. Intelligence officers—United States—Biography—Dictionaries. 5. World War, 1939–1945—Cryptography—Biography—Dictionaries.
  6. World War, 1939–1945—Campaigns—Japan. I. Title.
  D810.S7M2535 2016
  359.3'432092273—dc23

                                                                                    2015030516

∞™ The paper used in this publication meets the minimum requirements of American National Standard for Information Sciences—Permanence of Paper for Printed Library Materials, ANSI/NISO Z39.48-1992.

Printed in the United States of America

To my father,
Technical Sergeant Eugene P. Maffeo
32nd Infantry Regiment
7th Infantry Division
Army of the United States
Asia-Pacific Theater, 1944–1945

"A man is not dead while his name is still spoken."

—Sir Terence Pratchett, OBE

In 1923, upon his return from an intense language and cultural immersion program, future Rear Admiral Ellis Zacharias was eager to pursue an active intelligence career. Instead he found that

> nobody in the Navy Department showed other than slightly amused interest in my experiences and ideas. There was no one to take up seriously the question of my assignment to a post which would best utilize and justify the *three years in Japan*. There was little more than passing interest in the reports of my observations, and by calling attention to certain undeniable facts which I felt at least demanded consideration, I risked being called a daydreamer who sees ghosts.

In the 1920s and 1930s, both the U.S. Navy's cryptologic and intelligence organizations suffered greatly from a lack of funding, resources, and personnel. Part of this problem was, of course, due to the Great Depression, but there were other issues. Looking back from 1983, retired master cryptanalyst Captain "Tommy" Dyer said that

> in the first place very few people knew anything about it. And some who *knew* took a rather dim view of the activity. While we had some supporters here and there throughout the Navy, for the most part the people who might have been able to make personnel available thought we were a bunch of *blue-sky merchants*, indulging in a pipe dream.

Reflecting on the years before the war, from the vantage point of the 1960s, retired radioman and cryptanalyst Captain Prescott Currier remarked that the navy

> had only one intelligence target from 1921 on . . . that was Japan. Now, war plans were written to cover other nations, but the intelligence collection effort and all of the communications-intelligence collection effort was single target—just Japan and nothing else. It was just as well, because we only had 3½ cryptanalysts for most of that period, so that it [would have been] a problem to have done much of anything else!

Contents

The Blue Sky Merchants

Linguists, Translators, and Intelligence Officers

The "Hybrids"

Multiskilled and Multiproficient

Appendixes

Acronyms and Abbreviations

AFSA	Armed Forces Security Agency
ATIS	Allied Translator and Interpretation Section
CBR	chemical, biological, and radiological
CICFOR	Combat Intelligence Center, Forward
CINCNELM	Commander in Chief U.S. Naval Forces Eastern Atlantic and Mediterranean
CINCUS	Commander in Chief of the U.S. Fleet
CIO	Combat Intelligence Officer
CIU	Combat Intelligence Unit
CM	Cipher Machine
CNO	Chief of Naval Operations
COMINT	communications intelligence
CSS	Code and Signal Section
D/F	direction-finding
DD/CIA	deputy director of the Central Intelligence Agency
DEW	Distant Early Warning
DIO	district intelligence officer
DNI	director of naval intelligence
ECM Mk II	Electric Code Machine Mark II
EDO	Engineering Duty Only
FICPAC	Fleet Intelligence Center Pacific
FIO	fleet intelligence officer
FRUMel	Fleet Radio Unit Melbourne
FRUPac	Fleet Radio Unit Pacific
HF	high-frequency
ICPOA	Intelligence Center, Pacific Ocean Area

IO	intelligence officer
JCS	Joint Chiefs of Staff
JICPAC	Joint Intelligence Center Pacific
JICPOA	Joint Intelligence Center, Pacific Ocean Area
JIOCPAC	Joint Intelligence Operations Center Pacific
JMIC	Joint Military Intelligence College
MSTS	Military Sea Transportation Service
NCB	Navy Code Box (or Naval Cipher Box)
NCIS	Naval Criminal Investigative Service
NRL	Naval Research Laboratory
NSA	National Security Agency
OIC	officer in charge
ONI	Office of Naval Intelligence
OPNAV	Office of the Chief of Naval Operations
OSS	Office of Strategic Services
OWI	Office of War Information
PSIS	Pacific Strategic Intelligence Section
RAGFOR	Radio Analysis Group, Forward
RIU	Radio Intelligence Unit
SACO	Sino-American Cooperative Organization
SIS	Signal Intelligence Service
SupRadPac	Supplementary Radio Unit Pacific
UA	unauthorized absence
USA	U.S. Army
USAF	U.S. Air Force
USMC	U.S. Marine Corps
USN	U.S. Navy
USNA	U.S. Naval Academy
WAVE	Women Accepted for Volunteer Emergency Service

Foreword

Captain Maffeo has written a well-researched history of U.S. Navy cryptologic and intelligence development during the years 1910 through 1941. He explores this time frame with minibiographies of fifty-nine key people who contributed to this invaluable work. This small group struggled with some inept and self-centered senior leadership and small budgets to produce systems that were instrumental in the U.S. victory in World War II in the Pacific and laid the groundwork for the future. These key people could not have imagined what their original work has morphed into today; the Republic owes these pioneers a debt of gratitude.

In 1986 I played a small role in finally recognizing the labors of Captain Joseph Rochefort—who was a major architect in the crucial U.S. victory at the Battle of Midway—when President Reagan awarded him posthumously the Distinguished Service Medal and the Presidential Medal of Freedom.

Maffeo's book is a great contribution to naval history.

John M. Poindexter
Vice Admiral, U.S. Navy, Ret.
National Security Advisor to President Reagan

Author's Foreword

It might strain your credulity if I told you the idea of this book first appeared while watching a couple of Hollywood movies in the 1970s.

On the first day of Christmas vacation in December 1970, when I was sixteen years old, a couple of us went to see *Tora! Tora! Tora!*—a dramatic star-filled Hollywood production made in documentary style. The film depicts the Japanese naval aviation strike upon the U.S. Pacific Fleet at Pearl Harbor, and other targets, on December 7, 1941, as well as recounts the events leading up to that attack. In the early parts of the movie I was intrigued by the portrayal of several American intelligence officers and cryptanalysts who were energetically trying to puzzle through what was going to happen. Of course the screen was also full of cabinet-level secretaries, generals, and admirals trying to do the same, but I was particularly fascinated by two characters: Lt. Col. Rufus "Togo" Bratton, U.S. Army, a Japanese linguist and chief of army intelligence's Far Eastern Section (played by E. G. Marshall), and Lt. Cmdr. Alwin Kramer, U.S. Navy, also a Japanese linguist and head of the navy's Communications Security Group translations branch (played by Wesley Addy). Both characters were allocated considerable screen time as the film showed their seemingly futile efforts to alert higher-ups—on the night of December 6 and the morning of the seventh—that an attack appeared to be imminent. "Who *are* these guys?" I wondered. "How is it that they can speak Japanese and how can they read Japanese diplomatic codes?" What sort of background did they have—and how many years of preparation did it take—to be doing such things in December 1941?

Well, I pursued none of these questions at that time. But then in 1976 another Hollywood feature came out: *Midway*, a star-studded spectacle dominated by Charlton Heston and Henry Fonda. Similar to *Tora! Tora! Tora!*, this dramatic war movie was done in a semi-documentary style, depicting that monumental battle as well as the events leading up to it. Again, the character of an intelligence officer caught my attention: Cmdr. Joseph J. Rochefort, a Japanese linguist, cryptanalyst, and intelligence specialist (played in an overly folksy mode by Hal Holbrook), who was leading a special communications-intelligence group at Pearl Harbor called Station HYPO. In this role Holbrook, as Rochefort, also had considerable screen time. Again I wondered, "Who is *this* guy and the guys in his basement office?" What kind of background and experience did *he* have?

These questions remained in the back of my mind even as I became a naval intelligence officer myself, spending considerable time in support of the U.S. Pacific Fleet and the U.S. Pacific Command. Here and there, now and then, I heard little bits and pieces about the *old* days and the *old* guys, back before World War II—when for over a quarter century they all "knew" that the Japanese Empire would one day be our enemy and worked to prepare for it, and when the multiple facets of "radio intelligence" were our intelligence mainstay.

These same questions developed a little more focus for me about eighteen years ago, when I took a course on the history of intelligence as part of the master's program at the JMIC. Books such as John Prados's monumental *Combined Fleet Decoded: The Secret History of American Intelligence and the Japanese Navy in World War II*, Edwin Layton's *"And I Was There": Pearl Harbor and Midway—Breaking the Secrets*, and Gordon Prange's *Miracle at Midway* really opened my eyes to this subject. Then it all took a sharper edge around nine years ago, when I returned to the JMIC (which soon changed into the National Defense Intelligence College and has since further morphed into the National Intelligence University) to teach the history of intelligence for three years in their part-time program. The course covered a lot of ground, ranging all the way back to ancient times and then up to the first Gulf War, but within all that and with a renewed interest I really started seriously thinking about those nebulous pre–World War II intelligence and communications-intelligence people.

All that past was prologue, I guess. Three years ago I read Elliot Carlson's magnificent biography of Rochefort, *Joe Rochefort's War: The Odyssey of the Codebreaker Who Outwitted Yamamoto at Midway*, and I was delighted with the full story of that iconic, towering figure. It also reinforced to me that there were a goodly number of other people—like him—who likewise needed exposure. It was then that this book really took shape in my mind. I had become convinced that these unique people were singular and important, that there were more than just a handful of them, and that they were true pioneers and trailblazers. They had had the vision and the will to pursue this arcane business from the ground floor. They invented techniques, procedures, and equipment from scratch—and they wrote the rules as they went along. Although they are almost lost to history, we are hugely in their debt. Thus, I concluded that they needed exposure because they have drifted into almost complete obscurity—and they profoundly deserve being rescued from it.

Thus, I offer you fifty-nine profiles—or, if you will, minibiographies—of some of these very important people who essentially founded American naval intelligence and cryptanalysis as we know it today. Not only will you get to know Al Kramer and

Joe Rochefort (alas, not Togo Bratton, for I have focused exclusively upon the navy and the marines) but also a wide and robust group of their fellows.

In fact, as Capt. Duane Whitlock (one of these people himself) wrote many years after the war,

> A vital point, that should not be overlooked by historians and students of the war with Japan, is the fact that something more than 20 years was required to bring on-line the radio intelligence organization that ultimately gave commanders what was perhaps the greatest strategic and tactical advantage in the history of naval warfare.

This is echoed by Capt. Jack Holtwick (another one of these people) when he wrote that

> the foundations built during that [interwar] period were firm enough and well-enough designed that [when the war came] they could support a quantum increase in people, in real estate, in equipment, and in material.
>
> With the running start given to [intelligence] and to communications-intelligence productivity, the United States was able to hold its own in the Pacific despite the loss of most of its Fleet at Pearl Harbor; and to maneuver its remaining ships, aircraft, and submarines to advantage at Coral Sea, Midway, Guadalcanal, [etc.] and across Japanese merchant-shipping routes in the Western Pacific and the China Sea.
>
> To the appreciation expressed by our wartime admirals for the work of the Navy's [intelligence] organization, *during* the days and nights between December 1941 and October 1945, should be added a quiet "Well Done" *to those few who carried the load* from January [1910] *until* December 1941.

Steve Maffeo
Captain, U.S. Naval Reserve, Ret.
U.S. Air Force Academy
Colorado Springs, Colorado
April 2015

Acknowledgments

I could not have completed this project without spectacular assistance from a number of people around the country. So, working in a little fear that I'll overlook someone, and in no particular order, I gratefully thank the following:

At the Armed Forces Communications and Electronics Association, Santa Cruz, California: Mr. Lawrence J. Reeves, President of the Monterey Bay Chapter.

At the Naval Historical Foundation, Washington Navy Yard: Dr. David F. Winkler, Program Director; and Mr. Christopher Eckardt, Research Intern.

At the U.S. Naval Postgraduate School, Monterey, California: Ms. Eleanor S. Uhlinger, University Librarian, and Mr. John Sanders, Special Collections Manager, both at the Dudley Knox Library.

At the U.S. Naval War College, Newport, Rhode Island: Dr. John B. Hattendorf, the Ernest J. King Professor of Maritime History, Chairman, Maritime History Department, and Director, Naval War College Museum; Dr. Evelyn M. Cherpak, recently retired Head of the Naval Historical Collection; Mr. John W. Kennedy, Director of Education, Naval War College Museum; and Professor Robert E. Schnare, recently retired Director of the Henry E. Eccles Library.

At the U.S. Naval Cryptologic Veterans Association, Pensacola, Florida: Mr. Steve W. Roberts, retired master chief cryptologist, USN.

At the U.S. Naval Institute, Annapolis, Maryland: Ms. Janis D. Jorgensen, manager of the oral history program at the Institute's Heritage Group.

At the U.S. National Security Agency, Fort George G. Meade, Maryland: Dr. William J. Williams, Colonel, USAF, Ret., Chief of the Center for Cryptologic History; and Ms. Rene S. Stein, Librarian at the National Cryptographic Museum Library.

At the U.S. Office of Naval Intelligence, Suitland, Maryland: Dr. Randy Carol Goguen, Historian.

From the U.S. National Intelligence University, Washington, D.C.: Dr. John K. Rowland, Colonel, USAF, Ret., Emeritus Program Director and Associate Dean; and Colonel Terrence J. Finnegan, USAF, Ret., formerly a Course Director and a Deputy Director (and no relation to Captain Joseph F. Finnegan), Sacramento, California.

At the U.S. Air Force Academy, Colorado Springs, Colorado: Dr. Edward A. Scott, Director of the McDermott Library; Ms. Kelly A. Merriam, interlibrary loan technician, McDermott Library; Mr. Robert P. Toy, cataloging technician, McDermott Library; Dr. Elizabeth A. Muenger, USAFA Command Historian; Ms. Rhonda E. R. Maffeo, Project Lead, Warfighters Edge, Directorate of Education; and General Stephen R. Lorenz, USAF, Ret., President of the Air Force Academy Endowment.

And, last but not least: Cadet Micah E. Maffeo, AROTC, Fort Collins, Colorado; Vice Adm. John M. Poindexter, USN, Ret., National Security Advisor to President Reagan; Mr. Stephen Coonts, Colorado Springs, Colorado; Dr. Gregory Finnegan (son of Captain Joe Finnegan), Cambridge, Massachusetts; James E. Fahey, USCG, Ret., alas recently deceased, Braintree, Massachusetts; James Schlueter, FRUPac historian, Jefferson City, Missouri; CWO4 Albert J. Pelletier III, USN, Ret. (son of Capt. Albert J. Pelletier Jr.), Moncks Corner, South Carolina; Sally Ringle Hotchkiss, Andrew D. Ringle, and Kenneth A. Ringle (children of Rear Adm. Kenneth D. Ringle), Avery Island, Louisiana; Commander Michael E. Bennett, USCG, Washington, D.C.; Capt. Kenneth E. Green, USN, Ret., Baltimore, Maryland; Capt. Kenneth Newton, USN, Ret., Oshkosh, Wisconsin; Mr. Joel Omilda, Joint Intelligence Operations Center Pacific, Pearl Harbor, Hawaii; and at Rowman & Littlefield Publishers: senior acquisitions editor Marie-Claire Antoine; senior production editor Elaine McGarraugh; and assistant editor Monica Savaglia.

Introduction

No one who has not experienced it can realize how difficult it is to track the shadow of truth through the fog of war.

—Capt. W. J. "Jasper" Holmes, USN

Telling the story of intelligence feels odd because it is a story that desperately did not want to be told. Over the last century, thousands of people have worked to ensure that secret operations and findings would stay secret.

There exist few things as well known and as misunderstood as intelligence.

—Intelligence historian Prof. Michael Warner

One hundred years ago, in what was a relatively unsophisticated pre-computer and pre-electronics era, naval intelligence (and foreign intelligence in general) existed in rudimentary forms almost incomprehensible to us today. Despite the practice of information gathering for diplomacy and warfare being as old as mankind—some wags name it the "second oldest profession"—the pursuit of military and diplomatic intelligence shows, over the centuries, widespread ups and downs in activity based on a myriad of factors.

Founded in 1882, the U.S. Office of Naval Intelligence (ONI)—the world's "oldest continuously operating intelligence agency"—functioned for at least its first forty years with low manning, small budgets, low priority, and no prestige. It would take another twenty-five years and the Second World War before intelligence could even pretend to be a viable naval career field; hitherto, an officer inclined toward this business had to carefully alternate intelligence assignments with those in a "real" specialty—such as surface-ship sea duty, submarines, or aviation.

The navy's early steps into communications intelligence (COMINT), which included activities such as radio interception, radio traffic analysis, and cryptology came even later, essentially with the 1916 establishment of the Code and Signal Section (CSS) within the navy's Division of Communications. And, more practically, it came with the 1924 creation of the "Research Desk" as part of the CSS. Like ONI, this COMINT organization suffered from small budgets, low manning, low priority, and no prestige—as well as the curse of similarly being unsustainable as a career.

Nevertheless, what these organizations did have was a few people of talent, imagination, and drive—who were extraordinarily "forehanded," to use the old naval term. Between the two world wars they identified the Empire of Japan as the United States' largest potential future threat. They decided that a thorough knowledge of the Japanese language and culture was essential—so they created and funded a program which, from 1910 to 1941, ultimately ran fifty-one Navy and Marine Corps students through a three-year, full-immersion course. They realized that the newly developed techniques of radio direction finding and traffic analysis were extremely valuable and, beyond that, actually reading the messages would be even better—so they developed a cryptanalysis course which trained around twenty-five officers between 1924 and 1941. They saw that enlisted radiomen had to understand the specific nuances of Japanese Morse Code and had to be able to efficiently copy Japanese *kana* code, so from 1928 to 1941 they trained 176 navy and marine operators.

The pioneering work that these relatively few people did during this period was incredibly important; thus it's to the memory of those few that this book is dedicated. Unfortunately, those people are almost lost to history; their names are known only to professional historians of intelligence and cryptology—or perhaps to avid naval history buffs. Only a handful of them wrote memoirs or executed oral histories; even fewer have had biographies written about them. In 2013, I took an informal poll of some forty current naval intelligence and cryptology officers; the results showed virtually no recognition of any of these pioneers' names. This is a little surprising because many of these people went on, even after World War II, to important positions in the navy, the State Department, the Armed Forces Security Agency, the National Security Agency, and the Central Intelligence Agency.

* * *

In the preface to his classic book *Eminent Victorians*, British author Lytton Strachey wrote, "It has been my purpose to illustrate rather than explain," and so it is with me in *U.S. Navy Codebreakers, Linguists, and Intelligence Officers against Japan, 1910–1941*. My goal has been to simply acquaint the reader with my lost subjects, paint their portraits, and enable those remarkable people to once again—if only briefly—have some light shine upon them.

This book is not a definitive history of the prewar or wartime U.S. Navy, or naval communications, or naval intelligence. It certainly is not a complete study of radio intelligence, cryptology, or intelligence analysis. Neither is it a comprehensive account of the Office of Naval Intelligence, the Division of Naval Communications, the CSS, or the radio intelligence stations known as CAST, BELCONNEN, and

HYPO. The reader desiring such things can find them elsewhere fairly easily, and I hope my suggested readings list will facilitate just that.

In keeping with the notion of illustration versus explanation, this is a work meant to be popular rather than academic history. I have used original documents where possible. I have used considerable secondary works as well—which are based on primary sources and analyzed by scholars of quality. I have not guessed about what might still remain hidden. While I fully stand behind all of my facts, and while I've sourced the book with a robust bibliography and many chapter notes, I have not observed the rigorous and formal conventions of academic format nor scrupulously tagged every fact to a specific document, witness, or scholar.

* * *

In 1967, eminent cryptology historian David Kahn opened his monumental work, *The Codebreakers: The Story of Secret Writing*, with one of my select "fifty-nine" people: Lt. Cmdr. Alwin D. Kramer. On December 7, 1941, Kramer was a highly trained Japanese linguist working for the U.S. ONI. He was also cross-assigned as the head of the translation branch of OP-20-G—the U.S. Navy's secret communications-intelligence organization within the Division of Naval Communications. Having hand carried a briefcase of hot intercepts around Washington to the nation's leaders late the night before, Kramer set about another run early on Sunday morning. His briefcase now had several new MAGIC intercepts—MAGIC was the code word for intelligence gleaned from the Japanese diplomatic PURPLE machine code, which the United States had broken and could translate and read even *faster* than the Japanese diplomats for whom it was meant. Lieutenant Commander Kramer

> went first to Admiral Stark's office, where a conference was in session, and indicated to Commander McCollum [head of the Far Eastern Section of ONI], who took the key intercept from him . . . Kramer wheeled and hurried down the passageway. He emerged from the Navy Department building and . . . headed for the State Department eight blocks away. The urgency of the situation washed over him again, and he began to move on the double.
>
> This moment, with Kramer [literally] running through the empty streets of Washington bearing his crucial intercept, an hour before sleepy code clerks at the Japanese embassy had even deciphered it and an hour before Japanese planes roared off the carrier flight decks on their treacherous mission, is perhaps the finest hour in the history of cryptology.
>
> Kramer ran while an unconcerned nation slept late, ignored aggression in the hope that it would go away, begged the hollow gods of isolationism for peace, and refused to entertain—except humorously—the possibility that the "little yellow men" of Japan would dare attack the mighty United States.
>
> The American cryptanalytic organization swept through this miasma of apathy to reach a peak of alertness and accomplishment unmatched on that "day of infamy" by any other agency in the United States. That is its great achievement, and its glory.
>
> Kramer's sprint symbolizes it.

The causes of the Pearl Harbor disaster are many and complex, but no one has ever laid any of whatever blame there may be at the doors of the Navy's OP-20-G or the Army's Signals Intelligence Service. On the contrary, the Congressional committee that investigated the attack praised them for fulfilling their duty in a manner that "merits the highest commendation."

As the climax of war rushed near, the two agencies—together the most efficient and successful codebreaking organization that had ever existed—scaled heights of accomplishment greater than any they had ever achieved.

Aside from its focus upon the cryptanalytic organizations to the exclusion of the intelligence bureaus,[1] Kahn's words superbly set the stage for *U.S. Navy Codebreakers, Linguists, and Intelligence Officers against Japan, 1910–1941*. I thank Dr. Kahn as if he had custom written it just for me!

In fact, the inclusion of a few other brief quotations, from some other distinguished officers and historians, will further help set the stage:

The U.S. Navy had for a long time compiled special signal books [for use with signal-flag hoists], and it began inventing codes when telegraphic communications came into widespread use in the mid-nineteenth century. The Navy's first signal code dates from 1863. Between then and 1913 there would be at least eleven code or signal books adopted by the United States. Though *creating* all these codes, during this period the Navy exhibited little interest in delving into *others'* codes.—National security historian Dr. John Prados

The American Army or Navy cryptanalyst was a rare bird, in the service but not fully of it. No one knew exactly where he fitted in the scheme of things, for his was a shadow land south of Intelligence and north of Communications.—Historian Dr. Gordon Prange

Intelligence was not appreciated by the peace-time Army or Navy before Pearl Harbor. It was [too often viewed] as a chore, a tour of unpleasant duty that was either a dead end for one's career—or a punishment.

The Congressional investigation of Pearl Harbor found that the military was fundamentally guilty of not seeking out men for intelligence who possessed "the background, capacity, and penchant for such work." Moreover, the pre-war military was criticized for failing to promote its intelligence specialists.

[Because intelligence was not a viable career field], our intelligence specialists were forced to accept relatively low grades and pay scales, while less qualified officers [temporarily placed in intelligence] were promoted on the basis of having commanded a ship or battalion.

[However,] the man who can create a code-breaking machine . . . or who can decipher the enemy's codes and read the enemy's intentions, is [perhaps] worth far more to his nation than any mere admiral or general.—Pearl Harbor disaster special investigator Henry Clausen

It was a strange group. Impatient, intolerant, vibrant, and gregarious within the confines of their craft, they could also be rude in their relations outside their own circle. They were the "nuts" Joseph Rochefort once said made the best cryptanalysts. Though they were Regular Navy, they regarded themselves as anything but regular. . . . The young officers lacked a sense of reality, but regarded themselves as the most realistic of men. And they had a kind of superman complex that conceded no flaw or inferiority. . . . But whatever idiosyncrasies they had, they were superbly qualified for their assignment. —Intelligence officer and historian Ladislas Farago

Some of these people suffered from *cryptographitis*, which according to the great French code expert Colonel Étienne Bazèries, is "a sort of subtle, all-pervading, incurable malady." Moreover, Bazèries also wrote that *cryptographitis* also gives its victims delusions of grandeur; it subjects them to hallucinations; it wrecks them, makes them sad nuisances to their families and friends, and often nuisances to their governments.—Ladislas Farago

The five-year period before the war . . . was entirely a one-target period. As a matter of fact, the U.S. Navy had only one intelligence target from 1921 on. . . . That was Japan. Now, war plans were written to cover other nations, but the intelligence collection effort and all of the COMINT collection effort was single target—just Japan and nothing else. It was just as well because we only had 3½ cryptanalysts for most of that period, so that it was a problem to have done much of anything else![2]—Capt. Prescott Currier, USN

The volume, timeliness, and precision of information gained from radio intercepts, at all hours and in all weather, could not be matched by any other intelligence source.—Intelligence historian Prof. Michael Warner

The fate of the nation quite literally depended upon about a dozen men [at Pearl Harbor] who had devoted their lives and their careers, in peace and war, to radio intelligence.
    [In fact,] during this critical period of time [December 1941–June 1942] a team of eight experienced and dedicated communications intelligence veterans held in their hands the destiny of the war in the Pacific.[3]—Capt. "Jasper" Holmes, USN

The American victory over potentially overwhelming odds in the Battle of Midway (3–6 June 1942) was made possible mainly through cryptanalysis of radio transmissions the Japanese sent in their naval operational code. Information from this source reached Adm. Chester W. Nimitz, Commander in Chief, Pacific Fleet, via the Pearl Harbor radio intelligence unit. The unit was headed by Lt. Cmdr. Joseph J. Rochefort, who generally made contact with CinCPac headquarters by scrambler telephone to Lt. Cmdr. Edwin T. Layton, Nimitz's intelligence officer.
    For [his] plan to succeed, Nimitz had to know when and where to find Admiral Nagumo. He assigned the problem to Layton, who reviewed the intelligence findings of the previous three weeks, brooded over charts, and studied Pacific Ocean winds, weather, and currents. He repeatedly telephoned Rochefort to compare notes. At last he felt safe in reporting his estimates to Nimitz.
    Layton predicted that the enemy carriers would attack Midway on the morning of 4 June. "They'll come in from the northwest on bearing 325 degrees," he said, "and they'll be sighted at about 175 miles from Midway, and the time will be about 0600 Midway time." [Later, when the actual sighting did come, Nimitz famously] remarked to Layton, "Well, you were only five miles, five degrees, and five minutes off."—Professor E. B. Potter

Codebreaking did not assure the American victory at Midway but it made the victory possible. Midway was the greatest single success produced by intelligence in the war with Japan.—Dr. Ronald H. Spector

It is apparent that until the Japanese attack of December 7, 1941, most of the cryptanalytic work of the Navy fell upon the shoulders of a very few Regular Navy officers and men, and a handful of civilians at the Navy Department. Only about 400 persons were actively engaged in COMINT work at the time of the attack, and at least 200 of these were newcomers who had joined the group in the preceding 18 months.

Thus, the accomplishments of World War II in the COMINT field were built on the foundation laid between 1924 and 1941 by a score of officers and about one-hundred enlisted men.—Capt. Jack Holtwick, USN

[After the Battle of Midway, I] recommended that any awards that were to be made should go to the veterans who had long years in radio intelligence. I listed them by name, [particularly] remarking that Cmdr. Thomas Dyer's work and service had been outstanding. Not only had the old-timers, as individuals, contributed most by reason of their skill and experience, but *without the groundwork they had laid* [before the war] *we would have gotten nowhere.*—Capt. "Jasper" Holmes, USN

* * *

For all of my fifty-nine subjects I've tried to give the reader a reasonably complete sketch of their lives—prewar, wartime, and postwar. The sketch might be lengthy, approaching as many as forty or fifty pages, or it might be fairly brief—perhaps only five or six. In all but one case I've been able to do that fairly seamlessly. However, in so doing, I may have clouded my original intent—which was to paint pictures of intelligence and communications-intelligence people who were active *prior to* December 7, 1941, and who had thus laid the groundwork that was critically in place during the war. I know very well that there were many other individuals who put forth amazing intelligence contributions and did extraordinary work during and after the war, but from the outset my focus has been restricted to those who were *in place and engaged* prior to 1942. A stand-out example of the kind of person whom I've *not* included is the remarkable Rear Adm. Donald "Mac" Showers (1919–2012). He indeed served brilliantly in Joe Rochefort's Station HYPO and no one is more cognizant of his subsequent achievements than I am; but, he did not begin his naval intelligence career until several months after the attack on Pearl Harbor.

Lastly, some housekeeping notes. Although I cover many arcane terms in my chapter notes and in the glossary, there are a few terms and concepts which need explication right up front:

Boldface In any given chapter, the first time an individual is mentioned who is also part of this study—that is, has his or her own chapter elsewhere in the book—that person's surname is put in **bold**.

CINCUS Commander in Chief, *U.S. Fleet*. The second highest position—and largest command—in the pre–World War II U.S. Navy—second only to the Chief of Naval Operations. In 1922 the navy combined the Pacific Fleet and the Atlantic Fleet to form the United States Fleet. The main body of the ships, the *Battle Fleet*, was stationed in the Pacific Ocean and the *Scouting Fleet* was stationed in the Atlantic. During 1930 the Battle Fleet and Scouting Fleet were renamed the *Battle Force* and the *Scouting Force*. The title of CINCUS was officially replaced by *COMINCH* in December 1941 (as Commander in Chief, U.S. Navy).

Cipher A method of concealing plaintext by transposing its letters or numbers, or by substituting other letters or numbers according to a "key." Transforming plaintext into cipher is called "encryption." Breaking cipher back to plaintext is called "decryption."

Code A method in which arbitrary, and often fixed, groups of letters, numbers, phrases, or other symbols replace plaintext letters, words, numbers, or phrases for the purpose of concealment or brevity.

Communications Intelligence (COMINT) Measures taken to intercept, analyze, and report intelligence derived from all forms of communications. Similar to "radio intelligence."

Cryptology The study of both the making and breaking of codes and ciphers.

Main Navy The old, enormous, Navy Department Building in Washington, on Constitution Avenue, which sat for decades on the National Mall—about where the Vietnam Veterans Memorial sits today. It was the U.S. Navy's headquarters from 1918 until many offices were later moved to the Pentagon, and until it was finally torn down in 1970.

ONI The Office of Naval Intelligence. Founded in 1882, it is the oldest continuously operating intelligence agency in the world. Before and during the war it was located at Main Navy in Washington.

OP-20-G Within Naval Communications, the office symbol of the navy's Code and Signal Section, which became the Communications Security Group, which became the Radio Intelligence Section, and then which became the Communications Intelligence Organization. It was housed at Main Navy for many years, but in early 1943 it moved to the site of the former Mount Vernon Seminary on Nebraska Avenue. "Office of the Chief of Naval Operations (*OP*NAV); *20*th Division of the Office of Naval Communications, *G* Section."

Radio Intelligence A term commonly used during the two decades before the Pearl Harbor attack, usually referring to intelligence gathered from radio transmissions—but short of actual decoding or decryption of messages. Often synonymous with "communications intelligence."

Rank Abbreviations I have used abbreviations for rank or grade that are more in conformance with those used in the 1920s and 1930s than those used today, for example, Capt. or Cmdr. rather than CAPT or CDR. At times I've also titled junior officers as "Mr." rather than by their actual grade. Not very common today, this convention was widely used for centuries in the British and American navies. For example, Mr. Rochefort versus Lieutenant Rochefort.

Research Desk OP-20-GX. The specific division of Naval Communications focused upon cryptology, established in 1924 with Lt. Laurance Safford as head.

Station HYPO/FRUPac Early on there was no actual, official name for the U.S. Navy's Hawaiian COMINT group. The name HYPO (the standard name in those days for the "H" flag in the International Signal Code) was used in the beginning—"H" standing for He'eia where there was an intercept facility—and was often loosely used for the whole activity. Thus, "H" originally only applied to the actual Hawaiian radio intercept station. Later, when radio intelligence was placed directly under the operational Pacific Fleet (versus the administrative 14th Naval District), HYPO was renamed Fleet Radio Unit Pacific—FRUPac. The term FRUPac is anachronistic if used to refer to the unit prior to September 1943, but many historians do this for convenience. I have used HYPO and FRUPac somewhat interchangeably—probably HYPO being the more frequent. I have rarely employed the term Combat Intelligence Unit (or CIU), which for a time was also used.

The [ship's name] Unlike today's common usage, the bulk of the literature supports a preceding article used more often than not in the early twentieth century, so I have proceeded accordingly. For example, "he transferred to the *Arizona*" versus "he transferred to *Arizona*."

Tombstone Promotion Quite a few of the officers in this book received a promotion to the next grade at the time of retirement. An act of Congress in 1925 allowed officers in the navy, marine corps, and coast guard to be promoted one grade upon retirement if they had been specially commended for performance of duty in actual combat. Combat citation promotions were colloquially known as "tombstone promotions" because they conferred all the perks and prestige of the higher rank including the loftier title on their tombstones—but no additional retirement pay. An act of Congress in 1942 enabled tombstone promotions to three- and four-star grades. Tombstone promotions were subsequently restricted to citations issued before January 1, 1947, and finally eliminated altogether effective November 1, 1959. The practice was terminated in an effort to encourage senior officer retirements prior to the effective date of the change to relieve an overstrength in the senior ranks.

Traffic Analysis The analytic method or methods whereby intelligence is derived from the study of communications activity and the elements of messages—short of actual cryptanalysis.

*   *   *

It's my belief, or at least it's my hope, that while each profile or chapter might be read as a stand-alone account of its subject's engagement with prewar intelligence or cryptology, reading the volume as a whole will convey much more than just the sum of its parts.

In his autobiography, pioneering naval intelligence officer (and himself one of my fifty-nine profiled subjects in this book) Rear Adm. Ellis M. Zacharias virtually read my mind when he wrote:

> I hope that these lines will be recognized as my own modest tribute to these forgotten men and women of secret intelligence, if only by calling the nation's attention to their anonymous accomplishments.

Like Admiral Zach, I too hope I've accomplished just that in the pages of *this* book.

Sources

Carlson, in Hone, 269.
Clausen, 297.
Currier, NSA presentation.
Dyer, 207–8, 316.
Farago, *Broken Seal*, 44, 77–78.
Holmes, 54–55, 109, 167.
Holtwick, 372, 464.
Hone, 267–68.
Kahn, *Codebreakers*, 4–5.
Layton, *"And I Was There,"* 500.
Lundstrom, John B., in Hone, 234–35.
Potter, in Hone, 219–20, 224, 226–27.
Prados, 17, 73.
Prange, *Miracle*, 17.
Spector, *Eagle*, 450.
Warner, 3–7, 54.
Zacharias, Ellis, 84–90, 253.

Notes

1. Having written that, it must be noted that both Kramer and McCollum were technically Office of Naval Intelligence people rather than attached to the Division of Naval Communications. This is a complexity that will be examined in the following pages.
2. Capt. Jasper Holmes wrote that "in 1925, Rochefort, Safford, and Driscoll were the whole of the Navy's code-breaking crew."
3. Holmes's "eight" are Joe Rochefort, Tom Dyer, "Ham" Wright, Jack Holtwick, Tom Huckins, Jack Williams, Joe Finnegan, and "Red" Lasswell.

Illustrations

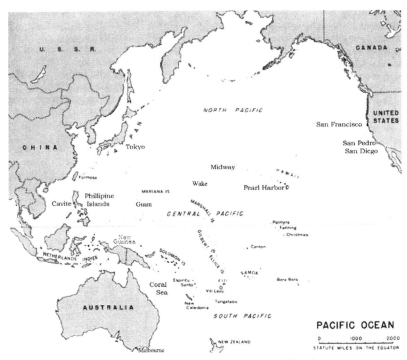

Chart: R. Johnstone, *U.S. Army in World War II* (with modifications).

"Main Navy" (the Navy Department Building) circa 1940. Constitution Avenue, Washington, D.C., located astride the Mall. Headquarters of the Navy for many decades, a great deal of what happened in this book took place within its walls. The building is no longer there; it was at the site of the current Vietnam Memorial. Naval Historical Foundation.

Building 251, what would become FRUPac, nearing completion in February 1943. It's still there on the rim of the Makalapa Crater, recently renovated and restored. NSA Library, Chiles/Weber Collection.

The Katakana Chart: A. - KANA C. PHONETIC
B. - MORSE D. STRUCTURE

COLUMN / LINE	A	I	U	E	O
SINGLE VOWEL	ア A (Ñ)	イ I (A)	ウ U	エ E (Y)	オ O (Ŝ)
K	カ KA (L)	キ KI (T)	ク KU (V)	ケ KE (V)	コ KO (—)
S	サ SA (C)	シ SHI (V)	ス SU (∞)	セ SE (>)	ソ SO (&)
T	タ TA (N)	チ CHI (F)	ツ TSU (P)	テ TE (A)	ト TO (E)
N	ナ NA (R)	ニ NI (C)	ヌ NU (H)	ネ NE (G)	ノ NO (J)
H	ハ HA (B)	ヒ HI (Z)	フ HU (=)	ヘ HE (E)	ホ HO (D)
M	マ MA (X)	ミ MI (U)	ム MU (T)	メ ME (=)	モ MO (/)
Y	ヤ YA (W)		ユ YU (R)		ヨ YO (M)
R	ラ RA (S)	リ RI (P)	ル RU (J)	レ RE (O)	ロ RO (Ā)
W	ワ WA (K)		ン N (+)		ヲ WO (J)

Part of the Katakana Morse code used by the Japanese military. Source: Sharon A. Maneki, *The Quiet Heroes of the Southwest Pacific Theater.*

The Scanners

Radio Direction Finders and Radio Traffic Analysts

CAPTAIN THOMAS AVERILL HUCKINS, U.S. NAVY (1901–1982)

Along with John Williams, solved both the strategic
and tactical Japanese naval communications structures
"One of the best traffic analysts in the Navy"
One of Rochefort's core team at Station HYPO
"Tom" "Huck"

Thomas Huckins was a "tall, fair-haired, well-built man who spoke with a careful drawl." After the usual surface-ship duty regimen he moved into communications and cryptanalysis. Sent to Station HYPO eighteen months before the war's start, Huckins joined in a partnership with John Williams and they subsequently formed an incomparable team of "scanners"—that is to say radio-traffic analysts. Serving at

HYPO and its successor organizations for the war's duration, Huckins's contributions to communications intelligence were extraordinary.

* * *

From the 1924 Annapolis yearbook, *The Lucky Bag*:

> *Huck* gave the Academy a rather boisterous welcome when he entered and, as a consequence, checked up twenty demerits for too much noise in ranks. He began running hurdles early Plebe Summer and, incidentally, still holds one record for the maximum number of hurdles knocked over in one race. He has been hurdling ever since and will have met them all before he gets through if he gets the chance. One of the high spots in *Huck*'s past centered around a little trip to Philly. He went to see "Sally" [*a musical comedy produced by Florenz Ziegfeld*] but, since he still has the ticket, we should say that he hadn't seen so much of the show. Every man has a Waterloo, but Huck prefers Guggenheimers [*unknown*] any day. He has always been connected with catboats, and one short Easter leave, he had a little extension of leave—whether the extension was granted or not remaining on the knees of the Duty Officers and the gods. However, his fitness for the service cannot be rated by his sailing adventures. Typical quote: "Got a match? My pipe's out." [Activities: track, track team captain; pentathlon winner; class football]

* * *

Thomas A. Huckins was born in Superior, Wisconsin, on September 12, 1901, but at some early point his family moved to the St. Louis area. As a result, when he was appointed to the Naval Academy in 1920, he claimed Kirkwood, Missouri as home.[1] He was subsequently graduated and commissioned in 1924, along with such distinguished classmates as Thomas H. **Dyer**, Edwin T. **Layton**, Ethelbert **Watts**, Daniel J. McCallum, John C. Waldron, and Hanson W. Baldwin. Later promotions were to lieutenant (junior grade), 1927; lieutenant, 1933; lieutenant commander, 1939; commander, 1942; and captain, 1943. Captain Huckins retired from the navy in 1954.

After his Annapolis graduation, Ensign Huckins began the normal surface-ship duty typical for junior officers of his generation. From 1924 through 1925 he was stationed on board the battleship *Texas*, and then he transferred to the destroyer *John D. Edwards*, serving on her from 1926 through early 1928.

Then, in March 1928, Lt. j.g. Huckins began the four-month cryptanalysis course at OP-20-G, along with Lt. Delwyn Hyatt, Ens. James Greenwald, and Ens. John Littig. For a brief period in 1929 he underwent some instruction at Naval Air Station Lakehurst, but was then transferred to the U.S. Fleet in the Pacific.

In 1930, in Fleet Problem XI, Lt. j.g. Tommy Dyer, Lt. j.g. Huckins, and Ens. William Leahy were assigned to a pioneering communications-intelligence section in

---

1. He was actually christened *Eugene* Averill Huckins, but for some reason legally changed his name to Thomas prior to going to Annapolis.

the Scouting Fleet, in which they had great success in obtaining solutions of all the ciphers which they attempted.

In November 1930, Lt. Cmdr. John **McClaran**, then head of OP-20-G, wrote that there were—realistically—only six officers in the entire navy who were trained and available for cryptanalytical work (less a few others who had other major qualifications such as aviator, submariner, or Japanese linguist): Lt. Cmdr. Laurance **Safford**, Ens. Bill Leahy, Lt. j.g. Tom Dyer, Lt. Bern **Anderson**, Lt. Joseph **Wenger**, and Lt. j.g. Tom Huckins. At that time McClaran was extremely concerned about his inability to fund or to acquire qualified and motivated students for the program.

In a similar analysis a year later, Huck was considered one of seven naval officers classed as competent cryptanalysts—the others being Tommy Dyer, Bern Anderson, Joe Wenger, Laurance Safford, and Joe **Rochefort**. Safford and Rochefort were the only ones qualified to instruct in the subject. It's interesting to note that Rochefort was often overlooked when analyzing the Naval Communications manning structure because he had left Naval Communications—and moved over to ONI—when he'd taken ONI's three-year Japanese language immersion training.

Mr. Huckins was ordered to OP-20-G for additional instruction in the summer of 1932, and then he relieved Lieutenant Dyer as head of OP-20-GX in 1933.

These were hard times for the country, the navy—and for esoteric naval offices which had shoestring budgets even in good times. At one point, due to the financial pinch of the Great Depression, Huckins informed his new boss (Cmdr. Howard **Kingman**) that he was going to have to return to the IBM Company his automated punch, sorter, and tabulator—for he didn't even have the $4,800 annual rental fee for these crucial pieces of machinery.

In mid-1934, Lieutenant Huckins and coworker Lt. Sid **Goodwin** transferred from OP-20-G; Goodwin went to the Sixteenth Naval District and Huckins to the Asiatic Fleet flagship—both arriving in August 1934.

There, Huckins replaced Lt. Joe Wenger as head of radio intelligence operations in the Asiatic area. On his way to the Philippines, Huck met Wenger in Los Angeles as Wenger had to return early due to ill health. Huckins drove Wenger to the naval hospital in San Diego to continue his medical treatments—which had started at the naval hospital at Canacao (close to Cavite). Wenger later remarked, "As it was a longish drive in those days, we had a good opportunity to discuss Asiatic problems and to pass on to him at least the highlights of my experience there." Obviously there was neither formal turnover nor opportunity to hand off notes and files.

Huck reported on board the Asiatic Fleet flagship *Augusta* in late summer 1934, and then was relieved by Sid Goodwin in November 1935. There were a lot of frustrations for communications-intelligence officers on the Asiatic Station in the years around when Huckins was there. As Lt. Ray **Lamb** wrote in 1936,

Asiatic C.I. service is handicapped by lack of understanding, interest, and appreciation of the purposes and possibilities on the part of seniors. . . . Under the past set-up on the Flag, with the various collateral duties [assigned], it has been impossible [to do C.I.] and has been the big kick of Huckins and Goodwin. They have had no time for *our activity* because of the collaterals. There are plenty of officers out here hanging [out in] bars who can take care of our own [general U.S. Navy] communications. I do not feel that [we] were detailed out here in order to take over odd jobs on the Flag.

In 1936, Huck was assigned to the staff of Destroyer Squadron Five, and then from 1937 through 1938 he became the assistant district communications officer in San Diego.

Lieutenant Huckins failed for selection to lieutenant commander in 1938, as did Lieutenants Tommy Dyer and Edward Crowe. In an earlier year Robert Densford was also passed over. Fortunately, all of these officers were later selected and promoted. The worry about promotion for officers specializing in communications intelligence was very well founded for a good number of years. In fact, a 1936 CNO letter to the Bureau of Navigation (which in those days managed naval personnel) stated that:

> insofar as officers are concerned, before full benefit can be expected from those having qualification and talent for language and cryptanalytic work, it would appear necessary to ensure that the promotion of such officers will be *assisted*—rather than *deterred*—thereby.

Cmdr. Laurance Safford, once again head of OP-20-G, was always concerned about this issue—for himself as well as his protégés. In a September 1938 letter he commented that "we have Dyer and Huckins to look out for. Rear Adm. Stanford C. Hooper [formerly director of naval communications] is going to do all he can for them, [as will] Rear Adm. Ralston S. Holmes [director of naval intelligence]." Dyer and Huckins were both selected as "fitted and retained" in February 1939. After passage of new promotion legislation that same year, they were subsequently promoted with others of their same dates of rank. This carried through for later promotions to commander and then to captain. To further help this issue, by keeping such officers from having to compete with all other line officers, a few—starting with Tommy Dyer in 1939—were designated as Engineering Duty Officers and later as Special Duty Officers (Communications) when that category was subsequently created in 1948.

In 1939, Lieutenant Commander Huckins was transferred to the battleship *Utah* as communications officer but then, in May 1940, Commander Safford recommended that Huck be ordered to communications-intelligence duty in the Fourteenth Naval District at Pearl Harbor.

> Huckins is a "fitted" officer designated for retention. He has had a total of five years communications-intelligence duty (2½ years in the Navy Department and 2½ years on the Asiatic Station), plus five or six more years of other communications duty. He is now serving on the *Utah* as communications officer. Huckins is a classmate of Dyer (1924), now on duty in the Hawaiian C.I. unit, but junior to him. He is not as good a cryptanalyst as Dyer or **Holtwick**, but is somewhat better than Lamb. He is better

qualified by training and experience to handle the direction finders and the intercept station than Lamb, Dyer, or Holtwick. Huckins has served only one year on his present cruise, but it is my understanding that "fitted" officers can be assigned wherever they will be of greatest value to the naval service. Lt. Cmdr. Huckins could remain in this billet for "Duration of War."

Accordingly, Mr. Huckins arrived at Station HYPO in July 1940, reporting in to the OIC, Lt. Cmdr. Tommy **Birtley**. Huck immediately relieved the overtasked Lt. Jack Holtwick of several duties. In an October 1940 letter, Huckins remarked that he "was spending about four to five hours per week on the planning of work in connection with the new Oahu combined traffic and R.I. station near Wahiawa," which he estimated would be ready for occupancy in July 1941. A year later, he wrote that it is "planned to move the intercept activities from He'eia into the new building on 15 November, and close the D.F. activity at Lualualei shortly thereafter." But in reality, as such things go, the move didn't occur until after the Pearl Harbor attack.[2]

As of June 1941, Huckins headed "GX" at HYPO—the Radio Section. With him were newly arrived Lt. Johnny **Williams**, reserve Lt. Cmdr. H. C. Moore, and two enlisted traffic analysts, Chief Radiomen George Hopkins and Richard Willis. Yeoman First Class C. W. Sawyer handled administrative office work.

When Lt. Jasper **Holmes** came to HYPO in mid-1941, he observed that HYPO traffic and intelligence summaries were produced by Tom Huckins, "a tall, fair-haired, well-built man who spoke with a careful drawl, and John Williams—a short, tense, very nervous lieutenant." Huckins had been in the same training company at Annapolis as had Holmes, but Huckins was two years junior. Holmes immediately noted that Huckins and Williams were interminably shuffling large volumes of messages.

> Each evening, their distilled observations of the day's traffic were typed out as a summary which had to be delivered to Lt. Cmdr. Edwin T. **Layton**, the fleet intelligence officer, before eight o'clock in the morning. Because I delivered a chart overlay of ships' positions every morning to Layton at CinCPac headquarters, I frequently acted as officer messenger for other secret material also. I soon learned of the importance Layton placed on the traffic intelligence summary for his intelligence briefings to the Commander in Chief, Pacific Fleet, Adm. Husband E. Kimmel, each morning at eight-thirty.

The importance of traffic analysis can't be overstated. "In the early stages of the Pacific War, before the cryptanalysts cracked Japan's main naval codes, traffic analysis was about all Joseph Rochefort [who had become HYPO's OIC in summer 1941] and his fellow analysts had to go on."

This point is further developed by Frederick D. Parker, author of *Pearl Harbor Revisited: U.S. Navy Communications Intelligence 1924–1941.*

> Collectively they revealed a wealth of information concerning Japanese naval activities. . . . In many respects [HYPO's] achievements in 1941 were similar to what had been

---

2. In late December 1941, both the DF station at Lualualei and the radio intercept station at He'eia were relocated and consolidated at Wahiawa, in the center of Oahu.

accomplished at Station CAST with traffic analysis against the Japanese Imperial Fleet maneuvers in the 1930s.

[HYPO's] daily summaries clearly showed that Lt. [Cmdr.] Thomas A. Huckins and Lt. John A. Williams, who headed the traffic analysis unit, had solved both the strategic and tactical Japanese naval communications structures. They understood the callsign generation system and were able to quickly reestablish order of battle data after routine callsign changes. This insight permitted unit identifications to the squadron level in ground-based air and destroyer units. It also allowed identifications to the individual ship level in battleships, cruisers, and carriers.

The capability to exploit these features of Japanese navy communications lasted until about three weeks prior to the attack on Pearl Harbor when callup and addressing procedures changed abruptly. Throughout the period they were also able to use their direction-finding capability to produce unique information as well as to support evidence from traffic analysis.

The traffic analysis unit was able to identify the Japanese Navy Combined Fleet Headquarters to principal line and staff subordinates within each of the fleets in both home and deployed locations.

Commander Rochefort was delighted with the quality of his cryptanalysis and linguistic staff, and "we had very excellent officers, too, for radio intelligence . . . that would be Tom Huckins and Jack Williams; these people were *very* difficult to beat for what we called radio intelligence."

In early November 1941, Huckins and Williams (aided by Capt. Red **Lasswell** and the other linguists) made a huge breakthrough as they studied an intercepted Japanese dispatch and interpreted the addressee as a relatively new organization: *Itikoukuu Kantai*—First Air Fleet. This operational unit consisted of all of Japan's fleet carriers (and support vessels) with a total of over 450 aircraft. This was a naval battle group with the single most powerful concentration of naval aviation in the world. It was the most critical component of what the Japanese called the *kido butai*, or *striking force*.

In the weeks prior to the attack on Pearl Harbor, Station HYPO was fed by the radio intercept station at Heʻeia and the direction-finding station at Lualualei. As the physical packages of messages came in, they first were handed to the traffic analysts, Lieutenant Commander Huckins and Lieutenant Williams, before being passed to the cryptanalysts—Lieutenant Commanders Tommy Dyer, Ham **Wright**, and Jack Holtwick.

In late November and early December 1941, Lieutenant Commander Huckins and Lieutenant Williams concurred that the absence of message traffic vis-à-vis the Japanese Navy's aircraft carriers was due to an abrupt change of Japanese fleet call signs, and it would take a little time to reestablish them. But within a few days they no longer agreed on what was going on. Huckins thought—as did most of the others in HYPO including the boss, Commander Rochefort—that no aircraft carrier radio traffic meant that the ships were idle in home ports. Williams, however, became certain that the carriers were on the move, and were maintaining strict radio silence as they moved.

After the attack on Pearl Harbor,

work at the codebreaking facility down at the Navy Yard proved arduous, and not only for cryptanalysts like Commanders Dyer or Wright, who would work for stretches of thirty hours at a time. Ens. Elmer Dickey was at Wahiawa until the fall of 1942, sent there by Jack Holtwick—then running the IBM machine room at HYPO. Dickey, a former enlisted radio operator at Bainbridge Island, Shanghai, Cavite, and He'eia, was quite happy in direction-finding work until traffic-analysis boss Thomas Huckins discovered him at Wahiawa and wanted him down at the Yard. Huckins called Dickey up one day and asked how he liked Wahiawa and what strings he had pulled to get there. Dickey replied that he liked it fine and had no desire to leave, to which Huckins countered that that was too bad since he would be cutting new orders for the ensign right after the weekend. Dickey spent the rest of the war working on the radio traffic analysis summaries that were compiled every night to be read by Admiral Nimitz the next morning. It was like the city desk of a large newspaper, Dickey recalled: "death was the only excuse" for not getting out the product, a five-to-seven page summary. Preparation began at about 2:00 A.M. and the thing had to be ready to leave in a sealed envelope by 7:30. Nimitz read the reports himself; they then formed the basis for Commander Layton's fleet intelligence summaries.

In charge of managing Imperial Japanese Navy direction-finding and message-traffic interception, Huck faced considerable challenges. As Jasper Holmes put it,

Only a fraction of the vast volume of Japanese radio traffic could be intercepted. Traffic analysts scanned the volume of traffic across the radio spectrum, and Huckins usually assigned the Japanese circuits to be guarded by the intercept station. More messages were intercepted than the cryptanalysts could profitably work on. Selection of those that were to receive primary attention was more of an art than a science. The identities of the originator and the addressees, the block of additives used in the encipherment, the priority given to the message, its length, the time of transmission, and [even the intuitive hunches of language officer Lt. Joe **Finnegan**] were all important elements to be considered.

Contrary to the standard procedure that had been developed regarding U.S. carrier operations, HYPO was not given advance warning about Vice Adm. Halsey's *Enterprise/Hornet* task force that launched Lt. Col. Jimmy Doolittle's sixteen B-25 bombers at Tokyo on April 18, 1942. This was because Admirals King and Nimitz clamped extraordinarily tight security on the operation. But this was unfortunate for several reasons, mostly because without extra staffing in place, HYPO was unable to exploit the large volume of Japanese naval radio traffic that naturally developed during and after the raid—that certainly would contain information on ship movements which would threaten the American task force. Lieutenant Commander Huckins was extremely disappointed and irritated. In charge of direction-finding and interception, he was responsible for staffing at Wahiawa. Always operating "on a shoestring" regarding material and staff, he nevertheless could have doubled the watch that night if he had known. As it was, he only had enough *kana* operators to cover just a few of the Japanese naval radio circuits.

By spring 1942, in the days immediately preceding the battles of the Coral Sea and of Midway, partners Huckins and Williams were working up to twenty hours per day—in parallel with the other members of HYPO's key group.

In a breakthrough on May 8, 1942, Huckins and Williams—through traffic analysis—were able to associate Vice Adm. Nagumo Chūichi's First Air Fleet with key elements of Vice Adm. Kondō Nobutake's Second Fleet—which meant the consolidation of an enormous, formidable naval force. This was crucial information with enormous relevance in the lead-up to the Battle of Midway in early June.

Huckins, promoted to commander in July 1942 and then to captain in July 1943, spent the war at Pearl Harbor, providing an enormous quantity of high-quality work at HYPO and then at its successor organizations.

Just one further example was his contribution in mid-April 1943. Traffic analysts Huckins and Williams worked the address information on a Japanese intercept of April 13, 1943, which was the itinerary message of Adm. Yamamoto Isoroku's trip to Ballale and Buin in the vicinity of Bougainville. In fact, it was the large number of addressees on the message which had drawn attention to it. After hours of mind-numbing decryption and translation effort, at FRUPac and OP-20-GY, this lucky intercept led to the shoot-down death of Yamamoto—the commander in chief of the Japanese Navy—on April 18.

As mentioned, Huck finished the war at Pearl Harbor. Then, by 1947, he had been given an afloat command—the attack transport *President Hayes*. During this time the ship was mainly used to move dependents of service personnel from station to station, mostly in the Pacific area.

In 1948, Captain Huckins was serving as an intelligence officer on the Alaskan Joint Staff. During May he was an "official passenger" on board the submarine *Sea Dog* as that boat conducted the first of a series of reconnaissance patrols close to the Siberian coast. Huck had brought on board known Soviet radio calls and frequencies, intelligence estimates on locations of Soviet air bases, and other materials—all of which he then passed on to the next submarine—the *Blackfin*—involved in this mission.

At this point, regretfully, Huck's trail fades. Currently it might be said that he "went off the grid"—whether purposefully or not isn't known. It could be on purpose; in the 1970s Jasper Holmes wrote that many of the people profiled in his book (*Double-Edged Secrets*), and now in this book, "had a passion for anonymity which concealed their genius and their accomplishments from all but the most discerning." Holmes very specifically named Tom Huckins in this assessment.[3]

Captain Huckins took a voluntary retirement in December 1954, closing his naval career after thirty and a half years. What he did for the next twenty-seven years is

---

3. Actually, I have been extraordinarily fortunate in gathering the life stories (and photographs) of my fifty-nine intelligence and cryptology pioneers. There have only been two that have been difficult—and they have not been difficult regarding their prewar and wartime careers, but only in their postwar lives. Coincidentally, those two are the key Station HYPO traffic analysis partners: Captains Tom Huckins and—to a lesser degree—John Williams.

unclear, although the record shows that he passed away in Phoenix, on May 5, 1982, at age eighty.

Huck had married Sue Leffingwell Edwards (1904–1982), at St. Louis, in 1930. Interestingly, she preceded him in death—also in Phoenix—just eleven days before his time came.[4]

Despite the other unknowns, it's clear that Captain Huckins's awards include the Bronze Star, awarded in October 1945, for his brilliant work in World War II communications intelligence.[5]

Sources

Carlson, 98–99, 112, 119, 130–31, 164, 300, 303, 274–75, 359, 536.
Dyer, 146–47, 197.
Holmes, 18, 22, 55, 69, 86, 167.
Holtwick, 47, 51, 70, 97, 117, 126, 136–38, 167–68, 197, 199, 312, 324, 361–62, 373–74, 402, 428, 431.
Lucky Bag, U.S. Naval Academy, 1924.
McGinnis, 10–11, 13.
Packard, 123.
Prados, 77–78, 177, 407, 459–61.
Rochefort, 103–4.
U.S. Navy, *Register of Commissioned and Warrant Officers.*

---

4. Even though Huck was twenty-nine years old and Sue was twenty-six when they were married in 1930, they may have known each other from earlier years. Like Huck, she also was from Kirkwood, Missouri; in fact, one of her Leffingwell ancestors was a cofounder of the town in 1853.

5. Bronze Star medals appear to be given reasonably frequently in modern times, but this was not really the case in World War II. Of the hundreds of Navy and Marine Corps COMINT officers who served—and fought—throughout the war, only forty-six received the Bronze Star.

CAPTAIN JOHN ALTON WILLIAMS, U.S. NAVY (1905–1962)

Along with Thomas Huckins, he solved both the strategic
and tactical Japanese naval communications structures
Station HYPO's premier traffic analyst
One of Rochefort's core team at Station HYPO
"Johnny" "Jack" "Guillaume"

A "short, tense, and" somewhat "nervous" junior officer, Johnny Williams was nevertheless Joe Rochefort's top traffic analyst. Prior to the Pearl Harbor attack, Williams
was alone—among the HYPO and Pacific fleet intelligence people—in thinking that
the silence of the Japanese aircraft carriers meant that they were actually at sea and

not anchored in home ports. During the war he turned in a spectacular performance at HYPO/FRUPac/JICPOA; unfortunately, medical issues curtailed his postwar career—as well as his life.

*   *   *

From the 1928 Annapolis yearbook, *The Lucky Bag*:

"Now up in New England"—on-and-on one hears a continuous flow of words about the dear old hills and lakes of Connecticut. "Who said New England wasn't the richest industrial district in the country?" But don't get the idea that the boy was the talkative sort of fellow. Silence was golden until someone made a wise crack about the old home town, and then—. Another peculiar thing, though he seldom ventured to the hops [*formal dances*], he was forever getting letters from some little girl. Who could she have been? Now, *Guillaume* wasn't always so hot when it came to the Academics, but he managed to spend two-thirds of the study hours pouring over aviation magazines and still be "sat." In fact, you could point to a speck on the horizon and quick as a flash he would tell you the type of plane, the kind of oil it used, and the color of the pilot's hair. Well, the best of luck, *Guillaume*—there is always room for new altitude records and maybe a chance for the moon. Where there are no Duty Officers. If *Guillaume* were writing this he would probably reply, "To hell with them; I'll stick it out." [Activities: track, swimming, water polo.]

*   *   *

John Williams was a New Englander, hailing from Willimantic, Connecticut. He received an appointment to the U.S. Naval Academy in 1924 and was subsequently graduated and commissioned an ensign as part of the class of 1928. Among his distinguished classmates were Joseph F. **Finnegan**, Philip D. Gallery, David L. McDonald, and William F. Raborn Jr. Further promotions were lieutenant (junior grade), 1931; lieutenant, 1937; lieutenant commander, June 1942; commander, September 1942; and captain, 1945. He received a medical retirement from the navy in 1953 as did his classmate—and fellow Station HYPO coworker—Joe Finnegan.

Despite his early interest in naval aviation, Ensign Williams undertook the normal surface-ship duty typical of junior officers of his generation. From 1928 through 1929 he served on board the battleship *Maryland*, and 1930 saw him doing staff work with the Battleship Divisions, Battle Fleet. He then transferred, 1931 through 1932, to the battleship *Oklahoma*, followed by a year on board the transport *Argonne* and then a year serving on the destroyer *Trever*.

In 1935, Williams transferred back to Annapolis for some postgraduate study. Directly after that, in mid-1936, Lt. j.g. Williams reported to OP-20-G as one of two new students admitted to that organization's cryptanalysis course.

In May 1937, Lt. Joseph **Wenger** (at OP-20-G) wrote to Lt. Jack **Holtwick** (at the Sixteenth Naval District at Cavite) that:

your relief, Williams . . . worked with me on the [1933 fleet maneuvers report] and is now taking charge of the '34. In addition, he is attending all the lectures given to the

R.I. [students] plus a course of instruction in the lingo. He should be the best equipped of any to plunge right into the mêlée. He seems like a good man, and I expect him to prove it when he relieves you.

On the way out to Cavite to relieve Holtwick, Williams was ordered to temporary duty at Station HYPO in Hawaii to assist them starting the recovery of new keys and sequences of the Japanese Navy's "ORANGE M-1 Naval Cryptographic System."

When Williams finally arrived in the Philippines in November 1937, he learned that one of his predecessors, Lt. Sid **Goodwin**, had set a pattern and foundation there for actual cryptanalysis (and not merely traffic analysis as originally intended). This focus had been continued by Jack Holtwick—and now would be actively followed by Williams and then in succession by Jefferson **Dennis**, Bernard **Roeder**, Rudolph **Fabian**, and John **Leitwiler**.

Of particular note during this time, Lieutenant Williams sent a memo to OP-20-G reporting the discovery of a well-organized high-frequency direction-finding network which the Japanese Navy had started operating in the area around November 1938. He detailed some of its activities—particularly the heavy focus upon the American and Australian cruiser detachments which had come to take part in the opening ceremonies for Singapore's new naval dockyard.

Mr. Williams was relieved, as OIC of the Sixteenth Naval District communications intelligence unit, by Lt. Jeff Dennis in January 1939—and then Dennis relieved him again, in February 1940, as assistant fleet communications officer on the staff of the commander in chief, U.S. Asiatic Fleet.

Lieutenant Williams then transferred to the destroyer *Craven*, serving on board from around February until December 1940. He then moved to the CINCUS intelligence unit, and then to the Fourteenth Naval District's COMINT unit around February 1941, although his movements and postings are a little confusing at this point.

Lt. Cmdr. Ham **Wright** and Lt. Johnny Williams, while technically attached to the CINCPAC staff, were assigned by the Fleet Communications Officer (Capt. Maurice "Germany" Curts) to work with the 14th District communications-intelligence unit. Mr. Wright worked with Lt. Cmdr. Tommy **Dyer**, and Mr. Williams with Lt. Cmdr. Thomas **Huckins**. In fact, though there were no formal orders assigning them, they became so much a part of the unit that they were assigned to coding duty in the Navy Yard Communications Office prior to 18 October, when the unit began standing its own duty.

When Lt. Jasper **Holmes** came to HYPO in mid-1941, he became reacquainted with Tom Huckins; they had been in the same company when midshipmen at Annapolis. Holmes observed that traffic analysts Huckins and Williams were seemingly interminably shuffling a large volume of messages.

Each evening their distilled observations of the day's traffic were typed out as a summary which had to be delivered to Lt. Cmdr. Edwin T. **Layton**, the fleet intelligence officer, before eight o'clock in the morning. Because I delivered a chart overlay of ships' positions every morning to Layton at CinCPac headquarters, I frequently acted as officer messenger for other secret material also. I soon learned of the importance Layton placed on the traffic intelligence summary for his intelligence briefings to the Commander in Chief, Pacific Fleet, Adm. Husband E. Kimmel, each morning at eight-thirty.

The importance of traffic analysis and direction-finding—the *forte* of "scanners" like Williams and Huckins—can't be overstated. "In the early stages of the Pacific War, before the cryptanalysts cracked Japan's main naval codes, traffic analysis was about all [Cmdr. Joseph] **Rochefort** and his fellow analysts had to go on."

This point is further developed by Frederick D. Parker, author of *Pearl Harbor Revisited: U.S. Navy Communications Intelligence 1924–1941.*

Collectively they revealed a wealth of information concerning Japanese naval activities. . . . In many respects [HYPO's] achievements in 1941 were similar to what had been accomplished at Station CAST with traffic analysis against the Japanese Imperial Fleet maneuvers in the 1930s.

[HYPO's] daily summaries clearly showed that Lt. [Cmdr.] Thomas A. Huckins and Lt. John A. Williams, who headed the traffic analysis unit, had solved both the strategic and tactical Japanese naval communications structures. They understood the callsign generation system and were able to quickly reestablish order of battle data after routine callsign changes. This insight permitted unit identifications to the squadron level in ground-based air and destroyer units. It also allowed identifications to the individual ship level in battleships, cruisers, and carriers.

The capability to exploit these features of Japanese navy communications lasted until about three weeks prior to the attack on Pearl Harbor when callup and addressing procedures changed abruptly. Throughout the period they were also able to use their direction-finding capability to produce unique information as well as to support evidence from traffic analysis.

The traffic analysis unit was able to identify the Japanese Navy Combined Fleet Headquarters to principal line and staff subordinates within each of the fleets in both home and deployed locations.

In early November 1941, Huckins and Williams (aided by Capt. Red **Lasswell** and the other linguists) made a huge breakthrough as they studied an intercepted Japanese dispatch and interpreted the addressee as a relatively new organization: *Itikoukuu Kantai*—First Air Fleet. This operational unit consisted of all of Japan's fleet carriers (and support vessels) with a total of over 450 aircraft. This was a naval battle group with the single most powerful concentration of naval aviation in the world. It was the most critical component of what the Japanese called the *kido butai*, or *striking force.*

In the weeks prior to the attack on Pearl Harbor, Station HYPO was fed by the radio intercept station at He'eia and the direction-finding station at Lualualei.[1] As the physical packages of messages came in, they first were handed to the traffic analysts, Lieutenant Commander Huckins and Lieutenant Williams, before being passed to the cryptanalysts—Lieutenant Commanders Dyer, Wright, and Holtwick.

---

1. In late December 1941, both the DF station at Lualualei and the radio intercept station at He'eia were relocated and consolidated at Wahiawa, in the center of Oahu.

In late November and early December 1941, Lieutenant Commander Huckins and Lieutenant Williams concurred that the absence of message traffic vis-à-vis the Japanese Navy's aircraft carriers was due to an abrupt change of Japanese fleet call signs, and it would take a little time to reestablish them. But within a few days they no longer agreed on what was going on. Huckins thought—as did most of the others in HYPO including the boss, Commander Rochefort—that no carrier traffic meant that the ships were idle in home ports. Williams, however, became certain that the carriers were on the move, and were maintaining strict radio silence as they moved.

On the morning of December 7, Johnny Williams and Ham Wright were having breakfast at the submarine-base galley, getting ready to go on duty at 0800. Upon hearing strange sounds, Williams went outside and then, as Ham later noted, "Johnny came back in and said, 'They're out there with the oranges'" on their wings. In fact, going outside

to see what the explosions and commotion were all about, Lt. Jack Williams was probably less surprised than most to see the cause. Alone among the Hypo and Fleet Intelligence people, he had been sure for days that the apparent silence of the Japanese carriers meant that they were at sea and not in home harbors. When he returned, he simply told Wright: "They're Japanese aircraft and they're attacking Pearl Harbor."

That morning's events drew Williams, along with everyone else in Rochefort's basement "dungeon," into frenetic wartime activity. In fact by spring 1942, in the days immediately preceding the battles of the Coral Sea and of Midway, partners Huckins and Williams worked up to twenty hours per day—again in parallel with the other members of HYPO's key group.

In a breakthrough on May 8, 1942, Williams and Huckins—through traffic analysis—were able to associate Vice Adm. Nagumo Chūichi's First Air Fleet with key elements of Vice Adm. Kondō Nobutake's Second Fleet—which meant the consolidation of an enormous, formidable naval force.

Williams, promoted to lieutenant commander in June 1942, and then to commander in September 1942, spent the war at Pearl Harbor, providing an enormous quantity of high-quality work at HYPO and then its successor organizations. Just one further example was his contribution as part of the team which, in April 1943, broke and analyzed the message containing the inspection-trip itinerary of Japanese Navy commander-in-chief Adm. Yamamoto Isoroku—which led to his shoot-down and death. Johnny's part, naturally in partnership with Tom Huckins, was working the address information. The huge number of addressees was both a flag to the message's importance as well as an extra challenge to unravel.

At war's end, Captain Williams moved on to other communications-intelligence assignments (he'd been promoted to captain in March 1945). In 1947 he was working in Washington at the Communications Supplementary Activity, OP-20-2, located at the Naval Communications Annex on Nebraska Avenue.

However, Johnny's career was cut short in 1953 when he was forced to take a temporary retirement. This was based on disability findings following several hospitalizations at Bethesda Naval Hospital. He continued medical treatments at the San Diego naval hospital after he returned there in 1954. In December 1957, Captain Williams appeared before a navy board for physical reevaluation; this board sustained his earlier medical retirement because his disability (a blood disease called primary polycythemia) was of a permanent nature and rendered him unfit to perform duties of his rank by reason of physical disability. The condition also prevented him from finding any regular employment at all.

John's wife, Vivian, had suffered for many years from her own poor health, and passed away in August 1960. In August 1961, Captain Williams remarried, to Viola Aileen Epperson of La Jolla, California.

John and Viola resided in La Jolla until John's death in the San Diego Naval Hospital on March 26, 1962. He was subsequently buried at Arlington National Cemetery.[2] After his death, Viola and his son John A. Williams Jr. established a "John A. Williams Memorial Fund" at the Stanford University School of Medicine, with the goal of advancing the study of blood diseases.

Captain Williams's awards include the Legion of Merit for his brilliant work and superlative accomplishments in World War II communications intelligence.

Sources

Carlson, 98–99, 113, 119, 130–31, 164, 187–88, 300, 303, 445, 483.
Holmes, 18, 55.
Holtwick, 137, 140, 182, 223–24, 248, 263, 281, 354, 408, 420, 428, 432–33, 439, 446.
Layton, *"And I Was There,"* 230, 313.
Lucky Bag, U.S. Naval Academy, 1928.
McGinnis, 14.
Parker, *Pearl Harbor Revisited*, 37–38.
Prados, 177, 459.
U.S. Navy, *Register of Commissioned and Warrant Officers.*

2. It's interesting how Johnny Williams's life parallels that of his Annapolis classmate Joe Finnegan— both class of 1928. After surface fleet duty, Williams took cryptanalytic training while Finnegan underwent language immersion training. But they both next served in the Philippines, and both spent the war at HYPO/FRUPac/JICPOA contributing incredibly important work in Pacific Theater communications intelligence. Then both had their careers cut short when they were forced to take early medical retirement in the same year, 1953.

The Book Breakers

Cryptographers, Cryptanalysts, and Codebreakers

REAR ADMIRAL BERN ANDERSON, U.S. NAVY (1900–1963)

First U.S. Navy Asiatic Station
communications-intelligence officer
"Andy"

Bern Anderson was one of the earliest navy cryptographic students and was the first communications-intelligence officer to be assigned to the important Asiatic Station. Moreover, he was one of the first three administrators of OP-20-G's Research Desk and thus very influential in the organization's formative years. Yet, similar to some others in this study, Anderson seemingly abandoned COMINT around 1934 and developed a fine reputation as a "black-shoe" surface-ship officer—which included the award of a high-level combat decoration in 1944. He ended his career as a graduate-level teacher of strategy and tactics with a PhD in history; he also published two books of naval history and was deeply involved helping Rear Adm. Samuel Eliot Morison put together Morison's monumental *History of U.S. Naval Operations in World War II.*

* * *

From the 1921 Annapolis yearbook, *The Lucky Bag*:

Andy blew into Uncle Sam's hospitable home from the wilds of Kansas City, having been attracted to the Severnside by the ad in 1917's *Lucky Bag*. He was extremely youthful and unsophisticated at first, but three years' close association has done wonders. He is one of those unfortunate youths who have been ruined by the Navy. As a Plebe, he learned to smoke; as a Youngster, he was converted into an oil burner [chewer of tobacco]; and First Class cruise completed his downfall. He has never been known to play anything more strenuous than a game of cuckoo under expert tutelage. There is one thing always taking the joy out of life for *Andy*—reveille. And haven, a finite quantity to him, is Sep leave [30 days] at home in an easy chair, an infinite quantity of Fats, and the latest copy of the *Parisienne*. As a classmate, he is a relief from books; as a friend, he is all that can be desired. Stripes, class standing, or grease are negative quantities with *Andy*. The trail he has left behind him will not soon be forgotten. Many a classmate has been sorely tried by his Bolshevik tendencies, yet we enjoy his exuberance and general carefree disposition—provided we are not his section leader.

* * *

Bern Anderson was born in Kansas City, Missouri, on June 12, 1900, to Andrew and Hattie Anderson. After a year at Kansas City Junior College, he entered the U.S. Naval Academy in 1917 and graduated in 1920 with the class of 1921-A. Among his noteworthy classmates were Walter F. Boone, Charles R. Brown, Daniel V. Gallery, and Arthur H. **McCollum**. Further promotions included lieutenant (junior grade), 1923; lieutenant, 1926; lieutenant commander, 1936; commander, 1940; and captain, 1942. He retired in June 1950 and was simultaneously promoted to rear admiral based on his World War II combat decoration.

From 1920 to 1921, Ensign Anderson served in the protected cruiser *Charleston* in the Pacific Fleet. Moving to the Atlantic Fleet in 1921, he was on board the destroyer *Jacob Jones*, the destroyer *Yarborough* (1921–1926), and the battleship *Texas*. For the U.S. Navy's Fleet Problem VI, in early 1926, Lieutenant (junior grade) Anderson in the *Texas* (part of the Black Force), and Lt. Laurance **Safford** in the destroyer *Hull* (part of the Blue Force) apparently stood-up temporary signals-decryption units to attempt interception of "enemy" radio traffic, but actual employment of these units is not confirmed by records.

In June 1926 he began the four-month course in cryptanalysis at OP-20-G. In September 1927 he married Elizabeth Stanton of Staten Island, New York, who was the daughter of mural painter and maritime historian Samuel Ward Stanton, the editor of *The Nautical Gazette.*

From October 1927 through September 1929, Lieutenant Anderson was OIC of the Research Desk (OP-20-G), at Main Navy, having relieved Lt. Joe **Rochefort**. By August 1928, Anderson had become convinced that all communications intelligence activities should be put under the ONI rather than Naval Communications—a common feeling among people in the business at that time. Of course, this view did not prevail nor did it apparently even reach the formal discussion stage. In due course Mr. Anderson was replaced by Lt. Cmdr. Laurance Safford—although there was a five-month gap before Safford was able to take over.

Next assigned to the Asiatic Station, Anderson reported to the Sixteenth Naval District at Cavite, and then to the commander in chief, Asiatic Fleet. He was the first of many OP-20-G officers to undertake this work on that station, and he was the first there to utilize formally trained enlisted radio-intercept operators. His position was titled "assistant fleet communications officer," but his main focus was really communications intelligence. His duty post was primarily on board the flagship, but for a time he and his wife lived in Shanghai where their daughter, Joan Elizabeth, was born in 1930.

In November 1930, Lt. Cmdr. John **McClaran** (then head of OP-20-G) wrote that there were only six officers trained and available for cryptanalytical work (less a few others who had other major qualifications such as aviator, submariner, or linguist): Lt. Cmdr. Safford, Ens. Leahy, Lt. j.g. **Dyer**, Lt. Anderson, Lt. **Wenger**, and Lt. j.g. **Huckins**. This list was validated again the next year, with the addition of Lt. Joe Rochefort (who sometimes was not included on such lists because he had officially become an ONI Japanese linguist). Of these Safford, Rochefort, and Anderson were the only ones considered qualified to instruct in cryptanalysis—with Anderson rated below the other two.

Lt. Joe Wenger replaced Lieutenant Anderson on the Asiatic Station around July 1932, although there was a gap of several months and thus no solid turnover of the position. Anderson was then assigned to the Radio and Sound Division of the Bureau of Engineering in Washington—actually replacing Wenger—so with travel time and other delays it's pretty apparent why there was a gap!

This seems to be the end of Bern Anderson's communications-intelligence and cryptanalytic involvement, because the rest of his career then focused upon surface-ship operations and later teaching at the Naval War College. Although Lieutenant Commander McClaran had not been particularly pleased with Lieutenant Anderson's tour of duty as head of the Research Desk (particularly in comparison to the iconic Safford and Rochefort), the record still shows that he was a pioneering and excellent COMINT officer. It could very well be that he himself requested no further COMINT duty—perhaps having lost interest in the business, or more likely because he saw a more viable future in conventional line-officer assignments.

In 1934, Anderson assumed command of the minesweeper *Swallow*, which was assigned to Alaskan waters. During this tour he received a Department of Commerce license as a Master of Ocean Vessels and an endorsement as a pilot for Alaskan waters. Then, from 1937 through 1939, he served as a recruit training officer at the Naval Training Station in Great Lakes, Illinois.

During the 1930s Anderson began a side career as an author, writing articles for the U.S. Naval Institute *Proceedings* on such topics as the political situation in China. His interest in history and historical writing continued throughout the rest of his naval career and well into retirement.

When the United States declared war on Japan in December 1941, Commander Anderson was serving as navigator of the battleship *Mississippi* with the Atlantic Fleet in Iceland; he'd reported on board in 1939. In May and June 1942 he served as commanding officer of the gunboat *Vixen*, the temporary flagship of Adm. Ernest King when he became the Commander in Chief, U.S. Fleet. Anderson then attended the senior course at the Naval War College in Newport.

During 1943 and 1944, Captain Anderson served as planning and control officer on the staff of the Commander, Seventh Amphibious Force, working for Rear Adm. Daniel E. Barbey. Anderson participated in Operation HOLLANDIA, the invasion of New Guinea, and subsequent invasions in the Admiralty Islands and at New Britain. In Task Force 77, he commanded the nine ships of the Special Service Vessels squadron at Aitape, Tanahmerah Bay, and Humbolt Bay—April and May 1944. For this service he was awarded the Legion of Merit with the combat "V" device.

From 1944 through 1946, Anderson took an assignment with the staff of the Naval War College's Strategy Department. After that, he served for two years with the Atlantic Fleet Amphibious Force, initially as commanding officer of Transportation Division 22. He then became chief of staff, and later commanding officer, of Amphibious Force 2. In 1949, Andy returned to the Naval War College, this time as head of the Strategy and Tactics Department. He retired in June 1950 and was simultaneously promoted to rear admiral.

In retirement, Rear Admiral Anderson pursued history studies at Harvard University, earning his master's in 1951 and a PhD in 1952. His dissertation was on the great explorer Vancouver and was expanded into a book, *Surveyor of the Sea: The Life and Voyages of Captain George Vancouver*.

Recalled to active duty, he was assigned to the Naval War College from 1952 through 1960. There he served as a research associate and "very able chief assistant" to Rear Adm. Samuel Eliot Morison in the writing of Morison's monumental and multivolume *The History of U.S. Naval Operations in World War II*. Later, in 1962, Anderson's own second book was published: *By Sea and by River: The Naval History of the Civil War*.

Anderson died on February 12, 1963, at the Naval Hospital in Newport. His widow, Mrs. Elizabeth Anderson, continued to live in Jamestown, Rhode Island, and his daughter, Joan Stickley, was then located in Washington, D.C.

Rear Admiral Anderson's decorations included the World War I Victory Medal with Atlantic Fleet clasp, the Yangtze Campaign Medal, the Navy Commendation Medal, and the Legion of Merit with the combat "V" device.

Sources

Cherpak, Evelyn, comp. *Register of the Papers of Bern Anderson.* Naval Historical Collection, U.S. Naval War College. Newport, RI: 1987.

Holtwick, 34, 47–48, 50, 61–62, 67, 69–71, 99, 105–6, 137, 199, 244, 291.

Lucky Bag, U.S. Naval Academy, 1921.

Morison, VI (15, 131), VIII (viii, 45, 65, 81, 87, 98, 111–12, 116, 123–24, 135, 404), IX (xiv), XI (ix–xi), XII (vii), XIII (ix), XIV (xi).

U.S. Navy, *Register of Commissioned and Warrant Officers.*

COMMANDER HENRY MUMFORD ANTHONY, U.S. COAST GUARD (1902–1991)

The Coast Guard's "gift to cryptanalysis"

Briefly serving in the navy before embarking upon a thirty-five-year career in the Coast Guard, Henry Anthony's contributions were as diverse as they were remarkable. He was consecutively a submariner, destroyerman, radio electrician, self-taught Japanese linguist, foreign merchant ship expert, and a "natural" cryptanalyst. During the war he was considered so valuable at FRUPac that for over two years the navy successfully stonewalled every effort to have him released back into Coast Guard service.

* * *

Henry M. Anthony was born on June 20, 1902, in Newport, Rhode Island. He began his naval career in 1920, as an enlisted man in the U.S. Navy, and saw service aboard submarines. After transferring to the U.S. Coast Guard in 1925 he specialized in breaking rumrunner codes during Prohibition. He served on board the cutters (formerly navy destroyers) *Wainwright* and *Cassin* during the Coast Guard's "Rum Patrol"—mostly on the East Coast. He then worked Coast Guard intelligence in New York City, followed by a move to the intelligence office in San Francisco.

Beginning in 1935, Anthony was at the Communications, Education, and Intelligence Office in Hawaii and formed a close association with the navy's Pacific Fleet intelligence officers there. He devoted considerable time to breaking simple Japanese "tuna clipper" codes; in fact, it was in 1937 that Chief Radio Electrician Henry Anthony made the acquaintance of Lt. Tommy **Dyer**, who was then the head of the Fourteenth Naval District's Communications Intelligence Unit at Pearl Harbor. Summer 1937 also saw him involved in the search for missing pilot Amelia Earhart when her aircraft disappeared in the Pacific Ocean during her attempted around-the-world flight.

During this time Anthony was teaching himself Japanese; the Coast Guard had always been on a shoestring budget and would not pay for language classes—so Anthony, on his own initiative and expense—learned Japanese. On official duty he boarded all Japanese merchant vessels calling at Hawaii, on the pretext of searching for smuggled narcotics, but in reality to check their routings and other sailing data. Over the years, Anthony became an authority—perhaps *the* authority—on the Japanese merchant marine. He was commissioned in 1941 and then, as an expert on merchant ship communications, he was instrumental in aiding the U.S. Navy's Fleet Radio Unit, Pacific (FRUPac) with its major codebreaking gains, working there almost continuously from the Pearl Harbor attack until September 1945. Such communications intelligence directly contributed to the U.S. submarine fleet decimating the Japanese merchant marine during the war.

Throughout the latter half of the war the Coast Guard wanted Mr. Anthony back from the navy and kept pressuring FRUPac to release him. FRUPac was reluctant for they valued his remarkable innate ability for cryptanalysis. The Coast Guard finally asked how long it would take to train a relief for him, and Tommy Dyer replied "about as long as it would take to train a relief for [internationally renowned pianist and conductor] José Iturbi." In a 1986 interview, Captain Dyer expanded on this. Mr. Anthony

> was what you think of as a "natural." He was largely self-taught, as most of us were. . . . He eventually took over the complete responsibility at Pearl Harbor for the Japanese "maru" [merchant ship] system and did a magnificent job with it. It's always a joy, in any line of work, to have a subordinate to whom you can turn over something and not have to give a second thought to what he's doing or how he's doing. . . . He was one of the shining examples of self-reliance in that respect.

After the war, Anthony was stationed at the USCG Supplementary Radio Station in Washington and then the Communications Security Office. He returned to Hawaii in the office of the Commander, Fourteenth Coast Guard District, Honolulu; his last station was in San Francisco, 1956 to 1959, on the staff of the Commander, Western Area, as communications officer.

Anthony was promoted to lieutenant commander in 1943 and then to commander in 1952. He retired on September 30, 1960; in retirement he lived in San Jose and then in Oakhurst, California. He worked in the insurance business and also as a newspaper reporter at large. For a number of years he served as commander of the local Veterans of Foreign Wars chapter.

Commander Anthony passed away in Fresno on July 7, 1991. He was survived by a daughter, Dolores Breazell.

He has been recognized by intelligence historian John Prados as a dedicated cryptanalyst whose name ought to be forever preserved for history: "Commander Henry M. Anthony, the Coast Guard's gift to cryptanalysis, specialized in Japanese merchant shipping codes."

He received a Bronze Star Medal for his World War II service at FRUPac, and the Coast Guard Commendation Ribbon and Pendant for his search-and-rescue planning work in the late 1950s. In the early 1980s, Anthony put in considerable effort helping Rear Adm. Edwin Layton (and his coauthors) work on Layton's reminisces, *"And I Was There": Pearl Harbor and Midway—Breaking the Secrets.*

At the time of this writing Commander Anthony is being looked at for inclusion in the NSA's Hall of Honor.

Sources

Anthony, Henry M. Military Service Information, National Personnel Records Center, Report No. 1-10800284603, April 20, 2012.

Dyer, 194, 226–27, 257, 296, 297.

Holmes, 128.

Layton, *"And I Was There,"* 6.

Obituary, "H. M. Anthony," *Madera* [California] *Tribune,* July 11, 1991.

Prados, 412.

U.S. Coast Guard. *Coast Guard Publication 2.0: Intelligence* (May 2010), 16.

U.S. Coast Guard official website; "Who Are Some of the Heroes of the U.S. Coast Guard?" FAQ, Coast Guard History.

U.S. Coast Guard, *Register of the Commissioned and Warrant Officers and Cadets.*

CAPTAIN PRESCOTT HUNT CURRIER, U.S. NAVY (1912–1994)

An early "On-the-Roof Gang" radioman, Prescott Currier was another "natural" for the communications-intelligence and cryptology business. Earning a commission in 1936, he went on to make significant contributions before and during World War II, rose to the grade of captain, and retired from the NSA in the 1960s.

*   *   *

Prescott Currier was born in Holbrook, Massachusetts, on June 4, 1912. He had hoped to attend the Naval Academy, starting with the academy's preparatory school, but was very underweight and did not get in. So, he enlisted in the U.S. Navy on

July 8, 1929, and then subsequently attended communications-intelligence training in Washington, graduating with On-the-Roof Gang Class Eight in July 1932. As a radioman third and second class, he served at the Asiatic Station in the Far East (under Chief Radioman Walter **McGregor**), and then received a discharge when his enlistment expired. Even as a junior radioman, Currier was identified as an extremely intelligent, industrious, and apt young man with the type of "cryptanalytic brain" for which OP-20-G was always searching. He had been doing excellent work, and receiving considerable praise, even prior to receiving formal cryptology or language training.

Currier then attended college at Dartmouth University (although one source indicates that he earned his degree in Romance languages at George Washington University). Invited to return to naval communications intelligence by Lt. Cmdr. Joseph **Wenger**, Currier took a federal civil service job with OP-20-G—as a junior cryptanalyst—and then received an inactive naval reserve commission as an ensign in April 1936. As a civilian, from June 1937 through October 1940, Currier worked in OP-20-GY (Cryptanalysis and Decryption), responsible for manual cipher systems—particularly tactical.

In spring of 1940, Cmdr. Laurance **Safford**, the head of OP-20-G, became concerned about some medical issues regarding Mr. Currier, unsure that "the medicos would pass him for active duty." Safford was planning to recall him and then send him out to Pearl Harbor to work for Lt. Cmdr. Tommy **Dyer** at Station HYPO. The medical question was resolved and Currier was promoted to lieutenant (junior grade) in November 1940. He was recalled to active duty that same year and remained with OP-20-G at least through early 1942. During this time he was working with—and most of the time for—Mrs. Agnes **Driscoll**.

In January 1941, Lt. j.g. Currier joined Lt. Robert H. **Weeks** (also of OP-20-G) and U.S. Army officers Capt. Abraham Sinkov and Lt. Leo Rosen (of the army's Signal Intelligence Service) on a ten-week mission to Great Britain. They delivered American communications-intelligence material to the British, including two copies of the PURPLE machine (which could decipher the current Japanese diplomatic code) and two RED machines (which could read the code of an earlier Japanese diplomatic enciphering machine). In return, the British supplied them with a little information about their exploitation of the German ENIGMA encryption system as well as considerable information concerning other nations' systems. The Americans were also provided with some state-of-the-art British direction-finding equipment. For the United States, this was one of the most significant signals-intelligence events of the prewar period.

While in England, Weeks and Currier traveled around the country to see various intercept stations and other places of interest. One day their car was stopped in a small village by a zealous local constable who was suspicious of foreigners. He announced that he was going to detain them and take them to the station, whereupon their British War Office driver jumped out of the car in a fury, accosted the constable, and shouted at the top of his voice, "Ye canna do this! They are *AMERICANS* and they are on a *SECRET MISSION!*"

Mr. Currier finally received orders to HYPO at Pearl, to report in July 1941—but they were subsequently rescinded. In November, Currier (accompanying his superiors Safford and Driscoll as well as Lt. Lee W. **Parke**) engaged with several MIT professors and representatives from the Bureau of Ships; at issue was the National Defense Research Committee project of designing and building high-speed analytical machinery for the navy's Communications Security Section.

In March 1942 a small group of British signals-intelligence experts visited OP-20-G in Washington. One of them, pioneering cryptanalyst Lt. Col. John Tiltman, wrote in his report that:

> Currier is a very good man with experience of Japanese naval ciphers extending over at least ten years. But he is the only man in [his] section who knows Japanese, and much of his time is occupied in trying to cope with unreciphered codebooks to the possible detriment of research on the "flag officer" and submarine ciphers.

Mr. Currier moved to OP-20-GZ (Language and Translation) during the spring of 1942. From then, until the end of the war, he was responsible for a huge volume of outgoing communications intelligence and other work on major Japanese naval systems.

He was promoted to commander in July 1945. In the postwar period he worked on both Soviet and then North Korean systems, and on several occasions served in a liaison capacity with the British.

From 1948 through 1950, Commander Currier was director of research at what became the Naval Security Group, and then from 1950 through 1951 he was assigned to the Office of Operations, Armed Forces Security Agency.

He then became the OIC at the Naval Radio Receiving Facility, Kami Seya, Japan, with duty from 1952 through 1954. He also was stationed in the Philippines, at the ONI, with the Armed Forces Security Agency, as assistant naval attaché in London, and at the NSA. He was promoted to captain in 1955, and in the mid-1950s he was the NSA's senior liaison officer to the United Kingdom. In the summer of 1958 he was made executive secretary of the U.S. Communications Intelligence Board.

In September 1962 he retired from active navy service. He then moved to England where he obtained an advanced academic degree (a diploma in comparative philology at the University of London). He later returned to the United States where he worked as a civilian at the NSA. In 1965 he became an agency-wide cryptologic consultant, and worked at that until he retired.

However, even in his retirement he continued to serve as a COMINT consultant. Moreover, he had long maintained a keen interest in the "Voynich Manuscript," and he therefore devoted an impressive amount of rigorously scientific analytic effort to that problem.[1]

---

1. The Voynich Manuscript is an illustrated codex handwritten in an unknown writing system. The book has been carbon-dated to the early fifteenth century (1404–1438), and may have been composed in northern Italy during the Italian Renaissance. The manuscript is named after Wilfrid Voynich, a book dealer

Captain Currier's awards and decorations included two Legions of Merit. He had earned formal naval qualifications in both the Japanese and Russian languages.

He passed away in Damariscotta, Maine, in 1994.

Sources

Bamford, 395, 401.

Benson, 19, 45.

Budiansky, 175–79.

Currier, Capt. Prescott H., Ret. "Presentation Given to Members of the Cryptanalysis Field." Ft. Meade, MD: National Security Agency, c. 1974. nsabackups.com.

Donovan and Mack, 59–60, 62, 141, 202, 204.

Farago, *Broken Seal*, 253.

Holtwick, 106, 141, 149–50, 224–25, 322, 340, 366, 376, 400, 408–9, 439, App. 91–97.

McGinnis, 13, 19.

Smith, *Emperor's Codes*, 74–79, 124.

Smith and Erskine, *Action This Day*, 164–65, 220.

Stinnett, 75–80, 333.

Toland, 62.

Van Der Rhoer, 71.

---

who purchased it in 1912. The pages of the codex are vellum. Some of the pages are missing, but about 240 remain. The text is written from left to right, and most of the pages have illustrations or diagrams.

Many people have speculated that the writing might be nonsense, but others have speculated that it might be a ciphertext with a message. The manuscript has been studied by many professional and amateur cryptographers, including American and British codebreakers from both world wars. No one has yet succeeded in deciphering the text, and it has become a famous case in the history of cryptography.

REAR ADMIRAL JEFFERSON RICE DENNIS, U.S. NAVY
(1909–1958)

"Jeff"

Jeff Dennis was an officer of remarkable technical ability and keen intelligence. He made significant communications, cryptologic, and signals-intelligence contributions to various naval operational forces, naval intelligence organizations, the Naval Security Group, the Armed Forces Security Agency, and the NSA. Sadly, he passed away far too young—common to many officers under consideration here—but he is only one of two to die while still serving on active duty.

*   *   *

From the 1930 Naval Academy yearbook, *The Lucky Bag*:

The myriad eyes of fellow Coloradoans opened in amazement, some four years ago, at the loss of one of their most promising sons. *Jeff* had deserted them, lured away from the peaks and plains of his native state by the rocks and shoals of the naval service. Now, *Jeff* is one man we have never been able to fathom. He will always do the thing least expected, and his closest friends can never tell what that will be. Who would have thought that he would be the one to give [the statue of] Tecumseh a coat of war paint before the Army game? It may be added that this occasion very clearly displayed his principles of honor, for when the Commandant asked for the guilty ones, *Jeff* gave a straightforward confession of having committed the deed.

Cares and tribulations, that wear most of us away to shells of our former selves, leave him bland and smiling. Never daunted, taking things as they came, he passed the four years with as little friction as possible. *Jeff* possesses a store of admirable qualities that have won him the most sincere respect here, and will win him more in the service years to follow. Just ask him how everything is, and he will say, "She's fine, thanks." [Activities: cross country, swimming, track]

*   *   *

Jefferson R. Dennis was born in Colorado Springs, Colorado, on April 10, 1909, son of Mrs. Charlotte Corday (Rice) Dennis and Dr. Frank L. Dennis. He attended Colorado Springs High School prior to his appointment to the U.S. Naval Academy. He graduated and was commissioned as an ensign in June 1930, along with such classmates as Dudley "Mush" Morton and Samuel D. Dealey. Jeff subsequently advanced in rank: lieutenant (junior grade), 1933; lieutenant, 1937; lieutenant commander, January 1942; commander, October 1942; and captain, 1945. He had been selected for the grade of rear admiral in the summer of 1957, but he unexpectedly died in early 1958 before he was authorized to pin it on; nevertheless, he was posthumously promoted to that grade to date from July 1957.

Following his academy graduation, Mr. Dennis joined the battleship *Oklahoma*, and then in May 1932 he transferred to the destroyer *Alden*. In 1933 he obtained a qualification as an interpreter in Spanish. Detached from the *Alden* in February 1934, he served for three months in the destroyer *Sicard*, prior to reporting for duty on board the destroyer *MacLeish*. From December 1935 until June 1936 he had submarine training at the Submarine Base, New London, and after qualification in submarines he served in the USS *S-21* until June 1937.

In July 1937 he was assigned to the Communications Division, Office of the CNO, for training in cryptology and communications intelligence at OP-20-G. He was joined by fellow new students Lts. j.g. Bernard F. **Roeder** and Allan L. Reed. Then, in January 1939, Dennis reported for communications duty at the Sixteenth Naval District, Cavite, Philippine Islands, relieving Lt. John A. **Williams**; this duty certainly included considerable Japanese traffic analysis, among other things. Upon arrival, he learned that Lt. Sid **Goodwin** had previously set a pattern and foundation at Cavite for cryptanalysis (and not just traffic analysis) which had then been followed by Jack **Holtwick** and Johnny Williams, and now would be followed by Dennis, Brute Roeder, Rudy **Fabian**, and John **Leitwiler** in turn. Mr. Dennis was assisted by, among other people, Capt. Alva B. **Lasswell**, USMC, a recent Japanese language/culture immersion graduate.

In April 1939 Dennis reported to OP-20-G that his primary mission (obtaining all information for CinCAF by traffic analysis and the decryption of messages in known systems) had—since November 1938—been subordinated to the effort to break into the new Japanese "AD" code.

> The most recent changes in Orange cipher systems result in a somewhat different problem confronting the decryption units than formerly. Assuming the AD Code to be "readily" solved (which it will *not* be for many months), there still remains the task of recovering 4,000 keys which are changed every four months, in addition to the solution of a new transposition form every ten days. . . . This system is so important, from the standpoint of current information desired, that one man's entire time must be devoted to it. And it might be added, the *same* man, for, as in all of these solutions, it is over-and-over again the "known word" that solves all the keys and forms; the "known word" is available only to the man who follows the traffic day-by-day.
>
> Referring again to the AD system, since 4,000 different keys of the same length must have been derived mathematically, there is no reason why 4,000,000 keys cannot and may not be introduced, each message presenting a new key for solution before it can be read. The problem then is one of quantity and time rather than difficulty, and dictates that serious consideration be given to increasing the number of cryptographic clerks assigned to [this] unit.

In January 1940, Lieutenant Roeder arrived from OP-20-GX to relieve Dennis as OIC of the Sixteenth Naval District communications intelligence unit. Then, in February, Dennis became assistant fleet communications officer on the staff of the commander in chief, U.S. Asiatic Fleet—again relieving Lt. John Williams. Working briefly for Adm. Harry E. Yarnell and then Adm. Thomas C. Hart, on board the flagships (heavy cruisers *Augusta* and later *Houston*), he remained in that assignment until October 1941.

While assistant fleet communications officer, in February 1941 Lt. Cmdr. Dennis participated in a U.S.-U.K. communications-intelligence conference in Singapore. There, the U.S. Navy released to the British a Japanese merchant ship code, a naval personnel code, and callsign information. In return, the British gave back valuable information about the Japanese JN-25 code.

In September 1941, Mr. Dennis was ready to depart the Asiatic station; he had remained an extra year beyond initial assignment "to do radio intelligence on the flagship." Thus, in the fall of 1941, Jeff was ordered to the Federal Shipbuilding and Dry Dock Company at Kearny, New Jersey. There he assisted in the fitting-out of the USS *Aaron Ward* and joined that destroyer, as executive officer, upon her commissioning in March 1942. Returning to duty ashore in May, he was again assigned to the Division of Naval Communications in Washington. In September 1944 he was transferred to Pearl Harbor for duty with the Fleet Radio Unit, Pacific (FRUPac), remaining there until September 1945 and the end of the war. For his work there he was awarded the Legion of Merit.

Between November 1945 and February 1950, Dennis served with the Communications Security Group in the navy's Communications Division in Washington. He was then assigned to the Armed Forces Security Agency, which shortly became the NSA.

In July 1953 he became the assistant chief of staff for intelligence for the Commander in Chief, U.S. Naval Forces Eastern Atlantic and Mediterranean. Then, from February 1955 until August 1957, he served as assistant director for communications security matters in the Office of the CNO. In addition, during this same period, he was head of the Naval Security Group.

On September 1957, having been relieved by Capt. Bernard F. Roeder, Dennis reported as assistant director of the NSA, and also as director of the NSA's intelligence production organization at Fort Meade, Maryland. He was serving in those capacities at the time of his death in February 1958, following an unexpected heart attack while shoveling snow at his home. He was subsequently buried at Arlington National Cemetery.

Captain Dennis had been selected for the grade of rear admiral; his selection had been approved by the president in the previous year. As a result, by posthumous promotion, his date of rank became July 1957. His awards included the Legion of Merit and the Navy Unit Commendation Ribbon; he was posthumously awarded the Distinguished Service Medal for his services 1955 through the time of his death.

Rear Admiral Dennis has been formally recognized and honored, by the U.S. Naval Cryptologic Veterans Association, as an officer who served as the head of the Naval Security Group or one of its predecessor organizations. He has also been named a Pioneer Officer of U.S. Naval Cryptology by the same organization.

Admiral Dennis was married to the former Jane M. Hall, of Seattle; they had two children, Capt. Jefferson R. Dennis Jr. (USNA class of 1957), and Charlotte M. Dennis.

Sources

Benson, 20.
Browne and McGinnis, *Communications Intelligence*, 236–37.
Donovan and Mack, 63, 144.
Dyer, 353.
Holtwick, 137, 140, 245–46, 305, 324, 327–29, 345, 351, 400, 431–32.
Lucky Bag, U.S. Naval Academy, 1930.
Prados, 214.
Rear Adm. Jefferson R. Dennis, USN, Deceased. Official Biography. U.S. Navy Office of Information, September 5, 1958. Courtesy of the Naval Historical Foundation.
U.S. Navy, *Register of Commissioned and Warrant Officers.*
Whitlock, 48.

MRS. AGNES MAY MEYER DRISCOLL,
U.S. NAVY CIVILIAN (1889–1971)

The "first lady" of naval cryptology
The navy's principal cryptanalyst for many years
"Miss Meyer" "Mrs. Driscoll" "Miss Aggie" "Madam X"

Agnes May Meyer Driscoll's career as a cryptanalyst—in which she was a breaker of a multitude of Japanese naval systems (as well as a contributor to early U.S. machine systems)—marks her as one of the true "originals" in American cryptology. Moreover, of all the pioneer American cryptologists, the enigmatic but brilliant Mrs. Driscoll remains as mysterious today as when she passed away over forty years ago—which is all the more ironic when one considers the range and number of her accomplishments as a groundbreaking cryptologist and that she was a woman working in an almost exclusively male domain.

In her thirty-year career with the navy, Mrs. Driscoll broke several major Japanese Navy codes and follow-on variants: these include the *Red Book Code* in the 1920s, then the *Blue Book Code* in 1930 and, in 1940, she made critical inroads into *JN-25*, the Japanese fleet's operational code, which the U.S. Navy exploited to great effect (after the attack on Pearl Harbor) during the Pacific War. And, no less significant, she gave a generation of Navy cryptologists—many of whom were brilliant in their own right—their introduction to, and initial education in, the business.

*   *   *

Agnes Meyer was born on July 24, 1889, in Genesco, Illinois—one of eight children—to Dr. Gustav F. and Lucy Andrews Meyer. She attended Otterbein College from 1907 to 1909 (where her father was a professor of music), and then in 1911 she completed an A.B. from Ohio State University, having majored in mathematics, music, physics, and foreign languages (German, French, Latin, and Japanese)—a curriculum which was very atypical of women's education in the post-Victorian era. Indeed, from her earliest days as a college student, Miss Meyer pursued technical and scientific studies not usually addressed by a woman of that time.

After college she moved to Amarillo, Texas. There she taught music at Lowry Phillips Military Academy from 1911 to 1914, and then other subjects in various high schools. By 1918 she was the head of the mathematics department at Amarillo High School—a position of some status. However, events were soon to change her career completely.

In April 1917, as a result of the unlimited U-boat campaign that the Germans had brought into play, and the revelations of the Zimmerman Telegram, the United States declared war on Germany and thus entered World War I. By early 1918 the U.S. Navy found that it had a serious personnel shortage as the war rapidly soaked up the pool of available manpower. To partially address this problem, the secretary of the navy—Josephus Daniels—made the far-reaching decision to allow women to enlist.[1] Subsequently, a large number of American women answered the call to arms, among them two of the Meyer sisters; Agnes thus resigned her position in Amarillo and enlisted in the navy in June 1918.

She began as a Chief Yeoman (F), the highest rank that could be achieved by a woman (the "F" stood for *female*, to ensure that such a person would be distinguished from a *male* yeoman). She was first assigned to the Postal and Cable Censorship Office in Washington, reviewing telegrams and letters for compromises or indications of espionage activity. She then was transferred to the Code and Signal Section of the Director of Naval Communications, which had the responsibility for developing operational codes and ciphers for the navy. At war's end, these naval reserve women were offered the opportunity to be discharged with an option to accept a civilian position within the Navy Department. So, in July 1919, Agnes Meyer

---

1. "Is there any law that says a yeoman must be a man?" Mr. Daniels asked his legal advisers. The answer was that there was not, but that only men had heretofore been enlisted. The law did not say "male." "Then enroll women in the Naval Reserve as yeomen," he said, "and we will have the best clerical assistance the country can provide."

took the offer and began working as a civilian in the same section, officially as a stenographer and then as a "clerk."

Shortly after this change, she was invited to spend some time at the Riverbank Laboratory in Geneva, Illinois (which was the same place where the iconic William and Elizebeth Friedman began their cryptologic careers). Miss Meyer joined a select group of people working at Riverbank's "Department of Ciphers," owned and overseen by millionaire George Fabyan. Fabyan paid her expenses—and a salary—and the navy gave its blessing to the venture. After she returned to Washington in March 1920, Mr. Fabyan wrote to Lt. Cmdr. Milo F. Draemel (at that time OIC of the CSS):

> We were very favorably impressed with the young lady and should the condition arise that it is deemed the part of wisdom to dispense with her services at Washington, I want to say . . . that you are authorized to send her [back] to Riverbank at my expense and I will give her employment in the Cipher Department at salary which is equal to that which she is now receiving and, furthermore, should occasion arise that you wanted her returned to the [Navy] Department, I will then release her for that purpose.

Later, in 1925, Lt. Laurance F. **Safford**—the first OIC of the Code and Signal Section's new "Research Desk"—wrote Fabyan to ask about purchasing some Riverbank publications, and also mentioned that

> Miss Meyer, who was trained at Riverbank, is back with us again and is doing excellent work. . . . The Navy was a trifle slow getting into the cipher game, but its importance is now realized and we will be grateful for such assistance as the Riverbank laboratories can give.

For several years there was correspondence between Mr. Fabyan and the navy, discussing the possibility of training other navy personnel, but it doesn't appear that anything came of it.

However, returning to 1920, toward the end of the year Miss Meyer is believed to have spent about five months at pioneering cryptologist Herbert O. Yardley's cryptanalytic organization (perhaps more popularly known as the American "Black Chamber" from the title of Yardley's subsequent 1931 book) in New York City. At that time, Yardley's bureau (officially known as MI-8, jointly funded by the army and the State Department) took on trainees from other government offices, so this was not unusual. In addition, Yardley's greatest successes were against Japanese systems; therefore, it's possible that the true foundation for Miss Meyer's later cryptanalytic exploits may have begun while at MI-8.

It's interesting to note that during this period the navy's communications intelligence effort was, for the most part, still more an idea than a reality. Some theoretical studies had been done before, during, and after World War I, but an organization designed explicitly to intercept, decrypt, and report intelligence from the radio traffic of other navies did not really exist. Much like the army, the navy's cryptologists (few and unsophisticated, such as they were) were producing systems to protect their own communications. So, Miss Meyer (or Miss Aggie, as she was also known) spent the next year working with the then head of the Code and Signal Section (Lt. Cmdr. William Gresham) on the development of a device known as the "CM" or the "Cipher Machine." In 1921 this device, which was a sort of mechanical cipher machine based on a sliding alphabet system, become one of the navy's standard cryptographic tools for most of the 1920s. According to retired Captain Safford—looking back from fifty years in the future—it was the first high-command cipher the navy had. But it had some problems.

> It was a machine which involved the cipher principal, and it was invented by Miss Aggie way, way back, and then the mechanical details were worked out by "Pop" Gresham. But I had to redesign the damn thing. We substituted aluminum for brass wherever we could; we changed the method of disengaging and re-engaging the racks. But it was the first system we had which dispensed with the codebook, and it stayed in effect for several years.

In 1937, in belated recognition for this pioneering accomplishment, the U.S. Congress awarded Miss Aggie (along with Mr. Gresham's widow) $15,000.

The year 1921 also saw a curious turn in Miss Meyer's career in cryptographic development. According to Laurance Safford, in her early days in the section she didn't "attempt any foreign solutions, but studied our own systems." In particular, "she solved all manner of commercial machine ciphers submitted to the Navy Department [by companies hoping for a government contract]. She solved them all, and none of them were accepted for the Navy." In a related activity, in 1922 Miss Aggie responded to a challenge published in a maritime magazine, concerning a supposedly invulnerable cipher message produced by a machine. She was able to solve it, much to the interest if not amazement of the machine's inventor, Edward H. Hebern.[2] In

---

2. Edward Hugh Hebern was born in Streator, Illinois, in 1869. He got a patent in 1919 for a rotor machine, shortly before three other inventors (in other countries) patented much the same thing. Hebern started a company to market his machine. By September 1922 Hebern was so sure of imminent huge orders from the navy and army that he began building a factory in Oakland. The striking three-story structure was built to accommodate 1,500 workers and had a luxurious office for Hebern. The 1923 stockholders' report said it was "one of the most beautiful structures in California and said to be the only building in the State of true Gothic architecture throughout." By the time it was completed the following year, it had cost somewhere between $380,000 and $400,000, and the company still had no income. Eventually Hebern would sell a few of his early machines to the navy, the army, the Pacific Steamship Company of Seattle, the Italian government, and a few other buyers, but the company went into bankruptcy and his ambitious building was repossessed. The Hebern-Code building still stands, at 829 Harrison Street in Oakland.

Hebern reorganized in Reno, calling his new business the International Code Machine Company. He *did* sell thirty-five machines to the navy in 1928 and 1931, which satisfactorily carried a huge load of traffic until most wore out by 1936. When Hebern tried to move forward with the navy, he was sent packing with "an abrupt and discourteous letter, discontinuing business with him," written by an officer who did not know him in Laurance Safford's absence. Safford, who had been his main navy point of contact, later wrote, "They pulled the rug out from under Hebern and were not even polite about it."

Later he, and then his estate, sued the government for claims that the U.S. "armed forces had adopted the rotor principle from Hebern and used it without just compensation in . . . thousands of high-security machines in World War II and in the Cold War—which they *had* unquestionably done.

fact, Hebern had invented what appears to be the first cipher machine to use rotors and was hopeful that the army and navy would have great interest in his device. After visiting Washington and pitching his invention, as well as meeting a number of people including Miss Meyer, Mr. Hebern decided that she might help him design an even better device. So, in 1922 he hired her away from the navy and brought her to his business in California as a technical advisor and navy liaison (interestingly, her place in the Code and Signal Section was temporarily filled by Elizebeth Friedman). According to Safford, it was actually

> upon the advice and recommendation of the section head—I think then it was Lt. Cmdr. Gresham—Miss Aggie resigned her Navy position and went to Mr. Hebern to look after the cryptologic end of his machines, leaving Hebern to be the inventor and mechanical designer.

Despite the Hebern Company's best efforts (and it must be noted that Hebern's work in rotor technology would affect machine cryptologic design for years to come) his machine could not provide sufficient cryptographic security; in fact, in 1924 an evaluation by William Friedman led to a successful attack on the system. The security issue, coupled with Hebern's inability to generate enough revenue to meet his enormous start-up costs, ultimately forced him into bankruptcy. Even before all of this completely played out, in 1925 Miss Meyer returned to Washington and the navy. At this point a number of circumstances had changed for her. In addition to the move from the West Coast back to the East, she got married—to Mr. Michael B. Driscoll, who was a lawyer for the Department of Commerce. How they met is unknown; the fact that they both originally hailed from Illinois may have something to do with it.

More important for the new Mrs. Driscoll's career, while she was in California the navy had created a serious cryptanalytic mission within the CSS. Initially to be known as the Research Desk, as mentioned earlier, its first head was Lt. Laurance Safford who found, upon his arrival in early January 1924, a tiny staff of one cryptanalyst—Mr. Claus Bogel—and four clerks, in Room 1621 on the ground floor of Main Navy's sixth wing. In fact, it was Miss Aggie's departure for California which was a cause for Mr. Safford to be brought in. "Her departure had left a hole in the organization," said Safford, looking back many years later. She had left even "before they got Bogel." Mr. Bogel was technically the navy's first cryptanalyst of record. "He'd been with the Army in World War I, and then later in an Army unit in New York City—Yardley's 'Black Chamber'—until 1923, when he was relieved due to shortage of funds; then the Navy picked him up." However, continued Safford, "Even with Bogel, the Navy decided not to rely on a civilian expert, but to get a

---

Ignored were the ethics of having obtained Hebern's best developmental efforts on the implied promise of large production contracts, which were awarded instead to the Teletype Corporation." In 1958 the government settled for the tiny sum of $30,000. "Hebern's contribution was worth . . . $1,000,000 at the least. Hebern deserved better. His story, tragic, unjust, and pathetic, does his country no honor." See Kahn, *Codebreakers*, 415–20.

commissioned officer to undertake the study—a person who could not go anywhere unless the Navy wanted to release him."

Shortly after Safford assumed control of the Research Desk, in 1925 Mrs. Driscoll was brought back into the group. Initially she taught Mr. Safford the science—and art—of cryptology. Then, for the next fifteen-plus years, Safford and Driscoll (joined with a succession of talented and dedicated colleagues) built up and honed OP-20-GX (it became "GY" in 1934): Office of the CNO, 20th Division of the Office of Naval Communications, G Section-Communications Security, X-Research Desk.[3] In this position "the enigmatic but brilliant" Miss Aggie, according to future Rear Admiral Edwin **Layton**, "not only trained most of the leading naval cryptanalysts of World War II, but they were all agreed that none exceeded her gifted accomplishments in the business." In fact, during the 1920s and 1930s, she taught an entire generation of navy cryptanalysts the business—cryptologists whose future contributions would influence the outcome of World War II in the Pacific. It's interesting to note that in 1925 she was a civil service CF-5 "clerk," making $1,860 per annum, and that Safford immediately recommended that she be reclassified to grade P-1-4, and raised to $2,400 per annum.

Lt. j.g. Joseph J. **Rochefort**, who in September 1925 arrived at OP-20-GX to learn cryptanalysis, certainly agreed with this assessment and years later even likened her to the iconic William Freidman, whose cryptanalytic skills, Rochefort thought, were incomparable. "There was considerable competition between her and Friedman—considerable competition."

In 1967, Ladislas Farago, a former wartime ONI section chief and later a bestselling military historian, wrote that

> among the experts Safford had . . . was a young woman, the daughter of a great patrician family whose name she bore but from whom she was separated by her compulsive love affair with cryptography. She was close to being the perfect cryptanalyst. She had what is called a "cipher brain," that unique quality of mind and sixth sense which go into the making of great cryptologists.[4]

In the early days, Mr. Safford organized the intercept and analytic efforts, while Miss Aggie provided the cryptanalytic and technical base for the navy's main communications intelligence program (Safford came and went, leaving the office and returning every few years for tours of required sea duty). Like Mr. Yardley's "Black Chamber," and later the army's codebreaking organizations, the navy concentrated on Japanese communications. This emphasis on Tokyo's communications originated in the high volume availability of Japanese message traffic, as well as a general feeling

---

3. Capt. Jasper Holmes wrote that "in 1925, Joseph Rochefort, Laurance Safford, and Agnes Driscoll were the whole of the Navy's code-breaking crew."

4. Without doubt, Mrs. Driscoll clearly is one of the people affected with a lifelong case of "*cryptographitis*" as defined by French Colonel Étienne Bazèries. It's interesting to note that Mr. Farago, as late as 1967, felt legally, morally, and ethically bound to *not* fully identify her in his book about Pearl Harbor—at all times simply calling her "Miss Aggie."

in government that real potential existed for future conflict between Japan and the United States—over China, colonies, influence, and trade.

The first break for the Research Desk was the exploitation of the Japanese Navy's current operational code, known as the *Red Book* (for the color of the binders in which the Research Desk organized the material). Actually, the Americans first got a handle on the code back in 1920, when ONI agents broke into the Japanese consulate in New York, cracked the safe, took photographs of pages of the codebook, and left—having put everything back as they had found it.[5] This "black-bag" job did not give the Research Desk everything on a silver platter, however. When she finally got tasked to work on the book, Mrs. Driscoll's problem was to recover the cipher systems used to encrypt the code groups—but it was a problem she solved. "It was Miss Aggie who was responsible for the initial solutions," wrote Layton years later, agreeing with a similar comment from Safford:

> This was no small achievement, because the two-volume *Red Book* contained some 100,000 code groups, with as many as three groups assigned to each Japanese word or expression. The Japanese instructions for the code stated that it was never to be used without super-encipherment.

Joe Rochefort also concurred with his colleagues: "She was mostly responsible for the first one we solved. . . . She deserves all the credit for that."

At first, the Japanese used relatively simple additive or transposition systems, but within a few years a dozen systems were being used with multiple keys. Unfortunately, very few of the decrypted messages were translated because the Research Desk (in fact the entire Naval Communications directorate) lacked Japanese translation ability. Indeed, even the ONI essentially had only one at Main Navy—Emerson J. Haworth, assisted by his stenographer wife; Dr. Haworth was a retired Japanese linguist, having formerly been a Quaker missionary and professor at Tokyo University.[6]

The *Red Book* breakthrough paid off in 1930 during the Imperial Japanese Navy's Grand Fleet Maneuvers. OP-20-G's analysis of the exercise indicated that Tokyo—alarmingly—had developed a good insight into American naval planning, specifically *U.S. War Plan Orange*, which called for U.S. Pacific Fleet operations near the Japanese home islands. Critical to this achievement was Mrs. Driscoll's cryptanalysis. For the maneuvers the Japanese made some extra coding efforts; nevertheless, she was soon able to exploit the system. Safford later wrote that

> the Japanese introduced a new cipher system for these maneuvers plus a daily change of key—but used the *good old "Red Book."* All hands turned-to on these messages; Mrs. Driscoll got the first break as usual, and the various daily keys were solved without too much effort.

---

5. The perpetrators were the district intelligence officer, a couple of ONI "gumshoes," a break-and-enter expert, and a locksmith/safecracker.

6. Regarding this period, it's fair to say that Naval Communications had the cryptanalysts, while Naval Intelligence had the linguists.

In this, and then in later system attacks, Miss Aggie would solve the ciphers and the first keys. Then the subsequent keys were given to a series of officers passing through the Research Desk for training—often under her supervision.

The importance of this feat of Miss Aggie and her associates can hardly be overstated. The solution was a tremendous achievement for "the Navy's entire cryptological effort, and it was especially . . . gratifying that it came so early in the game." Her unraveling of the code, and the input from traffic analysis by the U.S. naval listening station on Guam really—and probably for the first time—gained the attention of the higher leadership in the U.S. Navy. As Farago would remark, "The Research Desk became respectable overnight. Its value was recognized all the way up to the Chief of Naval Operations. Its continued existence was assured."

The section could actually only decipher a fraction of the intercepted messages available. However, through their efforts, the U.S. Navy was able to track the Imperial Navy in many day-to-day operations, its technological advancements, and to a degree observe its fledgling aviation arm.

Looking back from the perspective of 1943, Captain Safford would write that

> the work of solving these cipher systems and decrypting the messages was one of the most interesting duties ever undertaken by the section. We were literally exploring virgin territory. No one in the U.S. Navy had the slightest idea as to the professional concepts of the Japanese Navy.

And these professional concepts certainly included communications routines and even battle tactics.

In December 1930, the Japanese navy went to a new code which in due course became known as the "*Blue Book.*" This system entailed over 85,000 code groups that were further enciphered. The immense difficulty in breaking the *Blue Book* was that both the cipher and the code groups had to be recovered simultaneously. Layton later wrote that "the assault on *Blue* was led by Mrs. Driscoll, to whom it was an article of faith that any man-made code could be broken by a woman." There were no cribs or translations available this time; there was no ONI black-bag job at any Japanese consulate to provide any boilerplate information. Thus, according to Layton, "the *Blue* solution was a test," similar to a "wartime situation." Indeed,

> Miss Aggie and the OP-20-G team had "to work out their own salvation" by compiling the new code from scratch. The code groups had to be solved individually, one at a time. These were, and were then entered in the *Blue Book* [again, named for the color of its binding] with solutions added by hand in both Japanese characters (*kanji*) and English translations.

Layton later added that "no other codebreakers had ever achieved such a breakthrough. This was the greatest challenge and success in the unostentatious but spectacular career of Mrs. Driscoll."

Critical to Miss Aggie's breakthrough was her insight into the difference in the groupings of the code values. "She was the first to spot that a new code had been instituted," Layton continued.

This occurred in the fall of 1931, six months after Lt. j.g. Tommy **Dyer** . . . had joined OP-20-G as a trainee to work on solutions to the old *Red Code.* He was not making very fast progress the day that Mrs. Driscoll looked over his shoulder, took a work sheet from his hand, and remarked, "the reason you're not getting anywhere is because this is a new code." The *Red Book* was a three-*kana* system, and she recognized through her uncanny grasp of cryptology that the piece Dyer was working on had to be a four-*kana* system. Even with this discovery, it was slow, painful, laborious work before the code was broken.

One interesting piece of resulting intelligence concerned the postmodernization trials of the battleship *Nagato.* In particular it was noted that her new top speed was now 26 knots, which alarmed U.S. Navy leadership because this was greater than the top speed planned for the new U.S. battleships *Washington* and *North Carolina.* As a direct result of this intelligence, the navy raised the design requirements to 28 knots. Layton also observed that

> Lt. Joseph **Wenger** . . . discovered that Remington-Rand had just produced punch-card equipment that could handle alphabetic information, but investigation showed that it did not fill our requirements. It was Dyer, however, who after five months of pencil-pushing drudgery, came up with an ingenious labor-saving solution. He found a way to use IBM tabulating machines to ease the burden of sifting through the myriad possible solutions of the code group.

Thus, Miss Aggie's success was also important since this effort might well be the first time that state-of-the-art "tabulating machines" were used to keep track of cipher and code groups. The tabulating machinery was beginning to be a practical necessity. Cracking codes and ciphers was extremely difficult even for a top expert; thus, such machines were needed to help keep track of almost 85,000 code groups and cipher keys. "After ten years of pencil-pushing," Layton later commented,

> Mrs. Driscoll was initially unenthusiastic about having her task mechanized until the breakthrough into the Japanese Navy's *Blue* system came in September 1931 after she had worked out the key to the cipher's principal transposition . . . The use of the IBM tabulating machine made it easier to keep track of changing cipher keys and speeded up penetration of new systems.

In regard to Miss Aggie appearing to be slow to embrace machines, it's fair to say that her hesitation wasn't entirely due to merely a resistance to change. There were some essential steps in breaking a code, especially an enciphered code-book system such as the Japanese naval codes, which depended more on feel and insight than anything mechanical. "Others at OP-20-G may have taken the lead in making use of the tabulators, but Driscoll's analytical acumen and doggedness eventually broke the code." The *old guard,* such as Safford and Driscoll, had many years of experience under their belts, which had "taught them that cracking a code or cipher usually depended on the lightning strike of human intuition or some unpredictable entry into the system."[7]

In February 1933, Lieutenant Layton arrived at OP-20-G for a brief tour (leaving only four months later to become "captain" of a main turret on board the battleship *Pennsylvania*). He had already completed ONI's full three-year program of language and culture immersion in Japan. "I came to appreciate the magnitude of the contribution being made to our codebreaking effort by Mrs. Driscoll." Moreover,

I had been warned not to patronize Madam "X," as her colleagues sometimes referred to her, because she was sensitive to her role as a woman in a man's world. Because of this she kept to herself as much as possible and none of us were ever invited to socialize with her and her lawyer husband. While she could be warm and friendly, she usually affected an air of intense detachment, which was heightened by her tailored clothes and shunning of makeup. It was surprising to hear Miss Aggie curse, which she frequently did—as fluently as any sailor whom I have ever heard.

Eddie Layton's first real encounter with Miss Aggie occurred one day when she brought him a

large piece of graph paper and, not being a Japanese linguist, she asked, "Lieutenant Layton, does this make any sense?" She had marked the paper with zigzag staircases of letters in different colors of ink. She traced out a zigzag, and I told her it made sense—it could be a Japanese name, "Tomimura." When she shook her head, I suggested that the "mura," which means "town," has an alternate meaning of "son," so it might also be rendered Tomison or Thompson.

Somewhat later, Miss Aggie told Layton, "Lieutenant, I want to thank you. You helped me solve part of a cipher that's been bothering me for a long time. The name *is* Thompson." As it turned out, this name—intercepted in Japanese foreign office traffic—was identified as a former Pacific Fleet radioman; he was turning over navy engineering and gunnery information to the Japanese. Arrested and convicted in 1936 (the top secret cryptologic aspect was *not* exposed in court), he was sent to prison for violating federal espionage laws.

In 1935, Lt. j.g. Jack S. **Holtwick** had completed the Research Desk cryptanalyst course of instruction and took over—from Lt. Wesley A. "Ham" **Wright**—a task of systematically collecting and codifying the known but unrecorded data the section

---

7. In 1969, Rear Adm. Joseph Wenger recalled that, back in September 1930, "Mr. Safford and Miss Meyer discussed the idea at some length and expressed considerable doubt about the feasibility of using machines to perform what they regarded as the unpredictable nature and the variety of processes involved in cipher solution. As a result of the discussion, a [memo] to Captain Hooper [the DNC] was written, expressing in effect their appreciation of the desirability of having automatic machinery to perform cryptanalytic chores, but indicating skepticism as to the feasibility of the idea." But by 1931, they had become more interested.

had on ten years' worth of Japanese cryptologic systems. Holtwick later wrote that because of the tremendous workload—and low staffing levels—little time was spent

in maintaining a record of what had been done. Details of what had been solved, how they were solved, and what part each system played in the entire Japanese naval crypto-graphic system were available, if at all, only in the memory of Mrs. Driscoll. Fortunately, though, material . . . had accumulated over the years in a sort of "Fibber McGee's closet" in Room 1645, where odds-and-ends of incredible variety could be unearthed.

Lieutenant Wright had realized . . . the danger of having the entire background and continuity of a decade of effort available only in the brain cells of only one person. [His foreboding was forcefully proved warranted less than three years later when Mrs. Driscoll was seriously injured in an automobile accident in which two others were killed.]

Wright therefore set out systematically to identify each Japanese system of which we had any record, and to write a monograph containing all of the information he was able to accrue about it. . . . Holtwick, who took over this task on Wright's transfer, drew heav-ily upon Mrs. Driscoll's memory, and validated her recollections by actual application of the cryptographic details she remembered to the traffic stored in the closet. He was thus able to bring up to date and continue Wright's project of publishing a complete history of each type of system which the Japanese Navy and Foreign Office had used up to that time.

Miss Aggie's cryptanalytic successes were not limited just to paper codes and ciphers—which is to say manual systems. She never gave up her paper and pencil, but she was certainly involved in the introduction of early machine support against Japanese naval code systems—which was being applied to both making and break-ing ciphers. Toward the beginning of 1935, she led the attack on one of Japan's early machine cipher systems—the M-1, or ORANGE machine (not to be confused with the U.S. *War Plan Orange*), used to encrypt the messages of Japanese naval attachés around the world. This machine was derived from earlier ones such as those devel-oped for Germany by Alexander von Kryha, or those, mentioned earlier, by Edward Hebern. In this case, Mrs. Driscoll developed a manual method of decryption which used a diagram on cross-section paper against which she slid the recovered cipher sequence. This was a major accomplishment, which gave her and her associates "the confidence to tackle more sophisticated mechanical ciphers" including, ultimately, the German naval ENIGMA. As World War II approached, ciphers were more and more being generated by mechanical or machine methodology, but codes continued to be generally distributed in book form.

This M-1 breakthrough, however, led to a pair of issues. The first of these involved a dispute with some cryptanalysts in the army's codebreaking unit, the SIS. A group under Frank Rowlett had been working on the Japanese Foreign Ministry's cipher de-vice known as the RED machine—very similar to the ORANGE machine. Rowlett's breakthrough on RED came at about the same time as Mrs. Driscoll's breakthrough with ORANGE. Later on, some navy partisans would claim that the SIS had ben-efited from technical information provided by OP-20-G. The army team denied this and claimed they had received no help from the navy. The controversy was impossible to settle. At times the service cryptologic units were extremely reluctant to share any information with each other, and in any event technical exchanges often were made with one side not knowing upon what the other was working.

The second issue, for the navy, stemmed from its internal interpretation of Japanese naval cryptologic trends. The success against the ORANGE machine convinced some of the people in OP-20-G that the future was going to be dominated by machine systems. Anticipating this, the leadership assigned one of Miss Aggie's current associates, the previously mentioned Lieutenant Holtwick, to work on an analog device to replicate the ORANGE machine and possible future modifications. Building upon her work, and with great ingenuity of his own, he actually was able to do this, and his machine worked well enough to decrypt the cipher until the Japanese Navy discontinued its use around 1938.[8] As it turned out, however, the Japanese Navy remained wedded to paper codes and ciphers. The only other code machine it produced was the 1940 successor to the ORANGE machine, codenamed CORAL by the Americans; in fact, except for a few new machine systems—notably PURPLE, JADE, and GREEN—Japanese Empire cryptology used mostly manual paper systems.

Miss Aggie, at times, paid a price regarding her health as she fought these battles—a common thing for cryptanalysts, including such luminaries as William Friedman, Joseph Rochefort, Joseph Wenger, Joseph Desch, and a number of others. She faced periodic bouts of weight loss, and occasionally vacationed with her family in Westerville, Ohio, where the slower pace of life helped her rebuild her stamina. For a codebreaker, cryptanalysis was often a race between a solution and the individual's endurance.

Moreover, in 1937, Mrs. Driscoll was involved in a serious traffic accident in which two people were killed and she was seriously injured. Her jaw and leg were broken, and it took more than a year of convalescence (in which her leg never properly healed, bowing significantly outward; she was forced to walk with a cane and a very noticeable limp for the rest of her life) before she returned to OP-20-G. She was deeply religious, having become a Christian Scientist, and because of that had declined meaningful medical treatment. Some observers claimed that, upon her return, she appeared to have undergone a personality change in addition to her physical injuries; but this observation was disputed by other members of OP-20-G as well as her family. Commander Safford even mentioned the situation in a formal 1938 memo, stating that "Mrs. Driscoll is back on active duty once more and is herself in every respect."

Regardless, now her challenge was going to be the breaking of the new Japanese naval general-purpose operational code—JN-25. In June 1939, the Japanese Navy introduced this new code.[9] It was an extremely complicated system: it involved three

---

8. See the sections on Captain Jack Holtwick and Rear Adm. Ellis Zacharias for more information on this event.

9. "JN-25" was the name given by Allied codebreakers to the chief, and most secure, command-and-control communications scheme used by the Imperial Japanese Navy during World War II. It was the

separate codebooks, a three-hundred-page book of random additives, and an instruction book. The original codebook, designated the "A" by OP-20-G, contained over thirty thousand five-digit groups that represented numbers, place-names, and other meanings. A key characteristic was a self-check system for groups: when all of the digits of a group were added, the total was divisible by three. By late 1940, after a little over a year of work, good progress and some critical inroads had been made. A few thousand of the additive groups had been stripped away, and over five hundred of the code groups themselves had been recovered. At this point the navy could read some standard-format messages—such as weather reports—but the bulk of the messages remained to be discovered. Still, with the navy's best codebreaker leading the attack, there was every hope for rapid further successes. Indeed, by fall 1940, Mrs. Driscoll and her little group had solved the logic of the system, even though only a fraction was actually readable.

However, in October, Miss Aggie was moved off the JN-25 problem and assigned a small team to work against German systems, to particularly include the naval ENIGMA machine. The first two paragraphs of an OP-20-G memo—to the Director of Naval Communications—shows some insight into this new OP-20-GY division of work.

> Since November 1939, Mrs. Driscoll has been engaged in cryptanalytical attack on the current Orange Navy Operations code system [JN-25]. This attack has now progressed to the point where it can be pursued by others. Accordingly, it has been turned over to Lieutenant Bayley. He will be assisted by Lieutenant Chisholm full time, and by Lieutenant **Lietwiler** and Lieutenant Brotherhood for instruction. CRM **McGregor** and Y1C **Pelletier** will handle the actual code recovery, and two cryptographic clerks complete the group.
>
> Mrs. Driscoll, with two assistants, has begun an attack on the German Navy systems. Heretofore, they have resisted attack, but it is hoped that the employment of our best talent will produce results.

As it turned out, this and other curious moves, partially the result of a division in policy within OP-20-G, did not really benefit the attack on the German systems. Having said that—considering their lack of resources—they amazingly came very close to understanding how the naval ENIGMA worked without knowing enough to actually begin decryption. The move certainly weakened the effort against JN-25—though other talented codebreakers (many her former pupils) in Washington and in the Pacific theater would be able to exploit the code to great advantage *after* the U.S. entry into the war. Significantly, the move from working against JN-25 to the German ENIGMA also signaled the end of Agnes Driscoll's incredible string of

---

twenty-fifth Japanese Navy system identified. Introduced in 1939 to replace "Blue," it was an enciphered code, producing five-numeral groups for transmission. New code books or new super-enciphering books were introduced from time to time, each new version requiring a more-or-less fresh cryptanalytic attack. In particular, JN-25 was significantly changed on December 1, 1940, and again on December 4, 1941—just days before the attack on Pearl Harbor.

cryptanalytic successes for the U.S. Navy; she never again would match her accomplishments during the interwar period. As an aside, in 1941 she seems to have been classified as a civil service P-5, making around $4,400 per year.

When moving her to the German problem, neither she, Safford, nor the navy in general

> realized that it had asked her to defeat one of the most advanced encryption machines of the time. The 1940s naval ENIGMA was a *far* more difficult target than earlier versions of the device, and the German Navy was an even *more* cautious crypto-foe than that nation's army, air force, or intelligence agencies.

Ignorant of its own ignorance, OP-20-G began a "catalog attack"—the mainstay of Western codebreakers at the time—because it was logical and obvious, even if terribly labor intensive. Working with insufficient funding, personnel, and equipment, there wasn't much else they could do. "Driscoll and Safford seemed to have been cozily optimistic and dangerously ignorant about the ability of their small . . . crew to conquer the intricacies of the ENIGMA."

Two years into fighting against the Germans, the British were very well aware of this challenge and at least to an extent were willing to share some information. Accordingly, in August 1941 the head of the British codebreaking center at Bletcheley Park, Cmdr. Alastair G. Denniston, came to Washington to see Commander Safford and Mrs. Driscoll. Even though the United States was not yet at war, there had been some communications between British and American codebreaking operations—but up to this point it had only resulted in misunderstanding and tension. Denniston hoped to "smooth over the conflicts so far [and] to coordinate, appease, and control the Americans"—both U.S. Navy and U.S. Army.

However, at this meeting, Miss Aggie and Commander Safford surprised Commander Denniston by their disinterest in Britain's automated cryptologic attacks against the ENIGMA. They didn't think they needed or even wanted a British "bombe" (a complex, one-ton electro-mechanical "pre-computer" which aided cryptanalysis), nor was Mrs. Driscoll very interested in the statistical technique used by the machine. While admitting that she was currently somewhat "stumped" to fully understand the ENIGMA, she told Denniston that she thought she'd developed a nonmachine method which was probably better than the British, and that for health reasons she didn't care to accept his invitation to come to England—nor did she care to nominate anyone else in her stead.

This may have been a blunder on the part of OP-20-G, if Commander Denniston really were ready to share meaningful information; however, deeply fearful about the perceived lack of American security awareness, at this point the British weren't ready to reveal much. At age fifty-three, with a string of great successes behind her, Miss Aggie may have been overconfident and even inflexible. She may have shared in the prevailing U.S. Navy distrust of the Royal Navy and British Intelligence inherited from World War I experience (also shared, at this time, by her superiors Commander Safford and Rear Adm. Leigh Noyes) and particularly fueled by any signs of being played or treated as a very junior partner in the relationship. Or, it may be the result of too many years of isolation and restricted budgets at OP-20-G, which meant that Naval Communications had not seen very many bright, young, and well-trained people added to staff, "people who could stimulate new ideas and new methods—the way Agnes Driscoll had been able to do decades before." And it probably occurred to her that millions of dollars invested in bombes (even *if* any such funding could be found for OP-20-G) could be wasted overnight if the Germans significantly revamped the ENIGMA system.

In the spring of 1943 Miss Aggie was transferred back from the ENIGMA problem. Her attack had not been successful, although it's fair to say that later her technique did find "an important niche in OP-20-G's codebreaking operations—but it proved useful only after the harder work had been done by the bombes." *That* piece came about with leadership shake-ups at both OP-20-G and at Bletcheley Park, and only after the British and Americans forged close ties, with extensive cryptologic exchanges, to meet the incredible 1942–1943 challenges of the U-boat war.

Mrs. Driscoll now began work on the Japanese military attaché machine, known as CORAL. This system succumbed to cryptanalysis two months later, but it's unlikely that she decisively influenced the outcome. She and her assistants compiled mountains of statistics trying to understand the machine, but it took welcome help from another OP-20-G team (headed by Francis A. Raven) and some assistance from Bletcheley Park to complete the job.

Miss Aggie then appears to have moved into a machine support division—GM— within OP-20-G, and then in April 1944 she transferred to the Russian Language Section (OP-20-G-50), heading up a small machine support group. She had long since become a proponent of machines; even back in November 1941 she was one of three ONC people working with Commander Safford, and four scientists from MIT, concerning the design and manufacture of high-speed analytical machinery for the Communications Security Section. After months of frustration grappling with the ENIGMA, she was now more open-minded about automated help.

Mrs. Driscoll's activities are a little unclear for the next few years, but it seems she continued to work with Russian traffic in various ways. There's an amusing story from this period wherein Miss Aggie tangled with a gung-ho junior officer. The officious young man barged into her office and declared, "Ma'am, in this section [of her security clearance renewal paperwork] where you are required to list five references, you've listed the names of five *admirals*. You're supposed to list names of people who know you!" She is said to have looked him in the eye and replied, "Sonny, I knew all of them when they were ensigns and lieutenants, and if *you* don't straighten up, I'm going to tell them to never promote you."

In 1949, the Armed Forces Security Agency was formed, and both the army and navy transferred a number of their veterans over to the fledgling organization—one of whom was Agnes Driscoll. She moved through a series of offices, mostly special research areas, winding up in the Technical Consulting Group. Ironically, this group was led by Frank Raven, who years earlier had worked for her.

In 1952, when the NSA was formed, she was transferred to its Technical Projects/Services Group, which was an adjunct research office for operations. In 1954 she moved to the Pacific Division; there she developed some machine support for analysts working communications targets in Asia. In 1956 she was among the first contingents to move to NSA's new location at Fort Meade, Maryland. However, within a year, at age sixty-eight, she retired. Sadly, her retirement was not particularly noticed by the agency. By 1967 she was living with a sister in an apartment in northwest Washington, and her health had deteriorated to the point where she could hardly walk. She passed away in 1971—an event which also was overlooked by the agency. She was buried next to her husband at Arlington National Cemetery; he had been a World War I infantry captain who had died in 1964. (Her headstone is a typical one for a spouse in a national cemetery; lamentably, it conveys nothing of *her* lifetime of important national defense service: "His Wife / Agnes M / July 24, 1889–September 16, 1971.")

After considerable research for several biographical studies about Miss Aggie, NSA senior historian Robert J. Hanyok made this comment:

> For all her accomplishments, we really don't know much of anything about Agnes Driscoll, the person. She left no writings, not even technical reports; most of her knowledge and experience was preserved by officers determined to catalogue her accomplishments. Her private life remains a mystery, as well. Beyond that, there is virtually nothing. Many of her contemporaries can recall her cryptanalytic exploits, but no one seems to know anything about her personal life.

Always pleasant to others, she guarded her private life and remained something of a social recluse. For her entire career she figuratively avoided the spotlight and only allowed herself to be photographed on rare occasions. Moreover, even on the professional side, she left very little in the way of records concerning her cryptanalytic methods. The histories and technical documents produced by her associates essentially are the only sources, and these are often lacking in detail. Even what little we know is occasionally subject to dispute, as one sees when cross-checking one source against another.

Capt. Joe Rochefort, in a 1969 interview, said this: "I'll always remember that she used to turn the pages of a book or dictionary . . . with the rubber end of a pencil, always flipping over pages in the upper right-hand corner. She was very quiet. She was a first-class cryptanalyst . . . very talented—awfully good." Perhaps with some embarrassment he added, "I don't know where she is now." By 1970 Capt. Laurance Safford had also lost track of the woman with whom he worked for almost twenty years, and who he rated as "the principal cryptanalyst of the Navy for many, many years."

Mrs. Driscoll certainly commanded the respect of master cryptanalyst Capt. Tommy Dyer, who in 1983 speculated that her achievements weren't always fully recognized by the navy, perhaps because the navy might be "rather guilty of maybe male chauvinism." He thought that in addition to some general prejudice against all codebreakers, Miss Aggie's case was

> doubly compounded by the fact that she was a female. She was never given the status by the Navy that William Friedman was given by the Army. Certainly in the 1920s and early 1930s *she was fully his equal.* In the long term of history, I'd be hard-put to say that one was better than the other.

Writing in 2011, distinguished naval historian Craig Symonds wrote that

> in the interest of accuracy—not to mention fairness—it's important to note that one of the prime movers of [Navy cryptology] was Agnes Driscoll, who began working in the Code and Signal Section when Laurance Safford did in 1924. . . . She all but invented the science of cryptanalysis, and trained most of the [Navy] men who later played such a crucial role in American codebreaking.

But it's Rear Adm. Eddie Layton who's given, perhaps, the best summary of Miss Aggie's remarkable significance.

> In the Navy she was without peer as a cryptanalyst. Some of her pupils—like Wesley "Ham" Wright—were more able mathematicians, but she had taught cryptanalysis to all of them, and none ever questioned her superb talent and determination in breaking codes and ciphers. She understood machines and how to apply them—but her principal talent was her ability to get to the root of a problem, sort out its essential components, and find a way to solve it.
>
> Among her uniformed naval colleagues, she was held in the highest esteem through-out her long career, which continued from the Office of Naval Communications, to the Armed Forces Security Agency, and then to the National Security Agency.

Like her boss of so many years, Laurance Safford, she was a remarkable leader and forerunner in cryptanalysis, although—similar to Safford—she never really took the lead in pushing into highly automated cryptography. But—once again like Safford—she was totally dedicated to the country's (and the navy's) vital stake in the business, sensitive to OP-20-G's important place in that secret world.

It's good to report that Mrs. Driscoll did receive some belated, formal recognition. She has been designated a Pioneer Officer of U.S. Naval Cryptology by the U.S. Naval Cryptologic Veterans Association. Moreover, she was inducted into the NSA's official Hall of Honor in 2000.

She even was portrayed by actress Meg Brogan in the 2009 movie *The Red Machine*, which is indeed about U.S. naval intelligence and codebreaking, circa 1935. Interestingly, Brogan's "Agnes Driscoll" appears to be the single accurately-named real historical figure in the entire film.

Sources

A number of sources were key to this chapter; however, I'm particularly indebted to the work of NSA historian Robert J. Hanyok for considerable information and text.

Agnes Meyer Driscoll. Citation, NSA Cryptologic Hall of Honor.
Budiansky, 216.
Burke, 27.
Carlson, 37, 38, 41.
DeBrosse and Burke, xxix, 13, 23–53, 65, 68, 175–76.
Donovan and Mack, 58–60, 62–63, 115, 141, 147, 202, 204, 232.
Dyer, 126, 296.
Farago, *Broken Seal*, 45–46.
Hanyok, *Madame X: Agnes in Twilight.*
Hanyok, *Madame X: Agnes Meyer Driscoll.*
Hanyok, *Still Desperately Seeking "Miss Agnes."*
Holtwick, *History of the Naval Security Group*, 28, 29, 43, 80–81, 159–60, 309, 400, 439, 440.
Kahn, *Codebreakers*, 417–18.
Kahn, *Discovered*, 29, 31, 39.
Layton, *"And I Was There,"* 33–35, 45, 46, 58, 59, 79, 495.
Lujan, 50.
Pioneers in U.S. Cryptology, 13.
Rochefort, 30–31, 40.
Safford, *Interview with Captain L. F. Safford*, App. 210–14.
Symonds, 135.

CAPTAIN THOMAS "TOMMY" HAROLD DYER, U.S. NAVY (1902–1985)

The "father of machine cryptanalysis"
The navy's foremost officer cryptanalyst
One of Rochefort's core group at Station HYPO
"Tommy"

Alternately called "a consummate individualist," the "ultimate professional," and "a wizard at mathematics," Tommy Dyer had a mild and friendly personality combined with a tough and unrelenting mind. As a young man, new to the business, he developed procedures for using IBM tabulators to ease the burden of sorting through the myriad of possible solutions for breaking codes and ciphers. Later, as the lead crypt-analyst at Station HYPO in Hawaii from 1936 to 1945, Dyer led the team that was responsible for most of the breakthroughs in reading Japanese naval communications during the war in the Pacific. After the war he continued a brilliant career and went on to be one of the three primary cryptanalytic trainers for both the Armed Forces Security Agency and the NSA.

*   *   *

From the 1924 Annapolis yearbook, *The Lucky Bag*:

> On the whole, *Tommy* is a great worker, and we are sure will take on his youthful shoulders whatever ship is important enough for him to be assigned to. [Activities: *Masqueraders* (the drama club); Assistant Manager, *Lucky Bag*; Radiator Club (snack-bar club of non-athletes)]

*   *   *

Born in Osawatomie, Kansas, on May 23, 1902, Thomas Harold Dyer was the son of Thomas Henry and Belle Jamison Dyer. He attended the Manual Training High School in Kansas City and then entered the Naval Academy in 1921. Dyer graduated in 1924 along with such distinguished classmates as Edwin T. **Layton**, Thomas A. **Huckins**, Ethelbert **Watts**, Daniel J. McCallum, John C. Waldron, and Hanson W. Baldwin. Both Dyer and Layton were in the "Radiator Club" at An-napolis, a group of nonathletes who "sat on warm radiators on chilly days swapping stories." After graduation, future promotions included lieutenant (junior grade), 1927; lieutenant, 1932; lieutenant commander, 1939; commander, 1942; and cap-tain, 1943. He retired from the navy in 1955.

Leaving Annapolis, Ensign Dyer went directly to sea in the typical fashion for junior officers. From July 1924 through February 1925 he served as the assistant radio officer on board the battleship *New Mexico*. During this tour he began doing cryptograms found in the periodic *Naval Communications Bulletins* which very much intrigued him (of course, that was the whole idea; the cryptograms were put there by the "Research Desk" of the Office of Naval Communications in an attempt to attract officers with potential for cryptanalytic training). Dyer also read the groundbreaking book of early American cryptanalyst William Friedman, *The Elements of Cryptanaly-sis*—which apparently hooked him on the subject.

From February 1925 through April 1926, Mr. Dyer was assigned as the assistant communications officer of Battleship Division Four. Then, for three months, he worked as anti-aircraft control officer on board the *New Mexico*, and then briefly was a student at the Submarine School in New London, Connecticut. He next was sent to the cargo ship *Antares* as a watch and division officer, serving from August 1926 through spring 1927.

Then, from June through September, Mr. Dyer was present at the Office of Naval Communications, at the Main Navy building in Washington, to take their special "communications course"—reporting in to Lt. Joseph J. **Rochefort**. At that time, Rochefort was

> the officer in charge of what was known . . . as OP-20-GX. "20-G" embraced all of the things having to do with secret communications, registered publications, code compila-tion, and the signal book. "X" was the so-called "Research Desk." There were two other [students], Lt. j.g. Thomas **Birtley** and Lt. j.g. Frank Bond.

Unusually, Birtley was almost immediately selected, by the ONI, for transfer to Tokyo as an immersion language student. Lt. j.g. Dyer had very limited contact with Lieutenant Rochefort at this time as Rochefort had many other duties other than working with students; however, he did get to know the office's chief cryptanalyst Miss Aggie (Agnes Meyer **Driscoll**)—as well as her assistant, a former actor named Klaus Bogel.

Upon completion of the cryptanalysis course Tommy went back to sea. From October 1927 through May 1928 he was assistant communications officer, Battle-ship Divisions of the Battle Fleet, on board the USS *West Virginia*. From May 1928 through May 1929 he continued as a communications officer on the Battle Fleet Staff—on board the battleship *California*. Early in 1929, Lieutenant Rochefort transferred to the *California*, joining up with Lt. j.g. Dyer. They worked radio intel-ligence together in U.S. Fleet Problem IX along with Lt. Cmdr. Laurance **Safford**. They comprised the Battle Fleet's radio intelligence unit which succeeded in reading all the intercepted traffic of the opposing force and made considerable progress in solving the signal cipher. "We solved every key change that they had and read every message that we were able to intercept." As a result, the outcome of the problem was greatly influenced by the gained intelligence.

From August 1929 to May 1930, Mr. Dyer served as an assistant communications officer on the staff of the U.S. Fleet. Then, for two months, he worked as the first lieutenant of the destroyer *Pruitt*; subsequently he transferred to the destroyer *Badger* as communications and commissary officer—from June 1930 through May 1931.

In early 1930, U.S. Fleet Problem X found Tommy Dyer and Lt. j.g. Wesley "Ham" **Wright** together in the Battle Fleet's radio intelligence unit. They had no success in solving the major "enemy" system, which employed some seventy-eight alphabets, because the intercepted traffic was too scanty for a solution to be found in the time available.

In the second exercise of the year, executed in April, Fleet Problem XI saw Lt. j.g. Tom Dyer, Lt. j.g. Tom **Huckins**, and Ens. William Leahy assigned to the commu-nications-intelligence section in the Scouting Fleet. On this occasion they had great success in obtaining solutions of all the ciphers which they attempted.

In November 1930, Lt. Cmdr. John **McClaran** (then head of OP-20-G) wrote that there were only six officers trained and available for cryptanalytical work (less a few others who had other major qualifications such as aviator, submariner, or linguist): Lt. Cmdr. Safford, Ens. Leahy, Lt. j.g. Dyer, Lt. Bern **Anderson**, Lt. Joseph **Wenger**, and Lt. j.g. Huckins. This list was validated again the next year, with the addition of Lieutenant Rochefort (who at times was not included on such lists because he had officially become an ONI Japanese linguist). Of these, Safford, Rochefort, and Anderson were the only ones considered qualified to instruct in cryptanalysis—with Anderson rated below the other two.

Dyer was sent back to the cryptanalytic organization, OP-20-G, in May 1931. There he received further training under Miss Aggie and Lt. Cmdr. Safford. Since 1924, Safford had been the driving force behind the Research Desk, and now had returned once again.

Writing almost fifty years later, retired Rear Adm. Edwin **Layton** discussed the new Japanese "Blue Code," which had appeared in 1931. He said that Miss Aggie

> was the first to spot that a new code had been instituted. This occurred in the fall of 1931, six months after Tommy Dyer . . . had joined OP-20-G as a trainee to work on solutions to the old "Red Code." He was not making very fast progress the day that Mrs. Driscoll looked over his shoulder, took a work sheet from his hand, and remarked, "The reason you're not getting anywhere is because this is a new code." The Red Book was a three-*kana* system, and she recognized through her uncanny grasp of cryptology that the piece Dyer was working on had to be a four-*kana* system. Even with this discovery, it was slow, painful, laborious work before the code was broken.[1]

While this work went on, Dyer and Lt. Joseph Wenger—his immediate superior who had recently returned from running the Manila intercept station—looked for ways to improve the situation. Wenger had learned that the Remington-Rand Corporation had just produced punch-card equipment that could handle alphabetic information, "but investigation showed that it did not fill our requirements."

It was Dyer, however, who after "five months of pencil-pushing drudgery, came up with an ingenious labor-saving solution." He found a way to use IBM tabulating machines to ease the burden of sifting through the myriad possible solutions of the code group. This was in the hard times of the Great Depression, but Wenger and Dyer (and Commander McClaran) managed to get the Bureau of Ships to provide $5,000 to rent the necessary IBM equipment. Dyer worked out several cryptanalytic procedures for using the machines and, when they were also able to hire two key-punch operators, things began to look up. Dyer commented, in an interview in the 1980s, that

> in late 1931 we scouted around, discussed various possibilities, and finally discovered that Remington-Rand Corporation had developed a punch-card system that would

---

1. *Kana* are syllabic Japanese scripts, a part of the Japanese writing system contrasted with the logographic Chinese characters known in Japan as *kanji* (漢字). There are three *kana* scripts: modern cursive *hiragana* (ひらがな), modern angular *katakana* (カタカナ), and the old syllabic use of *kanji* known as *man'yōgana* (万葉仮名) that was ancestral to both. *Hentaigana* (変体仮名, "variant *kana*") are historical variants of modern standard *hiragana*. In modern Japanese, *hiragana* and *katakana* have directly corresponding character sets (different sets of characters representing the same sounds).

handle alphabetic information. We investigated that and then discovered that IBM had also developed alphabetic machinery. Because of the difference in underlying principles—Remington Rand was a purely mechanical device and IBM was electrical—IBM had a greater flexibility and would obviously be superior for our purposes.

Somehow (in the depth of the Depression), Commander McClaran succeeded in getting $5,000 for the first year's rental of IBM machines. We installed two key punches, a sorter, and a printing tabulator. Normally, when you install an IBM accounting system, you turn to the company and they give you all kinds of help. We could *not* do that; we didn't want them to know what we were going to do, so I had to design all the operating procedures, the method of punching the cards, and so on.

Eddie Layton later expanded on this.

After ten years of pencil-pushing, Mrs. Driscoll was initially unenthusiastic about having her task mechanized—until the breakthrough into the Japanese Navy's Blue system came in September 1931 after she had worked out the key to the cipher's principal transposition. By then it was clear that, although it was a two-part code unlike the predecessor, it used essentially the same vocabulary and phraseology as the old Red Book. The use of the IBM tabulating machine made it easier to keep track of changing cipher keys and speeded up penetration of new systems. Long before the introduction of computers, the sorting techniques that Dyer devised and pioneered enabled the U.S. to forge ahead of Britain in cryptology; it earned him the accolade "the Father of Machine Cryptanalysis."[2]

Looking back on this from the 1970s, retired Capt. Joe Rochefort gave enormous credit to the young Tom Dyer for this achievement.

Our whole operation [particularly during the war] depended on IBM machines. We were way ahead of anybody else. . . . Dyer [developed] the first installation [of collators and tabulators] that had ever been made. This was Dyer's idea. Without that, we couldn't have done anything. . . . Dyer developed the system, I would say, in the early Thirties. [He had] realized as time goes on we were not going to be able to do this thing *longhand* anymore.

As if he weren't busy enough, as Dyer himself commented, "Somewhere during the late fall or early winter 1931–1932, Lt. Cmdr. Safford went back to sea [on board the heavy cruiser *Portland*], and I became officer in charge of the Research Desk." His boss was the intrepid Commander McClaran. At this time, at the Research Desk, there were essentially just Mr. Dyer, Mrs. Driscoll, and two civil service clerks. Dyer also had a basic administrative charge over the navy's worldwide intercept-operator organization, and he was also in charge of the intercept-operator school on the roof of the Navy Department building. "All in all, I had quite a bit to do." Among other things, protecting U.S. Navy codes

---

2. It wasn't until 1936 that the U.S. Army began using machines for cryptanalysis.

was an assigned function of the Research Desk. A good bit had been done in working to try to develop a satisfactory cipher machine, particularly under Safford. Later, the development of the Electrical Cipher Machine by the Navy was largely under the Research Desk.

Somehow, in October and November 1932, Dyer also found the time and interest to take a language course of twenty lessons in Russian—and he subsequently completed twenty more.

In May 1933, Mr. Dyer was relieved at the Research Desk by Lt. Tom Huckins and then transferred to the battleship *Pennsylvania*; he was shortly followed there by Mr. Layton. According to Layton he was put in charge of Number Four turret, finding Tommy Dyer already there as his friendly rival as captain of Number Three. Then "Ham" Wright showed up in 1936, also transferring from the Research Desk. Finally, Joe Rochefort came on board, accompanying Adm. Joseph M. Reeves when the commander in chief transferred his staff to the *Pennsylvania* and made her his flagship. Layton later wrote that

> this curious coincidence brought together in the same ship the four of us who five years later would find ourselves working alongside each other in the critical months leading up to Pearl Harbor and on through the Battle of Midway. We always looked back on our battleship duty together as an interesting twist of fate. The coincidence was heightened by the fact that *Pennsylvania*'s skipper was Capt. Russell **Willson**, who had been the director of naval communications in World War I.

Unfortunately, during their mutual time on board the *Pennsylvania*, future captain Tommy Dyer had a fractious relationship with the ship's commanding officer, Capt. Russell "Fusser" Willson. Dyer believed that his failure to promote to lieutenant commander (the first time) was due to a poor fitness report from Captain Willson. He had crossed Willson by identifying that the *Pennsylvania*'s previous wardroom treasurer had apparently embezzled $2,000. As it turned out, that officer was indeed court-martialed, found guilty, and dismissed from the service, but Dyer sensed that Willson was clearly angry with *him* for bringing forth the issue—because it reflected poorly upon the ship—and thus upon her captain. Dyer lost further respect for Willson because he believed that Willson had also damaged the career of the ship's outstanding chief engineer (who had recently won the battleship division's "E" for engineering excellence) by inexplicably giving him a poor fitness report—despite the award of the "E."[3]

---

3. During World War I, Willson had invented a new strip form of Thomas Jefferson's coding disk or wheel cylinder, to which he included fixed indices as a super-encipherment system. It was called the Navy Code Box (or Naval Cipher Box), and commonly referred to as the NCB. For the NCB's invention, in 1935 Willson was awarded $15,000 by the U.S. Congress in lieu of a patent. Interestingly, the paperwork for Willson's proposed award passed through various offices in Washington, including OP-20-GX, when young Lieutenant Dyer briefly was officer in charge of the section. For whatever reason, Dyer recommended disapproval. Dyer never knew whether or not Willson was aware of his negative

At the end of 1935, OP-20-G boss John McClaran offered Joe Rochefort the job of OIC for the first decryption unit to be set up at Pearl Harbor—which would involve "pioneer organizing work." McClaran wrote to his old acquaintance that before he "went too far in this matter I should like first to hear from you." But Rochefort declined this opportunity to return to mainstream cryptanalysis, and suggested Tommy Dyer as a better candidate. As it turned out, McClaran did select Dyer, who then detached from the *Pennsylvania* and headed for Hawaii.

Thus, in July 1936, Dyer transferred to the Fourteenth Naval District at Pearl Harbor and there built a communications-intelligence organization essentially from scratch—which soon would be called Station HYPO. Dyer recollected dealing with Lt. Cmdr. Safford, at OP-20-G, rather than with Commander McClaran concerning this move, but no matter. What matters is that during the next nine years his accomplishments in Hawaii were extraordinary.

> When it became apparent that I would be going ashore in the summer of 1936, I corresponded with Laurance Safford. I was looking for a billet other than Washington. He finally suggested that there had been an arrangement between the CNO and the Commandant of the 14th Naval District to set up a unit in Pearl Harbor, and that they would like to have me go out and do that.

Upon arrival, and for many months after, Dyer was assigned a hodge-podge of duties by the district's chief of staff—who wasn't very interested in Dyer's real reason to be there.

> When Dyer arrived in Pearl Harbor early in July 1936, he was at first assigned as temporary relief for the registered publications issuing officer, and the communications officer, for Pearl Harbor. After about a month he was relieved of this duty and assigned by the chief of staff as assistant war plans officer. This was not intended by the chief of staff (Capt. David LeBreton) as a cover, despite the fact that the command had requested a radio intelligence officer. Adm. Harry Yarnell, who was the [district's] commandant, knew nothing of this, and it was not deemed political to go to him over the chief of staff's head.
>
> Consequently Dyer, on his own initiative, informed the chief clerk of the district that he had been assigned as assistant war plans officer and assistant district communications officer, and it was printed thus in the roster. Neither the war plans officer (Cmdr. William Heard), nor the district communications officer (Lt. Cmdr. Gale Poindexter) was ever informed that this dual assignment had not been officially made. They were, however, both informed of the purpose for which Dyer had been sent out by OPNAV—and both cooperated fully.
>
> When Adm. Orin Murfin relieved Admiral Yarnell as commandant, the situation deteriorated still further. While not hostile, Murfin was far from being sympathetic—with the result that Dyer fell heir to a number of conflicting assignments. . . . In addition, Lt. Cmdr. Poindexter had a couple of serious bouts with ulcers which left Dyer as Acting

recommendation, but when the award was finally granted Willson and Dyer were both on board the *Pennsylvania*—and Willson made a great point of showing Dyer the $15,000 check he'd received.

DCO. A third assignment as assistant district intelligence officer was added briefly in the summer of 1938. As a consequence of the above, very little of a constructive nature was accomplished during the first two years.

Intelligence historian John Prados has written that

Station HYPO evolved from . . . a simple direction-finding unit that existed at He'eia. Then Lieutenant Thomas H. Dyer added a codebreaking capability to HYPO while stationed at Pearl Harbor. . . . At the beginning Dyer alone was HYPO; it had none of the omniscience attributed to it later. That began in 1936. By 1938 Dyer had branched off from He'eia to found a processing office at Pearl, with both intercept and direction-finding stations at He'eia and Wahiawa. Nominally part of the 14th Naval District command, Station HYPO actually functioned under orders from OP-20-G, which established the division of labor for U.S. communications intelligence worldwide.

In 1937, after he had been in Hawaii for a year, Tommy was making some headway in obtaining a few machines to assist his cryptanalysis. In August 1938, company representatives installed several IBM machines at HYPO, including two punches with duplication attachments, one sorter, one reproducer, and one printer. Then, in November, OP-20-G assigned the HYPO unit the primary responsibility to work on a new Japanese code, designated "AD." At Pearl, Dyer's staff of one officer and two enlisted men was recognized as insufficient, so OP-20-G planned to increase personnel: Lieutenant Dyer was retained; Lt. Gill **Richardson** and a chief yeoman were sent out immediately; a new lieutenant (junior grade) and another chief yeoman were scheduled for early 1939; and another lieutenant was scheduled for mid-1939.

In November 1938 the Japanese Navy superseded their eight-year-old *Blue* system with a new code, requiring the Americans to scrap all previous code, keys, and cipher forms. OP-20-G now had to start from scratch. Commander Safford assigned the task to Tommy Dyer at HYPO, increasing his staff to four officers, but still the effort was enormous.

However, an increase to four officers "was considered temporary and not as a precedent for peacetime operations."

Lieutenant Dyer failed for selection to lieutenant commander in 1938, as did Lieutenants Tom Huckins and Edward Crowe. In an earlier year Robert Densford was also passed over. Fortunately, all of these officers were later selected and promoted. The worry about promotion for officers specializing in communications-intelligence was very well founded for a good number of years. In fact, a 1936 CNO letter to the Bureau of Navigation (which in those days managed naval personnel) stated that

insofar as officers are concerned, before full benefit can be expected from those having qualification and talent for language and cryptanalytic work, it would appear necessary to ensure that the promotion of such officers will be *assisted*—rather than *deterred*—thereby.

Cmdr. Laurance Safford, now head once again of OP-20-G, was always concerned about this issue—for himself as well as his protégés. In a September 1938 letter he commented that "we have Dyer and Huckins to look out for. Rear Adm. Stanford C. Hooper [formerly director of naval communications] is going to do all he can for them, [as will] Rear Adm. Ralston S. Holmes [director of naval intelligence]." Dyer and Huckins were both selected as "fitted and retained" in February 1939. After passage of new promotion legislation that same year they were subsequently promoted with others of their same dates of rank. This carried through for later promotions to commander and then to captain. To further help this issue, by keeping such officers from having to compete with all other line officers, a few—starting with Tommy Dyer and Alwin **Kramer** in 1939—were designated as Engineering Duty Officers: Cryptographic Duty. Dyer was later designated as a Special Duty Officer: Cryptologic Duty when that category was subsequently created in 1948.

Lt. Cmdr. Tommy Birtley came to HYPO in July 1939 and, as he was senior to Lt. Cmdr. Tommy Dyer, Birtley became OIC. Birtley (Dyer referred to him as "my old friend") was a rare "hybrid"—formally educated as a Japanese linguist and also formally trained as a cryptanalyst. Dyer then specifically focused upon the unit's GY (cryptanalysis) Section. When Birtley transferred to go to sea in mid-1941, Lt. Cmdr. Joe Rochefort (another of the rare hybrids) came in as OIC. Dyer wasn't offended by either officer taking charge of the unit he created—which both times relegated him to the subordinate position of assistant OIC—and, of course, continuing as chief cryptanalyst. Dyer knew and respected both of these officers. "I might have resented a total stranger coming in and upsetting my apple cart, but I was only interested in getting the job done." In December 1940, Dyer's old friend (and classmate) Lt. Cmdr. Edwin Layton arrived at Pearl Harbor as the FIO.

In early 1940, Lt. Cmdr. Dyer convinced the Fourteenth Naval District Commandant, now Rear Adm. Claude Bloch, that they absolutely had to have the headquarters building's basement for their operation—"5,000 square feet of glorious space." Years later he almost seemed surprised that he'd been successful. "Somehow, I don't know yet how I managed to do it, I wrangled it mostly." His wrangling wasn't just confined to square feet; by 1941 HYPO had an extremely respectable collection of IBM tabulating machines. "These electromechanical sorting devices (the precursors of modern computers) had somehow been acquired by Tommy Dyer" and were going to make an enormous impact during the forthcoming war.

At one point during this time Admiral Bloch said to Dyer, "They've told me I should have a Combat Intelligence Officer. I think there's a retired officer out at the University of Hawaii who would seem to fit the bill. What do you think?" Tommy didn't know Lt. Wilfred "Jasper" **Holmes**, but knew he wrote stories (under the name Alec Hudson) for the *Saturday Evening Post*. He thought Holmes would make a good choice. So they gave Holmes an office at the head of HYPO's stairway. Dyer thought it made a lot of sense to call the whole unit the Combat Intelligence Unit after Holmes's title because it didn't arouse too much curiosity. People knew it would have to be secret—a name sort of accurate and misleading at the same time. "We absorbed Jasper sort of by a process of osmosis." Holmes initially tracked merchant ship positions, and he gradually became aware of what the HYPO people were doing. He was different from the DIO, because the DIO was concerned broadly with intelligence. A "CIO focuses upon the tactical movements of an enemy that might be in his area."

With Joe Rochefort's arrival in mid-1941, and his close relationship with OP-20-G chief Cmdr. Laurance Safford, the HYPO team hoped he might win a reprieve from the fruitless slog against the AD code which had not been going well. However, on May 2, a directive from Washington reinforced that HYPO would stay exclusively focused upon the AD. This was frustrating for Rochefort as well as the navy's best cryptanalytic officers, Dyer and Wright. "It was also ultimately to prove [unfortunate] for the Pacific Fleet. For nine more months the HYPO team would obediently beat their heads against the stone wall of the [AD] code with negative results." It was a difficult code made impossible because it was little used—which meant there wasn't enough raw material coming in to work on and thus not enough to study to make any progress.

> By 1940 Dyer and his group were getting to the point where this system, "AD," was beginning to produce intelligible text. However, at this point the Japanese changed the underlying code. HYPO found that it now seemed to be limited to flag officers, and used very infrequently. From this point until mid-December 1941, HYPO struggled with this "admiral's code" and was never able to break it. There simply weren't enough intercepts to allow effective penetration of the system. Unfortunately, the attempt consumed countless hours of valuable cryptanalytic effort for no intelligence return.

However, Captain Dyer—looking back from 1970—said that the Japanese *were* using the AD, which

> indicated that it potentially contained information of the utmost value and justified fully the continued efforts of [myself] and the . . . unit to solve it. In retrospect, it might have been better had the Hawaiian Unit shifted over to JN-25 before 7 December, but it did not seem so obvious at the time.

He went on to say that Washington finally did stop HYPO from working on AD and switched their efforts to what had become the main Japanese naval operational code.

> Immediately after 7 December, [we were] assigned joint responsibility for JN-25. In reply to a request, a list of the 100 highest frequency groups was supplied by dispatch and used by Jack **Holtwick** as the basis of a "difference table" produced by machine which was invaluable in additive recovery. Within a matter of a very few days the cryptanalytic section of the unit was fully engaged in work on JN-25.[4]

---

4. In 1970, Captain Dyer commented that "it would be important to note that Washington and Pearl Harbor were *not* working on *current* JN-25 traffic in the fall of 1941, whereas Corregidor was—and [Corregidor was] also exchanging cipher recovery information with the British at Singapore."

It's interesting to note that in October 1941, Dyer's name was included on a list drawn up by Commander Safford at OP-20-G, identifying a small group of only eighteen officers that he considered fundamentally "qualified and acceptable" for communications intelligence and cryptanalysis.

Many years after the war, retired Capt. Joe Rochefort agreed, adding that

> the organization in Pearl, beginning in the fall of 1941 and extending until the time I left there—these people were the pick of the crop. I had Dyer, and a fellow named "Ham" Wright—these would be cryptanalysts and just about as good as they come.

In fact, Rochefort had only accepted the assignment with the assurance that Dyer would stay in the unit.

According to retired Capt. Jasper Holmes, who spent the entire war in HYPO and its successor organizations,

> Dyer's wife was a Honolulu resident who, unlike most other Navy dependents, had escaped evacuation. She would pack a laborer's large lunchbox full of sandwiches and send Dyer forth for a stint in the basement. When the sandwiches ran out, two or three days later, Rochefort would almost physically shove him up the stairs out of the basement to go home and get some decent rest away from the clack of the business machines.
>
> Rochefort knew that a top cryptanalyst with his teeth in a problem could never let it go. He might eat and converse or yield to exhaustion by taking short naps, but his mind would go right on shuffling combinations and permutations of code groups [and perhaps slide] into a nervous breakdown.
>
> Rochefort conserved Dyer's genius in a way a cruiser commander might husband his fuel supply against the hours when it would have to be lavishly expended.

Dyer himself later commented that another reason he left after twenty-four to twenty-eight hours of work was "so I could go home and my wife could have the car to go grocery shopping. Silly, but you have to eat."

Holmes observed that "next to Rochefort, Dyer was senior officer, both in regard to rank and length of service in communications intelligence. Until after the Battle of Midway either he or Rochefort was always in the basement, and usually both of them were there." In fact, "beginning in early 1942, Rochefort and Dyer alternated 24-on, 24-off, enabling one or the other always to be present in the basement." Dyer later commented that "we didn't see too much of each other the first six months of the war."

During the time he led HYPO, Dyer had developed a light touch in dealing with his subordinates. When Rochefort took over he was more of a forceful manager, but he continued much of Dyer's light style and tried to foster a collegial atmosphere.

According to intelligence historian John Prados, Lt. Cmdr. Dyer was totally surprised by the attack on Pearl Harbor. He was on duty the evening of December 6. Actually Dyer wasn't even supposed to be there, but his son was having a first piano recital the night of the fifth when he was scheduled for duty. Dyer traded with the officer scheduled for the fourth, then found himself invited to a party that night, [so] Dyer traded again and took the duty for the sixth. The night shift was himself and one enlisted man, Radioman Second Class Tony Ethier. Dyer spent the night working on the special cipher the Japanese were using in the Mandates. He received one of the messages [from the destroyer *Ward* in Pearl Harbor's mouth] about a possible submarine and called the district communications office . . . to make sure the message had been passed up the line.

About 7:00 a.m. Dyer knocked off for breakfast at a little Greek restaurant, returning a half-hour later to clean up his desk before going home, as scheduled, at eight o'clock. Then he heard noises outside the relatively soundproof basement offices of HYPO. At first he thought they were anti-aircraft guns, but Tommy Dyer could not understand why the Army should be firing anti-aircraft guns. Then he heard a louder explosion, which sounded like one of the Army's 14-inch coast-defense guns from Fort Kamehameha. . . . Chief Radioman Farnsley Woodward came downstairs to say planes were flying around dropping things. Dyer went up to see for himself.

"About three-hundred yards away," he recalled, "was a torpedo plane in a tight bank, a tight turn, and the 'rising suns' were shining right at me. I caught on fast." That was when Dyer went off to call Commander Rochefort.

As mentioned earlier, a few days after the attack on Pearl Harbor, HYPO was finally authorized to suspend work on the apparently impossible "AD" code and to start work on the important and now widely used Japanese navy operational code, JN-25-b. This fell primarily to Lieutenant Commanders Dyer, Wright, and Holtwick—with some assistance from Commander Rochefort. The hard work and the long hours in the basement became all-consuming. For the HYPO team the outside world—even other aspects of the war itself—faded. According to Dyer, "by and large, I would say, throughout the war, what I knew about U.S. operations was what I read in the *Honolulu Advertiser*." There was just not enough time. "There are only twenty-four hours in a day. . . . Trying to do a job [for which] thirty-two hours a day would not have been enough—you don't have time to waste on unessential things."

As historian Elliot Carlson explained it,

The way the system worked was that the cryptanalysts—Dyer, Wright, and Holtwick—handled the first phase: solving the puzzle that arrived on their desks in the form of a radio intercept. This was essentially a cryptogram concealing a coded message. Their job was to "break" the cryptogram and expose the unidentified code groups that constituted the message.

Cryptanalysts didn't need to know Japanese to do this; they had to be wizards at math, as were Dyer and Wright. But to attach meaning to the code groups required facility in Japanese, which was where the linguists came in.

Lt. Cmdr. Jack Holtwick also had the direct supervision of the IBM machines at this point, and thus had to juggle the multiple demands made upon that equipment.

According to Jasper Holmes, Tommy was his main customer. "Dyer, who used a punch-card sorter like a surgeon's scalpel to dissect both code and enciphering tables, needed unlimited access to the machinery."

In large measure due to Dyer's cryptanalysis, HYPO began contributing essential elements of information derived from JN-25 to Pacific Fleet commander in chief Adm. Chester Nimitz before the Battle of the Coral Sea. Then, by May 27, 1942, HYPO had developed such a detailed picture of the Japanese plan for the assault on and occupation of Midway that Nimitz's fleet intelligence officer—Dyer's classmate Eddie Layton—was able to predict almost precisely when and where the enemy would strike.

One day, after the Battle of the Coral Sea and in the run-up to the Battle of Midway, Lt. Cmdr. Holmes went upstairs to the *lanai* of the administration building for some fresh air. There he ran into an old friend who was currently assigned to the aircraft carrier *Yorktown*, which was undergoing emergency repairs. Just then Tommy Dyer came up out of the basement, on his way home, right after the successful conclusion of HYPO's intense time-date cipher blitz—trying to pin down the Japanese fleet's movement toward Midway Island.

> Under his arm was his old lunch box. His uniform looked as though he had slept in it for three days. He had. He was unshaven and his hair looked as though it had not been cut for a month. It had not. His eyes were bloodshot from lack of sleep, and his gait betrayed how close he was to utter exhaustion. With a seaman's contempt for a landlubber, my carrier friend remarked, "Now there goes a bird who should be sent to sea to get straightened out."
>
> For an instant my blood pressure soared to the bursting point and I nearly blurted out the truth. Dyer was one of the kingpins of the little band of officers whose genius and devotion to duty, over many years, had given us an opportunity to win a victory at last. If he wasted his time on spit, polish, and punctilio, the war would be much longer and cost many more lives. Fortunately, I regained control of myself in time and mumbled something like, "Oh, he's all right," feeling like Peter when he betrayed the Lord.
>
> Dyer would have been the first to condemn me if I had broken the secrecy that we all prized much more than any credit or the hope of reward.

During this time, due to a severe case of inflammatory colitis, Dyer's navy doctor had prescribed both "uppers" and "downers." The doctor "first gave me phenobarbital [but] I couldn't keep awake while sitting at my desk . . . so he gave me some Benzedrine sulfate. They were both, at that time, recommended for the symptoms I had." Even though it occurred to him that it might ruin his health, he "continued taking Benzedrine as necessary throughout the war. I figured there were people out there getting shot at . . . but I was living a rather bombproof existence." So, he concluded, if the Benzedrine should turn out "to inflict some injury on my health in the long run, so what? But I was very cautious with it; maybe one pill at night when on a 24-hour schedule."

Joe Rochefort has been widely quoted that Dyer had "energy" pills on his desk in a candy dish, for Dyer's *constant use and anyone else's*. But Tommy later forcefully denied it. "That's pure unadulterated fiction," he said in an interview. "I had *nothing on my desk* for the benefit of anybody else—or even myself. I did not supply anyone else with them. I did tell one other person about them, and that was a mistake, because he was not careful in their use."[5]

On the subject of Dyer's desk, Commander Layton had this observation.

> Under the glass on his desk resided what was reputed to be the best collection of pin-ups in the Pacific Fleet, which added its own touch to an unbelievably cluttered appearance. But Tommy Dyer knew exactly where everything was on it. A new yeoman once made the mistake of tidying up the legendary "Dyer desk" and it brought down Dyer's wrath after he was unable to locate a critical decrypt.

On his desk Dyer also had a lacquered abacus, called a *soroban*, which had been liberated from a previously held Japanese island. "Somebody in our outfit landing out there was thoughtful enough to bring it to me." As Rochefort's biographer Elliot Carlson noted, it was a perfect gift for a math wizard breaking the Japanese code.

As has been related several times elsewhere in this book, in October 1942, Cmdr. Joe Rochefort was summarily relieved as OIC of communications intelligence at Pearl Harbor. When the secret "plot" to sack Rochefort finally came to fruition—engineered by a few shallow-minded and unscrupulous officers in Washington—Dyer and the other denizens of the HYPO basement were astonished to suddenly be introduced to Rochefort's replacement, Capt. William **Goggins**. Dyer was at first wary of Goggins, thinking he must have been a participant in Rochefort's demise, but then revised his position.

> Initially I concluded that [Goggins] was in on the plot—if there was one. I think I treated him with the minimum politeness that a commander should show a captain. But I soon had to reform that opinion. I was forced to the conclusion that he was an innocent bystander who sort of got caught in a little jam.

They actually grew to be close colleagues and friends. In fact, at the war's conclusion in the fall of 1945, Captain Goggins hosted Captain Dyer on board his seagoing command, the battleship *Alabama*, as a special guest.

Dyer had been caught completely by surprise by Rochefort's removal.

> All of a sudden out of a clear sky, as far as I was concerned, they sent orders for Rochefort to come to Washington for temporary duty and conferences. At first I took it for a routine sort of thing, but before he left, he said, "I'll never be back." And he wasn't.

Commander Dyer very much missed Commander Rochefort, not so much for his leadership but because of his all-around prowess in every aspect of communications-intelligence—from cryptanalysis and communications to translation and analysis. "We were missing out on his expertise in analyzing and supporting the intelligence. We were bound to suffer to some extent. No one could step in his shoes."

---

5. This individual was very likely linguist Lt. Cmdr. Joseph Finnegan; see his chapter for more detail.

An often-repeated story from later in the war details how one day Ham Wright was invited, along with Tommy Dyer and Tom Steele, for an afternoon's rest at Admiral Nimitz's beach house on Oahu's north shore. Nimitz decided to just sit in the sun, but another guest—Vice Adm. Raymond Spruance—took the HYPO officers on a mile-long beach walk with an equivalent and exhausting swim back. At least one piece of business was covered: Spruance wanted to better understand the periodic blackouts that occurred when the Japanese changed codes. He thought there ought to be a way to have U.S. operations timed to go only when the codes were being solidly read; however, Dyer and Wright taught him some of the nuances of the challenge, including how unpredictable such code changes were.

Dyer's work throughout the war remained incredibly intense and extraordinarily valuable. Beyond the remarkable achievements involved in the run-ups to the Battles of the Coral Sea and of Midway, it's a little risky to try to choose some further specific accomplishments, for in so doing they might be viewed as disproportionally important among the whole. However, taking that risk, it's fair to note that in April 1943, Commander Dyer was directly involved with the interception, decryption, and subsequent intelligence reporting which led to the shootdown and death of Fleet Admiral Yamamoto Isoroku.

Dyer's work also resulted in the breaking of the Japanese merchant shipping and transport code as well as the main Japanese weather code. In fact, at what was now generally called FRUPac rather than Station HYPO, Tommy Dyer and Ham Wright made an entry into the so-called Japanese "Maru Code" (merchant ship code), and then turned it over to the unit's outstanding Coast Guard cryptanalyst, Lt. Cmdr. Henry M. **Anthony**, for complete exploitation. Rear Admiral Layton later expanded on this when he wrote that:

> while the Japanese never read our ciphers, we were able to maintain our penetration of their principal naval operational ciphers from early 1943 onward. This included the four-digit code used by the merchant shipping. The breakthrough into the so-called *maru* cipher used by the Japanese transports was the product of five months' sustained effort by the HYPO team led by Captain Dyer and Commander Wright. The Japanese modeled their merchant-ship communications system on British "reporting and routing" practice. So our ability to read the *maru* code allowed us to plot the Japanese convoy routes from their daily noon position reports. Their merchant skippers obligingly and methodically transmitted reports at 0800 and 2000 each day.
>
> Our ability to know exactly where their convoys were heading was to become the vital factor in running our successful submarine war which, by late 1944, had effectively severed the seaborne lifelines of Japan's scattered empire.

Captain Dyer (he'd been promoted to captain in the fall of 1943) finished the war in Pacific Theater radio intelligence. It had been a long trek since he'd first arrived in 1936 to set up his one-man shop. In November 1945, Tommy relieved Capt. John **Harper** as OIC of FRUPac—but this was only for two months as he, in turn, detached in December as the navy continued its massive demobilization.

From February 1946 to June 1949, Dyer was assigned to the Naval Security Station, Communications Support Activity, in Washington, D.C. (a precursor to the Naval Security Group) as chief of processing and technical director. In 1948 he was designated as one of the first Navy Special Duty Officers (Cryptology). Dyer was a leading member of the navy contingent that joined the fledgling AFSA in June 1949 and, along with Captain Safford, was in charge of all daily AFSA operations.

> Laurance Safford and I were—I can't remember what our title was—technical advisors or something. We shared an office, and reported directly to the director. I made a number of staff studies for the director and wrote his speeches for him.

In 1950, Dyer served as chairman of the site-selection committee for a relocation of the AFSA. They first selected Fort Knox, Kentucky; however, that decision was reversed with the later choice of Fort George G. Meade in Maryland.

After the AFSA had become the NSA, Captain Dyer established the agency's first academic training program (college and National Cryptologic School courses) for agency employees. Then, from October 1952 to January 1954, he was chief of station NSA Far East, Tokyo. He returned to NSA Washington in February 1954 to become—with very little enthusiasm—its first historian. He remained there until his retirement from the navy in February 1955. After that he moved out of Washington to teach at the University of Maryland. At this time he also became a fairly serious grower of orchids—at one point cultivating almost four hundred plants under special lights in his basement.

In the mid-1960s, both Tommy Dyer and Ham Wright were interviewed by David Kahn for Kahn's monumental book *The Codebreakers*. They were both subsequently censured by the director of naval intelligence for giving up too much information. This was a little ironic as they both had initially tried to bow out from the request but were pressured into it by the Defense Department's Office of Public Affairs. Fortunately, nothing came of the censure, for they had been careful to only discuss things that were already in the public record.

Captain Dyer began to suffer from arthritis around 1977, occasionally being laid up and "crippled up." At this point he had to abandon his orchid cultivation hobby.

Since Thomas Dyer was *so* extraordinary as a precomputer codebreaker, it's worth looking at him a little more closely in that regard before we complete his story.

In his book *The American Magic: Codes, Ciphers and the Defeat of Japan*, historian Ronald Lewin described Tommy as one of the very few "top" codebreakers in the U.S. Navy. Somewhat amusingly, Dyer only partially agreed, saying, "I think, without any false modesty, that—in cryptanalysis only—I was number one."

> With the single exception of the "Flag Officers' Code" [the unbroken AD code] we dealt with before the war, I don't remember a single problem that I came up against in actual Japanese that I wasn't able to cope with.

Dyer estimated that American cryptanalysts "demolished" around seventy-five Japanese naval codes and major code changes during the war. He went on to say, however, that

> in the total combination, in the value to the war effort and to the country, I unhesitatingly step aside for Joe Rochefort.
>
> But, purely as a cryptanalyst or codebreaker, I think unquestionably I was his superior. The only person that I know of, that came close to me in cryptanalysis, was Ham Wright.

In regard to Captain Rochefort, Dyer had more to say:

> He was outstanding. But his *really* outstanding quality was as an *intelligence analyst.* What he was taking was, after all, frequently fragmentary information and arriving at a correct analysis of what it said and what it meant.

Asked if he went along with Rochefort's contention that codebreakers are peculiar people, Dyer replied that:

> for a good part of the war there was a cartoon tacked up behind my desk with a very weird looking character. And it said, *You don't have to be crazy to work here, but it helps a hell of a lot.* Yes, I think all really successful cryptanalysts are a *little bit* odd, to say the least.

It needs to be mentioned that Captain Dyer also had an enormous regard for his former teacher, Agnes Driscoll, saying in an interview that:

> she was never given the status by the Navy that William Friedman was given by the Army. Certainly in the 1920s and early 1930s *she was fully his equal.* In the long term of history, I'd be hard-put to say that one was better than the other.

But Tommy might not have ranked her high with himself and Wright, as mentioned previously, because her glory was really of that earlier period, and not so much of the war itself.

People like Tommy Dyer, Ham Wright, and Agnes Driscoll were more "system breakers" than they were "code breakers." According to Dyer, the reality is that "you don't break messages; you break systems." Aside from his remarkable mathematical skills, Tommy had an uncanny ability to see patterns in the mass of letters and digits. He stated that:

> if you observe something long enough, you'll see something peculiar. If you can't see something peculiar, if you stare long enough, then that in itself is peculiar. And then you try to explain the peculiarity.

Just staring at the material was part of his method.

A lot of it is, I'm convinced, done by the subconscious. Sometimes when people ask me how I can solve messages, I say, "Well, you sit there and stare at it until you see what it says, and then you put it down." You look—it depends on what kind of a thing you're dealing with—but you look at it until you see something that attracts your attention, your curiosity. Maybe it doesn't suggest anything at all. You go on to something else. The next day you come back and look at it again.

One time Dyer joked about former Secretary of State Henry Stimson's famous remark, circa 1929, that it might be unethical to use cryptology in foreign relations, because "gentlemen don't read each others' mail." Tommy said that might very well be, but it didn't actually apply to cryptanalysts because "no one could accuse *us* of being *gentlemen*." He also addressed the common wisdom that musical ability and cryptology go together; he said he'd heard there's "an affinity between musical ability and cryptanalytic ability. If there is, I'm the great exception."

Concerning the overall business of cryptanalysis, he once keyed in on the term "MAGIC"—which was the designation of intelligence produced from decrypted diplomatic messages in the Japanese PURPLE code. He said that magic:

is too much the way that *laity*—and by laity I include a lot of people who *ought* to know better—view [codebreaking]. They don't think it's a scientific process of analysis and dealing with cause and effect. . . . They think that it's something that you can—well—if you have a *sixth sense*, you can just *do it*. A lot of people still think that whatever success [codebreakers] may have had was not due to a lot of *hard work*, but some kind of *intuitive* reasoning.

Moreover, he had this to say about the lack of support—particularly in the 1920s and 1930s, for signals intelligence.

In the first place *very few* people knew anything about it. And some who *knew* took a rather dim view of the activity. While we had some supporters here and there throughout the Navy, for the most part the people who might have been able to make personnel [and money] available thought we were a bunch of *blue-sky merchants*, indulging in a pipe dream.

In 1984, Tommy and Ham Wright helped Rear Adm. Eddie Layton's coauthors, Roger Pineau and John Costello, with interpreting final details in Layton's notes after Layton had a fatal stroke. Unfortunately, Layton had died prior to the completion of his book, *"And I Was There."*

In June 1930, Tommy Dyer had married Edith Miller (1901–1995) in Forest Grove, Oregon. They had actually met in high school in Kansas when both were on the yearbook staff. Interestingly, Mrs. Dyer didn't really find out that Captain Dyer was an ace cryptanalyst until the late 1960s when a couple of books such as Kahn's *The Codebreakers* were published; she essentially understood that Tommy was in the secret communications business but did not know the specifics. Apparently when Capt. Jasper Holmes wrote that "Dyer was one of a small group of officers whose passion for anonymity concealed their genius from all"—he had in mind Mrs. Dyer herself!

The Dyers had two children, Thomas Edward and Ann Leilani. Cmdr. Thomas Edward Dyer graduated from the Naval Academy in 1957 but prematurely died in 1981—after a major illness—to the great anguish of his parents.

Thomas Harold Dyer's awards included the Distinguished Service Medal, for his wartime contributions, as well as the Navy Unit Commendation Ribbon. He was one of only six radio intelligence officers in the navy or marines who received the DSM.[6]

Captain Dyer died on January 5, 1985, from cardio-pulmonary arrest. Edith passed away ten years later; they are buried together at Arlington National Cemetery. Tommy was designated a Pioneer Officer of U.S. Naval Cryptology by the U.S. Naval Cryptologic Veterans Association, and he was inducted into the NSA's Hall of Honor in 2002.

Sources

Bamford, 85.
Budiansky, 11, 213.
Capt. Thomas H. Dyer. U.S. National Security Agency. Cryptologic Hall of Honor. www.nsa. gov/about/cryptologic_heritage/hall_of_honor. Accessed 22 January 2013.
Carlson, 46, 74, 85–87, 91–92, 95–97, 102–5, 119–20, 187–88, 191, 205–7, 229, 258–59, 303, 334–35, 406, 413–15, 445, 448–49, 460, 500, 505, 536.
Donovan and Mack, 58.
Dyer, *Reminiscences,* 75–78, 83–84, 127–29, 135, 186, 192, 206, 207, 226, 228, 233, 249–51, 324.
Holmes, 22, 53–55, 86–87, 90, 94–96, 109, 115, 118, 125, 128, 167, 200, 242, 265, 267.
Holtwick, 47, 50–51, 70, 82, 86–89, 97, 104–7, 113, 126, 195–96, 202, 268, 312, 315–16, 319–20, 324, 327, 333, 341, 352, 362–63, 368, 398–99, 406, 428, 433, 439, 446.
Kahn, *Codebreakers,* 562–64, 593–95.
Kahn, *Discovered,* 23.
Layton, *"And I Was There,"* 6, 24, 45–47, 49, 52, 77, 93–94, 358, 413, 420–23, 468, 471, 474, 510.
Lewin, 102.
Lucky Bag, U.S. Naval Academy
McGinnis, 10–11, 20.
Prados, 78–79, 83, 171, 174, 176, 187–88, 284, 315, 319, 407–8, 459, 730.
Prange, *Miracle at Midway,* 18.
Rochefort, *Reminiscences,* 103, 127–28, 157–58.
Schom, 283–84.
Stillwell, "Lead Code-Breaker," 64.
Toll, 303–6, 312–14, 391–92.

---

6. After the Battle of Midway, Lt. Cmdr. Jasper Holmes was tasked to make recommendations for awards. He initially "recommended that any awards that were to be made should go to the veterans who had long years in radio intelligence. I listed them by name, [particularly] remarking that Dyer's work and service had been outstanding. Not only had the old-timers, as individuals, contributed most by reason of their skill and experience, but *without the groundwork they had laid* [before the war] *we would have gotten nowhere."* Furthermore, he believed, "it was most important that all of them be continued in radio intelligence work for the duration of the war and not be distracted from it by more glamorous or more rewarding opportunities. A little generosity in awards right [now] would make it easier to accomplish this." It did not happen. The decorations that were given came out at the end of the war.

CAPTAIN RUDOLPH JOSEPH FABIAN, U.S. NAVY (1908–1984)

The navy's second-best codebreaker
"Rudy" "Fabe"

Rudy Fabian was a master cryptanalyst, a superb administrator, and—even though he hailed from Butte, Montana—a "highly professional officer with an air of authority and a hint of Central European sophistication." His career differs from many of the others in this collection, in that once he became involved in communications-intelligence he spent very little time in "black shoe" surface-ship assignments. Shore-bound at secure bases, he thus received neither a high-level combat decoration nor the retirement "tombstone" promotion to rear admiral that would have followed such an award. Yet as a cryptanalyst his contributions were monumental, and he was ranked among the top three American naval codebreakers of the war.

*   *   *

From the 1931 Annapolis yearbook, *The Lucky Bag*:

A long-cherished dream was realized the day *Rudy* pitched his tent on the shores of the Severn. The call of the sea has lured many a man but no one more so than this candidate from the "wide open spaces." Not to be outdone by his brother, out of '23, he determined that a career at Uncle Sam's Cradle of Sea Power was not beyond his reach. Since the first odor of stencil ink, *Rudy* has been going ahead full speed. His formula includes conscientiousness mixed with the right amount of pleasant diversion. What could be a better means of attaining success? As a roommate he has no equal. When it comes to doing such favor as winding the Victrola, or giving you his last drop of hair tonic, he never flinches. He would even drag [date] your One-and-Only's girlfriend. As a result of continued and well-directed application he has maintained a high class standing. [Activities: Hop Committee chairman, Ring Dance Committee; vice president, Naval Academy Christian Association]

*   *   *

Rudolph Fabian was born in Butte, Montana, in 1908. After one year at the Montana School of Mines he entered the Naval Academy in 1927. He graduated and was commissioned an ensign in June 1931, along with such classmates as Bankson T. **Holcomb** Jr., John S. McCain Jr., Lawson "Red" Ramage, Horacio Rivero Jr., and Bernard F. **Roeder**. By subsequent promotion he attained the ranks of lieutenant (junior grade), 1934; lieutenant, 1938; lieutenant commander, June 1942; commander, November 1942; and captain, July 1950. He ultimately retired in July 1961.

As with most young officers in this period, Fabian saw several years of generic sea duty as his first assignments; from 1931 to 1933 he was on board the battleship *Tennessee*, followed by a tour on board the destroyer *John D. Edwards* from 1934 through 1935. In 1936 he transferred to the heavy cruiser *Chester*, and then moved to the submarine tender *Argonne*.

In 1938, Rudy was selected to report to OP-20-G at Main Navy for cryptanalysis instruction, along with Lt. j.g. William B. Braun and Lt. j.g. Merrill S. Holmes. Holmes and Fabian were retained another year for additional instruction in mathematical statistics and Japanese language. Fabian later wrote that:

I received a letter from Cmdr. Laurance **Safford** inviting me to Washington to work with his organization. I accepted the offer even though I did not know what he had in mind because I did not get accepted for graduate work in ordnance as I had hoped. . . . Commander Safford was a brilliant man. Many people disliked him because he was so quick. I was in a class of three people so our instruction was very intense. It was most fortuitous that Lt. Redfield **Mason**, a Japanese linguist, taught us Japanese telegraph codes as part of our class.

In addition to taking instruction, Fabian worked in OP-20-GY (the Crypto-Intelligence Subsection) from September 1939 through June 1940, along with Ernest S. L. **Goodwin**, Agnes M. **Driscoll**, and Chief Radioman Walter **McGregor**.

In late 1940 he was sent to the Philippines to command the radio intercept unit at Corregidor, relieving Lt. Bernard **Roeder** on September 29. In that role, at Station CAST, Fabian was involved in the intense search for information regarding Japanese plans as the relations with Japan deteriorated. Then, after the attack on Pearl Harbor, he had to cope with the difficulties created by the rapid Japanese advance through the Philippines in late 1941 and early 1942—which ultimately required total evacuation.

During late summer of 1940, Fabian and the personnel of Station CAST moved into new spaces at Monkey Point in Corregidor. Captain **Safford** later commented that while Station HYPO at Pearl Harbor had some of the best COMINT officers, with most of them having four to five years of radio intelligence experience, CAST's officers averaged just two to three years—but they were "young, enthusiastic, and capable." The seven officers and nineteen enlisted men of Fabian's cryptanalysis group exchanged possible recoveries of JN-25b code groups with Washington and a British unit in Singapore. Fabian later said that:

> I had twenty-six radio receivers, ranging from low to high frequency, a set of business machinery, and the appurtenances necessary for the interception of both high- and low-speed enemy transmissions. . . . We covered certain circuits from which we could get most of the information we desired, and the greatest volume of material.

It's fair to say that the obtaining of resources for CAST's attack on JN-25b is one of Fabian's greatest achievements.

CAST was the best site for intercepting Tokyo radio traffic, particularly Tokyo-Berlin.

> To cut the number of retransmissions of intercepts from Cavite to Washington (and thus reduce the danger of Japanese discovery of the MAGIC operation), in March [1941] the navy sent out a "B" PURPLE machine to the Philippines. OP-20-GY radioed the daily PURPLE and J19 keys to Fabian's unit; he applied these to the messages intercepted by his (and the army's) intercept stations. He was then to forward the important solutions by radio.

Up to December 7, 1941, JN-25 was targeted by Fabian on Corregidor, a British group at Singapore, and OP-20-G in Washington (Hawaii's Station HYPO was subsequently tasked onto JN-25 on 10 December). On December 4, the Japanese had engaged new additive books to the code. "Fabian's group broke into the new encipherment [on December 8], and by Christmas messages were again being read as before. But these readings were [still] tantalizingly fragmentary, and much remained to be done."

In the fall of 1940 dependents had been sent home—except Lieutenant Fabian's wife and son (she had a broken leg and could not travel); but, by January 1941 they had left as well. In the late summer of 1941 there were around sixty men at CAST altogether, including about ten cryptanalysts and six officers. Fabian still retained command, with Lt. John "Honest John" **Lietwiler** as his executive officer (Fabian and Lietwiler would later reverse roles for a time). Newly arrived language officers from Tokyo were Lt. Rufus **Taylor** and Lt. j.g. Thomas **Mackie**—just evacuated from the American embassy by naval attaché Cmdr. Henri **Smith-Hutton**—finding relative safety as conditions worsened.

Capt. Alwin **Kramer** later recalled that:

> the prime reason for ever having set up a cryptanalytical unit at Corregidor . . . was to keep the C-in-C, Asiatic Fleet (at that time Admiral Hart) as fully apprised as possible of political, military, and other developments of like nature in his sphere.

Captain Safford also commented that:

> the unit at Corregidor had been intercepting messages in the Japanese . . . diplomatic codes for several years and continued to do that up to and including December 7, 1941. Their main attention was on the local Asiatic circuits for the information of the Commander in Chief, Asiatic Fleet, but very late in November 1941, they were given the additional duty of covering the Berlin-Tokyo circuit, because we couldn't get adequate coverage from all the other stations combined.

However, the navy had decided that the now seventy-plus people at CAST amounted to a significant part of its overall accumulated expertise in both Japanese codes and the Japanese language, and thus the risk of leaving them in the path of the Japanese advance was too great. "Japanese ruthlessness in the interrogation of prisoners of war was well known, and the importance of keeping live COMINT people out of their hands was fully appreciated." Accordingly, newly promoted Lieutenant Commander Fabian headed the first CAST group taken off Corregidor. They left on February 5, 1942, aboard the battle-damaged submarine *Seadragon*, with sixteen men and fifteen boxes of equipment. The boat was so overcrowded that the men had to sleep in the narrow passageways. The *Seadragon* arrived at Surabaya in eastern Java around February 11; the CAST group then went by train to Bandung, in western Java, then on to a village where the Dutch had a well-established and very active radio intelligence organization (called KAMER 14).

There they shortly got back to work. The Americans were surprised at the level of expertise exhibited by the Indonesian senior noncommissioned officers that the Dutch loaned them. Fabian guarded his encryption materials, not letting the Dutch or Indonesians see them, but he very much appreciated their help. In the face of continual Japanese movement, for operational and security reasons the Asiatic Fleet intelligence officer, Lt. Cmdr. Rosie **Mason**, agreed to move Fabian and his group farther south and on to Melbourne, Australia. Thus, they packed up again and proceeded to Tjilatjap Harbor on the southern coast of Java; on February 21 the submarine *Snapper* evacuated them.

Mason soon joined Fabian in Melbourne; he had brought down a second group of CAST personnel. They combined with some Australian and British radio intelligence people at Victoria Barracks, and then moved to an apartment complex called the Monterey Flats on Queen's Road. Cmdr. Jack Newman, Royal Australian Navy, became deputy chief of the new unit. From all accounts, Commander Newman and Lieutenant Commander Fabian "worked together famously." The unit (still equipped with Station CAST's PURPLE machine) ultimately became known as FRUMel, but during this time as well as the period around the Battle of Midway, the unit was often referred to as Station BELCONNEN (the name taken from the Australian Belconnen Naval Transmitting Station). For a time Mason helped in the initial setup of Station BELCONNEN; after Fabian was in place and organized to take the lead, Mason returned to Main Navy in Washington.

BELCONNEN/FRUMel was made up of three main groups. First was what had been Fabian's Station CAST unit. The second was Commander Eric Nave's small Royal Australian Navy cryptography unit, which had moved to the Monterey Flats from the Victoria Barracks in February. Nave's unit was made up of a core of naval personnel, heavily assisted by university academics and graduates specializing in linguistics and mathematics. These included people like Arthur Dale Trendall, Athanasius Treweek, Eric Barnes, Jack Davies, and Ronald Bond. The third group was a trio of British Foreign Office linguists (Henry Archer, Arthur Cooper, and Hubert Graves), and some Royal Navy support staff evacuated from Singapore, particularly from the Far East Combined Bureau (FECB) there. Some IBM punch-card equipment was obtained to replace that left behind by Fabian's group on leaving Corregidor.

On March 5, Washington ordered Lieutenant Commander Lietwiler and the rest of Station CAST off Corregidor. A group of thirty-six men under Lt. j.g. Mackie left on the submarine *Permit*; then the last group (including Lieutenants Lietwiler and Taylor) left, once again utilizing the submarine *Seadragon*, arriving at Melbourne on May 6. Rudy Fabian reunited with his colleague Honest John Lietwiler, sharing a tiny office at the Monterey Flats, where they began a routine such that there was always one of them in the office at any time of the day or night. BELCONNEN was initially fed by a single Australian navy intercept station near Melbourne, with a second station near Darwin coming on line later. In addition, a large direction-finding network came into play. Fabian later said that:

with the start of war, my stint in the field turned out to be a long one. I [had] escaped from Corregidor and went to Melbourne in February 1942. . . . FRUMel [or BELCONNEN] was officially established on 12 March 1942. My counterpart from the Royal Australian Navy was Captain Jack Newman. The Australians were very helpful; their analysts and linguists were very talented. Our mission was navy communications. We did everything from beginning to end—decryption, translation, and processing. The JN-25 systems that we worked on were very complex. . . . To enhance our ability to solve the

Japanese naval systems, we shared information with our sister naval cryptologic units. We had a secure communications system called the COPEK system, which enabled us to share information with [Station HYPO or] the Fleet Radio Unit Pacific [FRUPac], Washington, London, and the British Eastern Fleet. These sites worked well together. As the commander of FRUMel, I kept our material circulating in the COPEK all the time.

Fabian was particularly concerned with security and constantly worried about exposure.

I was relieved when Commander Nave . . . left FRUMel. . . . He left because I reprimanded him for his lack of security.[1] I also had to get my admiral to remind General MacArthur about the need for security. MacArthur was so exuberant about our warning him that the Japanese were really going to attack Port Moresby, New Guinea, in [early] 1942, that I feared he was going to reveal the source. . . . The Japanese could have discovered our intercept capabilities, and the outcome of the war may have been very different.[2]

We distributed our information directly to Submarine Pacific Command and to the Fremantle unit. We also brought information once a day to the fleet intelligence officer at Brisbane. As MacArthur was the theater commander, we also supplied information directly to him. We strictly observed the need-to-know principle, but any commander who needed our information received it.

In fact, "the purpose of BELCONNEN was intelligence support for 'General MacArthur's Navy,' [which is to say] U.S. naval forces in the southern Pacific area, and as such was under the military control of the Commander, Southwest Pacific Force and its successor organization, the Seventh Fleet." As Fabian put it, he "received technical support and guidance from OP-20-G, but that guidance in no way detracted from our local responsibility to the fleet commander; the same as [had been] true for the CAST unit."

Fabian's position at BELCONNEN was "eased by having Washington's full support." He was held in high regard by the Redman brothers (Cmdr. Jack Redman, new head of OP-20-G; and Capt. Joe Redman, director of naval communications).

---

1. Commander, later Captain, Eric Nave of the RAN cryptographic unit arrived at the Monterey Flats in February 1942, as they had outgrown their cramped quarters at Melbourne's Victoria Barracks. A number of his unit were British code breakers who had escaped from Singapore before it was captured. According to some accounts, Commander Nave was a very secretive and mysterious person. He apparently did not get on well with Commander R. B. M. "Cocky" Long, the Australian director of naval intelligence, nor did he get on with Lieutenant Commander Fabian, USN. Nave and Fabian had a difficult relationship, and Nave eventually moved to the joint Australian-U.S. Army Central Bureau at Brisbane. According to historian David Jenkins, Fabian then wasted no time in getting rid of the civilian supernumeraries at Monterey, many of them British service wives who had been evacuated from Singapore. He also squeezed out the British diplomatic corps types like Cooper and Archer. However, men such as A. B. Jamieson and Athanasius Treweek, who had cordial relations with the Americans, remained with FRUMel throughout the war.
2. In fact, Fabian is said to have "regarded co-operation with anyone who was not in the U.S. Navy or under its command as poor security." One senior British officer said the atmosphere at FRUMel was "What is yours is mine, and what is mine is my own," and Fabian (backed by the Redman brothers, then heading naval communications in Washington) did not seem to be particularly interested in any exchange of material with the army Central Bureau.

He therefore escaped the drastic Redman-inspired changes (supported by vice chief of naval operations Adm. Frederick Horne) that were shortly going to sweep Capt. Laurance Safford and Cmdr. Joe **Rochefort** from their key positions—and strip away from the ONI any authority in communications-intelligence matters.

In April 1942, the Australian/American/British codebreakers in Australia made an enormous contribution by deciphering messages that detailed the organization of the Japanese forces prior to the Coral Sea operation. Fabian and Taylor are credited with discovering details about the Japanese striking force which contained the big carriers.

Moreover, BELCONNEN played a critical role in changing American strategy prior to the Battle of Midway—a rarely noted contribution. They determined that the Japanese had abandoned their plan for an amphibious landing at Port Moresby. This made Vice Admiral Halsey's carriers unnecessary in the South Pacific, enabling Admiral Nimitz to justify recalling them. BELCONNEN also decrypted a Japanese First Air Fleet order that showed when Adm. Nagumo Chūichi intended to leave his training bases and marshal his forces for the operation. BELCONNEN traffic analysis identified almost every ship in the Japanese order of battle, and concluded that the operation would either be against Hawaii or Midway. They essentially unraveled the planned date for the attack on Midway. BELCONNEN's analysis confirmed Cmdr. Joe Rochefort's analysis at Station HYPO; thus, Admiral King in Washington finally became convinced of this despite the contrary input he was receiving from OP-20-G. King cabled Nimitz, on May 17, 1942, that he had come to agree that Midway must be the target. (After the war, Captain Safford commented that had BELCONNEN and HYPO not *independently drawn the same conclusions*, then NEGAT's [OP-20-G's] diffuse fears for an operation against Alaska or somewhere else might have prevailed.)

In fact, BELCONNEN's credibility was already substantial. It's reported that, at one point during the lead-up to Midway, Fabian (or possibly Rufe Taylor) came into the codebreaking center and said, "Now you guys be sure of what you're writing—because they are *moving aircraft carriers* on the basis of what [we're] saying!" Fabian's unit first determined that Admiral Yamamoto's lengthy message of May 20, 1942, was a major operations order—but Rochefort's Station HYPO put out the first fragmentary solution of that message.

In September 1943, Rudy was relieved as OIC at FRUMel by Cmdr. Sid **Goodwin**. But then senior intelligence expert Capt. Arthur **McCollum** arrived at Brisbane to become the fleet intelligence officer for the Seventh Fleet, drafting Fabian to help him create an advanced intelligence center that Admiral King wanted put in place. Starting with just thirty men, it shortly grew to over three hundred. But, prior to the completion of that enormous expansion, Fabian had been sent on to Colombo, Ceylon [now Sri Lanka], to work as the U.S. Navy's liaison to an existing British radio intelligence unit, called Station ANDERSON. There Fabian discovered that intelligence sent from OP-20-G in Washington to Pearl Harbor, *then* to FRUMel, and *then* to ANDERSON arrived faster than the same intelligence sent in British channels from their center at Bletchley Park! He later wrote that:

I was sent to Colombo . . . as a liaison officer to provide COMINT to the British. [Then] I came back to the U.S. in 1945 and served as a staff officer at Nebraska Avenue at OP-20-G.

After the war, I went back to sea on a cruiser. I had to leave intelligence work and go to sea in order to get further promotion.

Commander Fabian finally did see promotion to captain, but it didn't happen until 1950. Subsequently he became the commanding officer of the replenishment oiler *Navasota*, from July 1953 through July 1954. During this time the *Navasota* conducted fueling operations in Korean waters and was also used as station ship at Kaohsiung, Formosa, where she fueled units of the Formosa Straits Patrol. She then deployed to the Western Pacific, providing fueling services to various fleet units.

Upon returning to the United States, Rudy began graduate work at the Naval War College in Newport. He graduated in June 1955, along with Captains Steve **Jurika** and Robert H. **Weeks**.

Captain Fabian brought his active duty career to a close in July 1961, and took retirement in Florida. He passed away in June 1984, at Port Charlotte. Fabian was always particularly proud of the work he and his unit had done in Australia, later commenting that:

BELCONNEN made major valuable contributions during the Coral Sea battle, the Midway battle, and the fighting at Port Moresby, New Guinea. We also contributed piecemeal information to all of the naval battles in the Pacific. It was difficult for us to function because the Atlantic war took precedence over us in terms of supplies and manpower. Nevertheless, we did our job extremely well and made valuable contributions to the war effort.

Rudolph Fabian had married Roberta Thorington and they had one son, Joseph. Roberta Fabian, who was the sister of Rear Adm. Alexander C. Thorington, predeceased Rudy when she passed away in 1975.

Captain Fabian was nominated, by General of the Army Douglas MacArthur, for the Distinguished Service Medal, but it was neither approved nor awarded. He did receive the Legion of Merit, the Navy Commendation Medal, the Army Unit Commendation ribbon, and the Army Distinguished Unit Emblem. He has also been designated, by the U.S. Naval Cryptologic Veterans Association, as a Pioneer Officer of U.S. Naval Cryptology. And, perhaps most significant, Capt. Laurance Safford—the "father of U.S. naval cryptology"—named Fabian as the navy's "second best" codebreaker of World War II.

Sources

Benson, 7, 20, 63.
Budiansky, 252–53.
Donovan and Mack, 38, 45, 57–58, 63–65, 144–45, 163, 291, 321–23, 147–48, 150–51.
Holmes, 45, 54.

Holtwick, Vol. I, 305, 325, 340, 360, 377, 416, 420, 426–27.
Holtwick, Vol. II, 112, 120.
Kahn, *Codebreakers*, 10, 25, 563, 568.
Lewin, 142.
Lucky Bag, U.S. Naval Academy, 1931.
Maneki, 78–82.
Prados, 211, 246–48, 267–70, 302–3, 317–18, 422.
Smith and Erskine, 140–41, 145, 148.
Spector, *Listening*, 108.
U.S. Navy, *Register of Commissioned and Warrant Officers.*
Worth, 41, 42, 76.

REAR ADMIRAL WILLIAM BERNARD GOGGINS, U.S. NAVY
(1898–1985)

"Bill" "Goo-Goo" "Goggles"

Bill Goggins was an outstanding black-shoe sailor with considerable experience in destroyers, cruisers, and battleships. He was also very experienced as a radio officer and with naval communications in general. What he was *not* was a cryptologist, nor a linguist, nor an intelligence officer, so it was a bit unusual that in 1942 he was assigned as the OIC of Hawaii's Station HYPO, and its follow-on organization, FRUPac. That he was very successful in this role is a tribute to his great professional acumen and also because he was "modest, reserved, a sensible administrator, and a gentleman."

* * *

From the Annapolis yearbook, *The Lucky Bag*:

Another name was added to Omak's long list of soldiers and sailors when *Goo-Goo* entered the Academy to obtain an education that would make him an officer of the Navy. Pink teas are not in *Goo-Goo*'s line, nor does the fairer sex hold any attraction for him. It is rumored that there is a certain little girl out in Washington, but what's the use of relating the usual stuff? *Goo-Goo* is satisfied to sit in his room for hours at a time, engaging with a slip-stick or a wireless outfit, or making his roommate [scream out loud] by banging on a typewriter or guitar. His one ambition in athletics is to swim. He easily won the Plebe championship his first year, and the Academy championship and gold medal Youngster year. The team captaincy came to him First Class year as a well-merited reward. Studying never bothered him for the reason that he never does any. Goggins is a man who has risen by his own efforts and fighting qualities. He is practical, self-reliant, capable, and ever ambitious. [Activities: Mandolin Club; track; swimming team captain; class swimming champion; Academy swimming champion]

* * *

William B. Goggins was born in Republic, Washington, on September 10, 1898, the son of William Goggins and Midge McCarter Goggins. He attended the University of Washington at Seattle for one semester before he was appointed to the Naval Academy in 1916, claiming Omak, Washington, as his home of record. While a midshipman, in the summers of 1917 and 1918, he had service aboard the battleships *Arkansas* and *Utah*. He was graduated and commissioned as an ensign on June 6, 1919 (his class of 1920 was graduated a year early because of a push for more officers due to World War I expansion). His classmates included such notables as Maurice E. Curts, Austin K. Doyle, Cato D. Glover Jr., Roscoe H. Hillenkoetter, Herbert G. Hopwood, Charles B. McVay III, Charles "Swede" Momsen, and Edmund T. Wooldridge. Subsequent promotions included lieutenant (junior grade), 1922; lieutenant, 1925; lieutenant commander, 1934; commander, 1939; and captain, 1942. On June 30, 1949, he was transferred to the retired list and simultaneously promoted to rear admiral—based on a high-level combat decoration.

Following graduation from the academy he joined the battleship *Idaho*, serving onboard until December 1920. After duty in the destroyer *Meade* he reported in March 1921, as assistant communications officer on the staff of the Commander, Destroyer Force and Flotilla Four, Pacific Fleet, onboard the cruiser *Charleston*. In October 1921 he transferred to the staff of Destroyer Squadron Twelve, Pacific Fleet (USS *McDermut*) as radio officer. He then was attached to the staff of the

Commander, Battleship Division Four, Battle Fleet, USS *Arizona*, from June 1923 to June 1924.

Returning to the United States, he had instruction in communications engineering at the Naval Postgraduate School at Annapolis, and continued the course at Yale University. Completing this instruction in October 1926, he joined the battleship *Florida*, and between October 1927 and August 1929 he was attached to the staff of Commander, Light Cruiser Divisions and Division Two, Scouting Fleet, as aide and radio officer. Thereafter he had duty in the Radio Division, Bureau of Engineering, Navy Department, Washington.

In June 1931 he joined the staff of the Commander, Scouting Force, U.S. Fleet, onboard the heavy cruiser *Augusta*, as aide and force radio officer. He remained in that assignment until June 1932 when he joined the destroyer *Hamilton* as executive officer. He transferred in July 1933, in the same capacity, to the USS *Noa*. Following a second tour of duty in the Bureau of Engineering, between June 1934 and June 1936 he commanded the USS *McCormick*, flagship, Destroyer Division Twenty-Seven, and later served as navigator of the light cruiser *Trenton*, flagship, Cruiser Division Two, Battle Force.

He returned to the Naval Academy, in 1939 through 1941, to teach electrical engineering. After that he had six months of duty as executive officer of the light cruiser *Marblehead* (supervising, among others, the navigator—Cmdr. Dick **Zern**) up through the Battle of the Java Sea in February 1942. The ship sustained heavy damage in action against the Japanese. Commander Goggins was severely burned and received a serious head wound. He and other casualties were landed on Java while the *Marblehead* sailed on to seek major, drydock-level repairs.

By the end of March, Japanese forces were going ashore on Java, so the American sailors hid until they escaped to Australia aboard small craft. These adventures formed the basis for a book by James Hilton and a 1944 movie, *The Story of Dr. Wassell*, which starred Gary Cooper and was directed by Cecil B. DeMille. As a result of the Java Sea action Goggins was awarded the Purple Heart; he was also entitled to the ribbon of the Navy Commendation awarded to the crew of the *Marblehead*.

Goggins was recalled to Washington after he had substantially recovered from his injuries. He was again assigned to the Radio Division of the Bureau of Ships (formerly the Bureau of Engineering), and shortly thereafter transferred to OP-20-G for a quick familiarization with codebreaking. Then, for only about a month, he was made OIC of OP-20-G when the incumbent, Capt. John Redman, was transferred to Pearl Harbor to be on the CinCPac staff. When Goggins was in turn sent to Pearl Harbor to relieve Cmdr. Joe **Rochefort** at Station HYPO, he was relieved by Capt. Earl **Stone** as OP-20-G. Unknown to Goggins, Rochefort's sacking was engineered by Rear Adm. Joe Redman, Capt. John Redman, and Cmdr. Joe **Wenger** for essentially personal issues.

When CinCPac (Adm. Chester Nimitz) and the commandant of the Fourteenth Naval District (Rear Adm. David Bagley) heard that Goggins was being sent to Pearl Harbor, they requested that he instead be ordered as deputy director of the newly established Intelligence Center, Pacific Ocean Area (ICPOA) under Capt. Roscoe Hillenkoetter—and not as OIC of HYPO. Thus, when Goggins reached Pearl he found himself in a state of limbo, briefed by his new, overall boss (Bagley) that his orders were going to be changed. As a result, Goggins kept his distance from the HYPO basement, unsure how the struggle over his role would be resolved. It's not really known how he and Rochefort got along during the short time before Rochefort left for Washington; they may not have had much—if any—contact.

Regardless of what admirals Nimitz and Bagley desired, the vice chief of naval operations, Vice Adm. Frederick J. Horne, got Admiral King's concurrence, confirmed Goggins's orders to HYPO, and so directed the Bureau of Personnel. Admiral Nimitz was extremely unhappy that Rochefort was removed—and that Goggins had replaced him—without even being given the courtesy of any notice or consultation. When Goggins was finally brought into the HYPO basement and introduced to the unit as the new OIC, he was met with no little astonishment by the HYPO crew.

But Commander Rochefort wrote a letter to Lt. Cmdr. Jasper **Holmes** in November 1942, not long after Rochefort had been transferred to Washington. It included an assurance that in his opinion Captain Goggins had nothing to do with Rochefort's dismissal, and that he hoped the team would "all be as loyal to Goggins as you have been to me." This comment

> facilitated Goggins's smooth takeover of an organization which had been badly shaken. Fortunately, Goggins was an able administrator and an expert in naval communications. He and I [Holmes] became close and enduring friends. . . . His knowledge of communications and his good relations with CinCPac staff were very important to FRUPac just when its own communications network had to be expanded and improved.

At HYPO, Cmdr. Tommy **Dyer** initially believed that Goggins was in on the plot to remove Rochefort (Goggins was at the moment sharing quarters with Captain Redman, who clearly *was* part of the plot). However, Dyer later concluded that the new head of HYPO was an innocent pawn in these machinations. At Pacific Fleet headquarters, fleet intelligence officer Cmdr. Eddie **Layton** knew that Goggins was a friend of the Redman brothers and so he too was very suspicious about how this had come about—since Goggins lacked experience in codebreaking, the Japanese language, traffic analysis, or intelligence evaluation.

However, Bill Goggins soon became well liked and respected within HYPO—which by now was often referred to as FRUPac. He did alter Rochefort's atmosphere of casual informality. Goggins was a strict, formal, by-the-book officer who essentially wanted things done the "old Navy" way. Nevertheless, he did gain the trust and confidence of HYPO's officers and men, and Holmes later commented that Goggins had indeed become an "able leader of FRUPac [after] Rochefort was detached."

Around February 1943, having split apart organizationally, ICPOA and FRUPac were reunited with Goggins as OIC of both.

Formal and by-the-book he may have been, but he occasionally joked around with his team. For example, by the end of 1943 they were becoming absolutely inundated by captured Japanese documents. Items were quickly evaluated, and things appearing to be of low interest or interest only as background information were left untranslated and were quickly shipped on to the Washington Documents Center—which Goggins liked to call the "Over the River Burial Association."

Captain Goggins later fully supported Commander Dyer in his dispute with OP-20-G (Station NEGAT) over the solving of a two-part Japanese tactical code. Goggins even wrote to NEGAT that "they [NEGAT] had delayed things by their reluctance to recognize that there could be *two* codes, and that Dyer was not in the habit of making idle statements." Goggins held Dyer in the highest esteem, at least once assessing him as "the navy's best cryptanalyst."

In early 1944, senior intelligence officer and Japanese expert Capt. Henri **Smith-Hutton**, working directly for Admiral King in Washington, organized an exchange between FRUPac and OP-20-G to see if there might be unnecessary duplication. Thus, Captain Goggins briefly came to Washington and Smith-Hutton sent naval reserve Cmdr. Bill **Sebald** to Pearl Harbor. It's not clear that a lot was accomplished by this exchange, but one result was that Sebald noted that FRUPac's order of battle intelligence regarding the Japanese naval air forces was clearly superior to Washington's.

When Goggins was detached in January 1945 he received a Legion of Merit for his FRUPac leadership. He then assumed command of the battleship *Alabama* while the ship was being overhauled at the Puget Sound Navy Yard. Upon completion of the overhaul and some training exercises, she headed for the Far East where she joined the fleet at Ulithi in May.

The *Alabama* supported the operations at Okinawa and Kyushu, and her gunners assisted in shooting down a number of *Kamikaze* aircraft. The *Alabama* then participated in the strikes against Japanese industrial installations and other facilities from Honshu to Hokkaido. On one occasion her principal target was an engineering works about fifty miles north of Tokyo against which she expended more than 1,500 tons of explosives. At this point, Goggins was awarded a gold star in lieu of a second Legion of Merit with the combat "V" device. At the war's conclusion, for a period in the fall of 1945, Bill Goggins invited Tommy Dyer as a special guest on board the *Alabama*.

After returning to the United States in January 1946, he reported for duty in the Office of the CNO in Washington, serving in that assignment until May 1947, when he assumed duty as Commanding Officer, Naval Administrative Command, Central Intelligence Group, Washington. From July 1947 to May 1949, when he was relieved of all active duty pending retirement, he served as chief of staff and aide to the Commandant, Fifteenth Naval District, Balboa, Canal Zone. On June 30, 1949, he was transferred to the retired list of the navy and simultaneously promoted to rear admiral.

His many awards included his two Legions of Merit, the Purple Heart, the Navy Unit Commendation Ribbon, the World War I Victory Medal, and the World War II Victory Medal.

After retirement from the navy, Admiral Goggins conducted research at Johns Hopkins University and was a staff consultant to the Army Research Association. He also operated his own firm, the General Kinetics Institute, which was a computer and communications company.

His wife of fifty-nine years, the former Etta Elgin, passed away in 1981. They had two children, Lt. Col. William B. Goggins Jr., USAF, and Jane G. Ryan.

Rear Adm. Goggins died of cardiac arrest in December 1985, in Arlington, Virginia. He and Mrs. Goggins are buried together at Arlington National Cemetery.

Sources

Carlson, 396, 402–5, 412–15.
Dyer, 253–54, 265–67, 306, 353.
Holmes, 115–16, 130, 168, 197.
Layton, *"And I Was There,"* 466.
Lucky Bag, U.S. Naval Academy, 1920.
Prados, 254, 411–12, 544.
U.S. Navy, *Register of Commissioned and Warrant Officers.*
USS *Alabama* information website, www.angelfire.com/va3/bb60/goggins.htm.

CAPTAIN ERNEST SIDNEY LEWIS GOODWIN, U.S. NAVY
(1904–1992)

"Sid"

Sid Goodwin spent a long and eventful career in the cryptologic field—and although he was never formally schooled in the Japanese language, he effectively taught himself and became very impressive as a translator. He pioneered cryptanalytic activity on the Asiatic station, and his noteworthy work there helped convince Washington to fully develop such functions in that area and in Hawaii. His contributions to the war effort were significant, including commanding the FRUMel during an important period. He went on, postwar, to major leadership positions in Washington—at the Office of Naval Communications, the AFSA, and the NSA.

*   *   *

From the 1925 Naval Academy yearbook, *The Lucky Bag*:

Dreams of dark-eyed senoritas and fair blue-eyed blondes of the north caused *Sid* to join the Navy at the tender age of sixteen. With such dreams, beans, slum, hammocks, and coal piles held no terror for him. Two twinkling stars have seen him through all academic difficulties. Before every Dago [foreign language] period, the entire deck rushed in to have him translate the lesson. It became such a regular thing that we sounded late blast for it. The Watch Officer sent his minions in search of a model midshipman and, as the best example of what others lack, Ernie was dragged up, photographed, and posted in conspicuous places. To him, taking a work-out is the next best thing to taking his drag [date] canoeing. [Activities: class gymnasium; gymnasium squad]

*   *   *

Born in New Orleans on October 1, 1904, Ernest S. L. Goodwin was the son of Frederick L. and Nora L. Goodwin. He graduated from the U.S. Naval Academy and was commissioned an ensign, on June 3, 1925, along with classmates such as Alwin D. **Kramer**, Redfield "Rosie" **Mason**, John F. Delaney Jr., Ernest "Judge" Eller, Robert E. Hogaboom, Morton C. Mumma Jr., and Linwood **Howeth**. He was promoted to lieutenant (junior grade) in 1928; lieutenant, 1934; lieutenant commander, 1939; commander, 1942; and captain, 1945.

Commencing the initial and typical heavy pattern of sea duty, Mr. Goodwin served on board the battleship *California* from June 1925 to July 1926, the destroyer *Yarborough* until April 1930, the destroyer *Tarbell* until June 1931, and the light cruiser *Omaha* from June 1931 to June 1932.

Goodwin then began his cryptologic career in the summer of 1932 when he reported for instruction to OP-20-G in Washington—along with Lt. j.g. Thomas A. **Huckins** and Lt. j.g. Victor D. Long. Other students there included Lt. j.g. Edward F. Crowe, Lt. j.g. Wayne N. Gamet, and Marine 1st Lt. Frank P. Pyzick. After studying cryptanalysis for one year, Sid became the head of OP-20-GC, the branch that created U.S. naval codes.

After a brief assignment with the radio intercept station at Wailupe, Territory of Hawaii, in 1933, Mr. Goodwin then transferred to the Sixteenth Naval District at Cavite in the Philippines, reporting in June 1934. He moved to Olongapo when the commander in chief of the Asiatic Fleet expressed willingness to have an additional radio intelligence officer on his staff; he was also promoted to lieutenant that same month. Mr. Goodwin worked as OIC of the Asiatic decryption unit until, in November 1935, he relieved Lt. j.g. Tom Huckins in the flagship *Augusta*. In effect, around February 1935, Goodwin essentially established Station CAST at the Mariveles Naval Reservation on the Bataan Peninsula.

Mr. Goodwin was thus the first of a series of six officers who came from training and duty at OP-20-G to the Asiatic Station—firstly as head of the Philippine on-shore decryption unit for a year, and then a year and a half as head of the Asiatic station's radio intelligence activities. This latter post was in the guise of assistant fleet communications officer, on the staff of the commander in chief, onboard the flagship. Goodwin was relieved in November 1935, from the on-shore billet, by Lt. j.g. Raymond S. **Lamb**; he was in turn relieved on the CinCAF staff by Lamb, in December 1936.

Initially, as an assistant to Mr. Huckins, it occurred to Goodwin that here was an opportunity to work on actual codebreaking—beyond just the existing routines of intercepting communications and radio traffic analysis.

> As I had no instructions from the commander in chief other than those which directed me to engage in radio intelligence work on shore under the supervision of Lt. Huckins, I realized that I was being given a free hand and that I was, at least for a time, to determine my own procedure to the best advantage of the Radio Intelligence Service.

Goodwin's resulting efforts on Japanese fleet maneuvers was praised in Washington. Lt. j.g. Ham **Wright**, in OP-20-G, stated in early 1935 that:

> Lieutenant Goodwin has done a remarkable piece of work from a cryptanalytic point of view. It clearly demonstrates that with adequate and capable personnel [the Asiatic unit] is capable of furnishing considerable information both to CinCAF and to the Navy Department.

As Goodwin himself wrote in a report,

> The value of an efficient and productive cryptanalytic bureau located on this station will be such as to make its establishment well worthwhile, and that no difficulties which block progress toward this end can be allowed to stand without a determined fight.

Thus, Lieutenant Goodwin established a precedent which soon led Lieutenant Commander **Safford**, the OP-20-G chief, to decide that it clearly had become important that the Pacific intercept stations should establish dedicated on-site cryptanalytic sections.

Apparently, Sid Goodwin did spectacular work in these assignments involving both code breaking and translating—which is all the more impressive as he was *not* a trained Japanese linguist. Indeed, in a March 1937 letter, Lt. Ray Lamb wrote that:

> The Admiral [CinCAF] himself recommended that we have got to have an additional officer out here to do the translating. In spite of what all our people say, the ORANGE [Japanese] language cannot be translated *accurately* by other than a qualified officer. We can break the stuff down, read it partially, but often we interpret it incorrectly or miss the important points. Goodwin did *wonders*, we all admit, but he was not always correct and he had to sacrifice all other projects in order to translate. [And,] there are no more *Goodwins* out here, and we cannot devote the time to translating with so many other projects on the list.

Lieutenant Goodwin went on to consecutive tours aboard the cruisers *Augusta*, November 1935 to March 1937, and *San Francisco*, March 1937 to June 1938. He then returned to Main Navy, relieving Lt. Cmdr. Joe **Wenger**. Thus, from 1938 to 1940 Goodwin was back in Washington, working under Safford, as the head of OP-20-GY—the cryptanalysis branch of OP-20-G. He later wrote that:

Commander Safford, although eccentric, was a genius. Safford introduced cryptanalysis to the Navy and established its intercept sites. Safford's greatest contributions were developing the Electric Code Machine and ensuring that this machine was ready when the war started. He was also responsible for the excellent communications security that the Navy had throughout the war.

There are many dimensions to communications intelligence; therefore, we should be careful in judging its effectiveness. In 1932, when I took the cryptanalysis course set up by Safford, I felt it was short on theory. My instructor was Tommy **Dyer**. We learned by just doing problems. However [I have to admit], when I was head of the cryptanalysis section, from 1938 to 1940, I did nothing to correct this situation.

But during this period, Goodwin did promote much better coordination among units. He

announced that a new "Information Section" had been established [to index] all information received, and as the contact point between OP-20-G and ONI in supplying desired back information, as well as making reports on currently translated messages to ONI. He requested that all units forward copies of all their translations for [GY's] consumption.

He also requested a free-flow of information from units to Washington and each other on what work was being done, how it was done, and general background of conditions under which it was done, including diagrams and photos of working spaces. This was to be forwarded by officer messenger in naval transports only—trans-Pacific air mail being regarded as too insecure for transmittal of unencrypted communications-intelligence material.

Mr. Goodwin was selected the first time he was considered for promotion to lieutenant commander, in 1938. Interestingly, the same promotion board passed over fellow communications-intelligence officers Tom Huckins, Tommy Dyer, and Ed Crowe.

In September 1940, Lieutenant Commander Goodwin became captain of the *Clemson*-class destroyer USS *Noa*, which spent much of the next two years on experimental assignments and on midshipman training operations out of Annapolis.

In September 1943 he became the OIC of FRUMel, primarily serving the U.S. Seventh Fleet.

In 1943, before going to Melbourne to relieve Rudy **Fabian**, I came to Washington to brush up on the business. . . . I was very impressed with the advances in code breaking that I saw in 1943.

As a joint military organization, FRUMel always had a U.S. commander and an Australian commander. Cmdr. Jack Newman was the Australian commander throughout the war. Newman's duties were to monitor FRUMel output for the Australians, help FRUMel obtain resources, assist FRUMel with the maintenance of good relationships with other sectors of the Australian government, and administer the two units of RAANs under FRUMel control. One unit of RAANs was stationed at Moorabbin and the other was at our headquarters in Melbourne. Melbourne was also the headquarters for the RAN, and Newman was responsible for all naval communications out of Melbourne. When Fabian was commander, there was a triumvirate of Fabian, **Lietwiler**, and Newman. Lietwiler was never commander of FRUMel by himself. All of us had excellent relations with Jack Newman. Working with the Australians was a great experience.

Our mission at FRUMel was to obtain and process intercept of Japanese naval communications from Moorabbin. During my watch, 90% of our traffic was Japanese submarine communications. We also identified targets for our ships, such as Japanese oil tankers and troop ships. We gave our intelligence to both U.S. and Australian navy commanders. Sometimes, because of atmospheric conditions, we intercepted FRUPac targets. Then we would radio this traffic to Station HYPO [FRUPac] in Hawaii.

In Australia, as in all British Commonwealth countries, the postmaster-general was in charge of telegraph communications. The Melbourne postmaster-general gave us control of a dedicated line to communicate with Hawaii and with Washington.

Working at FRUMel was challenging because of the push-pull relationship it had with the Office of Naval Intelligence (ONI) and the Office of Naval Communications (ONC). Arthur **McCollum**, the intelligence officer for the Seventh Fleet, wanted FRUMel under his jurisdiction.

Redman and Wenger, who were in ONC, strongly resisted McCollum's efforts. They maintained that FRUMel belonged under ONC because its mission was communication techniques, and it was manned by communicators who depended on contacts with other communications units and the assistance of Japanese language officers. FRUMel was established by an agreement between U.S. Navy communicators and the Australian Naval Board. A shift by the U.S. Navy to move FRUMel under ONI could disrupt this agreement.

How much did FRUMel contribute to the cryptologic effort in the Pacific? Those who worked in Hawaii say that they did 80% of the work. Others say that Washington did 75% of the work. Quantifying communications intelligence in this manner is incorrect. C.I. is multidimensional, not uni-dimensional. For instance, there are many categories of substantive contributions. Categories range from technical information to operational information. It is equally inappropriate to ask which site was number one in reading messages. Merely reading messages is not relevant. The important questions are, What messages were read? How timely were messages read? Which recipients got the messages? I believe that the entire team of FRUMel, Hawaii, and Washington performed an inestimable service for the war effort. My time and contacts at FRUMel were extremely gratifying and rewarding.

In December 1944, Commander Goodwin returned to Washington. Promoted to captain in 1945, he later helped Rear Adm. Samuel Eliot Morison with his epic history of U.S. naval operations in World War II. He "intensively" read the manuscript of volume 11: *The Invasion of France and Germany, 1944–1945*—a little surprising, as one might have expected him to look over Pacific operations rather than European.

In September 1946, Goodwin was made Assistant Chief of Naval Communications. Three years later he became Acting Head of the Supplementary Operations Branch (NavComDiv OP-202), relieving Capt. Joe Wenger—effectively the head of an early version of the Naval Security Group. He directed these efforts until September 1949, when he was relieved by Capt. Jack **Holtwick**.

Captain Goodwin represented the navy on the Communications Intelligence Coordinating Committee which assisted with the formation of the AFSA. He transferred to the staff of the AFSA as head of the Operations Section. He then assumed the duties of AFSA's Executive for Coordination and Compliance in September 1950, and the following August he became adjutant general for the same organization.

In 1952, Goodwin transferred to the NSA as an inspector, serving as such for both AFSA and NSA until August 1953. At that time, he became the head of the Office of Machine Processing for the NSA.

In September 1954, Captain Goodwin was designated as the first inspector general for the NSA, serving in that capacity until he retired on July 1, 1956.

His decorations and awards include the Bronze Star and the Second Nicaraguan Campaign Medal. In 1964, Sid earned a PhD in management from the University of Michigan. He taught first at Sacramento State University, and then at the Naval Postgraduate School in Monterey, California.

In 1933 he had married Elizabeth L. Zane of Nice, France. Captain Goodwin passed away in February 1992.

Sid Goodwin has been recognized and honored by the U.S. Naval Cryptologic Veterans Association as an officer who has served as the Commander, Naval Security Group, or one of its predecessor organizations. He has also been named a Pioneer Officer of U.S. Naval Cryptology by the same organization.

Sources

Browne and Carlson, *Echoes of Our Past*, 222–23.
Holtwick, 91, 105–6, 113, 117, 136–8, 147, 151, 153, 185, 216, 268, 305, 306, 340, 367, 410, 432, App. 6, 91.
Kahn, *Codebreakers*, 562.
Layton, *"And I Was There,"* 56, 78.
Lucky Bag, U.S. Naval Academy, 1925.
Maneki, 78–82.
Morison, XI, xi.
U.S. Navy, *Register of Commissioned and Warrant Officers*.

CAPTAIN JOHN SYLVESTER HARPER, U.S. NAVY (1900–1975)

"Bud" "Jack"

John Harper, like many people in this collection, successfully blended black-shoe destroyer and battleship service with duty in cryptology. However, in addition to his focus against the Japanese, he uniquely served in South America and against the Germans. Harper essentially backed into the business of cryptology, more active with communications security than with cryptanalysis. He was *not* identified, in the fall of 1941, as one of the eighteen officers "qualified and acceptable" for communications-intelligence—yet years later was designated a pioneer of naval cryptology by the Naval Cryptographic Veterans Association.

*   *   *

From the 1922 Annapolis yearbook, *The Lucky Bag*:

We've always wondered, and still do wonder for that matter, whatever induced J. Sylvester to enter the outfit. Look at his picture and you'll wonder, too. The Navy is the last organization on earth that one would suspect of having any charms for this youth. He knew more when he came in the place than lots of us will know when we get out. But when he did run into strange waters in the Academic Sea it was quite a task for him to bone [study]. He didn't know how. Fact is, he never learned. Take Dago [foreign languages] for instance. *Bud* figured that a knowledge of French wasn't essential to read drawings or converse with American girls, so why bone for it? We don't suppose any midshipman has read more magazines or books than *Bud* since Winston Churchill spoke the language. It's mighty convenient to be savvy. "Yes, that's Harper—number three in the front rank—he's always out of step."

*   *   *

John Harper was born on March 7, 1900, and grew up in Baltimore, Maryland. He graduated from the Naval Academy and was commissioned an ensign in June 1922, along with such classmates as Henri **Smith-Hutton**, Wilfred "Jasper" **Holmes**, William S. Parsons, William J. **Sebald**, and Hyman G. Rickover. Subsequent promotions included lieutenant (junior grade), 1925; lieutenant, 1928; lieutenant commander, 1937; commander, January 1942; and captain, June 1942. He retired from the navy in 1953.

After his Annapolis graduation he reported onboard the battleship *Pennsylvania*. This was followed by duty with the destroyer *McDermut* from 1924 through 1929— if the official *Navy Register* can be believed—which was an unusually long tour in just one ship for a junior officer in this time period. Then, during 1930 and 1931, Lt. Harper returned to the Naval Academy, assigned to the staff. From 1933 through 1935 he continued service in battleships, drawing duty on board the *Tennessee* and the *Maryland*.

In early 1932, Lt. Harper, Lt. j.g. Ham **Wright**, and Lt. j.g. Jack **Holtwick** were assigned temporary duty on board the battleship *California* to form a communications unit for the Fleet Exercise. The exercise was conducted in Hawaiian waters, and the communications unit utilized material obtained by simulated intercept—the analysts were furnished copies by the ship's radio room. Some success was achieved in solving the currently used contact code; however, more difficult and more significant was their complete break-in to the navy's real-world signal-code cipher—which later caused a complete revision of that system.

In early 1935, Lieutenant Harper was made head of OP-20-GX (Intercept and Tracking), under Cmdr. Howard **Kingman** (OP-20-G).

Harper was subsequently relieved at GX by Lt. Cmdr. August J. Detzer in the summer of 1936. Mr. Harper then replaced Joe **Rochefort** as OIC of the CinCUS communications-intelligence unit on board the flagship *Pennsylvania* (Lieutenant Wright was already there in the unit; Lt. Lee **Parke** arrived at the same time).

During his tour of duty as OIC of the CinCUS unit, Harper devoted almost all of its efforts to monitoring and maintaining the security of communications in the U.S. Fleet. In September 1937 he wrote Cmdr. Laurance **Safford**, once again the head of OP-20-G, outlining his efforts in this regard; he thus admitted to almost no activity at all in actual COMINT work against "ORANGE"—which is to say the Japanese. He reported that his three officers, five radiomen, and two yeomen were fully employed in maintaining cryptographic security, producing cryptographic aids, advancing radio security, administrating the registered publications program, and conducting censorship of ships' newspapers.

Interestingly, in the fall of 1938, Commander Safford was himself becoming very concerned about overall poor communications-security practices in the U.S. Navy—but he was not impressed with Mr. Harper's efforts. Safford seemed to feel that none of the recent CinCUS unit officers in charge had properly interpreted OP-20-G's COMSEC policies, and he was particularly concerned that the fleet may have "been misdirected during the past year by Harper and his assistants." He also felt that Harper's relief in the position, Lt. Wayne N. Gamet, was likewise "slow to see where the trouble was."

In June 1938, Lieutenant Commander Harper was given command of the destroyer *Hopkins*. In 1939, Harper detached from the *Hopkins* and was sent to South America as a member of the U.S. naval mission to Brazil. During this time he qualified as a translator of Portuguese.

Mr. Harper was assigned to the battleship *West Virginia* in 1941. At the time of the attack on Pearl Harbor he was serving as the damage control officer. As the attack began, Jack set about correcting the damage being inflicted upon the ship. He directed counter-flooding which probably prevented the *West Virginia* from capsizing and, when the attack was ended, he took charge of the fire-fighting on the upper decks until the fire was extinguished during the afternoon of the next day.

In early 1942, Harper was promoted to commander and sent back to OP-20-G. This was in preparation for returning to Brazil in order to establish a direction-finding network in that country. He established himself at the port of Recife, where he was responsible for constructing and operating an extension of the navy's high-frequency direction-finding net, from Recife to Belem to Bahia. Harper's network aided in the sinking of several German submarines and in the capture of three blockade runners. For this high-initiative activity, he was decorated by the commander, Fourth Fleet.

Harper was promoted to captain in 1943. In early 1944 he was assigned back to Washington where he served as head of the navy's Communications Security organization. He then was sent to the Pacific where he served during the remainder of World War II as OIC of FRUPac, from January 1944 to November 1945. There he relieved Capt. Bill **Goggins**, and was in turn relieved by Capt. Tommy **Dyer**. At FRUPac he was also pleased to find on his staff his friend and classmate Jasper **Holmes**.

After the war, Captain Harper was designated as the commanding officer of the Naval Security Station, at Nebraska Avenue, in Washington.[1] Then, toward the end of his career, he served at the NSA as director of research.

In 1953 he retired and stayed in Maryland where he was active with an electronics firm; he then was involved in real estate sales and promotion. Captain Harper passed away in 1975.

His decorations and awards included the Bronze Star. He was designated a Pioneer Officer of U.S. Naval Cryptology by the Naval Cryptologic Veterans Association, and intelligence historian John Prados, in his monumental work *Combined Fleet Decoded*, specifically named Harper as one of the FRUPac "cryppies" that should never be forgotten by history.

Sources

Holmes, 197.
Holtwick, 94, 138, 149, 153, 174, 182, 201, 212, 249–53, 305, 308, 380, 384, 432, App. 5.
Lucky Bag, U.S. Naval Academy, 1922.
McGinnis, 20.
Prados, 186, 412.
Toland, 197–98.
U.S. Navy, *Register of Commissioned and Warrant Officers.*

---

1. An interesting incident from this period comes from an interview conducted in 1977 with retired Chief Warrant Officer Ralph T. Briggs. Briggs stated that in December 1945, Captain Harper (as commanding officer of the station) ordered him to *not* testify at the current hearings about the Pearl Harbor disaster, and to *not* speak with Captain Laurance Safford any more than he already had. Safford was at that time trying to engage Briggs's support in his own testimony regarding having seen the Japanese "winds" execute message right before the Pearl Harbor attack. In December 1941, Briggs, then a petty officer, was an intercept operator at the navy's East Coast interception station—Station M (Cheltenham, Maryland). A trained *kata kana* instructor, he believed he had received the controversial "East Wind, Rain" message on December 4, which would have indicated an imminent major breach between the United States and Japan—although the message would not have specified the attack on Pearl Harbor. According to Briggs, Captain Harper told him that "too much" had already been revealed at the hearings, and that "perhaps someday you'll understand the reason for this."

CAPTAIN JACK SEBASTIAN HOLTWICK JR., U.S. NAVY
(1907–1987)

The cryppie with a knack for gadgets
One of Rochefort's core team at Station HYPO
Organized the first structure of the Naval Security Group
"Jack"

"Unusually seasoned, dapper, always natty," Jack S. Holtwick was an innovator and a trendsetter throughout his entire career. He excelled at cryptanalysis, machine cryptanalysis, organizational management, leadership, ship-handling (he commanded two ships), private-sector business administration, and historical compilation. He spent more than four years at Hawaii's Stations HYPO and FRUPac—in charge there at the war's end. He was a key member of Joe Rochefort's core group for over a year, but his extraordinary reputation in cryptology ranges far earlier—and later—than the war itself.

*   *   *

From the 1927 Annapolis yearbook *The Lucky Bag*:

"Let's see, who am I dragging next Saturday?" This question is asked as surely as the hop [*dance*] night draws near. That *Jack* is a Snake [*a midshipman who always has a date—often someone else's*], therefore, must be admitted, here and now. One would naturally think that such as he would not be much of anything else, but as it happens the rub comes here: *Jack* is something else. In fact, he's quite versatile. Not only have his heavenly aspirations been realized and his star secured, but he has won the position of Treasurer of the Trident Society [*founded in 1914, it produced a literary magazine and other publications*], and also feature editor of this annual. When these things are not occupying his time, Jack may be found in the boxing ring, or perhaps in the swimming pool. In fact, his proudest achievement in athletics is that he has been a charter member of the swimming sub-squad [remedial group] since his *entrée*. We must admit that he is a wee bit light, as the term is used in the Navy. This fact is well illustrated if one should pick up the *Log* [*midshipman humor magazine*] sometime and take note of his literary outbursts. He has to be toned down, or he would, in truth, make the publication float away. That he has been a good Samaritan to the dumb, an object of amusement to the bored, and a classmate to all is registered in our fondest memories, and when we are scattered throughout the Fleet, it will always be a pleasure to meet him again. [Activities: boxing, *Log* feature editor, *Lucky Bag* feature editor, *Trident* staff, musical club, class show director, sub-squad]

*   *   *

Jack Holtwick was born in the former Indian Territory, soon to be the state of Oklahoma, on February 27, 1907, son of Jack Sr. and Ida Muhl Holtwick. Jack Sr. once ran for president of the United States on an obscure third-party ticket. Jack Jr. attended San Pedro [California] High School and then entered the Naval Academy in 1923, graduating with distinction in 1927 along with such classmates as Richard D. **Zern**, George W. Anderson, Glynn "Donc" Donaho, Lee W. **Parke**, Gill M. **Richardson**, and U.S. Grant Sharp Jr. Subsequent promotions included lieutenant (junior grade), 1930; lieutenant, 1936; lieutenant commander, 1941; commander, 1942; and captain, 1945. He retired from the navy in 1957.

From September 1927 until February 1929, Mr. Holtwick served as junior plotting-room officer in the battleship *Tennessee*. He then underwent flight training at the Naval Air Station Pensacola, Florida, from March to July 1929, but did not graduate. He then served until April 1930 as the communications officer of the destroyer *Case*.

In early 1929, Ensign Holtwick—bored and broke in Philadelphia—onboard the soon-to-be-decommissioned *Case*, amused himself by working on cryptograms found in the *Naval Communications Bulletin* (cryptograms put in there by OP-20-G to hopefully attract officers with potential for cryptanalytic training). He sent his completed ones in to OP-20-G as the *Bulletin* requested—which caused his selection for OP-20-G's training program four years later.

However, his next two years of duty saw him as the gunnery and torpedo officer of the destroyer *Sicard*, which preceded a follow-on assignment—from June 1932 until June 1934—as radio officer of the battleship *Texas*.

In early 1932, Lt. John **Harper**, Lt. j.g. Wesley **Wright**, and Lt. j.g. Jack Holtwick were assigned temporary duty on board the battleship *California* to form a communications unit for that year's Fleet Exercise, which was conducted in Hawaiian waters. They utilized material obtained by simulated intercept—the unit being furnished copies by the ship's radio room. Some success was achieved in solving the currently used contact code, but more difficult and more significant was their complete break-in to the navy's signal-code cipher, which later caused a complete revision of this system.

In the spring of 1934, Mr. Holtwick applied for and received approval—and funding—to take twenty-five hours of Spanish instruction from the Berlitz Language School in Washington. He apparently did well, for the navy subsequently designated him as a qualified Spanish translator.

At that point Jack was assigned to OP-20-G, at Main Navy, for cryptanalysis training—one of five new trainees at that time. By the summer of 1935 he had finished the basic and most of the advanced cryptologic training. Holtwick was then selected, as a promising cryptology student, to take some specialized math courses (such as statistics, correlation, and probability and chance), commuting between Washington and Annapolis. In fact, Lt. j.g. Holtwick and Lt. j.g. Wright were among the first to do this, during 1934 and 1935.

Sometime after April 1935, Holtwick took over from Wright the supervision and installation of IBM equipment at OP-20-G. After some immersion in that role, Holtwick realized that considerable time and effort could be saved in sorting by a relatively simple change in the punching code; as a result the changes were made in the machines under Holtwick's hands-on supervision. In addition, Holtwick took over—again from Wright—a task of systematically collecting and codifying the known but unrecorded data the section had on ten years' worth of Japanese cryptologic systems. Holtwick later wrote that because of the tremendous workload—and low staffing levels—little time had been spent

in maintaining a record of what had been done. Details of what had been solved, how they were solved, and what part each system played in the entire Japanese naval cryptographic system were available, if at all, only in the memory of Mrs. Agnes **Driscoll**. Fortunately, though, material . . . had accumulated over the years in a sort of "Fibber McGee's closet" in Room 1645, where odds-and-ends of incredible variety could be unearthed.

Lieutenant Wright had realized . . . the danger of having the entire background and continuity of a decade of effort available only in the brain cells of only one person. [His foreboding was forcefully proved warranted less than three years later when Mrs. Driscoll was seriously injured in an automobile accident in which two others were killed.]

Wright therefore systematically set out to identify each Japanese system of which we had any record, and to write a monograph containing all of the information he was able to accrue about it. . . . Holtwick, who took over this task on Wright's transfer, drew heavily upon Mrs. Driscoll's memory, and validated her recollections by actual application of the cryptographic details she remembered to the traffic stored in the closet. He was thus able to bring up to date and continue Wright's project of publishing a complete history of each type of system which the Japanese Navy and Foreign Office had used up to that time.

This work gave Holtwick some valuable insights into the psychology of Japanese naval cryptographers which later greatly aided him in attacking Japanese naval codes.

His duties weren't just confined to a desk or the office. For example, in July 1935, during a dinner that ONI's Cmdr. Ellis **Zacharias** and his wife put on at their home for the Japanese naval attaché, at Zacharias's direction Mr. Holtwick and Chief Radioman Walter **McGregor** entered the attaché's apartment in the Alban Towers on Wisconsin Avenue. In the guise of overall-clad, toolbox-carrying electricians (*Jack* and *Mack*, as it were), they carefully examined Captain Yamaguchi's apartment—which also was his office. While pretending to fix a power failure in the suite, their covert mission was to determine whether—as ONI suspected—the attaché kept an electric cipher machine on his premises. Short of actually finding a machine, "the inspection by flashlight," Zacharias later wrote, "covered everything we desired," which included examining (but not taking) various crypto-paraphernalia and papers.

Holtwick also tried his hand at designing a mechanical device for cryptanalysis which had interlocking gears and pin-controlled stepping sequences. Lt. Joseph **Wenger**, then head of OP-20-GY, approved a project for the Naval Gun Factory's machine shop to construct a prototype of this cipher machine, also utilizing a custom-made *kana* typewriter as the printing element. Sometime later in 1937, when this imitative version of the M-1 Japanese cipher machine was actually finished (by that time Holtwick had transferred to the Sixteenth Naval District's communications-intelligence unit), it actually worked and worked as Holtwick conceived it. Unfortunately, the Japanese abandoned the M-1 system in 1938, so Holtwick's machine shortly lost its usefulness.

In addition to this activity, in 1935 Mr. Holtwick started producing a series of OP-20-G *RIPs* (*Radio Intelligence Publications*) specifically focused upon technical communications-intelligence information.

In September 1936, Lieutenant Holtwick was detached for communications-intelligence duty at the headquarters of the Sixteenth Naval District, Cavite, Philippine Islands, relieving Lt. Raymond **Lamb**; his cover title was "Assistant Issuing Officer, 16th N.D." On the way out he stopped in San Francisco to inspect the direction-finding setup at the Mare Island Navy Yard, and to investigate what was being done in the DF field by Pan American Airways. He also stopped at Pearl Harbor and spent a week in consultation with Lt. Thomas **Dyer** at the COMINT unit there.

When Holtwick arrived in Cavite he learned that Lt. Sid **Goodwin** had previously set a pattern and foundation there for doing actual cryptanalysis (versus just traffic analysis) which was followed by his successors, now including Holtwick.

At this point Holtwick wrote a letter back to Wenger in Washington, venting frustration over some issues—some of these frustrations may well have been more Ray Lamb's than Holtwick's, as Holtwick had just recently arrived. In any event, he mentioned discouragement about the failure (due to no funding) of the project to move radio intelligence from the Cavite Navy Yard to more secure spaces on Corregidor; problems with personnel; and hopes that new flag officers who may be assigned to administrative or actual control over COMINT activities be properly "sold" on the program.

> The matter of prestige comes in—it is very difficult for any high ranking officer to take the word of a lieutenant or j.g. concerning the tremendous importance of something of which the ranking officer has never even heard during his thirty or more years in the service. We have got, somehow, to overcome the lack of interest, lack of enthusiasm, and lack of co-operation and trust on the part of senior officers . . . for this branch of work.

> He mentioned also the collateral duties assigned to the R.I. officers that took badly needed time away from their [primary] duties, and the unsatisfactory situation with respect to enlisted personnel: lack of control of their assignments . . . discontent because of their belief they are held back in advancement; overwork; and inadequate quarters.

In May 1937, Lieutenant Holtwick and Radioman Meddie J. Royer experimented with new dipole combinations and then successfully developed an effective high-frequency direction-finding unit which was installed at Sangley Point, Philippines. This had taken many hours of laborious experimentation, which had been started by Holtwick's predecessor in the position, Lieutenant Lamb. Moreover, in early 1937, Holtwick was still interested in "mechanizing the clerical and pedestrian work of actual decryption of messages whose cryptographic systems had been solved." Thus, he "invented a device which introduced a mechanical twist to the normally pencil-and-paper task of performing the transposition necessary to decipher messages in the most frequently used enciphered Japanese naval codes." This device, called the "Holtwick Handy Cipher Solver," generated great excitement among his colleagues, but soon became obsolete when the Japanese discontinued the cipher for which it was designed.

Lieutenant Holtwick was relieved by Lt. John A. **Williams** regarding COMINT duties in November and then, from December 1937 until April 1939, Holtwick served as the assistant fleet communications officer on the staff of the Commander in Chief, U.S. Asiatic Fleet; he also picked up the extra duties of Fleet Camera Officer and Assistant Fleet Intelligence Officer. In late 1938, Holtwick spent some time in the hospital as he'd broke his ankle roller skating with Lt. (later Lt. Gen., USMC) Victor Krulak and their wives.

In April 1939, Holtwick left Manila on the SS *President Coolidge*, arriving at San Francisco. From June 1939 until May 1940 he served as the executive officer of the destroyer *Dewey*, which was a unit of Destroyer Squadron One. Then, reporting to the headquarters of the Fourteenth Naval District at Pearl Harbor, he was assigned to Station HYPO as a cryptanalyst—joining Tommy Dyer and Ham Wright who were already there. By 1941, in addition to working in the GY (Cryptanalysis) Section, Holtwick consulted with the GX (Radio) Section and headed the Statistical Section. He was in those roles, working under the iconic Cmdr. Joseph **Rochefort** (who had taken charge of HYPO in June 1941), when the Japanese attacked the U.S. fleet on December 7, 1941.

In the days before and immediately after the Pearl Harbor attack, Lieutenant Commander Holtwick also acted as liaison between the HYPO basement [or the "Dungeon" as it was often called] and "the Navy Yard, the Submarine Force, the CinCPac staff, and other outside agencies."

Then, according to Lieutenant Commander Dyer, "When we took over part of the responsibility for JN-25, Jack Holtwick completely organized the machine processing facilities and did an outstanding job of that. I was very grateful." Dyer called the machine room "the boiler factory." As described by historian Elliot Carlson,

> Jam-packed with a variety of IBM machines, cut-off from the rest of the basement and, mercifully, rendered soundproof by thick cinderblocks, the machine room would be Holtwick's domain. Used to discern patterns in encrypted messages transmitted by the Imperial Japanese Navy and speed the compromising of its codes and ciphers, the boiler factory in the months ahead would prove its worth.

Thus, Holtwick's primary duty became running the machine room, and as the volume of work rapidly increased, "the entire attention of this wiry, quick, and energetic officer was required to program and supervise the business machines and the very secret coding machine." As a result, Lt. Cmdr. Jasper **Holmes** took on many of Holtwick's other routine chores and external liaison tasks.

By the time of the Battle of the Coral Sea (May 4–8, 1942), the needs of the cryptanalysts and the translators exceeded the capabilities of the Dungeon's machines. Lieutenant Commander Dyer alone needed unlimited access to the machinery. "Holtwick had all the available machinery programmed twenty-four hours each day," but it was never enough, and often "the translators could not wait for machine time." Another Dungeon officer observed that in the lead-up to Midway, Holtwick "played the IBM machinery like a skilled pianist."

The Battle of the Coral Sea ended with the first carrier-vs.-carrier sea battle in naval history. In the Dungeon, during the battle, the men closely studied all intercepted Japanese messages for news.

> The Japanese used the word *gekichin* to report the destruction of an enemy ship, and *chimbotsu* to describe the sinking of one of their own ships. The Traffic-Analysis Desk flagged every important message and rushed it to Lieutenant Commander Holtwick in the machine room. As each printout rolled off the machines, hungry eyes searched for the code group for *chimbotsu*. When they spotted it, we learned that the "Ryukaku" was *chimbotsu*.

Although the loss of the carrier *Lexington* was a greater tactical blow to the United States than was the loss of the "Ryukaku" to the Japanese (in reality their carrier *Shōhō*), the blunting of the Japanese offensive—and the resulting safety of Port Moresby in Papua New Guinea—was very much a victory for the Allies on the strategic level.

Later, in the weeks and months after the Battle of Midway (June 4–7, 1942), the crew at Station HYPO hoped for some recognition for their contribution to the victory. That, as has already been discussed, was not going to happen because Rear Adm. Joe Redman (director of naval communications) and his brother Capt. John Redman (head of OP-20-G) in Washington were intent upon *not* commending Station HYPO—moreover, as Rear Adm. Edward **Layton** later wrote, they

> were determined to hide the facts about how badly *they* had blundered by predicting the wrong date and target of the Japanese operation . . . the Redman brothers, thanks to their ready access to senior members of the naval staff in Washington, circulated the word that [the Midway success] was the result of *their* outfit's work, and *not* that of Joe Rochefort's team. . . . They were soon boasting that without the efforts of the Station NEGAT [OP-20-G in Washington] cryptanalysts . . . Midway and the Hawaiian Islands would have been captured by the Japanese. Their campaign of disinformation worked.

There was also the issue of secrecy—it's difficult to give medals without disclosing what the activity was that earned them. Most of HYPO's officers and men took the news of no medals philosophically. Some took it satirically. Joe Rochefort's biographer, Elliot Carlson, wrote that:

> One was the basement's jokester, Jack Holtwick, known for his pranks. Sometimes showing up at parties with a monocle in one eye, he had a way of flipping it so it always ended up in his shirt pocket. When Holtwick heard the news, he rigged up a mock ribbon for himself. It had a veil over it indicating the decoration was for secret intelligence work that couldn't be revealed.

Eddie Layton further wrote that "we knew something of what was going on. . . . Just how successful the Redmans were at perpetrating their fraud didn't come to light for more than a year, when Commander Holtwick [visited at Washington] Rear Admiral Redman in October 1943." Redman made the comment that Station HYPO surely had "missed the boat at the Battle of Midway," but fortunately OP-20-G in Washington had gotten it right and "saved the day." Holtwick was stunned by the remark, not only because of its gross representation of the truth, but also because Redman had to know that Holtwick knew the exact opposite was true.

During the summer of 1942,

> work on the five-digit code [JN-25] continued to receive highest priority. Practically all of the time of Dyer, Wright, Finnegan, **Lasswell**, and most of the cryptographers, was occupied with that code. Holtwick gave it first precedence in the machine room.

In April 1943, Commander Holtwick was transferred and served for five months on the staff of the Commander, Southwest Pacific; there he was the OIC of FRUMel.

Holtwick was then reassigned, in November, to Chungking as chief of staff for security for the Commander, Naval Group China. Then, in June 1944, he was back to Pearl Harbor, now OIC of FRUPac—what had earlier been called Station HYPO or the Combat Intelligence Unit. Promoted to captain in March 1945, Holtwick continued duty as the OIC of the SupRadPac, which became the new name of the former FRUPac. He served in this role until the conclusion of the war.

For a brief period, from February through December 1947, Captain Holtwick served as the commanding officer of the fleet oiler USS *Platte*. His next assignment was back to Washington as the assistant chief, Office of Communications Security (OP-202-HO). He was detached from there in July 1949, and after brief duty as the comptroller of the new AFSA, became the head of the Security Branch, Navy Communications Division.

Holtwick was then assigned to the headquarters of the navy's communications-intelligence organization as the head of the personnel and administrative department. In that position, Captain Holtwick is credited with establishing the enlisted rating of "Communications Technician" for the navy. In addition, during this assignment, he founded the basic organizational structure of the Naval Security Group. With some satisfaction, he then became the head of the Group in January 1950.

From April 1950 until January 1951, Captain Holtwick served as the Navy Executive Secretary to the Secretary of Defense. He then became the chief of operations for the AFSA. In April 1952, he took the assignment as captain of the USS *Estes*, which was an amphibious force command ship. During that period, the *Estes* was overhauled at Mare Island Naval Shipyard in Vallejo, California. She then served as the flagship for the Commander Task Force 132, in *Operation Ivy*, which was the hydrogen bomb testing in the Marshall Islands. The *Estes* next became the flagship of the Commander Amphibious Forces Pacific during the exercise *PacPhibEx II*. With Rear Adm. Frederic S. Withington (Commander Amphibious Group 3 and Commander Task Force 9) embarked, the *Estes* set course for Kodiak, Alaska. This new mission, *Operation Blue Nose*, was to resupply government installations—specifically the DEW LINE—in the far north. In fact, the personnel of TF 9 were officially inducted into the "Honorary Order of the Arctic" as *Blue Noses* when the force crossed the Arctic Circle on July 19. While at anchor at Icy Cape, the task force received the news that a truce had been signed, ending the Korean War.

Captain Holtwick received a new assignment when the *Estes* came back to San Diego in September 1953. He returned to Washington for duty as the Special Assistant to the Director of the NSA—and remained in that role until his retirement in 1957.

Jack later affiliated with the research and development firm of Haller, Raymond, and Brown, which later became HRB-Singer. At that time the company provided signal processing equipment and expertise to the U.S. Department of Defense and to international clients in Europe and Asia. Holtwick retired from the company in

1965, having risen to the position of vice president for administrative and management services. He was subsequently recalled to active duty, from 1969 through 1971, for the purpose of compiling and editing a U.S. Navy–focused communications-intelligence history for the time leading up to World War II.[1]

Captain Holtwick was awarded the Legion of Merit medal, as well as the Navy Unit Commendation ribbon, for his cryptanalysis service in World War II. Ultimately, for his postwar service, he received a second Legion of Merit, the Navy Commendation Medal, and the Army Commendation Medal.

Jack Holtwick was married to the former Mary Elizabeth Casey (1907–1982) of Lynchburg, Virginia, with whom he had four children. They spent their later years in Hawaii where he passed away on January 8, 1987, at age seventy-nine. He and Mary are buried together in the National Memorial Cemetery of the Pacific in Honolulu.

Captain Holtwick has been recognized and honored, by the U.S. Naval Cryptologic Veterans Association, as an officer who has served as the Commander, Naval Security Group, or one of its predecessor organizations. He has also been named, by the same organization, as a Pioneer Officer of U.S. Naval Cryptology.

Sources

Budiansky, 23, 84.
Carlson, 97–98, 102, 188, 226, 303, 393–94, 423–24, 445, 483, 532–33.
Dyer, 221, 293–94, 301.
Farago, *Broken Seal*, 77, 79.
Holmes, 36, 45, 55, 73, 86–87, 118.
Holtwick, xx–xxii, 62–63, 78, 94, 114, 133, 135, 137–38, 140, 153, 156, 159–64, 168, 176–77, 182, 185, 195–96, 205, 208–10, 246–48, 257, 261–63, 281, 304, 312, 316–21, 326, 342, 361–62, 367–68, 377, 399, 406, 427, 439, 446, App. 6, 7, 11, 110.
Kahn, *Codebreakers*, 20.
Layton, *"And I Was There,"* 79, 449, 450.
Lucky Bag, U.S. Naval Academy, 1927.
McGinnis, 11, 13, 20.
Prados, 83, 163–64, 315.
U.S. Navy, *Register of Commissioned and Warrant Officers*.

---

1. With a number of modifications and edits, this work was republished in 2006 by the U.S. Naval Cryptologic Veterans Association in their special publications series. Titled *History of the Naval Security Group to World War II*, it's a massive two-volume administrative record/history, and has been absolutely invaluable to this author in the preparation of this book of short biographies.

CAPTAIN LINWOOD SYLVESTER HOWETH, U.S. NAVY (1902–1972)

"Lin" "Litewate"

Lin Howeth delivered a noteworthy career as a communications specialist and a cryptanalyst—which is a bit ironic in that he had gone on record, in the fall of 1941, as desiring no future communications-intelligence duty. Perhaps the attack on Pearl Harbor changed his mind, but for whatever reason he did, in fact, spend most of World War II, and almost all of his subsequent career, in the field. One of the very few authors in this collection of multi talented officers, his 1963 *magnum opus* is titled *History of Communications-Electronics in the United States Navy*, which is a remarkably detailed book still widely used today.

* * *

From the 1925 Annapolis yearbook, *The Lucky Bag*:

> Hailing from "across the bay" [Hurlock, Maryland], *Litewate* knew a great deal about the Navy, having seen it plying up and down the Chesapeake Bay. Notable quotation: "Aha! I see you've hidden my mail again. Come on, let's have it. What, is that all? Only three? Oh, well, there are two more deliveries today." Is he a *snake*? [*a midshipman who always has a date; often someone else's*] Not at all. Only dragged [dated] four weekends last month.

* * *

Linwood S. Howeth was born on February 19, 1902. Raised on Maryland's eastern shore, he traveled but a few miles to enter the Naval Academy in 1921. He graduated and was commissioned as an ensign in June 1925, along with such classmates as Redfield "Rosie" **Mason**, John F. Delaney Jr., Ernest "Judge" Eller, Ernest S. L. **Goodwin**, Robert E. Hogaboom, Morton C. Mumma Jr., and Alwin **Kramer**. Subsequent promotions included lieutenant (junior grade), 1928; lieutenant, 1935; lieutenant commander, 1939; commander, 1942; and captain, 1943.

Like many new Annapolis graduates of this period, Howeth began his career with a fairly intensive series of general sea-duty assignments: battleship *New York* (1926), destroyer *Preston* (1927), aircraft carrier *Lexington* (1928), destroyer *Billingsley* (1929–1930), and the store-ship *Arctic* (1931–1932). Then, for a very brief period, he taught midshipmen at Annapolis.

Lt. j.g. Howeth reported to OP-20-G for training in July 1933. He was one of six new cryptanalysis students starting at that time, including Lt. j.g. Wesley "Ham" **Wright**.

Upon completion in June 1934, Howeth was detached to a general service assignment which then led to a position on the staff of the Commander in Chief, U.S. Fleet, from 1935 to 1936. He then served at Naval Station Guantanamo Bay, Cuba, during 1937 and 1938.

Around this time, in a memo to the assistant director of naval communications—hoping to support several cryptologists for promotion to lieutenant commander—Cmdr. Laurance **Safford** wrote that:

> Lt. Linwood S. Howeth has never done any actual "communications intelligence" work, but is a good cryptanalyst and would be acceptable in event of war. Had one year's training in cryptanalysis. Had two year's duty in the "Security Unit of the Commander in Chief, U.S. Fleet," being in charge of the unit the second year. During

this period Howeth waged a successful campaign of espionage and instruction against the prevalent laxity and carelessness, [and due to his efforts] the fleet finally became [more] security conscious.

Whether due to Safford's memo or not, he did receive promotion, and so Lieutenant Commander Howeth joined the heavy cruiser *Salt Lake City*, in July 1939, as ship's secretary and communications officer. He was on board, under Captain Ellis **Zacharias**, when that ship operated as a key component of Vice Admiral Halsey's *Enterprise* task force in early 1942, when the *Salt Lake City* played a prominent part in the bombardment of the atoll of Wotje in the Marshalls—with Dr. Cecil **Coggins** on board as ad hoc IO—and then later shelled Wake Island.

Mr. Howeth was detached from the *Salt Lake City* in March 1942, right before she participated in Jimmy Doolittle's B-25 raid against Tokyo. He had been ordered to duty at Camden, New Jersey, in connection with the fitting-out of the light cruiser *Cleveland*. The *Cleveland* was commissioned on June 15, 1942; clearing the Chesapeake Bay on October 10, 1942, she joined a task force bound for the invasion of North Africa. Her firepower supported the landings in French Morocco in November, and after doing some patrolling duty, she then returned to Norfolk.

It's interesting to note that Mr. Howeth apparently had gone on record, in the fall of 1941, as not desiring future communications-intelligence duty—yet he spent most of World War II, and his subsequent career, in the field.

In January 1943, Commander Howeth reported to navy headquarters in Washington to take the position of administrative assistant to the Assistant Chief of Naval Communications for Communication Supplementary Activities.

But only three months later he was appointed as Assistant Officer in Charge, FRUPac, and Officer in Charge, Mid-Pacific Network, at Pearl Harbor. National-security historian John Prados has written that "among the dedicated 'cryppies' at FRUPac whose names ought to be recorded for history are Cmdr. (and then Capt.) Lin Howeth, [who] played a leading role at FRUPac until early 1945, when he led an advance detachment of codebreakers to a relocated CinCPac headquarters." Indeed, Howeth was appointed to supervise the creation of a forward joint-service communications correlation center on Guam, after that island was captured in August 1944. The Radio Analysis Group, Forward (RAGFOR) seems to have been started by late 1944; the Combat Intelligence Center, Forward (CICFOR) was in operation in January 1945. They were established as forward elements of FRUPac and CIC-JICPOA, and became extremely important when Admiral Nimitz moved to Guam in early 1945.

After the war Captain Howeth continued to work in communications and communications intelligence. He was designated as Head, Security Branch (OP-202) in June 1950, and was later relieved there by Capt. Dick **Zern** in February 1952.

In 1963, Captain Howeth published a groundbreaking and incredibly detailed (657 pages) study of communications-intelligence which continues to be studied to this day: *History of Communications-Electronics in the United States Navy*, with an introduction by Fleet Admiral Nimitz. It was a joint publication of the U.S. Navy's Bureau of Ships and the Office of Naval History.

Lin Howeth passed away in February 1972, in Easton, Maryland, and was buried with full military honors at Arlington National Cemetery. He was survived by his wife, Evelyn Noble Howeth (1907–1992), and several grandchildren, but unfortunately was predeceased by their only daughter, Virginia, in 1970.

Captain Howeth's decorations and awards include two Legion of Merit medals, the Navy Unit Commendation Ribbon, and the Second Nicaraguan Campaign Medal. He also has been recognized and honored, by the U.S. Naval Cryptologic Veterans Association, as an officer who has served as the Commander, Naval Security Group or one of its predecessor organizations.

Sources

Benson, 157.
Browne and McGinnis, *History of Communications Intelligence*, 228–29.
Dyer, 291.
Holtwick, 113, 138, 353, 432, 439, App. 7.
Lucky Bag, U.S. Naval Academy, 1925.
Prados, 412.
U.S. Navy, *Register of Commissioned and Warrant Officers.*

REAR ADMIRAL RAYMOND STARR LAMB, U.S. NAVY (1902–1957)

"Ray"

For about seven years, during the 1930s, Ray Lamb projected every appearance of being a natural, highly effective, and highly motivated COMINT "true-believer." He was excellent in the technical aspects of the business as well as the administrative. His mind ranged from cryptanalysis to direction-finding to communications security—and everything in between. He was a frequent correspondent with various leaders in OP-20-G, particularly Cmdr. Laurance Safford, all of whom expressed the highest confidence in his abilities and wisdom. That's why it's so strange that, right before World War II, he went on record desiring no further C.I. duty and spent the war—and the rest of his too-short life (he died at age fifty-five)—in submarines and destroyers. However, even though he absented himself from COMINT, a great deal of what he set in motion when he was active during those early years had significant and lasting impact.

* * *

From the 1926 Annapolis yearbook, *The Lucky Bag*:

What the Academy did to our *Ray* is exceeded only by what *Ray* did to our Academy. Hailing from the home port of the Eli's, he introduced much of the provincial worldliness of a New England college town, with the exception of anything concerning the *femmes*. He was, until Second Class year, when he underwent a radical change, the reddest of Red Mikes [professed bachelors]. However, it might be said "still water runs deep." This is a reminder of his adventures in the foggy city and of a rainy night at the Academy. Believing that his talent for cheerleading had been noticed and not wishing to take that honor away from someone else, *Ray* went out for class football. Ray has ever been a close follower of the footlights. It being said of him that his irresistible hair and his enticing smile have been too much for the stage celebrities, here and abroad, who have besieged him with letters, in futile attempts to gain such beauty secrets as the care of his profile and the kind of toothpaste he uses. He is also a great lover of nature, believing that a sunrise in Washington is worth two elsewhere; an ardent devotee of music, the latter being second only to his love for the weed [tobacco], for which he will go to such lengths as are known to but few—at a time. We wonder what *Ray* will do as Engineer Officer during a smokeless run. [Activities: class football]

* * *

Raymond Lamb was born in Connecticut on August 16, 1902. He reported to Annapolis, from New Haven, in 1922 and was subsequently graduated and commissioned as an ensign in 1926, along with such distinguished classmates as Wade McClusky Jr., Maxwell F. Leslie, Henri deB. **Claiborne**, Ranson **Fullinwider**, Frank P. Pyzick, Howard W. Gilmore, Lofton R. Henderson, Robert B. Pirie, James S. Russell, Wesley Ham **Wright**, and Paul D. Stroop. Subsequent promotions included lieutenant (junior grade), 1929; lieutenant, 1936; lieutenant commander, 1941; commander, 1942; and captain, 1943. He retired from the navy in 1956 and was simultaneously promoted to rear admiral, on the retired list, by reason of a combat citation, pursuant to Title 10, U.S. Code, Section 6150.

After his graduation from Annapolis, Ensign Lamb reported on board the light cruiser *Richmond*, and then in 1930 he moved to the submarine base at New London, Connecticut, for qualification training. He then was assigned to the submarine *V-5* in 1932; she was shortly renamed as the USS *Narwhal* and Lamb remained onboard until 1933.

In March of that year Cmdr. John W. **McClaran**, then OIC of OP-20-G, identified five of the class of 1926 as promising cryptography candidates; as a result, Lt. j.g. Lamb arrived at Main Navy in July as one of six new students. After completing the course and some on-the-job training, Lamb departed for the Philippine Islands in September 1935, onboard the SS *President Garfield*. He arrived in November to relieve Lt. Sid **Goodwin** and, working in several communications-intelligence billets, remained on the Asiatic Station from 1935 to 1937. Initially he served as the OIC of the Asiatic Fleet's decryption unit and assistant fleet communications officer—after Sid Goodwin and before Jack **Holtwick**. Goodwin had pioneered cryptanalytic activity on the Asiatic Station, and Lamb was happy to follow his lead and build upon his precedent.

Throughout 1936, Mr. Lamb and some of his men spent many hours in laborious experimentation at Sangley Point, engaged with the field testing of an XAB-RAB high-frequency direction-finding unit. Cmdr. Laurance **Safford**, now head of OP-20-G, gave Lamb frequent and considerable praise for this work. In fact, in September 1936, after that year's Japanese fleet maneuvers, Safford wrote, "You and your operators did a splendid job and you have my heartiest congratulations. You have made history, as this is the first occasion when a U.S. direction-finding station has tracked a foreign ship."

In December 1936, Lieutenant Holtwick relieved Lieutenant Lamb at the decryption unit, and then Lamb in turn relieved Lieutenant Goodwin on the CinCAF staff. It's interesting to note that at that same time both Lamb and Holtwick wrote letters to OP-20-G, putting on paper some concerns and frustrations about communications-intelligence field operations in general—and duty on the Asiatic Station in particular.

Holtwick mentioned discouragement about the failure (due to no funding) of the project to move radio intelligence from the Cavite Navy Yard to more secure spaces on Corregidor; problems with personnel; and hopes that new flag officers who may be assigned to administrative or actual control over COMINT activities be properly "sold" on the program.

"The matter of prestige comes in—it is very difficult for any high ranking officer to take the word of a lieutenant or j.g. concerning the tremendous importance of something of which the ranking officer has never even heard during his thirty or more years in the service. We have got, somehow, to overcome the lack of interest, lack of enthusiasm, and lack of co-operation and trust on the part of senior officers . . . for this branch of work."

He mentioned also the collateral duties assigned to the R.I. officers that took badly needed time away from their duties, and the unsatisfactory situation with respect to enlisted personnel: lack of control of their assignments . . . discontent because of their belief they are held back in advancement; overwork; and inadequate quarters.

Lamb covered some of the same concerns in his correspondence. He wrote that the Asiatic communications-intelligence unit was handicapped by lack of understanding, interest, and appreciation of possibilities on the part of seniors, and that it was difficult to obtain "hearing" due to the junior rank of C.I. officers. He considered it imperative that OPNAV clarify to CinCAF the impressive results previously obtained by the unit and emphasize mission, possibilities, personnel, duties, and setup. He also felt it crucial to clarify that the unit was not experimental but was fully operational and able to furnish accurate and complete data on ORANGE [Japanese] preparations, operations, and intentions. He also wanted explained the status of personnel, the necessity of adequate quarters, and the need to segregate R.I. radiomen from those in general service. Moreover,

> [We] have had no time for our activity because of the collateral duties. There are plenty of officers out here hanging out in bars who can take care of our own [routine] communications. I do not feel that I was detailed out here with a two-month-old baby in each arm [Mrs. Lamb had twins in mid-summer 1935], and had to sacrifice a submarine command, in order to take over *odd jobs* on the Flag.

The passionate pleas from these officers didn't seem to have much effect, and in fact many of these problems continued for years, which may have contributed to driving a wedge between personnel in the field activities and those in Washington—a wedge which to a degree hampered the joint effort during much of World War II.

Safford did respond to Lamb in January 1937. He hoped that Congress would release money for the Corregidor project. "We were downcast when this project fell through, but of course, I realize it must have made your position rather embarrassing." He also pushed back a little. Regarding the two R.I. officers on the station,

> The officer on the CinC's staff should be the front—should interpret results to the admiral and "sell" the ideas as necessary. The officer at Cavite should be the silent partner, and working member, of the firm. He should have no other duties. . . . The staff man may have to take on other duties. . . . He must have the admiral's confidence if he is to do a good job—also contacts with and the good will of the staff. For good and sufficient reasons, all R.I. activities on the Asiatic Station are under the CinCAF, and he has full authority to do anything he pleases.

Safford was no doubt more supportive than he sounded, and it's clear that he respected and liked both Holtwick and Lamb. But one has to also remember that Safford himself was only a lieutenant commander at this time, and that he had never personally served on the Asiatic Station or any other R.I. field activity; he thus may not have fully appreciated the difficulties that his field officers faced.

In late 1936, Lamb developed plans to visit Guam and the navy's COMINT Station A in Shanghai. Then in June 1937, he advanced another plan to cruise in a destroyer to Guam and back, pretending to take meteorological observations but really trying to intercept Japanese communications during their Fleet Grand Maneuvers. In this regard Lamb was hoping to duplicate what Ellis **Zacharias** had done in the cruiser *Marblehead* eleven years earlier. Lieutenant Lamb gained approval, but events forced the project's cancellation: in early fall 1937 there occurred the Battle of

Shanghai, wherein the Japanese landed in Woosung (across the river from Shanghai) and bombarded part of the city—as well as consolidated their positions in Peking, Tientsin, and Tsingtao.

Lamb then traveled to Shanghai, reviewing the situation there and inspecting Station A—which was in the compound of the 4th U.S. Marines. He planned to leave Shanghai in December, go back to Cavite, go work for a month at the station in Guam, return to Cavite, and then depart for the continental United States in March 1938. Then, Lt. Jack **Williams** would relieve him as Fleet C.I. Officer.

At this time Lamb needed sea duty for further promotion, and Safford thus didn't expect to get him back into COMINT until sometime in late 1939 at the earliest. Lamb became executive officer of the submarine *Cuttlefish*, being overhauled at the New York Navy Yard, in February 1938. It appears Lamb was happy to return to submarine duty but still kept thinking about communications; he sent Safford a letter to express his concerns about overall poor U.S. Navy communications security, advocating some innovative ideas.

For his part, Safford sent Lamb a letter in September 1938, reassuring him that a return to duty in COMINT would not be adverse to his further career or to further promotion. Safford mentioned letters of recommendation that were just executed which stressed each officer was performing highly important and highly classified duties, and commending each for the manner in which these duties were performed. "I believe that the recent letters from the C-in-C will fix things up pretty well for you, Dick **Zern**, and Jack Holtwick."

By November 1938, Lamb had received orders to OP-20-G requiring him to report in Spring 1939. He then was to travel to Hawaii, Station HYPO, leaving in August and hoping to arrive by October. While at Main Navy he outlined a new structure for HYPO—approved by Safford—which created three sections: Radio Intelligence (which Lamb himself would take over when he got there); Crypto Intelligence (headed by Lt. Tommy **Dyer**); and Enemy Information (headed by Lt. Cmdr. Tom **Birtley**).

In early fall Lamb wrote to Safford that he was in place at Pearl Harbor and that the new three-part structure was running smoothly. He was appalled, however, at where the Bureau of Engineering had placed the direction-finding station at Lualualei—physically inferior to many other potential sites, and totally surrounded by mountains.

By May 1940 he received orders to detach and report to the destroyer *Benham* as her executive officer. This left HYPO in some disarray as he and two other officers were detached simultaneously and only one was sent out as a replacement.

In May 1941, Mr. Lamb was promoted to lieutenant commander and then received follow-on orders to take command of the submarine *Stingray* at Cavite. It's not entirely clear what transpired at this time, but apparently Lamb then informed Commander Safford that he no longer desired to have any more communications-intelligence duties, and in fall 1941—when Safford published his short list of only eighteen officers "qualified and acceptable"—Lamb was not on it.[1] We can only guess at what drove Lamb's somewhat surprising decision. There is considerable evidence that for a number of years he had fully engaged himself in cryptanalysis and many other aspects of communications intelligence. His correspondence indicates such engagement, and the tone and subjects of Safford's letters to Lamb display Safford's respect for, and even reliance upon, Lamb's work and opinions. Nevertheless, once he joined the *Stingray* he stayed in submarines and destroyers—and apparently never looked back.

His tenure onboard the *Stingray* was fairly short (May through December 1941). When the war started, the boat was part of Submarine Division 22 under Commander, Submarines, Asiatic Fleet. On their first wartime cruise he had to return to port almost immediately due to mechanical issues. When the sub went into the shipyard, and then was damaged there by Japanese attacks, Lamb was detached and found himself associated with Lt. Rudy **Fabian** and the evacuees of Station CAST. He joined them at Bandung, Java, but shortly moved on—ordered to report to the submarine forces in the Southwest Pacific.

Mr. Lamb subsequently took command of the destroyer *Meade* and was onboard from June 1942 through June 1943. On November 15, 1942, during the naval battle of Guadalcanal, Commander Lamb and the *Meade* engaged four damaged Japanese transports—destroying them with five-inch gunfire. She then picked out of the water 266 survivors of the sunken U.S. destroyers *Walke* and *Preston*; Lamb was then ordered to proceed into an adjacent area and search for survivors of the light cruiser *Juneau* (including the to-be-famous five Sullivan brothers) but there had no success.

Subsequently the *Meade* was attached to Task Force 18, Destroyer Division 41, at the Battle of Rennell Island in January 1943—and then to Task Force 51 at the capture of Attu in May.

In August 1943, Lamb was promoted to captain. He traveled to New York City to take command of the new destroyer *Picking*, serving in that role from September 1943 to August 1944. Following shakedown off Bermuda, the *Picking* proceeded to Dutch Harbor, Alaska, where she arrived in December 1943 to serve with the North Pacific Fleet in Destroyer Squadron 49. She bombarded Paramushiro, Kuriles, in February 1944, Matsuwa Island, Kuriles, in June, and Paramushiro again in June. In August she steamed to San Francisco for upkeep, whereupon Lamb relinquished command.

Unfortunately, Captain Lamb's record becomes obscure at this point. He received a Bronze Star for his World War II combat service, and he retired from the navy in June 1956. Because of his combat decoration, as he retired he was simultaneously promoted to rear admiral. He passed away, far too young, on February 22, 1957.

---

1. Lamb certainly isn't the only very experienced and trained officer who backed out of COMINT before the start of the war, including future rear admirals Wayne N. Gamet and John A. Glick. It appears that Sid **Goodwin** and Lin **Howeth** also tried to quit, but as it turned out they spent most of the war—*and the rest of their careers*—in C.I. duty. Of course, the most prominent individual who started remarkably strong in C.I., and then abruptly walked away with disparaging remarks, was Vice Adm. Russell **Willson**.

Sources

Holtwick, 4, 112–13, 137–38, 140, 153, 168, 182, 185–87, 196–200, 228, 255, 263, 268, 286, 308, 312, 320, 327, 329, 332–33, 336–37, 343, 352, 361, 364–65, 367, 439, App. 113–14.
Lucky Bag, U.S. Naval Academy, 1926.
McGinnis, 11.
Morison, III, 158; V, 284, 353; VII, 335.
Prados, 246–47.
U.S. Navy, *Register of Commissioned and Warrant Officers.*

CAPTAIN JOHN MARION LIETWILER, U.S. NAVY (1908–1978)

"Liet" "Honest John"

John Lietwiler moved into cryptology early, with a focus upon the Pacific, before and during World War II. He was on board Station CAST in the Philippines when the war began, and in the face of the advancing Japanese was among the last of those evacuated to Australia, where he served at Station BELCONNEN and then later with Lord Louis Mountbatten in Ceylon. His postwar activity included work with the Naval Security Group and the NSA—and he closed out his career teaching high school French in Maryland.

*   *   *

From the 1932 Annapolis yearbook, *The Lucky Bag*:

When *Liet* answered the call of the Service, he had already spent two years at old Ohio U brushing up an acquaintance with Horace, Pliny, Xenophon and other popular novelists of that ancient day. Just what made him choose the Navy we cannot say—perhaps the dryness of Livy made wetness in huge chunks seem desirable. Or maybe some steamboat jaunts on the Ohio did it. Anyway, he came, he saw—he might even have conquered if it had not been for Math, Steam, Juice and other enemies of the language minded. He frankly admits that he regards chess and checkers as the finest sports—except perhaps the rope-climb and other small gymnastic feats. Ping-pong?—too strenuous! However, he has found time to take part in that classic sport of wrestling. He also belongs to that select group known as the Fusileers, having inherited somewhat of a shooting eye from his gran'dad. The Musical Clubs take up the rest of his spare moments. One thing we can say—John is no fusser—no parlor snake, and he rarely drags [dates]. [Activities: rifle, wrestling, musical clubs]

*   *   *

John Lietwiler was born in Spillman, West Virginia, on April 15, 1908, and grew up in Pomeroy, Ohio. He attended Ohio University for two years, and then entered the U.S. Naval Academy, graduating in 1932 along with such distinguished classmates as Robert H. **Weeks**, Alfred G. Ward, Bruce McCandless, and Lloyd M. Mustin. Subsequent promotions included lieutenant (junior grade), 1935; lieutenant, 1939; lieutenant commander, June 1942; commander, November 1942; and captain, 1951. He retired from the navy in 1960.

His first assignment after graduation was onboard the light cruiser *Cincinnati*, homeported in San Francisco, attached to the Battle Force, U.S. Fleet. His next assignment was the destroyer *Rathburne* out of Pearl Harbor. He then transferred to the minelayer *Oglala*.

Mr. Lietwiler came to Washington, in the summer of 1939, for duty with the Office of Naval Communications; this was for the full OP-20-G two-year course in cryptography. Here his classmates included lieutenants (junior grade) Robert Weeks and Herbert Coleman. In the spring of 1940, Lietwiler and Chief Radioman Harry Kidder took some time from study and visited Bermuda to observe the operations of the British Atlantic direction-finding network. By October 1940, although still under instruction, Lieutenant Lietwiler was also assisting naval reserve Lt. Francis Brotherhood and two other junior officers in OP-20-G's attack against the Japanese 5-numeral operations code, JN-25 (at this point OP-20-G's master Japanese cryptanalyst, Mrs. Agnes **Driscoll**, had been moved to work on German naval systems).

After course completion Lietwiler was sent out—on board the cruise liner *President Harrison*—to Corregidor in late summer 1941, to relieve Lt. Rudy **Fabian** as OIC of Station CAST. In October, Lietwiler was identified, in Capt. Laurance **Safford**'s official analysis, as one of only eighteen officers "qualified and acceptable" for communications-intelligence duty in the entire navy. Mr. Lietwiler was on watch at CAST when Pearl Harbor was attacked on December 7.

Lieutenant Lietwiler, along with his colleague Lieutenant Fabian (Fabian had remained on station to focus on radio intelligence technical work) and the rest of the CAST personnel, were evacuated by submarine to Australia in three stages. The last few days awaiting evacuation were incredibly nerve-wracking as the Japanese advance came closer. As Lietwiler later wrote, they ate their meals "with one eye for food and one for planes, but both ears cocked for shells." Lietwiler's was the last of the three groups to leave.

Mr. Lietwiler continued to serve in the Pacific Theater, notably at the new Station BELCONNEN (which shortly became FRUMel). During the final year of the war he was with the staff of Lord Louis Mountbatten in Colombo, Ceylon.

After brief service in Washington, he was assigned to the Naval Communications Station at Bainbridge Island in Washington State. There he relieved Cmdr. Wesley "Ham" **Wright**, in April 1946, as OIC, and was in turn relieved by Cmdr. Philip P. Leigh in July 1948. Commander Lietwiler's next assignments were in Guam, Wahiawa (Hawaii), and Great Lakes, Illinois.

Captain Lietwiler returned to Maryland in 1954 for a tour in the Office of the Inspector General of the Naval Security Station. He then became Acting Special Assistant to the Director of Naval Communications for Communications Security Matters, and head of the Naval Security Group, for a few months in mid-1955. In these roles he relieved Capt. James A. Morrison, and was in turn relieved by Capt. Jefferson **Dennis**.

Lietwiler's last navy assignment was with the NSA at Fort Meade, Maryland, after which he retired in 1960.

He then earned a master's degree from the University of Maryland, and taught French at Poolesville High School and North Bethesda Junior High School. He retired from teaching in 1973.

Captain Lietwiler suffered a heart attack and passed away in July 1978. He is buried at Arlington National Cemetery. He was survived by his wife, Helena Keehne Lietwiler, as well as two sons, Charles and Christian.

His awards and decorations include a Distinguished Service Medal and a Bronze Star Medal. Captain Lietwiler has also been recognized and honored, by the U.S. Naval Cryptologic Veterans Association, as an officer who has served as the Commander, Naval Security Group.

Sources

Browne and McGinnis, *Communications Intelligence*, 234–35.

Donovan and Mack, 61, 151, 161–63, 322.

Holtwick, 137, 325, 329, 340, 352, 368, 371, 376, 394, 400, 422, 425–28, 431, 433, 439, 441, App. 7, 12, 91–95, 111, 116, 123.

Lucky Bag, U.S. Naval Academy, 1932.

Prados, 211, 245, 267, 269–70, 421–22.

Stinnett, 62, 79.

U.S. Navy, *Register of Commissioned and Warrant Officers*.

CHIEF RADIOMAN WALTER JOSEPH McGREGOR, U.S. NAVY (1906–1941)

"Mack"

Mack McGregor is a superb representative for the large group of navy and Marine enlisted men (not to mention navy civilians) who were crucial to naval communications and intelligence—and then communications-intelligence—during this time. This period saw significant creation and expansion of naval direction-finding stations and radio intercept facilities manned with growing numbers of dedicated and technically savvy personnel. Indeed, without these people the other individuals featured in this study simply could not have operated—to say nothing about achieving the great successes that they did. Mack was among the first carefully selected radiomen to receive specialized COMINT training, which included the study of Japanese and Japanese *kana*, to support the growing need to best take advantage of available ORANGE communications. McGregor was unique in that he became one of the main instructors of that program, as well as uniquely sliding away from radio intelligence and into the mainstream of cryptanalysis right before the war. He was a multitalented and high-initiative professional; his premature death, at age thirty-five, was not only a personal tragedy but certainly a blow to the navy as well.

*   *   *

Walter McGregor was born in 1906 and first enlisted in the navy, at Boston, in October 1921. Serving in several ships and stations, he had advanced to Chief Radioman by February 1930.

He was one of the premier instructors of the navy and Marine Corps radio operators known as "The On-the-Roof Gang"—carefully selected radiomen who received intelligence and cryptologic training. This program had come about because, in 1928, the commander in chief of the Asiatic Fleet complained to the CNO about how few radiomen were qualified to copy Japanese *kana* code. The fleet had only nine qualified operators, all self-taught. CinCAF made the case that self-study and ad hoc operations were no longer sufficient to produce the needed number of qualified intercept operators. Therefore, in July 1928, the CNO announced the establishment of a school to instruct radio operators in intercept operations, particularly for Japanese *kana*. The first class began in October. Since these classes were held in a wooden structure set on top of the navy headquarters building in Washington (Main Navy), and since the radiomen could not explain their classwork to others, they eventually assumed the vague nickname of "The On-the-Roof Gang."

In 1932, McGregor graduated from OTR Class Seven and then went out to the Philippines to work as a radio intelligence operator on the Asiatic station. Lt. Sid **Goodwin** said that, when he arrived at Olongapo in the summer of 1934, he found the advice and information given to him by Chief McGregor and Radioman Second Class Prescott H. **Currier** of more value than anything else he was given.

Upon the death of OTR Class Sixteen's instructor (Chief Radioman J. B. Byrd), Mack returned to Main Navy and completed the instruction of that group. From that point he taught Classes Seventeen through Twenty, whose membership included many men who would become essential during World War II as well as to the future Navy Security Group. Of all the instructors, Chief McGregor taught the second-highest number of classes—while being continuously admitted for hospital treatments regarding a heart condition.

In fact, although he'd been in Vallejo, California, at the Mare Island Hospital in early 1935, he was back in Washington by July, teaching OTR classes. Mack's contributions weren't confined to teaching classes and sitting in front of consoles. In addition to those duties, he was always willing to moonlight. For example, during a 1935 dinner that ONI's Lt. Cmdr. Ellis **Zacharias** and his wife put on at their home for the Japanese naval attaché, at Zacharias's direction Lt. Jack **Holtwick** and Chief McGregor entered the attaché's apartment in the Alban Towers on Wisconsin Avenue. In the guise of overall-clad, toolbox-carrying electricians (*Jack* and *Mack*, as it were), they carefully examined Captain Yamaguchi Tamon's apartment—which also was his office. While pretending to fix a power failure in the suite, their covert mission was to determine whether—as ONI suspected—the attaché kept an electric cipher machine on the premises. Short of actually finding a machine, "the inspection by flashlight," Zacharias later wrote, "covered everything we desired," which included examining (but not taking) various crypto-paraphernalia and papers.

By early 1939, and all through 1940, Mack was working in OP-20-GY (the Crypto-Intelligence Subsection, Room 1643 of Main Navy), handling recoveries of the Japanese Navy's JN-25 code, and working with people such as Agnes **Driscoll**, Rudy **Fabian**, Albert **Pelletier**, and Sid **Goodwin**. As of January 1939 he had officially left radio intelligence duty and was fully engaged in cryptanalysis.

However, in February 1941, while working, Chief Radioman McGregor suddenly died of heart complications—at the far too young age of thirty-five. He is buried at Arlington National Cemetery.

A building was named for him at the Naval Technical Training Center in the Pensacola Naval Complex; he's one of five "On-the-Roof-Gang" people so honored.

Sources

Browne and McGinnis, *Communications Intelligence*, 17.
Holtwick, 141, 149, 154, 163–64, 322, 340, 376, 400, App. 91–94, 125, 127, 131, 134, 137, 140, 150, 157, 165.
Layton, *"And I Was There,"* 79.
McGinnis, 18.
Zacharias, Ellis, 181.

CAPTAIN LEE WOOD PARKE, U.S. NAVAL RESERVE (1904–1986)

"Lightnin'"

Lee Parke made solid contributions to the navy in battleship and destroyer service, as well as in cryptology. But it's perhaps in his subsequent twenty-years of service in the State Department, as a master cryptanalyst, where his real claim to fame lies.

* * *

From the 1927 Annapolis yearbook, *The Lucky Bag*:

Lee's elementary education was formed in Washington's graded and high schools. We first met him at Columbian Prep (usually known as Schadds), where we got our first impression. This impression has remained quite the same and today finds him neither higher nor lower in our estimation. Methodically igniting a cigarette, gracefully reclining in his little white cot, he often muses of his next leave, or more often his future. With Lee, anticipation is greater than realization, thus much of his time is spent in anticipation. *Lightnin'*, as he was christened Plebe Summer, stuck perhaps because of its applicability. To see his exactness of movement with that infinitesimal velocity would explain all. *Lightnin'*, always practical, has a lust for the exact sciences. Oft gazing with ardent admiration at the bit of feminine sweetness placed with such mathematical precision on his locker door, he recounts the number of days to June Week and plans how to make the most of that fifteen minutes after the Hop. Lee is a good friend. His natural quietness and gentlemanly manners make him, though not the life of the party, a desirable asset. He has much ambition, though covered with a comfortable cloak of laziness. Some day he'll throw that off, then we'll see big things of Lee. [Activities: crew, 150-pound football, Juice Gang]

*   *   *

Lee W. Parke, a descendent of Robert E. Lee, was born in Washington, D.C., on April 3, 1904. His father was Philip B. Parke and his mother was Mana (Mary) Lee. Parke graduated from the Naval Academy in 1927 along with such distinguished classmates as George W. Anderson, Glynn "Donc" Donaho, U.S. Grant Sharp, Jack S. **Holtwick**, Gill M. **Richardson**, and Richard D. **Zern**. Subsequent promotions included lieutenant (junior grade), 1930; lieutenant, 1936; lieutenant commander, January 1942; commander, September 1942; and captain, 1945. He transferred from the regular navy to the naval reserve around 1949, and then completely retired from the naval service in 1959.

From 1927 through 1931, Parke was a battleship sailor, serving on board the *New York*, the staff of the Battleship Divisions/Battle Fleet, and the *New Mexico*. At that point he then switched to destroyers, serving on board the *Bernadou* for a year and then the *Barney* from 1933 through 1934.

In the summer of 1934 he reported to OP-20-G at Main Navy for cryptologic instruction. A year later he had become the head of OP-20-GS (Communications Security), working under Cmdr. Howard **Kingman**. Then, in mid-1936, the newly promoted Lieutenant Parke reported to the CINCUS communications intelligence unit on board the battleship *Pennsylvania*; there he worked under Lt. John **Harper** and alongside Lt. Ham **Wright**.

In the summer of 1940, Mr. Parke was back at Main Navy in OP-20-GY (Cryptanalysis and Decryption), working European systems—particularly the Italian Navy. He was head of GY at least until early 1942.

In the fall of 1941, Parke was mentioned in Laurance **Safford**'s assessment document as one of only eighteen officers "qualified and acceptable" to work in communications-intelligence.

In November, Parke (accompanying his superiors Safford and Agnes **Driscoll** as well as Lt. Prescott **Currier**) engaged with several MIT professors and representatives from the Bureau of Ships; at issue was the National Defense Research Committee project of designing and building high-speed analytical machinery for the navy's Communications Security Section.

By December, GY was standing round-the-clock watches with five officers and a small support staff of chief petty officers, typists, and clerks.

Parke, promoted to lieutenant commander in January 1942, and then to commander in September 1942, served most of World War II in Washington—almost entirely in communications security.

In June 1944, Commander Parke was detailed from the navy to the Department of State. In November he became chief of their new Division of Cryptology, propelling State Department communications into a new and secure era of American diplomatic crypto-security. In the spring of 1945, Parke was promoted to captain, and in 1949 he moved from the regular navy to the naval reserve, and took a position in the federal civil service. By 1961 the cryptology staff was around thirty people; it was still headed by Parke, who by then was a special assistant to the deputy assistant secretary for operations.

Shortly after the 1962 Cuban Missile Crisis, "Parke developed a method of communicating overseas by a secure telephone system . . . referred to as the 'Red Phone' [or the Washington-Moscow hotline], the system allowed two heads of government to communicate within seconds."

Mr. Parke retired from the State Department in 1964. In a 1986 interview, the State Department's chief historian, William Slany, commented that "Parke left less of a record than many State Department employees because he was involved in such secret activity." This comment certainly explains the dearth of information on Mr. Parke—as well as many of the other people discussed in this book!

Parke died in July 1986, after a long illness, at the Bay Pines Veterans Administration Hospital in St. Petersburg, Florida. His wife, Cora Glassford Parke (1910–1986), had predeceased him by just two months. Captain Parke had been living with one of his sons, Thomas; he also was survived by two other sons, William and Robert, and a daughter, Betsi.

Sources

Benson, 45.

Farago, *Broken Seal*, 327.

Holtwick, 114, 133, 138, 152–53, 173, 182, 212, 299, 325, 367, 371, 376, 394, 400, 439, 444, 459, App. 5, 92–97.

Kahn, *Codebreakers*, 11, 501, 712.

Lucky Bag, U.S. Naval Academy, 1927.

Ovak, Kathleen. Obituaries: *St. Petersburg Times*, July 19, 1986.

U.S. Navy, *Register of Commissioned and Warrant Officers*.

LIEUTENANT JAMES WARREN PEARSON, U.S. NAVY (1910–1992)

"Jimmie"

Another On-the-Roof Gang member, Jimmie Pearson was also another fine representative of the navy and marine enlisted men—as well as Navy Department civilians—so crucial to the COMINT effort during the early years. He capped his navy career with a second, civilian career in COMINT, ultimately retiring from a high-level position at the NSA.

* * *

James W. Pearson was born on July 20, 1910, in Greer, South Carolina. He enlisted in the navy on July 20, 1928. Graduating with honors from the Navy Radio School, he then served with the fleet as a radioman. He completed special training (On-the-Roof

Gang Class Four), graduating in September 1930, and then began cryptologic service at the Asiatic Station in the Philippine Islands. In the latter part of 1933 he was one of a team of four enlisted men who began regular crossings of the Pacific Ocean conducting special intercept duties aboard vessels of the American Mail Line.[1]

As of 1932, Jimmie was a radioman second class at Olongapo; in 1934 a radioman first class at the Thirteenth Naval District in Seattle; in 1935 he had duty in Washington, D.C.; in 1937 he was still in Washington but now in training at the Radio Materiel School, Bellevue; 1938 saw Pearson advanced to radioman chief petty officer; by 1940 he was working in Guam; and in February 1941 he was back on the Asiatic Station in the Philippines.

He was promoted to warrant officer radio electrician and then was commissioned as an ensign—in May 1943—while serving at FRUPac in Pearl Harbor; he had reported on board Station HYPO shortly before the attack on Pearl Harbor. Mr. Pearson was subsequently promoted to lieutenant (junior grade) in August 1944, and then lieutenant in February 1946. He retired from the navy in August 1948.

Pearson continued his work in cryptology as a civilian employee with the Communication Supplementary Activity, the AFSA, and the NSA. He held a GS-16 position when he retired from the federal civil service.

Among his awards are the Bronze Star Medal and the Navy Unit Commendation. Jimmie and his wife, Marguerite, had one daughter, Judy. Mr. Pearson passed away in March 1992. His last home of record was in Deland, Florida.

Sources

Browne and McGinnis, *Communications Intelligence*, 71.
Holtwick, 54, 115–16, 354, 446, App. 47–48, 124, 127, 131, 134, 140, 144, 153, 161.
McGinnis, 172.
U.S. Navy, *Register of Commissioned and Warrant Officers.*

---

1. According to Capt. Jack **Holtwick**, this special project was initiated by a request from the Bureau of Aeronautics for a radioman to attach to each of four ships of the American Mail Line (which made round trips almost continually between Seattle and the Orient) to assist observers which were being placed on the ships by the Weather Bureau. The object was to make observations for one year of surface and upper air meteorological conditions over the Pacific Ocean. A radioman was needed because the two commercial operators assigned to each ship would not be able to handle the additional traffic. The radiomen were to have the status of passengers, and each would cost the government $30 per month for transportation and subsistence.

OP-20-G seized upon this as an excellent cover for four one-man mobile intercept stations which might be able to pick up some valuable transmissions while cruising past Japan and through the China Sea. So, four experienced and trustworthy men were briefed on the project and instructed on how to conceal their equipment as well as their real purpose. They were supplied with specially built receivers, which ultimately did not perform well; several of the men purchased more suitable receivers out of their own pockets. They were to wear civilian clothes and were given extra spending allowances of $15 per month, paid from secret ONI funds.

Considering that 1933 was a year for the Grand Maneuvers of the Japanese Navy, it was hoped that much valuable radio snooping could be performed. The project was not a great success due to equipment problems and the need to constantly hide antennas. Action was taken to obtain better "suitcase" receivers and to send them out, but the detail effectively terminated in May 1934. This was an interesting way for these men to see Seattle, Yokohama, Kobe, Shanghai, Hong Kong, and Manila—helping them to realize their recruitment enticement of "Join the Navy and See the World."

CAPTAIN ALBERT JOSEPH PELLETIER JR., U.S. NAVY
(1914–1999)

"Al"

Albert Pelletier's life spanned the time from World War I to well past the first Gulf War. As a sailor his career almost reads like a Horatio Alger story—from seaman to captain with duty spanning the globe. He was an early graduate of the famed "On-the-Roof-Gang" well before the war; he made significant contributions at OP-20-G and FRUPac just before and during the war; and he was active in postwar COMINT with such organizations as the AFSA, the Naval Security Group, and the NSA.

∗   ∗   ∗

Albert J. Pelletier was born on January 29, 1914, in Superior, Wisconsin. After graduation from high school, he enlisted in the navy in March 1932 and went to basic training at Great Lakes. He attended radio operator school at San Diego; then he was ordered to the battleship *Pennsylvania* for duty as a fleet radioman on the staff of the commander in chief, U.S. Fleet. He was advanced to radioman third class in 1934; further advancements and promotions included radioman second class, 1935; radioman first class, 1939; chief petty officer, 1942; ensign, 1943; lieutenant (junior grade), 1944; lieutenant, 1949; lieutenant commander, 1954; commander, 1958; and captain, 1965.

In January 1934, Pelletier transferred with the rest of the CINCUS staff to the battleship *New Mexico*, and then in 1936 he was selected for an embassy billet. However, after a period of temporary additional duty on board the destroyer *Babbitt*, the embassy assignment was changed to duty at Main Navy.

> One Sunday in May a Lieutenant **Harper** came aboard and offered me a job. While he wouldn't tell me anything about the job he so intrigued me that I accepted. The following Monday I had orders to Washington and reported to OP-20-G.

There Pelletier became a member of the pioneering "On-the-Roof-Gang," taking training as a radio intercept operator and learning Japanese Morse Code. He graduated from OTRG Class Eighteen.

In December 1936 he was assigned to Station CAST in the Philippine Islands; there he worked under Lt. John **Williams** and served as an intercept operator and radio traffic analyst—along with additional cryptologic duties. In November 1938 he transferred to Bainbridge Island, Washington, to assist in commissioning a new navy radio intercept facility—Station S.

January 1940 found Petty Officer Pelletier assigned back to OP-20-G, where he principally worked on the Japanese naval code JN-25. His arrival there coincided with a significant reorganization; the legendary Agnes **Driscoll** had just been moved from Japanese codes to German, and as discussed in a memo,

> Mrs. Driscoll has been engaged in cryptanalytical attack on the current Orange Navy Operations code system [JN-25]. This attack has now progressed to the point where it can be pursued by others. Accordingly, it has been turned over to Lieutenant Bayley. He will be assisted by Lieutenant Chisholm full time, and by Lieutenant **Lietwiler** and Lieutenant Brotherhood for instruction. CRM **McGregor** and [P.O.1] Pelletier will handle the actual code recovery, and two cryptographic clerks complete the group.

Pelletier remained at OP-20-GY and OP-20-GZ until June 1944. During that time he worked with several of the early stars of U.S. navy cryptography.

> My fellow workers were three very talented progeny of American missionaries who had grown up in Japan and were bilingual. They were Fred Woodrough, his sister Dorothy

Edgers, and Phil Cate. Our section . . . was headed by Lt. Cmdr. Alwin **Kramer**, a Japanese language officer.[1]

Pelletier later concurred with Rear Adm. Edwin **Layton** when Layton wrote that, by early December 1941, about 10 percent of JN-25 was readable.

> But it must be remembered that some messages such as movement reports and other routine activity for which traffic analysis was available were ninety percent readable, while other messages would have only a few groups recovered. . . .
>
> [After Pearl Harbor] we became a team that recovered JN-25 like mad. At this time Lt. Cmdr. Redfield **Mason** relieved Mr. Kramer. . . . Mr. Mason was a whirlwind and he really got us going. He was one of the most brilliant men I ever knew.
>
> Mr. Mason lived in Manassas, Virginia, and was able to obtain sufficient gasoline coupons to drive to work each day. I lived in . . . Falls Church and Mr. Mason was kind enough to stop by and give me a ride each day. This was an excellent arrangement for me but had one drawback: if he stayed late at work, so did I. The compensation was being able to talk "shop" to and from work and learn what was going on in the minds of the "brass."

By June 1944, Al Pelletier had been promoted to chief petty officer and then commissioned as an ensign. He was transferred to FRUPac at Pearl Harbor with no significant change in duty: cryptography working on code recovery. At Pearl he was reunited with some old colleagues and mentors from Station CAST: Capt. Joe **Finnegan**, Col. Red **Lasswell**, and Cmdr. Rufe **Taylor**. Not long after, Capt. Rosie Mason also transferred in from Washington and Pelletier was happy to work for him again.

Shortly after the war ended, Lt. j.g. Pelletier was transferred back to OP-20-G in Washington. In January 1949 he was sent to school at George Washington University. Lieutenant Pelletier then reported for duty, in October 1950, with the AFSA. Then, in January 1952 he was sent to Yokosuka, Japan, and later to the Naval Security Group Activity at Kami Seya. From September 1954 through August 1957, Lieutenant Commander Pelletier was assigned to the NSA.

In August 1957, Pelletier was transferred to London where he served on the staff of the Commander in Chief, U.S. Naval Forces Eastern Atlantic and Mediterranean. In mid-1960, after a month's training as an instructor, Commander Pelletier was back in the United States, now attached to the Naval Communications Training Center at Pensacola, serving as the training officer. He remained in that position until June 1963, when he was transferred to the Naval Communications Station, Guam, in the billet of executive officer.

---

1. Pelletier makes an interesting point in his autobiography. He wrote that "contrary to some claims, the U.S. Navy did not employ any *Nisei* in any cryptographic duties." Thus, navy cryptographers and translators were Caucasians with backgrounds such as Haworth, Woodrough, and Edgers; ONI full-immersion trained language and culture experts such as Rochefort, Kramer, and Mason; and then many graduates of the special ONI language program—as in the "Boulder Boys" from the University of Colorado.

In July 1965 he was selected for promotion to captain and assigned to the staff of the Commandant, Ninth Naval District, at Great Lakes; there he worked as the district officer for reserve training.

Captain Pelletier retired on September 1, 1968, after thirty-six years of service. Among his decorations and awards was the Legion of Merit for his remarkable cryptographic services during World War II.

Following his navy retirement he became active in, and was a frequent contributor to, the U.S. Naval Cryptologic Veterans Association—including working for a time as the association's president. He and his wife Dorothy lived for many years in Milton, Florida, and she also became very involved in USNCVA activities.

Captain Pelletier died on May 9, 1999, in Pensacola, at age eighty-five. His wife, Dorothy (1917–1994) predeceased him. They had married in 1936 and for the next thirty-two years she followed him around the world and raised four children: Ruth, Sally, Albert J. III (Spike), and Peggy. Al and Dorothy are buried together in Barrancas National Cemetery at Naval Air Station Pensacola.

Capt. Al Pelletier was a consummate COMINT pioneer and contributor. Even beyond that, he made indelible impressions upon many of his colleagues and students—such as "he was a hell of a guy, one you're glad you got to meet, and one you'll never forget," and "his laugh was infectious, and even in his later years his voice and laugh were his signature."

Sources

Browne, *Pelletier*, vi, 39, 132–33, 136, 139, 143, 145–47, 151, 161.
Holtwick, 400.
McGinnis, 29–32.
Pelletier, CWO4 Albert J. III, Ret., email correspondence, October 14–16, 2014.
Prados, 459.

VICE ADMIRAL BERNARD FRANKLIN ROEDER, U.S. NAVY
(1911–1971)

"Brute"

A talented technician, an inspirational leader, and an unusually multifaceted officer, Roeder contributed remarkable service in World War II, the Korean War, the Vietnam War, and the Cold War. A cryptologist and communications expert rather than an intelligence analyst or linguist, he also rose to high seagoing operational command, particularly with the amphibious forces. Roeder moved from pencils to computers and vacuum tubes to satellites—and remained on the leading edge all the way.

* * *

From the 1931 Annapolis yearbook, *The Lucky Bag*:

Brute took leave of the hills of western Maryland and sailed down to Annapolis with a determined air that brought him out of the fog sooner than the rest of us. His has been an eventful four years, and the Academy may feel justly proud of him. We need not say much about *Brute*. All of us know about him, as his rugged disposition makes him the center of any fest he happens to be in. He can land in more first sections per erg expended and can receive more mail per letter written than any man we know. His savviness is balanced by a broad grin and light-hearted nature that are all his own. During the spring, *Brute* lives out on the tennis courts, but he often takes a week-end off and drags [dates], thus always raising the average. He is so big-hearted that he will give you the shirt off his back, even though he has only five left in his locker—it's a fact. Notable quotation: "That's fruit [easy]. Wake me up five minutes before formation, will you?" [Activities: football, tennis, Reception Committee, Stage Gang, Glee Club]

* * *

Bernard F. Roeder was born in Cumberland, Maryland, on February 4, 1911, the son of William P. and Anna Roeder. Prior to entering the Naval Academy in 1927, he attended Allegheny High School in his hometown. He graduated from Annapolis with distinction, and was commissioned an ensign in June 1931, along with such notable classmates as Rudolph J. **Fabian**, Bankson T. **Holcomb** Jr., John S. McCain Jr., Lawson "Red" Ramage, and Horacio Rivero Jr. Further promotions included lieutenant (junior grade), 1934; lieutenant, 1938; lieutenant commander, June 1942; commander, November 1942; captain, 1949; rear admiral, 1958; and vice admiral, 1965. He was transferred to the retired list in 1969.

From August 1931 to June 1937, Mr. Roeder had the typical intensive general sea duty start to his career, serving successively aboard the light cruiser *Richmond* (1931–1932), the destroyer *Gilmer* (1933–1934), the destroyer *Farragut* (1935), and the aircraft carrier *Lexington* (1936–1937).

In July 1937, he was ordered to the Office of the CNO, Communications Division, at Main Navy, remaining there until November 1939. During this time he underwent instruction in OP-20-G's cryptology course, along with Lt. j.g. Jeff **Dennis** and Lt. j.g. Allan Reed. Upon completion of that training, in July 1938, Lieutenant Roeder briefly became OIC of OP-20-GC (Codes and Ciphers). He was relieved of that position, in turn, by Lt. Dick **Zern** in June 1939. In October—for only a month—he headed OP-20-GX (Cryptanalysis). Upon the arrival of Lt. Cmdr. Edward R. Gardner at GX, Roeder prepared to head to the Asiatic Station.

Between January and November 1940, Lieutenant Roeder was assigned as assistant communications officer for the Sixteenth Naval District at Cavite, Philippine Islands, relieving his colleague Jeff Dennis. Mr. Roeder then moved to the staff of the Commander in Chief, Asiatic Fleet, as security officer and assistant communications officer. He was engaged in these duties at the outbreak of the war with Japan and during the early defense of the Philippines. Much like Sid **Goodwin**, Ray **Lamb**, Jack **Holtwick**, John **Williams**, and Jeff Dennis before him, Roeder served as both the Philippines decryption station OIC ashore, and then as assistant fleet communications officer for CinCAF on board the flagship. Roeder materially built upon the precedent established by Lieutenant Goodwin, which had convinced Lieutenant Commander **Safford**, the OP-20-G chief back in Washington, to decide that it was important that the Pacific intercept stations should establish, maintain, and expand dedicated cryptanalytic sections. In early 1940, Roeder wrote a report for the commandant of the Sixteenth Naval District which underscored the importance of the Philippine station, stating that even resorting

> to strictly radio intelligence methods to obtain information of operations (intended and actual), dispositions, and intentions of the Orange Navy has, if nothing else demonstrated the ability of the Communication Intelligence Organization to function with considerable effectiveness under the same conditions which would . . . exist during an emergency in relations between the United States and Orange. . . . The apparent inability [of Orange] to conduct even minor operations involving coordination of attacking forces without resort to a great volume of radio traffic in preparation, and an abrupt rise of communications well beyond the capacity of normal circuits once operations have commenced, would probably continue to exist to a certain degree. Therefore, it is considered certain that the Asiatic Communication Intelligence Organization can continue to obtain positive advance information of operations.

Lieutenant Rudy Fabian relieved Lieutenant Roeder in late 1940. Roeder remained in the Philippines undertaking other duties than strictly intelligence or cryptology; in fact, in August 1941, Fabian commented in a letter that "Roeder may as well be considered as having practically no connection with R.I." However, he certainly was not done with radio intelligence; in a memo written in October 1941, OP-20-G head Laurance Safford listed Roeder as one of eighteen "qualified and acceptable" for wartime communications intelligence duties.

In January 1942, Mr. Roeder was assigned as communications officer for the U.S. naval forces at Surabaya, Java, and in February and March 1942, he was flag lieutenant and communications officer on the staff of the commander in chief, Asiatic Fleet. This latter was at the headquarters of the supreme commander of British-Dutch-American forces at Lembang, in western Java, which was then engaged in the defense of the Netherlands East Indies. Subsequently, Roeder was appointed as the assistant communications officer for the commander of U.S. naval forces at Perth, Australia. From May to November 1942, he continued in similar duty for the Commander, Southwest Pacific Forces, and the Commander, Seventh Fleet, at Melbourne and Brisbane.

His World War II service continued from January 1943 to August 1945 in the Office of the CNO in Washington, working in communications-intelligence duties. In fact, he was awarded the Legion of Merit while attached to the Division of Naval Communications.

From September 1945 to February 1947, Roeder served as executive officer of the battleship *New Jersey* (which was the flagship of the Commander, Fifth Fleet, based at Yokosuka) in support of the occupation of Japan. He then was assigned as commanding officer of the destroyer *Lowry*—operating with Task Force 38, cruising to Australia—and in June 1947 he was transferred to become commanding officer of the destroyer *Collett*.

Roeder returned to shore duty with the Communications Division in Washington. He then attended the Naval War College in Newport during 1949 and 1950, and in May 1950 was ordered to duty as Commander, Destroyer Division 112. That division was assigned to U.S. Naval Forces, Far East, and supported the UN action in Korea. Until its departure from the Far East in March 1951, DesDiv 112 operated with Task Force 77, conducted the Formosa Straits Patrol, and engaged in shore bombardment off the east coast of Korea. Roeder was in command of the ships which commenced the siege of Wonsan in February 1951, and then he and his ships continued operations in Korean waters until the armistice. For his Korean War service, Roeder was awarded gold stars in lieu of second and third Legion of Merit medals.

He was detached from his command in July 1951, and ordered to Washington to serve in naval intelligence.

From July 1953 until December 1954, he was assigned as operations officer on the staff of Commander, Battleship-Cruiser Force, U.S. Atlantic Fleet. While in that billet, he participated in the Naval Academy's midshipman cruise to Europe, and then a tour with the Sixth Fleet in the Mediterranean.

From February 1955 to January 1956, Captain Roeder commanded the attack transport *Pickaway*, which subsequently conducted training operations in the Far East and off the west coast of the United States. In February 1956, he assumed command of Transport Division Twelve, and then in August reported for duty as Commander, Transport Division Eleven—both divisions belonging to the Amphibious Force, U.S. Pacific Fleet. From March through August 1957, he served as chief of staff and aide to the Commander, Amphibious Training Command, Pacific Fleet.

In the fall, Captain Roeder reported back to Washington, and relieved Captain Jeff Dennis as assistant director for Naval Security Group Matters (Naval Communications Division) and head, Naval Security Group. In March 1959, Roeder was promoted to rear admiral. In May 1959, Roeder became OP-94-G, and his title was changed to Deputy Director of Naval Communications for Naval Security Group, and Head, NavSecGru. In June 1960 he was relieved by Capt. Lester R. Schulz and then, in July, Roeder reported for duty as Commander, Amphibious Group Three.

He was detached from that assignment, in October 1961, when he became Assistant CNO for Communications, and Director, Naval Communications. For his contributions in those positions he was awarded a fourth Legion of Merit, the citation of which praises him for exceptional leadership and technical expertise in "obtaining communications facilities and equipment incorporating monumental technological advances." He was also recognized as a remarkable proponent of the navy's use of communications satellites, which directly led to the first installation of COMSAT terminals in combatant ships of the fleet.

Another accomplishment, in 1963, was when Rear Admiral Roeder ordered staff to "Take Charge and Move Out" on the development of a secure, reliable communications system for the president of the United States to send orders to ballistic missile submarines in the ocean's depths. The solution was to deploy TACAMO EC-130Q aircraft flying in circles over the Atlantic and Pacific in order to receive very low-frequency data and high-frequency voice radio transmissions to relay Emergency Action Messages.

In May 1965, newly promoted Vice Admiral Roeder became Commander, Amphibious Force, U.S. Pacific Fleet. His performance in this assignment let to his fifth Legion of Merit medal.

July 1966 saw Roeder assume command of the U.S. First Fleet—relieving his Annapolis classmate Vice Adm. Lawson "Red" Ramage—on board the carrier *Kitty Hawk*. In this position he was particularly involved with coordinating training in the eastern and mid–Pacific Ocean Areas, and directly responsible for readying ships and squadrons for the demands of the war in Vietnam. His work included substantive improvements in electronic warfare capabilities and communications.

In September 1969, Vice Admiral Roeder was assigned temporary duty in the Eleventh Naval District at San Diego, and the next month he retired.

On September 3, 1971, at age sixty, "Brute" Roeder suffered a massive stroke. He was taken to the Naval Hospital in San Diego, where he subsequently passed away that afternoon. He is buried at El Camino Memorial Park, also in San Diego.

Roeder had married Kathleen Fitch, at Coronado, California, in 1936. They had a son, Lt. Cmdr. Bernard F. Roeder Jr. (USNA class of 1960), and three daughters: Franke, Anne, and Kathleen. Subsequent to Vice Admiral Roeder's death, Mrs. Roeder married again, to Vice Adm. Paul D. Stroop, who himself passed away in 1995. As of this writing, Kathleen F. R. Stroop is living in Coronado, aged ninety-nine.

Among Admiral Roeder's decorations and awards are the Distinguished Service Medal, five Legion of Merit medals with Combat "V" device, the Navy Commendation Medal, China Service Medal, the Korean Service Medal, and the Philippine Defense Ribbon.

Bernard Roeder has been recognized and honored, by the U.S. Naval Cryptologic Veterans Association, as an officer who has served as the Commander, Naval Security Group or one of its predecessor organizations. He has also been named a Pioneer Officer of U.S. Naval Cryptology by the same organization.

Sources

Holtwick, 137, 140, 245, 305, 329, 340, 345, 351, 356, 360, 431, 439, App. 7, 91, 109.
Lucky Bag, U.S. Naval Academy, 1931.
U.S. Navy Museum/Naval Historical Foundation, *Cold War Gallery.*
U.S. Navy, *Register of Commissioned and Warrant Officers.*
Vice Admiral Bernard Franklin Roeder, USN, Retired. Biography. Navy Office of Information, Internal Relations Division, April 28, 1970. Courtesy of the Naval Historical Foundation.

CAPTAIN LAURANCE FRYE SAFFORD, U.S. NAVY (1893–1973)

The "father" of U.S. Navy cryptology
"A code-and-cipher demon"
Excellent in mathematics, a mechanical genius, and a fancier of chess
Had a single-minded devotion to duty and an unshakable personal rectitude
Safford . . . singlehandedly . . . conceived, founded,
and built the navy's COMINT entity
"Sappho"

Laurance Safford, widely acknowledged as the "father" of U.S. Navy cryptology, established the navy's cryptologic organization after World War I and headed the effort more or less constantly until shortly after the Japanese attack on Pearl Harbor. His identification with the navy's effort was so close that he was effectively "the Friedman of the Navy," an allusion to the pioneering and brilliant army cryptologist William F. Friedman. Largely due to Safford, from 1924 to 1941 "the navy's cryptanalytic capability was one of constant growth; growth not only in size, but in proficiency, experience, and technical sophistication." Safford nurtured his office, OP-20-G, through the hard and lean interwar years. He was highly respected by other cryptologic and intelligence officers from both the navy and the army. From a technical standpoint Safford was an extremely talented officer, though his true ability lay in the collection, forwarding, and processing—the "frontend" of cryptology—and not as much in the analysis of the intercept or dissemination of COMINT. The year 1924 began his romance with cryptography; a passion which lasted throughout his career and in fact to the end of his life—for almost fifty years.

* * *

From the 1916 Annapolis yearbook *The Lucky Bag*:

Herewith we present the one and only. *Sappho* was not made for this world. He must have been born in a daze—ever since he entered the Academy he has lived in a perpetual haze of preoccupied alertness. He has an air of utter detachment mixed with an absolute knowledge of the concrete details of each and every occasion. Celestial lights simply radiate from him, and if there is some subject which he is not a greater authority than the inventor, discoverer, or whoever the high mogul would be for the . . . case under consideration, we have yet to locate it! With regard to congeniality, *Sappho* is right there. Whenever you see a small mob gathered in the murky dimness of Smoke Hall, you will find *Sappho* gesticulating like his roommate and sputtering like a Gnome engine. He speaks with [the] velocity of a Springfield rifle, but he thinks so much faster that his brain overleaps his tongue, and the resulting statement, although doubtless a gem of logical coordination, sounds like a Gatling gun in distress. *Sappho's* deepness of concentration has made him the last man to every formation since his entrance to this life of luxury and ease. It does a man a world of good to know *Sappho*. His ability to differentiate between what's right and what's wrong has kept him a clean, strong character, and you may bank on it—what he does is right. [Activities: Regimental Ordnance Officer; soccer]

* * *

Laurance Safford was born on October 22, 1893, in Somerville, Massachusetts. He secured an appointment to the Naval Academy in 1912, subsequently graduating in fifteenth place among the class of 1916. Among his prominent classmates were Russell S. Berkey, Robert B. Carney, William M. Fechteler, Charles Turner Joy, Arthur W. Radford, and Cassin Young. Because of the navy's expansion in World War I, Mr. Safford skipped the rank of lieutenant (junior grade) by receiving a temporary promotion to lieutenant in May 1917. Subsequent promotions included lieutenant commander, 1926; commander, 1937; and captain, 1942. He retired in mid-1951 but was immediately recalled to active duty; he finally finished his navy career in 1953.

The last years of World War I saw Mr. Safford at sea in the Atlantic, serving as the communications officer onboard an armed transport and then later a destroyer. He next attended submarine school in New London, Connecticut, where he qualified as a submariner. In 1921, Safford served as the navigator of the submarine USS *S-7* in her historic cruise from Portsmouth, New Hampshire to Cavite, Philippine Islands; this was historic in that the *S-7* and some other boats made the longest cruise on record for American submarines. At Cavite, in 1922, Mr. Safford was given command of the Asiatic Fleet's minesweeper *Finch*.

Safford's early sea-going career onboard ships as a conventional line officer gave no indication of the role he was to play in cryptologic history. But Safford was, in fact, very unconventional—a constantly rumpled uniform and hair often standing on end hid an excellence in mathematics and an affinity for machines, and he was attracted to chess and other such intellectual pursuits. Many years later, retired Rear Adm. Edwin **Layton** commented that Safford's "most remarkable feature was his eyes, which were constantly darting back and forth, as if watching out for some danger."[1]

In January 1924, "picked by the sheerest chance by the naval bureaucracy," he was called from command of his small minesweeper off the remote China coast to head the new "Research Desk" of the CSS within the Office of Naval Communications. Safford himself—fifty years later—recalled that

> I was selected upon the recommendation of several classmates, including Lt. John E. Reinburg, who had established the Registered Publications Section. They wanted somebody with an analytical mind who was slightly unusual. As Capt. Tommy **Dyer** has said, "you don't have to be crazy to be a good 'cryppie,' but it helps a lot." They wanted someone who they thought could make good in this arcane subject, and I was selected out of all the others who were available to come ashore at that time to start the thing off.

Earlier, a key staff member in the CSS (Miss Agnes Meyer **Driscoll**) had developed a device, known as the "Cipher Machine" or the "CM," along with the then head of the section (Lt. Cmdr. William Gresham). In 1921 this gadget, which was a mechanical cipher device based on a sliding alphabet system, become one of the navy's standard cryptographic tools for most of the 1920s. According to the retired Captain Safford—looking back from fifty years—it was the first high-command cipher the navy had.

But it had some problems. In fact, when Lt. Safford arrived to become head of the Research Desk (to be called OP-20-GX), the head of the Visual Signals Desk (OP-20-GS) in Naval Communications, Lt. Arthur "Rip" **Struble**, handed him the problem of taking the Gresham and Driscoll CM coding machine and making hardware modifications to improve its performance.

> It was a machine which involved the cipher principal, and it was invented by Miss Aggie way, way back, and then the mechanical details were worked out by "Pop" Gresham. But I had to redesign the damn thing. We substituted aluminum for brass wherever we could; we changed the method of disengaging and re-engaging the racks.

---

1. In addition, a long-time staff member once said that Safford "spoke in little bursts and unconnected phrases that unnerved his listeners," but that this also "brought universal admiration from us for his secretary's ability to produce a coherent memorandum from his dictation."

But it was the first system we had which dispensed with the codebook, and it stayed in effect for several years.

Once that had been done, Safford's sole task was to exploit a Japanese naval codebook that had been photographed—by ONI agents in a classic break-and-enter and safecrack job—at the Japanese consulate in New York. To help him, Safford had only a civilian cryptanalyst and four civilian clerical employees.

> I [had] reported for duty about 5 January 1924 and found these five people waiting for me. Cryptologist Claus Bogel was simply sitting around doing crossword puzzles, because he was not a good typist. But the four stenographers/typists (Miss Castleman, Miss Calnan, Mrs. Devirgy, and Mrs. Wilson) were very busy typing up the manuscript Mrs. Haworth was writing. She was hired because she was the only one who could read her husband's handwriting—Dr. Haworth, the Japanese translator. But her typing was so terrible that it was unusable, so these girls were busy typing copies of what later became known as the "Red Book."

Safford later emphasized the importance of the *Red Book* when he said it was truly "the foundation of our navy's penetration of Japanese naval secrets." But it was at this point that Safford also started thinking about improving interception of Japanese radio traffic. After considerable research, "done in a remarkably short time considering all the other pies in which he had fingers," Safford designed the specifications for a special "code machine." Among his other instances of foresight, he had recognized that the Japanese version of Morse Code posed a unique challenge to intercepting signals. Radio operators had to "learn a whole new set of long and short patterns, which involved actually unlearning the familiar ones." In 1924, the navy only had two operators who knew Japanese Morse. Safford contracted with the Underwood Typewriter Co. to custom-build special typewriters that printed in Japanese *kana*. Paid for out of an ONI slush fund, the forty or so incredibly valuable machines, ultimately called RIP-5s, cost about $160 apiece—very expensive at that time.

Moreover, later in 1928, the Research Desk began a secret training program that ultimately taught 176 Navy and Marine enlisted men the Japanese Morse. The three-month course took place in a blockhouse on top the Main Navy building. Final access was via a ladder, so the students called themselves the "On-the-Roof-Gang"—or "roofers."

Another thing Safford set in motion in 1924—another pie he stuck a finger in—was searching for people who might be interested in, and might develop capability in, cryptanalysis. Starting in July he began to publish a set of cryptograms, of varying degrees of difficulty, in the navy-wide *Communication Division Bulletin*. The names of officers who mailed back accurate solutions were earmarked for future duty at OP-20-G as space became available. Tommy Dyer, arguably the best of the World War II cryptanalysts, told an interviewer that this is how he was initially recruited.

> There was a little squib that said, "if you solve this, send in your solution to the Chief of Naval Operations, OP-20-G." So I did. . . . I think I sent in maybe not every one, but

ninety percent for the next couple of years. That led to my being ordered to the Navy Department for a three-month course.

Retired Capt. Joseph **Rochefort**, also looking back in time, said

I don't think it would be an exaggeration to say that, when Safford was ordered to the Navy Department to establish this cryptographic section, it was initially for the purpose of improving our own crypto systems. Then in order to do this, of course, it became very apparent to Safford that a knowledge of worldwide systems in use by, say, the British, the French, or the Japanese, or anyone else, would be very valuable. So he sort of drifted into a study of other systems. And, while still making every effort to improve our own systems (which were not very good at that time) he also was attacking other systems being used by other powers . . . in an attempt to interpret them.

Safford was perfect for the job. The infant Research Desk needed a "promoter" and he was just the man to do it. Moreover, his innate talent for cryptography immediately came to the surface. "His introduction and grounding in that arcane science was provided by his assistant, Miss Agnes Meyer [later Mrs. Driscoll]. She was an enigmatic but brilliant cryptanalyst."

Mr. Safford got to work on developing new codes for the navy. In those days,

no one in the navy was paying much attention to foreign countries' codes at the time, and they certainly weren't trying to break them. But Safford figured that to make a good code he ought to first see what other navies were doing. And so, the "Research Desk" was born in Room 1621 of the old Navy Department building [Main Navy] on the mall in Washington.

Safford promoted cryptologic efforts throughout the navy, attracting brilliant minds like his own. In addition to Miss Aggie, these included Joseph Rochefort, Joseph **Wenger**, Thomas Dyer, and several others who were to lead the business through World War II and into the postwar period. Joe Rochefort later said that

Safford really started this whole organization. . . . Safford laid all the groundwork. . . . He would be considered . . . the "father" of this whole thing which developed into the communications intelligence organization.

He was in communications; this is what he knew. These things just present a challenge and a true cryptanalyst will never give up until he has solved a particular system. A true cryptanalyst generally is not involved in subsequent use of the information. He's what you would call a technician who will solve a system just for the sake of solving the system. But he doesn't usually apply the results to any operation or need or purpose or anything else. This would be a true cryptanalyst. This would be Safford.[2]

---

2. Clearly, Safford is one of the people who caught a strong case of what the nineteenth-century French cryptanalyst Colonel Étienne Bazèries called *cryptographitis*— "a sort of subtle, all-pervading, incurable malady."

Inherent to that effort was his discovery of ONI's *cabinet noir* not far from his own office—which held their pilfered Japanese code books and Dr. Emerson J. Haworth, their sole translator.

> What he saw in Room 2646 determined Safford to burst the narrow confines of his Research Desk. He pleaded in his most persuasive manner for permission to branch out in two directions—to set up interception stations to obtain the Japanese dispatches which ONI needed to put its *Red Book* to practical use, and to add code-cracking to the functions of the Research Desk.

Thus, he was the first to organize the worldwide U.S. naval collection and radio direction-finding effort—so that when the United States entered World War II it had a system of intercept stations already in place and operational.

As it turned out, for almost twenty years,

> OP-20-G was the private fiefdom of the gifted and eccentric Commander Laurance F. Safford, a lugubrious, bespectacled 1916 Annapolis graduate . . . it was Safford who established the unit's two satellite stations, one in Manila called Station CAST, and Station HYPO in Hawaii. . . . It was also Safford who recruited the first team of analysts who became key players in the [World War II] codebreaking effort.

Initially, Safford got no help from the U.S. Army or the State Department. He later commented that

> when the newly established Research Desk began its study of Japanese diplomatic systems in 1924–25, the Army refused to give the Navy any assistance or to even admit that [their] "Yardley's Black Chamber" in New York City ever existed. In 1931, the Navy set an example of collaboration by giving the [Army] Signal Corps all Japanese diplomatic keys which had been recovered, plus full data on new systems which had come into being since that date. The Army more-or-less took over the Japanese diplomatic systems, leaving the Navy free to devote its efforts to Japanese naval systems. From that time on there was complete interchange between the Army and Navy regarding all technical features of Japanese systems as well as exchange of important translations.

It's pleasing to report that, despite some ups and downs, there generally were good relations between service cryptologists—at least at the working-man's level. Safford and his people were cooperative and willing, as were their army counterparts—led by the iconic cryptology pioneer William Friedman. This was particularly true after 1930; in fact, Friedman "had overcome the usual interservice animosities and developed a friendly, mutually beneficial collaboration with Safford." The two worked reasonably harmoniously for years—sometimes with their superiors' approval, sometimes despite their disapproval, and sometimes merely with their indifference.[3]

---

3. For the army, Friedman was much like Safford, "the master-mind, the organizer, the defender, the very personification of aggressive cryptology as a major instrument of intelligence." Intelligence historian Ladislas Farago later wrote that "Friedman's relations with Safford were excellent. Ties of close personal

In the early days at the Research Desk, Mr. Safford organized the intercept and analytic efforts, while Miss Aggie provided the cryptanalytic and technical base for the navy's main communications-intelligence program. Safford came and went, leaving the office and returning every few years for tours of required sea duty. In fact, he was wrenched out of the job in 1926 to later return in 1929; during that absence the office was run by Lt. Joe Rochefort, who'd just spent six months being trained in cryptanalysis.[4] Rochefort's crypto-schooling was also by Safford's design; early on he had organized a special sixteen-week course for cryptanalytics. Subjects included in the course were code breaking, cipher solutions, navy cryptographic systems, radio security, and radio intelligence.

In 1926, as mentioned earlier, Lieutenant Commander Safford was sent to the destroyer *Hull* as navigator and executive officer. Busy as he was at sea, he kept thinking about communications-intelligence, and in fact—during the winter of 1926–1927—Safford headed the Blue Force Radio Unit on board the *Hull*, opposing Lt. Bern **Anderson** who headed the Black Force unit in the battleship *Texas*. This was during the U.S. Navy Fleet Problem VII; both officers had embarked radio receiving equipment capable of continuous interception of "enemy" traffic.

In December 1929—after he returned to Main Navy from his sea duty—Safford reported that OP-20-GX had already accumulated five years of intercepted Japanese diplomatic traffic (which is to say ten thousand messages), as well as two years of Japanese naval traffic (two thousand messages)—all needing translation. That was the problem; at that time Naval Communications had no translators, and Naval Intelligence had only one—the eminent Dr. Haworth. Fortunately, that situation was to improve largely through ONI's full-immersion in-country language program.

The earlier *Red Book* breakthrough really paid off in 1930 during the Imperial Japanese Navy's Grand Fleet Maneuvers. OP-20-G's analysis of the exercise indicated that Tokyo—alarmingly—had developed a good insight into American naval planning, specifically *U.S. War Plan Orange*, which emphasized that U.S. Pacific Fleet operations would be near the Japanese home islands. Critical to this achievement was Mrs. Driscoll's cryptanalysis. For the maneuvers the Japanese made some extra coding efforts; nevertheless, she was soon able to exploit the system. Safford later wrote that:

> the Japanese introduced a new cipher system for these maneuvers plus a daily change of key—but [still] used the *good old* "Red Book." All hands turned-to on these messages; Mrs. Driscoll got the first break as usual, and the various daily keys were solved without too much effort.

---

friendship and a communion of interests bound them. . . . Safford, on his part, relegated himself to second place in this partnership. He was leaning heavily on his friend and colleague in whom he admired a rare combination of old-world sophistication and broad intellectual vision."

4. Capt. Jasper Holmes wrote that "in 1925, Joseph Rochefort, Laurance Safford, and Agnes Driscoll were the whole of the Navy's code-breaking crew."

In this, and then in later system attacks, Miss Aggie would solve the ciphers and the first keys. Then the subsequent keys were given to a series of officers passing through the Research Desk for training—often under her supervision. It's interesting to note that the Research Desk was still a very small unit in 1930: just Lt. Cmdr. Safford, Mrs. Driscoll, Lieutenant Wenger, and two to three typists.

The importance of this feat of Miss Aggie and her associates can hardly be over-stated. The solution was a tremendous achievement for "the Navy's entire cryptological effort, and it was especially . . . gratifying that it came so early in the game." Her unraveling of the code, and the input from traffic analysis by the U.S. naval listening station on Guam really—and probably for the first time—gained the attention of the leadership in the U.S. Navy. As intelligence historian Ladislas Farago would remark, "the Research Desk became respectable overnight. Its value was recognized all the way up to the Chief of Naval Operations. Its continued existence was assured."

The desk could actually only decipher a fraction of the intercepted messages available. However, through their efforts, the U.S. Navy was able to track the Imperial Navy in many day-to-day operations, its technological advancements and, to a degree, monitor its fledgling aviation arm.

Looking back from the perspective of 1943, Safford wrote that:

> the work of solving these cipher systems and decrypting the messages was one of the most interesting duties every undertaken by the section. We were literally exploring virgin territory. No one in the U.S. Navy had the slightest idea as to the professional concepts of the Japanese Navy.

And these professional concepts certainly included communications routines and even battle tactics.

One might think that, with his interest in mechanical devices, Lt. Cmdr. Safford might have aggressively rushed into the concept of automating cryptanalysis. However, looking back from 1969 to 1930, retired Rear Adm. Joe Wenger recalled that:

> Mr. Safford and Miss Meyer discussed the idea at some length and expressed considerable doubt about the feasibility of using machines to perform what they regarded as the unpredictable nature and the variety of processes involved in cipher solution. As a result of the discussion, a [memo] to Captain Hooper [the director of naval communications] was written, expressing in effect their appreciation of the desirability of having automatic machinery to perform cryptanalytic chores, but indicating skepticism as to the feasibility of the idea.

However, even by 1931 they had become more interested and had implemented some automation in-house, led by Lt. j.g. Tommy Dyer. Ten years beyond that they were actively seeking state-of-the-art assistance. In November 1941, Commander Safford, Mrs. Driscoll, and two other Naval Communications people began working with several professors and scientists from the MIT; the topic was the design and manufacture of high-speed analytical machinery for the Communications Security Section.

Back to November 1930, Mr. Safford was still caught in the shore-duty/sea-duty rotation. In fact, his then boss, Lt. Cmdr. John W. **McClaran**, addressed this by writing "Lt. Cmdr. Safford has attained a rank where he will be forced, for his own good, to drop [COMINT] and concentrate along other lines." McClaran was not only addressing the required sea rotation, he was also alluding to the fact that neither intelligence nor communications-intelligence were viable navy career fields in those days. If a person wanted to promote to commander and captain—and certainly if he had hopes of flag rank—he needed to abandon such "hobbies" and concentrate on the traditional patterns of naval officers—for then every line officer remained at core a sea officer, submariner, or aviator.

Accordingly, once again Safford went back to sea "somewhere during the late fall, early winter of 1931–32," to be on the commissioning crew of the cruiser *Portland* being built at Quincy, Massachusetts. At this time the young Lt. j.g. Dyer inherited the job of Research Desk OIC.

Even in his absence, "Safford's organization" broke more of Japanese naval codes and started to mechanize its operations with the addition of early IBM sorting and tabulating equipment.

In 1936, Safford returned from sea duty (cruiser *Portland*, 1933; battleship *New Mexico*, 1934–1935) to again take charge of "his" organization. But now he was not just running the Research Desk *within* the CSS; he was moved up to run *all* of OP-20-G, now called the Communications Security Group.

Aside from assaulting the crypto-systems of the Japanese, Safford redoubled his emphasis on U.S. Navy communications security.

> He modernized the existing equipment, adapted it to teletype and other rapid means of communication, developed various concealment and scrambler systems, started a program of miniaturization, and eliminated practically all the old paper-and-pencil systems.

Also during this period,

> one of his principal accomplishments, before the outbreak of war, was the establishment of the Mid-Pacific Strategic Direction-Finding Net—and of a similar net for the Atlantic, where it was to play a role of immense importance in the Battle of the Atlantic against the U-boats.

Safford was passed over for promotion to commander in 1936—underscoring the danger of spending too much time in non-career-enhancing duties. Fortunately, he was selected in the spring of 1937. In 1938, however, a newly created solution to the problem presented itself. Commander Safford's status was changed—at his request—from unrestricted line officer to a special subcategory of EDO: cryptographic duty. Lt. Cmdr. Tommy Dyer was assigned to this same category in 1939, as was Lt. Alwin **Kramer**—who actually was an ONI immersion-trained Japanese linguist. So far as known, they were the only officers ever to be so designated—not counting the Special Duty Officer categories which were created after World War II. This change also freed Safford from any further sea duty, so he stayed in COMINT and in Washington for the rest of his career.

As was mentioned earlier, Safford was personally involved with building cryptographic machines; among other things he collaborated on improving an army device which resulted in the SIGABA, or ECM Mk II. No successful cryptanalysis of this machine, during its service lifetime, is publicly known. Joe Rochefort later added that:

> Safford gradually got away from the dog work of cryptanalysis—he got away from this and this was left up to some other people, younger people. Safford gradually gave more and more attention to the security of our own system. He became more and more involved in secrecy—designing new machinery and this, that, and the other thing—rather than strictly cryptanalysis. He became quite intrigued with these new systems that were being developed.

Along these lines, Safford personally added improvements to civilian inventor Edward Hebern's early rotor mechanisms and gradually developed other cipher machines suitable for the navy's operational requirements of speed, reliability, and security. David Kahn, the American "dean" of cryptologic history, wrote that even so, Safford's "contributions to cryptanalytics were minor, since his talents [really] lay more in the administrative and mechanical fields." But Kahn contributes to a distinguished list of VIP testimonies when he emphasizes that, unquestionably, Safford "is the father of the Navy's . . . cryptologic organization."

It can't be overlooked that the years of the Great Depression were very hard for the American cryptologic services.

> OP-20-G and [Army] SIS were kept barely alive, mostly only by the zeal and dedication of the handful of people working in them. The fact that they were concentrating their attention on Japan did not make things any better [when] the eyes of America were focused on Europe.

In addition to looking for funding, Safford always made efforts to acquire more good people. As one of the best wartime cryptanalysts, Capt. Rudy **Fabian**, later said about his own recruitment,

> I received a letter from Cmdr. Laurance Safford inviting me to Washington to work with his organization. I accepted the offer, even though I did not know what he had in mind, because I did not get accepted for graduate work in ordnance as I had hoped. Safford had my name taken off the ordnance school list so that I could work in his program. Commander Safford was a brilliant man. Many people disliked him because he was so quick. I was in a class of three people so our instruction was very intense.

From 1938 to 1940, Lt. Cmdr. Sid **Goodwin** worked under Commander Safford—as the head of OP-20-GY. He later recalled Safford with a great deal of respect.

> Commander Safford, although eccentric, was a genius. Safford introduced cryptanalysis to the Navy and established its intercept sites. Safford's greatest contributions were de-

veloping the Electric Code Machine and ensuring that this machine was ready when the war started. He was also responsible for the excellent communications security that the Navy had throughout the war.

Safford was never insistent that cryptanalysis always be done "the hard way." Anything that helped cut corners or give an advantage was welcome; for example, he had rejoiced in the 1920 *Red Book* theft, and in 1938 was quite happy to utilize Japanese code books which had been recovered in China by Capt. James M. McHugh, USMC (McHugh was embedded with Chinese forces fighting against Japanese invaders). Safford also saw the advantage to allowing other groups to work on cryptanalysis rather than keeping it centralized in Washington. In the mid-1930s he decided that his main satellite intercept stations—HYPO and CAST—should establish their own cryptanalytic bureaus and not just collect signals.

He welcomed the army's activity in the business. The SIS actually broke the Japanese PURPLE diplomatic code, although for a time it was stymied by a lack of funds and resources. However, "at Safford's initiative, the navy underwrote the cost [and] OP-20-G absorbed some routine SIS work to free SIS's Frank Rowlett and his team for the main task."

In July 1940, Commander Safford and Col. Spencer Akin of the SIS began serious discussions on the division of interception, cryptanalysis, and other aspects of CO-MINT processing. But Safford had to report to Rear Adm. Leigh Noyes (the director of naval communications) that no agreement could be reached—the sticking point was not military or naval systems but rather the diplomatic.

In this wrangle over codebreaking responsibilities, Commander Safford proposed that the navy should take charge of all Japanese and Russian communications, and the army should take everything else. He further said it should be all one or the other. However, "veteran turf warriors in the higher ranks" of both services didn't see it that way. So, for those reasons—as well as for some legitimate technical ones—a strange plan was agreed upon: the navy would decipher the Japanese diplomatic PURPLE code on odd-numbered days; the army on even ones. And the two services would alternate by month the responsibility of disseminating important intelligence from the decrypts to other departments, including the White House and State Department. "Neither OP-20-G nor the SIS were happy with the arrangement—which was evidently forced upon them by higher-ups. The cryptanalysts from both services would share results and occasionally phone one another, but rarely met."

Wrangling wasn't always confined to the army; Safford occasionally took a dim view of his colleagues at ONI. While he acknowledged that there were some outstanding people in the organization, in retirement he also told an interviewer that "naval intelligence was kind of a dumping ground for the misfits in the navy for a long time." This attitude was not improved by periodic infighting and feuding between intelligence and communications.

As far back as August 1940, Safford had been opposed to any significant cryptographic exchange with the British—but the army's SIS was interested. In this situation, however, the one thing Laurance Safford and his army counterpart, William Friedman, did fully agree upon was there should be no release of information regarding American code *making*.

But by early 1941, higher authority—which is to say the president—had decided there would be exchanges. Accordingly, army Captain Abraham Sinkov, army Lieutenant Leo Rosen, navy Lieutenant Robert **Weeks**, and navy Lieutenant Prescott **Currier** traveled to London for a serious exchange of cryptographic information. The Americans gave away much—including two Japanese PURPLE diplomatic decryption machines—and received much—including a model of the British Marconi-Adcock radio direction-finder, which Safford called "generally superior to D/F in use in the United States at that time." However, the British did not provide a German naval ENIGMA machine which Safford believed had been part of the agreement. He was outraged and believed that the United States had been double-crossed, that the exchange was unbalanced, and that the United States gave up much more than it received. Safford agreed that the American delegation had been given good analytic notes and related materials on the ENIGMA cipher, but felt that withholding an actual machine violated the agreement of a fair exchange—although it's fair to say he may not have fully understood what the nature of such a machine was.

And, despite OP-20-G's historical focus upon Japanese systems, and despite the fact that the Japanese "Admiral's Code" and the new, main Japanese naval operational code—JN-25—were presenting resistance to full exploitation, Safford realized he was going to have to also throw effort onto German systems. Thus, in October 1940, Mrs. Driscoll was moved from work on the JN-25 problem and assigned a small team to work against German systems, particularly the naval ENIGMA machine. The first two paragraphs of an OP-20-G memo show some insight into this new OP-20-GY division of work.

> Since November 1939, Mrs. Driscoll has been engaged in cryptanalytical attack on the current Orange Navy Operations code system [JN-25]. This attack has now progressed to the point where it can be pursued by others. Accordingly, it has been turned over to Lieutenant Bayley. He will be assisted by Lieutenant Chisholm full time, and by Lieutenant **Lietwiler** and Lieutenant Brotherhood for instruction. CRM **McGregor** and Y1C **Pelletier** will handle the actual code recovery, and two cryptographic clerks complete the group.
>
> Mrs. Driscoll, with two assistants, has begun an attack on the German Navy systems. Heretofore, they have resisted attack, but it is hoped that the employment of our best talent will produce results.

However, when moving Miss Aggie to the German problem, neither she, Safford, nor the navy in general

> realized that [they] had asked her to defeat one of the most advanced encryption machines of the time. The 1940s naval ENIGMA was a *far* more difficult target than earlier versions of the device, and the German Navy was an even *more* cautious crypto-foe than that nation's army, air force, or intelligence agencies.

Ignorant of its own ignorance, OP-20-G began a "catalog attack"—the mainstay of Western codebreakers at the time—because it was logical and obvious, even if terribly labor intensive. Working with insufficient funding, personnel, and equipment, there wasn't much else they could do. Moreover, "Driscoll and Safford seemed to have been cozily optimistic and dangerously ignorant about the ability of their small . . . crew to conquer the intricacies of the ENIGMA."

Later, with some passage of time and the U-boat war not going all that well, British cryptographers decided to share more information with the Americans. Accordingly, in August 1941, the head of the British codebreaking center at Bletchley Park, Cmdr. Alastair G. Denniston, RN, came to Washington to see Commander Safford and Mrs. Driscoll. As mentioned, there had already been some interchange between British and American codebreaking operations—but it had precipitated some misunderstanding and tension. Denniston hoped to "smooth over the conflicts so far [and] to coordinate, appease, and control the Americans"—both U.S. Navy and U.S. Army.

However, at this meeting, Commander Safford and Mrs. Driscoll surprised Commander Denniston by their apparent disinterest in Britain's automated cryptologic attacks against the ENIGMA. They didn't seem to think they needed or even wanted a British *bombe* (a complex, one-ton electro-mechanical "pre-computer" which aided cryptanalysis), nor was Mrs. Driscoll very interested in the statistical technique used by the machine. While admitting that she was currently somewhat "stumped" to fully understand the ENIGMA, she told Denniston that she thought she'd developed a nonmachine method which might be better than the British, and that for health reasons she didn't care to accept his invitation to come to England—nor did she care to nominate anyone else in her stead.

If Commander Denniston really were ready to share meaningful information, this was a serious blunder on the part of OP-20-G. However, deeply fearful about American security awareness, it's not clear how much the British really were ready to reveal. Moreover, at age fifty-three, with a string of great successes behind her, Miss Aggie may have been a little overconfident and even inflexible. She may have also shared in the prevailing U.S. Navy distrust of the Royal Navy and British Intelligence inherited from World War I experience (certainly felt, at this time, by her superiors Commander Safford and Rear Admiral Noyes) and fueled by any signs of being played or treated as a junior partner in the relationship. Or, it may be the result of too many years of isolation and restricted budgets at OP-20-G, which meant that Naval Communications had seen too few bright, young, and well-trained people added to staff, "people who could stimulate new ideas and new methods—the way Agnes Driscoll had been able to do decades before." And it probably occurred to her and Safford that millions of dollars invested in *bombes* (even *if* any such funding could be found for OP-20-G) could overnight be wasted if the Germans significantly revamped the ENIGMA system.

As it turned out, OP-20-G's nonmachine effort did not really benefit the attack on the German systems, although—considering their lack of resources—they amazingly came very close to understanding how the naval ENIGMA worked without knowing enough to actually begin decryption. Throwing assets at ENIGMA certainly weakened the U.S. Navy's effort against JN-25—though other talented codebreakers (many of whom were Driscoll's former pupils) in Washington and in the Pacific Theater would be able to exploit the code to great advantage *after* the U.S. entry into the war.[5]

Through 1941, OP-20-G was working extensive cryptologic functions. It developed new systems for the U.S. Navy and printed and distributed new editions of codes and ciphers. It contracted with manufacturers for cypher machines. It encompassed subsections such as GI (which produced reports based on worldwide radio intelligence) and GL (which kept records and did historical research). However, OP-20-G's main interest was cryptanalysis. This included sections GX (intercept and direction-finding), GY (the old "Research Desk" which did cryptanalysis), and GZ (translation and dissemination). GY attacked new systems and recovered new keys for solved systems (PURPLE, for example). GZ would then do detailed recovery and code groups, this being more of a linguistic versus a mathematical challenge. By 1941, GY stood round-the-clock watches.

Aside from the activity at Main Navy in Washington, OP-20-G also owned the cryptanalysis units at Pearl Harbor and at Corregidor. OP-20-G at Washington (sometimes also called Station NEGAT) attacked Japanese systems, foreign diplomatic systems, and Atlantic Theater naval codes. Pearl (Station HYPO) worked on Japanese naval systems (*excluding* JN-25). Corregidor (Station CAST) worked some diplomatic deciphering and on JN-25. To give the reader an idea of scale, the remote CAST had seven officers and nineteen enlisted men, and used twenty-six radio receivers, a direction-finder, and some tabulating machinery.

Of Commander Safford's seven hundred officers and men at the start of the war (by the end of World War II the organization would number around six thousand), two-thirds were employed in radio interception or direction-finding activities, and one-third (including most of the eighty officers) focused upon cryptanalysis and translations. Safford thought that HYPO had some of the best officers, averaging four to five years of radio intelligence experience. CAST officers were "young, enthusiastic, and capable," with an average of two to three years of experience. NEGAT—which also had the main training responsibility—had a number of people with ten-plus years' experience, but it also had 90 percent of its personnel under one year's experience.

In October 1941, both Capt. Alan G. Kirk and Rear Adm. Theodore "Ping" Wilkinson (outgoing and incoming directors of naval intelligence) as well as Capt.

---

5. "JN-25" was the name given by Allied codebreakers to the chief, and most secure, command-and-control communications scheme used by the Imperial Japanese Navy during World War II. It was the twenty-fifth Japanese Navy system identified. Introduced in 1939 to replace "Blue," it was an enciphered code, producing five-numeral groups for transmission. New codebooks and/or new super-enciphering books were introduced from time to time, each new version requiring a more or less fresh cryptanalytic attack. In particular, JN-25 was significantly changed on December 1, 1940, and again on December 4, 1941—just days before the attack on Pearl Harbor.

Howard D. Bode (head, ONI foreign intelligence) wanted to inform Admirals Husband Kimmel and Claude Bloch, at Pearl Harbor, of the puzzling "bomb-plot" decrypt. This was a PURPLE message translated in Washington by the army on October 9; it requested a Japanese agent in Honolulu, when making reports, to divide (or plot) the waters of Pearl Harbor into five specific sectors—perhaps for targeting purposes. Commander Safford also wanted this information sent to the Pacific; he later said he'd additionally drafted a message for Cmdr. Joe Rochefort, which would direct him to decrypt traffic from the Japanese consulate in Honolulu. But this was all stopped by Rear Adm. Noyes, who said he "was not going to tell any district commandant [or fleet commander] how to run his job!"

In the lead-up to the Pearl Harbor attack, Safford and his entire organization worked themselves unsparingly. Two weeks of fifteen-hour days—prior to December 7—had left the head of OP-20-G physically drained and approaching a state of nervous exhaustion. In fact, he went home for the weekend of December 6—the first weekend he'd had to himself in a month. The unit had been overworked and overstretched, dividing limited manpower among Japanese diplomatic traffic, the nominally broken JN-25 naval code, and the tracking of potentially hostile U-boats in the Atlantic.

As previously discussed, Safford promoted collaboration with the army on several fronts and was largely responsible for the navy's entry into a joint effort on an assault against the Japanese diplomatic systems. He recognized the signs of approaching hostilities that appeared in the diplomatic traffic.

In early December 1941, when MAGIC intercepts indicated that Japanese diplomatic stations around the world were ordered to destroy codebooks and machines, the "Winds Code alert . . . assumed a vital new importance in the minds of certain ranking generals and admirals. It was regarded as the trigger by which Japan would communicate its final decision for peace or war." The Winds messages were innocuous plain-language weather reports, which were supposedly going to be sent out by Radio Tokyo, indicating dissolution of diplomatic relations. In fact, huge amounts of falsely identified "winds" alerts were relayed to Washington for analysis. This added to the workload of Captain Safford's already overburdened team, and it further diverted his attention and resources from the more critical work of penetrating the Japanese naval code systems. The pressure was such that Rear Admiral Noyes made a daily check for anything remotely resembling a "winds execute" message. As Safford put it, "*Higher Authority* began heckling me as to the possibility of having missed it."

However, Safford partially won one minor round in his efforts to create a true sense of urgency in the Pacific. Concerned that war was imminent, and worried about the potential capture of COMINT equipment and documents, he drafted an urgent warning to go out to the theater. But he wasn't able to get a message release from Capt. Joseph R. Redman, the assistant director of naval communications, nor could he gain it from Rear Admiral Noyes, the director. In fact, Noyes felt Safford was exceeding his authority and reportedly admonished him, saying, "What do you mean using such [alarmist] language as that?" Safford replied, "Admiral, the war is just a matter of days, if not hours." Noyes fired back, "You may think there's going to be a war, but I think they're bluffing." Safford then said, "Wake Island has all the Pacific crypto systems that we have printed. . . . If those systems fall into the hands of the Japanese it will go very hard with you and very hard with me, too."[6] Noyes took the point, but then considerably watered down the final message—fearful that the irascible director of navy war plans, Rear Adm. Richmond "Terrible" Turner, would in turn admonish Noyes for overstepping *his* authority.[7]

Needless to say, the early morning surprise attack on Pearl Harbor was psychologically devastating to Washington—and particularly so to those in Main Navy who had been trying to read the signs and make estimates. As one of those officers, ONI Far East expert Cmdr. Arthur **McCollum** described the situation, the CNO staff had a collective "nervous breakdown" in the wake of the attack.

Then, for some unknown reason, on January 23, 1942, Captain Safford wrote a memorandum to Rear Admiral Noyes suggesting a major reorganization of OP-20-G.

> Safford suggested the creation of OP-20-Q, a cryptographic division, under himself, while OP-20-G would be limited to communications intelligence. He suggested that Lt. Cmdr. George W. Welker assume control of OP-20-G. The reason for Safford's action is not clear.

Possibly Safford was forced out of his job; at least that was the view of many of his colleagues and all of his friends. As McCollum's institutional "nervous breakdown" ran its course in OPNAV, it may have run over Safford. "An excitable person himself, [maybe he] had to go," and

> perhaps Safford knew that he would be replaced and preempted his relief with a suggestion that would still leave him an important activity.
> Safford's suggestions were circulated for comments in OP-20/OP-20-G. The result was a new organization—but considerably different from what he had envisioned.

On February 12, 1942, Capt. Joseph Redman, the assistant DNC, directed a realignment, placing Cmdr. John Redman as head of OP-20-G, now called the Radio Intelligence Section. Commander Redman was an experienced communications officer but without any prior involvement in communications intelligence. "He got the job because he was available, because of political maneuvering, and undoubtedly because he was the brother of the assistant DNC." The reality would be that Cmdr. Joseph Wenger would effectively—if unofficially—run OP-20-G, which he did until he was officially put in charge in November 1944. Rear Adm. Edwin Layton later wrote,

---

6. Some sources have it as, "Well, Admiral, if all those publications on Wake Island are captured, we will never be able to explain it."
7. According to Safford, at the Battle of Savo Island (August 1942), Admiral Turner, in command of the amphibious force, sent out a call for help. Admiral Noyes, in command of the air support group, did not respond. "Both officers were good *haters*," Safford later commented. "Turner had his little victories in Washington, [then Noyes] had his revenge."

Outmaneuvered and outraged, Safford tried to salvage the outfit from dismemberment. In a memorandum eloquent with despair, he conceded the reorganization—but remained adamant in denying that "the senior officers concerned would be utilized to the best advantage." He challenged John Redman's ability . . . and proposed that he [Safford], not Wenger [his former student], be officer in charge.

But three days later "Safford found himself bounced as head of the navy's cryptographic and radio intelligence section, a cause that had occupied most of his thoughts and energies for the past seventeen years."

Thus, OP-20-G was reorganized. Safford was moved from control as a result of taking the institutional fall for the Pearl Harbor disaster, or because of internal Naval Communications political maneuvering, or because of the recognition that the work had become much too heavy for one man, or various combinations of these. Safford became the assistant director of naval communications for "cryptologic research," and was now specifically responsible for the development, production, and distribution of naval cryptosystems. In September, the development function was separated from production.

Safford retained control of the development work until the end of the war, devising such new devices as call-sign cipher machines, adapters for British and other cryptologic devices, and off-line equipment for automatic operation.

At Station HYPO, out in Hawaii, Joe Rochefort was not happy with the turn of events.

As long as Safford was in Washington, I just about knew what to expect from him, and he knew what he could expect from me. It worked very nicely on a personal basis. It was only when other people became involved in it as a part of the wartime expansion that we began to have trouble.

Safford was sort of eased out of the job that he had, and he was stuck over in a corner somewhere; I know we didn't [properly] utilize his talents.

On the other hand, as pointed out by NSA historians Robert Hanyok and David Mowry,

While Safford had fostered the development of OP-20-G and in 1936 had become its permanently assigned commander, by the time of Pearl Harbor he probably had come to be overmatched by the enormous demands in time and resources made upon his organization. The rapidly multiplying targets and the simultaneously growing workforce overwhelmed the prewar structure he had built.

The OP-20-G mission was stretched globally, with two centers of interest—the ongoing U-boat struggle in the Atlantic, and the Pacific crisis that vied for the scarce resources of the section. The multiple demands may have simply outstripped Safford's ability to effectively manage OP-20-G.[8]

8. "The informal style in which Captain Safford had run the [relatively small] OP-20-G organization may have worked in peacetime but it was less appropriate for coping with the rapid expansion that was

Organizationally, Safford had promoted a decentralized system with naval communications-intelligence sections in Washington, D.C., Pearl Harbor, T.H., and Manila, P.I. He gave the chief Japanese naval code problem to the organization in Hawaii, and named the brilliant naval officer Joseph Rochefort to head that effort. He also gave Rochefort a blank check to obtain the very best navy cryptanalysts. This all paid off handsomely in the spring of 1942, when Rochefort's team sufficiently broke JN-25—in time to greatly assist in winning the Battle of Midway.

Safford has been retrospectively criticized for keeping the brilliant HYPO cryptanalysts on the extremely difficult Japanese "Admirals Code" too long—it was actually *never* broken—and not allowing them to sooner attack the operational code JN-25. However, the potential information gains would have been huge if they'd succeeded, justifying the effort. As Safford later said, "If we could have solved the Flag Officers System, Admiral Kimmel would probably have known of the Japanese plans, and the Pacific Fleet would not have been surprised on December 7, 1941."

But to his credit, Safford essentially was the engineer of the accurate support provided by Rochefort and his unit concerning the Battle of Midway—generally considered the turning point of the war in the Pacific. When Safford finally directed them to cease work on the "Admirals Code" and to focus on JN-25, they were subsequently able to break enough to allow Admiral Nimitz to make informed decisions about positioning forces to best advantage—for both Midway and also for the preceding Battle of the Coral Sea. Then, Station HYPO and its successor organizations went on to provide accurate and timely intelligence for the rest of the Pacific War.

Of course, it can't be overlooked that it was Lt. Cmdr. Safford who, in 1936, sent his old friend Tommy Dyer to Pearl Harbor to establish and build a cryptanalytic unit (what became Station HYPO). And, as already stated, it was Commander Safford who, in 1941, talked his old friend Joe Rochefort into taking the post at HYPO and then manipulated the system to make it happen—thus placing two of the navy's best COMINT officers in position. Moreover, as Rochefort later said,

> The reason, I think, that HYPO was successful—I'm trying now to be—not modest and not immodest—but it was because part of my arrangement with Safford was that I'll undertake this job, but I'll get my pick of the personnel: I'll take this job providing I can keep Lt. Cmdr. Dyer and I can get first shot at anybody else who I need and I get all the language officers. These were the conditions. Safford said, "You can have anything you want."

However, as already shown, institutional infighting and disputes over organization in Washington led to Safford's ouster in early 1942. The word of this was apparently not quickly disseminated through the system; his protégé Rudy Fabian wrote him this note in July after the victory at the Battle of Midway:

---

necessary in wartime." For example, "he wanted to assign even *more* independence to his friend Joe Rochefort in Station HYPO at Pearl, but this infuriated certain ambitious naval communications officers."

My congratulations for the most remarkable success of the organization *you alone* are responsible for. Justifying it through the lean years must have been a job—but I bet they almost eat out of your hand now.

One can only imagine Fabian's reaction when he learned that Safford was essentially to be shunted to the side for the remainder of the war. This was the beginning of the end for Rochefort, too.

Safford and Rochefort had enjoyed a relationship based on personal trust, with the understanding that the different units in the system would not vie for credit. With Safford purged, the trust and rapport were gone, and relations between HYPO and Washington quickly turned sour.

Purged he may have been, but "Safford was still destined to play a key role in efforts to maintain the integrity of U.S. codes." Despite his focus upon cryptanalysis, he had always "understood the vulnerability of ciphers and codes, and worked tirelessly to protect American ones with increasingly sophisticated means." However, it is fair to say that OP-20-G, "the positive intelligence force he had created, [went on to] fight the war without him."

Later during the war, Safford could take some pride in observing that his Atlantic Ocean

arc of high-frequency direction-finders were very effective in exploiting U-boat radio communications. As many as twenty-five high-frequency stations might get bearings on a transmission and immediately report to the net control center in Maryland. From there they were flashed to the naval communications-intelligence organization in Washington, where they were combined into positional fixes and flashed to the Combat Intelligence Division's Atlantic Section, which then rapidly pushed the information to operational anti-submarine forces.

Safford was also very significant, in another aspect, in reducing the heavy toll of Allied shipping losses to German U-boats in the Atlantic. According to historian John Toland, Safford believed the Germans were reading U.S.-British communications despite encryption, and wanted to modify the American crypto devices. Incredibly, he met significant financial and other resistance. Safford nevertheless proceeded—even to the point of scrounging parts—and developed a new device. When copies of it were finally deployed, beginning in December 1943, losses sharply declined.

Dissatisfied with his own career marginalization—as well as the subsequent dismissal of his friend Joe Rochefort from Station HYPO—Captain Safford struck back. In 1944, he seems to have been the author of a very critical twenty-one-page anonymous memorandum titled *The Inside Story of the Battle of Midway and the Ousting of Commander Rochefort*, which was widely circulated among members of the naval intelligence and communications organizations.

Safford continued to serve as assistant director of naval communications for cryptographic research until January 1949. At that point he became a special assistant to the director of the AFSA. There he worked with his old colleague Capt. Tommy Dyer. "Laurance Safford and I were—I can't remember what our title was—technical advisors or something. We shared an office, and reported directly to the director."

Captain Safford retired from the navy in June 1951, but was immediately recalled to active duty. In January 1952 he was appointed the special assistant to the head of the Security Branch in the Division of Naval Communications. He then fully retired from active duty in 1953, remaining in the Washington, D.C., area.

As we consider his career, it's difficult to overstate Laurance Safford's incredible impact. In addition to the pioneering creation and guidance of the navy's COMINT organization for nearly twenty years, he had a hand in an enormous number of component pieces to this important business.

> He [oversaw] the recruitment, training, and formation of the corps of radio-intercept operators who manned the navy's monitoring sites around the world and in the United States. Safford played a role in the establishment of the navy's constellation of monitoring and direction-finding sites in the Pacific region from the mid- to late 1930s.
>
> He had also recruited and staffed the Research Desk of the Code and Signal Section with such notables of naval cryptanalysis as Agnes Meyer Driscoll, Joseph Rochefort, and Thomas Dyer. Safford had set up a program of training in cryptanalysis of selected naval and Marine officers, rotating them into the Research Desk for periods of on-the-job training before they returned to positions in the fleet. Safford also had allowed, albeit reluctantly, the early experimental use of machine aids in cryptanalysis—among them early IBM punch-card sorters to tabulate and inventory code groups and specialized typewriters modified to copy Japanese *kana* characters sent by Morse code.

Intelligence historian John Prados further emphasizes that:

> Safford also innovated a machine the navy used to encrypt its own messages, contributing importantly to American communications-security throughout the war.

Intelligence historians Roger Pineau and John Costello have written that:

> it was Safford who singlehandedly . . . conceived, founded, and built the navy's CO-MINT entity. . . . It was Wenger who [then] harnessed the power and drive of [Joe and Jack Redman] to organize radio intelligence for the navy's, and the nation's, long-term goals. [However] the HYPO team of Rochefort-Dyer-Wright was to prove the Redman-Wenger philosophy of a centrally controlled and directed radio-intelligence operation *was not applicable* to a tactical command [such as the Pacific Fleet].

Unfortunately, a number of people remember Laurance Safford less for his remarkable professional achievements, but more for his Pearl Harbor–attack investigation activities. Prados writes that:

> swirling controversy over whether there was a conspiracy to conceal intelligence about Pearl Harbor, over the "Winds" code messages, and so on, engulfed Laurance F. Safford and Alwin D. Kramer.

For Safford, the core issue was the "Winds Message" or "Winds Code." As briefly mentioned earlier, before the commencement of hostilities,

innocuous phrases were to be inserted into regular weather reports sent by Radio Tokyo, indicating whether diplomatic relations were in danger. The Winds code provided for problems not only with the United States, but also with England or Russia. Two Tokyo cables on November 19th, 1941, the so-called "Winds Set-up" messages, established that such signals might be sent and the phrases of the open code.

These were "East Wind Rain," meaning danger in Japan-U.S. relations; "North Wind Cloudy," meaning Japan-Russia relations in danger, and "West Wind Clear," meaning Japan-Britain relations in danger. Upon receiving any of these messages, Japanese embassies and consulates affected were to burn documents and destroy their last codes and cipher equipment.

The controversy lay in whether any of the enumerated phrases was ever broadcast and if so, which one or ones. Such a broadcast would have been the "Winds Execute."

And the controversy was ideological in that Captain Safford—among some others—became obsessively driven to help exonerate Admiral Kimmel and General Short for taking the full blame for the disaster. Safford believed that there had been a Winds "execute" message, but that it had been suppressed. He also believed that a delay in disclosing the fourteenth part of the last Japanese diplomatic intercept the night before the attack showed that many high-level people in Washington were even more to blame than were the Hawaiian commanders. He felt that the Washington leadership did not pass any of this information—as well as other intelligence analyses—to the Hawaiian commanders. He also believed that there later had been a destruction of documents and other evidence to cover up these failures. The Winds issue had been pumped up—mostly by Safford—"into a major controversy that fixated a number of the Pearl Harbor investigations, and later engaged a number of historians and the public for decades."

It's fair to say that Captain Safford became shrill—embarrassingly so—stressing that a Winds "execute" message was indeed sent, that it was an actual war signal, and that it constituted an announcement that Tokyo had decided to attack the United States. But it just does not appear to be the case. Even if—and there is great doubt—there had been an authentic "execute" message sent out and intercepted, it really would have told Washington nothing that American leaders didn't already know. It certainly would not have specified an actual strike on Pearl Harbor or any other American installation.

The same is true about the timeliness of distributing the long Japanese diplomatic message which came that fateful weekend. The decryption of the thirteen-part message—and even the final fourteenth part—did not expose an imminent attack on any particular location. But Safford just could not let the matter rest. Even after the war and the closure of the Pearl Harbor investigations, "unyielding in his conviction, during his retirement he orchestrated a massive research effort to prove he had been correct all along." Yet in the final analysis, Captain Safford's "evidence" for the existence of a conspiracy to cover up the Winds Execute message appears to have no substance. It's somewhat of a mystery as to why he spent such incredible amounts of time and energy on it, and exposed himself to great stress and even ridicule.

While angst over intelligence and the attack didn't quite "destroy" Safford or his reputation—as it effectively did his friend and colleague Capt. Al Kramer—it took its toll, and even more so it took its toll on Mrs. Safford. It completely wore her out and rubbed her nerves raw. In later years just the mention of "Pearl Harbor" would often provoke her to tears or screams of rage and frustration, provoke her to throw visitors out of the house, and cause her to destroy "suspicious-looking" correspondence.

In 1967, Captain Safford, while working as a research specialist at the Library of Congress, developed an interest in the 1937 flight across the Pacific Ocean on which aviator Amelia Earhart disappeared. He wrote that Earhart's

> Oakland-to-Honolulu flight in March 1937 [had at the time] afforded me the chance for competitive testing of two different experimental types of navy high-frequency direction finders plus a third type in actual use by the Pan American Airways. Unfortunately, the test could not be carried out because both sets of Navy HF/DFs were disabled at the time. Then [she] disappeared in July 1937. . . .
>
> My interest . . . was renewed in 1967 when I read a book titled *Daughter of the Sky*, in which it was stated: "A high-frequency direction finder had been obtained from the Navy and installed on Howland Island." Now it so happened that in 1937 the Navy's high frequency direction finders were under my cognizance, and I had no recollection of any such installation. My opposite number in the Bureau of Engineering was unable to throw any light on the subject, yet there were a dozen references to a "Navy emergency direction finder" in another book called *The Search for Amelia Earhart*. My curiosity being aroused, I decided to solve this enigma and write a technical article for the Naval Institute.

His article became the draft of a book, but he died before he could complete it. However, the manuscript was edited and reworked by others and published in 2003: *Earhart's Flight into Yesterday: The Facts without the Fiction* by Laurance Safford with Cameron Warren and Robert Payne.[9]

Captain Safford passed away at Bethesda Naval Hospital on May 15, 1973. He had been married to Ruth Perkins Safford (1897–1979); they are buried together in a known but unmarked grave at Oak Hill Cemetery, Washington, D.C.

---

9. Safford's basic thesis was that the management of the radio aspects of Earhart's flight was incompetent and disastrous; that she ran out of fuel and crashed in the ocean relatively close to Howland Island; greater-than-expected headwinds and/or an unknown engine management error/failure caused the aircraft to burn excess fuel; and that that the U.S. government gave Earhart whatever she asked for but utterly failed to take any initiative to stave off a foreseeable disaster. Safford was contemptuous of the "Japanese capture and spy mission hypotheses," arguing that Earhart lacked the time/fuel/speed to make it to any mandated island.

He had been awarded the Legion of Merit for his wartime service, covering the period March 1942 to September 1945.[10]

He was also awarded $100,000 by the government, in 1958, as compensation for various cryptologic inventions which he had come up with over the years—inventions which he was not allowed to patent for reasons of national security. When initially proposed by Sen. Leverett Saltonstall, the bill called for payment of $150,000; however, this was ultimately reduced to $100,000 by the Congress.

Captain Safford has been recognized and honored, by the U.S. Naval Cryptologic Veterans Association, as an officer who has served as the Commander, Naval Security Group, or one of its predecessor organizations. He has also been named a "Pioneer Officer of U.S. Naval Cryptology" by the same organization.

Perhaps most important, he was inducted into the NSA's Hall of Honor in 1999.

Sources

Benson, 10–12, 17, 43, 155.
Bryden, 257–72.
Budiansky, 4, 36–37, 138, 167–68.
Burns, 7, 62.
Capt. Laurance Safford. NSA Cryptologic Hall of Honor citation.
Carlson, 31–35, 42, 50, 85–89, 104, 114, 117, 120–21, 172, 203, 213–16, 267, 322, 397–98, 435–38, 455, 495, 502–3.
Clausen, 29, 42, 45, 70, 173, 211, 219–21, 278, 305–6.
Costello, 189, 200–201, 278–79, 281, 294.
Donovan and Mack, 27, 57–58, 60–61, 97, 106, 146–47.
Dorwart, *Conflict of Duty*, 93.
Dyer, 53, 85, 186, 306, 324.
Farago, *Broken Seal*, 41–45, 52–53, 63, 76, 87, 96–97, 106–7, 162–64, 197–98, 252–53, 280, 290, 318, 326, 328, 340.
Hanyok and Mowry, 53–54, 77, 99.
Haufler, 114.
Holtwick, 34, 36–38, 40–46, 48, 50, 61–62, 69–72, 80–82, 88–92, 105, 184, 187, 199–200, 205, 212, 224–25, 260, 267–68, 312, 320, 339, 343–44, 422, 425, 431, 439, 444, 450–52, 458, 460–61; App. 3, 5, 10, 91–97.
Kahn, *Codebreakers*, 10–11, 388, 503–4, 573–74.
Layton, *"And I Was There,"* 32–36, 47, 56, 58, 77, 95, 166, 231, 256, 264–65, 268, 285–87, 329, 367–68.
Lewin, 24.
Lucky Bag, U.S. Naval Academy, 1916.
McGinnis, 9, 17, 21–22, 35.
Prados, 77, 79, 164, 166–69, 176, 226, 300, 318, 731.

---

10. Safford's Legion of Merit citation reads in part, "A dynamic leader combining strong purpose and creative imagination with a profound knowledge of mechanical and electrical science and their cryptographic applications. Captain Safford was the driving force behind the development of the perfected machines which today give the United States Navy the finest system of encipherment in the world."

Prange, *At Dawn*, 82, 448–49, 455–56, 458, 464–65, 474, 555, 585, 621–22, 666–67, 670, 714–15.
Prange, *Miracle*, 17.
Rochefort, 6–8, 10–13, 21, 27–28, 98–101, 103, 140–41, 252–53, 256, 298.
Safford, *Brief History*, 25.
Safford, *Interview with Captain L. F. Safford*, App. 210–12.
Smith, *Emperor's Codes*, 74.
Smith and Erskine, *Action This Day*, 152, 216, 221.
Spector, *Eagle*, 5–7, 10–11.
Symonds, 135–37.
Toland, 52–53, 61–68, 74–75, 95, 102, 135–37, 194–203, 207–17, 223–24, 244–45, 286–87, 297–98, 322.
U.S. Navy, *Register of Commissioned and Warrant Officers*.
Wohlstetter, 171, 218.
Worth, 16–17, 19–20, 25, 104, 113, 218.

REAR ADMIRAL EARL EVERETT STONE, U.S. NAVY (1895–1989)

"Schlitz" "Stoney"

Earl Stone was neither a linguist, an intelligence officer, nor a cryptologist—yet he holds a significant place in cryptologic history. His primary focus during his naval career was communications. In fact, early on he completed a master's degree in communications engineering from Harvard—a very unique accomplishment for a naval officer in 1925. He seems to have skillfully balanced his communications assignments with black-shoe surface ship duty, ultimately earning promotion to flag rank a year after the end of the war. He held two crucial communications jobs during the war: assistant director of naval communications in Washington, and assistant chief of staff for communications in Nimitz's Pacific Ocean Area command. However, he's probably best known for his postwar leadership of the "Stone Board," and for the challenging assignment as the first director of the AFSA—the forerunner of the NSA.

*   *   *

From the 1918 Annapolis yearbook, *The Lucky Bag*:

Earl came to us a shy, modest, and intensely conscientious lad, and has changed little which is rather remarkable, for he roomed with "Red" Hoffman. A happily-mated family, the twain, for "Red" enjoys shocking Earl and leaving the room an inviting paradise for the pap [demerit] sheet, while *Stoney* takes a housewifely interest in keeping the place neat, even to sewing buttons on his leggings and swabbing the dust from behind the radiator. Youngster [sophomore] year, *Schlitz* appeared at the first hop [dance]. His magnetic smile and smooth dancing were in evidence regularly after the first plunge. Plebe year some first classman, noticing *Schlitz's* beefy stanchions, suggested that he try out for crew. Well, he wasn't tall enough for this sport, but he gave it a thorough trial. He worked because he felt that he ought to, and this spirit has actuated him in all his endeavors. Being desirous of "doing his bit" in getting out the *Lucky Bag*, he sacrificed his time many a night in order to typewrite the brainstorms turned in. Such an unselfish and willing attitude is bound to spell success. Earl's one source of discontent here is that his friends persist in ascribing pro-German symptoms to his acts. "By golly, I'm not a Dutchman. My folks are all *Americans*." [Activities: crew squad, *Lucky Bag* staff]

*   *   *

Earl Stone was born in Milwaukee, Wisconsin, on December 2, 1895. He attended East Side High School and completed his freshman year at the University of Wisconsin's journalism course at the Milwaukee State Normal School. He was appointed to the U.S. Naval Academy in 1914. Stone was graduated and commissioned an ensign in June 1917 (but a year early as the class of 1918 was graduated early due to World War I pressures). Some of his classmates were Jerauld Wright, Miles R. Browning, Joseph "Jocko" Clark, James Fife Jr., Leland P. Lovette, William "Sol" Phillips, Forrest P. Sherman, Clifton "Ziggy" Sprague, and Thomas L. Sprague. Subsequent promotions included lieutenant (junior grade), 1918; lieutenant, 1920; lieutenant commander, 1930; commander, 1937; captain, 1942; commodore, 1945; and rear admiral, 1946.

After graduation from the Academy he joined the USS *Cleveland*, which was employed on escort duty during World War I. Detached from that cruiser in March 1919, after serving briefly as her engineering officer, he then served until June 1923 as aide and radio officer on the staff of the Commander, Training, Pacific Fleet (redesignated in 1922 as Commander, Base Force, Pacific Fleet). He then went under instruction in communication engineering at the Naval

Postgraduate School (located at Annapolis in those days), and then at Harvard University, where he received the degree of master's of science in communications engineering in June 1925. Stone then took more training, for four months, at the Naval Research Laboratory in Washington.

In October 1925, Mr. Stone joined the battleship *California*, flagship of the Commander, Battle Fleet, and then a year later was assigned duty as aide and radio officer on the staff of Commander, Battleship Division Four, on board the USS *New Mexico*. He next served in the Office of Naval Communications in Washington from summer 1928 until summer 1930. During the next two years he was aide and fleet communications officer on the staff of the Commander in Chief, U.S. Fleet, on board the flagships *Texas* and *Pennsylvania*. In August 1932, Stone transferred to the cruiser *Cincinnati*, serving as her first lieutenant until June 1933.

After a second tour of duty in the Office of Naval Communications, he successively commanded the destroyer *Long* and then the destroyer *Aylwin* from June 1935 until June 1938. He then returned to Washington to serve as Communications War Plans Officer, Office of the CNO, and as the naval member of the Coordinating Committee of the Defense Communications Board.

In February 1941, Stone joined the USS *California* as executive officer, and after that battleship was sunk during the attack on Pearl Harbor, he was transferred to similar duty on board the cruiser *Salt Lake City*—under Capt. Ellis **Zacharias**. In February 1942 he was designated as prospective commanding officer of the troop transport *Thomas Stone*, which was then fitting out, but he was soon detached to duty as communications officer on the staff of the Commander, Eastern Sea Frontier (at the time Rear Adm. Adolphus Andrews).

In October 1942, Captain Stone reported for duty back in Washington, relieving Cmdr. John Redman as assistant director of Naval Communications for Communications Intelligence, and Head, Communication Intelligence Organization (OP-20-G).

Stone shortly learned of clandestine message traffic flowing between John Redman (who had transferred out to Pearl Harbor) and Stone's subordinate in Washington, Joe **Wenger**—messages mostly about their secret plan to get Joe **Rochefort** terminated as OIC at HYPO. Stone was troubled by what he discovered and apparently refused to have anything to do with it, recognizing—among other things—that use of a navy cipher system for personal communications was improper if not illegal.

When Rochefort soon reported in at Washington on temporary orders—which, by the Redman-Wenger plan, were going to be permanent—Rochefort confronted Stone and Wenger. They both told him that they were ignorant of the whole thing and that "they were both satisfied with combat intelligence at Pearl and did not desire any changes." Stone was telling the truth; Wenger was dissembling. Stone appears to have been baffled about the whole situation. "I never quite understood the personal animosity that existed between some of the people on duty in Washington and those in Hawaii." He did not know him well, but he liked and respected Rochefort—later commenting, "He was one of the most able people we had," and thus was puzzled by the sentiment against him. "I knew there was an argument going on and I must say I didn't realize that it was [as] serious as it proved to be when Rochefort was summarily relieved—*which was an awful mistake.* But . . . I had no part in that."

However in 1943, in his position as head of OP-20-G, Captain Stone very much antagonized the Hawaii unit when he sent a four-page letter to Capt. Bill Goggins, who had replaced Joe Rochefort as head of Station HYPO. Two of the pages, Tommy **Dyer** was certain, were written by HYPO nemesis Rosie **Mason** and asserted that a current decryption disagreement between HYPO and OP-20-G was all due to Dyer being "confused," leading Stone to suggest that Dyer possibly needed to be transferred someplace else. Dyer and Goggins found the letter infuriating, due not only to the personal attack but also because—in reality—it was again *Washington* which was mistaken in its analysis, "causing considerable loss of effort" and delay. Stone then irritated Dyer further by transferring his main cryptanalytical partner, Ham **Wright**, away from HYPO to Washington. Many years later in an interview, Dyer somewhat grudgingly expressed respect for Stone as a communications officer, but felt that he "didn't know beans" about the cryptology business.

Nevertheless, Schlitz Stone led the organization through some of the most challenging days of World War II, including the move of OP-20-G from the old Main Navy building to its new home at 3801 Nebraska Avenue. In early 1943, Stone alerted the director of naval communications to "determined efforts" being made by the army to consolidate army-navy COMINT. Stone advised his superiors that "the navy will lose in any merger." There was agreement against such a plan at the top level (Admirals Frederick Horne and Ernest King), although there does appear to have been an increased effort by each service to upgrade the quantity of exchanges. In late 1943, Stone also ran into some conflict with J. Edgar Hoover; the FBI aggressively complained (and threatened repercussions) that it was not getting navy COMINT which it needed, particularly for counter-espionage efforts in Central and South America.

Captain Stone was relieved at OP-20-G by Capt. Philip R. Kinney in March 1944. He then took charge of fitting-out the battleship *Wisconsin* and then commanded that ship from April 1944 until March 1945. He promoted to commodore and ordered to duty as assistant chief of staff for communications on the staff of the Commander in Chief, Pacific Fleet and Pacific Ocean Areas (Adm. Chester Nimitz), then located at the advance headquarters on Guam. During that period, and during a period of great expansion of fleet communications, he was responsible for the coordination, planning, construction, maintenance, and use of communication facilities and policies in the Pacific Ocean Areas. Nimitz later wrote that Stone had performed this gigantic task in an outstanding and extremely efficient manner.

In January 1946, Commodore Stone was promoted to rear admiral and then reported for duty as Chief of Naval Communications in Washington.

Rear Admiral Stone is perhaps best remembered for his leadership of the "Stone Board" and for arguably his most challenging job—taking charge as the first director of the AFSA. As a historical study done by the NSA has it, Stone was the chairman of a joint committee, appointed in August 1948, to make recommendations for reforming and reorganizing cryptologic activities. The Army supported consolidation, but the Navy and Air Force opposed unification. In December the Stone Board—named for its chairman, issued a report that recommended maintaining the status quo. A few months later, with the advent of a new secretary of defense and a change of position by the Air Force, the Navy grudgingly went along with the concept. The AFSA was created in May 1949.

Just six months earlier, Stone had been an ardent opponent of the unification and centralization concept. Now, ironically, he was appointed chief of the new organization. Stone directed the AFSA from July 1949 to July 1951. As the first director, he presided over the initial and stormy U.S. government attempts to centralize the country's cryptologic efforts. He attacked the problem with the zeal of a true convert. Admiral Stone cajoled the services into cooperation by using the same arguments that he himself had ignored in 1948.

The impact of the AFSA on the services was immediate and severe. Besides turning over more than 600,000 square feet of space to the new organization, the Army and Navy had to donate about 80% of their existing Washington billets—79% for the Army Security Agency and 86% for the Naval Security Group. Although the Army kept many of its uniformed service people, its corps of over 2,500 civilian experts was turned over to the AFSA virtually intact. This made the service cryptologic agencies little more than collection organizations, with practically no central processing. . . . This revolution was accomplished virtually overnight with only minimal dissension and was AFSA's most noteworthy success.

However, in other ways in these early years of sparring with the various military cryptologic organizations, Stone's consolidation efforts met with only limited success.

The structural weaknesses within the AFSA itself reduced the effectiveness of Stone's efforts. He did not have the authority to suppress conflicts and duplications. AFSA was a military organization that reported to the Joint Chiefs of Staff. Thus, he spent most of his time negotiating with the services over what AFSA could do because he could not direct the services. This military organization slighted the intelligence needs of civilian organizations such as the CIA and the Department of State. Poor performance [later] during the Korean War made further reform urgent. Many of the structural weaknesses in the AFSA were corrected by the creation of the National Security Agency in 1952. Stone's contribution was that he laid the groundwork for successful centralization in the early years of NSA's existence.

In August 1951, Rear Admiral Stone left the Defense Department and returned to navy duty, assuming command of Cruiser Division One. In that position, and concurrently as Commander, Task Group 77, Stone commanded the heavy-support ships which provided surface interdiction and gunfire strikes against enemy fortifications and facilities on the east coast of North Korea. For his contributions and leadership, Stone received a third Legion of Merit with a Combat "V" device.

Detached from CruDiv One in August 1952, Stone was then assigned to the joint staff of the Commander in Chief, U.S. European Command. In September 1953 he became Commander, Training Command, U.S. Pacific Fleet. His final tour of duty was as Superintendent, U.S. Naval Postgraduate School, in Monterey, from December 1955 until his retirement on January 1, 1958.

He had married Eleanor N. Pritchard; she predeceased him in 1963. Rear Adm. Stone took his retirement in the Monterey area, and he became the first director of the Allen Knight Maritime Museum there. He passed away at age ninety-three, in Carmel, California, on September 29, 1989; he'd been going in to the office just a few days preceding his death.

Among his many decorations and awards, Admiral Stone had three Legion of Merit medals (one with the Combat "V" device), a Navy Unit Commendation Ribbon, the Korean Service Medal, the United Nations Service Medal, and the Philippine Liberation Ribbon.

Rear Admiral Stone was also honored by the U.S. Naval Cryptologic Veterans Association as an officer who had headed the Naval Security Group or one of its predecessor organizations.

Sources

Benson, 90, 92, 127.
Browne and McGinnis, *Communications Intelligence*, 216–17.
Carlson, 405, 408.
Dyer, 254, 329.
Holtwick, 460, 463.
Howeth, Introduction, xi.
Kahn, *Codebreakers*, 702.
Layton, *"And I Was There,"* 467.
Lucky Bag, U.S. Naval Academy, 1917.
Maneki, Sharon A. *Rear Admiral Earl Everett Stone: A Convert to Cryptographic Centralization.* DOCID 3575729. Cryptologic Almanac 50th Anniversary Series. Center for Cryptologic History, National Security Agency, date unknown. Last reviewed February 2003; released in June 2009, FOIA Case No. 52567.
Morison, XIII (317), XIV (385).
Rear Admiral Earl Everett Stone, U.S.N., Retired. Biography. Navy Office of Information, Biographies Branch, January 28, 1958. Courtesy of the Naval Historical Foundation.
U.S. Navy, *Register of Commissioned and Warrant Officers.*

ADMIRAL ARTHUR DEWEY STRUBLE, U.S. NAVY (1894–1983)

"Ripples" "Rip"

Arthur Struble was always sunny-natured, a perfect gentleman with the ladies (who seemed to have universally adored him), and a "splendid fellow and a great talker." At the same time, he was superbly competent and sharply focused on business when the occasion required. At the flag level, Struble was a spectacular two-war combat commander. In addition, as a younger man, "Rip" also contributed noteworthy leadership service in cryptographic and communications positions—particularly during 1927–1930 as OIC of the navy's CSS, OP-20-G. In fact, he was much respected and later praised for his early communications intelligence savvy and activity by the "Father of U.S. Navy Cryptology"—Capt. Laurance Safford.

*   *   *

From the 1915 Annapolis yearbook, *The Lucky Bag*:

"We have with us tonight 'Arthur dear'—the envy of the women, the pride of the Navy, and the hope of the American people. Oregon is noted for red-cheeked apples, and she sent us her best when she sent us the *Ripples*. For two years he was regarded merely as a precocious infant, and then the Academy awoke to the fact that he was a savoir of the first magnitude. If he had not spent so much time helping [his roommate, R. J. Jondreau] he would have *starred* long ago; as it is, he lingers contentedly on the edge of a 3.4. Plebe year he started out to be the bold, bad man of the Third Company—and was ragged the first time he *frenched* [went into town without permission]. When he heard the report read out, he laughed—which is a custom of his [*Ripples* is short for *Ripples of Laughter*]. But he did not reform. Ripples is a fusser [*smooth, careful, extremely concerned with appearance*], not from choice but from necessity. You see, all the ladies admire his pink cheeks, and he is too much of a gentleman to deny them the pleasure of seeing him frequently at the hops [dances], where he chooses remarkably pretty partners—which is also a custom of his. But when *Ripples* goes aboard ship, he forgets all about girls and frivolities and concentrates on the day's work—which is likewise a custom of his." [Activities: *Masqueraders*, lacrosse]

*   *   *

Arthur Dewey Struble was born in Portland, Oregon, on June 28, 1894, son of Walter Burr and Hannah Wadsworth (Fairchild) Struble. He attended Lincoln High School in Portland before his appointment to the U.S. Naval Academy in 1911. From there he graduated and was commissioned an ensign in June 1915. Subsequent promotions include lieutenant (junior grade), 1917; lieutenant, 1920; lieutenant commander, 1925; commander, 1935; captain, 1941; rear admiral, 1942; and vice admiral, 1948. In July 1956 he was transferred to the retired list of the navy and was simultaneously promoted to the rank of admiral on the basis of his many combat awards.

Following graduation from the academy, he served consecutively—until September 1917—in the armored cruiser *South Dakota*, the protected cruiser *St. Louis*, and the store ship *Glacier*. After assisting in fitting out the destroyer *Stevens* at Quincy, Massachusetts, he joined that ship as engineering officer upon her commissioning in May 1918. In May 1919, off Newfoundland, the *Stevens* served as one of the picket ships posted along the route of the navy's Curtiss flying boat *NC-4* on her record-setting transatlantic flight. During his tour of duty, "as engineering officer of the *Stevens*, by applying certain newly understood principles of thermodynamics," Struble "was able to achieve significant improvements in the performance and fuel efficiency of the ship's engineering plant."

In October 1919 Mr. Struble reported as executive officer onboard the new destroyer *Shubrick*, and as such participated in the Haitian Campaign. He later commanded that vessel, and in April 1920 he transferred to the destroyer *Meyer*, in which he had duty as the executive officer until September 1921.

His demonstrated competence, first as an engineering officer, and then as XO and CO of destroyers, was in large part the basis for his appointment to the faculty at Annapolis. Thus, he was next assigned as an instructor in "Steam" (the Department of Marine Engineering and Naval Construction) at the Naval Academy—interestingly working alongside his former roommate, Jondreau, whom he'd had to help so much with studies when they were midshipmen. This assignment continued until June 1923, when Struble joined the battleship *California*.

The record is a little obscure here, but it appears that at some point during this time he spent at least a few months in Washington, in charge of the Visual Signals Desk (OP-20-GS) in Naval Communications. In fact, when Lt. Laurance **Safford** arrived in 1924, to become head of the Research Desk (OP-20-GX), Mr. Struble handed him the problem of taking the Gresham/Driscoll "CM" coding machine and making hardware modifications to improve its performance.

From October 1925 until September 1927, Struble served successively as aide and flag lieutenant on the staff of the Commander, Battleship Division, Battle Fleet, and then on the staff of the Commander, Battle Fleet. In both cases, the admiral was Richard Harrison Jackson, with whom Struble maintained contact until Jackson died, in 1971, at the age of 105.

Rear Adm. Joseph **Wenger** commented, in 1970, about working with Struble during the large 1926 U.S. Navy "Fleet Problem."

> It was during these maneuvers, while I was a coding and communications watch officer on the staff of [the] Commander, Battleships, that I came into direct contact with communications intelligence work again. Lieutenant Commander Struble, who was flag lieutenant at that time and had been in 20-G when I was there, put the finger on me to attack the "enemy" radio traffic.

In October 1927—relieving Lt. Cmdr. Lewis W. Comstock—Lieutenant Commander Struble was assigned to the Office of Naval Communications, at Main Navy, as head of the CSS (OP-20-G). Admiral Jackson, mentioned earlier, had become a mentor to Struble, and had years before served as a naval attaché and at ONI in Washington; he was a key influence in Struble's decision to seek this assignment. This was a fairly lengthy tour, ending in May 1930. He, in turn, was relieved by Lt. Cmdr. John W. **McClaran**.

During the following two years Struble had duty on the staff of the Commander, Battleship Division Three as aide and flag secretary. In June 1932 he reported as gunnery officer on board the battleship *New York*, and in June 1933 he was detached for a two-year tour of duty as the district communications officer, Twelfth Naval District, San Francisco.

Commander Struble reported onboard the heavy cruiser *Portland* in June 1935, and served as her first lieutenant and damage control officer until June 1936. He then joined the staff of the Commander, Cruisers, Scouting Force, as damage control officer, and on being detached from that assignment a year later, he reported to the Central Division, Office of the CNO, Main Navy.[1]

He joined the battleship *Arizona* in June 1940 (*Arizona* was "a happy ship" he later commented), and served as executive officer until January 1941 when he assumed command of the light cruiser *Trenton*. Upon the outbreak of World War II he was in command of that vessel, cruising in the Southeast Pacific. He continued in that position until May 1942.

Captain Struble was next assigned to the Office of the CNO as director of the Central Division. For this duty he received a letter of commendation with authorization to wear the Commendation Ribbon from the secretary of the navy. In October 1942 he was selected for the grade of rear admiral.

In November 1943 he reported as chief of staff and aide to the Commander, Task Force 122, Twelfth Fleet (Rear Adm. Alan G. Kirk, a former director of naval intelligence). Struble was subsequently awarded the Legion of Merit with the Combat V, for operations in Europe,

> for exceptionally meritorious conduct as Chief of Staff to the Western Naval Task Force, previous to—and during—the amphibious assault on the enemy German-held coast of Normandy commencing June 6, 1944 [Operation "Overlord"].

In August he was assigned duty as the Commander, Amphibious Group Nine, Seventh Amphibious Force. While serving in that command, and back in the Pacific, he directed the initial landings at the entrance to Leyte Gulf, then the assault landings at Ormoc Bay (his flagship then the destroyer *Hughes*), and lastly the successful amphibious assault on Mindoro in the Philippines. He also conducted numerous landings in the Central Visayas, having been appointed commander of the Visayan Attack Force. At this point the light cruiser *Nashville* became his flagship. On December 13, 1944, as Struble's force approached the Sulu Sea, a *kamikaze* "Val" dive-bomber hit the *Nashville*, wrecking the flag bridge, the combat information center, and the communications office. Around 130 people were killed, and another 190 were wounded. Struble's chief of staff (Capt. Everett W. Abdill) was among those killed; Struble had to transfer his flag to the destroyer *Dashiell*.

On January 29, 1945, his flag now in the amphibious force command ship *Mount McKinley*, Rear Admiral Struble's force capably put ashore the XI Corps in the San Narciso area at Zambales, northwest of Subic Bay. Forces under him captured Subic Bay, Mariveles, and Corregidor.

In March 1945, Struble was commander of Task Group 74.3 (embarked in the U.S. Coast Guard Cutter *Ingham*) for the liberation of Panay and the West Negros in the southern Philippine islands.

---

1. The CNO Central Division and its predecessors provided administrative assistance; acted as liaison with navy bureaus, government agencies, and the Congress; and administered island governments and places occupied by naval forces.

As commander of Amphibious Group Nine, he was subsequently awarded a Gold Star in lieu of a second Legion of Merit (with Combat "V"), for "exceptionally meritorious conduct . . . in action against enemy Japanese forces in the Philippine Islands, from 17 November to December 8, 1944." He received a second Gold Star in lieu of a third Legion of Merit (with Combat "V") for outstanding services in action against enemy Japanese forces in the Philippine Islands, from December 8, 1944, to January 2, 1945.

In addition, Rear Admiral Struble was awarded the Distinguished Service Medal for services

in the Philippine Islands Area from January to August 15, 1945. As Attack Group Commander, [he] demonstrated brilliant leadership and resourcefulness in the tactical execution of operational plans for the amphibious landings at Zambales, Bataan, and Corregidor on the Island of Luzon; on the Islands of Negros and Panay; and at Macajalar Bay on the Island of Mindanao. His sound judgment in the preparation of assault plans, his tact in coordinating the joint operations of the Allied Military Forces, and his professional skill in the discharge of his duties were major factors in the success of the Philippine Islands operation and in the ultimate regaining of complete control in the Southwest Pacific Area.

He was also awarded the Distinguished Service Medal by the U.S. Army for

service to the government in a position of great responsibility, from 30 August to 17 November 1944, as an Amphibious Attack Group Commander during operations against enemy Japanese forces in the Philippine Islands during the liberation of that area from Japanese domination.

In September 1945, after the surrender of the Japanese, Rear Adm. Struble assumed command of Minecraft, Pacific Fleet, in which duty he was responsible for clearing mines in the Western Pacific Ocean. He received a Commendation Ribbon from the secretary of the navy for service in this assignment, from August 30, 1945, to June 1, 1946. He then transferred to command the Amphibious Force, Pacific Fleet, in June 1946. Elements of the forces under his command, together with an army infantry division, an army engineer brigade, and army, navy and Marine Corps aircraft, participated in the first full-scale peacetime amphibious training exercises, held in late November and early December 1946. These exercises were conducted off the coast of Southern California and were brought to a successful conclusion on December 14.

In April 1948, Rear Admiral Struble was detached from command of the Amphibious Force, Pacific Fleet, and assumed duty as Deputy Chief of Naval Operations (for Operations), in Washington. He was also selected for promotion to vice admiral. In that capacity he was the naval deputy on the Joint Chiefs of Staff. He remained in that assignment until May 1950, when he became the Commander, Seventh Fleet. In July 1950 he directed the initial Korean War aircraft carrier operations in the Yellow Sea and the Sea of Japan. He was also responsible for preparing plans and for the conduct of operations in connection with the security of Formosa.

On August 24, 1950, he began work on the joint operation plan for the Inchon invasion. He commanded the 261 ships of the UN forces, plus the U.S. X Corps consisting of the First Marine Division and the Seventh U.S. Army Infantry Division, for that invasion. On September 15, this force carried out a highly successful amphibious assault against Inchon under very difficult hydrographic conditions. Under the overall direction of General of the Army Douglas MacArthur, the assault and landings were successfully completed, and the occupation of this area by UN forces turned the tide in Korea and forced the eventual withdrawal of North Korean forces from South Korea.

About one month later Vice Admiral Struble commanded a large landing at Wonsan. Later in the year his forces furnished close air support and gun support for the UN troops operating in North Korea; this facilitated the now-famous evacuation of the First Marine Division from the Chosin Reservoir area, and for the redeployment of the X Corps from Hungnam.

Until March 28, 1951, the Seventh Fleet continued support of UN operations in Korea, providing gunfire and close air support—in addition to bombardment and air interdiction missions—against the enemy's transportation systems in North Korea.

For his performance against an armed enemy, as commander of the Seventh Fleet during the period September 15 to October 19, 1950, Vice Admiral Struble was awarded the Distinguished Service Cross by the Department of the Army.

He was also awarded a Gold Star in lieu of a second Distinguished Service Medal for exceptionally meritorious service as the Commander, Seventh Fleet, during operations from June 27, 1950, to January 1, 1951.

Detached from command of the Seventh Fleet, he reported on March 28, 1951, as Commander, First Fleet. He served as such until March 24, 1952, and then proceeded to duty with the Joint Chiefs of Staff in Washington.

On May 14, 1952, Rip Struble became the U.S. naval representative on the Military Staff Committee of the UN, and on July 1, 1953, he assumed the duties of Chairman of the U.S. Military Delegation to the Military Staff Committee of the UN. On June 1, 1955, he reported as Commander, Eastern Sea Frontier and Commander, Atlantic Reserve Fleet, and continued to serve in this latter assignment at the UN Headquarters. On July 1, 1956, Vice Admiral Struble was transferred to the retired list of the U.S. Navy, and because of his high-level combat decorations was simultaneously promoted to full admiral on that list.

Admiral Struble's many decorations and awards included the Navy Distinguished Service Medal with Gold Star, the Army Distinguished Service Cross and Distinguished Service Medal, the Legion of Merit with two Gold Stars, and the Commendation Ribbon with Bronze Star. Among other things, he also had been awarded the Mexican Service Medal, World War I Victory Medal, Haitian Campaign Medal, China Service Medal, and the Philippine Liberation Ribbon with two stars.

From other nations he'd been awarded the *Legion d'Honneur*, Rank of Officer, and the *Croix de Guerre* with Palm, from France; the Royal Order of the Phoenix, Higher Commander, from Greece; Commander of the Order of Leopold with Palm and the *Croix de Guerre* with Palm from Belgium; and the Order of Military Merit, Silver Star, from Korea.

Struble was married to the former Hazel L. Ralston, also of Portland. They had three children; Arthur Jr. (USNA class of 1943), Nancy, and Elizabeth. Hazel Struble passed away in April 1962. Subsequently, Admiral Struble married the widow of Rear Adm. Kenneth D. **Ringle** (Margaret Avery Ringle) in 1967. Interestingly, even after long careers in the navy and with many mutual friends, Admirals Ringle and Struble had never actually met.

Beginning in mid-1978 Struble suffered a series of strokes which progressively incapacitated him; he died in May 1983 at his home in Chevy Chase, Maryland. He's buried at Arlington National Cemetery with his first wife, Hazel; Margaret Ringle Struble died in 1999, and was interred in the family cemetery at Avery Island, Louisiana.

Admiral Struble has also been recognized and honored, by the U.S. Naval Cryptologic Veterans Association, as an officer who has served as the Commander, Naval Security Group, or one of its predecessor organizations.

Sources

Admiral Arthur D. Struble, Biographical Sketch, Navy Biographies Branch. Adapted from OI-430, May 9, 1966.

Holtwick, Vol. 1, 50.

Longines Chronoscope with VADM Arthur D. Struble. Longines Chronoscope: A Television Journal of the Important Issues of the Hour. 12m 11s. William B. Hugey and Elliott Haynes, interviewers. National Archives and Records Administration 1953-02-09—ARC 96074, LI LW-LW-530—DVD Copied by Thomas Gideon. www.youtube.com.

Lucky Bag, U.S. Naval Academy, 1915.

McCollum, interview, Vol. 2, 665.

Morison, XI, 30; XII, 119, 377; XIII, 18–19, 24, 323.

Ringle, Andrew D., e-mail correspondence, July–August 2013.

Ringle, Kenneth A., e-mail correspondence, July–August 2013.

Safford, in Holtwick, App. 214, 220.

U.S. Navy, *Register of Commissioned and Warrant Officers.*

REAR ADMIRAL ROBERT HARPER WEEKS, U.S. NAVY (1909–2003)

"Bob"

Robert Weeks finessed a remarkable career, making significant contributions as a submariner, cryptanalyst, destroyerman, communicator, and in senior leadership as a flag officer. A pre–World War II cryptologist as a junior officer, he closed out his career as vice director of the Defense Communications Agency.

*   *   *

From the 1932 Annapolis yearbook, *The Lucky Bag*:

Coming from Massachusetts, *Bob* proved capable of upholding the Bay State's standard of producing saviors. He had no trouble in conquering what proved to be the downfall of many. Always up toward the top of his class, never worrying, never complaining, *Bob* is one of those lucky mortals who make the best of everything and find contentment in a job well done. He whiled away most of his time in reading, and the library found him a frequent borrower. Those that knew *Bob* from Plebe year noticed a great change that was made in him. He was a misogynist pure and simple until a bit of femininity broke through his reserve during Second Class Sep leave. Athletically, Bob spent most of his time on the cross-country and track teams, helping his class teams win several times in both sports. Modesty is one of *Bob*'s virtues; he never boasts of his conquests or accomplishments. Those who know him, and there are but few who don't, have little doubt that to him will come the fruits deserved by one so upright and loyal. [Activities: track, cross-country, soccer]

*   *   *

Bob Weeks was born November 2, 1909, in Springfield, Massachusetts. He earned an appointment to the Naval Academy in 1928 and graduated in 1932 along with such classmates as John M. **Lietwiler**, Alfred G. Ward, Bruce McCandless, and Lloyd M. Mustin. Subsequent promotions included lieutenant (junior grade), 1935; lieutenant, 1939; lieutenant commander, June 1942; commander, November 1942; captain, 1951, and rear admiral, 1960. He transferred to the retired list in 1971.

From 1933 through 1934 he served on board the heavy cruisers *Chester* and *Portland*. In 1935 he qualified as a submariner and then served in submarines until 1938, first in the *S-43* and then in the *S-25*. In 1938, Mr. Weeks was briefly attached to the staff of the commander in chief, U.S. Fleet.

Lt. j.g. Weeks was then identified for cryptographic training at Main Navy with OP-20-G. By the late 1930s such training had evolved into a two-year course. He started in June 1939, along with Lieutenants (junior grade) Herbert Coleman and John Lietwiler.

One day in early 1941, fellow OP-20-G officer Lt. Cmdr. Alwin **Kramer**, who coincidentally was Mr. Weeks's next-door neighbor, brought him into his house to see Kramer's latest "haul" from an ONI "black-bag job" against the Japanese consulate in New York City. Kramer had personally developed the resulting spy-camera photos of documents in his basement darkroom. However, they had to hurriedly hide it all after they heard a knock on the door—good thing, as the unexpected caller just happened to be the Japanese naval attaché in Washington, with whom Kramer was friendly.

In January 1941, Lieutenant Weeks joined Lt. j.g. Prescott **Currier** (also of OP-20-G) and U.S. Army officers Capt. Abraham Sinkov and Lt. Leo Rosen (of the army's Signal Intelligence Service) on a ten-week mission to Great Britain. They delivered American communications-intelligence material to the British, including two copies of the PURPLE machine and two RED machines. In return, the British supplied them with a small amount of information about their exploitation of the German ENIGMA—as well as considerable information concerning other nations' systems. The Americans were also provided with some state-of-the-art British direction-finding equipment. Even with the miniscule disclosure of ENIGMA information, for the United States this was one of the most significant signals-intelligence events of the prewar period.

While in England, Weeks and Currier traveled around the country to see various intercept stations and other places of interest. One day their car was stopped in a small village by a zealous local constable who was suspicious of foreigners. He announced that he was going to detain them and take them to the station, whereupon their British War Office driver jumped out of the car in a fury, and shouted at the top of his voice, "Ye canna do this! They are *Americans* and they are on a *secret mission!*"

Before they left England, at the insistence of their hosts, Mr. Weeks had to write out and sign a handwritten commitment to preserve the secrecy of the information gathered, informing "by word of mouth only the head of our section, Cmdr. L. F. **Safford**, USN." The army officers executed a similar document.

Not long after returning from this mission to the United Kingdom, Weeks was detached from OP-20-G. He was assigned to the newly activated CinCLant communications security unit, which was located onboard the Atlantic Fleet flagship, the heavy cruiser *Augusta*—which he joined in Newport, Rhode Island. At that time the commander in chief Atlantic was Adm. Ernest J. King.

In October 1941, Weeks's name was included on a list drawn up by Safford, identifying a small group of only eighteen officers that he considered "qualified and acceptable" for communications intelligence and cryptanalysis.

During World War II, Weeks held several naval communications-security positions in Washington, at least one of which included carrying coded information on board President Roosevelt's yacht on the Potomac River. In fact, in August 1941, Weeks had traveled with Roosevelt to Newfoundland for the president's historic meeting with British Prime Minister Winston S. Churchill—where they produced the pivotal policy statement known as the Atlantic Charter.

In 1947 and 1948, Weeks served as the commanding officer of the destroyer *James C. Owens* when she supported the UN's Palestine/Israel Mediation Force. He then commanded the oiler *Sabine* during 1953 and 1954.

Weeks then attended the Naval War College, graduating in June 1955, along with Captains Stephen **Jurika** and Rudolph **Fabian**.

Then, as the commodore of Destroyer Squadron Ten (during 1958 and 1959, onboard the USS *Forrest Sherman*), he commanded an Atlantic task force which transited the Suez Canal to join Pacific forces protecting Formosa from communist China.

After selection for rear admiral in 1960, Weeks became the commander of Cruiser/Destroyer Flotilla Ten, serving as such during 1961 and 1962. He then became Deputy for Communications and Electronics, European Command, based in Paris from 1963 to 1965. Rear Admiral Weeks served as the director of Naval Communications from 1965 to 1968, and then finished his career as vice director of the Defense Communications Agency, retiring in 1971.

In retirement Admiral Weeks tutored English as a second language to children in the Arlington school system. He had long been interested in languages; early in his career he had obtained a qualification as an interpreter of French.

In the early 1980s, Weeks put in considerable effort helping Rear Adm. Edwin Layton (and his coauthors) work on Layton's reminisces, *"And I Was There": Pearl Harbor and Midway—Breaking the Secrets.*

Weeks had married Reina Sigrid Alvord of Long Meadow, Massachusetts, in 1934. Mrs. Weeks, born in 1912, predeceased him in 1994.

Admiral Weeks died of pneumonia on June 11, 2003, at the Arleigh Burke Pavilion in McLean, Virginia. He was ninety-three years old. He left a daughter, Sigrid Weeks Benson, and a son, John Alvord Weeks, as well as several grandchildren and great-grandchildren. He is buried at Arlington National Cemetery. His decorations and awards include a Legion of Merit.

Sources

Benson, 19.
Budiansky, 175–76, 178–79.
Farago, *Broken Seal*, 253.
Holtwick, 245, 305, 325, 329, 340, 352, 371, 425, 428, 439, App. 91–92.
Layton, *"And I Was There,"* 6, 284.
Lucky Bag, U.S. Naval Academy, 1932.
Smith, *Emperor's Codes*, 74–77.
Smith and Erskine, *Action This Day*, 164–65, 220–21.
Stinnett, 78–80.
U.S. Navy, *Register of Commissioned and Warrant Officers.*
www.arlingtoncemetery.net/rhweeks.htm

REAR ADMIRAL JOSEPH NUMA WENGER, U.S. NAVY
(1901–1970)

First special duty communications officer to make flag rank
"Joe" "Skinny"

An early entrant, and certainly an "original" in the U.S. Navy's radio intelligence business, Joseph Wenger was also involved in the first development of machines for use in cryptanalysis. He was early to see the role of communications intelligence and its value—particularly in radio-traffic analysis—to military planners.[1] On the down side, early in the war he was very involved in the deposing of Capt. Laurance **Safford** (the "father of U.S. naval cryptology") as head of OP-20-G; he was also an active participant in the post-Midway sacking of Cmdr. Joseph **Rochefort**—who

---

1. He was right to extoll the virtues of traffic analysis, but he often—at least in the old days—emphasized TA *over* cryptanalysis. In the early 1930s he told Tommy **Dyer** that codebreaking would yield little information of value in any future war! It does appear that he altered that view as time passed.

was perhaps the most brilliant of the navy's communications-intelligence practitioners and leaders. That aside, Wenger was an extremely influential figure in American cryptologic history; after the war he played a large role in the development of both the Naval Security Group Command and the NSA.

*   *   *

From the 1923 Naval Academy yearbook, *The Lucky Bag*:

"Say, Jig, wait a minute and I'll be with you." The scuttlebutt [*drinking fountain*], is the only object in sight; a strange attraction, you wonder. The minute's up, he's ready and raring to go; for an explanation of the delay, he'll offer, "It's a motto, that's all." But living up to mottoes isn't his only attainment, because he's a disciple of art—discovered Plebe year by a mere sketch on a long-forgotten hop-card. Under observation since then, he has thought, studied, practiced, and slept art to the edification and amusement of us all. Odd books and papers, full of inspirations or palpitations, an avidity for "dago" [*foreign languages*], a pen or brush ever wet, are conclusive evidence that *Skinny* has an aim to create and display his "oeuvres" in the Latin Quarter of gay Paris, where it's considered good form to wander about with the flowing tie, the trailing locks, and the hungry where-do-I-get-my-next-meal attitude. A friend ever dearer, a companion of highest ideals, Joe has a bright future ahead. "Say, Jig, guess I'll stay in the Navy!" [Activities: crew squad]

*   *   *

Joseph N. Wenger was born in Patterson, Louisiana, on June 7, 1901. He was admitted to the Naval Academy in 1919 and graduated in 1923; among his distinguished classmates were Thomas B. **Birtley**, Arleigh A. Burke, Kenneth D. **Ringle**, Edward S. Pearce, and Melville Bell Grosvenor. Subsequent promotions included lieutenant (junior grade), 1926; lieutenant, 1930; lieutenant commander, 1938; commander, 1942; captain, 1943; and rear admiral 1951. Unexpected hospitalization in October 1957 led to his unplanned retirement in February 1958.

Wenger's career, between the two world wars, was typical of many future naval cryptologic officers—which is to say he rotated between sea duty and OP-20-G, the navy's early cryptologic element, in Washington. He was associated with OP-20-G primarily when on shore duty, and his early association with cryptology was via participation in training courses in 1925 and 1929—as well as some correspondence with Laurance **Safford** (head of OP-20-G when *he* wasn't on sea duty) about the subject.

Following graduation from the Academy, Ensign Wenger was briefly assigned to the Bureau of Ordnance and then joined the battleship *Arkansas* in September 1923. From November 1924 until June 1925 he underwent initial cryptographic training at OP-20-G (in fact, he was the first student to undertake the sixteen-week course as developed by Lieutenant Safford). Up to this point Wenger had seen a career for himself in gunnery. He later said that his commanding officer nominated him for cryptography training because he was the only eligible candidate whose family lived in Washington and could therefore "afford to live there on an ensign's pay." Nevertheless, after his cryptologic training he then became the communications watch officer on the staff of the Commander, Battleship Divisions, Battle Fleet. Continuing duty on that capacity until September 1926, he subsequently had sea service as radio officer in the cruiser *Pittsburgh*, and then in 1928 the cruiser *Milwaukee*. In those days he rarely found any staff or time to work on cryptanalysis, but was very engaged in interception and traffic analysis.

Wenger commented, in 1970, about working with Lt. Cmdr. Arthur **Struble** during the large 1926 U.S. Navy "Fleet Problem."

> It was during these maneuvers, while I was a coding and communications watch officer on the staff of [the] Commander, Battleships, that I came into direct contact with communications intelligence work again. [Mr.] Struble, who was flag lieutenant at that time and had been in 20-G when I was there, put the finger on me to attack the "enemy" radio traffic.

Detached from the *Milwaukee* in March 1929, he undertook further cryptologic training (an expanded course which was finalized in 1930) under the guidance of Agnes **Driscoll**, focused almost entirely on practical work. He did well; in November 1930, Lt. Cmdr. John **McClaran** (then head of OP-20-G) wrote that there were only six officers trained and available for cryptanalytical work (less a few others who had other major qualifications such as aviator, submariner, or Japanese linguist): Lt. Cmdr. Laurance Safford, Ens. William Leahy, Lt. j.g. Thomas Dyer, Lt. Bern **Anderson**, Lt. Joseph Wenger, and Lt. j.g. Thomas **Huckins**. The next year he starred in another report; Wenger was considered, in 1931, one of only seven naval officers classed as competent cryptanalysts—the others being Dyer, Anderson, Huckins, Safford, and Joseph **Rochefort** (Safford and Rochefort were the only ones considered qualified to instruct in the subject). At this time Mr. Wenger was the only officer who had more than six months' training in cryptography.

He did considerable work on the Japanese "Red Code" during this tour. Moreover, while at the Research Desk, Wenger played a role along with Tommy Dyer in the introduction of sorting machines to navy decoding work. In fact, Lt. j.g. Eddie **Layton**, also in the office at that time, observed that

> Lieutenant Wenger . . . learned that Remington-Rand had just produced punch-card equipment that could handle alphabetic information, but investigation showed that it did not fill our requirements. It was Dyer, however, who after five months of pencil-pushing drudgery, came up with an ingenious labor-saving solution. He found a way to use IBM tabulating machines to ease the burden of sifting through the myriad possible solutions of the code group. This was in the biting days of the Depression, but Wenger and Dyer managed to talk the Bureau of Ships into providing $5,000 to rent the IBM equipment. They were also able to hire two key-punch operators, and things began looking up.

In August 1931, Wenger was assigned to the Bureau of Engineering. He then had brief duty, during May and June 1932, at the American embassies in London, Paris, Berlin, and Zurich—where he investigated various European "cipher machines." Wenger then joined the staff of the Commander in Chief, Asiatic Fleet (having to pay his own way from Naples on a Japanese passenger liner!), serving from 1932 through June 1934 as assistant fleet communications officer and radio intelligence officer.

During 1931 and 1932, Lt. Henri **Smith-Hutton** served onboard the *Houston* as aide and flag lieutenant, and later as aide and fleet intelligence officer on the staff of the Commander in Chief, Asiatic Fleet. There he worked alongside, and became friends with, Joe Wenger.

Other than his OP-20-G training, this was Wenger's first real operational involvement with communications intelligence. In 1933 or early 1934 he began to assemble the reports of the various radio intelligence elements which had participated in obtaining information on the Japanese Imperial Fleet maneuvers of 1933; he and Lt. j.g. John **Williams** worked together on that project. Wenger's analysis and consolidation of these reports into a major study of his own crystallized his thinking on the value of COMINT and particularly the importance of traffic analysis in a military environment. He gained an appreciation of the valuable information which could be gained from studying Japanese communications procedures, traffic associations, systems, call signs, and other message externals, and he recognized that this information could be extraordinarily important—and at times just as important as information derived from actually reading the message texts. He also understood the critical need to establish multiple intercept stations to collect Japanese naval signals, and he helped create OP-20-G's Pacific Ocean collection network.

Lieutenant Wenger returned to the United States in July 1934. Lt. Tom Huckins left OP-20-G to replace Wenger as head of radio intelligence operations in the Asiatic area. Huckins, on his way to the Philippines, met Wenger in Los Angeles as an ill Wenger was returning early. Huckins drove him to the naval hospital in San Diego to continue medical treatment which had started at the naval hospital at Canacao (close to Cavite). Wenger later remarked, "as it was a longish drive in those days, we had a good opportunity to discuss Asiatic problems and to pass on to him at least the highlights of my experience there." Obviously, there was neither formal turnover nor opportunity to hand off notes and files. After a brief period of hospitalization (for the removal of an inflamed appendix), Wenger reported in October to the cargo ship *Sirius*. He continued sea service on that ship until January 1935, when he transferred to the cargo ship *Antares*.

After three months' duty as the navigator of the *Antares*, Lieutenant Wenger was detached and ordered to the Office Naval Communications where he remained until mid-1938. In this assignment he took charge of the "Research Desk" or Cryptanalytic Section (OP-20-GY) in the navy's nascent communications-intelligence organization. While in this position he helped launch the navy's effort in the field of machine processing and aided in the development and refinement of cipher devices which were adopted by the service.

In 1936, the chief of naval operations commended Mr. Wenger for "devising and developing a new and improved type of mechanized cipher device . . . the initiative, zeal, and technical ability displayed by you . . . merit special notation by a letter in your record." In June 1937, Wenger produced a "Military Study of Communications Intelligence Research Activities," which was an exhaustive study of all elements of law, regulation, and policy which set forth or bore on the COMINT mission. It was an extremely important document in its effect on plans and operations up to World War II.

Wenger was also fully engaged in an intense rivalry with the U.S. Army's cryptologic unit, at times withholding some of the navy's advances from the army's chief cryptanalyst, William F. Friedman.[2] In June 1938, Lieutenant Commander Wenger was relieved by Lt. Sid **Goodwin**.

Following an assignment as commanding officer of the destroyer *Tillman*, in April 1939 Wenger joined the light cruiser *Honolulu* as her navigator.

In July 1941—and present there at the outbreak of World War II—Wenger was again in Washington, in the War Plans Division (OP-20-WP), and then back to OP-20-G by February 1942. He immediately designed a plan for a sweeping reorganization of the naval COMINT structure. This reorganization—rightly or wrongly—was an attempt to change the nature of OP-20-G from a decentralized organization to a more centralized one. The plan was approved at the highest levels, and Wenger emerged as the deputy and then the head of OP-20-G, effectively deposing and pushing aside Capt. Laurance Safford—who had essentially created the unit and the COMINT program, and who had been consumed in its mission for the past seventeen years.[3] Wenger remained at 20-G throughout World War II and up through mid-1949; in the latter part of this period he also served as deputy director of naval communications.

Prior to the Battle of Midway in early June 1942, Cmdr. John Redman and Cmdr. Joe Wenger were part of a major disagreement between Stations HYPO and NEGAT (the call sign for OP-20-G) as to the intentions of the Japanese; as events played out, it became clear that HYPO had correctly worked it out and that NEGAT had been profoundly mistaken.

Turning his attention to the east, in August 1942 Commander Wenger came to the conclusion that the British were concealing their cryptologic successes against the "SHARK" key to the German naval ENIGMA machine. The truth is that the British were not having much success, even with their early mechanized "bombes."[4] A month

---

2. In fact, as late as September 1942, British cryptologist Dr. George McVittie was surprised that Wenger would reveal secrets to him *which he had not* also passed to the U.S. Army.

3. Intelligence historians Roger Pineau and John Costello have written that Joe Wenger was a talented communications-intelligence officer as well as something of an "opportunist." They also wrote, "It was Safford who singlehandedly . . . conceived, founded, and built the navy's COMINT entity. . . . It was Wenger who [then] harnessed the power and drive of [Rear Adm. Joe Redman and Cmdr. Jack Redman] to organize radio intelligence for the navy's, and the nation's, long-term goals." However, "the HYPO team of Rochefort-Dyer-Wright was to prove the Redman-Wenger philosophy of a centrally controlled and directed radio intelligence operation *was not applicable* to a tactical command [such as the Pacific Fleet.]"

4. A "bombe" was a large, single-purpose computing machine, better than contemporary IBM sorters and tabulators, but not really a computer in the modern sense.

later Wenger proposed to his superiors that the U.S. Navy should give up on the British and build a considerable number of four-wheel bombes for itself, at the cost of more than $2 million. He did stress that "it must be understood that it is a gamble." But by summer 1943 six bombes per week were being delivered from the National Cash Register facility in Dayton—the prime contractor for the project. By December 1943 seventy-five of the machines were running successfully, to great effect.

However, returning to fall 1942, Commander Wenger also became involved in the unprofessional rivalry conspiracy of Rear Adm. Joseph Redman and Cmdr. John Redman to remove Cmdr. Joseph Rochefort from his key post as head of Station HYPO/FRUPac. In October 1942, Capt. Earl **Stone** relieved Commander Redman as assistant director of Naval Communications for Communications Intelligence, and head of OP-20-G. Stone shortly learned of clandestine message traffic flowing between John Redman (who had transferred out to Pearl Harbor) and Stone's deputy in Washington, Joe Wenger—messages mostly about their secret plan to get Rochefort terminated as OIC at HYPO. Stone was troubled by what he discovered and apparently refused to have anything to do with it, recognizing—among other things—that use of a navy cipher system for personal communications was improper if not actually illegal. Wenger was then ordered by the new director of naval communications, Capt. Carl Holden, to destroy the secret cipher; at Pearl Harbor, Admiral Nimitz told Jack Redman to cease all such "intolerable" activity, and refused to speak to him for weeks.

When Joe Rochefort then reported in at Washington on temporary orders—which, by the secret plan, were actually permanent—he assertively confronted Stone and Wenger. They both told him that they were ignorant of the whole thing and that "they were both satisfied with combat intelligence at Pearl and did not desire any changes." Stone was telling the truth; Wenger was not—on both points. Stone appears to have been genuinely baffled about the whole situation. "I never quite understood the *personal animosity* that existed between some of the people on duty in Washington and those in Hawaii." He did not know him well, but he liked and respected Rochefort—later commenting that "he was one of the most able people we had," and thus was puzzled by the intense sentiment against him. "I knew there was an argument going on and I must say I didn't realize that it was [as] serious as it proved to be when Rochefort was summarily relieved—*which was an awful mistake.*"

Later in the fall of 1942, Wenger was the driving force behind the navy using wartime authority to actually "commandeer" Mount Vernon Seminary on Nebraska Avenue in northwest Washington (this was a finishing school for girls from wealthy families); so it was that OP-20-G left the old Main Navy building and moved during February 1943, and this is why for many years navy COMINT personnel informally referred to headquarters as "Nebraska Avenue."

In 1943, in a lecture on "Future Cooperation between the Army and Navy," Commander Wenger remarked that

the value of radio intelligence has been demonstrated to the extent that we can never again afford to neglect it as we did before the war. Furthermore, the difficulties of obtaining intelligence have increased so greatly that we shall have to maintain an organization constantly at work on high-speed electronic equipment if we are to be prepared for any future wars. The equipment necessary to obtain radio intelligence is growing so complicated that we cannot wait until war comes to provide it.

After the war, in the words of NSA historian Robert Hanyok, regardless of his occasional "Byzantine practices" Wenger "turned out to be very important because he helped set up post-war cryptological organizations." At the end of World War II, Captain Wenger worked to ensure the continuity of the navy's cryptologic efforts—which were threatened by demobilization—by retaining experienced personnel and promoting a reservoir of reservists. Wenger also strongly supported the creation of a company, Engineering Research Associates of St. Paul, Minnesota, which helped lay the foundations for the modern computer industry. In the late 1940s he initiated a computer-based research project which became one of the first major programs undertaken by the IBM company for the U.S. government. During this time Wenger had become head of the Supplementary Operations Branch (NavComDiv OP-202)—effectively an early version of the Naval Security Group. He was once again relieved by Sid Goodwin.

In July 1949, Captain Wenger became a deputy director for COMINT at the new AFSA, and also served as the deputy coordinator of joint operations for the U.S. Communications Intelligence Board. In June 1951, Wenger was promoted to rear admiral, the first navy COMINT officer to attain flag rank on active duty, resulting from the creation of the Special Duty Officer designator in communications. When the NSA was established in 1952, Wenger became its vice director in December of that year and served there until August 1953.

He then became director of communications-electronics on the Joint Staff of the U.S. European Command, and as coordinator of both U.S. and NATO communications-electronics plans and programs. In October 1956, Wenger was appointed as deputy director of communications-electronics for the JCS, and in December 1956 he became chairman of the Joint Communications-Electronics Committee of the JCS. In May 1957 he was designated as the chairman and U.S. member of the Communications-Electronics Board, Standing Group, NATO. Unfortunately, Rear Admiral Wenger's active-duty career then ended in collapse and emergency hospitalization; he entered the hospital in October 1957, and then retired in February 1958.

After his retirement he continued to serve as a member of NSA's Scientific Advisory Board. He was also a technical consultant for RCA and the Syracuse University Research Corporation. Rear Admiral Wenger's involvement in cryptology and communications electronics ended only with his death on September 21, 1970, in Jackson, New Hampshire. He was subsequently buried at Arlington National Cemetery.

Admiral Wenger had married Mary Crippen in 1932 and they had one son, Jeffrey J. Wenger.

As perhaps forecast in his Annapolis yearbook commentary, early on Wenger qualified as a foreign-language interpreter—although it was in French, not Japanese. He also pursued a keen interest in drawing, etching, and watercolor throughout his life. He had illustrated several periodicals and books in his youth. He held a substantial one-man photographic exhibition at the Smithsonian Institute in 1934. He designed his family's summer home in New Hampshire, upon which construction had just started when he unexpectedly died.

Admiral Wenger received the Distinguished Service Medal at the end of World War II—one of only six navy people in the radio intelligence world so recognized. He also received the National Security Medal from President Eisenhower in 1953. His other decorations and awards include the Yangtze Service Medal, and the Order of the British Empire (Honorary Commander) from Great Britain.

Wenger was also recognized, by the U.S. Naval Cryptologic Veterans Association, as an officer who has served as the Commander, Naval Security Group, or one of its predecessor organizations, and he has also been named a Pioneer Officer of U.S. Naval Cryptology by the same organization. He was inducted into the NSA's Hall of Honor in 2005.

Sources

I'm particularly indebted to the work of NSA historian Thomas Johnson for considerable information.

Benson, 44, 46, 48–49, 52–53, 55, 60, 87–88, 92, 119, 126, 129, 133–38, 155–56.
Browne and McGinnis, *Communications Intelligence*, 220–21.
Budiansky, 27, 87, 223–24, 238, 294–95, 359.
Carlson, 50, 214–16, 220, 339, 387–88, 393, 400–10, 444–48, 455, 503, 529.
Donovan and Mack, 106.
Dyer, 263, 290, 352.
Holtwick, 45–46, 48, 50, 61, 68–69, 70–74, 80–82, 88, 97–99, 105–8, 122–23, 127–29, 131–32, 136–37, 140–42, 147, 150, 152–53, 155, 158, 160–62, 164, 178–80, 182–83, 199–201, 210, 216, 222–24, 229–30, 246–47, 257–58, 268–70, 277–78, 294–95, 297, 305, 312, 342, 368, 379, 387–88, 390, 392–93, 404, 429, 439–40, 445, 450, 453–58, 460–63, App. 5–6, 11, 103.
Johnson, Thomas R. *Joseph N. Wenger.* In the "Cryptologic Almanac 50th Anniversary Series." Center for Cryptologic History. U.S. National Security Agency. DOCID: 3575736. Approved for public release on 12 June 2009, FOIA Case No. 52567.
Layton, *"And I Was There,"* 34–35, 46, 56, 367–68, 378, 466–67, 525.
Lucky Bag, U.S. Naval Academy, 1923.
McGinnis, 9–10, 22.
Prados, 45, 77–79, 213, 300–1, 317, 319, 410–11, 592, 711, 731.
Rear Adm. Joseph N. Wenger. U.S. National Security Agency. Cryptologic Hall of Honor. www.nsa.gov/about/cryptologic_heritage/hall_of_honor, accessed 22 January 2013.
Rear Admiral Joseph N. Wenger, United States Navy, Retired. Official Biography. Biographies Branch, U.S. Navy Office of Information, February 13, 1958.
Smith and Erskine, *Action This Day*, 191, 212, 227.
Toll, 310, 312, 481.
U.S. Navy, *Register of Commissioned and Warrant Officers.*
Winton, 123–24.

CAPTAIN DUANE LEWIS WHITLOCK, U.S. NAVY (1917–2007)

A "Roofer"—an enlisted On-the-Roof-Gang alumnus
Decorated for Coral Sea and Midway support

With a modest start to his naval career, Duane Whitlock moved from junior enlisted radioman all the way to captain. Along the way he mastered radio interception, traffic analysis, operational intelligence, and cryptology.

* * *

Duane Whitlock was born on January 29, 1917, in Beloit, Wisconsin, son of Duane and Martha Whitlock. He joined the navy in 1935 as an apprentice seaman, trained as a radioman at Naval Training Station, San Diego, and served onboard the cruiser *Richmond*. Selected for intelligence duties, he was trained as a Japanese intercept operator at Main Navy in "On-the-Roof-Gang" Class Twenty, 1937 to 1938. He went out into the fleet serving as an intercept operator in Hawaii, Guam, and at Cavite—and then as a traffic analyst producing radio intelligence at Corregidor (Station CAST), and at Melbourne (Station FRUMel).[1]

He was a radioman second class when he came to the Philippines; he worked with Lt. Jeff **Dennis** at CAST, who became a mentor then and for years to come. By 1942, Whitlock had advanced to chief radioman. In Hawaii during the war, he received a commission in August 1943, and was promoted to lieutenant (junior grade) in December 1944. He was awarded the Bronze Star for his intelligence contributions relative to the battles of Coral Sea and Midway. Further postwar promotions were lieutenant, 1949; lieutenant commander, 1954; commander, 1958, and captain, 1964.

Whitlock attended George Washington University under the navy's auspices. After a tour of duty in Japan, interposed between service at the AFSA and the NSA, he completed a course at the Naval War College and was assigned to the staff of CinCPacFlt. He then served for four years at ONI as an operational intelligence analyst. In his final two years in the navy he served the commander of the Naval Security Group as assistant chief of staff for special operations. He retired in June 1967, but returned briefly to the NavSecGru as a civilian from 1968 to 1969. In 1988, he published a universal theory of systems in a book titled *Critical Thoughts and Notions*. He published another book shortly before his death, *The Search for Intelligent Design*.

Looking back fifty-some years, Whitlock made this summarization in a 1995 *Naval War College Review* article:

> A vital point, that should not be overlooked by historians and students of the war with Japan, is the fact that something more than 20 years was required to bring on-line the radio intelligence organization that ultimately gave commanders what was perhaps the greatest strategic and tactical advantage in the history of naval warfare.

Captain Whitlock passed away April 7, 2007, in Mill Valley, California, and is buried with his wife of fifty-two years, Gertrude (1916–1992) at Holy Cross Catho-

1. Whitlock is another voice pushing back against those who insist that the U.S. was reading quantities of Imperial Japanese Navy coded messages right before the Pearl Harbor attack. In 1986 he wrote, in reference to his time on Corregidor:

I can attest from first-hand experience that as of 1 December 1941 the recovery of the JN-25B had not progressed to the point that it was productive of any appreciable intelligence—not even enough to be pieced together by traffic analysis. The reason that *not one single* JN-25 decryption made prior to Pearl Harbor has ever been found or declassified is that no such decrypt ever existed. It simply was not within the realm of our combined cryptologic capability to produce a usable decrypt at that particular time.

A senior NSA historian, Donald M. Gish, has said that there was *some* penetration (few in number and confined to ship movement reports) but agrees that it didn't amount to "meaningful intelligence."

lic Cemetery in St. Helena, California. He and Gertrude had two daughters and one son. In 1995 he had remarried, to Evelyn Elliot-Whitlock (1923–2013).

Sources

Browne and McGinnis, *Communications Intelligence*, 23.
Budiansky, 253.
Costello, 323.
Donovan and Mack, 58.
Duane L. Whitlock (1917–2007), "Find a Grave Memorial," www.findagrave.com
Holtwick, 355, 360, 371, App. 118, 122, 145, 154, 161.
McGinnis, 200.
Prados, 214, 268–69, 507.
Stinnett, 72.

VICE ADMIRAL RUSSELL WILLSON, U.S. NAVY (1883–1948)

"Russ" "Fusser"

Russell Willson was an interesting and very capable officer—albeit one with a remarkable contradiction. He'd performed impressively as the first director of Naval Communications' new CSS, 1917–18, and during that same period invented an encryption device which was used, with modifications, for almost twenty years—these were both extremely important achievements for which he was rapidly promoted *and* awarded the prestigious Navy Cross. Moreover, his daughter also became a Navy cryptanalyst during World War II. But around 1919, Willson inexplicably "walked away from cryptology, calling the subject a professional dead-end" and for the rest of his career tended to disparage those who remained in the communications intelligence field.

*   *   *

From the 1906 Annapolis yearbook, *The Lucky Bag*:

A noble character, famed throughout for his fussing capabilities [*being smooth, careful, excessively concerned with unimportant matters*]. Makes a hit with the fair sex by his kindly manner in throwing them bouquets; has a large bill at the florists. Hasn't missed a hop [dance] since plebe year, and has dates enough ahead to keep him going for some time. Does a little in art. Declares he would rather be chairman of the hop committee than class president. With the aid of handkerchiefs attains a sylph-like form when fussing. Wears kid gloves to Steam [marine engineering] drill. [Activities: chairman, hop committee; Farewell Ball committee; *Lucky Bag* committee; chairman class crest committee]

*   *   *

Russell Willson was born on December 27, 1883, in Fredonia, New York. The son of Sidney Louis Willson and Lucy Fenton Staats Willson, "Russ" briefly attended MIT during 1901–1902, and unsuccessfully tried to obtain an appointment to West Point. He then went on to graduate from the U.S. Naval Academy in 1906, along with such classmates as Aubrey W. Fitch, Leigh Noyes, Frank Jack Fletcher, Milo F. Draemel, Isaac C. Kidd, John H. Towers, Fred F. **Rogers**, Robert L. Ghormley, and John S. McCain. After graduating from the academy as a "passed midshipman"—the usual scenario over a hundred years ago—Willson received a commission as an ensign in 1908. Subsequent promotions included lieutenant (junior grade), 1911; lieutenant, 1913; lieutenant commander, 1917; commander, 1918; captain, 1929; rear admiral, 1939; and vice admiral, 1942.

Mr. Willson served in the battleship USS *New York* during the 1914 Vera Cruz Incident in Mexico, and later as flag lieutenant to Adm. Henry Mayo, who was then commander in chief of the U.S. Atlantic Fleet.

Early during World War I, Lieutenant Willson organized and developed the U.S. Navy's CSS at Main Navy. Initially this was OP-58, the Confidential Publications Section, Division of Operations, Office of the CNO; later it became the CSS in the same division. He was charged with updating navy signals and codes, organizing critical functions of the Naval Communications System, and coordinating with the British Navy.

Mr. Willson also invented a new strip form of Thomas Jefferson's coding disk or wheel cylinder, to which he included fixed indices as a super-encipherment system. It was identified as the Navy Code Box (or Naval Cipher Box), commonly called the NCB.[1] He then oversaw production and fleet-wide distribution of the NCB as

---

1. First invented by Thomas Jefferson in 1795, this cipher did not become well known. It was independently invented by French Colonel Étienne Bazèries (as the "Bazèries Cylinder") almost a century later. A similar system was used by the U.S. Army from 1923 until 1942, known as the M-94. For the NCB's invention, in 1935 Willson was awarded $15,000 by the U.S. Congress in lieu of a patent. Interestingly, the paperwork for Willson's proposed award passed through various offices in Washington, including OP-20-GX, when young Lieutenant Tommy Dyer briefly was in charge of the office. For whatever reason,

well as some associated cryptographic systems. His very respectable contributions to secure signaling and cryptology helped bring about unusually rapid promotion to lieutenant commander (May 1917) and commander (July 1918)—as well as the award of the Navy Cross.

Commander Willson finished World War I service with the Sixth Battle Squadron of the Royal Navy's Grand Fleet, including special temporary duty in connection with signals.

In 1921, future vice admirals Russell Willson and Wilson Brown, and future marine general Holland Smith (among others), worked for the extremely astute Rear Adm. Clarence "Parson" Williams in the navy's War Plans Division; these officers recast *U.S. War Plan Orange*—including the first subsection focused upon Central Pacific operations against the Japanese. Later that same year Willson took command of the destroyer USS *Mason*.

In 1923, Russ was momentarily drawn back to the cryptology business. The CNO convened a board of former cryptographic officers to evaluate the Hebern Electric Cipher Machine, invented in California by a civilian entrepreneur named Edward Hebern. This board consisted of future vice admirals Willson and W. W. "Poco" Smith, as well as future rear admiral Royal Ingersoll; after some study and experimentation, they recommended the machine's adoption for the navy when perfected.

Willson attended the Naval War College later in 1924, and then served onboard the battleships *Florida* and *Pennsylvania*, 1925–1926. He was a member of the U.S. Naval Mission to Brazil from 1927 to 1930, during which time he was promoted to captain. In 1931 he was commander of Destroyer Division Ten, and in 1932 commanded Destroyer Division Six. From late 1932 through 1934, Willson was back at the Naval Academy as head of the Department of Seamanship and Navigation.

In 1935–1936, Captain Willson was commanding officer of the battleship *Pennsylvania*, which then was flagship of the Pacific Fleet under Adm. Joseph M. Reeves. There he met notable future linguists/cryptanalysts/intelligence analysts Eddie **Layton**, Tommy **Dyer**, and Ham **Wright** (in the ship's company), as well as Joe **Rochefort** (on the admiral's staff as intelligence officer). For a number of reasons, Willson and Rochefort took an immediate dislike to each other. Willson was smooth, dignified, genteel, and always well-groomed and careful in his speech; Rochefort held him in low esteem, thinking him pompous and "a stuffed shirt." On the other hand, Willson thought Rochefort brash, unpolished, and too full of himself working in an unimportant dead end field—and much too visible as Admiral Reeves's favorite protégé.

An incident illustrates the situation. Rochefort had been told by the Coast Guard that Japanese fishing boats off the fleet's San Pedro, California, anchorage were constantly radioing to each other in a code. Rochefort challenged Ham Wright—newly trained at OP-20-G—to figure it out. Working all through the night on intercepts

---

Dyer recommended disapproval. Dyer never knew whether or not Willson was aware of that action, but when the award was finally granted, Willson did make a great point of showing Dyer the $15,000 check he'd received while they were both on board the *Pennsylvania*.

provided by the Coast Guard, Wright solved it around dawn—and found nothing more insidious than shared intelligence as to locations of schools of fish. Totally exhausted, Wright missed a Saturday morning inspection and, perhaps unsurprisingly, Captain Willson was furious. Wright explained what he'd been doing; he then received a further dressing-down for "fooling around with that stuff." Still not sensing he held a completely losing hand, Wright tried to respectfully point out that the captain had once led OP-20-G, that he'd invented the Navy Code Box, and that he'd received the Navy Cross for his outstanding work in cryptology. Willson instantly snapped back, "Yes, but then I had the *good sense to get out!*" This is a remarkable insight into Willson's mind, and it's also very indicative of the general lack of regard (and even lack of respect) that cryptology and radio intelligence had in that period—particularly coming from an officer as experienced, knowledgeable, and capable as was Willson. Yet it's remarkable to consider that during World War II, Willson's daughter, Eunice Willson Rice, made her own reputation as a theoretical cryptanalyst at OP-20-G, particularly looking at German systems.

Concerning the friction between Captain Willson and Lieutenant Commander Rochefort, Willson was going to have two significant opportunities to put Rochefort in his place. In December 1939, Rochefort came up for promotion to commander. Willson was one of nine rear admirals on the selection board; despite an enormous number of open commander slots, Rochefort failed for selection. It's unclear exactly why this happened; there were several possible factors, but Rochefort came to believe that Willson likely convinced the other admirals that this impertinent officer—who had *not* attended Annapolis—was not commander material. What is very clear, however, is that in mid-1942, Willson had another opportunity to negatively influence Rochefort's career. After the Battle of Midway, Admiral Nimitz (CinCPac) and Rear Admiral Bagley (Commandant, Fourteenth Naval District) jointly recommended to Admiral King (CominCh, U.S. Fleet) that Rochefort be awarded the Distinguished Service Medal. Rear Admiral Willson, then King's chief of staff, submitted a lengthy memo in which he powerfully argued against the award; King, unfortunately for Rochefort—and to the irritation of Nimitz—concurred with his chief of staff with no further discussion.

During their mutual time onboard the *Pennsylvania*, future captain Tommy Dyer also had a fractious relationship with "Fusser." Dyer believed that his failure to promote to lieutenant commander (the first time) was due to a poor fitness report from Captain Willson. He had crossed Willson by identifying that the previous wardroom treasurer had apparently embezzled $2,000. As it turned out, that officer was indeed court-martialed, found guilty, and dismissed from the service, but Dyer sensed that Willson was clearly angry with *him* for bringing forth the issue—because it reflected poorly upon the ship—and thus upon her captain. Dyer lost further respect for Willson because he believed that Willson had also damaged the career of the ship's outstanding chief engineer (who had recently won the battleship division's "E" for engineering excellence) by inexplicitly giving him a poor fitness report—despite the award of the "E."

In any event, after Captain Willson left the command of the *Pennsylvania* in late 1936, he then moved on to serve for three years as naval attaché at the U.S. Embassy in London. He liked this posting to England; he later said, "There are a few shore jobs I'd rather have had, but not many."

Now a rear admiral, Willson became the last peacetime commander of Battleship Division One prior to the start of World War II. In May 1939, he relieved Rear Adm. Chester Nimitz as ComBatDivOne, and then in turn was relieved in January 1941 by his classmate Rear Adm. Isaac Kidd—who subsequently was killed onboard the division flagship, USS *Arizona*, during the Japanese attack on Pearl Harbor.

In early 1941, Willson became the superintendent of the U.S. Naval Academy. Then, after the start of World War II, Rear Adm. Willson (who had served on Adm. Henry Mayo's staff with Ernest J. King prior to World War I) became the chief of staff to King in his role as Commander in Chief, U.S. Fleet. A practical destroyer/ battleship seaman, he made solid contributions on King's staff, and was promoted to vice admiral in March 1942. However, during this time, he began to see a decline in his health.

In mid-1942, Willson looked into the navy's inspection service, and subsequently "blew the roof" off the Bureau of Ships—in the pressure of high-tempo production too many smaller vessels were being delivered incomplete or with poor workmanship, which was not being detected and corrected.

In August 1942, Willson was detached for duty with the Pacific Fleet; but, before he could report to his new assignment he was officially found medically unfit for sea. As a result, he was retired in January 1943 but was immediately recalled to active duty and retained in Washington, still on King's staff, for the duration of the war. He also served as the naval member of the influential Joint Strategic Survey Committee—a new "think tank" for the JCS. Willson participated in several of the wartime conferences between President Roosevelt and Prime Minister Churchill. Vice Admiral Willson was also a member of the U.S. delegation at the Dumbarton Oaks Conference in 1944, and then a military advisor at the San Francisco UN Conference on International Organization in 1945. He was relieved of all active duty in February 1946.

After World War II, Willson became an associate editor of *World Report*, which later became *U.S. News and World Report*.

An Episcopalian, Russell Willson had married Eunice Westcott Willson (1884–1962) in June 1911. They had one son, Russell, and two daughters, Eunice and Mary. Vice Admiral Willson passed away June 6, 1948, in Chevy Chase, Maryland. He and his wife, as well as Lt. Russell Willson Jr. (their only son, a naval aviator who died in an airplane crash in 1945), are buried together in the Naval Academy Cemetery at Annapolis.

In addition to his Navy Cross, Vice Adm. Willson was awarded two Distinguished Service Medals (from both the navy and the army), the Mexican Service Medal, the World War I Victory Medal, the American Defense Service Medal with Fleet Clasp, the American Campaign Medal, and the World War II Victory Medal.

Admiral Willson has also been recognized and honored, by the U.S. Naval Cryptologic Veterans Association, as an officer who has served as the Commander, Naval Security Group, or one of its predecessor organizations.

Sources

Browne and Carlson, *Echoes of Our Past*, 190.

Carlson, 28, 65–66.

Dorwart, *Conflict of Duty*, 139.

Dyer, 168–74.

Holtwick, *History of the NavSecGru*, 10, 12, 17–18, 23, 27, 157, 224–25, 376, 400, App. 1, 2, 9, 17.

Kahn, *Codebreakers*, 387, 418.

Layton, *"And I Was There,"* 49–50.

Lucky Bag, U.S. Naval Academy, 1906.

Morison, I, 116, 236.

Schmidt, Raymond P. "Russell Willson: Creative Cryptologist," in Browne, *Echoes of Our Past*, 3–10.

U.S. Navy, *Register of Commissioned and Warrant Officers*.

CAPTAIN WESLEY ARNOLD "HAM" WRIGHT, U.S. NAVY
(1902–1986)

The navy's second best codebreaker
A wizard at math
One of Rochefort's core group at Station HYPO
"Ham" "Hammy"

Endowed with extraordinary mathematical skills, Ham Wright was a natural to go into cryptology. A "broad-shouldered redhead with craggy features and big hands," he was often "rambunctious" and playful as well as unfailingly courteous. He bore a strong resemblance to Depression-era screen actor Wallace Berry. Once he abandoned general "black-shoe" surface-ship duties for cryptology, around age thirty, he apparently never looked back. He achieved incredibly valuable cryptanalytical contributions throughout the war and remained in the business for the rest of his working life. He was named, by both Laurance Safford (the "father of U.S. Navy cryptology") and Thomas Dyer ("the father of machine cryptanalysis") as among the navy's best codebreakers of the war, perhaps second only to Dyer.

* * *

From the 1926 Annapolis yearbook, *The Lucky Bag*:

> *Hammy* was a member of the Old Navy in the capacity of a yeoman. However, things around Crabtown [*Annapolis*] came natural to him and he soon found himself entirely at home. *Hammy* has most of the virtues of the men in blue, but he is not without his faults. He has his weaknesses, the outstanding one being the weaker sex, or more appropriately, the week-end sex. It is rather difficult to say whether the *femmes* have got him or whether he has the *femmes*. *Hammy* has set a pretty good stride in athletics but his love for chow overbalances his desire to become a second Jim Thorpe, and it is only after much endeavor that he has been able to break loose from his appetite and get down to actual participation. He has a natural gift for making friends, and his ready wit and quick response to an S.O.S. for help in math have placed him high in the estimation of his classmates. *Hammy* is the kind of fellow who never needs a friend because they are all his friends. With his natural genius for math he should easily be able to compete with the best of them in the Construction Corps, and we all hope that he makes his mark. [Activities: football, baseball]

* * *

Wesley A. Wright was born in Brooklyn, New York, in 1902. He initially enlisted in the navy and became a yeoman, serving three years onboard the battleship *Florida* before obtaining an appointment to the Naval Academy. He graduated in 1926 and was commissioned as an ensign, along with such classmates as C. Wade McClusky Jr., Maxwell F. Leslie, Henri de B. **Claiborne**, Ranson **Fullinwider**, Frank P. Pyzick, Howard W. Gilmore, Lofton R. Henderson, Robert B. Pirie, James S. Russell, Raymond S. **Lamb**, and Paul D. Stroop. Subsequent promotions were lieutenant (junior grade), 1929; lieutenant, 1936; lieutenant commander, 1941; commander, 1942; and captain, 1948.

Mr. Wright followed the usual intense sea-duty pattern for young officers in this period. He was onboard the battleship *Texas* from 1927 to 1928, and then transferred to the destroyer *Melvin* during 1929 through 1930. He moved to the destroyer *Alden* in 1931, followed by service as gunnery officer in the battleship *New York* during 1932.

But it was in 1929, when he was attached to the *Melvin*, that Wesley Wright found himself on a rifle range shared by Lt. Cmdr. Laurance **Safford**, who was then a fellow officer in a destroyer division. Ham had previously and easily solved a series of ciphers inserted in the navy's fleet-wide communications bulletins, placed there by Safford when he was head of OP-20-G. Unsurprisingly, Safford now had no great difficulty in convincing Wright that he should specialize in cryptology.

In fact, just a year later, U.S. Fleet Problem X found Tommy **Dyer** and Wesley Wright together in the Battle Fleet's radio_intelligence unit. Even though they had previously served together onboard the flagships *New Mexico* and *Pennsylvania*, this was the first time they had actually worked together. They had no success in solving the major "enemy" system, which employed some seventy-eight alphabets, because the intercepted traffic was too scanty for a solution to be found in the time available.

In early 1932, a similar communications-intelligence unit was formed for the flagship of one of the exercise fleets; this was right before the fleet departed the West Coast en route to Hawaii—off of which the Fleet Problem XIII maneuvers were to take place. The officers temporarily ordered onboard the *California* for this purpose were Lt. John **Harper** as well as Lts. j.g. Ham Wright and Jack **Holtwick**. They used material obtained by simulated intercept—being furnished copies of pertinent messages by the ship's radio room. During the maneuvers they had some success in solving the current contact code; more difficult and more significant was their complete break-in to the signal code cipher—which later caused a real-world cryptologic revision of the system.[1]

In June 1932, Cmdr. John **McClaran** (head of OP-20-G) nominated Wright to take the formal one-year course at Main Navy. "Wright has made more progress in cryptanalysis than any other officer in the Navy who has not had a special course of instruction in this subject." So, after Wright completed the general line officer postgraduate course, which he had started in 1932, he reported to OP-20-G in summer 1933—along with several others, including Lt. j.g. Lin **Howeth** and Lt. j.g. Ray **Lamb**.

In the summer of 1934, Wright had moved to the staff of OP-20-G under Cmdr. Howard **Kingman**. In July, Kingman and Wright met with the head of the Naval Postgraduate School (Capt. J. H. Newton) and some of his staff to discuss a plan to have promising cryptology students take some specialized math courses (such as statistics, correlation, and probability and chance), commuting between Washington and Annapolis. Jack Holtwick and Ham Wright were among the first to do this, during 1934 and 1935.

---

1. "Fleet Problem" was the term used by the U.S. Navy to describe each of twenty-one large-scale naval exercises conducted between 1923 and 1940. They were labeled with Roman numerals, running from Fleet Problem I through Fleet Problem XXI. A twenty-second Fleet Problem exercise, scheduled for 1941, was canceled because of the tensions before the start of World War II. The fleet problems were usually once-a-year exercises in which U.S. naval forces would engage in mock battles. One or more of the forces would play the part of a European or Asian navy. They were the culmination of the navy's annual training maneuvers.

Sometime after April 1935, Lt. j.g. Holtwick took over, from Lt. j.g. Wright, the supervision and installation of IBM equipment at OP-20-G. In addition, Holtwick completed the Research Desk cryptanalyst course of instruction and then took over—again from Wright—a task of systematically collecting and codifying the known but unrecorded data the section had on ten years' worth of Japanese crypto-logic systems. Holtwick later wrote that because of the tremendous workload—and low staffing levels—little time was spent

in maintaining a record of what had been done. Details of what had been solved, how they were solved, and what part each system played in the entire Japanese naval cryp-tographic system were available, if at all, only in the memory of Mrs. Agnes **Driscoll**. Fortunately, though, material . . . had accumulated over the years in a sort of "Fibber McGee's closet" in Room 1645, where odds-and-ends of incredible variety could be unearthed.

Lieutenant Wright had realized . . . the danger of having the entire background and continuity of a decade of effort available only in the brain cells of only one person. [His foreboding was forcefully proved warranted less than three years later when Mrs. Driscoll was seriously injured in an automobile accident in which two others were killed.]

Wright therefore set out systematically to identify each Japanese system of which we had any record, and to write a monograph containing all of the information he was able to accrue about it . . . Holtwick, who took over this task on Wright's transfer, drew heav-ily upon Mrs. Driscoll's memory, and validated her recollections by actual application of the cryptographic details she remembered to the traffic stored in the closet. He was thus able to bring up to date and continue Wright's project of publishing a complete history of each type of system which the Japanese Navy and Foreign Office had used up to that time.

In 1935, fresh from cryptanalysis training in Washington, Ham Wright joined Joe **Rochefort**, Tommy Dyer, and Eddie **Layton** on board the CinCUS flagship *New Mexico*. Then, the flag shifted to the battleship *Pennsylvania*. Rochefort and Wright were in the staff intelligence office (Rochefort was OIC); Dyer and Layton were in the ship's gunnery department. Shortly after Wright's arrival, Rochefort was in-formed by the Coast Guard that Japanese fishing boats off the fleet's San Pedro, Cali-fornia, anchorage were constantly radioing to each other in some kind of code. So, Rochefort challenged Wright—freshly trained at OP-20-G—to figure it out. Work-ing all through the night on intercepts provided by the Coast Guard, Ham solved it around dawn—and found nothing more insidious than shared intelligence as to locations of schools of fish. Totally exhausted, Wright missed a Saturday morning inspection, and the ship's captain, Russell **Willson**, was furious. Wright explained what he'd been doing; he then received a further dressing-down for "fooling around with that stuff." Still not sensing he held a completely losing hand, Wright tried to respectfully point out that the captain himself had once been in charge of OP-20-G, that he'd invented the "Navy Code Box," and that he'd received the Navy Cross for his outstanding work in cryptology. Willson instantly snapped back, "Yes, but then I had the *good sense to get out!*"

In April 1937, Wright was still in the CinCUS communications-intelligence unit, but now under Lt. Cmdr. John Harper. Fourteen months later he returned to Main Navy, to relieve Lt. Wayne N. Gamet in charge of the Statistical Section, OP-20-GYR.

By late 1938, out in Pearl Harbor, Tommy Dyer was working on the new Japanese "Black Book" code, and Ham Wright was also working on it at OP-20-G. Wright made a "first entry," but with an error. Dyer was able to straighten it out—an incredible five-thousand-mile collaboration via encrypted messages—to get a firm entry into the basic code.

In spring 1939, OP-20-GYT (Training) and GYR (Research) were reformed as GR (Research and Training) under Lieutenant Wright, assisted by Lt. j.g. M. S. Holmes.

In January 1940, Cmdr. Laurance Safford (again head of OP-20-G) wrote to the assistant director of naval communications, hoping to get support for several officers going up for promotion—including Wright.

> Wright is one of the Navy's outstanding cryptanalysts. He has exceptional natural ability as a mathematician. He had 3½ years duty in communications intelligence, and has contributed materially to the solution of foreign codes and ciphers. Also had 2 years duty in the "security unit" on the staff of CINCUS—all of which was devoted to defensive measures to protect and improve our own systems. He designed the signal cipher and ECM cipher now in use. Was "drafted" from the P.G. Ordnance Course after one year to become a cryptanalyst.

In May 1940, Lieutenant Wright issued what was apparently intended to be the first of a series: "Communications Intelligence Enlisted Personnel Letter #1-1940." In it he pointed out problems managing equal-length tours, a tentative slate for cryptographic personnel, and the like. But then he left OP-20-GR in mid-June 1940, assigned to the light cruiser *Philadelphia*, flagship of Cruiser Division Eight.

Then, in December 1940 at OP-20-G's request, the Bureau of Navigation transferred Mr. Wright from the *Philadelphia* to the CINCUS staff—as well as transferring Lt. John **Williams** from the destroyer *Craven*. Thus, they both moved to the CINCUS intelligence unit, and then to the Fourteenth Naval District's COMINT unit (Station HYPO) in February or March 1941, although their movements and postings are a little confusing at this point.

> Lt. Cmdr. Ham Wright and Lt. Johnny Williams, while technically attached to the CinCPac staff, were assigned by the Fleet Communications Officer (Capt. Maurice "Germany" Curts) to work with the 14th District communications-intelligence unit. Mr. Wright worked with Lt. Cmdr. Tommy Dyer, and Mr. Williams with Lt. Cmdr. Thomas **Huckins**. In fact, though there were no formal orders assigning them, they became so much a part of the unit that they were assigned to coding duty in the Navy Yard Communications Office prior to 18 October, when the unit began standing its own duty.

By early 1941, the "AD" or Japanese administrative code (the "admiral's" or "flag-officers' code") was the main assignment of Station HYPO cryptanalysts Dyer, Holtwick, and Wright—to their continual, enormous frustration. It was so little used that the cryppies had insufficient intercepted material to study. In fact, it was the only Japanese code never broken by the Allies ("nobody *ever* got into this thing"). Dyer and Wright asked to be relieved of this task and to be assigned to the dominant Japanese operational code, JN-25b. However, Commander Safford believed that the AD could be broken, and so Station CAST (Corregidor) and Station NEGAT (Washington) were to focus on JN-25, and HYPO's skilled cryptanalysts were needed to stay on AD, for Safford felt if it could be broken the value would be incredible.

So, as of June 1941, Mr. Wright was in the Fourteenth Naval District's communications-intelligence unit, but attached to the CinCPac staff. A few months later, Wright appears as one of the few (eighteen) officers officially documented by Laurance Safford as "qualified and acceptable" for COMINT and cryptology.

On the morning of December 7, 1941, Lt. Cmdr. Ham Wright and Lt. John Williams were having breakfast at the Pearl Harbor submarine base galley, getting ready to go on duty at 0800. Upon hearing gunfire and explosions, Williams ran outside, and then "Johnny came back in and said, 'They're out there with the oranges'" on their wings. They then "dashed over to headquarters, dodging all the rifle fire. All the sailors were out from the sub base, shooting rifles at these planes, hand guns, and anything they could get ahold of."

Station HYPO's main, modern direction-finding unit, the big CXK unit at Lualualei, was—incredibly—suffering technical difficulties on December 7, and so it was offline—leaving only the older models operational. Toward the end of the attack, Wright placed a call to Lt. Cmdr. Eddie Layton (the fleet intelligence officer) to report they had a DF bearing on Japanese radio signals—but it was from one of the older, bilateral systems, which could only give a two-way reading. Thus, the enemy was bearing either 363 degrees or 183 degrees—not very useful even if the Americans had had any assets to deploy right then.

Right after the Pearl Harbor attack, Safford went ahead and allowed HYPO to work on JN-25b, and by early March 1942, the ability of Tommy Dyer and Ham Wright to read more and more of the code was growing. In late May they were recovering about a third of the code groups—compared with only around one-fifth in April. It wasn't very easy, and they knew it wouldn't be. In an oral history that Ham did years later he commented that:

> The Blue-Book preceded JN-25. [It was] in force for about four years. We did pretty good with that. Then they dropped it and went into that numerical thing [JN-25] and we had a hell of a time getting into that.

On May 20, Station HYPO intercepted Admiral Yamamoto's final operations order for the Midway offensive, and practically the entire staff jumped on it. On that fateful occasion Wright, ready to leave after a twelve-hour shift, stayed on to work the time-date groups. Joe **Finnegan** had brought the part with date-time cipher to Wright, and said "Ham, we're stuck on the date and time." Shaking off his fatigue, Wright sat at an empty desk in the traffic analysis section, and took the garbled text as well as the three previous uses of the cipher (one of them in a message that had led to the Battle of the Coral Sea). Wright put four people on a search for other instances of the cipher, and he and Finnegan got to work. For a good while a flaw in one corrupt cryptogram frustrated their efforts, but as the night wore on Wright worked it out.

> He discovered that the date-and-time cipher comprised a polyalphabetic with independent mixed-cipher alphabets and with the exterior plain and key alphabets in two different systems of Japanese syllabic writing—one the older, formal *kata kana*, the other the cursive *hira gana*. Each has 47 syllables, making the polyalphabetic tableau a gigantic one of 2,209 cells.
>
> By about 5:30 the next morning, he had a solution. His inability to apply symmetry of position to the unrelated alphabets gave it a certain amount of slack, but he regarded it as essentially sound. He showed it to [Cmdr. Joe] Rochefort. That expert noted the weak spots and said to Wright, in mock rebuke, "I can't send this out."
>
> "If you don't," Wright replied firmly, "I will." Rochefort laughed. He'd only been testing Wright's faith in the solution, and Wright knew it. "Go ahead," he said.
>
> Wright took it up to communications for transmission, via the COPEK channel, to the other COMINT units. He then headed once again for home, and on the way saw Eddie Layton about 7:45 and told him about it. Within hours, Admiral Nimitz knew that the Japanese had ordered that the Midway operation was to commence June 2 against the Aleutian Islands and June 3 against Midway atoll. [Layton's] intelligence staff had [earlier] forecasted correctly—but what a relief it was to know for sure; to work on fact instead of theory.

Various historians have given credit to Tommy Dyer for helping, but he said in a 1983 interview that he had *not*. He did comment that as the internal time-date cipher had appeared in Japanese messages only three times, Finnegan's and Wright's solution was "a brilliant piece of work." To find the essential missing date, "Lieutenant Commanders Wright and Finnegan stayed up all night in the Dungeon, trying to crack the various layers of encipherment in the messages. At 5:30 the next morning, Wright reported to Rochefort that . . . the attack would begin on June 4th, Tokyo time." They were correct, though the Japanese later postponed the attack by one day.[2]

For months there had been a growing conflict between OP-20-G (Station NEGAT) and Station HYPO concerning interpretations of intercepts and enemy intentions. By the spring of 1942 it had become both amazing and tragic. In fact, during the run-up before the Battle of Midway it actually became bitter, ugly, and even personal. Perhaps the most obvious and important example was the disagreement over the identity of the Japanese code-designator "AF" as Midway or somewhere else. "It was a mess," wrote Ham Wright later on. "We would fight with OP-20-G all the time; we could not get together." It became a feud and a war of words. "Some of it was not too polite," he said. "Washington wanted to take complete charge and

---

2. Although most histories want to give Wright the lion's share of credit for this work—similar to what I wrote earlier—in an interview long after the war Wright himself generously said, "Finnegan worked that out," and did not elucidate his own role. (Finnegan would appear to agree, saying in a postwar oral history, "I solved it.")

tell us what to do in detail, but Rochefort would have no part of it." Wright was briefly sent to Washington to try to hammer out a truce. "It boiled down to who was going to do the work and who was going to get the credit," he recalled. "The NEGAT (OP-20-G) cryptanalysts did not want to trust *our* additives and would not use them. This attitude reached down to OP-20-G's radio operators—the lists we sent in would often wind up in the waste basket. It was very easy to get additives wrong. We were certainly most reluctant to trust *theirs*, so we worked out our own."

During the April 1943 incident which led to the shoot-down and death of the commander of the Japanese Combined Fleet, Adm. Yamamoto Isoroku, it was HYPO which had "engendered what is probably the most spectacular single incident ever to result from cryptanalysis." They intercepted Yamamoto's inspection-tour itinerary message, immediately recognized its importance due to the many address-ees, broke the code which was the current edition of JN-25, and then translated it. Wright figured out the meaning of its internal geographic code groups. After considerable discussion and thought, Admiral Nimitz decided to act upon it. (See Appendix N, "Operation VENGEANCE.")

In early 1942 Wright had occupied quarters near the submarine base—very close to CinCPac headquarters at that time. His place

> served as a kind of ersatz lounge for the basement crew. Wright himself idled away many hours listening to his opera records, very often with a lot of company. Refugees from the "Dungeon"—sometimes even Admiral Nimitz—routinely dropped in to listen to his records and play the slot machine he had on the premises. Wright maintained an "open house for everyone to come in, any time of day, play the slot machine, have a drink and leave a quarter" recalled HYPO linguist Lt. John Roenigk.

Then, for a time Wright shared a small house with Alva **Lasswell** and Tom Steele in Makalapa officer housing, just down from Admiral Nimitz's house and four hundred yards from CinCPac headquarters. All three loved to play chess and would while away some of their rare downtime with this activity—while also drinking Old Fashioneds.

An oft-repeated story details how one day Ham Wright was invited, along with Tommy Dyer and Tom Steele, for an afternoon's rest at Admiral Nimitz's beach house on Oahu's north shore. Nimitz decided to just sit in the sun, but another guest, Admiral Raymond Spruance, took the HYPO officers on a mile-long beach walk with an equivalent and exhausting swim back. At least one piece of business was covered: Spruance wanted to better understand the periodic blackouts that occurred when the Japanese changed codes. He thought there ought to be a way to have U.S. operations timed to go only when the codes were being solidly read; however, Dyer and Wright taught him some of the nuances of the challenge, including how unpre-dictable such code changes were.

At HYPO, which was beginning to be called FRUPac, Tommy Dyer and Ham Wright got a start in the Japanese "Maru Code" (merchant ship code), and then turned it over to the unit's outstanding Coast Guard cryptanalyst, Lt. Cmdr. Henry M. **Anthony**, for complete exploitation.

Later in 1943, OP-20-G (at that time headed by Capt. Earl E. **Stone**) transferred Commander Wright back to Main Navy and replaced him at FRUPac with a reserve lieutenant commander with relatively little experience. As lead cryptanalyst, Dyer was, unsurprisingly, stunned. Wright "was my great support," Dyer later told an interviewer. "From that day on, for some reason, I never had a great deal of love for Earl Stone."

In 1944, Ham was assigned as OIC of the Naval Communications Station Bainbridge Island, Washington, where he was very involved in the training of enlisted cryptologic personnel. He was relieved by Cmdr. John **Lietwiler** in April 1946.

He then returned to Washington and served in OP-20-G at the Nebraska Avenue building, where it had moved from the old Main Navy. Wright's next assignment was as commanding officer of the Naval Communications Facility at Yokosuka, Japan. He was instrumental in that organization's move to Kami Seya; in December 1952, U.S. Naval Radio Receiving Facility Kami Seya was completed, and the Security Group Department and general-service receivers were also moved there. Shortly thereafter the rest of NavComFac Yokosuka also moved to that site.

Captain Wright then headed the AFSA, Far East. Captain Dyer was sent out to Tokyo to relieve him—but Wright was suddenly returned to the United States due to a diagnosis of stomach cancer—fortunately it was a false alarm, but it also meant that they had no face-to-face turnover.

Moving back to Washington, Ham worked first at the AFSA headquarters, and then at the NSA. From 1954 to 1956 he served as chief of the NSA Field Detachment, Pacific. He then returned to Washington, where he retired in 1957.

In the mid-1960s, both Tommy Dyer and Ham Wright were interviewed by David Kahn for Kahn's monumental book *The Codebreakers*. They were both subsequently censured by the director of naval intelligence for giving up too much information. This was a little ironic as they both had initially tried to bow out from the request but were pressured into it by the Defense Department's Office of Public Affairs. Fortunately, nothing came of it, for they had been careful to only discuss things that were already in the public record.

During the war, and then later, Capt. Joe Rochefort always attributed HYPO's 1942 successes not to himself, but to the fact that he was given the cream of naval communications personnel. In fact, he named his "key staff" as Dyer, Wright, Finnegan, Lasswell, Huckins, and Williams. "So the organization in Pearl, beginning in the fall of 1941 and extending until the time I left there—these people were the pick of the crop. [Among these] I had Dyer and a fellow named 'Ham' Wright—these [were] cryptanalysts and just about as good as they come."

Forrest "Tex" **Biard**, a HYPO linguist who came to the unit in September 1941 and who eventually retired as a captain after the war, later wrote that one of the "top five 'greats' at HYPO was Wesley A. Wright, better known as 'Ham'. . . . Ham worked with and under Tom Dyer . . . solving many knotty problems in the codebreaking area."

Historian Ronald Lewin described Tommy Dyer as one of the very few "top" codebreakers in the U.S. Navy. Dyer essentially agreed, saying, "I think, without any false modesty, that—in cryptanalysis only—I was 'number one.'" The only person that I know of that came close to me in cryptanalysis was Ham Wright."

Capt. Laurance Safford, the "father of U.S. naval cryptology," agreed when he called Ham Wright the wartime navy's second-best codebreaker.

In the early 1980s, Wright put in considerable effort helping Rear Adm. Edwin Layton (and his coauthors) work on Layton's reminisces, *"And I Was There": Pearl Harbor and Midway—Breaking the Secrets.*

Among Captain Wright's awards and decorations are two Legion of Merit medals, one of which was for his World War II contributions. In addition, he has been recognized and honored, by the U.S. Naval Cryptologic Veterans Association, as a Pioneer Officer of U.S. Naval Cryptology.

Ham Wright passed away in January 1986. He had been married to Elizabeth Oulahan Wright (1903–2003); they are buried together in Arlington National Cemetery.

Sources

Biard, 151–58.

Carlson, 65, 72, 97, 104, 120, 187–88, 191, 198, 206–7, 245, 260–61, 303, 325, 346–47, 445, 520.

Donovan and Mack, 63, 106, 144, 149–50, 156, 163, 279.

Dyer, 97, 195, 244, 250–51, 254, 257, 281–82, 308–9, 331–32.

Farago, *Broken Seal*, 106, 164.

Holmes, 94, 135, 167.

Holtwick, 51, 94, 102–3, 113, 134–35, 138, 153, 160, 176, 182, 212, 268, 305, 326, 339, 352–53, 363, 367–68, 408, 420, 428, 432, 433, 439, 446, App. 91–92.

Kahn, *Codebreakers*, 562, 564, 570, 595.

Layton, *"And I Was There,"* 6, 49–50, 94, 316–17, 413–14, 474.

Prados, 69, 315, 318–19, 408, 412.

Rochefort, 103.

Smith, *Emperor's Codes*, 140.

Symonds, 188.

Toll, 386.

REAR ADMIRAL RICHARD DEWEY ZERN, U.S. NAVY (1905–1958)

"Dick"

Dick Zern, like many of the officers under consideration here, balanced a traditional "black shoe" surface-ship career with several contributory tours of duty in communications intelligence. A cryptologist rather than a linguist or intelligence officer, he curiously doesn't seem to have done much cryptanalysis after initial training, and once the war began he served almost exclusively in surface warfare operations.[1] Yet, after the war, navy superiors had the confidence to assign him communications electronics duties at the JCSs level, to lead Naval Communications' security division—and to lead the early Navy Security Group.

* * *

From the 1927 Annapolis yearbook, *The Lucky Bag*:

> It has been said by a critic of speech makers that a fast talker as a speech maker is more enjoyed than a slow talker. *Dick* always has something to say about everything and he gets it over in a very short time—but it is always good, sensible stuff, coming from sound, well-trained material above the shoulders. *Dick* has a wonderful way of making friends. Knowing everybody in a class of 600 is quite an accomplishment—*Dick* does. He is full of ready wit and humor, and has a pleasing and attractive personality which makes everyone like him. He is gifted with much pep and fight, and is always found engaging in some form of athletics. Like most of us, he has had his difficulties with the Academic Department, but by sheer grit and hard, well-directed effort, he has shown that he has in him the qualities which tend to make a leader of men. In his uniform of blue, and brass buttons, with his golden hair shining, and his blue eyes at full power, *Dick* has raised havoc among the fair sex in every port and every hop [dance] that he visits. His two pet worries are getting fat and bilging [flunking out], but by hard workouts in the gym and study hours he has given us a more enjoyable four years here at the Academy by being our loyal classmate. A firm believer in naval traditions and customs, one may rest assured that *Dick* will be a credit to his country, flag, and the Navy. [Activities: track, swimming, Glee Club, *Lucky Bag* staff, choir]

* * *

Richard D. Zern was born in Viola, Illinois, on January 10, 1905, the son of John G. and Nellie Dewey Zern. He attended Western Illinois State Teachers College at Macomb, Illinois, for over a year before entering the U.S. Naval Academy. He was graduated and commissioned an ensign in June 1927, along with such classmates as George W. Anderson, Glynn "Donc" Donaho, Lee W. **Parke**, U. S. Grant Sharp, Gill M. **Richardson**, and Jack S. **Holtwick**. Further promotions included lieutenant (junior grade), 1930; lieutenant, 1936; lieutenant commander, 1941; commander 1942; and captain, 1945. He retired in 1957 and was simultaneously promoted to rear admiral on the retired list—on the basis of a high decoration for service in combat during World War II.

After graduation, he remained at Annapolis for a two-month course in aviation ground training. He then reported to the battleship *Arizona*, serving in the gunnery

---

1. Zern's Annapolis classmate Capt. Jack Holtwick, in his detailed history of the Naval Security Group prior to World War II, identifies Zern as one of eighteen naval officers who were "qualified and acceptable" as cryptologists as of October 1941. But, interestingly, he is *not* one of the five who had gone on record as "not desiring further C.I. duty."

department. He transferred to the destroyer *Corry* in 1928 as communications officer—with additional duties as ship's service officer and assistant gunnery officer. In February 1930, the *Corry* was decommissioned, and Zern moved to the destroyer *Broome* with essentially the same duties.

From June 1931 until May 1933, Lt. j.g. Zern was on board the battleship *New York*, serving as watch and division officer, ship's secretary, and anti-aircraft battery junior officer. During the following year he was assigned to the submarine tender *Holland* as watch and division officer, second deck officer, and five-inch gun officer.

In the summer and fall of 1934, Mr. Zern was at Main Navy, where he undertook instruction as a cryptanalysis student at OP-20-G; he was subsequently selected for the advanced class in December 1934. He then served some duty in the Division of Naval Communications, but in June 1936 he was assigned to the light cruiser *Milwaukee* as radio and signal communications officer as well as watch and division officer.

In 1937 Lieutenant Zern was designated as flag lieutenant and aide to the commander of Battleship Division Two, and then in January 1938 he began a similar assignment with the Commander Battleships, Battle Force, attached successively to flagships *Arizona*, *Maryland*, *Tennessee*, and *West Virginia*.

In July 1939, Zern returned to Main Navy and to OP-20-GC, relieving Lt. Bernard F. **Roeder**, in charge of designing and producing specialized naval cryptologic publications.

October 1941 saw Lieutenant Commander Zern embarked onboard the SS *President Van Buren*, en route to the Philippine Islands and the U.S. Asiatic Fleet. In November he reported to the light cruiser *Marblehead* as navigator. Soon after the Japanese attack on Pearl Harbor, the *Marblehead* and other American warships joined with ships of the Royal Netherlands Navy and the Royal Australian Navy to patrol the waters surrounding the Netherlands East Indies and to screen Allied shipping moving south from the Philippines. Subsequently, the *Marblehead* was heavily damaged at the Battle of Makassar Strait. As a result, with Mr. Zern onboard, the cruiser began what turned out to be a sixteen-thousand-mile voyage to New York— via South Africa—searching for sufficient dry dock facilities; the first half of the voyage was done without use of the rudder, necessitating steering by engines alone.

During the period August 1942 through May 1945, Commander and then Captain Zern served successively as aide and flag secretary to the Commander, Battleship Division Six; Commander, Battleships, Pacific Fleet; and Commander, Battleship Squadron Two. In these assignments he was attached to the flagships *Washington*, *Massachusetts*, *North Carolina*, and *South Dakota*. In addition, during August and September 1943, he served as surface operations officer on the staff of the Commander, Carrier Division Eleven. Involved in numerous actions against the enemy, Dick was awarded the Legion of Merit with the Combat "V" device.

Captain Zern returned to the United States in May 1945, and after brief duty in Washington at the Bureau of Naval Personnel, he was designated as OIC of the Navy Unit, Armed Forces Radio Service, at Los Angeles. In that capacity he was concerned with producing, recording, and distributing radio transmissions for its Broadcast Center—programs consisting of information, education, and entertainment for U.S. forces serving outside the continental limits of the United States. Detached in June 1947, he then became a student at the Naval War College in Newport, graduating the next year along with Cmdr. Gilven M. **Slonim**.

In June 1948, Captain Zern assumed command of the fleet oiler *Chikaskia* and was tasked to transport bulk petroleum products from the Persian Gulf to U.S. activities in Sicily, Ceylon, and Japan. He then returned to Washington for duty as the Chief of Naval Communications coordinator with the Joint Communications-Electronics Committee (of the JCS).

From February through April 1952, Zern was head of the Security Branch, Naval Communications Division, as well as head of the Naval Security Group.

In May he was placed in command of Destroyer Squadron Four as well as De-stroyer Division Forty-One. In October 1953, he began an assignment as chief of staff and aide to the Commander, Training Command, U.S. Atlantic Fleet.

Captain Zern's last assignment was as the professor of naval science, with the Naval Reserve Officers Training Corps, at the University of Michigan at Ann Arbor. He retired in June 1957, and was simultaneously promoted to rear admiral due to his high-level combat decoration during World War II.

Richard D. Zern had an elder brother, Shelton C. Zern, who was a marine of-ficer—Naval Academy class of 1923. Like Dick, he also studied cryptanalysis at OP-20-G during the early 1930s, and he was subsequently stationed in the Far East. Shelton had additionally applied for ONI's Japanese language/culture immersion program, but for whatever reason was not accepted. In 1947, subsequent to World War II service, Shelton was promoted to full colonel. He passed away in 1959, one year after his brother.

Dick Zern was married to the former Thelda Irene Burnett of Long Beach, California. The couple had one son, Richard B. Zern. In February 1958, Admiral Zern passed away at Ann Arbor where the family had remained in retirement; Mrs. Zern died a decade later in 1968. They are buried together at Arlington National Cemetery.

Rear Admiral Zern has been specifically recognized and honored, by the U.S. Na-val Cryptologic Veterans Association, as an officer who served in charge of the Naval Security Group or one of its predecessor organizations.

Sources

Browne and McGinnis, *Communications Intelligence*, 230–31.
Holtwick, 113, 138, 148, 153, 320, 439.
Lucky Bag, U.S. Naval Academy, 1927.
Rear Adm. Richard D. Zern, USN: Official Biography. Navy Office of Information, Biographies Branch, February 25, 1958. Courtesy of Naval Historical Foundation.
U.S. Navy, *Register of Commissioned and Warrant Officers.*

The Blue Sky Merchants

Linguists, Translators, and Intelligence Officers

CAPTAIN FORREST ROSECRANS "TEX" BIARD, U.S. NAVY
(1912–2009)

Served at Stations HYPO, NEGAT, and FRUMel
One of the first combat radio-interception officers on board a flagship
"Tex" "Jack"

Passing away at age ninety-six in 2009, Forrest Biard was the last surviving prewar trained Japanese crypto-linguist of the U.S. Navy's World War II codebreaking organizations. He underwent ONI's full-immersion language and culture course from 1939 to 1941. He then affiliated with Station HYPO at Pearl Harbor, transferred to Station NEGAT (OP-20-G) in Washington, and finally was attached to Station

FRUMel at Melbourne. In early 1942 he was among the first to lead small radio-interception units on board Pacific Fleet flagships in combat. Described as intense and somewhat abrasive, he didn't always gel with superiors; nevertheless, he was always a sharp, knowledgeable, and high-performing analyst.[1] Captain Biard retained a lifelong fascination with the Japanese language and Japanese military history, yet after the war he turned his focus to engineering, nuclear engineering, and physics— ultimately teaching physics at the college level.

*   *   *

From the 1934 Annapolis yearbook, *The Lucky Bag*:

> *Jack* arrived at the Naval Academy the morning of June 19, 1930 with a letter from the Navy Department telling him he couldn't get in, but he got in anyway. On the way in he was told to leave all guns and spurs and boots at the main gate. He missed them terribly for a while, but he soon became accustomed to eating at a table instead of a chuck wagon, and at the end of three years he had almost forgotten about the cactus and mesquite of his native state. We have often wondered how he managed to pull himself away from the cactus-covered plains of the cow country to see what the Navy had to offer and those of us who know can tell how fondly he still remembers those good old days in the state where men are six feet tall (except *Jack*, who has long regretted being a sandblower [short]) . . . Second Class Year, before it ended, found him giving more than due share to Radio and Radio Stations. Between Radio Stations and the weight loft in the gym, it is almost impossible to find *Jack* in the off hours. . . . The end of Second Class Year found this young man from Texas taking voyages in the Merchant marine on leave. He says he wants to be a sailor" [Activities: expert rifleman]

*   *   *

Forrest R. Biard was born on December 21, 1912, in Bonham, Texas, son of Robert J. and Forest Lynn Biard. The family moved to Dallas when he was eleven years old, and he graduated from North Dallas High School before entering the Naval Academy in 1930. He graduated high in his class and was commissioned an ensign in 1934, along with such distinguished classmates as Jackson D. Arnold, Bernard A. Clarey, John J. Hyland, Victor H. Krulak, Richard H. O'Kane, and John G. **Roenigk**. Subsequent promotions included lieutenant (junior grade), 1937; lieutenant, 1941; lieutenant commander, 1943; and commander, 1944. In 1955 he left the naval service and was simultaneously promoted to captain, on the retired list, by reason of a World War II combat citation pursuant to Title 10, U.S. Code, Section 6150.

Typically for the time period, Ensign Biard went to sea immediately after graduation, at first serving onboard the heavy cruiser *New Orleans* from 1935 to 1937. There he rubbed shoulders with Lt. Joseph **Finnegan**, who inspired Biard and

---

1. Many years after the war Rear Adm. Edwin Layton claimed Biard as a colleague and a friend— which is a pretty strong endorsement from an extremely noteworthy superior.

turned his interest toward Japanese language studies. Mr. Biard then transferred to the destroyer *Manley* and remained there until his selection for ONI's full-immersion Japanese language and culture course. He thus went to Japan, and in theory he would have stayed there around three years, but because of the rising tensions as war approached he left in September 1941. This was almost a year early—he was pushed out of the country along with several other fellow students by naval attaché Cmdr. Henri **Smith-Hutton**. Biard helped the last ten of the group escape, getting them to the port of Kobe to board a Japanese liner—using Tex's Model-A Ford and a large supply of "tinned" gasoline.

Lieutenant Biard then reported to Station HYPO at Pearl Harbor, along with Lt. Allyn Cole, Lt. j.g. Gilven **Slonim**, Lt. j.g. John Roenigk, Lt. j.g. Arthur Benedict, Lt. j.g. John Bromley, and Marine Capt. Bankson **Holcomb**. Biard always remembered his first day in "The Dungeon"—the basement rooms where HYPO was then located. The OIC, Cmdr. Joe **Rochefort**, took his new linguists over to where Capt. "Red" **Lasswell** and Lt. Cmdr. "Fully" **Fullinwider** were working and said, only partially kidding, "Gentlemen, here are your desks. Start breaking Japanese codes." The new linguists faced an enormous challenge. "Fortunately," Biard later said, "my desk was near Rochefort's. People in the basement came to him with problems or just to discuss the day's developments. By eavesdropping on these conversations I learned much."

Among other initial tasks that Rochefort assigned his new radio intelligence officers was handling the OP-20-G-mandated priority to listen for the Japanese "East Wind, Rain" execute message—which presumably would indicate an imminent break in U.S.-Japan relations. Thus, on November 29, Rochefort sent Slonim, Bromley, Cole, and Biard to the intercept site at He'eia to stand round-the-clock watches solely to listen for the message—which apparently never was transmitted. As it turned out, Slonim had just been relieved by Biard when the Pearl Harbor attack began on December 7.

In early 1942, Rochefort was directed to detach some of his key men to form afloat radio intercept units with various task forces. As valuable as this initiative turned out to be, HYPO acutely felt the loss of these highly trained specialists.[2] Thus, from February 15 to May 27, Tex and a small group of radiomen were temporarily assigned to the carrier *Yorktown*—Biard as the radio intelligence officer. Biard shortly fell into conflict with his boss, Task Force 17 commander Rear Adm. Frank Jack Fletcher. He refused Fletcher's request to brief the entire staff on the nature of the highly secret communications-intelligence mission.

2. According to Capt. Jasper Holmes, "When the first radio intelligence teams proved valuable to the carrier task force commanders, the argument became academic. FRUPac had to provide the service, and the only way to do it was gracefully and efficiently. The radio operators could pick up the earliest signs of alarm at the target of a raid, and the language officer could gauge the magnitude of the defending forces by the flow of radio traffic. Armed with a list of the major Japanese units' radio calls, the team also had the potential ability to detect the presence of major Japanese naval forces within strategic distance. Radio intelligence teams with the task forces could sometimes copy Japanese messages that escaped the shore-based intercept station."

To do so would have been a clear violation of security measures designed to protect [such "ULTRA" sources and methods]. Though Biard was clearly in the right, Fletcher did not relish being defied by a lowly lieutenant, and the exchange appears to have poisoned [their] relationship before it ever had a chance to develop.

Onboard the *Yorktown*, Biard participated in several small strikes in the South Pacific, and then was of course present at the significant Battle of the Coral Sea, May 4–8, 1942. During this action, after the sinking of the Japanese carrier *Shōhō*, Admiral Fletcher decided to retire his force to the south and assess the situation. Utilizing several radio sources, Lieutenant Biard analyzed that the Japanese carriers were off to the east and within range, but as he could neither determine an *exact* bearing nor distance he failed to convince the admiral to launch aircraft. It didn't help that "Fletcher and the intense and abrasive Biard did not get along well." Lieutenant Biard had identified that the enemy carriers were on a course of 280 degrees and were at speed of 20 knots, and therefore felt it was quite possible to deduce their location. However, Admiral Fletcher chose to believe the analysis of Lieutenant Commander Fullinwider, onboard the carrier *Lexington*, rather than Lieutenant Biard's; unfortunately, Fully had mistranslated the key interception—and thus an opportunity for a decisive strike was lost to the Americans. Later, both the *Lexington* and *Yorktown* were aggressively attacked; luckily Fullinwider and his unit escaped injury when the *Lexington* had to be abandoned prior to her sinking. Although she was badly damaged, the *Yorktown* did not have to be abandoned and was able to return to Hawaii.

Back at Pearl Harbor, Lieutenant Commander Fullinwider replaced Lieutenant Biard on the *Yorktown*. After rapid repairs were made on the carrier, she sailed to her own destiny at the extraordinary Battle of Midway during the first week of June.

Mr. Biard returned to the Station HYPO "dungeon" and essentially worked there on translations and cryptanalysis for around fourteen months. When the first contingent of "Boulder Boys" arrived at Pearl Harbor in 1943, Tex was put in charge of them and began to organize a translation and interrogation center. These new linguists were recent graduates of ONI's Japanese/Oriental Language School at the University of Colorado at Boulder.[3] In the summer, newly promoted Lieutenant Commander Biard sent seven of these officers to Vice Adm. Thomas Kinkaid, the Commander, North Pacific Force, for duty in the Aleutian Islands.

In August 1943, Tex himself was briefly transferred to OP-20-G (Station NEGAT) in Washington. Later in the fall he was sent back out to the Pacific and attached to Station FRUMel at Melbourne for further translation and cryptanalysis work. At first he was not happy there, immediately developing a remarkable dislike for the OIC, Cmdr.

---

3. In the fall of 1941, realizing that their outstanding and progressive Japanese full-immersion program had not generated nearly enough linguists and cultural experts, ONI started a Japanese-language training program at Harvard University and the University of California. It then was moved to the University of Colorado at Boulder in July 1942. In fact, ONI Deputy Director Ellis **Zacharias** spoke at the graduation ceremony of the first class of the school, in July 1943, in Boulder's Mackey Auditorium; one of several speakers, Zach confounded many of the 142 graduates "with a rapid-fire speech in Japanese—that he then translated for the broader audience." By the war's end, around 1,200 men and women had gone into the program.

Rudy **Fabian**, and Fabian's deputy, Cmdr. John **Lietwiler**. Biard, known to be a bit prickly himself, found the two commanders particularly unpleasant and even abusive. Fortunately for him they were shortly changed-out in routine rotations, which in his opinion created a much better command climate.[4] All unpleasantness aside, he did have one enormous intelligence triumph during this period.

In February 1944, Tex was promoted to commander. Almost simultaneously he and Lt. Cmdr. Tom Mackie were dispatched to help Gen. Douglas MacArthur's intelligence center in Brisbane. MacArthur's cryptanalysts and linguists at the Southwest Pacific Command were buried in messages which now might be interpreted because they had been done in systems exposed by Japanese Army code books captured in New Guinea. Capt. Arthur **McCollum** at Brisbane called Cmdr. Sid **Goodwin**, who had replaced Fabian as OIC at FRUMel, to see if they could borrow a couple of language officers. Goodwin sent out Biard and Mackie.

> The first morning . . . remains one of the most memorable events of my entire life. . . . Tom and I took the top two messages and started to read. Neither of us said a word for a minute or two but very soon I leaned over to see what Tom had, and he leaned my way to see what I was reading. Both of us had eyes as big as mill wheels. It was almost unbelievable. Mackie and I stumbled all over the words in our haste to tell our hosts that we had just read two parts of a thirteen-part message that was hotter and more explosive than Vesuvius.

The thirteen-part message gave precise details for Japanese defensive plans regarding New Guinea, the Bismarck Archipelago, the Admiralty Islands, and the Solomon Islands. This information, translated and analyzed at Brisbane, enabled General MacArthur to understand Japanese strengths and weaknesses in these areas and rearrange his own plans, which significantly accelerated Allied operations and reduced Allied casualties. In fact, later on, U.S. Army authorities expressed the thought that the aid of Mackie and Biard had shaved perhaps three months off the time it took to capture the Bismarck Archipelago.

During September to November 1944, Commander Biard was assigned to the amphibious command ship *Wasatch*, first at New Guinea and then at the Philip-

---

4. Retired Rear Adm. Gill **Richardson** (and some others) have written that having senior linguists (such as himself and Spencer Carlson) commanded by more junior officers for management and leadership details (such as Fabian and Lietwiler) was quite satisfactory—at both CAST and FRUMel—as it allowed them to fully concentrate on translation and cryptanalysis work. Strangely, Tex Biard certainly had a different view when he came to FRUMel in late 1943: "Three of these officers were captains, while the officer in charge of them was a commander. This could have worked without tremendous friction had the officer in charge and his executive officer been well chosen. But somewhere up the line things went quite amiss. I hasten to add that the crypto-linguist captains who had the misfortune of having to serve under the despotic commander and his equally unfriendly executive officer, both quite junior to these captains, will always have my undying respect. They tolerated the daily and almost hourly insults so frequently given us in the linguistic section by their juniors, yet they still managed to perform their vitally important crypto-linguistical jobs most creditably. The insults some of us had to endure did not add to our ability to perform in that manner. Station [FRUMel] did its job and did it well, not because of the officers in charge, but in spite of them."

pines; he received the Bronze Star with Combat "V" device for his work while on-board, interrogating prisoners from ships sunk during the Battle of Leyte Gulf. He then returned to Melbourne, but was detached from FRUMel in April 1945.

After World War II ended, Commander Biard attended the navy's postgraduate school which was then located in Annapolis. While there he studied nuclear engineering, nuclear physics, and radiation hazards. From there he went on to pursue a master's degree in physics at The Ohio State University. While working on that degree he was called away to serve as the operations officer for the first hydrogen bomb test, but he subsequently returned to Ohio State University and finished the program in 1953.

Commander Biard then had an opportunity to go back to Japan—as the captain of the engine repair ship *Luzon*. Departing Long Beach in May 1953, the *Luzon* deployed to the western Pacific and arrived at Sasebo in June. Except for a run to Pusan, South Korea, she provided repair facilities at Sasebo until sailing to Yokosuka in January 1954. She departed the Far East in February and returned to Long Beach.

As he retired from the navy in January 1955, Biard was simultaneously promoted to captain due to his high-level combat decoration from World War II. Tex then began teaching physics at Long Beach City College. He remained on the faculty there until his final retirement in the 1980s. While at Long Beach, he originated an innovative course that used a variety of musical tools, including the human voice, to illustrate the physics aspects of acoustics; that class was later filmed and shown on public television.

In his senior years, Captain Biard's hobbies included studying and discussing physics—including quantum theory, the big bang theory, and astrophysics. He also read and translated Japanese history books, particularly those about World War II.

A distinguished alumnus of Ohio State University's Department of Physics, Captain Biard donated funds to create the *R. Jack and Forest Lynn Biard Lectureship in Cosmology and Astrophysics*, named in honor of his parents. In the early 1980s, Biard put in considerable effort helping Rear Adm. Edwin Layton (and his coauthors) work on Layton's reminisces, *"And I Was There": Pearl Harbor and Midway—Breaking the Secrets.*

Tex Biard passed away on November 2, 2009, at age ninety-six. He was preceded in death by his wife, Winifred Mary Stevens Biard (1914–1996). They are buried together at Arlington National Cemetery.

Captain Biard's awards and decorations include the Bronze Star with Combat "V" device, the Purple Heart, the Navy Commendation Medal, the Presidential Unit Citation, and the Navy Unit Citation.

Sources

Carlson, 94, 101–2.
Dingman, 113, 115, 123.
Drea, 92–93.

"Forrest R. Biard," obituary. *Dallas Morning News*, November 8, 2009.

Holmes, 36, 58, 121, 125.

Layton, *"And I Was There,"* 6, 51, 395, 398–401.

Lucky Bag, U.S. Naval Academy, 1934.

McGinnis, 39, 63.

Oral History Interview with Forrest R. Biard. Forrest R. Biard, Ronald E. Marcello. World War II Pacific Theater (Naval Engagements) Oral History Project. University of North Texas. Oral History Collection, 1992.

Prados, 306, 309, 423.

R. Jack and Forest Lynn Biard Lectureship in Cosmology and Astrophysics. The Ohio State University's Center for Cosmology and AstroParticle Physics. ccapp.osu.edu/biardlecture.html

Smith, *Emperor's Codes*, 213, 253–54.

Spector, *Listening*, 80.

Symonds, 165.

Toll, 337, 341, 346.

U.S. Navy, *Register of Commissioned and Warrant Officers.*

CAPTAIN HENRI DE BALATHIER CLAIBORNE, U.S. NAVY (1903–1969)

"A classic, formal, New Orleans Creole of the old school—and a great raconteur"
District intelligence officer, San Pedro, 1938–1939
Intelligence officer, ONI Far Eastern Section, 1943–1944
Fleet Intelligence Officer, 7th Fleet, 1945–1946

On top of his ability to speak French, Henri Claiborne also had an affinity for Japanese, completing the ONI three-year full-immersion program in 1934. He then managed an impressive career alternating between surface-ship duty and intelligence.

He served as a district intelligence officer, on staff at ONI's Far Eastern Section, and as Fleet Intelligence Officer, 7th Fleet. Then, right after the war, he took the twenty-year navy retirement, moved to Virginia, and cultivated grapes.

* * *

From the 1926 Annapolis yearbook, *The Lucky Bag*:

One drowsy afternoon several years ago during his customary serene and languid siesta, this gay cavaliero bethought to himself, "I am a man of the world, of nature too expansive to be confined by four office walls." So he joined the Navy and for four years has been confined by four bulkheads. During that time he reigned supreme over the Combined Radiator Clubs [snack-bar clubs of nonathletes]. He was a versatile talker and with his trenchant wit probed subjects of all descriptions from the lightest to the heaviest. For information concerning the relative merits of the Irish, Swedes, and French see Henri. You might also pick up a few tips on the turf for, theoretically, Henri has made several track fortunes. Epicures who would fain know the secret of success with "French drip" should do well to drop in on him when he has his "java pot" primed and ready for action. Henri's versatility in other endeavors was wont to seep out on occasions when he overcame his inertia and propensity toward work-outs on the "Johnston bars." There is nothing, claims this young buck, to be more desired than a soft but firm horizontal support on which to brace one's shoulders while he listens with insatiable ear to the mellow crooning of old Morpheus.

* * *

Henri de B. Claiborne was born in New Orleans, Louisiana, on August 11, 1903, to Fernand C. Claiborne and Marie Louise Villere Claiborne. He had at least one sibling, a sister named Clarisse. Henri attended the Jesuit College and the New Orleans Academy, and then the Severn School at Severna Park, Maryland. He was appointed to the U.S. Naval Academy in 1922 and was graduated from there and commissioned an ensign in June 1926. Among his distinguished classmates were C. Wade McClusky Jr., Maxwell F. Leslie, Ranson **Fullinwider**, Frank P. Pyzick, Howard W. Gilmore, Lofton R. Henderson, Robert B. Pirie, James S. Russell, Raymond S. **Lamb**, Paul D. Stroop, and Wesley "Ham" **Wright**. Subsequent promotions were lieutenant (junior grade), 1929; lieutenant, 1936; lieutenant commander, 1940; commander, 1942; and captain, 1943. He retired from the navy in 1947.

After graduation, Ensign Claiborne remained at the academy for a few months and then joined the gunboat *Tulsa* in early 1927. At this time the *Tulsa* saw some repair at the Charlestown Navy Yard and then cruised in the Atlantic with the Special Service Squadron. When civil strife broke out in Nicaragua, parties of Marines and bluejackets from the squadron landed to protect lives and preserve property. At one point during the Second Nicaraguan Campaign, Ensign Claiborne commanded a landing force at Barra Rio Grande. When not engaged in these kinds of operations, the *Tulsa* conducted routine training exercises in waters near the Panama Canal Zone and visited ports in Honduras.

Claiborne returned to the United States and, after a course of instruction at the Naval Operating Base, Hampton Roads, Virginia, he reported onboard the battleship *Texas* in 1929. Subsequently he was assigned duty at Cavite in the Philippine Islands, and then from 1930 through 1931 served on the gunboat *Helena* on the South China Patrol of the Asiatic Fleet. Among other things, the *Helena* was there to observe politician Wang Ching-wei and his activities against political and military leader Chiang Kai-shek.

Around 1930, Lt. j.g. Claiborne received a formal navy qualification as an interpreter of French—which might not be too surprising considering his New Orleans and family backgrounds. Moreover, in 1931, Henri was selected for ONI's Japanese full-immersion language and culture program; for that duty he was attached to the American embassy in Tokyo from 1931 through 1934.

Upon his return to the United States, he briefly served in Washington with ONI. In 1935, Mr. Claiborne was ordered to the light cruiser *Marblehead*; he shortly transferred to the light cruiser *Richmond* in 1936. At that time the *Richmond* operated off the U.S. West Coast as part of the Scouting Fleet. Then, Lieutenant Claiborne came ashore in 1938 to serve as the intelligence officer of the Eleventh Naval District in San Pedro, California.

In 1940, Henri went back to sea, attached to the light cruiser *Omaha* as the gunnery officer. Just a month before the United States entered the war, the *Omaha*, while on neutrality patrol in the mid-Atlantic Ocean, encountered a merchant ship which aroused suspicion. Refusing to satisfactorily identify herself, and taking evasive action, the stranger was ordered to heave-to. She flew the American flag and carried the inscription "*Willmoto* of Philadelphia" on her stern. As the *Omaha*'s crew dispatched a boarding party to this freighter, her crew took to their lifeboats. When the boarding party pulled alongside they could hear explosions from within the hull, and one of the fleeing crewmen shouted, "This is a German ship and she is sinking!" In short order the men of the *Omaha*—despite the extreme risk—salvaged the vessel and brought her in to Puerto Rico. The *Willmoto*, as it turned out, was really the German freighter *Odenwald* carrying a cargo of rubber.[1]

After the United States entered the war, in December 1941, the *Omaha* continued patrols in the mid- and South Atlantic. However, Henri detached from the cruiser in August 1942, transferring to Washington. There, Commander Claiborne served with the Far East Section of ONI as well as with the Joint Intelligence Staff.

---

1. An admiralty court ruled that since the ship was falsely and illegally claiming American registration there were sufficient grounds for confiscation. A case was started claiming that the crews of the two American ships (the destroyer *Somers* was present with the *Omaha*) had salvage rights because the *Odenwald*'s crew—attempting to scuttle the ship—effectively abandoned her. The court case, not settled until 1947, ruled that the members of the boarding party and the prize crew were entitled to $3,000 apiece, while all the other crewmen onboard the *Omaha* and *Somers* were entitled to two months' pay and allowances. As an aside, this was the last "prize money" awarded by the U.S. Navy.

Captain Claiborne left Washington for the Southwest Pacific, serving there from 1945 through 1946, assigned to the Seventh Fleet as the fleet intelligence officer—with a fellow Tokyo-immersion language officer, Capt. Martin R. "Mert" Stone, as his deputy. At this point in the war it was an extraordinarily busy and challenging assignment. For example, in 1945, FRUMel was "at full stride, and aerial reconnaissance was at 1,500 sorties or more per month." The Seventh Fleet intelligence center ended the war as an enormous organization with over 180 officers and 225 enlisted personnel assigned.

In January 1947, shortly after leaving that post and returning to the United States, Captain Claiborne retired from the navy.

Sometime later he and his wife settled in the Northern Neck of Virginia. Claiborne developed a small vineyard and made his own wine, becoming somewhat of a pioneer in the wine industry in that area.

Henri was distantly related to fashion designer Liz Claiborne. Coincidentally, he was also a shirt-tail relation to fellow Tokyo immersion-language officer Rear Adm. Kenneth Duval **Ringle**. Admiral Ringle's mother was a DuVal from Kentucky; a DuVal ancestor had married an offspring of the Honorable William C. C. Claiborne, who was the governor of Louisiana in the early 1800s—including 1815 when the famous Battle of New Orleans occurred. Rear Admiral and Mrs. Ringle were very fond of Captain Claiborne; moreover, Ken Ringle was "somewhat amused and intrigued by Claiborne's chosen role in retirement as some sort of French country squire."[2]

Henri was very proud to be the great-great grandson of the famous Governor Claiborne (Ringle "used to scoff good-naturedly at such Southern ancestor worship as *Shintoism*"). Because of this family pride, when the epic Hollywood movie *The Buccaneer* came out in 1958, Henri prepared a lawsuit against Paramount Pictures. The movie's story takes place during the War of 1812 and tells a very creative version of how the privateer Jean Lafitte helped in the Battle of New Orleans, choosing to fight for America on principle rather than for the likely victor, Great Britain. The movie includes a romance between the criminal Lafitte and a fictionalized daughter of Governor Claiborne. Henri saw this portrayal as "a defamation and misrepresentation of the Claiborne family's good reputation" and felt he needed to take action; however, it doesn't appear that the lawsuit went anywhere.

Captain Claiborne passed away on May 8, 1969, at Bethesda Naval Hospital and is buried at Arlington National Cemetery. Even though she was a Virginian, his wife, Harriot Carter Claiborne (1910–1997), is buried at Palm Cemetery in Winter Park, Florida. Henri's tombstone is all business in the usual style of Arlington, but Harriot's has the pleasing epitaph, "she lived with gusto and grace."

---

2. It's interesting to note that Admiral Ringle's children clearly remember the retired Captain Claiborne—from the late 1950s and early 1960s—when he would visit the Ringles at Avery Island, Louisiana, or they would visit him in Virginia. They were aware that he had been a naval officer, and he told them stories about being on a cruiser chasing German raiders in the South Atlantic. Strangely, they don't recall any discussion of his time as an immersion student in Japan, or that he was a Japanese linguist and worked in ONI—as had their father. As Andrew Ringle wrote, "If he and Dad discussed it, it was [always] out of my hearing."

Captain Claiborne's awards included, among other things, the Legion of Merit for his wartime work, as well as the Nicaraguan Campaign Medal from the 1920s.

Sources

Captain Henri de Balathier Claiborne, U.S. Navy. Official [draft] U.S. Navy biography dated March 2, 1945. Courtesy of Dr. Gregory Finnegan.

Lucky Bag, U.S. Naval Academy, 1926.

Packard, 369.

Prados, 424.

Ringle, Kenneth A., Sally Ringle Hotchkiss, and Andrew D. Ringle. Email correspondence, August 5, 2013, March 27, 2014, and March 28, 2014.

U.S. Navy, *Register of Commissioned and Warrant Officers.*

REAR ADMIRAL CECIL HENGY COGGINS, M.C., U.S. NAVY (1902–1987)

A man of unbounded energy and enthusiasm
The Navy's first chemical and biological warfare officer
The Navy's first psychological warfare officer
The "founder" of the Naval Criminal Investigative Service

It's probably safe to say that Cecil Coggins may be *the* most unusual character in this book—which says a lot considering the remarkable people filling these pages. Very much like his mentor and close friend Ellis **Zacharias**, Coggins was a self-taught intelligence pioneer of extraordinary imagination and initiative. However, unlike Zach and the majority of individuals under study here, Coggins was neither an Annapolis graduate nor an experienced, conventional naval officer of the line: he was a physician who had—of all things—initially specialized in obstetrics. But whether one considers counter-espionage, aviator debriefing, photo interpretation, undercover activity, biological and chemical warfare, prisoner interrogation, or psychological warfare, Dr. Coggins mastered it all—largely teaching himself (and then teaching others) as he evolved in the profession. Cecil Coggins was truly a man of immense energy and diverse interests. From the navy's Bureau of Medicine and Surgery to the ONI to the Office of Strategic Services; from medicine to intelligence to psychological warfare; and from Missouri to Hawaii to China, Dr. Coggins's life journey was remarkably unusual and unconventional. Coggins's work left a significant mark in the fields of naval intelligence, medicine, and unconventional warfare. In fact, "None of his various . . . assignments lacked controversy and, in all of them, Coggins exhibited a typical dash of color, and occasionally, he effected surprising impact."

*   *   *

Cecil Hengy Coggins was born an identical twin—his brother was named Cyril—on April 10, 1902, in Kirkwood, Missouri (they would be joined by a sister, Lucille, in 1912). Their parents were Lucius B. Coggins and Jesse Hengy Coggins. The brothers went to Columbia High School in Columbia, Missouri. They roamed widely for summer jobs, including venturing out of state, and worked in such places as mines, cattle ranches, and lumber camps. Upon graduation they both traveled to New Orleans where Cecil got a job with a printing company—but he then abruptly shipped out as an unrated seaman onboard the freighter SS *Jefferson Davis*. He "jumped ship" with two friends in Salonika, Greece; they ineffectively disguised themselves and made for the front in the Greco-Turkish War of 1919–1922. Caught and imprisoned by the Greek police, they eventually rejoined the *Jefferson Davis* in Bizerte, Tunisia, and then subsequently returned to New Orleans in a nonpay status.

Shortly thereafter, Coggins talked his way into the office of Mr. Percy Parks, a vice president of the United Fruit Company. Parks took an instant like to the young man and offered him a supervisor's job at a banana plant in Honduras. After only three months as a plantation assistant manager, Coggins was offered his own farm to run with around one hundred workers deeper in the jungle. He did well, but two incidents there helped change his life's path: a boy in his employ was bitten by a viper and died before Coggins could get him to a clinic; later, he unsuccessfully tried to save a man whose arm had been severed in a machete fight. "I felt then that I wanted to become a doctor." Within a few weeks, he was on a steamer, bound for the United States.

In 1922, Coggins enrolled in the University of Missouri at Columbia as a pre-medical student and worked at a part-time job as a hospital orderly (later becoming a laboratory technician and then an assistant in the radiology section). He also took another part-time job as an assistant instructor in zoology.

Coggins completed a BA in medicine in 1925, began medical school (also at Missouri) the following semester, and in 1926 married another student—Dorothy

Hammond. He interrupted his studies and took a one-year appointment in Macon, Missouri, teaching high school physics and physical education as well as coaching football. He then returned to the university in the fall of 1927 as a second-year medical student. Then, in 1928, Cecil and Dorothy moved to Philadelphia for him to finish studies at Thomas Jefferson University.

In June 1930, Coggins graduated and joined the U.S. Navy as a lieutenant (junior grade) with the additional formal title of Assistant Surgeon. Earlier that year he had competed in a rigorous five-day examination given by the navy's Bureau of Medicine and Surgery, and as a result was one of only seventy-five young MDs offered a commission. He then completed an internship at Philadelphia's League Island Naval Hospital, followed by residency work in obstetrics and gynecology (at BuMed's direction) at Lankenan Hospital. At that point Coggins was assigned to sea duty, and so he and Dorothy moved to Long Beach, California, and he began his naval career in earnest. Subsequent promotions would be lieutenant (Passed Assistant Surgeon), 1936; lieutenant commander (Surgeon), 1942; commander (Medical Inspector), 1942; captain (Medical Director), 1945; and, because of a World War II combat decoration, he was promoted to rear admiral upon retirement in 1959.

Based out of Long Beach in 1932, Assistant Surgeon Coggins served about one year each onboard the light cruiser *Concord*, the light cruiser *Raleigh*, and the battleship *Arizona*. Obviously these billets offered no opportunity for Cecil to work in his navy-directed specialty of obstetrics; moreover, onboard the *Concord* he was assigned a myriad of nonmedical duties such as Red Cross Officer, Navy Relief Officer, and secretary for the ship's punitive and disciplinary boards. On the plus side, he traveled to such places as Cuba and Haiti. On March 10, 1933, a considerable earthquake hit Long Beach; Coggins immediately went on shore with the *Arizona*'s fire and rescue team and worked nonstop for forty-eight hours giving emergency treatment.

In June 1933, Coggins was assigned to the naval dispensary in San Pedro. The following November, Dorothy gave birth to their first child, also named Cecil (they eventually had three boys, Cecil, John, and William). It was about this time that Coggins began a leisure-time hobby of watching the activities of Japanese fishing boats operating around Long Beach and Los Angeles (over eight hundred fishermen crewed around sixty boats in the Long Beach-San Pedro-San Diego areas). He had come to suspect that some of these boats were shadowing U.S. Navy vessels as they conducted maneuvers offshore. (At this time the U.S. Pacific Fleet was primarily based here; the fleet's move to Pearl Harbor would not occur until 1940.)

He also continued to read everything he could find on intelligence and espionage, an interest which had begun in childhood when he read Rudyard Kipling's novel *Kim*—which is a tale of an orphan who becomes a master spy in nineteenth-century British colonial India. By the mid-1930s, Coggins's personal intelligence library had grown to about one hundred books. "I had unwittingly acquired, during my teen years and all my college years, a fairly good knowledge of counter-espionage." He was also reading everything he could find on the culture and politics of Japan.

One of the themes of his intense study was the use of intelligence in the preparation for war upon an enemy, and Coggins gradually became convinced that the Japanese had targeted the United States for this kind of intelligence collection as early as 1930—if not before.

In the fall of 1934, it was Dr. Coggins who brought about the first undercover mission for a future Pacific Fleet intelligence officer, Lt. Edwin **Layton**. Coggins, who had started working with the Eleventh Naval District intelligence office and ONI's local undercover organization, discovered that a just-arrived Japanese naval tanker had brought some films to show to the local Japanese Citizens Patriotic Society in Long Beach. They suspected that it was subversive material and wanted Layton, as an educated Japanese linguist, to check it out. Posing as a fire insurance inspector, Mr. Layton attended the showing and found the films indeed subversive—as well as "corny."

Helped by a friend who was a ham radio operator, Coggins began to focus upon radio traffic between ships of the Japanese fishing fleet. He observed that some vessels did seem to shadow American warships. Moreover, he noticed that some of the boats came back to port with crewmen different than those who had sailed out. Coggins found local U.S. immigration officials unhelpful. Frustrated, in October 1935 he summed-up his observations and concerns in an unsolicited formal report to ONI in Washington; he sent it via the chain of command but he expected to be reprimanded for exceeding his duty as a medical officer.

However, his report was received with great interest; in fact, ONI's Lt. Arthur **McCollum**, a Japanese linguist and specialist, immediately requested that Coggins send him anything else he might have. ONI already had a rising concern about civilian-owned alien shipping off the coasts of the United States, and it also realized that it had very little information on the issue. Coggins's report had gone from his medical commanding officer, to the commander of the Pacific Fleet (Adm. Joseph M. Reeves), to ONI. The Eleventh Naval District's intelligence officer then had two officers interview Coggins in depth; as a result the commander of the district became convinced that there was an espionage problem. Even FBI director J. Edgar Hoover (apparently ONI copied him with Coggins's report) jumped into the discussion with *his* concerns. The navy and local California authorities began to increase efforts regarding fishing-boat observation and control.

Unfortunately, amidst the Great Depression, this was a difficult budgetary time for ONI. With significantly decreased funding, the director of naval intelligence, Capt. William Puleston, was having to rely more on retired officers and other kinds of volunteers—rather than paid, full-time naval and civilian analysts. Thus, in many ways this was a good time for Dr. Coggins to step forward. Finding a welcoming organization, "the naval surgeon had leapt into the murky field of intelligence largely under the influence of his personal library of intelligence books, his own imagination," his unusual analytical skills, and his driving energy. Furthermore, "Coggins' grounding in science and his medical doctorate differentiated him from the typical *dilettante* image which tainted many volunteers in the intelligence services during this period."

He continued his work in the naval dispensary, seeing many patients by day and delivering around forty to forty-five babies per month—many at night. The district intelligence officer at first called upon Coggins to investigate a couple of people (a British expatriate chemist claiming unusual expertise in explosives, and a *Nisei* radio expert who appeared to be a spy). He then was specially called in by Admiral Reeves (via his intelligence officer, Lt. Joseph **Rochefort**) to investigate an apparently serious case of espionage by a dishonorably discharged navy veteran. In this case (also discussed in the sections on Agnes **Driscoll**, Edwin Layton, and Ellis **Zacharias**), Dr. Coggins shortly determined that the suspect, Harry Thompson, was boarding docked American warships disguised as a chief petty officer. Once onboard, he was frequently being successful in stealing various papers and even manuals or a variety of technical and operational subjects. He then was selling them to a Japanese naval officer, Miyazaki Toshio, whose cover was a university language student.

Coggins displayed great skills in working with an informant, tailing, observing, copying documents, interfacing with postal inspectors, and compiling evidence. He then engineered Thompson's arrest, flew to Washington to brief Commander Zacharias (presumably their first meeting which led to a quarter-century of close friendship and professional teamwork), and ultimately testified at the trial. It was a complex case even involving some codebreaking in Washington. Zacharias called it the first big case of counter-espionage since World War I, and it ultimately led to Miyazaki's flight to Japan and Thompson's sentence of fifteen years in the penitentiary. "Coggins gained a small amount of notoriety" but also considerable "official recognition and approval."

At this point Dr. Coggins was due for sea duty and thus did a two-year tour as a medical officer onboard the battleship *California*. Then, in September 1938, Coggins was ordered to take a course in orthopedic surgery at San Diego Naval Hospital—with additional duty in the Eleventh Naval District's intelligence office. He welcomed the move away from obstetrics to a medical specialty with more relevance to military needs. He also had experienced the death of a patient's baby at the moment of delivery, and although he was fully exonerated by the subsequent investigation, this incident likely cemented his existing urge to move on.

During this period Zacharias, who had transferred out to San Diego as the district intelligence officer, asked Coggins to prepare some lectures to be given to other officers. The subjects included intelligence theory, techniques of surveillance, counterintelligence, detection and prevention of sabotage, and the like. He also took part in some work with existing and new colleagues, such as Lt. Eddie Layton, Lt. Cmdr. Joe Rochefort, and Lt. Cmdr. Ken **Ringle**.

In September 1940, ONI invited Coggins to Washington for the purpose of writing a manual on counter-intelligence. ONI's leadership had come to realize that he was probably the subject's most well-read and knowledgeable officer in the entire navy. So, Coggins brought his family to Washington for three months. He "intended the manual to be a primer on investigative procedures." When finished, it was "215 pages of basic ground rules, suggestions, and experience for ONI's team of investigators." The work actually broke no new ground, "but it did lay the foundation for an organization later known as the Naval Investigative Service [or as it is known today, the Naval Criminal Investigative Service—NCIS]." Coggins thus helped to define the mission of a small investigative section (OP-16-B-3) of ONI's Domestic Intelligence Branch.[1] While in Washington, he solidified his relationship with Captain Zacharias, who had rotated back to ONI; Cecil and Dorothy socialized quite a bit with Zach and his wife, Claire.

Dr. Coggins and his family returned to San Diego in November 1940, whereupon he resumed his medical duties. He also resumed additional work in the naval intelligence office, but then Lieutenant Coggins received orders to Pearl Harbor, at which he arrived in January 1941. Dorothy and their seven-year-old son arrived soon thereafter and then, in August, she gave birth to their second son, John. Coggins was then assigned to the Fourteenth Naval District's intelligence officer (Capt. Irving H. Mayfield) with the title of Pacific Fleet Counter-Espionage Officer. As such he reported both to Mayfield and to his friend Lieutenant Commander Layton, who was now the Fleet Intelligence Officer, Pacific Fleet. Mayfield immediately tasked him to help train local *Nisei* in counter-espionage. Coggins was also given a collateral duty as Fleet Health, Recreation, and Morale Officer.

Dr. Coggins was impressed with the apparently smooth mixture of different racial cultures in Hawaii. The territory seemed to him a "huge and quietly efficient melting pot for nearly half-a-million people." Japanese Americans, according to the 1940 census, constituted the largest ethnic group in the islands—about 158,000 people—approximately 40 percent of the territory's population. Coggins's goal "became one of ascertaining the loyalty of the local *Nisei*, and also of strengthening the security of the military establishment."

Coggins was partnered with Lt. William Stephenson, a lawyer who led a group of junior naval reserve intelligence officers. Coggins, Stephenson, and this team compiled a card index of several hundred Japanese "believed to pose a threat." Between January and December 1941, these officers also recruited a web of about 120 undercover agents, trained them, and assigned them to watch their own neighborhoods. Coggins also focused upon "plant security" in regard to potential sabotage of civilian factories as well as the naval bases. He submitted his reports and criticisms to Lieutenant Commander Layton, who in turn passed them to Rear Adm. Claude C. Bloch, commandant of the Fourteenth Naval District. An old-school officer, Bloch found the tireless and earnest Coggins profoundly irritating, not at all impressed by this maverick physician-turned-sleuth. Bloch shortly

1. The manual was *Training Manual for Personnel Assigned to Investigations Sections of Naval Intelligence Service* (ONI-T-8-10). Office of Naval Intelligence, Navy Department. Washington, DC: Government Printing Office, 1941. The navy initially printed and distributed around 1,300 copies.

ordered all sentries to specifically watch for the doctor—and arrest him if he were caught poking around in any unauthorized areas.

Much like Lt. Cmdr. Ken Ringle—now drawing similar conclusions in southern California—Coggins quickly decided that there was overwhelming evidence that the vast majority of Japanese Americans living in Hawaii were in fact loyal to the United States.

On the morning of the Pearl Harbor attack, Coggins rushed to the district intelligence office—in those days, interestingly, located in the Alexander Young Hotel in Honolulu. He was torn by the idea that he should instead proceed to a hospital to offer medical help for the casualties he knew would be streaming in, but he stayed at the DIO and began working intelligence issues. In later years, however, he was inclined to think he'd made the wrong choice that day and instead should have contributed his medical expertise where needed.

Parallel to ONI, FBI, and local police efforts in southern California, these same organizations now began rounding up preidentified suspects in Hawaii. For several days Coggins was extremely busy running leads, investigating reports, and working with the FBI, the army, and the police. He interviewed the first prisoner of war taken by the United States—a junior officer from a Japanese midget submarine which had foundered on a reef.

In January 1942, Captain Zacharias (now the commanding officer of the heavy cruiser *Salt Lake City*) invited Dr. Coggins to sail with him as they had become "close friends and indefatigable coworkers in intelligence." The ship was attached to a task force, under Vice Adm. William "Bull" Halsey, which proceeded to the Marshall Islands, targeting the atolls of Kwajalein and Wotje. Cecil was introduced to the wardroom as an intelligence officer rather than a surgeon. With Zach's enthusiastic support, Coggins volunteered to coordinate intelligence collection as they proceeded against enemy seaplane bases. He gathered up several privately owned cameras which he gave to the pilots of the *Salt Lake City*'s two reconnaissance aircraft, along with suggestions about various shots they should take. The resulting maps which were created, as well as the photos—which Coggins analyzed and annotated—were published and distributed to the rest of the task force and used to great effect, marking Coggins's entry into combat and operational intelligence.

In February, President Franklin D. Roosevelt signed Executive Order 9066 which implemented the relocation of Japanese Americans away from coastal areas. Hawaii was included in the order.

In April 1942, Coggins's wife and sons evacuated to California to stay with some of her relatives. At about the same time—back from his adventures on board the *Salt Lake City*—Coggins received a plea for help from the Honolulu Japanese Civic Association. This motivated him to approach Hawaiian transportation and land-reclamation magnate Walter F. Dillingham. As a result, at a special dinner, Dillingham presented a petition from the *Nisei* community requesting that the U.S. government allow Japanese Americans to enlist and fight for the United States. The select attendees at the dinner included the relatively new Pacific Fleet commander, Adm. Chester

W. Nimitz, and the relatively new military governor, Lt. Gen. Delos C. Emmons.[2] Both officers were very impressed, and in turn passed the petition to the secretaries of the navy and of war. Coggins also sent a memorandum to ONI recommending the inclusion of *Nisei* volunteers into the armed forces to fight in other areas than the Pacific. He wrote that this was an operational concept at least as old as the Roman Empire, and one that history showed often worked.

General Emmons worked toward implementing the inclusion of *Nisei* into the military, and in addition held off attempts to relocate Hawaii's Japanese Americans. His position was based on two compelling reasons: "*Issei* and *Nisei* had exhibited no disloyal behavior (indeed, just the opposite), and Japanese residents constituted an irreplaceably large fraction of Hawaii's vital work force." Only 2,000 of the approximately 158,000 Japanese Americans in the Territory of Hawaii were interned— mostly due to Emmons's efforts. In this regard he was totally different from his counterpart in California, Lt. Gen. John DeWitt, who was remarkably eager to implement massive relocation. Emmons faced considerable opposition to his position, including such people as U.S. attorney Angus Taylor (about whom Coggins wrote, "although we are good friends, I feel that in this matter Angus has rather gone off the deep end"), and John A. Balch, chairman of the Hawaiian Telephone Company, who wanted to relocate the Japanese to the island of Moloka'i—the same place where many Hawaiian victims of Hansen's disease (leprosy) were forcibly quarantined.

Again, similar to Lieutenant Commander Ringle in southern California, Coggins wrote an article for *Harper's Magazine* which was eventually published in June 1943. Echoing Ringle, Coggins argued for tolerance and a case-by-case assessment of individuals—and against widespread "racial profiling," to use a more modern term.

Coggins journeyed twice to Washington in 1942. One of the trips focused upon the relatively new concern over biological warfare. In July he was directed to meet with chemist and businessman George W. Merck, who had been appointed by FDR to head the War Research Service, and examine the feasibility of offensive biological weapons. The conference with Merck and his senior board concluded that the concept of biological warfare was workable, that it presented a real threat to U.S. forces, and that further research should be pursued. Coggins was appointed as the navy's new Biological Warfare Officer. After taking an army course on the subject at Camp Detrick, Maryland, Coggins was expected to advise navy officials on whether U.S. forces were prepared to defend against—or employ—chemical and biological weaponry.

Upon Coggins's transfer to Washington, Captain Zacharias, now the deputy director of ONI, approached him and asked him if he'd like to create—apparently in his *spare time*—a unit of psychological warfare for the navy.

In fact, for Cecil Coggins, 1943 was going to be the start of an incredibly busy and fascinating period. "Within the space of three years, Coggins spearheaded his own

---

2. Among them was Admiral Nimitz's chief of staff, Rear Adm. Milo F. Draemel. It's interesting to note that during the period 1918 to 1921, Lieutenant Commander Draemel was the officer in charge of the Code and Signal Section at Main Navy, OP-20-G.

military radio propaganda unit and became a recognized expert on chemical warfare and biological warfare."

> His job as chief of navy psychological warfare was only one of several roles he performed [beginning in 1943]. His other duties included work as a planner for the new, covert Office of Strategic Services and as a navy delegate to a supervising panel for the Office of War Information. Finally, Coggins filled the role of the navy's biological warfare officer—a minor post which threatened periodically to become one of greater concern to U.S. officials.

Coggins enthusiastically agreed to Zacharias's request. In fact, he had—on his own initiative—recently sent a suggestion directly to chief of naval operations Adm. Ernest J. King, proposing a program of propaganda radio transmissions to the Japanese-occupied Philippine Islands. Zach got approval from the navy's surgeon general (as Cecil was still to retain his biological warfare position) for the doctor to again formally work for ONI. He immediately began to recruit for the Special Warfare Branch (OP-16-W). Coggins shortly decided that there were two men he needed: a Hungarian émigré named Ladislas Farago, who had written a book titled *German Psychological Warfare*; and an American officer, Lt. Cmdr. Ralph G. Albrecht, who was fluent in German, an interrogator, and familiar with the British navy's radio propaganda programs.

Coggins traveled to New York City where Farago was director of research for an organization called the Committee for National Morale. Cecil wanted him as chief of research and general "idea man" for OP-16-W. Farago was a perfect choice and subsequently made significant contributions to the war effort. He acquired extensive intelligence experience and later became a prominent intelligence and military historian. From his point of view, Farago in turn considered Coggins one of the Navy's most extraordinary officers.

> Lt. Cmdr. Cecil Hengy Coggins [was] a naval surgeon specializing in obstetrics whenever he served in the Medical Corps. But most of the time he was off on special assignments, dabbling in all sorts of intelligence work. Dr. Coggins [was] a slight, crew-cut, narrow-eyed, humorless man of unbounded energy and enthusiasm, [and was] like Allen Dulles, an espionage buff.[3]

---

3. Farago later wrote that: "Early in 1942, Dr. Coggins happened to read my book, *German Psychological Warfare*, and decided to become the Navy's pioneer psychological warrior. He envisaged the application of this kind of assault on the enemy navies, using persuasion instead of the compulsion of arms to paralyze the fingers, as he was wont to put it, that pulled the triggers.

I first met Coggins in August 1942, when he called upon me in New York unannounced at the Committee for National Morale, where I then worked as director of research. He introduced himself, sat down at my desk and outlined to me in super-charged words an elaborate plan he had hatched to organize a psychological warfare branch inside Naval Intelligence. He invited me to join him as his chief of research and general idea man. I told him I could not very well hope to be accepted in ONI because I was then still a citizen of Hungary and had been in this country less than five years. Moreover, [since] little Hungary had seen fit to declare war on the United States, my status was that of an enemy alien."

"'Never mind,' Coggins said. 'I'll fix that.' He gave me my instructions, as strange as this strange man was himself. This was in August, on a hot summer day, but Coggins told me: 'Be in Washington on

In December 1942, Coggins was sent to a joint four-day conference on military intelligence matters at Camp Ritchie, Maryland. For Cecil this signaled his "full and official immersion into the national intelligence community." Then, in the spring of 1943, he was sent to London to conduct liaison regarding propaganda and other issues; among the officers he met with was an aide to the head of British naval intelligence—a reserve commander named Ian Fleming. Coggins was extremely impressed by British intelligence activities and personnel. "[British officers] were all clearly *intelligence-minded* which, sadly, cannot be said for the vast majority of our own officers." Coggins's British venture was then followed by an excursion to Oshawa, Canada, to a British-run secret intelligence training camp.

Back at ONI, Cecil divided the new OP-16-W into three desks: German, Italian, and Japanese. The focus was initially upon the effort against the German U-boats due to their enormous threat as well as President Franklin Roosevelt's emphasis on the "Germany First" strategy. Coggins's group targeted the crews of the *Kriegsmarine*'s submarine fleet through their ears, hearts, and minds. Thus, the "Norden Broadcasts" became the Special Warfare Branch's first major project, fully backed by Admiral King who was feeling desperate about the U-boat war. They created a radio character for the real Lieutenant Commander Albrecht, a *persona* called *Cmdr. Robert Norden*, who made brief, regular broadcasts via multiple channels and frequencies in virtually perfect German. First broadcast in January 1943 (and continuing into 1945), and using real or at least realistic facts, events, and names, the regularly scheduled transmissions targeted the submariners' morale on a variety of nuanced subjects. "Norden" stressed that the crews were, in the eyes of the German high command, unappreciated and expendable pawns, that they were often lied to by commanders, and that the task of the U-boat arm was ultimately hopeless in the face of overwhelming Allied manpower and industrial might. There is credible evidence that Norden not only reached his target, he even achieved an odd, cult-like following in some areas of the German audience. As the war ended, captured *Kriegsmarine* documents indicated that the broadcasts had created a worrisome deterioration of morale.

By August 1943, Coggins was deeply engrossed in all his myriad responsibilities, but enjoyed living in the capital with his family—which now included his twin brother; Cyril had left a managerial job in advertising in New York and was now an

---

December 4. Go straight from the Union Station to the Fairfax Hotel. Don't register, but go directly to Room 307 and enter without knocking. The door will be unlocked. Be there at 5 p.m. sharp. I'm now going somewhere in the Pacific, but will see you in Washington.'

More than three months later, at the exact time, I was on the third floor of the hotel, standing outside Room 307, when the door opened. There was Coggins, and inside the parlor of the suite I found three more people. They were Captain Zacharias; Joseph Riheldaffer, an elderly commander; and a young lieutenant named Booth. Three hours later I was hired as a 'secret agent,' because my status as an enemy alien made any other entry into ONI administratively impossible."

"Coggins solved my draft status in a similarly melodramatic fashion. I was then classified as 1-A, but Coggins called on my draft board in New York, identified himself as a physician, and told them I had suffered a nervous breakdown and had to be committed to a psychiatric institution. I was promptly reclassified 4-F and remained in that category until my 38th birthday, in September 1944, when I ceased to be eligible for the draft and Coggins could take me 'out' of the institution."

army first lieutenant on duty in Washington. Cecil began to look more closely at chemical and biological warfare. He was concerned to learn that the Japanese were claiming that U.S. forces had used poison gas on them; although this was false, Coggins believed it might be used as "justification" for the Japanese to begin their own real chemical offensive.

In early 1943, Cecil had begun attending meetings for the planning boards of both the OWI and the OSS. He was assigned to look at finding people for open billets in Naval Group China; this navy organization had combined with army and OSS groups to form the Sino-American Cooperative Organization (SACO). Collaborative intelligence was under navy Capt. Milton E. Miles, some OSS officers, and Chiang Kai-shek's intelligence and secret police chief, General Tai Li. Coggins noticed that there was an opening for a senior medical officer—and of course saw himself as a natural. He wanted to get into the thick of this "good-sized war" and try his hand at active combat surgery. He also feared—rightly—that soon his mentor Ellis Zacharias was going to be transferred from ONI and back to sea. Thus, in late 1943, Cecil moved his family to Oroville, California, and left for China "with considerable eagerness."

On November 22, 1943, Commander Coggins arrived at Kunming, China. Traveling on to Chungking, he met up with SACO personnel and moved to their headquarters. He was tasked as a field surgeon, and started to accompany mobile hospitals in close support of *guerrilla* forces. He received a commission and the uniform of a colonel in the Chinese Army—and was named Colonel *Koh-jin-ssu*. He was then assigned to teach at an intelligence school established by Tai Li at Kienow. There he taught sanitation, hygiene, first aid, counter-espionage, and assassination. He also medically screened officer candidates for recruitment into the Chinese Army and its intelligence organization. Despite very poor communications with the United States, he learned of the birth of his third son—William Frederick—in February 1944. At one point, returning to Washington with Captain Miles (who was actually deputy director of SACO and theater OSS chief), Coggins brought an idea to the head of the OSS's research and development division, Dr. Stanley Lovell. The idea was to use poison against high-ranking Japanese officers who visited Chinese prostitutes in Peking, Shanghai, and other cities. The poison would have to be cleverly designed and packaged such that the women could easily conceal it; fortunately for many Japanese officers the chosen poison failed in testing, so the project was canceled.

In the spring of 1944, Coggins established a field hospital near Changsha. It was during this time that he became one of the few U.S. intelligence officers who focused upon Japan's biological warfare activities against the Chinese—even before a great deal of information came to light at the end of the war. Conducting field trips from Changsha, Coggins and his enlisted navy pharmacist's mates became aware of evidence of Japanese biological (perhaps) and chemical (certainly) activity. It was impossible to nail down, but finding large numbers of dead soldiers and civilians, with no visible wounds, was a huge indication—as were various reports of other OSS personnel and missionary doctors. Coggins was on the right track; however, he "never discovered conclusive evidence of either chemical or biological attacks on a systematic basis," and conclusive evidence was extremely hard to document in a country rampant with natural disease. The Japanese military indeed had an aggressive chemical and biological program underway, but it was really centered far away in Manchuria and elsewhere—the Sagami Navy Yard being one location—in the Japanese home islands.

In May 1944, at Changsha, Coggins had to evacuate himself, his men, medical supplies, and some British and American missionaries in the face of advancing Japanese army units. In the fall he was in the field with Chinese guerillas, and in December he and a couple of pharmacist's mates were running another field hospital deep in rural territory. At one point Cecil traded a navy-issue .38 pistol for a U.S. Army officer's jeep to better bring in wounded; but even with the jeep the guerrillas had to walk several days to where they could be picked up, and in the deep winter such casualties were suffering not only from gunshot wounds and malaria, but also from frozen feet. That same December, Captain Miles gave command of the main SACO hospital to a junior lieutenant commander. Miles may have felt that Coggins had a greater impact as the senior *field* surgeon, but Cecil had wanted the hospital position and failure to get it was a significant disappointment.

March 1945 saw Dr. Coggins promoted to captain (and to the associated title of medical director) and then, coincidentally, the next month brought urgent orders demanding Coggins's quick return to Washington. He was allowed a few weeks rest in Oroville with his family, which including shaking off some health problems acquired in China. His new, high-priority assignment was to prepare for some specific chemical warfare activity: he was to inspect, package, and transport a new defoliating agent to the West Coast for further delivery to the West Pacific. In mid-July, Coggins was busy preparing 1,200 pounds of the agent at an army base in Oakland; however, the project was abruptly terminated with the Japanese surrender in August.

In 1946, Captain Coggins returned to China, in the vicinity of Tsingtao, as the chief medical officer onboard the hospital ship USS *Repose*. That year Cecil also was awarded the Bronze Star, with the Combat "V" device, for his field service with SACO during the war.

Dr. Coggins was then assigned as chief of atomic, biological, and chemical warfare on the staff of the NATO headquarters in Paris. In this capacity he established schools of warfare defense in NATO nations, coordinated their research, and devised a way to quickly and effectively report biological and chemical attacks.

Captain Coggins probably continued his association with the OSS, the Central Intelligence Group, and later perhaps even the CIA. He was designated the navy's chief of CBR warfare in the late 1940s; it was designed to be a general line officer's job, but only a medical officer with Coggins's background carried the necessary qualifications. In 1950 he personally directed a joint military test in which a "harmless" bacteria strain in aerosol form was sprayed from San Francisco Bay toward the heart of the city—fortunately there were no identified illnesses connected with the experiment.

Cecil also proposed a concept in CBR defense to architects and engineers in the navy's Bureau of Ships that remains part of ship operational capability even today—rigging a system of water pipes to the highest points on board. The result is a ship-wide device that can bathe the exterior of the entire vessel in a steady shower of sea water, thereby protecting it from many kinds of CBR assault.

Dr. Coggins retired from the navy in 1959 and was simultaneously promoted to rear admiral due to his high-level World War II combat decoration. Following his retirement, for several years, he served as the medical chief of civil defense for the state of California.

Interestingly, unlike his mentor Zacharias and many of his other intelligence colleagues, Coggins was ever the unsuccessful linguist. During his lifetime he studied German, Spanish, Chinese, and Russian—mastering none of them. He was, however, extremely proficient in just about everything else he attempted: banana plantation manager, physician, self-taught counter-espionage expert, "cofounder" of the NCIS, overhead-imagery analyst, champion of the *Nisei*, the navy's first chemical and biological warfare officer, and the navy's first head of psychological warfare.

As his eminent biographer, William Scaring, has written,

> Coggins' highly specialized knowledge, his advanced degree, and the mystique of being a physician all allowed him access to senior officers and to intelligence work that might have been denied to peers of his junior rank. His work's significance reached far beyond his place in the chain.
>
> Coggins' work in counter-espionage was seminal in the United States, laying the foundation for a naval agency responsible for pursuing spies and other threats to national security. His work in this field also brought him into close contact with the Japanese-American (*Nisei*) community in Hawaii. Coggins became an ally of this beleaguered ethnic group just as the U.S. government was in the process of relocating many *nisei* against their will. Finally, Coggins' examination and later development of chemical, biological, and psychological weaponry during and after the war contributed a dark and fascinating chapter to the evolution of modern warfare in the Cold War.
>
> Coggins believed strongly that there was a parallel between medical diagnosis, deductive investigation, and intelligence analysis: each field required a highly trained practitioner who was capable of assembling seemingly unrelated symptoms, clues, or trends in order to produce an overall observation about hidden conditions.[4]

---

4. There have been a number of medical doctors in U.S. military history who've also dabbled in intelligence and espionage. Among them are Drs. Benjamin Church and Edward Bancroft during the American Revolution; Church (the senior Continental Army physician and a provisional congressman) actively spied for the British while espousing colonial rhetoric, while Bancroft spied for the British against Continental officials Silas Deane and Benjamin Franklin. U.S. Navy Fleet Surgeon William M. Wood, later the navy's surgeon general, collected intelligence in Mexico during the Mexican War. Major General Ralph Van Deman was a physician who eventually entered the army's Military Intelligence Division—and later became its director. In the 1930s Cecil Coggins visited the retired Van Deman in San Diego. And we shouldn't overlook Dr. Furusawa Takashi, in Los Angeles in the mid-1930s; he headed a circle of Japanese intelligence agents. Coggins did bring Harry Thompson (who was in Furusawa's organization) to justice, but could not build up enough evidence to have a workable case against Furusawa.

Cecil intended to write his memoirs in retirement, but for some reason just did not get around to it. He had organized a great deal of material and had selected a tentative title: *Say "Ah."* The title reflects perhaps a double meaning—a doctor's first instruction to a patient, as well as the expression of wonderment he so often used himself upon discovery of new things.

Rear Admiral Coggins passed away on May 1, 1987, in Monterey, California. He was truly an original and a pioneer in several fields and known to all as a man of "unbounded energy and enthusiasm." At a party given for him as he left for China in 1943, his wife Dorothy was asked, "How do you ever live with this man?" She replied, "Oh, I just hang on to the tail of the kite!"

Sources

A number of sources give valuable insights on the remarkable career of Rear Admiral Coggins, but I'm particularly indebted to what's essentially a five-hundred-page biography in the form of an unpublished PhD dissertation: *Cecil Coggins and United States Military Intelligence in World War Two*, written by William E. Scaring, Boston College, 1996.

Breuer, 130–32.
Dorwart, *Conflict of Duty*, 66, 122, 201.
Farago, *Burn after Reading*, 276–77.
Layton, *"And I Was There,"* 50.
Miles, 220, 224, 352–53.
Moon, 89, 95–96.
Nakamura, Kelli Y. "Cecil Coggins." *Densho Encyclopedia*. encyclopedia.densho.org/Cecil%20 Coggins/.
ncis.navy.mil/aboutNCIS/history/pages/1935-1945.
Prados, 67.
Scaring, i, ii, iv, 1, 24–25, 32, 34–35, 38, 45–46, 48, 58–59, 64–65, 68, 71, 76–77, 82–83, 85, 87, 91–95, 103–23, 125–26, 130–33, 136–39, 141–43, 147–55, 159, 161–63, 165–66, 169, 174–77, 182, 190–92, 194, 198, 205–31, 233, 235, 238, 244, 252–57, 261, 278, 291, 301, 306, 316, 319, 322, 326–29, 331, 345–46, 357–61, 366, 409, 442–57, 477, 479, 489.
U.S. Navy, *Register of Commissioned and Warrant Officers*.
Wilhelm, 83–84, 125–27.
Zacharias, Ellis, 167, 274, 304–5.

CAPTAIN JOSEPH FRANCIS FINNEGAN, U.S. NAVY
(1905–1980)

Intuitive, brilliant, and volatile
One of Rochefort's core group at Station HYPO
One of the two "ace translators" at HYPO
"Joe" "Trench"

Joe Finnegan was a superb intelligence officer as well as one who certainly marched to the sound of his own drummer. He started out with the normal surface-ship early career—although it might be said that service on a Yangtze River gunboat might be considered a little unusual. He underwent the ONI-sponsored full-immersion Japanese language and culture training, which directly led to duty at radio intelligence Station CAST in the Philippines. Later, after his ship was put out of commission during the Pearl Harbor attack, Finnegan attached to Hawaii's Station HYPO and there, for the duration of the war, he delivered a spectacular—if at times a flamboyant—performance.

* * *

From the 1928 Naval Academy yearbook *The Lucky Bag*:

This dark haired boy early heard the call of the sea. Finding the "Hub" [*a nickname for Boston*] too small, he climbed out on one of the spokes and in time found himself in our midst. Hailing from the "Savoir State," he had no trouble with the Academic Department. Every study hour he may be heard to say: "Have you anything to read? . . . Oh, I've read all those." Finding time hanging heavily on his hands, he used his literary ability to advantage in "Log" [the midshipman humor magazine] work. *Joe* likes nothing better than to be managing something, even in the mess hall. He manages to keep the Filipinos [the enlisted mess stewards] busy filling the dishes. Whenever a political discussion is in progress, *Joe* will be found somewhere near. He should have been a lawyer. Since he didn't choose that profession the Navy is the winner, because we all want him with us in the fleet. Notable quotation: "Say! What time is it?" as the bell rung, "What's the lesson?" [Activities: Gymkhana [*a spectacular show put on just before spring exams*] business manager; swimming manager; "Log" staff]

* * *

Joe Finnegan was born on August 5, 1905, at Fields Corner, Dorchester, Massachusetts.[1] His parents were Peter Joseph Finnegan and Marion Catherine Connor Finnegan, who also had another son and four daughters. Joe went to the Boston Latin School but had to drop out in the ninth grade and seek various minor employments due to the family's poverty. He later told his son that he then came up with a plan to become a naval officer; but at this point it's hard to confirm whether it really was a deliberate plan or not. Regardless, in December 1922 he enlisted in the navy as an apprentice seaman; later, as a third class yeoman, he served onboard the battleship *Mississippi*. He then gained entry to the naval academy preparatory school in San Diego, from which he graduated first in his class. He subsequently received an appointment to the U.S. Naval Academy in 1924, and was graduated and commissioned an ensign as part of the class of 1928. Ensign Finnegan finished fifteenth out of 153 in class standings. Among his distinguished classmates were David L. McDonald, Philip D. Gallery, William F. Raborn Jr., and John A. **Williams**.

---

1. "Francis" might not have been Joseph's real middle name, and in fact he might not have had one at all. His son Gregory sheds some doubt on the issue, and some official navy records clearly show him as "NMN." Interestingly, toward the end of his life, there's at least one document where he wrote "Joseph Gregory Finnegan"—perhaps in honor of his son. It could be, like President Harry S Truman, he felt his birth name lacked something and so decided to add to it on his own.

Subsequent promotions were lieutenant (junior grade), 1931; lieutenant, 1936; lieutenant commander, January 1942; commander, September 1942; and captain, 1945. He retired from the navy in 1953 for medical reasons—just as did his classmate (and Station HYPO coworker) Jack Williams.

For two months after graduation Ensign Finnegan took aviation indoctrination training. Then, from August 1928 through November 1930, he served onboard the battleship *Florida*—and was part of her decommissioning crew as she was taken out of service and scrapped as part of the terms of the London Naval Treaty. In early 1931 Joe was briefly sent to the Asiatic Station and attached to the USS *Peary*, which was part of Destroyer Squadron Fifteen. Then, from December 1931 through October 1933, he had duty onboard the shallow-draft Yangtze River gunboat *Monocacy*. This was unusual and adventurous duty, for such gunboats mixed station-ship duties with river patrolling—and supplied armed guard details to U.S.-flagged merchantmen transiting unsecure stretches of the river. In 1933 the *Monocacy* began serving as a station ship in various Chinese treaty ports during the cruising season, with her crew serving as a landing force in case of trouble.

Joe then helped commission the heavy cruiser *New Orleans* at New York, and then briefly served onboard as radio officer; there he became acquainted with and befriended Ens. Forrest "Tex" **Biard** and another future Japanese linguist, Ens. John R. Bromley.

Lieutenant Finnegan was then selected for ONI's full-immersion Japanese language and culture training, which for him ran from fall 1934 through fall 1937 (Mr. Biard later said that Finnegan's example had inspired him to also apply for the Tokyo immersion). In Japan, Joe made the acquaintance of fellow students Lt. Ranson **Fullinwider** and Marine Capt. Alva "Red" **Lasswell**.

Joe immediately made good use of this training, for his next assignment was with the Sixteenth Naval District at Cavite, starting in early October 1937. There Finnegan was the first language officer attached to the secret radio intelligence unit called Station CAST, where he quickly proved of great value. In fact, in 1938, his fellow COMINT colleague and Annapolis classmate Jack Williams wrote a very positive note about him.

> Here is one officer of whom the communications intelligence service should not lose sight. He is enthusiastic to the "nth" degree. His knowledge of Japanese is practically perfect and he took to the telegraphic language like a duck to water. He will read meanings in messages that I don't believe could be duplicated by any other language officer. By this I mean that he not only reads the words that are there but also gets at the essential idea behind the message. He can recover keys and forms to a high degree of ability. Give him a couple of groups in a message and he will give you the entire thing. . . . On code work I don't believe we have his equal, much less his superior, in the service.

In the fall of 1938, Lieutenant Finnegan was relieved as the CAST language officer by Red Lasswell. Joe was next attached to the engineering division of the battleship *Tennessee*, December 1938 through May 1941. Mr. Finnegan was then sent to the FBI in Washington, for two months, for a military intelligence officer training class. After that he returned to Pearl Harbor—and the *Tennessee*—as aide and flag lieutenant to Rear Adm. David W. Bagley, who was the Commander, Battleship Division Two. Finnegan was serving in that billet the morning of December 7, 1941, when the Japanese attacked Pearl Harbor. He had been on liberty ashore, so was not onboard during the strike.

Shortly after the attack, Joe—a "burly, black-haired Irishman"—was ordered to the basement offices of Station HYPO, or the Combat Intelligence Unit of the Fourteenth Naval District. He made his entrance on December 8, straight from duty with the *Tennessee* which had been damaged and put out of commission during the attack. He was very welcome as an excellent Japanese linguist and experienced cryptanalyst. He already knew many of the people at HYPO, having been part of the navy's small community of linguists and cryptologists for about seven years. Finnegan naturally knew Lieutenant Commander Fullinwider and Captain Lasswell from language immersion training in Japan. He also knew Lt. Cmdr. Jack **Holtwick** from his assignment at Station CAST, and he certainly knew Lt. Forrest Biard from previous service on the *New Orleans*. In fact, sixty years later, Biard gave a presentation in which he said that one of the few good things that happened on December 7 was that in hitting the *Tennessee*, the Japanese

> made one fatal mistake. They spared a very special one of her officers, a certain Lt. Cmdr. Joseph Finnegan, U.S.N.A. Class of 1928, Tokyo-trained Japanese linguist, usually gregarious but sometimes reclusive, intuitive, brilliant, volatile, and a "professional" U.S. Irishman from Boston. The Japanese paid a high price for that mistake. It cost them the war.[2]

On his first night at HYPO, he was walking across the navy yard in the dark; the yard naturally under strict blackout. According to Lt. j.g. Gil **Slonim**, he fell "ass over elbow" into a newly dug slit trench, which earned him the nickname "Trench." Recalling his first day at HYPO, Mr. Finnegan later said that

---

2. It might be fair to say that if Joe Finnegan had a fan club, Tex Biard must rank as its "chairman"—apparently all the way from 1934 to Biard's death in 2009. In Biard's opinion, Finnegan's wartime value was only exceeded by Joe Rochefort's: "Of the brilliant officers at HYPO, second in line after Rochefort for honors is the incomparable human dynamo, the top-notch linguist, intuitive codebreaker, brilliant thinker, strategic analyst, and, along with Joe Rochefort, an outstanding mind-reader of the Japanese high command, the professional U.S. Irishman from Boston, Joe Finnegan. I knew Joe well for years prior to working with him in the [HYPO] Dungeon. . . . In our team Finnegan was a 'Babe Ruth'—always a star, always spectacular, a home-run hitter and always a fantastic threat to the enemy—who hadn't the slightest idea that he was batting so effectively against them." If Biard has any serious competition in singing Finnegan's praises, it was retired university professor William H. Amos. Bill had lived in Japan and also went through ONI's University of Colorado language program. As a naval reserve lieutenant he worked at FRUPac and JICPOA in translations from 1943 to 1945; for two years he worked under Finnegan on a daily basis. Almost to the present day, Bill remembered Joe as brilliant and as his "hero." As this book was being edited, Bill passed away at ninety-four years of age and may have been the last of the HYPO/FRUPac officers.

when I arrived, Commander **Rochefort** was under terrific pressure because of the attack the day before. At 5:00 on the morning of the 8th, Pearl Harbor went to general quarters in a full red alert, standing by for another attack. It didn't take much imagination to know how tense things were. . . . [a lot of responsibility] was dumped willy-nilly on Rochefort for lack of any other facility.

HYPO's OIC, Joe Rochefort, immediately assigned Joe Finnegan to work on Japanese consulate cables which had just been made available to the unit. Finnegan returned to fleet duty on December 20, but came back to the basement—or "the Dungeon"—permanently in mid-February. During his brief time at HYPO in early December, he'd liked the work in the Dungeon and had made a strong impression on Rochefort. When he came back, Finnegan gravitated to his old friend "Lasswell, to form one of the most effective partnerships in Rochefort's basement." In fact Lieutenant Commander Finnegan and Major Lasswell, wrote colleague Jasper **Holmes**, "became the most productive of the cryptographer-translators." As noted by HYPO historian Elliot Carlson, "steeped in Japanese and familiar with the elements of cryptology, Finnegan was a perfect fit in the basement." Rochefort never regretted his decision: "I had possibly the two best language officers—I like to think, besides me—this would be Joe Finnegan and . . . Alva Lasswell. [Accurate translation] would be the crux of the whole thing. You can assign values and all that sort of thing, but unless you do a good job of translating then the whole [effort] is lost."

HYPO's chief cryptanalyst, Lt. Cmdr. Thomas **Dyer**, agreed. "Our two top translators were very good. They balanced each other."

Many years later retired Capt. Jasper Holmes, who worked very closely with both officers, made an interesting comparison between the two.

Lasswell approached cryptanalysis like a chess-player maneuvering relentlessly to untangle his problem. His desk was usually clear of everything but his current puzzle. He worked sitting upright at his desk, wearing a carefully pressed Marine Corps uniform of the day, his sole deviation being a green eyeshade for protection against the hours under fluorescent lights.

Finnegan barricaded himself behind a desk with two flanking tables, all piled high with IBM printouts, newspapers, messages, crumpled cigarette packs, coffee cups, apple cores, and sundry material, through which he searched intently, usually with success, for some stray bit of corroboratory evidence he remembered having seen days or weeks before. He paid little attention to the hours of the day, or days of the week, and not infrequently he worked himself into such a state of exhaustion that his head dropped into the rat's nest on his desk and he reluctantly fell asleep.

Rochefort was a master at matching the talents of these two translators. A Finnegan hunch checked out by Lasswell's siege tactics made a firm foundation on which to build.

Holmes had some other interesting things to say about Finnegan in his invaluable 1979 book, *Double-Edged Secrets: U.S. Naval Intelligence Operations in the Pacific during World War II.*

When work on the [Japanese Navy JN-25] code reached the state where language-officer cryptanalysts could read a few code groups, they frequently wanted background information. Finnegan, in particular, would sometimes demand information that was difficult to get and often seemed completely irrelevant. He was very inarticulate and sometimes unable to explain his requirements or his reasoning, but so many times he was right in his conclusions that I did my utmost to get whatever he wanted. He conducted cryptanalysis by hunches and intuition. He had the ability to take off in an illogical direction from a shaky premise and land squarely on a firm conclusion. *En route*, he might want . . . me to produce charts of remote areas, find the eight-letter name of a place for which he had the middle four letters, and tell him what news had been broadcast from Honolulu three days back.

In fact, Holmes was very protective of Finnegan. In the early months of the war, Finnegan roomed with Lt. j.g. Gil Slonim in the latter's apartment. According to Finnegan's son, Dr. Gregory Finnegan, who talked with Slonim in the late 1990s,

They worked opposite shifts at HYPO. . . . Gil recalled trying to get to sleep after grueling shifts and not being able to because Finnegan had a neurotic tic such that he couldn't go to work without hearing the sign-off song on Gracie Fields' radio program.

Unfortunately for Slonim, Finnegan had already displayed some invaluable brilliance in his work, so

When Lt. j.g. Gil Slonim complained about this to Lt. Cmdr. Jasper Holmes, he said Holmes' reply was that "if Joe Finnegan needed a brass band to be able to work, he'd get it."

Joe was the first in the Dungeon to voice concern that the Japanese were about to try "a power play around the southern end of the allied defense line in the area of New Guinea." He identified a new aircraft carrier associated with the Japanese 4th Fleet at Rabaul (but he read it as the *Ryukaku* rather than its real name of *Shōhō*). On April 24, 1942, Lieutenant Commander Finnegan also discovered a reference to a new organization, the "MO Covering Force" and references to an "MO Occupation Force." He assessed that MO meant Port Moresby and an associated Port Moresby operation. After a few days of careful digging and thinking, Major Lasswell and Commander Rochefort agreed. This all turned out to partially reveal the Japanese plan to move down and around the eastern end of New Guinea and go through the Coral Sea to occupy Port Moresby, while another force would seize an advance base in the Solomon Islands. This and other information persuaded Admiral Nimitz to position forces for what came to be the Battle of the Coral Sea.

Prior to the Battle of Midway, as American intelligence was trying to determine what the Japanese symbol "AF" meant in radio interceptions, Lieutenant Holmes observed that fresh water was a constant problem at Midway, and that a breakdown of the main distillation plant would be of great interest to the Japanese if they planned to invade there. Knowing that Pearl Harbor could securely communicate with Midway via an underwater cable, Finnegan then remarked that Midway could be secretly instructed, using the cable, to report such a breakdown via a plain-language radio message. Then, if the Japanese intercepted that report, they'd likely report it in turn to Tokyo, and American radio intelligence would catch it. Rochefort looked at Finnegan for a moment, and then said, "That's *all right*, Joe." The idea was implemented, the Japanese caught the message and reported it, and American radio intelligence intercepted their report—ending the uncertainty that "AF" was Midway.[3]

Mr. Finnegan and his colleagues found great profit in milking reports from Japanese radio intelligence for actionable information, particularly transmissions from their Wake Island R.I. unit. On one instance, Finnegan believed that he had broken an intelligence report based on a radio news broadcast from Honolulu, but it had gaps. The radio stations did not keep transcripts, so Finnegan wanted to see all the local newspapers to perhaps piece it together. As luck would have it, that morning a brand-new and intense young man named Ens. Donald M. Showers reported to the Dungeon—and was instantly sent back into town to get a complete set of papers since December 7. A day later he returned, weary and bedraggled, but with bound volumes of the *Honolulu Advertiser* and the *Honolulu Star-Bulletin* under his arms.[4]

One of Finnegan's colleagues at Station HYPO, Arthur Benedict, later said that

in the two to three weeks before Midway—I can never get over the way Finnegan worked. He never left the building, hardly slept, and lived on "bennies." The Benzedrine [an amphetamine] helped Finnegan maintain his 84-hour work-weeks, but he paid for it with an addiction.

On May 20, Station HYPO intercepted what seemed to be Japanese Admiral Yamamoto Isoroku's operations order for the Midway offensive, and practically the entire staff jumped on it. Lt. Cmdr. Wesley **Wright**, ready to leave after a twelve-hour shift, stayed to work on the date-time groups. Joe Finnegan had brought the part with the date-time cipher to Wright, and said "Ham, we're stuck on the date and time." Shaking off his fatigue, Wright sat at an empty desk in the traffic analysis section, and took the garbled text as well as the three previous uses of the cipher (one of them in a message that had led to the Battle of the Coral Sea). Wright put four people on a search for other instances of the cipher, and he and Finnegan got to work. For a good while a flaw in one corrupt cryptogram frustrated their efforts, but as the night wore on Wright worked it out.

---

3. When the message about Midway's malfunctioning water evaporator came into HYPO, it surprised Lt. Cmdr. Tommy Dyer, who had not been let in on the secret. "I happened to read the Japanese interception of the water message, and I was so ignorant of the whole affair that I told Rochefort, 'Those stupid bastards on Midway. What do they ever mean by sending out a message like this in plain language?'"

4. "Mac" Showers spent the entire war in Pacific Theater combat intelligence, and then followed that with a distinguished career in naval intelligence. "Of all the officers and men working in the basement during the Battle of Midway, Showers was the only one eventually to reach the rank of rear admiral" on active duty. He was instrumental in getting the long-overdue Distinguished Service Medal awarded to Joe Rochefort's family in 1986. Rear Adm. Showers died in October 2012.

By about 5:30 the next morning, he had a solution. His inability to apply symmetry of position to the unrelated alphabets gave it a certain amount of slack, but he regarded it as essentially sound. He showed it to Rochefort. That expert noted the weak spots and said to Wright, in mock rebuke, "I can't send this out."

"If you don't," Wright replied firmly, "I will." Rochefort laughed. He'd only been testing Wright's faith in the solution, and Wright knew it. "Go ahead," he said.

Wright took it up to communications for transmission, via the COPEK channel, to the other COMINT units. He then headed once again for home, and on the way saw [fleet intelligence officer] Eddie **Layton** about 7:45 and told him about it. Within hours, Admiral Nimitz knew that the Japanese had ordered that the Midway operation was to commence June 2 against the Aleutian Islands and June 3 against Midway atoll. [Layton's] intelligence staff had [earlier] forecast correctly—but what a relief it was to know for sure; to work on fact instead of theory.

Various historians have given credit to chief cryptanalyst Lt. Cmdr. Tommy Dyer for helping, but he said in a 1983 interview that he had not. He did comment that because the internal time-date cipher had appeared in Japanese messages only three times, Finnegan and Wright's solution was "a brilliant piece of work." To find the essential missing date, "Lieutenant Commanders Wright and Finnegan stayed up all night in the Dungeon, trying to crack the various layers of encipherment in the messages. At 5:30 the next morning, Wright reported to Rochefort that . . . the attack would begin on June 4th, Tokyo time." They were correct, though the Japanese later postponed the attack by one day.[5]

Right before the Battle of Midway, the Japanese made a substantial code change on June 1, 1942, making it impossible for HYPO to follow all their movements. Joe Finnegan

> went around muttering "The big boy is out there," meaning that [Admiral] Yamamoto, with most of the Japanese Combined Fleet, was in the central Pacific hunting for [Admiral] Spruance. Finnegan was right, but he had nothing tangible to go on. Information to confirm his hunch was not available until much later.

After the incredible American victory at Midway, Finnegan actually disappeared for a few days. Jasper Holmes began to be alarmed, but Rochefort said, "'I know where Joe is. Relax.' Sure enough, Finnegan was at his desk the next day, red-eyed and surly and more demanding than ever."

Holmes seems to have been fascinated by Finnegan, and had many stories about him. For example, at Christmas 1942, Holmes's wife Isabelle held a party at their Diamond Head home for about fifteen Dungeon personnel (she had not been

---

5. Although most histories want to give Wright the lion's share of credit for this work, in an interview long after the war Wright himself generously said, "Finnegan worked that out," and did not elucidate his own role. Finnegan would appear to agree, stating in a postwar interview, "I solved it, and it was of the greatest importance because it provided the actual date of the Midway attack and the dates for the noon positions of the Occupation Force." Retired Rear Adm. Edwin Layton later wrote that "it was Lt. Joe Finnegan, a linguist-cryptanalyst, who finally hit upon the method that the Japanese had used to lock up their date-time groups."

evacuated to the mainland because the Holmeses were permanent Oahu residents from before the war). Lieutenant Commander Holmes became alarmed that they were all going to be arrested for breaking curfew because at one point "Finnegan stood up and led the language officers in an emotional rendition of *Kaigun Kōshin Kyoku*, the Japanese Navy song, in Japanese [and] his Irish tenor must have been heard to the uttermost limits of [nearby] Black Point."

In mid-1944, Commander Holmes and a new officer named Lt. Alex Johnson were stuck working on a message which directed the moving of a line of Japanese submarines.

> I asked Commander Finnegan to look at what we had plotted, and he was soon "hooked" on the problem. It was the kind of thing at which he was a genius, involving research of back traffic, plugging holes in old messages with newly recovered cipher numbers, and confirming or rejecting guesses derived from the plot. In a day or two, Johnson had a plot of the new line that passed every test for consistency and probability.

Promoted to captain in 1945, Joe Finnegan remained at Station HYPO and its successor organizations until November of that year. He then transferred to Norfolk to become commanding officer of the attack cargo ship *Winston*; that tour of duty ran from June 1946 until August 1947. Under Captain Finnegan the ship plied the waters of the western Atlantic, participating in amphibious maneuvers with the Marines from the Central American coast in the south to the shores of Greenland in the north.

In September 1947, Joe became the chief of the Advisory Council at the new Central Intelligence Agency, retaining that post until September 1950. At that point he was given command of the attack transport *Menard*. She had been in mothballs, but in light of the Korean War she was recommissioned. After an intensive shakedown, the *Menard* steamed to the Far East in early 1951 to support the movement of men and supplies to the Korean Peninsula. For more than three years she operated between Japanese and South Korean ports, and from the West Coast to the Far East, to bolster the ocean supply lines to ground forces in South Korea. In May 1952, Captain Finnegan left the ship at San Francisco.

After the change of command ceremony, Joe—incredibly—disappeared for about six weeks, going "UA" (unauthorized absence; the navy's term for AWOL). He was subsequently recognized and taken into custody at Rough-and-Ready Island—a naval supply annex near Stockton. He then was confined at Naval Station Treasure Island in San Francisco. Not only had he vanished without permission, he had taken nearly $30,000 of ship's money and gone on a travel and gambling spree in parts of California and Nevada—including Las Vegas. However, an inquiry chose not to pursue charges because it became evident that Captain Finnegan had suffered a significant mental breakdown, precipitated by an addiction to the amphetamine trade-named Benzedrine which—as mentioned earlier—he'd acquired during the incredible high-stress periods at FRUPac during World War II.[6] He was tentatively placed on disability retirement, in January 1953, and discharged into the custody of one of his sisters in Boston. There appears to have been some debate over his case between the Office of the Judge Advocate General and the Bureau of Medicine and Surgery—criminality versus illness. However, it was resolved by October 1954 when Captain Finnegan received a full retirement by reason of permanent physical disability. From then on Joe essentially lived in the Boston area for the rest of his life. At some point in the 1960s he traveled to Washington and went before a medical board, at Bethesda Naval Hospital, which declared him "competent." At that time he may have been drug free and competent, but it's fair to say that his alcohol consumption was high—as it had been for years.

Captain Finnegan was recalled to active duty from July through November 1969, which involved work at the Naval Historical Division in the Washington Navy Yard. There he was interviewed for eleven volumes of oral history but, after review, most were deemed highly classified and given up to the NSA. Historian Elliot Carlson mentions that Finnegan was engaged in some correspondence with Joe Rochefort during that same time—in which they both discussed, among other things, their respective unhappy medical situations.

Captain Finnegan had married twice. His first wife was the nationally ranked tennis player and minor Hollywood actress Mercedes Marlowe (1914–1987), whom he wed in 1938. The union didn't last very long and they were divorced in May 1941.[7] Joe's second wife was Phyllis Liebman (1919–1972). In early 1941, Phyllis had moved from San Francisco to Oahu where she found a civilian job with the army. She and Joe both lived in Waikiki; she from 1941, and he from around 1944. They saw each other during the latter part of the war as best as Joe could get breaks away from FRUPac and JICPOA.[8] They had one son, Dr. Gregory Finnegan, who at the

---

6. During the war, use of such drugs to stay awake and sharp during high-intensity work was by no means unknown. Finnegan's FRUPac colleague Tommy Dyer used them. In fact, Joe Rochefort suggested that, during 1942, Dyer had lots of pills on his desk for anyone to use—a remark that Dyer flatly denies. But Dyer did say, in his USNI oral history, that he "did tell one other person about them, and that was a mistake, because he was not careful in their use." It very well could be that the person whom Dyer would not name was Joe Finnegan.

In regard to the mental stress and strain of cryptography, intelligence expert Capt. Arthur McCollum made this comment at a Congressional hearing: "This type of work is one of the most trying mental exercises you can have. We have had a number of our officers and a number of our civil people break down rather badly under continual punching on this sort of thing and it is a continual concern of officers who handle these people to keep them from coming to a mental breakdown on this type of work."

7. Mercedes Marlowe only appeared in a few films, including *Escape from Hell Island* (1963), *For Love or Money* (1963), and *Gomer Pyle, USMC* (1964). Joe's son says that the decision to part was Joe's, but in order not to damage his naval career she agreed to formally initiate the divorce, which she did in Las Vegas. At that time there was a story that she was leaving Lieutenant Commander Finnegan to take up with professional boxer Jack Dempsey, but it's hard to connect her name to the three-times married Dempsey. Captain Finnegan appears to have paid alimony to her until he passed away in 1980.

8. Finnegan's son, Gregory, provides this interesting comment: "Because of the irregular hours worked by the HYPO/FRUPac people, they had to get—over and over and over—exemptions from general travel regulations regarding being out after curfew and the mandate for carpooling to save gas. [This was made more difficult,] of course, without being able to explain WHY such special treatment was necessary!"

time of this writing is retired from Harvard University (anthropology and librarianship) and is living in Cambridge. Joe and Phyllis separated in 1952 at the time of his breakdown, but they never divorced.

Joseph Finnegan passed away from multiple ailments—principally pneumonia—on September 8, 1980, in Brighton, Massachusetts. He is buried at Arlington National Cemetery. His obituary, published in the *Boston Globe*, said that he was "the most successful initial translator in all the Navy's communication intelligence stations . . . his contributions were essential, especially his intuition, during the critical Pearl Harbor-Guadalcanal period."

Captain Finnegan's awards include the Legion of Merit for his brilliant work and superlative accomplishments in World War II communications intelligence.

Sources

Amos, Prof. William H., email, February 1, 2014.
Biard, 151–58.
Carlson, 200, 256, 277–79, 286, 303, 346, 439, 445, 500, 520.
Dyer, 206–7, 244, 265–66.
Farago, *Broken Seal*, 335.
Finnegan, Dr. Gregory A. Telephone interview, February 8, 2014.
Holmes, 37, 55, 62–64, 69–70, 86, 88, 90–94, 98, 101, 119–20, 167, 172.
Holtwick, 263, 318–19.
Layton, *"And I Was There,"* 427, 452, 471.
Lucky Bag, U.S. Naval Academy, 1928.
Prados, 315, 319, 408, 730.
Prange, *Miracle*, 18.
Rochefort, 103, 105.
Schom, 27, 283.
Slesnick, 54.
Smith, *Emperor's Codes*, 139–40.
Symonds, 188.
U.S. Navy, *Register of Commissioned and Warrant Officers*.

REAR ADMIRAL RANSON FULLINWIDER, U.S. NAVY
(1905–1969)

A long-term pre-war Station HYPO veteran
One of the original at-sea flagship combat radio intelligence officers
"Fully"

Known as a courtly and quiet-spoken gentleman, Ranson Fullinwider was fairly typical of the Japanese language officers profiled in this book. He started out as a "black-shoe" surface ship officer; he later was sent to Japan as an ONI immersion language and culture student—from 1932 to 1935. He did three more years in a battleship and then began a long run in radio intelligence, including a considerable period at Hawaii's Station HYPO. He was one of the first to lead a flagship-based radio interception unit in combat and in this role survived the sinking of both the *Lexington* and the *Yorktown*. After further wartime communications-intelligence work, his postwar years saw him involved in diplomatic liaison activities in Argentina, Pakistan, Portugal, and Spain.

*   *   *

From the 1926 Annapolis yearbook, *The Lucky Bag*:

> "Hey, Mister, what state are you from?" But Mid'n Fullinwider, Fourth Class, didn't know what to say, because he was from the District of Columbia. *Fully* soon overcame his bashful stage and became one of the stellar members of that non-reg organization, the Wine, Women, and Song Club. If you doubt his ability at handling the *femmes*, just get him to tell you about the time he dragged [brought] two of them to the same hop [dance] and didn't get his lines twisted. It's just his way of trying anything once. However, don't get the idea that our hero isn't a real he-man because he likes to drag and knows how to gargle tea—for pacing a rollicking quarterdeck and busting Texas broncos are his favorite pastimes. . . . *Fully* kept his [grade point] average down to a happy medium, and spent all of his spare time reading the paper. Here's wishing you luck, *Fully*, wherever you go, whether it be selling snow shoes in Savannah, or swimming suits in Archangel. [Activities: Sub-Squad]

*   *   *

Ranson Fullinwider was born in Washington, D.C., on October 23, 1905, to Bettie G. and Commander Simon P. Fullinwider, U.S. Navy. He attended the Army and Navy Preparatory School and then entered the Naval Academy in 1922. He graduated in 1926, along with such distinguished classmates as Clarence Wade McClusky Jr., Maxwell F. Leslie, Wesley "Ham" **Wright**, Henri deB. **Claiborne**, Frank P. Pyzick, Howard W. Gilmore, Lofton R. Henderson, Robert B. Pirie, James S. Russell, and Paul D. Stroop. Subsequent promotions included lieutenant (junior grade), 1929; lieutenant, 1936; lieutenant commander, 1941; commander, 1942, and captain, 1944. In 1956 he was placed on the disability retired list and simultaneously promoted to rear admiral by reason of special commendation for performance of duty in combat.

Like so many junior officers of his generation, Mr. Fullinwider began a career as a general line officer in surface ships—in his case initially serving onboard the battleship *New Mexico* from August 1926 through June 1927. He then was attached to the oiler *Ramapo* until March 1928. From that time until May 1932 he was onboard the destroyer *Borie*, and then he reported for a month's orientation at OP-20-G at Main Navy.

Having been selected as one of ONI's Japanese language and cultural immersion students, he moved to Japan and studied there from July 1932 until September 1935. While in Japan he became acquainted with Lt. j.g. Joe **Finnegan** and Marine 1st Lt. Alva "Red" **Lasswell**, with whom he would later serve at Station HYPO in Hawaii. In the fall of 1935, Lieutenant Fullinwider returned to Main Navy for about nine months' duty, and then was attached once again to the *New Mexico* from June 1936 to April 1939. In April 1936, Fully was one of thirteen Japanese language officers whom ONI offered to Naval Communications for duty in decryption units. Accordingly, in the spring of 1939, he took a month's orientation at OP-20-G before being sent out to the Fourteenth Naval District headquarters at Pearl Harbor.

There, as a barely oriented cryptographer but a thoroughly trained linguist, he affiliated with Station HYPO. Arriving in June 1939, his duties were to assist the new OIC (Lt. Cmdr. Thomas **Birtley**), perform as a language officer, and work in HYPO's new "Enemy Information Division." By the spring of 1941, Mr. Birtley and Mr. Fullinwider remained the only Japanese translators at HYPO; new fleet intelligence officer Lt. Cmdr. Edwin **Layton** found them "very much understaffed and overworked." By that summer Fullinwider was the longest-serving member of HYPO, excluding Lt. Cmdr. Thomas **Dyer**.

Right before Cmdr. Joseph **Rochefort** arrived to take over as HYPO's OIC in June 1941, Capt. Red Lasswell had attached in May. Lasswell was immediately assigned to lead a two-man language team—himself and his old friend from Japanese immersion, Lieutenant Commander Fullinwider—but fortunately in September they were augmented by linguists Lt. "Tex" **Biard**, Lt. Allyn Cole, Lt. j.g. Gil **Slonim**, Lt. j.g. John Bromley, and Marine Capt. Banks **Holcomb**.

After the attack on Pearl Harbor in December, Rochefort was directed to form several teams and put them onboard select aircraft carriers as new radio interception units. Thus, in early 1942, Biard and several radio operators went out with the *Yorktown*, Slonim likewise on the *Enterprise*, and Fullinwider similarly on the *Lexington*. In early May 1942 the *Yorktown* and *Lexington* were engaged at the Battle of the Coral Sea. During the action, Fully mistranslated a Japanese signal regarding the enemy task force's course and speed. Rear Adm. Frank Jack Fletcher, the overall U.S. commander onboard the *Yorktown*, was not getting along with Lieutenant Biard and was not confident in him. As a result, the admiral took Fullinwider's assessment over Biard's; however, due to Fully's error, this unfortunately resulted in a lost opportunity to hit the Japanese carriers while they were servicing their aircraft. Later, the Japanese attacked both the *Lexington* and *Yorktown*; luckily Fullinwider and his unit escaped injury when the *Lexington* had to be abandoned prior to her sinking.

Back at Pearl Harbor, Lieutenant Commander Fullinwider replaced Lieutenant Biard on the *Yorktown*. As that ship and her escorts moved toward Midway Island, where she was shortly going to be in the midst of the enormous Battle of Midway, Fully and his unit intercepted several enemy transmissions which indicated that the Japanese were attempting to seed the area with submarines. Fortunately for the Americans, nothing came of it.

During the battle itself, which began on June 4, 1942, the teams of Fullinwider in the *Yorktown*, and Slonim in the *Enterprise*, provided extremely valuable information after initial contact was made with the Japanese—particularly through the interception of Japanese plain-language reports. Once again the *Yorktown* was severely damaged, but unlike her experience at the Coral Sea, this time she was beyond saving. The Radio Intercept Unit stayed onboard as long as possible, destroying documents and dropping equipment over the side. Mr. Fullinwider was one of the last to leave the burning ship and facilitated moving his men—as well as Admiral Fletcher—to the nearby cruiser *Astoria*. Fully remarked to Fletcher that the admiral could count on him because he was becoming an old hand at abandoning sinking aircraft carriers. After the battle, and upon their return to Pearl Harbor, Fullinwider and his unit were then "grounded" due to the shortage of carrier flagships.

Promoted to commander in December 1942, Mr. Fullinwider remained at HYPO—which was becoming more widely known as FRUPac—until March 1943. He then transferred back to Washington, working in the office of the CNO until September 1944. He was promoted to captain in August, and a month later he returned to the Pacific Theater for a year, attached to Pacific Radio Unit 128. At the end of the war, in September 1945, he saw service in the attack transport *Bosque*.

In March 1946, Captain Fullinwider once again returned to Washington and then in August he became the naval attaché—and naval attaché for air—at the U.S. embassy in Buenos Aires. In August 1949 he transferred to the Ninth Naval District at Great Lakes, Illinois. From 1951 through June 1952 he was at the Naval War College in Newport, Rhode Island, where he completed the naval warfare senior course. In August 1952, Fully was in the office of the U.S. Naval Attaché in Karachi, Pakistan. Then, after a few months back in Washington, Captain Fullinwider was sent as part of the Military Assistance Advisory Group in Portugal and Spain. In March 1956, Fullinwider reported to the headquarters of the Potomac River Naval Command, but was there only until his retirement a few months later.

On July 1, 1956, Captain Fullinwider was placed on the navy's disability retired list and was simultaneously promoted to the rank of rear admiral—by reason of special commendation for combat performance in World War II.

Fully was related to quite a collection of Naval Academy alumni, some of whom include his father, Capt. Simon Peter Fullinwider (1894); his two brothers, Rear Adm. Edwin G. Fullinwider (1921) and Capt. Simon Pendleton Fullinwider (1917); and two nephews, Simon Pendleton Fullinwider Jr. (1955) and Capt. Peter Lansing Fullinwider (1949).

On September 6, 1969, at age sixty-four, Ranson Fullinwider unexpectedly died from a heart attack. This happened in Highlands, South Carolina; he collapsed while driving with his wife from their home in Fort Lauderdale on the way to visit his brother, Edwin, in Washington.

Among his awards are the Navy Commendation Medal with the Combat "V" device, the Navy Unit Citation, and several foreign decorations.

Fully is buried along with his wife at Arlington National Cemetery. Mrs. Fullinwider was Gabie Marie DeLores Fullinwider (1908–1969); she passed on just a month after he did.

Sources

Carlson, 101, 105, 140, 200, 243, 256, 375, 483.

Holmes, 22, 58.

Holtwick, 104, 181, 327, 329, 333, 406, 428, 446.

Layton, *"And I Was There,"* 52, 395, 400.

Lucky Bag, U.S. Naval Academy.

Obituary, Rear Admiral Ranson Fullinwider. *Navy Times*, September 21, 1969.

Prados, 175, 306, 309, 322, 328.

Rear Admiral Ranson Fullinwider, USN, Retired. Transcript of Naval Service. BuPers-E24-DRH, August 22, 1956.

Spector, *Listening*, 80.

Toll, 346.

BRIGADIER GENERAL BANKSON TAYLOR HOLCOMB JR., U.S. MARINE CORPS (1908–2000)

Fluent in both Japanese and Chinese
In Rochefort's group at Station HYPO
"Banks" "Chink"

As part of a long and remarkable career, Banks Holcomb served for almost twelve years in the Far East, and could speak both Chinese and Japanese—*very* difficult languages—fluently. General Holcomb served in Rochefort's Station HYPO, as well as in Shanghai, Peking, Tokyo, Korea, at sea, and at various posts in the United States including the ONI in Washington.

*   *   *

From the 1931 Annapolis yearbook, the *Lucky Bag*:

> *Chink* is first, last, and always a Pekinese. He knows more about the China Station than does the admiral in command, a fact which is shown in his undying interest in *orientalia*. Though he is reputed to be able to carry on a conversation with any given laundry man, one of course cannot vouch for his being Chinese. In the immediate past his ambitions and efforts have been directed toward the Marine Corps—and none know it better than those who have maligned the marines within hearing distance of him. *Chink* doesn't talk a great deal, but he does things. When he can find a moment not filled with boning [studying] or radio, he builds ship models which are worthy of a naval constructor. [Activities: Cross country, track, Radio Club, choir.]

*   *   *

Bankson Holcomb was born in Wilmington, Delaware, on April 14, 1908. He first went to China in 1921 with his businessman father, and after five years became very proficient in the Chinese language. During that time he also became interested in amateur radio and built some basic equipment for himself. He graduated from the Peking American High School, and then served in the Marine Corps as an enlisted man from April 1925 through June 1927, having enlisted with the Marine Detachment, Peking. After six months he was ordered to the Naval Academy Preparatory School in San Diego, where he promptly failed Ancient History. He was then assigned to the Virginia Preparatory School in Hampton Roads, and was subsequently appointed to the Naval Academy. He graduated from the academy in June 1931, along with classmates Rudolph J. **Fabian**, John S. McCain Jr., Lawson "Red" Ramage, Horacio Rivero Jr., and Bernard F. **Roeder**. He was promoted to first lieutenant in 1934; captain, 1939; major and lieutenant colonel, 1942; and colonel, 1948. He was made a brigadier general on the retired list in 1959. He was the cousin of Gen. Thomas Holcomb, who was Commandant of the Marine Corps from 1936 to 1943.

After a period at the Marine Barracks in the Philadelphia Navy Yard, in 1932 Banks returned to the Orient as a platoon leader with the 4th Marine Regiment at Shanghai. After two years at the former capital, he undertook a Chinese language course at the American Embassy in Peking. In 1937 he was ordered to Quantico, promoted, and given command of a company of Marines. He passed through the ONI in Washington, and then was sent to Japan, 1939–1941, to take the ONI full-immersion language and culture program, working out of the American embassy in Tokyo.

Shortly before the attack on Pearl Harbor, he was moved out of Japan and sent to Hawaii, assigned to Station HYPO under Cmdr. Joseph **Rochefort** to work as an intelligence officer and translator. Holcomb was on Rochefort's team mainly as a linguist, and as such was detached with three radio operators to be on board the carrier *Enterprise*, translating enemy radio traffic for Vice Admiral Halsey and Task Force 8;

this assignment was in early 1942, during the Kwajalein raid. Banks then returned to Pearl Harbor to work at HYPO in translations and cryptanalysis support. Captain Jasper **Holmes** later wrote that when Holcomb came back to HYPO his description of the raid and Halsey's aggressive spirit "brought a ray of hope into the basement."

In December 1942, Holcomb was sent to China as OIC, Communications Intelligence Activities. He also became a member of the special U.S. Naval Advisory Group in Chungking, assisting the Chinese government in planning the expulsion of the invaders. In 1944, Holcomb came back to Washington as a language officer. Working in OP-20-GZ, he was assigned by Captain Rosie **Mason** to focus upon that section's responsibilities dealing with China. While there he impressed a young ensign named Edward Van Der Rhoer as a remarkable linguist, as well as "a stocky, friendly man with wavy black hair."

In 1945 he returned to the Pacific where he worked radio intelligence and translations for Admiral Spruance, Task Force 58, onboard the flagship. In the last stages of the war he participated in the bitter campaigns for Iwo Jima and Okinawa and, later, returned to Japan for occupation duty.

In 1948, Holcomb was promoted to colonel and assigned duties in Norfolk. He remained as an intelligence officer, but did not return to the communications-intelligence field for the remainder of his career.

In 1949 he once again returned to the Asiatic-Pacific theater, after attending the Armed Forces Staff College at Norfolk, to become chief of staff of the Pacific Fleet Marine Forces at Guam. When war erupted in Korea, Holcomb was assigned as the G-2 (Intelligence) to the 1st Marine Division, fighting with it from Pusan to Chongjin. One day, as he was interrogating Chinese prisoners, one of them shocked him by saying, "Don't you know me, Colonel?" Holcomb then did recognize him as a person he frequently worked with in Chungking—back in 1942.

After the Korean War, Holcomb assumed duties as Assistant Chief of Staff, G-2 Section, Fleet Marine Force, Atlantic.

During World War II, Holcomb garnered seven battle stars on his Asiatic-Pacific ribbon, and earned three more battle stars during the Korean War. Upon his retirement, in 1959, he received a "tombstone" promotion to brigadier general due to his high-level combat citations. After his retirement he and his wife lived in Inverness, Scotland, from where he involved himself in the FRUPac veterans' amateur radio unit. In the early 1980s, General Holcomb put in considerable effort helping Rear Adm. Edwin Layton (and his coauthors) work on Layton's reminisces, *"And I Was There": Pearl Harbor and Midway—Breaking the Secrets.*

Banks died in Scotland, in 2000, at the age of ninety-two.

His many awards include the Bronze Star and two Legions of Merit (one for World War II service and one for the Korean War). General Holcomb has also been designated a Pioneer Officer of U.S. Naval Cryptology by the U.S. Naval Cryptologic Veterans Association.

Sources

Carlson, 94, 101, 164, 239–43, 508.
Holmes, 57–58.
Layton, *"And I Was There,"* 6, 361–62.
Lucky Bag, U.S. Naval Academy, 1931.
McGinnis, 20.
Military Times "Hall of Honor" Website.
Official Biography: *Brigadier General Bankson T. Holcomb, Jr.*
    https://slsp.manpower.usmc.mil/gosa/biographies/rptBiography.asp
Smith, *U.S. Marines*, 218–19.
U.S. Navy, *Register of Commissioned and Warrant Officers.*
Van Der Rhoer, 119–21.

CAPTAIN WILFRED JAY "JASPER" HOLMES, U.S. NAVY (1900–1986)

"Indefatigable"
Officer in charge, Fourteenth Naval District's
Combat Intelligence Unit, 1941–1943
Deputy officer in charge,
Joint Intelligence Center Pacific Ocean Area, 1943–1945
"Jasper"

Jasper Holmes was a technocrat—a career submariner and an engineer with a master's degree. In fact, he narrowly qualifies for inclusion in this study because his involvement in intelligence didn't begin until spring 1941. Yet his affiliation with Station HYPO—eight months before the Pearl Harbor attack—led to extraordinary intelligence contributions during the war at HYPO, ICPOA, and JICPOA. He then spent the following twenty years on the faculty of the University of Hawaii, rising to the position of Dean of Engineering. Moreover, we owe him a considerable debt for illuminating the Pacific's intelligence war via the official history that he wrote—as well as his insightful book, *Double-Edged Secrets*.

* * *

From the 1922 Naval Academy yearbook *The Lucky Bag*:

> No, ladies and gentlemen, this is not a walking advertisement for the world-renowned Rubberset Shaving Brushes [*refers to Holmes's brush-cut hair style in his yearbook photo*], but a dashing young Swede from Hudson, N.Y. One would never guess that beneath this placid countenance lies the aesthetic soul of an ardent devotee of Terpsichore; yet, each time he emerged from the shower during Plebe Year he would gracefully flit to and fro in an impressionistic dance of the muses. Curses, have we failed to mention the bath towel? That towel was just as necessary to *Jasper* as tulle is to Eva Tanguay [*a very popular vaudeville singer who favored extravagant costumes*]. The combination of Navy life and love, however, has changed him to a sadder but wiser man, and his only pastime is writing the nightly wail of his everlasting love in a *billet-doux* to Hudson, N.Y. Frequently heard saying, "Any mail for me, Assistant?" *Jasper* is a true salt from the heels up, and with a little practice he'll be able to hold his liquor with the best of 'em. [Activities: water polo, track, swimming]

* * *

Wilfred Holmes was born in Stockport, New York, on April 4, 1900. He attended Hudson High School in the adjacent town of the same name, and then entered the Naval Academy in 1918. He graduated and was commissioned an ensign in 1922, along with such notable classmates as John S. **Harper**, William S. Parsons, Hyman G. Rickover, William J. **Sebald**, and Henri H. **Smith-Hutton**. Subsequent promotions included lieutenant (junior grade), 1925; lieutenant, 1928; lieutenant commander, 1941; commander, 1943; and captain, 1944. His naval career was extremely unusual in that he was medically retired as a lieutenant in 1936; however, he was recalled to active duty at the Fourteenth Naval District a few months before the attack on Pearl Harbor. Holmes served the entire war in Pacific Theater intelligence, receiving three more promotions and a Distinguished Service Medal before retiring from the navy in 1946 for a second—and final—time.

Typical for his generation of officers, after graduation from Annapolis, Ensign Holmes was initially sent for battleship duty on board the USS *Nevada*. He then qualified in submarines and was posted to the sub *O-11*—just in time to be on her decommissioning crew in 1924. Mr. Holmes then transferred to the submarine *S-32*. In 1925, the *S-32*'s division moved from San Pedro to the Asiatic Fleet. She thus arrived at Cavite, Philippine Islands, in mid-summer and through the winter of 1926 conducted local exercises in the Luzon area. That spring she deployed to the China coast, conducting exercises both en route to and from her summer base, the former German installation at Tsingtao.

The year 1928 saw Mr. Holmes back at the Naval Academy for postgraduate instruction—as well as promotion to lieutenant. He then was sent to Columbia University in New York City where he earned a master's degree in electrical engineering.

In 1930 he crossed the country to San Diego to serve with Submarine Division 20, where he met Capt. Chester W. Nimitz, the division's commander.

Lieutenant Holmes was assigned to the submarine V-6 in 1931—which was renamed the USS Nautilus that same year. The Nautilus was attached to the Pacific Fleet at Pearl Harbor where she became the flagship of Submarine Division 12. The submarine Barracuda was Holmes's next posting, where he served as engineering officer during 1932. In 1933, Mr. Holmes returned to the East Coast and a short assignment at the Naval Research Laboratory, and then returned to take command of the submarine S-30 at Pearl Harbor.

However, 1935 saw Mr. Holmes spending much of his time in the naval hospital at Pearl, undergoing treatment for a significant degree of arthritis in his spine. Unfortunately, his case did not really improve with treatment, so he was retired from the navy, in March 1936, due to medical disability. Fortunately, he had considerable experience as a practical engineer, had the graduate degree in electrical engineering, and had completed another postgraduate course in diesel engineering. As a result he was shortly able to land a faculty position, at the University of Hawaii, as an assistant professor of engineering and mathematics.

He had considerable skill as a writer, too—he'd written the prize-winning essay in the U.S. Naval Institute's annual competition in 1934—and began publishing essays and short stories under the pen name Alec Hudson, several of which were published in the Saturday Evening Post. These often had a naval theme, and Holmes' descriptions of naval equipment and procedure were detailed enough that another aspiring writer, Naval Academy midshipman Edward L. Beach Jr., recognized that "Alec Hudson" must be a naval officer.[1]

In early 1941, the Fourteenth District commandant, Rear Adm. Claude Bloch, remarked to Lt. Cmdr. Tommy **Dyer**, "They've told me I should have a Combat Intelligence Officer. I think there's a retired officer out at the University of Hawaii who would seem to fit the bill. What do you think?" Dyer, lead cryptanalyst of the district's extremely secret Station HYPO, didn't really know retired Lt. Wilfred Holmes, but did know he wrote stories (as Alec Hudson) for the Saturday Evening Post. However, Admiral Bloch apparently knew more about Holmes's suitability than he let on. According to Holmes,

years before, when I was a communications officer in a small submarine, I became interested in cryptography. I solved some of the exercise cryptograms in the monthly communications bulletins and I read a few books on the subject, including an Army pamphlet, Elements of Cryptanalysis, and Herbert O. Yardley's American Black Chamber. A book by Fletcher Pratt, Secret and Urgent, recounted several incidents when Union forces

---

1. No doubt the name "Hudson" came from Holmes' high school. Capt. Ned Beach later earned the Navy Cross in World War II, commanded six submarines and ships, commanded the first submerged circumnavigation of the world, and wrote over a dozen books, including the best-seller Run Silent, Run Deep.

obtained important information from the decryption of Confederate secret messages. There were also stories of the achievements of British cryptanalysts in World War I.

Knowing none of this background, Dyer still agreed that Holmes would make a good choice. Bloch also consulted Cmdr. Joseph **Rochefort**, the new OIC of HYPO. Rochefort was not particularly enthusiastic, not knowing what he would do with an ex-submariner. Yet, if nothing else, "Bloch wanted an officer with knowledge of navigation who could write readable reports," and so brought him on active duty to do ship plotting. At first Holmes was physically stashed here and there, but they finally thought of actually putting him with HYPO. As a newfangled CIO, he was different than the DIO or the fleet intelligence officer, because those officers were concerned more broadly with intelligence. But a CIO was to focus "upon the tactical movements of an enemy that might be in his area."

They eventually gave Holmes an office at the head of the stairway to HYPO's basement rooms. At that point Rochefort actually decided that it made a lot of sense to officially call HYPO the Combat Intelligence Unit, or CIU—after Holmes's title—because it would partially disguise what HYPO was doing and wouldn't arouse too much curiosity. Other people would realize they were doing something secret, but the term CIU didn't really hint at just how secret—the name was "sort of accurate and misleading at the same time."[2]

Holmes initially tracked U.S. and foreign merchant ship and other noncombatant ship positions, plotting their estimated noon positions each day. By collating several sources of information he "soon had charts that furnished a picture of ship movements which was of service to several different offices around Pearl Harbor." Even after Holmes and his assistant—an enlisted yeoman named William Dunbar—moved into HYPO's basement, they were clearly with, but not of, HYPO. Neither had an intelligence nor even a significant communications background. "We were not told anything about [HYPO] and were cautioned not to be curious." That changed after a while. Rochefort shortly saw value in Holmes's work and incorporated him and Dunbar into the overall operation. Rochefort soon included Holmes in the HYPO watch list and started giving him radio traffic analysis summaries to get him up to speed. He gradually became aware of what the HYPO people were doing. As Lieutenant Commander Dyer later said, "We absorbed Jasper sort of by a process of osmosis." Still,

> from the beginning there was confusion as to how my activity fitted into the standard organization chart. . . . Sometimes this was a handicap, but generally it was an asset,

---

2. Early on there was not actual, official name for the Hawaii COMINT group. The name HYPO (the standard name in those days for the "H" flag in the International Signal Code) was used in the beginning—"H" standing for He'eia—and was often loosely used for the whole activity although, strictly speaking, "H" originally only applied to the actual Hawaiian radio intercept station. Later, when radio intelligence was placed directly under the Pacific Fleet (versus the Fourteenth Naval District), it was renamed Fleet Radio Unit Pacific—FRUPac. Technically, the term FRUPac is anachronistic if used to refer to the unit prior to September 1943, but many historians do this for convenience. I have used HYPO and FRUPac somewhat interchangeably—probably HYPO being the more frequent. I have rarely used the term CIU.

because I could often call on several different sources for assistance and could innocently remain ignorant of much inhibiting red tape.

Holmes's desks were moved into the center of the basement. There,

he filled up his new space, creating a nest of file boxes, all holding cards with data provided by the basement's various analysts. Near Holmes' desk was a makeshift plot table constructed out of planks and sawhorses. Soon steel backing was placed on the planks, permitting Holmes to indicate ship movements with small magnets.

He delivered chart overlays of ship positions to the fleet intelligence officer, Lt. Cmdr. Edwin **Layton**; after a while he also started to currier traffic intelligence summaries and other secret materials. Among other reports, Rochefort reviewed the traffic analysis summary every morning "and then passed it to his designated liaison officer, Lieutenant Holmes, who delivered it by car to FIO Layton at Kimmel's headquarters."

Holmes later wrote that "early in November 1941, the situation in the Pacific became alarming. We realized that war was imminent, and the CIU began to maintain a continuous watch." On November 7, Holmes wrote in the unit's Communications Intelligence Summary that the "greatest effort is being made to increase the number of identifiable calls to facilitate analysis of the traffic, but ORANGE [the prewar code name for the Japanese] changes in methods of handling fleet traffic renders this more difficult than had been hoped." By mid-November he had to write that "the large number of alternate calls used by major forces renders analysis of traffic headings very slow and difficult." By the end of November his frustration level was very high; his daily entry now often said nothing more than "no information on submarines or carriers."

By December first, Jasper had made some progress in lining up the calls that had changed in early November, but then they changed again. He decided that "the fact that they lasted only one month indicates an additional progressive step in preparation for active operations on a large scale. It appears that the Japanese Navy is adopting more and more security provisions."

Jasper lived with his wife, Isabelle, and son, Eric, at Black Point, close to Diamond Head, in a community then mostly consisting of artists and submarine officers. He was off duty on Sunday morning, December 7, 1941. Holmes was surprised to be awakened by his son and told of the attack. He told Eric that the report must be wrong, that if the Japanese are attacking anything today they must be "thousands of miles away, taking an island in the Dutch East Indies" or in the South China Sea. On the way in to Pearl Harbor, Jasper saw considerable smoke coming from the base and a lot of anti-aircraft fire in the skies above the harbor. The sights and sounds of battle within the navy yard were enormous, and when Holmes climbed down into the HYPO basement the boss, Joe Rochefort, gave him the bad news: "Japanese air attack on Battleship Row. It looks bad."

Among the events of that hard Sunday, Holmes ironically observed that "the most important contribution of communications intelligence that day" was to cause orders being sent to Vice Adm. William Halsey to search for the Japanese strike force to the south of Oahu. This was the wrong direction, because the only direction-finding units operational that day were unable to distinguish between the real and the reciprocal bearing of radio transmissions—and with a fifty/fifty chance, the wrong direction was picked by CinCPac Fleet. However, this was actually fortunate, because had north been chosen, and had Halsey gone north and encountered the six Japanese aircraft carriers with only his single carrier *Enterprise*, things might not have gone well for him.

In the days right after the attack Holmes continued to track Allied noncombatant ships, which were already at sea, until he was sure that they had reached port. He then shifted more effort on trying to keep track of Japanese submarines.

As is widely known and has been recounted elsewhere, the commander in chief of the Pacific Fleet, Adm. Husband Kimmel, was relieved of command after the attack and Adm. Chester Nimitz was sent out from Washington to replace him. Years before, Holmes had worked as a junior engineering officer in a submarine division commanded by Nimitz. "He had little reason to remember me," but when they met in a passageway shortly after Nimitz's arrival at Pearl on Christmas Day, the new commander in chief greeted Holmes by name and even knew some details about his medical retirement and subsequent activities. Holmes was an admirer of both Kimmel and Nimitz. Holmes felt that it was inevitable that Kimmel would be replaced but he believed it was done unfairly and too harshly. Perhaps Kimmel "should have been relieved of command, but not in disgrace." However, Holmes also thought that the fact "that Nimitz was the one chosen to replace Kimmel was the great good fortune of the United States."[3]

One afternoon at the very end of 1941, Associate Supreme Court Justice Owen Roberts—the head of the first official and large-scale Pearl Harbor disaster investigation—came to the HYPO basement, accompanied by his colleagues Admirals Joseph Reeves and William Standley. The admirals focused their discussion with Joe Rochefort, while Justice Roberts spent time with Jasper Holmes.

As HYPO fell deep into the ever-increasing stress of wartime operations, Holmes grew progressively impressed with the unit's officers. "They had more detailed knowledge of Japanese naval communications systems than I had acquired of American naval communications systems in twenty years of naval experience." Moreover, he went on, "Had I not witnessed it, I never would have believed that any group of men was capable of such sustained mental effort under such constant pressure for

---

3. Jasper not only knew Admiral Nimitz from earlier in his career, but also Admiral Ernest J. King, the wartime navy's overall commander in chief and CNO. King had been commander of the submarine school at New London when Holmes was a student. He recalled that a fellow student had dated one of King's daughters. The story was that she defended her father's strict discipline and exacting demands with this statement: "He is the most even-tempered man in the Navy. He is *always* in a rage."

such a length of time." He finally concluded that "the fate of the nation quite literally depended upon about a dozen men who had devoted their lives and their careers, in peace and war, to radio intelligence."

As the wartime tempo grew Holmes collected more and more duties. Since Rochefort and the other technical experts were buried in work only they could do, Holmes tried to take administrative details off their hands. He inherited liaison duties with the navy yard, the submarine force, CinCPac staff, the naval district, and the like. In the early stages of the war there was no way to promote a retired officer recalled to active duty, so he remained a lieutenant for quite a while.

> My low rank made no difference while I was in the basement, but sometimes it was a minor handicap in my negotiations with the Navy Yard. Fortunately I had many personal friends in the yard and I knew all the ways and byways of its organization. Sometimes even this did not help. Frustration was a minor price to pay for the privilege of making a small contribution to what was cooking in the basement. I did not have the ability [at that time] to stir the pot or taste the broth, but I could chop wood and carry water.

He also became a sort of "odd bits of information" source to support the analysts, finding for them place-name references, charts, maps, news reports, positions of Allied forces, and the like. When the language-officer cryptanalysts could read a few code groups, they often needed background information. Lt. Cmdr. Joseph **Finnegan**, in particular,

> would sometimes demand information that was difficult to get and often seemed completely irrelevant. He was very inarticulate and sometimes unable to explain his requirements or his reasoning, but so many times he was right in his conclusions that I did my utmost to get whatever he wanted. He conducted cryptanalysis by hunches and intuition. He had the ability to take off in an illogical direction from a shaky premise and land squarely on a firm conclusion. *En route*, he might want Dunbar and me to produce charts of remote areas, find the eight-letter name of a place for which he had the middle four letters, and tell him what news had been broadcast from Honolulu three days back.

In fact, Holmes was very protective of Finnegan. In the early months of the war, Finnegan roomed with Lt. j.g. Gil **Slonim** in the latter's apartment. According to Finnegan's son, Dr. Gregory Finnegan, who talked with Slonim in the late 1990s,

> They worked opposite shifts at HYPO. . . . Gil recalled trying to get to sleep after grueling shifts and not being able to because Finnegan had a neurotic tic such that he couldn't go to work without hearing the sign-off song on Gracie Fields' radio program.

Unfortunately for Slonim, Finnegan had already displayed some invaluable brilliance in his work, so

> When Lt. j.g. Gil Slonim complained about this to Lt. Cmdr. Jasper Holmes, he said Holmes' reply was that "if Joe Finnegan needed a brass band to be able to work, he'd get it."

From time to time Jasper tried his hand at both Japanese language and cryptography, but felt that he was a poor student. Maj. "Red" **Lasswell**

> undertook to teach me the *kana* syllabary in both *katakana* and *romaji*. "First thing a Japanese kindergarten kid learns," Rochefort said—by way of encouragement. One afternoon Finnegan gave me part of a place-name that he wanted completed. I tried various combinations of *kana* but none of them fit any names on the charts or in the gazetteers. I had pieced together WO-DO-RA-KU and sat surveying it in disgust when Rochefort happened to look over my shoulder. "That's all right, Jasper," he remarked. "You've got it." I was not only a slow learner, I was so retarded I could not recognize that "Wodoraku" was the *kana* spelling of Woodlark [as in Woodlark Island in New Guinea].

He later wrote that:

> I was invariably frustrated by the Japanese language, and never acquired a knowledge of more than the *katakana* syllabary and a few special Chinese characters, or *kanji*. Had the U.S. Navy been dependent on people like me, Japanese secrets would have been safe; but [fortunately] it was not.

On March 4, 1942, there was a second small attack on Pearl Harbor. "Operation K" was a Japanese naval operation intended as both a reconnaissance of Pearl Harbor and also a disruption of repair and salvage operations. It culminated with an unsuccessful attack (the few bombs dropped completely missed the harbor and caused only minor damage) carried out by two "Emily" flying boats. This was the longest distance ever undertaken by a two-plane bombing mission, and the longest bombing sortie ever planned without fighter escort. The fleet intelligence officer, Eddie Layton, whimsically suggested that it was Jasper who had planned the attack, since it closely followed a fictional story he had written as "Alec Hudson" for the *Saturday Evening Post* before the war. Of course no one took that seriously, and in fact several years after the war Jasper had the opportunity to talk to a Japanese naval officer who had planned the raid—he had never heard of Alec Hudson nor that story.

Prior to the Battle of Midway, as American naval intelligence was trying to determine what the Japanese symbol "AF" meant in radio interceptions, Lieutenant Holmes observed that fresh water was a constant problem at Midway, and that a breakdown of the main distillation plant would be of great interest to the Japanese if they planned to invade there. Knowing that Pearl Harbor could securely communicate with Midway via an underwater cable, Joe Finnegan then remarked that Midway could be secretly instructed, using the cable, to report such a breakdown via a plain-language radio message. Then, if the Japanese intercepted that report, they'd likely report it in turn to Tokyo, and American radio intelligence would catch it. Rochefort looked at Finnegan for a moment, and then said, "That's *all right*, Joe." The idea was implemented, the Japanese caught the message and reported it, and American radio intelligence intercepted their report—ending the uncertainty that "AF" was Midway.

About this time Ens. Donald "Mac" Showers, fresh from the mainland, was assigned to HYPO and reported to Holmes as his assistant. Holmes was thoroughly impressed by this eager and intense young man who had a brilliant intelligence career ahead of him; in fact, many years later, Showers would be the only denizen of the HYPO basement to eventually be promoted to rear admiral on active duty.

In April 1942, Cmdr. Arthur **McCollum** was sent from ONI to CinCPac to discuss some plans then being formulated by the Commandant of the Marine Corps and ONI. The commandant at that time was Lt. Gen. Thomas Holcomb (and coincidentally a cousin of Station HYPO's Maj. Bankson **Holcomb**). Mac presented the plan to Admiral Nimitz—a plan which he and ONI's senior planner, Capt. Arthur **Struble**, had put together. Commander McCollum was an early advocate of full-scale operational intelligence centers, and later wrote that:

> the plan was to establish [an] intelligence center at Pearl Harbor with a rather large staff. The center would receive and interpret all types of intelligence bearing on CinCPac's sphere of operations. Admiral Nimitz liked the idea but, disliking large staffs, was somewhat resistant on personnel grounds. There followed a great deal of correspondence between Pearl Harbor and Washington. The Intelligence Center Pacific Ocean Area [ICPOA] was, however, created, with Cmdr. Roscoe Hillenkoetter from ONI as officer in charge. ICPOA was detached from the CinCPac staff and placed under the command of the Fourteenth Naval District. The ICPOA concept was warmly received by Cmdr. Joseph Rochefort, if less so by Nimitz's fleet intelligence officer, Lt. Cmdr. Edwin Layton.

It may be that McCollum was optimistic about his friend Rochefort's warm interest. Jasper saw it differently when

> ComFourteen bucked the job of officer-in-charge of ICPOA to Rochefort, who was already overworked in communications intelligence.

Around the time of the Battle of the Coral Sea, the challenge to HYPO was enormous. Holmes commented that

> only a fraction of the vast volume of Japanese radio traffic could be intercepted. Traffic analysts scanned the volume of traffic across the radio spectrum, and [Tom] **Huckins** usually assigned the Japanese circuits to be guarded by the intercept station. More messages were intercepted than the cryptanalysts could profitably work on. Selection of these that were to receive primary attention was more of an art than a science. The identities of the originator and the addressees, the block of additives used in the encipherment, the priority given to the message, its length, the time of transmission, and [even] Lt. Cmdr. Finnegan's hunches were all important elements to be considered.

Keeping track of information fragments and correlating them with each other became a problem. Holmes said that

I went to a friend of mine who was the chief clerk of the Navy Yard, and cajoled him into giving me a couple of visual file cabinets of the type used by supply officers for ready reference to inventory cards. We then transcribed pertinent portions of translated messages, traffic-analysis reports, and other data on five-by-eight-inch index cards, making a separate card for each ship, organization, and place-name. The coordinated information would then be available at the flip of a finger. . . .

Eventually we progressed to making multiple copies of each translation. . . . It would have been much simpler if xerography had been invented, but we had to use the hectograph process of duplication. Dunbar soon needed a couple of yeomen to help him type and duplicate the slips. The purple ink used in the hectographing became our trademark, emblazoned impartially on product and producers.

Until Midway, communications intelligence dominated combat intelligence, but when the action shifted to the Solomon Islands there was also a change in the nature of combat intelligence.

The Japanese, being now on the defensive and having their forces concentrated in Rabaul, no longer needed to transmit plans by radio and this, together with [changes] in their code, made it impossible for radio intelligence to determine specific details of their dispositions and timing. . . . RI had been highly successful in strategically defensive operations. For offensive operations additional intelligence services were required.

After the Battle of Midway, essentially at Holmes's initiative and with Rochefort's agreement, Lt. Cmdr. Holmes, Lt. Cmdr. Jack **Holtwick**, and Lt. Tom Steele met several times to discuss recommending some awards for basement members. Holmes strongly felt that the unit had "spearheaded one of the greatest naval intelligence successes in history" and that such recognition could "strengthen the organization for the hard work ahead." He also was concerned that some well-earned recognition might encourage these naval "national treasures" to "continue in radio intelligence work for the duration of the war and not be distracted from it by more glamorous or more rewarding opportunities" which might come along. Locally, this initiative received some traction, with Rear Adm. David W. Bagley (the new commandant of the Fourteenth Naval District) and Admiral Nimitz concurring. But, Admiral King, in Washington, shortly decided that there would be no awards for radio intelligence until after the war was over.

After the great Midway victory, according to Holmes, there was really no great moment of exhilaration in the basement. Work continued at a dogged pace. "Absenteeism was no problem, rather the reverse. There was always danger that some key man would work himself into a nervous breakdown just when he was needed most."

In the summer of 1942, Jasper had a terrible flare-up of his spinal arthritis, for which he blamed the faulty air conditioning in the basement—which often made it too cold. Fortunately, he discovered a naval reserve doctor who was an arthritis specialist; he determined that Holmes had an infection on top of the arthritis, which he defeated with a new antibiotic.

July saw the establishment of the Intelligence Center Pacific Ocean Area, the idea of which had started back in April with Cmdr. Arthur McCollum's pitch to Admiral Nimitz. Joe Rochefort was drafted to run it. Holmes recalled that

> one morning, late in July, Rochefort dropped a mass of papers on my desk and told me to find some space to put the new organization. I was relieved to discover that only seventeen officers and twenty-nine men had been ordered to ICPOA by Washington, but even that number created problems. [HYPO] had expanded to fill all available space in the basement. The cryptanalysts were justly concerned that bringing a number of new people into the basement would erode the security essential for their work.
>
> My section of the old Combat Intelligence-HYPO organization became the Combat Intelligence Unit (later the Estimate Section) of ICPOA. With its charts, files, the hectograph, and the scrambler telephone to the fleet intelligence officer, it was moved to the far end of the basement. This provided space for a few desks in the CIU for the earliest ICPOA arrivals and isolated them somewhat from the production areas of radio intelligence.

With ICPOA's establishment in July 1942, Holmes continued as head of the Combat Intelligence Unit—screening and passing on to appropriate users intelligence of operational value. Holmes also continued an intimate relationship with HYPO.

In September 1942, Capt. Roscoe Hillenkoetter (an intelligence officer with considerable European background) reported as OIC of ICPOA, relieving Cmdr. Rochefort of this extra duty. On September 25, ICPOA moved into offices totaling six thousand square feet in the navy yard's supply building—and Holmes moved with them. "Holmes gradually slid from being solely with one outfit to being almost entirely with the other."

When two naval reserve lieutenants arrived to run ICPOA's administrative section, Holmes was effectively freed of admin duties and could fully concentrate on intelligence matters.

HYPO became a nominal part of ICPOA—as the Radio Intelligence Section—but it remained in its basement with Joe Rochefort still in charge. Then, Rochefort received temporary orders to Washington in October; Holmes at first thought this was a great opportunity to straighten out some issues with OP-20-G and lobby for more cryptographers, translators, *kana* radio operators, and equipment. But Rochefort apparently didn't have a good feeling about the situation, and gave Holmes a package of personal papers and the keys to his desk; Jasper didn't even suspect he'd never see Joe Rochefort again until long after the war was over.

Thus, a couple of weeks after Rochefort had gone, when Capt. William **Goggins** was brought into the basement and introduced to the unit by Captain Hillenkoetter as the new HYPO OIC, he was met with no little astonishment by Holmes and the rest of the HYPO crew. They realized that "Rochefort had been summarily relieved as OIC of COMINT in Hawaii. It was another blow to our morale. . . . Rochefort became the victim of a Navy Department internal political coup." His friends at HYPO were stunned; Holmes summed up the feeling when he wrote:

All the charges could have been easily disproved but, instead of being decorated or given a spot-promotion to captain for the greatest intelligence achievement in the Navy's history, he was relieved of duty in radio intelligence and ordered to sea. [Then] for more than a year his unsurpassed technical qualifications and his exceptional analytical ability were lost to RI at a time when the Navy needed them badly.

But Commander Rochefort wrote a letter to Lt. Cmdr. Holmes in November 1942. It included an assurance that in Rochefort's opinion Captain Goggins had nothing to do with Rochefort's dismissal, and that he hoped the CIU team would "all be as loyal to Goggins as you have been to me." This comment

> facilitated Goggins' smooth takeover of an organization which had been badly shaken. Fortunately, Goggins was an able administrator and an expert in naval communications. He and I [Holmes] became close and enduring friends. . . . His knowledge of communications and his good relations with CinCPac staff were very important to [HYPO] just when its own communications network had to be expanded and improved.

Bill Goggins soon became well liked and respected within HYPO—which by now was frequently being called FRUPac. He did alter Rochefort's atmosphere of casual informality. Goggins was a strict, formal, by-the-book officer who essentially wanted things done the "old navy" way. Nevertheless, he did gain the trust and confidence of HYPO's officers and men, and Holmes later commented that Goggins had indeed become an "able leader of FRUPac [after] Rochefort was detached." After Rochefort left, Holmes "more or less took over the business of communicating with Layton."

Christmas 1942 was not as grim in Honolulu as had been Christmas 1941. "In appreciation of the privilege of being allowed to stay . . . [Mrs. Holmes] decided to have as many of our homesick friends to Christmas dinner as she could possibly manage. That Christmas she managed about fifteen guests—all male."

When the new year began, FRUPac was [again] reading many Japanese messages in the five-digit code. For most of these messages, the CIU of ICPOA served as a middle man between FRUPac and Fleet Intelligence.

ICPOA had no translation or interrogation section until February 1943, when

> the first contingent of twenty graduates of the Navy's language school arrived. . . . These young reserve officers had received eleven months of intensive instruction in Japanese at the language school in Boulder, Colorado. . . . What captured documents fell into our hands before the translation section became functional were exploited by Cmdr. Edwin Layton or his assistant, Lt. Robert Hudson, in the Fleet Intelligence Office—or by the overworked translator-cryptanalysts in FRUPac.

Around March, having split apart organizationally, ICPOA and FRUPac were reunited with Captain Goggins as OIC of both; this was after Captain Hillenkoetter departed.

In April, FRUPac and ICPOA moved from the Pearl Harbor navy yard to a new two-story wooden building that had been built for them on the rim of the Makalapa

Crater, a short distance from CinCPac headquarters. "The new building was isolated on a dead-end road and surrounded by a high chain-link fence, with a Marine sentry always posted at the gate. Everybody was happy with the move."

Holmes later wrote that

> the fortunes of ICPOA had waxed and waned during its nine-month existence. FRUPac and the CIU continued to supply most of the information concerning the enemy because, until the second half of 1943, operations in the central Pacific were defensive. No large-scale offensive operations were yet being planned in detail and ICPOA, therefore, had few assigned responsibilities.

The CIU had grown along with FRUPac. Holmes's plotting facilities, his charts and maps, and his file of hectographed Japanese messages grew to occupy more space than had originally been allotted to the entire unit. His file of place names had grown to more than twenty thousand cards. With the addition of more new officers—never forgetting the redoubtable Mac Showers, already in place—there now were enough lieutenants to stand a continuous watch, so that Holmes could stop personally standing a night watch even though he worked seven days per week. "Each week the CIU turned out an estimate of the distribution of Japanese naval forces. It was mainly based on Japanese naval radio communications. We might have been misled by radio silence or deception but it was the best information we had."

Amidst the normal, frantic activity and workload as the war was fought, one day in the spring of 1943 good fortune, fine processes, and excellent cryptanalysis delivered a gift to the Americans. It was the Solomon Islands inspection itinerary of Admiral Yamamoto Isoroku, the commander in chief of the Japanese Combined Fleet. It was Holmes who called FIO Layton with the news of this success, and then Lasswell and Holmes carried the finished translation to Layton. Then, Commander Layton's analysis and advice were key to Admiral Nimitz's decision to attempt a shoot-down of Yamamoto's aircraft. Layton summed up the situation by observing that

> Yamamoto was preeminent in all categories, that any successor would be personally and professionally inferior and, finally, that the death of the commander in chief would demoralize the Japanese, who venerate their captains much more than Occidentals do.

The attempt was made and Yamamoto was killed—to the severe detriment of the Japanese war effort. (See Appendix N, "Operation VENGEANCE".)

There were nights when nearly every American submarine on patrol in the central Pacific was working on the basis of information derived from cryptanalysis.

> Holmes' work brought him into contact with units from all over the Pacific Fleet, but he remained a submarine officer in spirit, if not in assignment. Holmes developed a close working relationship with the operations officer of the Pacific submarine fleet. This officer would come by HYPO every morning around nine o'clock, where he and Holmes would compare the current positions of U.S. submarines with decrypted messages concerning Japanese fleet movements. Most days this information was somewhat general

in nature, but from time to time intercepted and decoded messages provided enough detail to put an American submarine in exactly the right spot to intercept a major target.

Some of the veteran COMINT professionals considered passing information to the submarine force was dangerous to their operation. However, for quite a while Holmes had been passing on a considerable amount of sensitive intelligence to the submarines with no tangible results. Still,

> everyone was apprehensive of the Japanese becoming suspicious that their code was compromised. A change of code could throw us completely in the dark at just the time when information was of the greatest importance. I began to realize the weight of responsibility Commander Rochefort had assumed by permitting me to converse with the Submarine Force.

Holmes secretly developed a private ritual which eventually became known among the submariners at Pearl Harbor. Ned Beach, the Naval Academy midshipman who had recognized "Alec Hudson" as the pen name of a naval officer, went into submarines himself and soon learned of the practice. An account attributed to Beach, written many years after the war, said that Holmes

> had become an intelligence officer at Pearl Harbor and, after the attack on the Day of Infamy, had taken on himself the particular and personal dedication to see the destruction of every ship that had participated in it. During the war, from time to time, commanders of submarines would receive by messenger, without explanation, a bottle of fine whiskey. Little by little the word got around that one of the ships sunk on a recent patrol had carried special significance for someone. In this way Jasper Holmes never left submarines. It was through him that we would receive orders to be somewhere at a certain time—and on occasion there was a bottle of booze at the end of the trail.

Holmes later wrote, "I confess that I always felt personally vindictive toward every ship that participated in the attack on Pearl Harbor. I kept a carefully verified list of their names and ceremoniously crossed each name off the list with great satisfaction as we confirmed its owner's sinking." He did regret that circumstances prevented him getting a bottle of Scotch to future rear admiral Herman Lossler, the captain of the submarine *Cavalla*, after that boat sank the carrier *Shokaku* on June 19, 1944.

Throughout the war Holmes kept working with the submarine force. When Rear Adm. Charles Lockwood became ComSubPac in early 1943, his relations became even closer. "I proudly wore the submarine insignia I had earned before the war, and Admiral Lockwood treated me as one of his own staff. Sometimes I thought he believed that producing intelligence for submarines was our only function—but it was not."

> When we had information that might enable a submarine to make contact with a Japanese aircraft carrier or a task force, I went directly to the chief of staff of ComSubPac and delivered it orally. I did not tell him how the information was obtained, but he must have guessed. We kept no records. If I had a position in latitude and longitude,

I wrote the figure in ink on the palm of my hand, and scrubbed my hands after I had delivered the message.

After the "*maru* code"—the Japanese merchant ship code—was broken, Commander Holmes started to meet daily with an old friend, Cmdr. Richard Voge, who had become operations officer of ComSubPac. "We added to the submarine situation plot the tracks and routes of all known Japanese convoys at sea, and any other pertinent enemy information." They would then decide which targets would be allocated to each submarine patrol.

In fact, Admiral Nimitz directed Holmes to "mastermind the offensive," in the summer of 1943, and to push intelligence to ComSubPac. "Orders would be flashed out with up-to-date information on the courses of Japanese convoys. "Sometimes it was only a matter of hours between decryption of a *maru* message and one of our submarines reporting a sinking." Then, the installation of a hand-powered telephone link, with the commander of the submarine force, completed what Holmes described as "the basis of almost perfect coordination between operations and intelligence." The breaking of the *maru* code was a major factor in sending the annual "sinking rate up by the end of 1943 to a million and a half tons." By January 1944, American subs were sending enemy merchantmen to the bottom at a rate of almost a third of a million tons per month. "There was no way for the Japanese shipbuilding industry to keep pace." As Holmes wrote long after the war,

> the limited risk taken in allowing submarines to use liberally information from the *maru* code was justified by the large potential gain.
> Intelligence, like money, may be secure when it is unused and locked up in a safe. It yields no dividends until it is invested.

In September 1943, the intelligence operation of Admiral Nimitz's staff was reorganized to deal with the ever-increasing workload. As Holmes described it, the Radio Intelligence Section was separated from ICPOA and transferred to the Pacific Fleet as Fleet Radio Unit Pacific—so now, for the first time, HYPO officially became "FRUPac."

ICPOA was placed directly under the assistant chief of staff for intelligence of a *joint* staff, which now reflected Nimitz's expanded role as CinC Pacific Fleet and CinC Pacific Ocean Area. It was renamed the Joint Intelligence Center, Pacific Ocean Area, or JICPOA. Newly promoted Brig. Gen. Joseph J. Twitty, U.S. Army, was appointed the J-2 and OIC of JICPOA. Twitty was a cartographer, topographer, and Japanese linguist; he'd been Army intelligence's liaison with ICPOA since fall 1942.

Edwin Layton, promoted to captain in June 1943, remained the FIO. The CIU of ICPOA now became the Estimate Section of JICPOA. Promoted to commander also in June, Jasper remained chief of the Estimate Section and also was appointed deputy OIC of JICPOA—which meant he was also a member of the new joint staff. Holmes and the Estimate Section remained in the new FRUPac building at the Makalapa crater until the end of the war, which continued to help bridge organizational gaps.

The codebreaking group, now officially titled FRUPac, remained outside the Joint Intelligence Center under the Pacific Fleet's communications officer. The link between the FRU and the JIC was the latter's Estimates Section, headed by Wilfred J. Holmes. Housed in the same building as the FRU, the Estimates Section received all decrypted messages from OP-20-G, FRU, and other naval cryptographic centers, then processed the information for dissemination to CinCPac commands.

Mrs. Holmes's 1942 Christmas dinner had been a great success, so they decided to double-up in 1943 by having as many JICPOA-FRUPac men as the house would hold—twice—one group at Thanksgiving and then another group at Christmas. At Thanksgiving, by stretching out the extended dining-room table with the library table and card tables, they seated about twenty guests—but the party was subdued with the news of the taking of the island of Tarawa (Operation GALVANIC). It had been a great U.S. victory, but had cost the Marine Corps almost one thousand killed and two thousand wounded, while the navy lost the escort carrier *Liscome Bay* and approximately seven hundred men.

The primary responsibility of JICPOA was the preparation of intelligence for CinCPac, but it produced much material for distribution to intelligence officers in all echelons. By the end of 1943 more than seventy JICPOA bulletins, on many subjects, had been prepared and distributed.

Also, toward the end of 1943, JICPOA started to issue information bulletins and air target folders on each of the major atolls in the Marshall Islands. All the bulletins and folders carried a standard yellow cover, which became JICPOA's trademark throughout the Pacific. Such documents were commonly called "yellow devils." Later, when Admiral Nimitz was promoted to fleet admiral in December 1944, his five-star insignia was printed in dark red on the covers of JICPOA publications. Holmes said that

> one of my first actions, when I acquired greater responsibility for JICPOA, was to create a Distribution Section, whose duty it was to withhold critical information from the merely curious, but to expedite delivery of all JICPOA publications to those who needed them. I believed that distribution based strictly on a "need to know" principle would greatly reduce the number of copies issued. . . .
>
> Intelligence derived from decryption of enemy radio messages was classified "ULTRA" or "TOP SECRET ULTRA," and was not handled by the Distribution Section. Practically everything produced by the Estimate Section was classified ULTRA and was distributed by the fleet intelligence officer or directly by the Estimate Section in accordance with the FIO's direction.[4]

---

4. ULTRA was the overall Allied codeword for wartime signals intelligence obtained by breaking high-level encrypted enemy radio communications—used in all theaters of the war. The entire notion of obtaining intelligence via cryptanalysis was incredibly tightly controlled during the war and for many years after. Prior to the 1970s, many fine books and articles were written about the war but were inaccurate—or incomplete—because their authors had no idea of the actual existence or effectiveness of ULTRA activities.

Early in 1944, plans were made for a new three-story JICPOA building right next to FRUPac at the Makalapa Crater. Holmes later wrote that

> consolidation of intelligence and close cooperation between JICPOA and CinCPac's Plans and Operations Division paid big dividends. . . . The results of aerial and submarine reconnaissance and photography arrived promptly at JICPOA. . . . This intelligence was incorporated into thousands of maps, charts, bombardment grids, and air target folders then in preparation for . . . forthcoming operations.

At this point, groups of about thirty officers at a time were arriving at regular intervals from the language school at Boulder. Most of them went to the Translation Section until there were more than 200 language officers at JICPOA. Even so, from the end of 1943 forward, Holmes stated that it was impossible to translate every document that came in. "In one shipment from Saipan we received *fifty tons* of Japanese documents." Moreover, to show the scale of products coming out of JICPOA, by the end of the war it had issued thirty-nine volumes of CinCPac-CinCPOA translations and about ninety special translations. JICPOA's Translation Section operated in three shifts, each shift eight hours a day, seven days a week. "The language officers called it the 'Salt Mines,' or the 'Zoo Section.'"

The new JICPOA was completed in May 1944. Except for the Estimate Section, JICPOA moved from the FRUPac building into the new one.[5]

> Because of the security requirements for the ULTRA material it filed and the necessity for its close cooperation with FRUPac, the Estimate Section remained on the first floor of the FRUPac building. As chief of the Estimate Section I retained my desk in the old building, and as deputy officer-in-charge of JICPOA I acquired an office alongside General Twitty's in the new building. It was fortunate for me that my two offices were so close together.

Photo-interpretation had come into its own during the war—though of course it was far from being a World War II invention.

> Photo-interpretation was the major source of information available to the enemy Bases Section in producing the yellow-covered information bulletins on the Mariana and Caroline Islands. It became equal with communications intelligence and translations as a primary source of intelligence. . . . In 1944 the demand for photo-interpreters greatly exceeded the supply. The number on duty at JICPOA varied from fifteen to more than ninety.

The quantity of intelligence products generated by the unit was staggering. For example, in mid-1944, JICPOA supplied the Fifth Fleet and the Joint Expedition-

---

5. Reused for many years after the war in various non-intelligence roles, Facilities 251 and 258 gradually deteriorated. In fact, as a junior officer at FICPAC in the mid-1980s, I occasionally mailed letters at the U.S. Post Office in one of the buildings; I always came away happy that my foot hadn't gone through the deteriorating wooden porch. However, the buildings were both restored, in 2004–2005, and have gained new life as offices for the Commander Pacific Fleet organization.

ary Force with literally tons of maps, charts, air target folders, information bulletins, photographs, estimates, and translations.

Toward mid-1944, JICPOA got some unanticipated help.

> In the Marianas we took some prisoners who elected surrender rather than suicide. They appeared to be convinced that early surrender was a better course for Japan than the death and destruction that further resistance would entail. From ostensibly patriotic motives, they were willing to work with JICPOA's new Psychological Warfare Section in writing leaflets urging surrender. Millions of these leaflets were dropped on Japan.

Starting in July 1944, JICPOA began producing a weekly intelligence bulletin. The first print order was for two thousand copies, and demand almost immediately jumped to six thousand. By the end of the war, the weekly circulation was fourteen thousand copies.

Holmes wrote that one of the important functions of his Estimate Section was the *realistic* assessment and appraisal (and constant reappraisal) of damage American forces had supposedly inflicted upon the Japanese. "I was thankful, however, that our task was only to ascertain the truth. Captain Layton at CinCPac, and Commander Voge at ComSubPac, had the unpopular job of convincing battle-hardened veterans that many of what they believed to be honest reports of damage to the enemy were . . . over-optimistic."

December 1944 saw Jasper's promotion to captain, as well as a huge Christmas dinner at his house.

> Izzy baked a big ham to go with the turkey. She improvised tables to turn the living room into a second dining room, and we invited thirty guests from JICPOA and FRU-Pac. . . . Victory seemed distant, but assured. The road ahead might be rocky, but when a toast was offered to "the Golden Gate in '48," the optimists replied "back alive in '45."

By January 1945, JICPOA had five hundred officers and eight hundred enlisted men. FRUPac, separately organized and administered, "probably had as many more." There was also a great deal of change. Mac Showers took over most of the responsibility of the Estimate Section. Moreover, as Holmes later summarized,

> Jack Holtwick went to Chungking, China. Tom **Birtley**, who had been in charge of [HYPO] before the war, returned to FRUPac after a tour of sea duty and a long siege in the hospital. Capt. Redfield **Mason** and, later, Cmdr. Rufus **Taylor** (another language officer and expert cryptanalyst) came out from Washington. Captain Goggins, who had been the able leader of FRUPac since Commander Rochefort was detached, left to take command of the battleship *Alabama*. He was relieved by Capt. John **Harper**, my friend and classmate.

Greater changes in JICPOA followed the establishment of CinCPac's advanced headquarters on Guam in January 1945. Then, when Admiral Nimitz himself moved to Guam, Capt. Eddie Layton—his steadfast fleet intelligence officer—went with him. CinCPac took to Guam most of JICPOA's enlisted male yeoman, leaving the unit understaffed. Jasper wrote a letter to Vice Adm. Charles "Soc" McMorris, Nimitz's chief of staff, asking for permission to employ female yeomen. Admiral Nimitz had a standing rule of no women on his staff. This decision wasn't merely old-fashioned conservatism or bias; the admiral long maintained a vision of embarking his staff onto ships or into combat zones; bringing women, in his view, would be both immoral and illegal. In any event, Jasper received a note back in Admiral Nimitz's copperplate handwriting: "Tell Captain Holmes he can employ one female yeoman for every male yeoman he has sent to Guam." Jasper later wrote that this turned out very well, and that he was convinced that JICPOA would have actually worked more smoothly "if we had started out with a solid core of women in many of the stable jobs."

After the Okinawa campaign, JICPOA faced its largest challenge—producing intelligence for Operation OLYMPIC, the proposed invasion and capture of the southern third of the southernmost main Japanese island, Kyūshū. For this operation, JICPOA became a factory geared to producing all types of intelligence materials; during this time it averaged two million sheets of printed intelligence and more than 150,000 photographic prints each week. However, the invasion became unnecessary with atomic bombs being dropped on Hiroshima and Nagasaki, and the subsequent Japanese surrender in mid-August 1945. Holmes felt that it was fortunate that it turned out that way. Regarding the planned invasion, JICPOA's estimate was that "the total of American casualties could well have been [over three million]—and the Japanese casualties would have been several times greater."

Captain Holmes retired from the navy, for the second time, in 1946. He returned to the University of Hawaii and progressively held a number of posts—including Dean of Engineering—before he retired from there in 1965. Holmes Hall, the engineering building at the university, is named for him. After retiring from the university, Jasper reengaged his interest in communications intelligence and the attack on Pearl Harbor. Among other things, he studied the entire thirty-nine-volume report of the 79th Congress' *Hearings before the Joint Committee on the Investigation of the Pearl Harbor Attack.*

At one point, in 1957, Jasper visited retired Fleet Admiral Nimitz in California and convinced him to revisit the matter of a Distinguished Service Medal for Joe Rochefort. Nimitz wrote to the secretary of the navy but surprisingly was rebuffed for several reasons that—at that time—seemed logical to the navy department.

In 1966, Captain Holmes authored a significant five-hundred-page book of naval history, titled *Undersea Victory: The Influence of Submarine Operations on the War in the Pacific*, which was published by Doubleday. Then, when the highly classified existence of ULTRA information was finally made public in the early 1970s, Holmes wrote a detailed memoir of his Pacific war experiences at HYPO, ICPOA, and JICPOA. Brought out in 1979 by the Naval Institute Press, and quoted frequently in this collection of biographies, the book was titled *Double-Edged Secrets: U.S. Naval Intelligence Operations during World War II.*

It's a fascinating account of a central, essential part of the war that's gotten relatively little attention. Holmes writes with considerable modesty describing his role at HYPO; in fact, he was deeply and intimately involved in many of the critical episodes that took place there, and one suspects he gives himself too little credit.

We certainly owe Jasper Holmes a great deal for his insights into Pacific Theater wartime intelligence. As Fleet Admiral Nimitz later wrote,

> Captain Holmes had an unequalled opportunity to observe and take part in the development throughout the war of intelligence for high command. He played an able part in this development and his recorded observations and opinions are therefore of unusual value.

Historian Ronald Lewin expanded on this when he wrote that Holmes—via his end-of-war report and his book—gives us a unique and

> authoritative account of how the signals intelligence outstation at Hawaii, diminutive at the time of [the Pearl Harbor attack], grew into an enormous tri-service intelligence factory capable of feeding the Americans' combat forces as they too expanded, advanced, and splayed out over the Pacific Ocean Areas.

In the early 1980s, Jasper also put in considerable effort helping Rear Adm. Edwin Layton (and his coauthors) work on Layton's reminisces, *"And I Was There": Pearl Harbor and Midway—Breaking the Secrets*.

Captain Holmes received a Distinguished Service Medal at the end of World War II—one of only six navy people in the radio intelligence world so recognized. It's also satisfactory to report that—in addition to Holmes Hall being named for him at the university—the navy named an important building for him at Pearl Harbor. Building 352, which is just down the Makalapa hill and very close to the World War II–era Commander Pacific Fleet headquarters, was dedicated in his honor in July 1991: The Captain Wilfred Jay "Jasper" Holmes, USN (Ret) Intelligence Building (interestingly, its interior auditorium is named for Brig. Gen. Joe Twitty). The building's occupants almost never refer to it by name, instead usually calling it by the name of the organization it houses, which have been FICPAC, JICPAC, and, more recently, JIOCPAC.

Jasper did not live to enjoy that particular honor, but it's pleasing to note that just two months prior to his death (at that point he was in a nursing home), Jasper heard other news about recognition which truly delighted him: Capt. Joe Rochefort's family was going to finally receive the long-overdue Distinguished Service Medal from President Ronald Reagan.

Jasper passed away on January 7, 1986; he's buried with his wife, Isabelle (Izzy) W. Holmes (1900–1972), and alongside their son, Dr. John Eric Holmes (1930–2010), at the National Memorial Cemetery of the Pacific, in Honolulu. It would appear that Isabelle had been the young lady to whom Midshipman Holmes wrote love letters from Annapolis, as mentioned in his 1922 yearbook writeup. Made of stern stuff, during the war she was the air-raid warden for Black Point—fully equipped with helmet, gas mask, and flashlight. Because the Holmes family was permanently residing in Hawaii prewar, they were not subject to evacuation to the mainland as most service families were. As a result, Izzy made their house a comfortable place for socialization for families of officers awaiting evacuation—as well as for Jasper's wartime bachelor colleagues.

Perhaps it's fitting to leave Captain Holmes's story with one of his oft-quoted conclusions about the business of wartime intelligence: "No one, who has not experienced it, can realize how difficult it is to track the shadow of truth through the fog of war."

Sources

As mentioned earlier, Holmes's own book *Double-Edged Secrets* is not only a primary resource for Jasper's personal story, but also for the stories of many others in this volume; as such, it's most highly recommended to the reader. It's still readily available in paper or as an ebook.

Carlson, x, 94–95, 99–100, 106, 113, 132, 178, 189–91, 241, 262, 276–77, 281, 333–35, 395, 406–7, 414, 418–19, 445, 449–51, 453.
Clausen, 121.
Farago, *Broken Seal*, 269, 313–14.
"Herm Kossler's Bottle of Scotch [article about Jasper Holmes]," by "Andy," January 16, 2010. *Maritime Texas: An Eclectic Blog of People, Places, and Events.* maritimetexas.net/wordpress/?tag=jasper-holmes. Accessed January 23, 2013.
Holmes, 1–3, 6, 9–11, 14–15, 18–21, 30, 36, 40–43, 46, 55, 61–63, 65, 75, 86–87, 90, 101, 103, 108–16, 119–121, 125, 129–132, 140, 142, 144, 147, 152, 158–59, 161, 167–69, 177, 181, 183–84, 191, 195, 197–98, 203, 211, 215–16.
Holmes, "Narrative, Combat Intelligence Center, Joint Intelligence Center, Pacific Ocean Area." In Spector, *Listening*, 160–61, 164, 169.
Kahn, *Codebreakers*, 566.
Layton, *"And I Was There,"* 6, 350, 374, 421, 423, 468, 470, 473–74, 492.
Lewin, 93, 101–2, 133–35, 139–40.
Lucky Bag, U.S. Naval Academy, 1934.
Packard, 369.
Prados, 305, 318, 369, 400–1, 410–11, 459–60, 543–44, 596–97, 600, 611, 679.
Prange, *Miracle*, 18.
Rochefort, 180.
Smith, *Emperor's Codes*, 138.
Spector, *Eagle*, 458.
Symonds, 185, 206, 209, 387.
Toland, 33.
Toll, 158, 305–6, 312–13, 387.
U.S. Navy. *Register of Commissioned and Warrant Officers.*

CAPTAIN STEPHEN JURIKA JR., U.S. NAVY (1910–1993)

Raised and educated in Asia
Fluent in five languages
Had an unusual understanding of the Orient not common for an Occidental
The only naval aviator in pre-war intelligence
"Steve"

Stephen Jurika stands apart from most of the other people in this study: first, as the only officer in the group who was a naval aviator; and second, while he certainly was an extremely proficient Japanese language officer, he was *not* one of ONI's language and culture immersion students. He also could claim having Douglas MacArthur as a family friend, and he'd played cards with Franklin Roosevelt. Steve Jurika smoothly combined aviation and intelligence in a spectacular career, ranging from pre–World

War II through the mid-1980s. As the navigator of the carrier *Franklin* in spring 1945, he was awarded the Navy Cross for heroism during a devastating aerial attack. His last government employment was as a civilian professor of national security affairs and intelligence at the Naval Postgraduate School.

*   *   *

From the 1933 *Lucky Bag*, the Naval Academy yearbook:

> Born in sunny California and reared in the Orient, *Steve* came to us through the Service, thereby learning first-hand the ways of the Navy. Widely read and travelled, he is possessed of a philosophy which defines happiness as its air. Ideals have meant much to him, and he has adhered to them these four years. Studies hold no terrors for him; his chief occupation during study hours is letter writing. He is gifted with an easy flow of speech and tact, makes friends easily, and retains them indefinitely. With a keen and appreciative sense of humor, impulsive, sound judgment, and a willingness to question anything, *Steve* is eminently qualified to handle one of Uncle Sam's battle canoes. *Steve's* drags [dates] are a constant source of interest to him—each one something new—each one a puzzle to be solved in a definite way. His One-and-Only is subject to change without notice. An officer and a gentleman, whose *forte* is rifle, whose pastime is swimming, and whose obsession is smallbore, we know he will attain success in his field. [Activities: Rifle, Radio Club]

*   *   *

Stephen Jurika was born in Los Angeles on June 10, 1910, while his parents were travelling; he actually grew up in the Philippine Islands. He was the second of the four children of Stefan Jurika and Blanche Anna Walker. Blanche was from Oxnard, California, but Stefan was a naturalized American citizen originally from Bohemia (which later became Czechoslovakia), and had fought in the U.S. Army in the Spanish-American War. Stefan founded a south-seas trading company in 1902 on the island of Jolo between the Philippines and Borneo, and then later moved to Zamboanga, P.I., and established branches of the business in Cotabato and Davao, as well as Jolo.[1]

---

1. Stephen's mother, Blanche Walker Jurika (a graduate of Cornell University in 1905) lived most of her life in Philippines, arriving in 1908. After her husband Stefan died in 1928, Blanche established a coconut plantation on her own at Panabutan Bay to the north of Zamboanga, later moving to Manila and building a home overlooking Lake Taal at Tagaytay, to be closer to her two daughters and grandchildren. She became well known as "The Story Lady," the radio voice of *The Children's Hour* on KZRH, reading evening bedtime tales to young listeners. When World War II broke out her daughter's family was able to get out, but Blanche stayed because she had family members remaining in the Philippines, including a son in the Santo Tomas Internment Camp. She was not put in the camp, but worked with other local residents to assist the prisoners from the outside. She also was said to have raised funds for guerrilla camps outside of Manila. A spy infiltrated the group, betraying her and others, and she was arrested in February 1944 by the *Kempetai*, the Japanese secret police. She was executed—actually *beheaded*—on or about August 29, 1944.

Stephen attended schools in the Philippines and China, and then high school in Kobe, Japan. A natural linguist, he had become fluent in Japanese, Spanish, Filipino, Czech, and Chinese (he later was to be officially designated a U.S. Navy Spanish interpreter). After high school, he went to the San Diego Army and Navy Academy. He then enlisted in the navy and underwent boot camp at Naval Training Center San Diego; in September 1927 he joined the collier/freighter/tender USS *Jason* in the Asiatic Fleet. Steve transferred to the Naval Academy Preparatory School in San Diego, from which he finally gained entrance to the Naval Academy in 1929. He graduated and was commissioned as an ensign in 1933—along with distinguished classmates such as John D. Bulkeley, Ignatius J. Galantin, David McCampbell, Thomas H. Moorer, Rufus L. **Taylor**, and Draper L. Kauffman. Subsequent promotions would be to lieutenant (junior grade), 1936; lieutenant, 1941, lieutenant commander, 1942, commander, 1944, and captain, 1952. Captain Jurika retired from the navy in 1962 and although his award of the Navy Cross in 1945 would have allowed him to receive promotion to rear admiral on the retired list (as so many others in this book did), that program was terminated in 1959.

After his Academy graduation, Mr. Jurika first served on board the cruisers *Louisville* (in the engineering division) and *Houston* (in the gunnery division). He made the acquaintance of—and actually socialized a little with—President Franklin D. Roosevelt while onboard the *Houston*. During Jurika's assignment the cruiser transported the president on a trip through the Caribbean, Central America, and Hawaii.

Steve then qualified as a naval aviator in 1936 after graduation from flight school at Naval Air Station Pensacola. His initial aviation assignment was with Torpedo Squadron 3, attached to the carrier *Saratoga*. At this same time, much like Lt. (Doctor) Cecil **Coggins**, it occurred to Lt. j.g. Jurika that the vessels of the huge Japanese fishing fleet off Los Angeles, San Pedro, and San Diego might have intelligence personnel onboard, keeping tabs on the movements of the U.S. fleet—which was then based in that area.

From June 1939 until August 1941, Mr. Jurika served as the naval attaché for air, at the American Embassy in Tokyo, working under chief naval attaché Cmdr. Henri **Smith-Hutton**. He was the first aviator—army or navy—to draw embassy duty in Japan. By all accounts he was a very capable assistant attaché, doing excellent work,

---

Steve was the brother-in-law of Lt. Cmdr. Charles "Chick" Parsons, USNR (holder of two Navy Crosses, the Distinguished Service Cross, and the Bronze Star). Born in Tennessee, Parsons spent most of his life in the Philippines. While at Zamboanga, in about 1927, he met and married Katrushka (Katsy) Jurika, daughter of Stefan and Blanche Jurika. Parsons fought creatively and tenaciously against the Japanese in many capacities, and became a legend in the large Philippine guerrilla movement.

Steve's brother, Major Thomas W. Jurika, was born in Zamboanga, Mindanao, in 1914. The youngest of Stefan and Blanche Jurika's children, Tommy had grown up sailing his bamboo-outrigger around the Sulu Sea like a native, which indeed he almost was. Tom became his brother-in-law Chick Parsons's right-hand man while Chick was directing guerrilla operations. The Japanese had been looking for Tom ever since he had burned and destroyed equipment and war materiel useful to them during the defense of Cebu in April 1942; he was wanted dead or alive, and the price tag on his head was second only to the price on Chick's head. Tom and Chick both survived the war, and eventually found the mass grave where the *Kempetai* had buried Blanche Jurika and over two dozen other people.

and in turn he was extremely impressed by his boss. "I admired Smith-Hutton very much." Jurika's command of Japanese and other Far Eastern languages—as well as his solid cultural understanding of the Far East—proved immensely valuable in his intelligence collection and analysis. He smoothly interacted with Japanese naval officers, learning from and enjoying the experience. Early on he met navy minister Mitsumasa Yonai, commenting later that

> he was not only gracious—remember, I was a lieutenant junior grade and he was an admiral—but he considered every American naval officer he came into contact with . . . as a representative of a great country.

Language and cultural expertise aside, Jurika proved himself as an active, assertive, and high-initiative intelligence officer. He collected significant information about Japanese military, naval, and industrial capabilities, doing considerable photography of sensitive sites.

> Jurika played a great deal of golf in Japan, particularly in groups with members of the British embassy. His British friends, with their own intelligence interests, readily agreed to play at courses near Japanese military and naval airfields, but kept wondering why Jurika didn't concentrate on his game [until] it became obvious the American was really observing Japanese aircraft operating around these bases.

He took every advantage to collect as much information as possible. He mingled and shared information with other attachés.

> I thought the Soviets had the best intelligence networks in Japan [better than the Germans or the British]—using Japanese communist party members—but I also felt that, based on intelligence exchanges, Soviet information collection was haphazard.

Jurika creatively developed a technique for taking photographs of warships under construction at the Mitsubishi yard at Kobe.

> As a pilot, Jurika had to log a certain number of hours in the air to maintain his proficiency rating, so the embassy had an arrangement with the Asiatic Fleet whereby air attachés would go to the Philippines several times a year to fly. On these trips Jurika took U.S.-owned ocean liners from Kobe both because the captains were naval reserve officers and because the vessels were U.S. territory. . . . Jurika would identify himself to the captains and ask that as they exited harbor into the Bungo Strait they sail as close to shore as possible. The Mitsubishi yard happened to be located right near the Bungo entrance. Jurika would get a cabin on the port side of the liner; on a tripod a few feet back from the porthole stood his Leica camera with its telephoto lens. . . . As the ship steamed past the yard, Jurika would snap as fast as he could wind film. His pictures showed vessels behind netting or fitting out, but were good enough over time to show the progress of construction. Later ONI could go back and calculate just how long it had taken to construct a given warship and could then apply this information to other vessels of the same type.

Onboard one of these American liners in April 1940, Jurika was able to clearly watch a Japanese aircraft carrier conduct flight operations as they went by. He noted that the tempo of operations was significantly slower than that of U.S. carriers.

Interestingly, he was frequently invited to ship launchings at Kobe, and always stayed at the German "Tor" Hotel overlooking the harbor, or at the Oriental Hotel downtown, where he could get rooms overlooking the Mitsubishi yard. At other times he would visit and take observations from some houses on the bluffs above the Mitsubishi yard at Yokohama—houses owned by Americans employed by the U.S. consulate and by the Standard Oil Company.

In January 1941, Mr. Jurika received an intelligence officer's break of a lifetime when he heard that the Japanese Army was sponsoring an air show at Haneda field outside Tokyo. He went, of course and

> there in front of him stood a static display—a parked aircraft of novel configuration. It was the *Zero* fighter, developed in the usual Japanese secrecy by the veteran Mitsubishi design team. . . . Jurika walked right up to the plane and climbed into the cockpit. He found a plaque *in English* bearing such essential specifications as the plane's weight and engine horsepower. Jurika also looked at the metal used, the type of landing gear, the construction of wing covers, and other features. . . . Attaché Smith-Hutton forwarded Jurika's report to ONI. Several months later a note came back saying that the attaché ought to be more careful in reporting characteristics of aircraft . . . Washington assumed the report had to be wrong.

Jurika recalled later that this was about the only time ONI ever responded to any report sent from Tokyo. He journeyed about as much as he could, including out of Japan and over to China. He liked to visit Shanghai, where he

> garnered Asiatic Fleet scuttlebutt, observed the Japanese in a setting where they, too, were away from home, and got news, magazines, books, and all manner of information in a place free of Japanese press controls. In fact, what Stephen Jurika did on a small scale later became an official activity for the U.S. naval attaché in Japan. Wholly apart from the American attachés assigned to China, the Tokyo attachés began to make Shanghai visits specifically to watch the Japanese . . . but unlike Jurika's informal sojourns, these visits were made with the cognizance and specific approval of the Japanese Navy Ministry.

As part of his proactive desire to travel about collecting information, Steve decided he needed to visit the "Mandates." The South Sea Mandate was the Japanese territory granted by the League of Nations; it consisted of several groups of islands (the modern-day Palau, Northern Marianas, Federated States of Micronesia, and the Marshall Islands) which came under the administration of Japan after the defeat of the German Empire in World War I. The Japanese had stopped filing reports with the League of Nations in 1938; so, reasoned Jurika, clearly a visit was necessary to see what might be going on there. Attaché Smith-Hutton gave his permission. ("I don't think you'll make it, but fine.") So Mr. Jurika sent his Japanese clerk over to the South Seas Development Company office to buy a ticket on their weekly flight. He was told the plane had engine trouble. After several weeks of various similar excuses, Jurika tried himself, but also was told the flying boat was grounded. He returned with a newspaper clipping showing that the aircraft was making trips to Truk and Ponape. The Japanese had no real answer, but then put in writing (completely contrary to League of Nations guidelines) that American naval officers were not eligible to visit the Mandates. Jurika never got to make his trip—tensions were rapidly increasing.

In fact, fearful of a break in relations at any time, Commander Smith-Hutton proceeded to get all his language officers and other assistants out of Japan in the summer of 1941. Mrs. Jurika and their daughter had already left, in November 1940. Accordingly, in the summer of 1941, Mr. Jurika received orders to join the new aircraft carrier *Hornet*. First, though, he spent several weeks at ONI, and found that they had done a fair job of writing up intelligence (at least the information *that its staff believed*) from the attachés in Tokyo. He wrote several updates to supplement that information, and waited for someone to debrief him regarding his tour in Japan. Surprisingly, no one did, exactly echoing Ellis **Zacharias's** experience—eighteen years earlier—when no one at ONI was interested in debriefing *him* after *his* three-year tour. With great understatement, Smith-Hutton later commented that this kind of thing happened far too often, and that "it's most unfortunate that the reports sent back to our Navy Department by experienced observers . . . didn't receive wider circulation."

Among the people Jurika met with in Washington was Capt. Donald B. "Woo" Duncan, who was the air operations officer to the COMINCH, Adm. Ernest King. Captain Duncan was instrumental in planning Lt. Col. Jimmy Doolittle's B-25 operation to attack Tokyo. Duncan made discreet inquiries of the army concerning its medium bombers, especially the B-25 and B-26, asking for such information as take-off speed, dimensions, range, and load capabilities. He checked with navy sources for deck space data, experience with heavily loaded take-offs, and Pacific weather patterns to determine the best time for raids against Japan. By January 16, 1942, Duncan had produced a thirty-page handwritten analysis that concluded that the B-25 was the only plane that could possibly be used. It could carry two thousand pounds of bombs and make a two-thousand-mile flight if extra gas tanks were installed. Captain Duncan proposed that the *Hornet*, the newest carrier in the navy, would be the ideal ship to carry the planes. He proposed that by using a screening force of another carrier and some cruisers and destroyers, the *Hornet* could be brought within five hundred miles of Japan. After bombing Japan the bombers could escape to China, and the navy task force would withdraw to safer waters. Steve Jurika advised Woo Duncan on some of the particulars, discussed the potential effects of such a raid, and helped finalize some crucial details. Then, in October 1941, Lieutenant Jurika reported onboard the *Hornet* as part of her commissioning crew. And not coincidentally, he was the ship's intelligence and operations officer on the Doolittle Raid, February–April 1942.

During the *Hornet*'s voyage toward Japan, Mr. Jurika briefed the Army fliers about Tokyo and evasion scenarios, and lectured on

Japanese anti-aircraft defense methods, and told those *willing to listen* what he could about the Japanese and their attitudes toward prisoners, and what the fliers' chances might be in a situation like this—not good, thought Jurika.

Some of the army officers referred to his briefings as the "how to make friends and influence the Japs" lectures. Steve thought they seemed very nonchalant, even a bit "undisciplined." At one point, when he thought they were not taking him seriously, he mentioned that they were likely to be beheaded if taken prisoner. "This seemed to settle them down quite a bit."

Shortly before the raiders took off, at Doolittle's suggestion, Jurika provided a Japanese medal he had been awarded (when he was naval attaché for air in Tokyo), which was then affixed to one of Doolittle's bombs. Then, on the day of the event, Steve worked as a flight-deck officer to help launch the B-25s. The sea-state was not cooperative for the launch; the *Hornet* dipped and rose "until the flat deck was a crazy seesaw." Jurika later commented that "you would actually launch them into the air at least horizontal but on the upswing, in fact, giving them a boost up into the air."

Several months later Steve was still in place as the *Hornet*'s (and Rear Adm. [selectee] Marc Mitscher's) intelligence officer, and served as such at the Battle of Midway. He briefed the *Hornet*'s pilots the night before the battle. "There [are] at least two carriers, two battleships, several cruisers and about five destroyers in the attack force which will attempt to take Midway. The support force some distance behind contains the rest of their forces."

The *Hornet* wasn't as effective at Midway as her crew had hoped. Her dive bombers followed an incorrect heading and did not find the enemy fleet, and several bombers and escorting fighters were forced to ditch when they ran out of fuel attempting to return to the ship. Fifteen torpedo bombers of Torpedo Squadron Eight did find the enemy and pressed home an attack, but they were met by overwhelming fighter opposition about nine miles out, and with no escorts to protect them they were shot down one by one. Ens. George Gay was the only survivor of thirty men. Later, *Hornet* aircraft, launching late due to the necessity of recovering planes from the *Yorktown* and faulty communications, attacked a battleship and other escorts but failed to score any hits. However, *Hornet* planes attacked the fleeing Japanese on June 6, 1942, and they assisted in sinking a heavy cruiser and damaging a destroyer and another heavy cruiser.

After Midway, the *Hornet* proceeded to the sea approaches of bitterly contested Guadalcanal in the Solomon Islands. In October 1942, she and the *Enterprise* intercepted a Japanese force in what became the Battle of Santa Cruz. The battle was a tactical win for the Japanese, but in many ways a strategic loss. Terribly damaged and judged unrecoverable, the *Hornet* had to be sunk by U.S. forces after her crew was taken off; during the attack Mr. Jurika was thrown into a bulkhead on the flag bridge—which required him to undergo two months of rehabilitation in a hospital at Auckland.

In December 1942, Lieutenant Commander Jurika had been reassigned ashore at Guadalcanal as gunnery officer for the Commander, Fleet Air Noumea—and then Commander, Aircraft, Solomon Islands; once again he was working for Rear Admiral Mitscher. At one point he was sent to New Georgia to covertly scout for a better airfield site than the Japanese field at Munda. Wearing out several pairs of boots, sporting fatigues dyed with coffee as camouflage, and being plagued with insects, he and his associate (Cmdr. Bill Painter) avoided strong Japanese patrols to finally determine that a site at Segi Point might suffice. It wasn't all dangerous, hard work, however; at least once they did get to sip some Scotch on Australian coast-watcher David Kennedy's hilltop house in the relative cool of the evening.

At this point Lieutenant Commander Jurika was transferred back to the United States, serving from August 1943 until December 1944 as a Torpedo Training Officer. He was stationed first at Naval Air Station Ft. Lauderdale and then at Naval Air Operational Training Command Jacksonville.

Jurika had become "somewhat of a legend" to a good number of navy men during this time, due to his participation in the battles at Midway and Santa Cruz, as well as the Doolittle raid on Tokyo; in fact, he had been identified by name and portrayed by actor Leon Ames in the major Hollywood movie *Thirty Seconds over Tokyo*, which had been released in November 1944.

Steve next reported onboard the aircraft carrier *Franklin* as the ship's navigator. On March 19, 1945, he was on the *Franklin*'s bridge when she suffered grievous damage from a massive air attack while her task force prepared to strike at the Japanese mainland. In addition to damage from enemy ordnance, the ship was also on the verge of destruction by the explosion of her own munitions and aviation stores. Jurika maintained his post on the bridge, closely advising the commanding officer (Capt. Leslie Gehres), and helping to maneuver the ship to control the conflagration. At the worst moment he was the only officer consulted by the captain when the idea of abandoning ship seemed appropriate. The ship ultimately was saved and, among the awards that were given out, Steve was decorated with a Navy Cross—the navy's second highest medal. He stayed onboard until the *Franklin* was brought into the Brooklyn Navy Yard.

While at New York, Commander Jurika received orders sending him back to the Pacific as chief of staff to the Commander, Carrier Division 26. Then, from January 1946 through July 1947, he worked in the Pentagon for the deputy chief of naval operations, Vice Adm. Forrest Sherman. During 1948 and 1949, Steve was naval attaché for air to Australia and New Zealand. In the spring of 1950, he then was transferred to Naval Air Station Corpus Christi; there he served as the station's executive officer.

In June 1951, Jurika was again sent back into the Pacific, on the staff of Carrier Division 1, based at Yokosuka, Japan. He then became a liaison to the Japanese Air Defense Force from 1951 through 1952; for this service he was awarded the Legion of Merit—from the U.S. Air Force. January 1953 saw Captain Jurika back in Hawaii, as head of the Pacific Fleet Evaluation Group, analyzing naval operations in the just-ended Korean War.

Steve was then sent to the Naval War College, from which he graduated in June 1955—along with Captains Rudy **Fabian** and Robert **Weeks**. He transferred back to

Washington, once again working in the offices of OPNAV. Among other things, he wrote CNO policy papers for the JCS. On top of his navy work, he also completed a master's degree in geography and political science at George Washington University.

In the period 1957 to 1959 he was assigned as commanding officer of Fleet Air Wing 14 in San Diego. He finished his naval career as commanding officer of the NROTC unit at Stanford University. While working at Stanford, he completed PhD degrees in both geography and political science. Steve retired from the navy in July 1962.[2]

He then taught political science at the University of Santa Clara for several years. Then, from 1975–1986, he worked as a professor of national security affairs and intelligence at the Naval Postgraduate School in Monterey; concurrently he was a research fellow at the Hoover Institution.

Dr. Jurika was the author, coauthor, or editor of a half-dozen books, including *From Pearl Harbor to Vietnam: The Memoirs of Admiral Arthur W. Radford*; *The President and National Security: His Role as Commander in Chief*; and *A Geography of Southern Asia*.[3]

Steve was married to Lillian Ursula Marie Smith Jurika (1920–2011), who was originally from Coronado, California. They had three daughters, Lillian, Jane, and Anne.

Stephen Jurika died from cancer on July 15, 1993, and was buried in the Gate of Heaven Catholic Cemetery in Los Altos. Mrs. Jurika was interred with him upon her death.

Captain Jurika's decorations included the Navy Cross, the Legion of Merit, and a Navy Commendation Medal.

---

2. Unlike a number of officers in this study, Captain Jurika never felt that his work in intelligence had detracted from his career as a line officer in aviation, nor held him back from promotion. In reality, his serious intelligence work lasted only from June 1939 through August 1941—while he was an assistant attaché in Tokyo—so this makes sense. However, in his U.S. Naval Institute oral history he does comment—and he comments at length—about a different issue. He says that in 1957 he had been selected to command an aircraft carrier, which may well have led to promotion to rear admiral. However, he was accosted by the vice chief of naval operations, Adm. Harry Donald Felt, who demanded that Jurika recommit himself to being a hard-charging naval officer, and quit being distracted by unimportant things. Felt had learned that Jurika had just earned a master's degree and was considering pursuing a doctorate. Apparently Steve's response was unsatisfactory, for Felt had him deselected for carrier command. Jurika said in his interview that he has no regrets as to what happened. What did puzzle him is that Felt had been his friend and mentor since 1935, and had never before done anything other than help him!

Moreover, because Steve had been awarded the Navy Cross in combat, he was fully eligible to be given an honorary promotion to rear admiral upon his retirement. However, that provision in the law expired in November 1959, so when Captain Jurika decided it was time to retire in July 1962, that honor was no longer available to him. Steve Jurika was a particularly sharp individual, and he surely knew the rules. He doesn't mention it in his oral history. My guess is that he wasn't particularly interested.

3. Admiral Arthur W. Radford served for over forty years and held a variety of posts including vice chief of naval operations, commander in chief, U.S. Pacific Fleet, and later chairman of the JCS. Radford and Jurika had been close over the years.

Sources

The Doolittle Raid—Key U.S. Navy Participants; Captain Stephen Jurika. www.uss-hornet.org.
Jurika, Vol. I: 2–7, 13, 26, 37, 57, 116, 135, 163, 212, 246, 299, 320, 330, 332, 337–41,
    344, 347, 357, 360, 370, 389–90, 394–98, 414–16, 456, 461, 465–67, 487. Vol. II: 22,
    33, 38, 143, 157, 432.
Lucky Bag, U.S. Naval Academy, 1933.
Mahnken, 65, 81
Morison, III, 391.
Prados, 18, 23, 26–27, 30, 38–39, 53–54, 96, 287, 498–500.
Symonds, 258–59.
Tull, 282–83, 286–87, 291.
U.S. Navy, *Register of Commissioned and Warrant Officers.*

COLONEL ALVA BRYAN "RED" LASSWELL, U.S. MARINE CORPS (1905–1988)

One of Rochefort's core group at Station HYPO
One of two "ace translators" at HYPO
"Admiral Yamamoto's nemesis"
"Red"

"A tall, sandy-haired, cigar-smoking Marine," Alva B. Lasswell was a gifted linguist known for his precise and industrious work habits. He started his military career as a

Marine private; in fact, he and Cmdr. Joseph **Rochefort** were the only regular officers at HYPO who hadn't gone to Annapolis. Lasswell is one of the few Marines selected for ONI's full-immersion Japanese language and culture training program. Then, informally schooled in cryptanalysis at Station CAST in the Philippines, he was attached to HYPO just before the war. Partnered with Lt. Cmdr. Joseph **Finnegan**, the two officers became a phenomenal team of translators-analysts. After the war, "Red" completed a long Marine Corps career with no further COMINT assignments, but his remarkable accomplishments at HYPO ensure his singular reputation.

*   *   *

"Red" Lasswell was born on January 5, 1905, in Walpole, Illinois, the son of Charles S. and Leanna Russell Lasswell. He attended high school in Piggott and then Rector, Arkansas, but did not graduate from either of them. He received considerable homeschooling from his father, who was a teacher. In 1921, Lasswell moved to Oklahoma and worked as an accountant. In the fall of 1925 he enlisted in the Marine Corps at Kansas City and then was sent to Parris Island for recruit training. After graduation he spent some time as a bookkeeper at the post exchange because of his mathematics ability. He also took some correspondence courses to improve his general education. Lasswell was accepted for officers' candidate school at Washington, and was graduated and commissioned as a second lieutenant in September 1929. Further promotions included first lieutenant, 1934; captain, 1936; major, April 1942; lieutenant colonel, August 1942; and colonel, 1943.

Lieutenant Lasswell was assigned duty at the Marine Barracks in Philadelphia during 1930, and then at the Marine Barracks in Hampton Roads during 1931. In 1932 and 1933 Lasswell was transferred to the Marine detachment on board the battleship *Arizona*. In 1934 he was promoted to first lieutenant and posted to Naval Air Station, Pensacola, Florida, followed by duty with the 5th Marines at Quantico, Virginia, where he taught FBI agents small-arms marksmanship. For this duty he received a letter of commendation from FBI director J. Edgar Hoover. It was about at this time that Lasswell mentioned to his commanding officer that he was interested in foreign language training; as a result, his CO generated a letter of recommendation which he hand carried to Washington. "Red" shortly found himself in Washington at ONI, where he was accepted for its full-immersion language and culture training in Japan. Thus, Lasswell spent 1935 through the first half of 1938 in Japan—attached to the embassy but with no other duties than study.

Captain Lasswell then reported to the Marine Barracks, Cavite Navy Yard, in September 1938, with the cover title of Assistant War Plans Officer for the Sixteenth Naval District—but in reality he was the language officer for the Station CAST decryption unit, relieving Lt. Joseph Finnegan. Lasswell was trained in basic cryptology—on the job—by Lt. Jefferson **Dennis**, the OIC. This tour proved crucial for Lasswell, giving him extensive insight into Japanese cryptosystems which were invaluable to him during the forthcoming war.

In June 1939, Captain Lasswell left Cavite for Shanghai onboard the transport *Henderson*. He reported for duty with the 4th Marines with the cover title of Assistant Regimental Intelligence Officer—but really as officer in charge of the secret Shanghai radio intelligence station. He stayed there until around July 1940.

He then reported to the 8th Marines at Camp Elliott on the outskirts of San Diego; his duties there were infantry rather than language or communications, first as a company commander and then as a battalion commander.

Anticipating the coming of the war with Japan, and recognizing that they did not have enough people with expertise, the Marines set up a Japanese language school at the University of Hawaii in May 1941. In April, Captain Lasswell was ordered as the OIC. In the winter of 1940–1941, Lasswell interviewed possible candidates with Japanese language backgrounds. However, Lt. Jack **Holtwick** at Pearl Harbor's Station HYPO essentially intercepted him, requesting that Lasswell be reassigned back into the COMINT environment. Holtwick may have been operating under the direction of Cmdr. Joseph Rochefort, who was just coming in to take over HYPO as OIC. Lasswell had developed a good reputation as a linguist, and Rochefort had been given a free hand in recruiting the best people in the community. When Lasswell reported to HYPO he initially was paired with Lt. Cmdr. Ranson **Fullinwider** in the translation section. Many years later, Lasswell wrote in his memoirs that the work—for the linguists—was somewhat boring in the months leading up to the Pearl Harbor attack because there wasn't a great deal of message traffic to work on; this was because Station HYPO was not yet assigned to study the Japanese Navy's JN-25 operational code and was bogged down in the infrequently used and ultimately unbreakable "Admiral's Code."

A couple of days before the attack on Pearl Harbor, Lasswell was fully engaged helping Warrant Officer Farnsley Woodward with some recently obtained Japanese cables encoded in their "LA" diplomatic system. However, it wasn't until several days after the attack that they were able to break it and render it readable.

Lasswell was on watch early on December 7, 1941, and was ready to be relieved—which was not going to happen. Those who had been there on duty overnight, as well as everyone else who were now called in, were going to be there for a long while. Like some others did, Lasswell found a cot and put it behind his desk. Later that same day he was outside for some reason and several blocks away from HYPO; he saw that a Japanese plane had crashed near the eastern bank of the Pearl Harbor channel. Lasswell was among those who pulled the dead pilot out of the cockpit. He noted that the pilot was wearing heavy woolen clothing under his flight suit. "I rushed back to call [fleet intelligence officer Edwin] **Layton**," who was desperately trying to confirm whether the attack had come from the north or the south. "I told him this aviator came from the north. He was in heavy clothing, and I [said] I think you can feel very certain that his plane came from the north."

A few days later, Lt. Joseph Finnegan came in to HYPO to find something useful to do because his ship, the battleship *Tennessee*, had been badly damaged and put out of action. Finnegan was an outstanding Japanese linguist and reasonably experienced cryptanalyst. He only stayed a few days before being called away, but came back to HYPO in February 1942 for a long-term assignment. He and Lasswell were paired together, and they became "a phenomenal team of translator-cryptanalysts," even though they had very different styles. According to Capt. Jasper **Holmes**, who knew and worked closely with them both, Lasswell liked cheap Cuban cigars which contributed to the constant tobacco smoke in the Dungeon. Holmes wrote that

> Lasswell approached cryptanalysis like a chess-player maneuvering relentlessly to untangle his problem. His desk was usually clear of everything but his current puzzle. He worked sitting upright at his desk, wearing a carefully pressed Marine Corps uniform of the day, his sole deviation being a green eyeshade for protection against the hours under fluorescent lights.

Capt. Tommy **Dyer** wrote, long after the war, "Our two top translators were very good. They balanced each other; Lasswell was very precise and methodical, and Finnegan was given to wild flights of fantasy."

Similarly, in a 1969 interview, retired Capt. Joe Rochefort said, "I had possibly the two best language officers—I like to think, besides me—this would be Joe Finnegan and a Marine, a fellow named Alva Lasswell. [Translation] would be the crux of the whole thing. You can assign values and all that sort of thing, but unless you do a good job of translating then the whole value is lost."

As mentioned earlier, just before the war began the Marine Corps felt handicapped by having too few Japanese language specialists, so it began to seek (as well as train) linguists. As historian John Prados wrote,

> The most natural recruiting grounds were right in California and Hawaii, where many *nisei* resided. [Captain] Alva Lasswell was sent several times to San Francisco on temporary duty to interview prospective linguists who were brought to brush up their Japanese and learn technical terminology in a class at the University of Hawaii. [But] after the exclusion order [Executive Order 9066 which implemented the relocation of Japanese-Americans away from coastal areas], the Marines could no longer recruit on the West Coast.

On May 19, 1942, Station HYPO was swamped by a particularly large volume of traffic, including about fifty intercepts which appeared to be of very high priority. Major Lasswell took on the priority package and shortly got the impression that this might be the order of battle and main operations order for the large Japanese Navy campaign which the unit knew was in progress—a movement that ultimately led to the U.S. Navy's incredible victory at the Battle of Midway. Whether Lasswell's intercepts were or were not literally those documents, the large amount of information obtained was incredibly detailed and important. "I knew I detected something important that night. I spent the whole night on it. . . . There were several problems involved, such as the area codes and grid. . . . I don't think that Rochefort even knew I was working on this thing 'til the next day." Commander Rochefort reviewed and sent out Lasswell's findings, but "the element of doubt was thrown into it by the Washington office; [they] thought I was wrong. . . . Lt. Cmdr. Rosie **Mason**, my counterpart at Station NEGAT . . . agreed with my translation but thought the target [was not Midway but rather] elsewhere in the Pacific." The argument lasted several days. "I stuck to my guns. I saw no reason to [change my mind]." Of course, as related elsewhere, Lasswell and HYPO were proven to be correct and Mason and NEGAT embarrassingly wrong. For the rest of his life, Lasswell remembered the long Midway message break as his greatest wartime achievement.

For a time Red Lasswell shared a small house with Ham **Wright** and Tom Steele in Makalapa officer housing, just down from Admiral Nimitz's house and four hundred yards from CinCPac headquarters. All three loved to play chess and would while away some of their rare downtime with this activity—while also drinking *Old Fashioneds*. There were frequent mornings that Lasswell joined up with Nimitz as he walked by and accompanied the admiral on his path toward headquarters.

Lasswell's family moved from the East Coast to California to be closer to him in case he got any extended time off. That hardly ever happened, although once he hitched a ride in the tail of a B-24 going stateside from Oahu. There was another time Lasswell was sent to Washington predominantly for a break—but upon arrival he was told to report to Main Navy to cover for the absent Rosie Mason. Unbelievably, the reason Mason was gone is because he'd been sent to Pearl Harbor to fill in for Lasswell!

Amidst the normal, frantic activity and workload as the war was fought, one day in the spring of 1943 good fortune, fine processes, and excellent cryptanalysis delivered to the Americans the Solomon Islands inspection itinerary of Admiral Yamamoto, the commander in chief of the Japanese Combined Fleet. Lieutenant Colonel Lasswell had the duty, and FRUPac (as HYPO was now generally known) was the first (rather than FRUMel at Melbourne, or NEGAT at Washington) to break the message. As the eminent cryptologic historian David Kahn wrote, when the machine-assisted cryptanalysis of the Yamamoto message produced Japanese plain text, it

> went to a translator of more than ordinary competence, a 38-year-old Marine Corps lieutenant colonel named Alva Bryan Lasswell. . . . Lasswell [produced an] almost minute-by-minute listing of [Yamamoto's] activities on a day during which the admiral would come closer to the combat zone than he had probably ever done before! The cryptanalyzed intercept amounted to a death warrant for the highest enemy commander.

"We've hit the jackpot!" Lasswell shouted after initially scanning the message. He later wrote that the original intercept had been received by FRUPac's net, and that he "personally did the whole thing overnight." In many ways, this incident could have seemed more noteworthy than his 1942 Midway message decipherment and translation, but "I didn't feel, somehow or the other, the joy in [the Yamamoto decryption] that I did in the other, because I sort of felt more of a snooper." He was also very happy that he had no part in Admiral Nimitz's follow-on decision to take action on the information and order the shoot-down. Rear Adm. Eddie Layton later summed up the situation by observing that

Yamamoto was preeminent in all categories, that any successor would be personally and professionally inferior and, finally, that the death of the commander in chief would demoralize the Japanese, who venerate their captains much more than Occidentals do.

The attempt was made and Yamamoto was killed—to the severe detriment of the Japanese war effort.[1]

Colonel Lasswell had another particularly important achievement during his HYPO tour.

In 1944 Lasswell decoded and translated a Japanese message concerning their submarines. They had set up seven subs located seven miles apart around the coast of New Guinea—anticipating that this would be the route taken by Gen. Douglas MacArthur on his return to the Philippines. This [potential] ambush ended with the U.S. Navy destroying all of the submarines, for Lasswell had decoded their exact locations.

Colonel Lasswell was transferred to Station NEGAT in Washington in October 1944, continuing similar work there for the remainder of the war.

From October 1945 until July 1946, Red was OIC of the Marine Corps Separation Center at Naval Station Bainbridge, Maryland. He then became chief of staff, First Marine Division, at Tientsin, China. From July 1947 until May 1948, Colonel Lasswell served as commanding officer of the 7th Marine Regiment at Camp Pendleton, California.

Then, from June 1948 through June 1950, Lasswell was assigned as commanding officer, Marine Barracks, Yokosuka, Japan. He was next attached to the Industrial College of the Armed Forces, as a student, until July 1951. For the next two years, Colonel Lasswell served as the assignments officer, for colonels and generals, at Headquarters Marine Corps. He then went back to the Pacific in 1953, first as commanding officer of a major supply depot in Korea, and then as an advisor to the commanding general of the Korean Marine Brigade. Lasswell's last assignment began in 1954 as chief of staff, Marine Corps Recruit Depot, San Diego. He retired from active duty in April 1956, after thirty-one years of service.

In retirement, Lasswell lived in southern California and for some years was in the banking and real estate business. He passed away after battling lung cancer on October 28, 1988, at his home in Vista, California.

In 1938, Captain Lasswell had married Elizabeth Louise Pearce (1916–2006) while in Japan. They had two sons, James (USNA 1963) and John (USNA 1967), who both later retired as navy commanders.

Colonel Lasswell received the Legion of Merit medal, in March 1946, for his remarkable contributions during World War II. He also has been officially recognized by the U.S. Naval Cryptologic Veterans Association as a Pioneer Officer of U.S. Naval Cryptology.

---

1. Rudy **Fabian** at FRUMel was against the ambush on Admiral Yamamoto, thinking that the Japanese would surely deduce that prior knowledge of his flight plan had been obtained. Years later, in an oral history, he said that "it could have compromised the hell out of us."

Sources

Carlson, 94, 100–1, 130, 140, 176–77, 187, 191, 196–98, 278–79, 286, 303, 308, 327–29, 342–45, 445, 483, 496, 519.
Dyer, 265.
Holmes, 37–38, 55, 64–65, 118, 124, 135–36.
Holtwick, 304, 327–28, 360, 402, 427, 446.
Hunnicutt, 1–11.
Kahn, *Codebreakers*, 595–96.
Layton, *"And I Was There,"* 6, 474.
McGinnis, 20–21, 39, 49.
Prados, 315, 319, 352, 406, 408, 412, 459–60.
Rochefort, 103, 105.
Smith, *Emperor's Codes*, 182–83.
U.S. Navy, *Register of Commissioned and Warrant Officers.*

REAR ADMIRAL EDWIN THOMAS LAYTON, U.S. NAVY (1903–1984)

Fleet Intelligence Officer for Admirals Richardson, Kimmel, and Nimitz
The first special-duty intelligence officer to make flag rank
"Eddie"

Edwin Layton remains a central figure in any discussion of the pre-war and wartime U.S. Navy's efforts toward intelligence and communications-intelligence. Almost always competitive, at times pugnacious, and even occasionally abrasive, Layton was also extremely sharp, remarkably intuitive, quick-thinking, and hard-working. After the usual junior officer start in surface ships, he volunteered for ONI's full-immersion Japanese language and culture course. He then undertook normal Pacific-oriented tours, alternately, in intelligence duties ashore and nonintelligence duties at sea. He was one of the few intelligence-oriented language officers to also undertake formal—if brief—cryptology training at OP-20-G. His outstanding linguistic ability and fluency in Japanese proved to be assets as his career progressed and as World War II loomed on the horizon. A Tokyo embassy assignment, and then more sea time, led to his posting as FIO, Pacific—serving three successive commanders-in-chief—during the entire 1940–1945 period. Postwar assignments included tours as a DIO, once again the Pacific Fleet's intelligence officer, the director of the Naval Intelligence School, and the deputy director for intelligence at the JCS level.

*   *   *

From the 1924 Naval Academy yearbook, *The Lucky Bag*:

The fame of [*Eddie*] (also known as *Seventeen*) began with his portrayal of a certain femme role in the Masqueraders [the midshipmen's drama club]. Some still believe that it was Marilyn Miller, incognito. But truly it was our "Gwendolyn" giving the boys a treat. Since then he has rested on his laurels and become strongly affiliated with the Radiator Club [snack-bar club of nonathletes]. His two great failings are a thorough belief in the constancy and infallibility of women, and an inveterate susceptibility to blind drags [dates]. The elusive two-five [satisfactory grade-point average] is winged by *Seventeen* with little or no effort. With a never-failing source of humor and a ray of happiness that follows wherever he goes, his success cannot be disputed. [Activities: Masqueraders; Radiator Club]

*   *   *

Edwin Layton was born in Nauvoo, Illinois, on April 7, 1903, son of George E. and Mary C. Layton. After graduation from Galesburg High School, in 1920, he entered the U.S. Naval Academy. Eddie graduated from the academy, and was commissioned an ensign, in 1924 along with such distinguished classmates as Thomas H. **Dyer**, Thomas A. **Huckins**, Ethelbert **Watts**, Daniel J. McCallum, John C. Waldron, and Hanson W. Baldwin. Further promotions included lieutenant (junior grade), 1927; lieutenant, 1933; lieutenant commander, 1938; commander, 1942; captain, 1943; and rear admiral, 1953. He retired from the navy in 1959.

After his academy graduation, Mr. Layton served for the next five years in the Pacific Fleet onboard the battleship *West Virginia* and the destroyer *Chase*. At one point Ens. Layton was assigned to escort a group of Japanese naval officers around San Francisco; he was amazed to hear that they almost all spoke excellent American English and most could also speak French. He wondered how many U.S. Navy officers could speak Japanese and was dismayed to learn there were hardly any, so he subsequently volunteered for ONI's full-immersion study program.

Thus, in 1929, he was one of the few officers selected for that Japanese language and culture training. One of his fellow students was Lt. Joseph J. **Rochefort**. They liked each other instantly. Layton later wrote that "our lifelong friendship began . . . on board the steamer *President Adams* when the long Pacific crossing gave me a chance to get acquainted with him." They were assigned to the American Embassy in Tokyo where they remained for three years, sharing living quarters for most of that time. During their stay in Japan, assistant naval attaché Lt. Cmdr. Arthur

McCollum took them under his wing and showed them "the ropes." Both young officers excelled in their study of the language and culture. The last four months of the tour Layton spent in Peking, China, as assistant naval attaché at the American Legation. Then, in February 1933, Layton returned to the United States for a short five-month tour at ONI.

In June 1933, Eddie transferred to the battleship *Pennsylvania*, in charge of Number Four gun turret (Lt. Tommy **Dyer** was his friendly rival as captain of Number Three). Lt. j.g. Ham **Wright** arrived in 1936, transferring from OP-20-G. And Joe Rochefort came onboard when the CINCUS, Adm. Joseph M. Reeves, transferred his staff to the *Pennsylvania* and made her his flagship.

> This curious coincidence brought together in the same ship the four of us who five years later would find ourselves working alongside each other in the critical months leading up to Pearl Harbor and on through the Battle of Midway. We always looked back on our battleship duty together as an interesting twist of fate. The coincidence was heightened by the fact that *Pennsylvania*'s skipper was Capt. Russell **Willson**, who had been the director of naval communications in World War I.

Lieutenant Layton served onboard the *Pennsylvania* until June 1936. He received letters of commendation from the secretary of the navy and from the commander in chief, U.S. Fleet, in 1934 and 1935 respectively, for gunnery excellence and for special performance in Fleet Problem XVI.

In the fall of 1934, Lt. j.g. (Dr.) Cecil **Coggins** brought about the first intelligence undercover mission for Mr. Layton. Coggins, who had been working with the Eleventh Naval District's intelligence office and ONI's local undercover organization, discovered that a just-arrived Japanese naval tanker had brought some films to show to the local Japanese Citizens Patriotic Society in Long Beach, California. They suspected that it was subversive material and wanted Layton, as an educated Japanese linguist, to check it out. Posing as a fire-insurance inspector, Mr. Layton attended the showing and found the films indeed subversive—as well as "corny."

Layton returned to Main Navy at Washington, relieved Lt. Tommy **Birtley** at OP-20-GZ, and served there at Main Navy until February 1937. Much of that time he worked at ONI, rubbing shoulders with the head of the Far Eastern section, Cmdr. Ellis **Zacharias**. There Layton worked on a study of Japanese industry and the "strategic power grid." But for approximately eight months he also worked in Naval Communications at the OP-20-G Research Desk. There he met the legendary Mrs. Agnes **Driscoll**, who helped him learn the art and science of cryptography. His first encounter with "Miss Aggie"

> occurred one morning when she brought me a large piece of graph paper and asked, "Lieutenant Layton, does this make any sense?" She had marked the paper with zigzag staircases of letters in different colors of ink. Not being a Japanese linguist . . . she traced out a zigzag, and I told her it made sense—it could be a Japanese name, "Tomimura." When she shook her head, I suggested that the "mura," which means "town," has an

alternate meaning of "son," so it might also be rendered Tomison or Thompson. Somewhat later, Miss Aggie told me, "Lieutenant, I want to thank you. You helped me solve part of a cipher that's been bothering me for a long time. The name *is* Thompson."

As it turned out, this name—intercepted in Japanese foreign office traffic—was identified as belonging to a former Pacific Fleet radioman; he and an accomplice were turning over navy engineering and gunnery information to the Japanese in the San Diego area. As also discussed in the chapters on Ellis Zacharias and Cecil Coggins—who were engaged in the local investigation of the case—Thompson was arrested and convicted in 1936 (the cryptologic aspect of the investigation was *not* exposed in court), and he was sent to prison for violating federal espionage laws.

Layton was relieved of duty by Lt. Redfield **Mason** and then returned to Tokyo, in 1937, for a two-year period as assistant naval attaché at the American embassy. There he relieved Lt. Ethelbert **Watts** in that position. Interestingly, during this time, he had the opportunity to get to know the prominent Japanese admiral Yamamoto Isoroku and periodically played cards with him.[1] In April 1939, Layton was assigned as the captain of the Pacific Fleet's auxiliary ship-minesweeper *Boggs*, commanding her while she operated with Mobile Target Division One, Battle Force, until December 1940.

In the summer of 1939, Lieutenant Commander Layton visited with Captain Zacharias in San Diego; Zach was now the IO for the Eleventh Naval District. While drinking daiquiris, Zacharias asked Layton if he'd like to be FIO for the Pacific Fleet. Zacharias believed that war was just over the horizon, and that the Pacific Fleet needed an outstanding IO who was also an excellent Japanese linguist—and needed an assistant IO who was one as well. As a result Layton later wrote that

> I was not surprised when the following year orders came to me to report to flagship *Pennsylvania* as FIO—and Bob Hudson joined shortly after as my assistant. Of all my colleagues, [Robert E.] Hudson knew the Japanese people and psychology best.

Thus, in July 1940, Mr. Layton reported to the commander in chief, U.S. Fleet, as staff intelligence officer for Adm. James O. Richardson. Subsequently, when war was declared on December 8, 1941, Layton was present as the Fleet Intelligence Officer on the staff of Adm. Husband E. Kimmel—who had replaced Admiral Richardson as CINCUS at Pearl Harbor. Fortunately, when Chester Nimitz came to Pearl Harbor to relieve Kimmel, Layton was asked to stay on.

Heretofore, with the conservatism typical of the old-school senior leaders, intelligence and cryptographic officers did not have great sway on events—as bemoaned by new and dynamic intelligence professionals such as Captain Zacharias. Zach wrote that, up through 1941, many such officers were of relatively low rank, understaffed,

---

1. As did Ellis Zacharias, when Yamamoto was an attaché in Washington in the 1920s. Poker seemed to be the Japanese officer's favorite game. Layton told Admiral Kimmel that Yamamoto "could win at poker among good poker players, and could play better bridge than most good bridge players, and . . . was a champion . . . of the Japanese chess game, 'Go.'"

and generally held at arm's length by their superiors. So, just prior to the war's beginning, Zach's evaluation of the situation was that at that time

> it was not [an intelligence officer's privilege] to [predict] enemy intentions from the information they gathered. This function was usurped by the planners, whose main preoccupation should have been to take appropriate countermeasures to the Japanese moves culled from the incoming material, promptly submitted to higher echelons, and highlighted by those who knew the Japanese.
>
> Layton . . . had his own ideas and drew his own conclusions. But he could not present them with the force necessary since he was only a lieutenant commander. He himself felt that his ears were pinned back too often for comfort and [became] reluctant to provoke the ire of superior officers who disliked intensely a junior officer interfering with their own ideas, especially when the junior was "only an intelligence officer."

It's pretty fair to say that the worst example of this kind of thing was personified by Rear Adm. Richmond K. "Terrible" Turner, who before the Pearl Harbor attack was War Plans Officer at Main Navy in Washington. In that role, Turner essentially channeled information coming from Naval Intelligence and Naval Communications to himself, and then reserved all rights of analysis and estimation for himself. He told the head of naval intelligence that "ONI [will] make no estimate of prospective enemy intentions . . . but furnish information to War Plans who would make the required estimates."[2]

But it's also fair to say that as the prewar situation got worse, Admiral Kimmel (and most certainly Admiral Nimitz after the war began) soon developed a great deal of trust in the intelligence process and in intelligence personnel—and understood the nuances of what realistically could and could not be assessed. A good example is the famous exchange between Layton and Kimmel on December 2, 1941.

Kimmel: "What! You don't know where the Japanese carriers are?"

Layton: "No, sir."

Kimmel: "You haven't any idea where they are?"

---

2. Layton never learned to like Terrible Turner due to what Layton believed was Turner's withholding of information before the Pearl Harbor attack. Moreover, he did not enjoy staff work with him when he came to the Pacific Theater to command amphibious forces. "Few who worked closely with him in these operations could forget—or forgive—his stormy temper, overbearing ego, and celebrated bouts with the bottle." Finally, they had a nasty confrontation on the eve of the Japanese surrender in Tokyo Bay. According to Layton, Turner staggered into the crowded wardroom of the battleship *South Dakota*, clearly inebriated. Turner was delighted to announce that the navy had released some findings from the Pearl Harbor attack court of inquiry. He boomed out, "They said that goddamned Kimmel had all the information and didn't do anything about it. They should hang him higher than a kite!" At that time Turner was probably nervous that his own actions and inactions as head of the navy's War Plans Office right before the attack would be questioned, so he very much wanted all blame to land on Kimmel. This was a very sore subject for Layton; he lost his temper and interrupted Turner in mid-rant, telling him he was wrong, and that Kimmel certainly hadn't had anything like full information. Turner bellowed across the wardroom "Are you calling me a liar?" and moved to grab Layton by the collar. "Only the prompt intervention of the *South Dakota*'s skipper, Capt. Emmet Forrestel, prevented a 'four-striper' captain from exchanging blows with a four-star admiral."

Layton: "No, sir. That's why I have 'home waters' on the report with a question mark. I don't know."

Kimmel: "You mean to say that you are the Intelligence Officer of the Pacific Fleet and you don't know where the carriers are?"

Layton: "No, sir, I don't."

Kimmel: "For all you know, they could be coming around Diamond Head, and you wouldn't know it?"

Layton: "Yes, sir. But I hope they'd have been sighted by now."

Kimmel, smiling: "Yes, I understand."

Layton realized that Admiral Kimmel appreciated that the intelligence system was good, albeit not perfect, and if the honest answer was "I don't know," then he had to take a commensurate course of action. It seems that it will be debated forever, but at that time analysis at Pearl Harbor, reinforced by alerts from Washington, precipitated a credible intelligence picture: Japanese forces were assembling for strikes in the Far East, not in the mid-Pacific. Layton was convinced that the Japanese would push southward. They might strike the British, and if anything they might strike at the Philippines, not wanting to "risk leaving our forces [there] on their flank."[3] As he told Kimmel, Layton believed that Japan could not afford to initially "gamble too much, wherein she might lose the war in the first battle when she had larger stakes—more vital stakes—at hand."

Admiral Kimmel had repeatedly asked Washington whether the Pacific Fleet was receiving all relevant intelligence—including diplomatic—and had been assured by the CNO that it was. "We believed that we were receiving it," Layton later wrote. But with the advantage of hindsight and full postwar information, he concluded that "the failure to relay . . . vital pieces of intelligence [particularly diplomatic] deprived us of essential facts and misled us when it came to our assessing the possibility of a Japanese attack on Pearl Harbor."

Even without full input from Washington, Layton did have other sources. He later outlined that

> the main sources of information were from . . . ONI, who forwarded us reports from naval observers, naval attaches, other competent observers, State Department, consular agents. Also from CNO via the Office of Naval Communications certain highly secret information under the classification of communications intelligence.
>
> Also local reports from the local district intelligence office [at Pearl] regarding local security conditions; through liaison with British intelligence of the Secret Intelligence Service, intelligence as to Japan's activities in the Far East. Also from the commandants

---

3. That being written, it's probably fair to say that had Mr. Layton, Admiral Kimmel, or even General Short had access to MAGIC (Japanese *diplomatic* radio intelligence)—which they essentially didn't—they might have raised the level of readiness in the Hawaiian commands. Such intelligence would have made them more aware of Japan's rapid march toward hostilities, as well as some issues concerning activities at the Japanese consulate in Honolulu.

of the Twelfth [San Francisco] and Sixteenth [Philippines] Naval Districts and Panama Sea Frontier regarding movements of Japanese merchant vessels; reports also from the commandant of the Third Naval District [New York City] regarding movements of Japanese merchant vessels.

Built upon their close friendship, Layton had a remarkably good relationship with Joe Rochefort who had recently come to Pearl Harbor as OIC at Station HYPO (the Fourteenth Naval District's radio intelligence and cryptanalysis office), facilitating intelligence integration between the two organizations which—it must be emphasized— were not under the same chain of command. Years after the war, Layton wrote that

> Joe Rochefort and I were old and close friends both professionally and socially. We conferred many times daily—via a secure sound-powered telephone; he was at one end at "his shop" and I at my end—about material arriving in the COMINT channel. He would always call me when they came across a "hot" item, and would ask my views about problems as they arose—blanks in the text, garbles and the like—to see if we could guess a meaning or value for the benefit of the cryptanalysts and translators.

This relationship created great and obvious efficiencies; however, the partnership essentially bypassed Washington and brought intelligence estimates directly to the fleet commander—a situation that bureaucratically minded officers resented at Naval Communications headquarters in Washington.

Of course Pearl Harbor, and other military installations on Oahu, were indeed targeted by the Japanese in an effort to deliver a surprise knock-out blow to the U.S. fleet—despite the considerable indicators to the contrary.

> "Pearl Harbor is under air attack, sir," was how Commander Layton's yeoman broke the news by telephone to his chief at his home overlooking Manalua Bay, fifteen miles to the east of the naval base. The curtain drop of Diamond Head had shut him off from sight and sound of the raging attack. He jumped into the Cadillac roadster of his neighbor Lt. Paul Crossley, and they hurtled off, taking the road through downtown Honolulu, with Mrs. Crossley at the wheel. "The nightmare grew larger and louder the closer we came to the naval base, which radiated terrible explosions," Layton was to recall.

Upon taking command of the Pacific Fleet after the Pearl Harbor attack, Admiral Nimitz soon came to appreciate the intelligence organization he inherited—and the people in it. Nimitz emphasized to Layton that on top of correlating, analyzing, and presenting the information he had, the admiral also wanted Layton to put himself in the minds of the Japanese admirals—and then tell Nimitz what they intended to do. "I want you to be the Admiral Nagumo on my staff, where your every thought, every instinct, will be that of Admiral Nagumo's; you are to see the war, their operations, their aims, from the Japanese viewpoint and keep me advised about what you (as a Japanese) are thinking."

In this vein, relying on solid multi-source intelligence and cryptographic information—as well as his personal intuition, experience, and assessment skills—he gave Nimitz just such an estimate prior to the Battle of Midway. "Layton and Rochefort, having correctly foretold the Japanese move against Port Moresby [prior to the Battle of the Coral Sea], now enjoyed the CinCPac's full attention." At first Layton tried to demur when Nimitz asked him to predict exactly how the coming battle would unfold. "Sir, I have a difficult time being specific." But Nimitz insisted. "I want you to be specific. After all, this is the job I have given you—to be the admiral commanding the Japanese forces, and tell me what is going on." So, Layton predicted that the enemy carriers would attack Midway on the morning of June 4, 1942. "They'll come in from the northwest on bearing 325 degrees," he said, "and they'll be sighted at about 175 miles from Midway, and the time will be about 0600 Midway time." Days later, when the actual sighting did come—and after some calculations—Nimitz famously remarked to Layton, "Well, you were only five miles, five degrees, and five minutes off."

In fact, in the lead-up to Midway, Admiral King in Washington had suggested to Admiral Nimitz that the apparent Japanese interest in Midway was intended "to divert our forces away from [their real objectives in the] South Pacific." But Nimitz was willing to push back against King "because he was confident that Layton and Rochefort knew what they were talking about." In fact, Rochefort and Layton were impressed and energized by the confidence Nimitz showed in them. "We were aware that by challenging King and his [Washington] intelligence staff head-on, Nimitz had put himself out on a limb—and we were clinging onto it behind him."

At all times, those very few in the know about the vital radio and cryptanalysis intelligence program had to religiously keep it secret, coming up with various other explanations—coast-watcher sightings, chance aerial or submarine sightings, prisoner interrogations, spies, and the like. Some people assumed that naval intelligence must have a "mole" in Japan; once an officer from the carrier *Enterprise* said to Layton, "That man of ours in Tokyo is worth every cent we pay him," to which Layton must have just smiled and changed the subject.

In the fall of 1942, despite (or perhaps because of) his incredible contributions to the successful battles at the Coral Sea and at Midway, Commander Rochefort was removed from his billet by the political machinations of professional enemies he had at Main Navy. The reader is invited to read the chapters on Joseph Rochefort and Joseph **Wenger** for more detail on that incredible story, but for here suffice it to say that these same people persuaded Admiral King to also take a swipe at Layton. King told Nimitz that "the attitude of Commander Layton also seems not to have been very helpful. I suggest you consider what should be done in [his case]." Nimitz called Layton into his office and informed him he apparently had an enemy in Washington. Layton was dumbfounded, but then was reassured; Nimitz said, "Go back to your office and don't think any more about it."[4] Admiral Nimitz could and did shield Commander Layton. But, as much as it angered him, Nimitz could not save Rochefort because he

---

4. After Admiral Nimitz told Layton that Washington expected Nimitz to "take care of Layton" in a negative sense (like Washington had engineered the removal of Rochefort), the admiral reassured him nothing of the sort was going to happen. "He pulled from his desk a portrait photograph, which he signed

was technically in the navy's administrative command structure—and thus beyond Nimitz's span of control as operational head of the fleet.

As FIO, Layton was virtually in charge of all intelligence in the Pacific Ocean area and, with his staff, evaluated Japanese naval, air, and sea capabilities—and then projected their intentions. His efforts over the next few years were hugely augmented by the creation and growth of the ICPOA, the JICPOA, and the morphing of Station HYPO into the FRUPac. All of this intelligence effort was vital in planning naval campaigns against the enemy and significantly contributed to the success and ultimate victory of American fighting forces in the Pacific theater of war. Layton "had a standing invitation to walk into Nimitz's office at any hour of any day if he believed he had important information for the C-in-C; no one else on the staff, except perhaps the chief of staff, had this privilege."

Amidst the normal, frantic activity and workload as the war was fought, one day in the spring of 1943 good fortune, fine processes, and excellent cryptanalysis delivered to the Americans the Solomon Islands inspection itinerary of Admiral Yamamoto, the commander in chief of the Japanese Combined Fleet. Commander Layton's analysis and advice were key to Admiral Nimitz's decision to attempt a shoot-down of Yamamoto's aircraft. Layton summed up the situation by observing that

> Yamamoto was preeminent in all categories, that any successor would be personally and professionally inferior and, finally, that the death of the commander in chief would demoralize the Japanese, who venerate their captains much more than Occidentals do.

The attempt was made and Yamamoto was killed—to the severe detriment of the Japanese war effort. (For more details, see Appendix N, "Operation VENGEANCE.")

Promoted twice during the war, Captain Layton accompanied Fleet Admiral Nimitz to Tokyo Bay when the Japanese formally surrendered on September 2, 1945.

Eddie Layton remained on the staff of the Pacific Fleet until February 1946, and then returned to the United States for a two-year tour of duty as commander of the U.S. Naval Net Depot at Tiburon, California. Intelligence work beckoned again, this time a two-year assignment as the first director of the Naval Intelligence School at Naval Air Station Anacostia, from September 1948 to June 1950.

When the Korean War broke out in 1950, Layton's vast Pacific-area experience and intelligence expertise were again required, so he spent six months as DIO for the Commandant, Fourteenth Naval District, in Hawaii. His evaluative skills and keen interpretation of events were of tremendous value, particularly during the early stages of the conflict. In January 1951 he once again assumed the position of FIO for the Commander in Chief, Pacific Fleet, for a two-year period.

In 1953, with the Korean War over, he was promoted to rear admiral (the first career intelligence officer to make flag rank on active duty) and assigned to the staff of the Joint Chiefs where he was Assistant Director—and then Deputy Director—for Intelligence. From 1956 to 1958, Layton served as assistant chief of staff, CinCPac,

---

then and there: 'To Commander Edwin T. Layton. As my intelligence officer you are more valuable to me than any division of cruisers.'"

at Pearl Harbor. His last duty before retirement was director of the Naval Intelligence School at the Naval Receiving Station, Washington, D.C.

Rear Admiral Layton retired from the navy in November 1959. He immediately joined the Northrop Corporation as Director of Far East Operations in Tokyo, remaining in that position through 1963. He retired from Northrop in 1964 and moved to Carmel, California. There he read, wrote, built model ships, worked in scrimshaw, and watched birds and whales.

Admiral Layton was married three times. His first wife was Virginia Yarnell from Los Angeles; they had one son, Professor Edwin T. Layton Jr. Married in 1927, Virginia and Eddie were divorced in 1928. His second wife was Dagne Wickstrom from Duluth; they had two children, Daniel and Carol. Married in 1936, Dagne and Eddie were divorced in 1956. His third wife was Miriam Reid, whom he married in 1959; she had three children from a previous marriage.

Miriam Layton strongly encouraged Eddie to put his story in print, and thus was key in the creation of his reminisces, *"And I Was There": Pearl Harbor and Midway— Breaking the Secrets*, written with coauthors Capt. Roger Pineau and British historian Mr. John Costello. She assisted with the preparation of early drafts, and even after Layton's death sustained his collaborators by making available all his notes and papers in addition to providing them with the hospitality of her home. According to Mrs. Layton, Eddie

> fairly seethed with pent-up emotions surrounding the trauma of having gone through all but one of the Pearl Harbor investigations, and of hearing some of his fellow officers verbally coerced into testifying falsely. Our countless evenings of conversation fulfilled his need to give vent to his outrage at the cover-up in Washington, and at the sacrifice of Admiral Kimmel and General Short.

Ever since the beginning of World War II, Layton had been concerned by what he felt were erroneous accounts and interpretations of the reasons the United States was caught off guard at Pearl Harbor—and particularly by verbal and print attacks on his former commander.

> Layton had always suspected that Admiral Kimmel had been given a "raw deal" by Washington, but it was not until after the war that he discovered just how Kimmel had been framed. Layton knew that the fundamental cause of the Pearl Harbor disaster was Washington's failure to properly evaluate and disseminate radio intelligence information.

Layton and his coauthors covered considerable ground in *"And I Was There,"* certainly including communications intelligence. Writing from Layton's very unique position, they detailed the major contributions that radio intelligence made to winning the Pacific war, including the Battle of Midway, the death of Admiral Yamamoto, the "Great Marianas Turkey Shoot" during the Battle of the Philippine Sea, and the incredible success of the U.S. Navy's submarine war against Japan. Before that, they highlighted the incredible advances in intelligence and cryptology in the years leading up to World War II. Finally, they extolled Admiral Nimitz's effective application of radio intelligence which "made him the understated and unsung hero of the Pacific War."

Years earlier, Rear Admiral Layton had helped Rear Adm. Samuel Eliot Morison with proofreading and other assistance on Morison's epic history of U.S. naval operations in World War II, particularly on Volume IV: *Coral Sea, Midway, and Submarine Actions, May–August 1942*. In addition, in the early 1960s, Layton and retired Rear Adm. Arthur McCollum had helped Professor Roberta Wohlstetter understand the nuances of the 1945 congressional investigations as she wrote her powerful study, *Pearl Harbor: Warning and Decision*.

Rear Admiral Layton died from a stroke in Carmel on April 12, 1984, aged eighty-one, a year before his book was finished. He's buried at the Garden of Memories Memorial Park in Salinas, California.

Capt. Forrest "Tex" **Biard**, who had served at Stations HYPO and FRUMel during the war, and whom Layton recognized as a colleague and a friend, evaluated Layton in 2002.

> He was [a] human dynamo, sharp, quick thinking, fast acting, intuitive, fast to comprehend, and extremely aggressive. Layton and Rochefort were close friends of long standing. At Pearl Harbor they worked together in complete harmony, forming an almost perfect team. Rochefort gave Layton remarkably clear and reliable estimates and analyses; the quick-witted Layton [then added] comments and suggestions or more analysis. After that he had to sell the final product to Admiral Nimitz.

Rear Adm. Ellis Zacharias, who knew him for decades, saw Layton in a similar vein, writing that Layton was always "alert and imaginative with a tremendous capacity for work."

Language and intelligence historians Irwin and Carole Slesnick had this interesting observation: "Eddie Layton was a complex person . . . some people thought him cold, insensitive, and friendless. Yet, after the Japanese fleet was devastated at Midway in June 1942, Layton cried over the loss of his Japanese friends."

Capt. Jasper **Holmes**, who served at HYPO, FRUPac, and JICPOA through the entire war, observed that

> if Admiral Nimitz had not had Eddie Layton as his intelligence officer, he might not have had the confidence to risk everything on the conclusion of what many other senior officers considered to be a bunch of nuts, in a basement, dreaming up wild hallucinations.

And as former chief of naval operations, Adm. Arleigh Burke, has said, "Layton, by keeping his job above his personality, contributed the necessary rapport that someone else might not have been able to provide."

Rear Admiral Layton's many decorations include the Distinguished Service Medal, the Navy Commendation Medal, and the United Nations Service Medal.

The U.S. Naval War College in Newport, Rhode Island, honored Layton in the 1960s by naming its Chair of Naval Intelligence after him.

Sources

As it is with every figure profiled in this book, it's impossible to distill a career—or an entire lifetime—of remarkable service into a mere handful of pages. However, unlike most subjects of this book, it is possible to recommend considerable and easily obtainable further reading for Rear Admiral Layton. His enormous memoir, *And I Was There* (six hundred pages), is widely available; likewise are his U.S. Naval Institute Oral History interviews (two hundred pages). Thus, a reader intrigued by the admiral can be fully immersed in his first-person accounts and reflections.

Biard, 151–58.
Budiansky, 12–13, 18, 29, 42, 319.
Carlson, 50–53, 57, 65, 86, 88, 91, 109, 113–14, 124–25, 131–34, 165–67, 178, 181, 189, 193–94, 197–98, 202–3, 224–25, 230, 235, 238, 270–71, 273–74, 285, 293, 295–96, 309–10, 316, 318, 335, 337–38, 343, 351, 369, 388, 390–91, 394, 397–98, 404, 412, 428, 493, 504, 508.
Costello, 153–55, 162–79, 183–84, 192–93, 233, 236–37, 295–96.
Donovan and Mack, 147, 150, 152, 346.
Dorwart, *Conflict of Duty*, 62.
Dyer, 165, 215, 263, 284–86, 353–53.
Holmes, 18–19, 60–61, 89–90, 121, 132, 135–36, 140, 178–79, 184, 192, 197, 216.
Hone, 267–68.
Kahn, *Codebreakers*, 39–40, 598.
Layton, *Reminisces*, 88.
Layton, Pineau, and Costello, *"And I Was There,"* 6–8, 49, 58–59, 68–69, 496, 502–3, 510–11.
Lewin, 26, 61–62, 86, 89, 93, 103–4.
Lucky Bag, U.S. Naval Academy, 1924.
Lundstrom, John B., in Hone, 242, 244.
Morison, IV, xi.
Potter, E. B., in Hone, 220, 224, 235.
Prados, 101–2, 175, 177, 301, 320–22, 324, 370, 380, 390, 404, 414, 459–60, 495, 730–31.
Prange, *At Dawn*, 68, 87, 291, 439–40, 449, 469–71, 511, 590, 717.
Prange, *Miracle*, 18–20, 46, 102, 104.
"Rear Admiral Edwin T. Layton," in *The Course to Midway*. www.navy.mil/midway/ncb.html, accessed 23 January 2013.
Rear Admiral Edwin T. Layton, USN, Retired. Official Biography. Biographies Branch, Office of Information, U.S. Navy, December 9, 1959.
Rochefort, 145–48, 160, 180–84, 213.
Schom, 284, 488.
Slesnick, 55.
Symonds, 143–45, 182–83.
Toland, 33–34.
Toll, 307–9, 316, 385, 387–90, 401.
U.S. Navy, *Register of Commissioned and Warrant Officers*.
Winton, 116–19.
Wohlstetter, 33–40, 42–49, 55–59, 65, 313.
Worth, 31, 33–34, 52–53, 82, 138.
Zacharias, Ellis, 224, 252–54.

REAR ADMIRAL ARTHUR HOWARD McCOLLUM, U.S. NAVY
(1898–1976)

"Bright, confident, and dynamic"
Head of ONI's Japan Desk, 1934–1935
Head of ONI's Far Eastern Section, 1939–1942
"Mac" "Deacon"

Arthur McCollum had remarkable and remarkably successful careers in intelligence and as a surface-ship officer. Much like his mentor Rear Adm. Ellis Zacharias, "Mac" seems to have been everywhere, known everybody, and done everything—before the war, during the war, and then afterward. As intelligence historian John Prados wrote, "It's virtually impossible to say enough about the pre-war intelligence pioneers like Henri Smith-Hutton, Arthur McCollum, and the others. Without their language experience and intelligence savvy, the Pacific war would have gone on longer and been a great deal bloodier even than it was." McCollum capped his career with two tours of duty with the early CIA.

*   *   *

From the Naval Academy 1921 yearbook, *The Lucky Bag*:

Here he is, Ladies and Gentlemen, not exactly as he came to us, but still serviceable. The story of his life at the Academy would differ little from the average, but the narration of his heroic efforts to conquer the Great White Way would be interesting beyond a doubt; however, this is neither the time nor the place to relate it. What could you expect from a man with a Scotch name who was born in Japan, lived in Seattle, and claims Alabama as his home? *Deacon* has the manners, politics, and smooth line of the world-famous Southern Gentleman, the last of which has helped him keep well on the weather side of a 2.5 [satisfactory grade point average] without much effort. If he doesn't know what he is talking about he throws out such a smoke screen that no one else is aware of the fact, hence that savvy smile when the marks go up. If there is anything you want, from the loan of a dollar on up the scale, to someone to drag a friend's friend, go see *Mac*. He will help you if it can possibly be done. His one failing is his passion for Red Hair and the Drama.

*   *   *

Arthur H. McCollum was born on August 4, 1898, in Nagasaki, and in early childhood lived in Fukuoka, Japan. He was the middle of five children born to John W. and Drucilla Collins McCollum, who were Southern Baptist missionaries. He was educated by private tutors and public schools abroad and then in the United States, including public school at Marion, Alabama, and the Perry County (Alabama) High School. He also attended, from 1915 to 1917, the Marion Institute preparatory school. He was admitted to the Naval Academy in 1917 and then was graduated and commissioned as an ensign in 1921. Among his noteworthy classmates were Bern **Anderson**, Walter F. Boone, Charles R. Brown, and Daniel V. Gallery. Further promotions included lieutenant (junior grade), 1924; lieutenant, 1927; lieutenant commander, 1937; commander, 1941; and captain, 1942. McCollum retired from the navy in 1951 and was simultaneously promoted to rear admiral due to a high combat decoration from World War II service.

After his Annapolis graduation, Ensign McCollum went directly to sea duty, as was the norm, first onboard the battleship *Arkansas* and then attached to the transport *Argonne*. Then, in 1922, he was selected for the ONI full-immersion language and cultural program and was accordingly sent to Tokyo. Fortunately,

Lt. Cmdr. Ellis **Zacharias** very kindly took me in to live with him. He and the former assistant naval attaché had rented a house and acquired a couple of servants out in one of the suburbs of Tokyo; there was a little colony of language students there. Zach very kindly took me under his wing because I didn't know anything, and he said, "Well now, the first thing we have to do with you is get you a suit of clothes. You need a dinner jacket and you've got to have a set of white tie and tails. Out here when you go to dinner after six o'clock, you wear a black tie—a tux—and if it's after eight you put on a white tie and tails." That was the social thing, so we went down and Zach pawned his credit and I pawned mine and acquired this rig from a Chinese tailor in Yokohama.

It's fair to say that from this point forward McCollum viewed Zacharias as a mentor and was always an admirer—a prominent ONI historian even called him one of Zach's "disciples."

McCollum had forgotten most of the Japanese he'd learned as a child, so in many ways he started his studies from scratch.

We got some books, the standard book of grammar of the Japanese language, one written by a German and the other by a Professor Basil Chamberlain—the Mojino Shirube *Introduction to the Study of Japanese Characters.* [Then] you went out with one of the students that had been there before and if you could, you got one of their instructors—a tutor—and most of us would take about two hours a day with two different tutors. You had one come in the morning and one in the afternoon. [At first such students used a primary school reader. There was really no supervision of the students, but] you had an examination to pass every six months, given by a man called the Japanese secretary of the American embassy; a Japanese-speaking official of the embassy. If you didn't make it, you would be sent home.

McCollum was present for the massive Great Kanto Earthquake in September 1923, which killed over 100,000 people and devastated Tokyo, Yokohama, and many other communities. Mac became a liaison between U.S. warships at Yokohama, which were trying to lend assistance, and the American ambassador.

In 1924, Lt. j.g. McCollum also briefly served on board the USS *John D. Ford* as a liaison with Japanese naval units. Completing his language immersion time in Japan in 1925, he was then sent to the Naval Submarine School at New London, Connecticut. After graduating from the course, he was briefly transferred to Washington to work at the new "Research Desk" in Naval Communications, OP-20-G.

By 1926 there was a slow but steady stream of ORANGE [Japanese Navy] traffic flowing across Lt. Cmdr. Laurance **Safford**'s desk. The plain text was quickly sorted by him and forwarded to his part-time linguist assigned by ONI, Lt. j.g. Arthur H. McCollum. . . . The decrypted dispatches were worked by Mrs. Agnes **Driscoll** and then also passed for translation.

Lieutenant McCollum was shortly relieved in the translation work by his old friend and mentor from Japan, Lieutenant Commander Zacharias. McCollum then reported onboard the submarine *O-7*, and after a year was reassigned as the *O-7*'s commanding officer; this duty ran from July 1927 through April 1928. Mac then transferred, for four months, to the submarine *S-11* as her executive officer.

From October 1928 through June 1930, Mr. McCollum returned to Japan and language duties as an assistant naval attaché. From the mid-1920s through the mid-1930s, attachés and their staffs did their best to visit Japanese naval bases, air stations, and aircraft factories to see what they could see. Accordingly, Mac made regular trips to Kure, Sasebo, and Yokosuka, albeit under close Japanese scrutiny. At this time Lt. j.g. Edwin **Layton** and Lt. Joseph **Rochefort** appeared in Tokyo as new immersion students. McCollum took them under his wing, just as Lieutenant Commander Zacharias had taken *him* in 1922. Layton found Mac an affable man, "the kind who'd give a newcomer a cold, dry martini and add a warm invitation to dinner." McCollum and Rochefort later became good friends, but at first McCollum wasn't happy to see Rochefort, who very unusually was accompanied by his wife and son. Mac didn't see how anyone could succeed in this difficult assignment, cope with living in Japan, and still manage a family. He sent a dispatch back to Main Navy recommending Rochefort's recall. The response was negative; Rochefort was staying. Several months later Mac had come to understand ONI's thinking—Rochefort was an individual of unusual ability.

McCollum came to know the future emperor Hirohito when he was prince regent; in fact, back in the spring of 1923, Mac had helped teach the prince "how to dance in our style." McCollum also became acquainted with Hirohito's brother Prince Takamatsu, as well as admirals Nomura and Yamamoto. In the fall of 1928, McCollum made the arrangements for U.S. naval participation in the coronation ceremonies of Emperor Hirohito.

From September 1930 through June 1933, McCollum was assigned onboard the battleship *West Virginia*, where his various duties included command of a gun turret.

Then, during the period August 1933 through February 1935, Lieutenant McCollum returned to intelligence, heading ONI's Japan Desk. Among other things, "he gathered photos of Japanese ships and had scale models built from which identification data could be produced in what was apparently a 'first' for that technique." When he returned to ONI in 1939, he worked on updating the Japanese ship-recognition publications that he had produced earlier. "His new recognition publications, with pictures and updated speed-curve data, were issued in 1941 and proved to be of considerable value to submarine operations after the United States entered the war." In 1934, as an interesting break in routine, Mac served as a naval aide to Japanese Prince Kaya during his visit to Washington.

During this tour at ONI, in 1934 and 1935 Mac again rubbed shoulders with Cmdr. Ellis Zacharias and Lt. Edwin Layton. According to Lt. Joe Rochefort, who was the intelligence officer at San Pedro in the mid-1930s, Zach suggested to him that Rochefort put "spies" on U.S. Navy ships to look for "disloyalty." Both Rochefort *and* Admiral Reeves (the commander in chief) rejected this overly aggressive suggestion—but Rochefort did persuade director of naval intelligence, Capt. William "Pulie" Puleston, to send out their mutual friend Lieutenant McCollum. Mac was assigned to the Hydrographic Office at San Pedro for the purpose of going undercover in "special intelligence duties," which included counter-espionage. This assignment ran from February 1935 through June 1936. Puleston (DNI from 1934–1937) wanted ONI to be more than an office of static information for policy makers. He wanted a broader, "operational" intelligence stance. McCollum liked this shift. "The idea of ONI being an outfit to serve the fleet in outlying areas was a thing that was elaborated and established by Captain Puleston."

From June 1936 through January 1938, Mac was attached to the staff of the U.S. Fleet as assistant operations officer, acting operations officer, and FIO; the commander in chief at that time had become Adm. Arthur J. Hepburn. McCollum and Rochefort had essentially traded billets, with Rochefort now fleet liaison officer in San Pedro. In February 1938, Lieutenant Commander McCollum returned to Main Navy before taking command of the destroyer *Jacob Jones*, from April 1938 through September 1939. Onboard the *Jacob Jones*, Mac assisted in the evacuation of American nationals from Barcelona as that city was captured by the Spanish nationalist forces of Gen. Francisco Franco.

In the period November 1939 through October 1942, McCollum served as the head of OP-16-FE, ONI's Far Eastern Section. "Because of my presumptive capabilities in relation to the Far East, I was frequently consulted on policy matters." For some months in 1939 and 1940, DNI Rear Adm. Walter S. Anderson lent him and his language expertise to FBI director J. Edgar Hoover, to assist the FBI in its surveillance of Japanese Americans and Japanese visitors.

Nothing seemed beyond Mac's interest in those years. Once, "as ONI's Far Eastern Desk head, McCollum claimed an entire shipload of war junk from the Far East, which" came from the fighting between the Japanese and Chinese. As might be said today, McCollum was always thinking out of the box. Realizing that the progressive ONI immersion program—which he had gone through himself—had only generated a small number of graduates,

In June 1940, McCollum . . . recruited Professor Albert E. Hindmarsh to formulate and implement a program to train . . . hundreds of Japanese language officers [that] the navy would need in the event of war with Japan. The aim was to produce in the shortest possible time a large population of intelligence officers able to speak, read, and write Japanese. . . .

Hindmarsh submitted [his] plan to the Director of ONI, the Chief of the Bureau of Personnel, and the Chief of Naval Operations. The plan called for the establishment of a center at Harvard University and another at the University of California at Berkeley to train Japanese translators and interpreters. Approximately 50 students would be selected to complete a 12-month program of study beginning in the fall of 1941.

In June 1942, the school moved to the University of Colorado at Boulder.

Class was held at Berkeley on Friday, 12 June, after which the students were dismissed and ordered to reassemble in Boulder on 24 June.

In July 1943, ONI deputy director—and Mac's mentor—Capt. Ellis Zacharias, spoke at the graduation ceremony of the first class of the school in Boulder's Mackey Auditorium. One of several speakers, Zach confounded many of the 142 graduates "with a rapid-fire speech in Japanese—that he then translated for the broader audience." By the war's end, around 1,200 men and women had gone into the program.

In October 1940, Mac drafted a six-page memo that—almost fifty-five years later and almost twenty years after his death—has brought him considerable notoriety and a degree of ill fame. It only came to light with a Freedom of Information Act request by a revisionist historian working on a book about the attack on Pearl Harbor. Now commonly referred to as the "McCollum Memo," or the "Eight Action Memo," Mac addressed it to DNI Rear Admiral Anderson and to Capt. Dudley Knox (head, historical branch, ONI). In it he "outlined the general situation and possible courses of action available to the United States in response to the actions of the Japanese Empire in Asia and its relations to the Axis Powers in Europe." The memo has nine paragraphs focused upon countering rising Japanese hegemony over East Asia and exploring possible responses. The ninth paragraph is where some controversy lies, because in that section McCollum outlined eight points or steps that, in his opinion, would provoke the Japanese *if* that's what the United States would want to do. The Pearl Harbor conspiracy advocates take this as a recommendation for action, and many believe that this document was shown to President Roosevelt who adopted it as a plan. However, the memo is a "what if" analysis by—technically—a junior naval officer. There's no real evidence that the document moved beyond Anderson and Knox—to say nothing of reaching the president. That being said, it would have been useful had McCollum chosen to discuss it in his U.S. Naval Institute historical interviews during 1970–1971.[1]

Running the ONI Far Eastern Desk, McCollum was responsible for analyzing MAGIC and other COMINT derived from Japanese naval communications.[2] Mac

---

1. The McCollum memo was first widely disseminated with the publication of Robert Stinnett's book *Day of Deceit: The Truth about FDR and Pearl Harbor.* Stinnett is a conspiracy theorist who presents the memo as part of his argument that the Roosevelt administration conspired to provoke the Japanese to attack the United States, pursuant to a complex scheme to bring the United States into the European war, without "generating ado" over broken political promises. Roosevelt had recently issued a campaign promise that the United States would not become entangled in Europe's war under his watch. Subsequent to its publication, almost all historians reject the notion that McCollum's memo was a blueprint for war, that McCollum personally advocated provoking the Japanese, or that Roosevelt even saw it. Here is the final part, which the conspiracy advocates find intriguing:

It is not believed that in the present state of political opinion the U.S. government is capable of declaring war against Japan without more ado; and it is barely possible that vigorous action on our part might lead the Japanese to modify their attitude. Therefore, the following course of action is suggested:

   a. Make an arrangement with Britain for the use of British bases in the Pacific, particularly Singapore.
   b. Make an arrangement with Holland for use of base facilities and acquisition of supplies in the Dutch East Indies.
   c. Give all possible aid to the Chinese government of Chiang Kai-shek.
   d. Send a division of long-range heavy cruisers to the Orient, Philippines, or Singapore.
   e. Send two divisions of submarines to the Orient.
   f. Keep the main strength of the US Fleet, now in the Pacific, in the vicinity of the Hawaiian Islands.
   g. Insist that the Dutch refuse to grant Japanese demands for undue economic concessions, particularly oil.
   h. Completely embargo all trade with Japan, in collaboration with a similar embargo imposed by the British Empire.

If by these means Japan could be led to commit an overt act of war, so much the better. At all events we must be fully prepared to accept the threat of war."

2. MAGIC is the compartmentation code assigned to intelligence derived from Japanese diplomatic traffic that was intercepted by the United States as a result of the 1940 breaking of PURPLE, the Japanese diplomatic code. In everyday discussion, they would have said, "Bill is cleared for MAGIC," rather than

and his associate, Lt. Cmdr. Alwin **Kramer** (an ONI language officer but actually head of the OP-20-G translation and dissemination branch in Naval Communications), had fairly complete control of what MAGIC messages—out of a very large volume—were selected as important for naval leaders as well as national and policy-makers. Their judgment in this role was highly regarded.

On July 2, 1941, McCollum produced a strategic estimate titled "The Possibility of Early Aggressive Action by Japan," the gist of which was sent to the Pacific Fleet. Shortly thereafter, Pacific Fleet intelligence officer Lt. Cmdr. Edwin Layton asked Washington if he could be fed considerably more diplomatic intelligence. The response from his old mentor and friend, Commander McCollum, was not what he wanted.

> I thoroughly appreciate that you would probably be much helped in your daily estimates if you had at your disposal the DIP [diplomatic intelligence].
>
> This, however, brings up matters of security, etc., which would be very difficult to solve. While I appreciate your position fully in the matter, still I cannot agree that this material should be forwarded to you in the way you suggest. . . .
>
> I should think that the forces afloat should, in general, confine themselves to the estimates of the strategic and tactical situations with which they will be confronted when the time of action arrives. The material you mentioned can necessarily have but passing and transient interest [because] action in the political sphere is determined by the Government as a whole and not by the forces afloat. . . .
>
> In other words, while you and the Fleet may be highly interested in politics, there is nothing you can do about it. Therefore, information of political significance, except as it affects immediate action by the Fleet, is merely of interest to you and not a matter of utility.

In August 1941, McCollum traveled to the Admiralty in London. He visited several sections of the Naval Intelligence Division and was given access by Adm. Sir Dudley Pound—the First Sea Lord—to British COMINT. Mac then visited various British sites involved in COMINT production.

Upon his return from London in October, McCollum found that an ONI publication,

> the *Intelligence Digest*, had projected an attack on Siberia by the Japanese. The interpretation had been published at the direction of the Director of War Plans, Rear Adm. Kelly Turner. McCollum saw no change in the situation to warrant the projection. Accordingly, the next *Digest* went out *without* the Siberian fairy tale. The omission did not sit well with Turner, and soon a directive came out that ONI could not send out any evaluations; it could only report facts.

---

say, "Bill is cleared for PURPLE." Rear Adm. McCollum, in retirement, had this to say about MAGIC: "We may call it MAGIC, but it's not always 'magic.' Sometimes it's just the blathering of some Japanese diplomat we're getting. Some people thought because we're 'reading the mail,' that the information had an aura of authenticity that it didn't necessarily deserve. Under the Japanese system any consular or diplomatic official could send out their opinion on something, and it wasn't necessarily any sort of official information or point of view."

Turner persuaded the CNO, Adm. Harold R. Stark, to strip the jobs of intelligence analysis and evaluation from ONI and give them to him. Moreover, beyond regular intelligence matters, the challenges of handling COMINT were compounded for the navy by this struggle. "Turner won out . . . but he proved to be incapable as an intelligence analyst. To the professional intelligence officers who [after the war] gave testimony before Congress, Admiral Turner was the 'villain' in the navy's use—or non-use—of COMINT" during that period. Additionally, "Turner's confidence in his exclusive ability to forecast Japan's moves . . . provoked Kirk and McCollum to fury." Capt. Alan G. Kirk was director of naval intelligence from March through October 1941; he was succeeded by Rear Adm. Theodore "Ping" Wilkinson, who had equal frustrations with Admiral Turner.

Turner appointed three officers to assist him with intelligence analysis, but they were also extremely inexperienced. Nevertheless, Rear Admiral Turner had a stranglehold on the whole naval intelligence process. Turner's control of OP-20-G wasn't as total as his hold on ONI; nevertheless, he did have his thumb on the dissemination of MAGIC to the Pacific Fleet. He made it clear that neither ONI nor OP-20-G could send "out any information which would initiate any operations on the part of the fleet, or fleets, anywhere." The process of evaluation and dissemination of intelligence was topsy-turvy.

Commander McCollum requested that the change in responsibility be formalized. He asked Royal E. Ingersoll, the assistant CNO, "Admiral, how about issuing an order in writing amending that part of the ONI manual?" Apparently Ingersoll lost his temper. "Get out of here!" he roared. "A verbal order is enough!" Thus, ONI officially and legally continued to bear the responsibility of intelligence analysis and evaluation, but they were prohibited to actually do it in practice.

In early November 1941, McCollum put the Far Eastern Section on a twenty-four-hour-a-day watch rotation. He "felt that the situation between us and Japan was extremely explosive and would erupt at any time."

On the first of December, Mac drafted a memo with his analysis and concerns about the southward movements of Japanese forces, and showed it to Admirals Stark, Ingersoll, Turner, Noyes, and Wilkinson. Judging from the last two months' activity, Commander McCollum felt that the Japanese were principally looking at "control or occupation of Thailand, followed almost immediately by an attack against British possessions, possibly Burma and Singapore." In his opinion "war or a rupture of diplomatic communications was imminent," and he requested to know "whether or not the fleets [Pacific and Asiatic] had been adequately alerted." He received a "categorical assurance" from Turner and Stark that "dispatches fully alerting the fleets and placing them on a war basis had been sent." But then, when McCollum saw further MAGIC intercepts which indicated that Japanese diplomats were directed to destroy their codes and code machines, he drafted another warning—which Turner would not approve and Wilkinson would not support.

Mac did "arrange for the destruction of certain codes and classified documents held in various far Eastern naval stations." McCollum suggested that "Commander

Safford draw up these messages to naval attachés because they involved codes—a communications responsibility." Safford drafted the dispatches and released them on the third and fourth of December.

It's interesting to note that, from reading messages which Admiral Turner had shown him, Commander McCollum was under the distinct impression that the Pacific Fleet had left Pearl Harbor and gone to sea around December 5. This, of course, was not the case.

Mac came in to Main Navy at 0800 on Sunday, December 7, to relieve Lt. Cmdr. Ethelbert **Watts**, who'd been on watch overnight. Watts was an assistant to McCollum, covering the Japan Desk and supervising (along with McCollum) the communications intelligence pipeline to President Roosevelt—through Rear Adm. John R. Beardall, FDR's naval aide. McCollum, Watts, and Cmdr. Hartwell C. Davis were particularly good at rapidly translating Japanese messages into workable English.[3] Mr. Watts was the ONI Far Eastern Section night-watch duty officer on the evening of December 6 and early morning of December 7, 1941. Years later, retired Rear Adm. McCollum remembered:

> Around ten o'clock or maybe a little bit before, [Lt. Cmdr.] Kramer came in with the fourteenth part. That was *the end.* In other words, diplomatic relations were being broken. The fourteenth part was the final. In other words, in spite of everything [the Japanese were saying], "You people have wronged us" and so on, summing up the case and breaking up diplomatic relations.
>
> Kramer hot-footed [he literally ran] it over to the White House, along with Admiral Beardall . . . and tried to get it to the President, which they did—or someone did—and also to the secretary of state, the secretary of the navy, and so on. I continued to haunt the CNO's outer office. Kramer came back in around 10:30 and he said, "We have the final—we've got the instructions for delivery," and it repeated over and over that it must be delivered to Mr. Hull at precisely one-o'clock Washington time. Kramer and I thought about it for a minute, and he said let's see what the times are.

It was obvious that one o'clock in Washington was dawn or early morning at several key Pacific locations, including the Malay Peninsula, the Philippine Islands, and the Hawaiian Islands. But there were no conclusions made by anyone that there was going to be an actual attack, let alone where any such attack might be delivered. In fact, Al Kramer was more concerned about Kota Bharu in Malaysia—where the Japanese did indeed attack on December 8.

Shortly, Commander McCollum found himself part of a conference in the CNO's inner office: Admiral Stark, Admiral Ingersoll, Rear Adm. Beardall, Rear Adm. Wilkinson, Rear Adm. Noyes [head of naval communications], and Captain "Pinky" Schuirmann [liaison to the Department of State]. The consensus was that the major threat was to Singapore, the Gulf of Siam, the Malay Peninsula, or the East Indies

---

3. H. C. Davis had been one of the earlier ONI Japan immersion students, having been a contemporary of Ellis Zacharias.

in general. However, perhaps more intuitively than rationally, Admiral Wilkinson suggested that the CNO might telephone Admiral Kimmel at Pearl Harbor. Admiral Stark lifted the receiver, but then decided to call the president instead, dismissing the group. McCollum later recalled that the CNO remained unalarmed during the discussion, with an almost "so what" attitude. The group continued to talk about the situation in another room, but without any action being taken by the CNO, further staff-level talk was "neither of substance nor consequence." At that point McCollum thought "that the feeling in the office of the CNO was that we've done everything we can and now it's just in the hands of the gods."

Thus, naval reaction to the last-minute Japanese signals was not at all frenzied, although, to their credit, it was characterized by some urgency on the part of the Far Eastern specialists—particularly Lieutenant Commander Kramer and Commander McCollum. Unfortunately, "the fact that Naval Intelligence had so little influence with War Plans and the CNO, and so little responsibility to the operating forces, partly accounted for the lack of alarm." Regardless, eminent Pearl Harbor historian Gordon Prange remarked that after studying the record concerning McCollum, he was left "with the pleasing impression that a firm, knowledgeable hand had been on the tiller in ONI's Far Eastern Section in 1941."

In summing up the Pearl Harbor disaster, groundbreaking historian Roberta Wohlstetter observed that one problem was that

a general prejudice against intellectuals and specialists, not confined to the military but unfortunately widely held in America, also made it difficult for intelligence experts to be heard. Commander McCollum, [Lieutenant Commander Kramer], Lieutenant Colonel Bratton,[4] Lieutenant Colonel Sadtler, and a few others—who felt that the signal picture was ominous enough to warrant more urgent warnings—had no power to influence decision. The Far Eastern code analysts, for example, were believed to be too immersed in the "Oriental point of view." Low budgets for American intelligence departments reflected the low prestige of this activity—whereas in England, Germany, and Japan, 1941 budgets reached a height that was regarded by the American Congress as quite beyond reason.

The other thing that must be remembered is that while Japan was the primary focus of U.S. intelligence, it certainly—in late 1941—was not the only focus. Admiral Wilkinson's staff in ONI were also worrying about

the immediate threats to the Atlantic coast from Nazi U-boats, saboteurs and spies, and from suspicious fishing boats lurking around the Panama Canal waters. In some ways it seemed more important to track the Fascist-owned, transatlantic LATI airliners, which pinpointed Allied convoys for German submarines, than to keep an exact plot of each Japanese aircraft carrier in the remote Sea of Japan.

---

4. A number of histories, and the movie *Tora! Tora! Tora!*, show Rufus Bratton as a full colonel at the time of the Pearl Harbor attack. But according to the *Army Register*, his date of rank as a colonel is December 1, 1942, not 1941.

In the afternoon of December 7, 1941, former naval intelligence officer William J. **Sebald** called his friend McCollum at ONI and volunteered to come on active duty. Mac immediately had him appointed a "civilian agent" and started working on getting him a reserve commission. Bill Sebald had been an immersion language student but then had resigned from the navy to practice law in Japan and then in Washington. Sebald subsequently did outstanding work in naval intelligence during the war, rising to captain; after the war he became U.S. political advisor to Japan, ambassador to Burma, and then ambassador to Australia.

In April 1942, Commander McCollum was sent to CinCPac to discuss plans then being formulated in the office of the Commandant of the Marine Corps and at ONI. The commandant at that time was Lt. Gen. Thomas Holcomb (and coincidentally a cousin of Station HYPO's Major Bankson **Holcomb**). Mac presented the plan to Admiral Nimitz—a plan which he and ONI's senior planner, Capt. Arthur **Struble**, had put together. Commander McCollum was an early advocate of full-scale operational intelligence centers, and so

the plan was to establish [an] intelligence center at Pearl Harbor with a rather large staff. The center would receive and interpret all types of intelligence bearing on CINCPac's sphere of operations. Admiral Nimitz liked the idea but, disliking large staffs, was somewhat resistant on personnel grounds. There followed a great deal of correspondence between Pearl Harbor and Washington. The Intelligence Center Pacific Ocean Areas [ICPOA] was, however, created, with Cmdr. Roscoe Hillenkoetter from ONI as officer in charge. ICPOA was detached from the CINCPac staff and placed under the command of the Fourteenth Naval District. The ICPOA concept was warmly received by Cmdr. Joseph Rochefort [head of Station HYPO], if less so by Nimitz's fleet intelligence officer, Lt. Cmdr. Edwin Layton.

In 1942, newly promoted Captain McCollum was sent to the southwest Pacific. He briefly worked as the deputy commander of Gen. Douglas MacArthur's ATIS, which was a joint Australian-American operation. The commander was Col. Sidney Mashbir, U.S. Army. McCollum and Mashbir apparently did not get along well at all and had very different styles as intelligence officers. McCollum called Mashbir "that Syrian rug merchant," while Mashbir referred to McCollum as "Nick Carter, master spy," referring to a character in a dime-novel series.

By March 1943, Captain McCollum had acquired a dual role. He was the intelligence officer for U.S. naval forces in the South West Pacific Area/Seventh Fleet, and also commanding officer of the semi-independent Seventh Fleet Intelligence Center (SEFIC), which was initially located at Brisbane—but later moved to Hollandia (in Dutch New Guinea, later known as Jayapura, Indonesia) and then to Leyte.

At SEFIC . . . McCollum corralled every scrap of information a fleet commander might want: prisoner-of-war interrogation reports, comments from naval radio intercept facilities, and eventually the full range of naval signals intelligence. To work on this treasure trove, he pirated away some of ATIS's best naval talent. . . . They and his other recruits quickly discovered that while McCollum was not an easy man to work for, he made those who were on his good side feel that they could do no wrong. That won their loyalty, boosted their morale, and fueled their eagerness to move ever-closer to the front lines.

Mac was never shy about trying to shape things to fit his vision, though he wasn't always successful in his efforts.

Arthur McCollum, the intelligence officer for the Seventh Fleet, wanted FRUMel under his—and ONI's—jurisdiction. However, [the leadership] in Naval Communications strongly resisted McCollum's efforts.
   They maintained that FRUMel belonged under [the Office of Naval Communications] because its mission was communication techniques, and it was manned by communicators who depended on contacts with other communications units and the assistance of Japanese language officers. FRUMel was established by an agreement between U.S. Navy communicators and the Australian Naval Board. A shift by the U.S. Navy to move FRUMel under ONI could disrupt this agreement.

In later 1943, when Captain McCollum arrived at Brisbane to become the fleet intelligence officer for the Seventh Fleet, he drafted Cmdr. Rudy **Fabian** to help him create an advanced intelligence center that Admiral King wanted put in place. Starting with just thirty men, it shortly grew to over three hundred. At that time McCollum worked for Vice Adm. Arthur "Chips" Carpender and Adm. Thomas C. Kinkaid. Mac's organization provided intelligence support for campaigns in the northern Solomons, New Guinea, the Bismarck Archipelago, and the Philippine Islands—and helped develop guerilla forces in the Philippines and in southern Asia.
   In May 1945, Captain McCollum was transferred back to Washington to work at the Bureau of Personnel. In June he served as the naval aide to Abdul Illah, the crown prince of Iraq, during a state visit. Mac then supervised the final details of construction regarding the heavy cruiser *Helena*, accepted her for the government, and took command in September. Initially he served as flag captain to the commander in chief, U.S. Naval Forces Europe (Adm. H. Kent Hewitt). From May through June 1946, he took the *Helena* to the Far East, and then from June through October he served on the China Coast as flag captain to Rear Adm. Willard A. Kitts III.
   Captain McCollum then was assigned to duty in the new Central Intelligence Group—which of course later became the CIA. In May 1948, Mac was ordered to sea as the commander of the Fleet Training Group and Underway Training Center, Chesapeake Bay. In this assignment he was responsible for the first-stage training of all types of ships. Then, in October 1949, he was ordered to New York City to organize the Atlantic Division of the newly created Military Sea Transportation Service, and then took command of the "MSTS Atlantic"—forty-five ships and over 8,500 personnel.
   Mac retired from active duty in June 1951 and was simultaneously promoted to rear admiral due to a high-level World War II combat decoration. He was then immediately recalled to active duty and assigned as a consultant to the CIA. He "re-

retired" from that work in fall, 1953. From then until 1964 he worked in real estate and insurance in Northern Virginia.

In the early 1960s, retired rear admirals Layton and McCollum helped Professor Roberta Wohlstetter understand the nuances of the 1945 congressional investigations as she wrote her powerful study, *Pearl Harbor: Warning and Decision.*

Commander McCollum was portrayed by actor Francis A. De Sales in the 1970 Hollywood movie *Tora! Tora! Tora!* In a brief but powerful scene, during the morning of December 7, McCollum tells the CNO and other senior Washington naval officers, "Sir, the fourteenth part of this intercept, which [Lt. Cmdr. Alwin] Kramer just delivered, indicates to me that the Japanese are going to attack."

Mac had married Margaret Lois Benninghoff on October 2, 1925, in Rochester, New York, while he was attending submarine school. Like Arthur, Margaret was the child of a missionary and had likewise been born in Japan. They had one son, Arthur H. McCollum Jr., who retired as a navy commander.

Rear Admiral McCollum's decorations and awards include the Legion of Merit with the Combat "V," the Navy Commendation Medal, the Asiatic Pacific Campaign Medal with five battle stars, the China Service Medal, and the Order of Al Rafidain, Class III, from Iraq.

Mac died on April 1, 1976. He predeceased Margaret (1901–1985), but they are buried together at Arlington National Cemetery.

Sources

Benson, 21, 23, 64.

Bryden, 267–70.

Budiansky, 233, 255–56.

Carlson, 52–53, 70–73, 75, 91, 357, 385–86.

Clausen, 217–18, 305.

Costello, 187–89, 191–92, 194, 216, 218–19.

Dingman, 4–5, 8–15, 21–22, 61, 102, 105–6, 127–28, 221.

Donovan and Mack, 28, 192.

Dorwart, *Conflict of Duty*, 62, 63, 91, 118, 159–60, 174, 176–77, 179–81, 191–92, 195, 203.

Farago, *Broken Seal*, 102, 135–36, 167, 231, 325–26, 358, 366, 368.

Farago, *Burn after Reading*, 213.

Holtwick, 43f, 55.

Kahn, *Discovered*, 23–24.

Layton, *"And I Was There,"* 39, 91, 97–98, 100–1, 123–24, 142–43, 166, 239–40, 251–52, 256, 267–69, 300, 303, 343, 408, 465, 500, 507.

Lewin, 72–73.

Lucky Bag, U.S. Naval Academy, 1921.

Mahnken, 62.

McCollum Memo, http://www.conservapedia.com/McCollum_memo. Accessed March 15, 2014.

The McCollum Memo—Analysis: Blueprint, No; Important Clue, Yes, http://12-7-9-11.
  blogspot.com/2009/03/mccollum-memo-analysis.html. Accessed March 15, 2014.
The McCollum Memo: Conspiracy or . . . ? http://todayshistorylesson.wordpress.com
  /2009/10/07/the-mccollum-memo-conspiracy-or/. Accessed March 15, 2014.
McCollum, *Reminiscences*, Vol. I 39–42, 56, 79–81, 414, Index 22; Vol. II 482, 495, 787.
McGinnis, 9.
Packard, 22, 145, 320, 347, 349, 368, 409.
Prados, 5, 8–9, 167, 349–54, 404, 422, 544.
Prange, *At Dawn*, 32–34, 86–87, 251, 356–57, 441, 448, 455, 457, 485, 664–65, 713.
Schom, 132.
Schuon, 158–59.
Slesnick, 71–73, 139–40.
Stinnett, 6–9, 231–32, 259.
Toland, 57–58, 62, 74.
U.S. Navy, *Register of Commissioned and Warrant Officers.*
Wohlstetter, 39–40, 127–28, 172, 270, 311–14, 328–32, 334, 336, 395.
Zacharias, Ellis, 287.

REAR ADMIRAL KENNETH DUVAL RINGLE, U.S. NAVY
(1900–1963)

The champion of the *Issei* and the *Nisei*
Adm. Arleigh Burke's best friend
"Ken"

Kenneth Ringle was another outstanding product of ONI's Japanese language and culture immersion program, a superb intelligence officer, and an outstanding blue-water seaman. His prewar investigations of the Hawaiian and particularly the

California Japanese American communities convinced him that only a fraction of those people posed security risks, and thus he aggressively opposed the subsequent mass removal and internment of those groups—unfortunately to no avail. He later commanded at the ship and division level, and was awarded a Legion of Merit with Combat "V" at the Battle of Leyte Gulf. Although he was intensely proud of his intelligence work, and although he was promoted to rear admiral at the time of his retirement, he felt that his years in intelligence had effectively derailed his career progression regarding high operational sea command and active-duty flag rank. From 1942 through the rest of his life, he did take great satisfaction in receiving many letters of thanks and appreciation from grateful Japanese Americans for his considerable help and understanding during their most difficult time.

*   *   *

From the 1923 Annapolis yearbook, *The Lucky Bag*:

He was an innocent young thing when he entered this he-outfit, but his roommate taught him to smoke, whereupon he collected probation Youngster year. He was the best-looking girl *The Masqueraders* [drama club] ever had—"Of course this is Joan, don't you recognize my voice?" The *New York Times* printed his picture alongside that of King George in the Pictorial Section. As a Yard Engineer, he was a chief machinist's mate [yard engines were daughters of faculty and staff who lived at the academy]. He dragged [took dates to dances] always, and fell for every drag [date]. He fished for "crabs" [Annapolis girls] for a solid year, but his miniature went west to his O.A.O. His education was gratefully deficient because he missed Second Class Cruise, with its exhibits so enlightening to the technical mind. He spent the summer navigating a canoe on the Severn River and piloting 30–30s out across Lake Erie with the Rifle Team. Notable quotation: "Oh for Gaw-awd sake!" [Activities: *Masqueraders*; *Masqueraders* president; rifle squad; expert team rifleman; 1921 national rifle matches; assistant rifle coach]

*   *   *

Kenneth Ringle was born in Hutchinson, Kansas, on September 30, 1900. After attending Westport High School in Kansas City, he was appointed to the Naval Academy from which he graduated in 1923 and was commissioned an ensign—along with such classmates as Arleigh A. Burke, Thomas B. **Birtley**, Edward S. Pearce, Joseph N. **Wenger**, and Melville Bell Grosvenor. Ringle had become an extremely accomplished rifle marksman at the academy; a passion which he carried forward for many years. His further promotions included lieutenant (junior grade), 1926; lieutenant, 1931; lieutenant commander, 1938; commander, 1942; and captain 1943. He ended his navy career in 1953, and was simultaneously promoted to rear admiral on the retired list due to having received a high-level wartime decoration.

Kenneth Ringle and future chief of naval operations Arleigh A. Burke became close friends, first meeting at an academy preparatory school in Columbia, Missouri.

The families of both aspiring midshipmen paid $100 per month for three months, for which they received focused instruction from a former congressman and his daughter. The course ended just before the official nationwide entrance examination in April 1919, which both young men fortunately passed with high enough grades to enable their admission. Burke and Ringle remained fast friends throughout their time at Annapolis; Ringle frequently helped Burke with Spanish and some other courses. In fact, they remained extremely close for the rest of their lives; Burke told Ringle, many years down the line, that Ringle was "the best friend I've ever had," and he became godfather to Ringle's eldest son. (Likewise, Burke's wife, Roberta, and Ringle's wife, Margaret, became each other's closest friends from about 1932 until Bobbie's passing in 1997.)

Upon graduation from the academy, Ensign Ringle served on board the battleship *Arkansas* through 1924, and then was assigned to the destroyer *Isherwood* as engineering officer from 1925 to1928; this latter assignment included a 1926 good-will cruise to various British, French, and Mediterranean ports.

He had always envisioned a career as a sea officer—a boy on the plains of Kansas dreaming of commanding warships—and certainly that's how his post-Annapolis career began. But no one is assigned to sea duty all the time; normally every other assignment is on shore. Ringle wasn't enamored with a lot of the usual postings; many years later he told one of his two sons (also named Ken) he originally looked into intelligence because he disliked the usual choices for shore duty.

In the late 1920s, during a trip to Spain and Portugal (where, incidentally, he met Mother during a horseback picnic in Estoril; she was living for a time with her eldest sister), he encountered the U.S. naval attaché in Madrid and, as he told me, "I thought that was a pretty good way to spend shore duty—dinner parties, pretty women, and interesting diplomatic stuff." Since he spoke Spanish fluently, he applied for the job in Madrid, but was told people *far* senior to him were lined up for it for *years*. But the Bureau of Navigation (which handled personnel in those days) and the Office of Naval Intelligence had noticed his gift for languages, and informed him about another program he might like.

In fact, he jumped at it. He was indeed "intrigued by the idea of extended time abroad [so he] parlayed [his] gift for languages into a special three-year assignment" as one of ONI's Japanese language/culture immersion students, and went off to study in Tokyo from 1928 to 1931. During that period both the navy and the army were particularly invested in Japanese language programs: in 1930 the students (officially "language officers" attached to the embassy) included Lieutenants Ringle, **Rochefort**, and **Layton**; Lieutenants junior grade Pearce, **Birtley**, **Watts**, and **Mason**; Marine First Lieutenant Pyzick; and eight army officers. Ringle's son Ken has an interesting insight on this experience.

After an intensive year or so of schooling in Tokyo, language students like my dad were dispersed to distant points in Japan where they would be out of touch with any occidentals. My father lived for at least a year in Beppu (on the island of Kyushu). According to one of his USNA classmates who touched base with him over there, one of my father's specialties was proficiency in the "woman's language" of Japanese, which apparently is or was something more than a dialect—almost its own language with subtle shadings and the like. The very respectable *geishas* of Beppu were highly amused that he could speak their particular "language" and apparently doted on Dad. Some of these ladies delighted in telling my father about braggarts in the Japanese military who would come to the *geisha* house, get drunk and noisy, and seek to impress the girls by spouting useful military intelligence. This information was very useful to Dad.

Ringle also told his son about another unique experience he had while an immersion student.

> Dad experienced a tragic incident where he struck and killed a Japanese child who had run in front of his car. This was somewhere in Honshu, I think, while he was touring this largest island of Japan. The death was an obvious and unavoidable accident, but he was devastated by the incident and sought guidance from the embassy on how to best handle it. They told him to ask to be the chief mourner in the little girl's Buddhist funeral, hire other mourners to walk with him in the procession, pay the cost of the funeral, and do several other related things. He was very fascinated by the experience which, despite the overwhelming sadness involved, provided him a rare window into Japanese culture.

Upon his return from Japan, Ringle was assigned as gunnery officer to the Pacific Fleet's heavy cruiser *Chester*, 1932–1934. Mr. Ringle and the new Mrs. Ringle spent their honeymoon driving from Avery Island, Louisiana, through Pascagoula and then up to the Brooklyn Navy Yard where he was to meet the *Chester*. Their son Andrew states that

> memorable to me is Mom's recounting of Dad taking her out to dinner to a dark Japanese restaurant in Brooklyn where, fresh back from Japan, he not only demonstrated to the staff his fluency in Japanese, but according to her his demeanor turned "inscrutable" in the darkness and his eyes appeared to become more and more slanted. "Who is this man I married?" was her alarmed reaction.

This tour of duty included participating in a Presidential Naval Review at New York; at that time the *Chester* was the flagship for the Commander, Special Service Squadron. Then, in 1935, Lieutenant Ringle took a course of instruction at the Naval War College in Newport.

For about a year, beginning in July 1936, he served as assistant IO for the Fourteenth Naval District in Honolulu. The younger Ken Ringle shared this insight from that period:

> Sometime in the 1990s I got a phone call and then a long, handwritten letter from a very old Japanese-American in Hawaii who was then in his 90s. He had somehow found my name and address and wanted me to know of my father's role in making him the first Japanese-American officer in the U.S. Navy.

It turns out that sometime in the late 1930s, while he was with ONI in Hawaii, my father enrolled as a student at the university, apparently as a cover. In a class he met a Japanese guy who thought my father was just another student. One day they were having lunch or coffee and bemoaning—as students will—the cost of college and the difficulty of making ends meet. My father asked if the guy was interested in a job, saying he had heard there might be an opening if he showed up at such-and-such a building and knocked on such-and-such a door. This Nisei guy did so and encountered a secretary, to whom he gave his name and asked about work. She smiled and showed him into the inner office. And there, to the astonishment of the Nisei, sat my father in his dress-white uniform. Dad told him that it had been brought to the attention of ONI that this man, who had dual citizenship—U.S. and Japan—had taken the unusual step of surrendering his Japanese citizenship. Dad asked why. The Nisei told him he had been born in Hawaii, felt himself an American, and didn't want anything to do with the Japanese government then dominated by the militarists. Dad had checked the guy out, and then offered him a job keeping his eyes open in Hawaii and looking out for provocateurs in the Japanese community who were loyal to the emperor.

This Nisei went on to work in translation, interpretation, interrogation, counterespionage, war crimes prosecution, and many other things. The fact that he was made a naval officer, he insisted, was almost entirely due to the strong recommendation of K.D. Ringle, and he was profoundly grateful.

This man was Douglas T. Wada, the only Nisei specifically recruited to serve in U.S. naval intelligence before World War II. After thirty-eight years of service, he retired from the navy in 1975 in the grade of commander.

After the close of this district intelligence assignment in Hawaii, ending in July 1937, Ringle served as the communications officer on board the aircraft carrier *Ranger*. During this tour, on a cruise to Peru, Ringle first crossed the equator and became a "shellback"; his son Andrew still has his certificate, which is signed by the *Ranger*'s commanding officer, Captain (later Admiral) John S. "Slew" McCain—the grandfather of Senator John S. McCain III.

In July 1940, Lieutenant Commander Ringle's next assignment began as assistant district intelligence officer for the Eleventh Naval District in southern California. He initially worked out of a small office in the San Pedro YMCA building. In this job, Mr. Ringle worked general counter-espionage throughout southern California with a focus upon the security of naval and Marine Corps bases, but he also was tasked to gauge the danger—if any—of "Fifth Column" activity among California's American-born Japanese population. He thus moved among the vegetable farmers, tuna fishermen, and small businessmen of southern California, using his considerable language skills to ask questions and observe the Japanese American way of life. He started out small, but by the time the war started eighteen months later, he controlled five branch offices and around seventy-five men, ranging from the Mexican border all the way up to Sacramento, and from the West Coast eastward into Nevada. He built a network of informants within the Japanese American community, including members of the Japanese American Citizens League. Such people were grateful that a military official, representing the U.S. government, sought them out and trusted them, and for the most part were concerned themselves about the apparent militarist ambitions of the Japanese government. In 1981, the younger Ken (an award-winning writer, editor, and critic at the *Washington Post*) wrote a lengthy article about the senior Ken for the *Washington Post Magazine*; in it he detailed that, to promote cooperation and avoid suspicion,

> my father functioned with the disarming candor of a prairie-born rationalist. Although he wore civilian clothes and drove an inconspicuous rumble-seat coupe, he always made it perfectly clear who he was and, in most cases, what he was doing. . . . He knew his listeners, as loyal Americans, shared his concern[s].

He found out which community organizations were pro-American, and which were militaristic Japanese. He was even given the full membership list of the "Black Dragon Society," a particularly right-wing organization espousing full loyalty to the emperor. Ringle was frequently invited to meetings, community activities, and into homes. He concluded that there were, of course, genuine spies within the Japanese communities—but those numbered less than 3 percent of the total.

It was to further refine and develop his knowledge of the true threat that Ringle—acting largely on his own initiative—decided to break into the Japanese consulate in Los Angeles. Seventeen years after the caper, Ringle told his son Ken about it, much to the young man's amazement—he was alarmed that his dad might have been caught and punished. Not a chance, because

> we couldn't possibly have been caught. We had the police outside watching. We had the FBI. We even had our own safecracker—we checked him out of prison for the job.

They opened the safe, removed everything, photographed the documents, and replaced each item just as it had been. "The processed films . . . yielded lists of agents, codes, and contact points for Japan's entire West Coast spy network—a network headed by a Japanese naval officer named Itaru Tachibana," who was pretending to be an English-language student. Later on Ringle, two other ONI officers, and the FBI trapped and deported Tachibana and an associate for attempting to purchase military secrets. At that time they also got their hands on a "truckload" of documents which helped them dismantle the entire Japanese espionage effort on the West Coast. But the preceding consulate break-in had also yielded something else which Ringle considered extremely valuable:

> evidence that Tachibana and other official agents of Imperial Japan looked upon most American Japanese—both resident aliens (*issei*) and American-born (*nisei*)—not as potential *allies*, but as cultural *traitors* [and thus] not to be trusted.

A letter dated July 18, 1941, from Secretary of the Navy Frank Knox, informed Ringle that Knox had sent a commendation about the Tachibana case for his record. Later in 1944, Ringle wrote to an ONI colleague to state that "while there are many things I'm proud of . . . the Tachibana affair and the *Nisei* work are two that are peculiarly my own."

During the summer of 1941, confidential presidential investigator Curtis Munson consulted with Lieutenant Commander Ringle, staying twice at his house. Munson's subsequent reports told President Roosevelt that in case of war Japanese Americans will keep very quiet, that 90 percent like the American way of life best, and if there would be any sabotage, it will be largely from imported agents because the Japanese government is actually "afraid of—and does not trust—the *Nisei*."

When the attack on Pearl Harbor came, Mr. Ringle and his team worked with the FBI for forty-eight hours straight, rounding up nearly 450 known agents of Imperial Japan. To do so, they used very accurate information obtained in the consulate break-in, as well as data previously gathered by ONI and the FBI. By December 19, Mr. Munson was rushing a program to Washington which could maintain the loyalty of Japanese Americans and reinforce "wholesome race relations." The program was largely based on ONI proposals, which were mostly Lieutenant Commander Ringle's—strongly supported by fellow Japanese and intelligence expert Lt. (Dr.) Cecil **Coggins** (and to a lesser degree Capt. Ellis **Zacharias**); Coggins was actively focused upon the plight of Japanese Americans in Hawaii.

At the request of the CNO, Mr. Ringle put together a report at the end of January; this was the first of the "Ringle Reports," analyzing the West Coast Japanese question, stressing that the "'Japanese problem' has been magnified out of its true proportions." Each case "should be handled on the basis of the *individual* . . . and *not on a racial basis*."

But the U.S. Army, personified by provost-marshal Maj. Gen. Allen W. Gullion (he'd been an aggressive prosecutor during Brig. Gen. Billy Mitchell's court-martial in 1925), pushed to have full authority of all aliens on the Pacific Coast. And the army's attitude was perhaps too much aligned with Lt. Gen. John L. DeWitt, in charge of defending the West Coast; when asked about the loyalty of Japanese Americans, Dewitt once said, "A Jap is a Jap. . . . We must worry about the Japanese all the time until he is wiped off the map." *Issei* and *Nisei* were soon being fired from jobs, evicted from homes and farms, barred from travel and commercial fishing, and even attacked on the streets. Then, despite President Roosevelt's (and certainly Mrs. Roosevelt's) distaste for the mass internment proposal, in February 1942 the president did sign into effect Executive Order 9066, enabling the relocation program. He tried to soften it by adding, "be as reasonable as you can"; however, every person of Japanese ancestry was ordered to be off the Pacific Coast, and be east of the Sierra Madre Mountains, by April.

Ringle was distraught at the turn of events. He tried to meet with General DeWitt and with Maj. Karl R. Bendetsen, who had been assigned to coordinate the enemy alien issue within DeWitt's West Coast command; both officers refused to see him. Amazingly, Bendetsen's plans for the internment were even more severe than what the radical DeWitt had originally envisioned. In addition to Coggins and Zacharias, colleagues and superiors at ONI generally supported Ringle, but he later wrote that the Navy Department . . . did not desire to invade the Army's field of responsibility and stir up any dissension at home in the early stages of the most serious war ever faced by this country.

At this time, and since the outbreak of the war, the Ringle family had a Nisei teenager working for them named Yamashita Michiko. When it was time for her to be relocated,

> Dad and Mom insisted on personally escorting her to the Santa Anita collection point for the internment—rather than have her thrown on a train at bayonet point. The Army insisted Dad be armed since she was considered an enemy alien; so, he got his .45 automatic and threw it in the glove compartment of the car.

The younger Ken later wrote that at this point his father was "drained, depressed, and feeling somehow an inadvertent accomplice to the betrayal of America's Japanese." He wondered if it might have made a difference if he had finished the "Ringle Report" sooner, although that seems unlikely in retrospect. He did take some satisfaction in facilitating Miss Yamashita's release from her internment camp, by recommending her for a job he'd identified in Chicago.

Ringle also started to realize that his three years in Japan, plus his years working for ONI in Hawaii and Southern California, had essentially derailed his navy career from the mainstream—delaying or potentially capping his potential for promotion. "I have already been informed by the grapevine that I'm an *old* man . . . and can't have my destroyer [command] because I'm over 40," he wrote to a friend in Washington. Nevertheless, he applied for sea duty at the end of February.

But before he got to sea, the director of ONI loaned Ringle to Milton Eisenhower, director of the new War Relocation Authority—at Eisenhower's request. For a month in early summer Ringle expanded his original reports, trying to raise the cultural consciousness of those working with the Japanese Americans and suggesting specific approaches and programs within the camps. Ringle's son Ken later wrote that

> many of my father's recommendations were put into effect in the camps. They may have ameliorated, to some small degree, the injustice of their existence in the first place. I am confident, at least, that his efforts helped—probably more than he ever knew—to provoke second thoughts about the internment.

Later, in October 1942, his report was anonymously published in *Harper's Magazine* as "The Japanese in America—The Problem and the Solution," by "An Intelligence Officer." (In June 1943, Cecil Coggins would also write a piece for *Harper's* on the same subject.) Ringle's daughter Sally has stated that, in his frustration over the internment, he told the family he would never again use his Japanese language skills on behalf of the government. In fact, she recalls, he went for a considerable period not speaking Japanese for any reason. "I really believe until we were in Coronado (after the transport trip through the canal some six years later), and he spoke to our yardman, he did not do so."

All things considered, Mr. Ringle was very eager to get to sea and out into the war. Very soon, and newly promoted to commander, he got his wish; he was on board the light cruiser *Honolulu* as the navigator.

At one point on December 1, 1942, during high-speed maneuvering during the Battle of Tassafaronga (sometimes called the Fourth Battle of Savo Island), the *Honolulu* steered extremely close to the island. Official naval historian Samuel Eliot Morison was on board the ship and later included this scene in his book: On the bridge, Commander Ringle reported to the skipper that a hard left turn would be very advisable. Captain Robert W. Hayler offered to turn *ten* degrees left, to which Ringle replied, "Captain, you'll turn *twenty-five* degrees—or you'll have to take her over the mountain!"

In early January 1943, Rear Adm. Walden "Pug" Ainsworth, then on board the *Honolulu* as commander, Task Force 67, selected Ringle to be his chief of staff—in which position he remained through October 1944, seeing considerable action. Under Pug's leadership, this cruiser-destroyer force soon won renown as the "Ainsworth Express" for its fierce fighting in support of the final drive to push Japanese troops off Guadalcanal. Its bombardment of the Japanese air base at Munda, on the island of New Georgia, would be, again in the words of historian Morison, "long regarded as a model."

In July 1943, Ringle was promoted to captain. Shortly thereafter he was awarded the Legion of Merit with the Combat "V" for outstanding performance as Ainsworth's chief of staff. This was particularly for the Battles of Kula Gulf and Kolombangara (this latter also known as the Second Battle of Kula Gulf); these actions were in July, in the Solomon Islands. At some point during this time, he was also awarded the Purple Heart after being struck by a flying five-inch shell casing which broke his ankle.

On October 20, 1944, while screening landings in Leyte Gulf, the *Honolulu* was struck by an aerial torpedo, which took her out of the battle—and sent her entirely out of the war for major repairs in the United States.

In early February 1945, Ringle was appointed captain of the amphibious force command ship *Wasatch*. In April the *Wasatch*'s force embarked the XXIV and the XXXI Infantry Divisions; this was part of Task Group 78.2, Amphibious Group 8, commanded by Rear Adm. Albert G. Noble. This force took part in the liberation of Mindanao, Morotai, and northern Borneo. After V-J Day, the *Wasatch* took part in the occupation of Wakayama and Nagoya (Japan) and Taku (China), which extended into the fall of 1945. Underway from Taku on November 7, the ship sailed for the United States, via Pearl Harbor, and arrived at San Francisco on December 10.

After the war, Ringle's first assigned shore duty was with ONI in Washington. However, even more convinced that intelligence duty had not been, and would not be, conducive to advancement in the "black-shoe" mainstream surface-ship navy, he immediately asked for a transfer and was put into the War Plans Division.

During 1948–1949, Captain Ringle became commodore of a division of transport ships stationed in the Pacific, with his flagship the attack-transport USS *Henrico*. He was thrilled to go back to sea after being in Washington; he booked his whole family aboard the attack-transport *President Hayes*, sailing to the West Coast from Norfolk, via Guantanamo and the Panama Canal.

> His fellow officers told him he was crazy, that the navy would fly his family out or send them via train in railroad luxury. They told him the whole ship would be filled with pregnant sailors' wives and yowling children and he and his wife would have to share a cabin with their kids until Panama. He didn't care; he always said it was the best idea he ever had for his family. Although his youngest son Andy was just an infant, his older son Ken and daughter Sally had the run of the ship.[1]

After he took command, Ringle's division of transports then proceeded to the Chinese coast, where they operated off Tsingtao in support of U.S. troops which were there, as well as aiding in the evacuation of U.S. nationals in the face of advancing communist forces.

After the division returned to California, Ringle's son Ken remembers that his dad later

> took great satisfaction in dispatching from his flagship an LCPR, a pint-sized landing craft, to ferry my Cub Scout pack to a beach picnic—where we could drop the ramp and hit the beach like John Wayne.

In the latter part of 1949, Captain Ringle participated in advance preparations for Operation *Miki*, a joint Army-Navy amphibious training exercise; *Miki* was a war game which simulated the recapture of an enemy-occupied Oahu. Ringle and his division worked on beach landings on the "Silver Strand" south of Coronado, practicing the handling of landing craft in the surf.

Captain Ringle's last assignment was as a U.S. naval liaison with NATO. He was with the North Atlantic Ocean Regional Planning Group, tasked with the establishment of the Supreme Allied Commander Atlantic command. Ringle considered this a high point in his career and was very happy and proud of his NATO work. His wife Margaret was happily engaged as well, since they did a lot of the diplomatic aspects together. "She dusted off her old French and Portuguese and, as she would say, 'tried to get the accent right and just let the verbs fall as they may.'" Ringle's son Ken again provides an interesting take on this period:

> Around 1989 I got a call at the *Washington Post* from some harried officer at the Pentagon (he may have been Air Force—I don't think he was Navy) who had been assigned to quickly throw together a history of NATO for its fortieth anniversary. He asked what I knew about my Dad's work as naval liaison to NATO. I told him I had very clear memories of how much he enjoyed the work, even though the many warm friends he

---

1. At this time, the skipper of the *President Hayes* may well have been former HYPO "scanner" Capt. Thomas A. **Huckins**. Yet other records indicated it might have been Capt. Richard H. Woodfin. It's hard to nail down conclusively at this point, and it doesn't really matter—though it would be an interesting coincidence if it indeed had been Huck.

and Mother made in other navies—particularly the British—didn't think a multinational naval force could ever be made to work.

"Well, nobody thought it could work except your father," the officer told me. "From all I can tell, he wrote the naval provisions of the NATO treaty almost single-handed. And that's the only portion of the NATO treaty that has never had to be changed in forty years!"

Captain Ringle left active duty in 1953. Simultaneously, he received promotion to rear admiral on the retired list due to his combat-earned Legion of Merit. He initially took a job as executive secretary of the Foreign Relations Association in New Orleans, but he resigned after a year as it turned out to be largely a figurehead position with no substantive role. He then spent most of his time on Avery Island at the house he had named "Fiddler's Green," having in mind the term's traditional maritime connotation of an old sailor's heaven. There he mostly read, golfed, and fished. Much to his satisfaction, considerable numbers of old navy friends and shipmates came by to visit.

Rear Adm. Ringle saw some brief reengagement with the active navy in the late 1950s, with the creation nearby of Naval Auxiliary Air Station New Iberia. The station hosted a training squadron for advanced multi-engine students. Ringle's old friend Adm. Arleigh Burke, as chief of naval operations, came down to open the base, and shortly seized upon an opportunity to tease his old friend. The front page of the local newspaper, *The Daily Iberian*, had a picture of Ringle and a feature article on him keyed to the creation of the base ("New Iberia Welcomes Navy"), but juxtaposed to that article was a lengthy and heavily illustrated story on a brothel raid. The CNO couldn't refrain from jest, expressing concern about just what kind of welcome for the navy had been planned—and about just what kinds of things retired rear admirals do for amusement in rural Louisiana.

Ringle participated with activities at the base and enjoyed the connection. In turn, he was looked on by the station personnel as having *a lot of stroke*—the student pilots were clearly directed to not fly over Avery Island "and disturb the admiral's egrets."

Rear Admiral Ringle died of a heart attack, in Louisiana, on March 23, 1963. From 1942 to the time of his death he continued to receive friendly and warm correspondence from various Japanese Americans, thanking him for all his efforts on their behalf. His daughter Sally writes that she "will never forget returning after his funeral . . . and finding a beautiful floral arrangement 'From the Farmers of Portuguese Bend.'"

Ringle remained a little frustrated that he hadn't made flag rank on active duty, but he certainly wasn't embittered about it. He had hoped that would happen; he loved the navy through and through, and aspired to serve longer and at higher operational levels. The couples who were the closest friends that he and his wife had for decades—the men all former classmates—all were promoted to rear admiral on active duty: Arleigh "31-Knot" Burke (ultimately a full admiral and later chief of naval operations); Frederick "Freddie" Withington (later commander, U.S. Forces Japan), and William "Goat" Mendenhall (later deputy chief of staff, U.S. European

Command). It was being, in a way, odd man out of this intimate group that disappointed him the most—and disappointed those friends as well.

Among Admiral Ringle's many decorations and awards are the Legion of Merit with Combat "V," the Purple Heart, and, rarely seen, some significant rifle marksmanship awards—not the least of which are the 1923 U.S. National Match Medal for Excellence in Team Marksmanship, the 1928 U.S. Scouting Force Winning Team Auckland Cup Match Medal, and the 1932 U.S. Scouting Force Small Arms Medal.

In 1932, Lt. Kenneth D. Ringle had married Miss Margaret Johnston Avery, who was from Avery Island, Louisiana; they had three children: Kenneth, Andrew, and Sally. In 1967, four years after Admiral Ringle passed away, Mrs. Ringle married again, coincidentally to Adm. Arthur D. **Struble**, whose first wife had died in 1962. Interestingly, despite lengthy navy careers, admirals Ringle and Struble had never met each other. Arthur Struble subsequently passed away in 1983.

For a time during the late 1990s, when both Margaret and Admiral Arleigh Burke's widow, Bobbie, had become extremely frail and a bit forgetful, Margaret's daughter Sally had both of them at her home at Avery Island, where they often held hands and gazed fondly at each other. Bobbie passed away in 1997, age ninety-eight; Margaret carried on until 1999, having achieved the age of ninety-one. Ken and Margaret are buried together in "The Grove"—the Avery family cemetery—on the island.

Sources

Coffman, 81, 86, 97.
Hotchkiss, Sally Ringle, e-mail correspondence.
Lowman, 14, 16, 76–77, 80, 96–99, 114, 210, 248.
Lucky Bag, U.S. Naval Academy, 1923.
Morison, V, 308; XIII, 324;
Niiya, 1–3.
Official Congressional Directory, 1930.
Ringle, Andrew D., e-mail correspondence.
Ringle, Kenneth A., e-mail correspondence.
Ringle, Kenneth A., *Washington Post Magazine*, 54–62.
Scaring, 103, 122, 180–82.
Slesnick, 40–42, 241.
U.S. Navy, *Register of Commissioned and Warrant Officers*.

CAPTAIN FRED FREMONT ROGERS, U.S. NAVY (1884–1952)

The pioneer in ONI's full-immersion Japanese language program
Mentor to Ellis Zacharias
"A very quiet, excellent officer, hard-working and efficient"
"Fred" "Rogé"

Fred Rogers was the very first naval officer to undergo ONI's full-immersion language and culture study in Japan, and therefore was a true pioneer in the navy's attempt to profoundly understand the Japanese language and culture. He is also important in that he fired the imagination of a young Ens. Ellis Zacharias, setting him on the course of Japanese language mastery as well as the mastery of the intelligence profession. Rogers later made good use of his Japanese skills and knowledge, both at ONI and as naval attaché in Tokyo. Retired before the start of the Second World War, he was brought back on active duty—not in intelligence but in training Seabees for action in the Pacific Theater.

* * *

From the 1906 Annapolis yearbook, *The Lucky Bag*:

Small—but his pompous presence lends to the air of distinction given by those raven locks and sparkling black eyes. He recites with that assurance that comes of high intellectual attainments, and is responsible for the hypothesis that metal lifeboats are not used because they sink. Of a somewhat inventive turn of mind, and has taken out a patent on his cast-iron boiler with copper tubes. Received a pretty picture postal card on first class cruise, but the mystery remains unsolved.

* * *

Fred F. Rogers was born in Clinton, Illinois, on September 21, 1884, where he attended grade and high school. His father was John B. Rogers. Fred was appointed to the Naval Academy in 1902 and graduated as a passed midshipman with the class of 1906. Distinguished classmates included Arthur L. Bristol Jr., William L. Calhoun, Milo F. Draemel, Aubrey W. Fitch, Frank Jack Fletcher, Robert L. Ghormley, Isaac C. Kidd, John S. McCain, Leigh Noyes, John H. Towers, and Russell **Willson**. Subsequent promotions included ensign, 1908; lieutenant (junior grade), 1911; lieutenant, 1913; lieutenant commander, 1917; commander; 1918; and captain, 1931. He retired in February 1940, but was brought back onto active duty in May 1942 to serve during World War II.

After leaving Annapolis in 1906, Mr. Rogers was ordered to the Asiatic Station where he had consecutive duty in the battleship *Wisconsin*, the gunboat *Quiros*, the gunboat *Samar*, and the battleship *Alabama*. In November 1908 he was transferred to the gunboat/dispatch vessel *Dolphin*. During his service on board the *Dolphin*, he was present when she cruised to Venezuela to transport Ambassador William I. Buchanan to negotiate the settlement of Venezuela's foreign loans.

Then, in April 1910, Ensign Rogers was sent as an assistant naval attaché at the American embassy in Tokyo—but in reality he was the first U.S. navy officer ordered to Japan for ONI's full-immersion language and culture program. Completing that intense educational experience, Lieutenant Rogers reported to the battleship *Virginia* in July 1913, where he served as watch officer and first lieutenant.

One fall day in 1913, in the ship's wardroom, an ensign named Ellis **Zacharias** listened in fascination as the mess treasurer, Lieutenant Rogers, discussed why lunch was very late with the senior mess steward—a lengthy discussion *in fluent Japanese*. Coincidentally—fortuitously for his messmates—Rogers was the only certified Japanese language officer in the entire U.S. Navy. This scene became an epiphany for Zacharias, who soon decided that he too wanted to become a language officer and an expert on Japan. Seven years later, Commander Rogers (at the Japan Desk at ONI) cabled Lieutenant Zacharias (who was at that time accompanying a midshipman training cruise) to ask if he still were interested. "Your message, affirmative," Zacharias immediately replied.

In March 1916, Lieutenant Rogers transferred from the *Virginia* to the gunboat *Castine* as executive officer and navigator. Detached from the *Castine* in January 1917, Rogers then served consecutively as navigator for the battleships *Illinois* and then the *Oklahoma* during the First World War. From February 1919 until June 1921, Fred was on duty in the ONI in Washington.

Returning to sea duty, Commander Rogers served as FIO of the Asiatic Fleet, from July 1921 until August 1922, when he subsequently assumed command of the destroyer *Barker*. In June 1923, Rogers began the senior course at the Naval War College. Then, he served on the War College's staff until September 1926 when he assumed command of the cargo ship *Sirius*. In October 1927 he transferred to the light cruiser *Concord*, serving as her executive officer until June 1928. From that date until May 1931, Fred again was on staff at the Naval War College. From June 1931 until May 1933, Captain Rogers was commander of Destroyer Division 8 in the Scouting Force.

After brief duty at ONI, Fred returned to Tokyo, where he was the naval attaché at the American embassy from September 1933 until September 1936. During this time he reported that the Japanese were working designs for warships of 45,000 to 55,000 tons. He was also stunned to witness "the abortive *coup d'état* of February 2, 1936, which was one of several key turning-points that sent Japan on a course for war, first with China, then with the United States and Britain." A precipitate of the attempted coup was a great increase of the military's influence upon the civilian government.

Henri **Smith-Hutton**, an assistant naval attaché at this time, later wrote that Rogers had some sort of personality clash with Ambassador Joseph C. Grew. For whatever reason, Smith-Hutton didn't think Grew consulted Rogers as much as he had his predecessor, Capt. Isaac C. Johnson Jr. However, in Smith-Hutton's view, Rogers had a very impressive tour of duty. "Rogers was one of the more successful naval attaches from a diplomatic-social point of view that we ever had in Tokyo." In the social arena he was particularly well regarded, because "he and Mrs. Rogers entertained a lot, as they were wealthy."

After his return to the United States, Captain Rogers commanded the battleship *Texas*, from November 1936 until June 1938. The following year he completed the advanced course at the Naval War College. Then, from June to November 1939, he served on the Naval Examining Board in Washington.

Captain Rogers retired from active duty in February 1940. However, after the start of the Second World War, he did some work in the Newport area (where he had maintained a home since 1924) in the line of formal civil defense preparations. He then was recalled to active duty in May 1942, assuming command of the Advanced Base Depot, as well as the Naval Construction Training Center, both located at

Davisville, Rhode Island. During the course of the war, this Construction Battalion (Seabee) training center sent almost 130,000 personnel into forward Pacific areas. Henri Smith-Hutton later wrote that Rogers told him "he wished that he might have been given something to do with Japan and the Far East on recall," but he did realize his Seabee assignment was very important and appreciated the opportunity. Captain Rogers was awarded the Legion of Merit for his activity and leadership in this program, and was relieved of active duty in August 1945.

Fred continued his retirement in Newport, and after a lengthy illness passed away there on November 6, 1952. He predeceased his wife, Winifred Warner Rogers (1882–1976); they are buried together at Woodlawn Cemetery in Clinton, Illinois— where they both had been born.

Among Captain Rogers's decorations and awards are the Legion of Merit, the Bronze Star, the Mexican Service Medal, and the Dominican Campaign Medal. He was also presented with the Bust of Bolivar and Diploma by the government of Venezuela, and was made a commander of the Military Order of Avis by the government of Portugal.

Sources

Captain Fred Fremont Rogers, U.S.N., Retired. Official Biography. U.S. Department of the Navy, August 13, 1945.
"Captain Fred Rogers Dies," Obituary, *Newport Daily News*, p. 2, November 6, 1952.
Dingman, 3.
Lucky Bag, U.S. Naval Academy, 1906.
Packard, 347, 365, 367.
Prados, 7–8, 21.
Smith-Hutton, Vol. I, 160–61; Vol. II, 623.
U.S. Navy, *Register of Commissioned and Warrant Officers.*
Zacharias, Ellis, 16.

LIEUTENANT COMMANDER DURWOOD GARLAND "TEX" RORIE, U.S. NAVY (1909–1987)

Rochefort's right-hand man at Station HYPO
"Tex"

Starting out World War II as a chief petty officer, Tex Rorie was already a veteran in radio intelligence. He served at Station HYPO before and during the war, and was Cmdr. Joe Rochefort's invaluable "go-to" man and general troubleshooter. He received an officer's commission in 1943 and ultimately served thirty-two years in the navy—before retiring to the trucking business in Maryland.

*   *   *

Durwood "Tex" Rorie, from Wichita Falls, Texas, was born on March 2, 1909. He joined the navy in 1927 and served aboard several ships as a communicator before attending Japanese language and communications-intelligence training in 1940. He was assigned to the Philippines and at Hawaii before World War II, and attached to Station HYPO before and during the war. At that time he and his family were living not far from Pearl Harbor; in fact he later told an interviewer that after the December 7 attack his kids picked up a quantity of shell casings in their backyard.

As a chief petty officer (yeoman), he served as Cmdr. Joe **Rochefort**'s right-hand man and all-around problem solver in 1941 and 1942, staffing Station HYPO and attending to the many administrative details. According to retired Captain Jasper **Holmes**, CPO Rorie was

> an old-timer in communications intelligence [and] supervised the work assignments, security, janitorial service, and supplies. [For example,] at two o'clock every morning Rorie mustered the yeomen to swab down the deck for the new day.

Joe Rochefort particularly appreciated his supply acumen.

> Supply details I left to the chief we had. He was quite capable of getting the things we wanted, and I never inquired where he got them or anything else. He produced these things from somewhere, being a good CPO.

Rorie handled much of Rochefort's dealings with the Fourteenth Naval District. As Rochefort's biographer Elliot Carlson described it,

> he was Rochefort's troubleshooter and exercised uncommon authority, which rested on their strong relationship of absolute trust. "I could get to [him] anytime with anything, talk to him, get anything signed that I put in front of him," Rorie said. "He never looked at it. He would just sign it. And I made sure that he never signed anything that he shouldn't have been signing."

Chief Rorie was particularly useful in assuring that the specialized equipment (such as punchers, sorters, collators, machine printers, etc.) constantly coming to HYPO was received, properly signed-off, *not* commandeered by others, and moved down into the basement. At the highest levels, including district commandant Admiral Bloch, HYPO was totally approved and supported. But a good number of lower-level officers and chiefs, unbriefed because of not having a need to know, were resentful of the "secret" unit in the basement. According to Rorie, it was fair to say that Rochefort "wasn't liked and they didn't like the [unit]. . . . Everybody resented us. We had . . . part of the basement of the main building. They wanted us out of there."

In terms of security, Rorie was the mainstay in lieu of fence, barricade, or sentry. He was the "gatekeeper" to the HYPO basement. As Carlson put it:

> Husky, gruff, and very able-bodied, Rorie maintained a commanding presence at his desk by the door. He screened every visitor. No stranger, no unwanted person, regardless of rank, ever got past Rorie or one of his equally formidable assistants.

CPO Rorie was largely responsible for recruiting new enlisted men for the ever-growing unit, constantly trying to meet Rochefort's rising need for manpower. In a 1983 interview, retired Capt. **Dyer** complimented him in this regard:

> Rorie had an uncanny knack for being able to pick good men from a new draft of recruits . . . to the best of my knowledge there wasn't a one of them . . . who didn't turn out to be perfectly satisfactory for our purposes.

According to Carlson, Rorie was aided by his own network of chiefs around the base.

> Some [of these CPOs] were located at the Pearl Harbor receiving station through which all [new] enlisted men arriving from the west coast were required to pass. . . . Rochefort had a deal with [Admiral Bloch] that HYPO would have the first pick of new sailors.

Rorie implemented the policy. Whenever a new batch came in, one of his pals alerted him, so Rorie would drive over to the receiving station and look the group over. One day, at the end of December 1941, Admiral Bloch offered Rochefort the twenty-member band of the sunken battleship *California*. Their instruments were destroyed or at the bottom of the harbor, and the men remained unassigned. Rochefort jumped at the opportunity and sent the chief to recruit them. Rorie lined them up and then,

> I just walked out there and I said "Any of you keep your damn mouth shut?" Well, they all held up their hand. I said, "Any of you want a good job?" They all held up their hand. I said, "We can get even with the Japs. Maybe we can give you a job that can give some satisfaction [now] that your instruments have been blown up."

They all indicated that they wanted the so-far unnamed job. However, the local navy security office and the local FBI butted in. They were concerned with some bandsmen with "foreign" names, such as Garbuschewski, DeStalinska, and Palchefsky, and they decided such individuals would not be allowed in the "top-secret" basement. Rorie then had the unpleasant task of explaining this to the *California*'s bandmaster, Lovine "Red" Luckenbach. "We'll take these guys, but I can't take [those specific] guys; the FBI won't allow us to do it." Luckenbach, a subordinate petty officer, replied, "Like hell. Either you take [us] all or you're not going to get any." Chief Rorie held back his own "ferocious" temper and went to consult the "manpower-hungry" Commander Rochefort. Characteristically, Rochefort said, "The hell with the FBI; bring those guys in here." Thus, just after the first of the year, the whole band came filing into HYPO's unventilated, tobacco-smoke-filled basement. Starting with clerical chores, in time they became vital participants in "HYPO's code-breaking efforts, [many] taking over the job of running the IBM tabulating machines and transferring information from intercepted messages into punch cards."

Tex Rorie started the war out as a chief petty officer. He was subsequently commissioned as an ensign in May 1943; promoted to lieutenant (junior grade) in August 1944; to lieutenant in February 1946; and to lieutenant commander in May 1953. He had a thirty-two-year naval career, retiring in January 1959. After leaving the navy he worked for the Preston Trucking Company of Preston, Maryland, as a terminal manager and general manager. Mr. Rorie passed away on December 24, 1987; his last known residence was in Winter Springs, Florida.

Sources

Carlson, 95, 106, 227–29, 483, 505.
Dyer, 272–74.
Holmes, 3, 36, 56.
Oral History Interview with Tex Rorie dated October 1984. NSA-OH-27-84, via the U.S. Naval Cryptologic Veterans Association.
Rochefort, 154.
U.S. Navy, *Register of Commissioned and Warrant Officers.*

CAPTAIN WILLIAM JOSEPH SEBALD, U.S. NAVAL RESERVE (1901–1980)

Wartime head of COMINCH's Japan Combat Intelligence Section
Postwar U.S. political advisor for Japan
Postwar U.S. ambassador to Burma
Postwar U.S. ambassador to Australia
"Bill"

Bill Sebald took a different path than most of his peers in this collection, stepping completely out of the navy in the early 1930s, coming back in during the war, and then going on to very high rank in the diplomatic corps. His view of Japan before the war was also unique when his first period of service, beginning in 1925, "brought me as a young U.S. Navy language officer to a country marked by peace and quiet, order and friendliness. During the thirties, while practicing law in Kobe, I observed the growth of nationalism and rampant imperialism which led to Pearl Harbor and to Japan's inevitable collapse."

* * *

From the 1922 Annapolis yearbook, *The Lucky Bag*:

"Say, mister, where ya' from?" "Baltimore, sir." "Baltimore, well that's the worst place on earth, isn't it?" "Yes, sir." "What?" "No, sir." "That's better. What ya' got in that suitcase?" "A zither, sir." "Never heard of that one, let's see it. Oh, it's a musical instrument, eh? Well, let's hear it—Out! OUT! Are hymns all you know? You win!" It was thus that *Bill* started his naval career by using to advantage the principal qualification of the naval profession: strategy. He has further successfully demonstrated that skill out in the boxing ring—not to mention the barber shop, store, and pay office. "Say, *Bill*, get me a drag [date] for next Saturday?" "Sure, blonde or brunette?" [Activities: rifle squad, expert rifleman, boxing squad, Featherweight Boxing Champion, class lacrosse]

* * *

William Sebald was born in Baltimore on November 5, 1901, the youngest of the four children of Dr. and Mrs. Frank J. Sebald. He attended the Baltimore Polytechnic Institute prior to entering the U.S. Naval Academy in 1918. He graduated and was commissioned an ensign in 1922, along with such notable classmates as John S. **Harper**, Wilfred "Jasper" **Holmes**, William S. Parsons, Hyman G. Rickover, and Henri H. **Smith-Hutton**. Subsequent promotions included lieutenant (junior grade), 1925; lieutenant, 1928; lieutenant commander, 1942; commander, 1943; and captain, 1945. He retired from the inactive reserve in 1960.

Mr. Sebald initially followed the usual pattern of a junior officer, serving in the battleship *Texas* from 1923 through 1925.

However, in 1925, Bill was selected for ONI's total immersion Japanese language and culture program, and as a result spent the next three years in Tokyo and other parts of Japan. One of his instructors was Naganuma Naoe, who had also taught Lt. j.g. Redfield **Mason** and Lt. j.g. Henri **Smith-Hutton**. In May 1927, Sebald married Edith Frances de Becker of Kobe, Japan.[1] She was the daughter of the international lawyer and long-time resident of Japan, Dr. Joseph Ernest de Becker, and of Kobayashi Ei, a Japanese artist.

Mr. Sebald then briefly served on board the battleship *Oklahoma* and the light cruiser *Cincinnati*. For a few weeks he served as an aide to the Japanese admiral Nomura Kichisaburō, who was visiting the United States. At that point, seeing a unique

---

1. Interestingly, Edith's sister, Marie Antoinette De Becker, had married Maj. Gen. Charles A. Willoughby. Willoughby served as Gen. Douglas MacArthur's chief of intelligence during most of World War II and the Korean War.

opportunity, he resigned from the navy in October 1930. Bill moved back to his home state and entered the school of law at the University of Maryland, from which he graduated with the degree of Juris Doctor. Returning to Japan, he practiced law in Kobe from 1933 until shortly before the outbreak of war in Europe; he operated his father-in-law's firm in Kobe, as Dr. de Becker had died in 1929. For a while Bill retained a commission in the naval reserve, but gave it up because it seemed to attract the attention of the *Kempetai*, the Japanese Army's secret police. While in Japan, Sebald specialized in international law in banking, shipping and maritime matters, and Japanese law. However, in early 1939 he and his wife moved to Washington and practiced law there until the start of the war with Japan.

Around October 1939, Sebald was asked to give his views about things in Japan at a USNA class of 1922 luncheon held at the Army-Navy Club in Virginia. He remarked that the Japanese Navy was large and well run, and that they would be a "first-class enemy" in case of war. He also stated that Japanese military aviation appeared to be much better than most Westerners thought. Afterward he was dismayed by the general reaction of his listeners; many appeared not to believe what he'd said, didn't want to believe what he said, thought he'd gone *Asiatic*, and shouldn't be listened to as "he's pro-Japanese."

The afternoon of December 7, 1941, Sebald called his friend Cmdr. Arthur **McCollum**, at ONI, and volunteered to come on active duty. Mac immediately had him appointed a civilian "agent" and started working on getting him a reserve commission. However, *because* of his substantial Japanese background and close relationships with so many Japanese people, some officials at ONI were actually afraid to bring him back as an officer—apparently worried that he actually *had* gone *Asiatic*. Mac had no patience with this attitude and aggressively campaigned on Bill's behalf. While all of this was churning, one day in late December 1941 the FBI searched Sebald's home and took some items because they considered his wife to be an "enemy alien." When informed, McCollum "hit the roof" and appealed to the ONI director; after some phone calls the same agents revisited the house, brought back the items, and apologized. Sometime later, ironically, Mrs. Sebald was actually asked to join the OSS as a consultant on Japanese psychology—which she did for a six-month period. She was appalled at how the OSS people she worked for were so ignorant about Japan.

McCollum's efforts on Sebald's behalf came to fruition in May 1942, when he was sworn in as a lieutenant commander, U.S. Naval Reserve. Initially he worked with Cmdr. Ethelbert **Watts** in the Japanese Section of the Far East Division. He started out by writing the ONI director's daily summary and building the subsection on Japanese naval aviation.

At one point, Commander McCollum decided that it might be good for Sebald to go over to Naval Communications, with OP-20-G, and work cryptographic translations for Lt. Cmdr. Rosie Mason. However, despite his formidable Japanese language skills, he just "couldn't get the hang of" cryptanalysis and was "very unhappy" in the work, so all parties concerned agreed it would be best to have Sebald back at ONI. Not long after, Watts went to sea duty, so Mr. Sebald replaced him as head of the Japan Section. From his nineteen months in ONI, Sebald later observed, "It's fellows who are usually in [a] basement who do the work of filing away and having cross-files, cross-indexes, and careful analyses, who [often] come up with the *proper answers*."

In July 1943, Bill was ordered onto the staff of the Commander in Chief, U.S. Fleet (COMINCH)—which is to say Adm. Ernest J. King. He and his Annapolis classmate Cmdr. Henri Smith-Hutton, who was already there, decided to organize a Combat Intelligence Division for COMINCH (Sebald later said it was really all Smith-Hutton's idea). Organizationally, Henri was F-2, and Bill was F-22 (F-21 was the Atlantic Theater, and F-23 was Operational Summaries). They got raw and finished intelligence from all kinds of sources and places—certainly including Cmdr. Rosie Mason at OP-20-G.

Sebald concentrated on the war with Japan and saw himself (and his small staff) as analysts or "evaluators of all intelligence concerned with the Pacific Ocean Area." The focus was upon operational intelligence to keep COMINCH "informed so that they could plan intelligently, operate intelligently, and know what the situation was or what to expect at any given time." F-22 worked seven days per week, with long hours, but typically did not man the office overnight. Ultimately, Sebald's staff grew to about twenty people, including a half-dozen women in the WAVE program. One of his staff was a young officer named Byron "Whizzer" White, who had been a star football player at the University of Colorado and years later would become an associate justice on the U.S. Supreme Court.

Thus, Sebald spent almost all of the war in Washington, despite requesting theater if not actual sea duty; however, no one in his chain of command thought he could be spared—or risked. He did travel a little; for example, at one time he spent a month at FRUPac/JICPOA, comparing notes and procedures, while FRUPac's Capt. Bill **Goggins** came to Washington in a sort of exchange visit. Sebald came back to F-22 feeling that between the two organizations, CinCPac had the better air order of battle intelligence. Commander Sebald did, of course, have a constant flow of communication with key individuals in the theater, certainly including Captains Ed **Layton** and Jasper **Holmes** at CinCPac, and Capt. Mac McCollum—now at Seventh Fleet.

Later on, he also had considerable dealings with a former Pearl Harbor COMINT expert. Historian Elliot Carlson relates that in the fall of 1944, Capt. Joe **Rochefort** was in Washington and back into the intelligence business—head of OP-20-G50 (Pacific Strategic Intelligence Section). With a large team,

> he was besieged with requests for insight into important but hitherto neglected aspects of the Pacific War. One of his most demanding customers was Commander Sebald, representing COMINCH, [for] things such as a study on the present oil situation in Japan, and a study showing what success the Japanese have had in sweeping acoustic mines.

At one point, Commander Sebald scolded PSIS for their naïveté about power relations inside Japan's leadership; one can only imagine how the knowledgeable and confident Captain Rochefort enjoyed that memo from a more junior officer.

Toward the end of the war, Bill was tasked to analyze what the Far East would look like after the Japanese surrendered, and to estimate to what degree the Soviet Union would push into the area. In June 1945, Sebald estimated that the Japanese economy would collapse by August or September. He later commented that there was no reason to welcome the Soviets into the Pacific war at the last minute, to drop the atomic bombs, or to launch a ground-force invasion of the homeland. He, like Capt. Ellis **Zacharias** (Sebald very much admired and respected Zacharias), did not think the Japanese would fanatically "fight to the end," but would rationally surrender when they soon concluded there was no other option—unless, of course, the home islands were actually invaded, at which point fanatical resistance probably *would* be seen.

However, the bombs *were* dropped and the Japanese surrendered in August. The COMINCH organization was stood down as part of the general demobilization. Sebald quickly wrote some final reports and a brief history of the organization. In several documents he stressed, for the future, that the fields of intelligence and cryptology needed to be advanced as viable full-time careers, that peacetime funding be provided to maintain good intelligence organizations, and that analysts (he called them "evaluators") be highly screened and highly trained.

Sebald was promoted to captain in October, and as he prepared to go back to civilian life Admiral King gave him an inscribed photograph of himself—which said, "To Commander William J. Sebald with *appreciation* and regards." King made a particular effort to make sure that Bill understood that the admiral had never underlined the word "appreciation" to anyone before this. Sebald was of course greatly honored, and thought that this recognition might stem from how he had worked his assignments. When he came into the COMINCH organization he was told that his expertise was recognized, so he should speak and write freely and hold nothing back. That's how he operated, knowing at times his views were not always in line with current policy or conventional thinking. Yet he never received any pushback or criticism for his observations and recommendations—and apparently they must have been *appreciated* all the way to the top.

At the end of November, Sebald transitioned to inactive naval reserve status and returned to civilian life. He was immediately taken into the Foreign Service, and at the request of Gen. Douglas MacArthur, the Supreme Commander of the Allied Powers (SCAP), Sebald returned to Japan in January 1946. One stopover on the way was Honolulu, where he was able to visit with his old friend Capt. Jasper Holmes.

Bill had been appointed a special assistant to George Atcheson, the acting political advisor to MacArthur; he was also made head of the State Department's contingent in Japan. He assisted Atcheson in making weekly reports for MacArthur on the political situation in Japan. In August 1947, Atcheson was killed in a plane crash, and Sebald succeeded him—being picked by MacArthur without consulting the State Department.

He kept this position until the end of the occupation in April 1952, owing to his unusually good relationship with MacArthur. Firstly, he was able to keep the Soviet Union, in particular, from interfering in MacArthur's policies, and secondly he had useful personal contacts with leading Japanese; finally, he was a valuable channel to Washington from which MacArthur wanted to maintain as much independence as possible. For these reasons he gained MacArthur's confidence, and at the same time he knew how to cope with his boss's difficult character and never tried to overstep his own limited role.[2]

Sebald had entered the State Department's career foreign service and, rising rapidly, attained the ranks of minister plenipotentiary in 1948, and ambassador in 1950. However, back to September 1947, Bill was made the deputy for the supreme commander as well as chairman and U.S. member of the Allied Council for Japan. In that capacity he served for almost five years. During this period of the Cold War, he carried the brunt of the diplomatic battle in the Allied Council in order to expedite and bring about the repatriation of more than a half-million Japanese prisoners of war from Siberia and other Soviet-controlled areas. He was also the chief of the Diplomatic Section—similar to a Foreign Office—of General Headquarters, SCAP, and in October 1950, he became the U.S. Political Adviser for Japan.

In his three-hatted job, he was one of the key advisers on the formulation of the Japanese peace treaty and worked closely with General MacArthur and Secretary of State John Foster Dulles—albeit in the background—in developing the philosophy and policies upon which much of the eventual treaty was based.

> At first Sebald was able to get MacArthur's general support for the State Department's policy, and he persuaded him to introduce the policy of shifting more responsibility to the Japanese government in the meantime. He was also able to persuade MacArthur, who saw Japan as a "Switzerland of the Far East," to accept the maintenance of U.S. military bases, perhaps in view of the communist expansion in Asia. All this was possible because of the relationship he had built with MacArthur. He also contributed to formulating the peace treaty through arranging for John Foster Dulles to meet as many Japanese leaders as possible, and it was on Sebald that Dulles relied for help in negotiating with the Japanese.
>
> Sebald was not in a position to decide the grand strategy of U.S. policy, but with his rich experience and knowledge of Japan, his language ability, and his wide-ranging connections with Japanese society, he did as much as any area specialist to help the decision-makers formulate their strategy.

Shortly before the peace treaty with Japan became effective in April 1952, Bill was appointed as the U.S. ambassador to Burma—in which capacity he served until November 1954. At that time he returned to Washington as the Deputy Assistant Secretary for Far Eastern Affairs.

---

2. "[However,] he could not discuss the whole occupation policy with MacArthur and was finally rebuffed when he tried to give his opinion on some critical issues, such as the purge of Japanese officials. Yet the relationship between Sebald and MacArthur was to be a valuable asset for the State Department when it began to move towards concluding a peace treaty with Japan in 1949, since MacArthur was a key figure in developing U.S. policy."

In March 1957, he was assigned as U.S. ambassador to Australia, where he served until his voluntary retirement from the Foreign Service in December 1961.

Ambassador Sebald wrote a number of books on Japanese law, including original translations of the Japanese civil, criminal, and commercial codes with annotations. In 1949, he was awarded the degree of Doctor of Laws by the University of Maryland for his work in Japanese law. Although a member of the bar of Maryland, the District of Colombia—and the U.S. Supreme Court—with the outbreak of the war with Japan he had given up his law career and never returned to active practice.

In 1965 he published a book, *With MacArthur in Japan: A Personal History of the Occupation of Japan.* Then, in 1966, he was the coauthor (with Dr. C. Nelson Spinks) of another book, *Japan: Prospects, Options, and Opportunities.* Moreover, during the 1930s, he had published several books on various aspects of Japanese law.

After his retirement, Ambassador Sebald and his wife lived in Washington until they moved to Naples, Florida, in 1966. They had never had any children. Bill became a member of the Naples Yacht Club and served a term as president of the Asiatic Society of Japan. He also served a term as president of the Japan-America Society in Washington.

Captain Sebald had been decorated with the Legion of Merit for his contributions on the wartime staff of COMINCH. Moreover, in recognition of his efforts to improve friendly relations and understanding between the United States and Japan, Ambassador Sebald was awarded the First Class Order of the Rising Sun with Grand Cordon by the Emperor of Japan, the highest decoration that could be given to a non-Japanese.

Ambassador William J. Sebald passed away from emphysema, at Naples, in August 1980. Mrs. Edith de Becker Sebald passed away a year later. They are buried together in Washington at Rock Creek Cemetery, where an observer might find their tombstone engraving to be charming. The single inference of rank or accomplishment is the simple abbreviation of "Amb." in front of William's name. Rather, the lengthy inscription emphasizes that they were together for fifty-three years—and that he was her loving husband, and that she was his loving wife.

Sources

Carlson, 426–27.

Dorwart, *Conflict of Duty*, 181, 195, 218.

Kusunoki, Dr. Ayako. "William J. Sebald and the Occupation of Japan" synopsis of the article. *The Asiatic Society of Japan.* www.asjapan.org.

Lucky Bag, U.S. Naval Academy, 1922.

Prados, 8–10, 26–28, 498, 544–45, 596, 611, 705.

Sebald, *Reminiscences*, Vol. 1, 253–63, 266, 270–72, 275, 279, 291, 293, 295, 298, 301, 306, 309, 323–24, 332–34, 345, 355.

U.S. Navy, *Register of Commissioned and Warrant Officers.*

William J. Sebald. Career Summary, Office of the Historian, U.S. Department of State, www.history.state.gov.

CAPTAIN GILVEN MAX SLONIM, U.S. NAVY (1913–2000)

"Gil"

Gil Slonim had barely completed his ONI-sponsored Japanese-language immersion training before the start of World War II. He then spent the war attached to Station HYPO/FRUPac—but that attachment saw him uniquely serving most of those years afloat, leading mobile radio intelligence units, on board a number of flagships and advising several admirals during combat actions. Present at Pearl Harbor the day the war started, he also was on board the battleship *Missouri* in Tokyo Bay on the day the war ended, where he witnessed the actual Japanese surrender ceremony.

* * *

From the 1936 Annapolis yearbook, *The Lucky Bag*:

> Despite a very bad case of *mal de mer* aboard the USS *Paducah* back on the Great Lakes,
> Gil decided that the Navy was the life for him, so he tossed a pair of boxing gloves, shoes,
> and trunks in a suitcase and headed for the Naval College. He K.O.'d everything in sight
> except Plebe Steam [marine engineering], which had him down for the count of nine on
> a few occasions. . . . Gil's capacity for work coupled with an ambition to get someplace
> have been the keynotes of his success and these same valuable attributes will win him
> his place in the Fleet. [Activities: boxing; reception committee; Quarter-Deck Society]

* * *

Gilven Slonim was born in Duluth, on September 29, 1913, to Sam and Susie
Slonim. He attended Duluth's Central High School and then the U.S. Naval Academy. He graduated and was commissioned as an ensign in 1936, along with such
noteworthy classmates such as John K. Fyfe, Chester W. Nimitz Jr., Richard R.
Pratt, and David C. Richardson. Subsequent promotions included lieutenant (junior
grade), 1939; lieutenant, 1942; lieutenant commander, 1943; commander, 1944;
and captain, 1955. He transferred to the navy's retired list in 1965.

Mr. Slonim's initial assignments are typical of the time. From 1936 through
1937 he was attached to the battleship *Maryland*, and then he was assigned to the
destroyer *Barry* during 1938 to 1939.

In 1939, Lt. j.g. Slonim reported to the U.S. embassy in Tokyo, having been
selected as one of ONI's language and cultural immersion students. His tour was
cut short by a few months, when naval attaché Cmdr. Henri **Smith-Hutton** sent
him and a few others out of the country—in late summer 1941—due to the great
instability and deterioration of the diplomatic situation.

Unlike several of the evacuation immersion students, Slonim and three others (lieutenants junior grade John Bromley, Allyn Cole, and "Tex" **Biard**) were sent to Hawaii
rather than Corregidor. Accordingly, he reported to Station HYPO—in the basement
of the Fourteenth Naval District's headquarters building—in September 1941 to work
for Cmdr. Joe **Rochefort**. Among other initial tasks that Rochefort assigned his new
radio intelligence officers was handling the OP-20-G-mandated priority to listen for
the Japanese "East Wind, Rain" execute message—which presumably would indicate
an imminent break in US-Japan relations. Thus, on November 29, Rochefort sent
Slonim and his former immersion-training colleagues Bromley, Cole, and Biard to the
intercept site at He'eia to stand round-the-clock watches solely to listen for the message—which apparently was never transmitted. As it turned out, Slonim had just been
relieved by Biard when the Pearl Harbor attack began on December 7.

Lt. Cmdr. Joe **Finnegan** roomed with Gil in the latter's apartment for the first
months of the war. According to Finnegan's son, Dr. Gregory Finnegan, who talked
with Slonim in the late 1990s,

They worked opposite shifts at HYPO. . . . Gil recalled trying to get to sleep after grueling shifts and not being able to because Finnegan had a neurotic tic such that he couldn't go to work without hearing the sign-off song on Gracie Fields' radio program.

Unfortunately for Slonim, Finnegan had already displayed some invaluable brilliance in his work, so

when Lt. j.g. Gil Slonim complained about this to Lt. Cmdr. Jasper Holmes, he said Holmes' reply was that "if Joe Finnegan needed a brass band to be able to work, he'd get it."

In early 1942, Rochefort was directed to detach some of his key men to form afloat radio intercept units with various task forces. As valuable as this initiative turned out to be, HYPO acutely felt the loss of these highly trained specialists.[1]

Lieutenant Slonim was attached to Admiral Halsey's staff [on the *Enterprise*] for the Wake-Marcus strikes in late February-early March 1942. He took the first intercept unit, consisting of two radio operators, into action. This unit, despite its small size and scant equipment, was able to provide the admiral with target weather information at both Wake and Marcus Islands. He was able to inform the admiral what success the U.S. cruiser force bombarding Wake had attained when the radio station on Marcus was placed out of commission . . .

Slonim's unit, increased to three operators, continued serving with Admiral Halsey. Interception of contact reports on the force by this unit influenced the time of launching [of Lt. Col. Jimmy Doolittle's B-25s against Tokyo from the carrier *Hornet*] in April 1942. The admiral decided to launch the strike immediately upon detection.[2]

Later, during the Battle of Midway, Lieutenant Slonim's unit on the *Enterprise* (now advising Rear Adm. Raymond Spruance) intercepted and translated the first sighting reports of the Japanese search planes—thus anticipating the attack which came against the *Yorktown*.

Mr. Slonim was attached to HYPO/FRUPac from 1941 through 1945, but spent the majority of the time afloat leading similar radio intelligence teams and translating interceptions for various task force and fleet commanders—rising from lieutenant to commander along the way. Of course, a number of other officers, such as Tex

---

1. According to Capt. Jasper Holmes, "When the first radio intelligence teams proved valuable to the carrier task force commanders, the argument became academic. FRUPac had to provide the service, and the only way to do it was gracefully and efficiently. The radio operators could pick up the earliest signs of alarm at the target of a raid, and the language officer could gauge the magnitude of the defending forces by the flow of radio traffic. Armed with a list of the major Japanese units' radio calls, the team also had the potential ability to detect the presence of major Japanese naval forces within strategic distance. Radio intelligence teams with the task forces could sometimes copy Japanese messages that escaped the shore-based intercept station."

2. Also according to Captain Holmes, upon the task force being sighted by Japanese picket boats, "Slonim picked up frantic and garbled Japanese conversations on the radio. . . . Any doubts that the boats' alarm got through were soon dispelled. Within minutes, the Japanese civil defense circuits were on the air, and Slonim could hear excited Japanese conversation about carriers, planes, and gunfire." As a result, "Halsey . . . had little choice but to launch the Army air strike immediately [much earlier than desired] and retreat."

Biard, Ranson **Fullinwider**, and Bankson **Holcomb** led similar units at sea, but apparently none quite as much as did Slonim. Some of his adventures leading afloat radio intelligence teams are as follows:

On board the *Enterprise* at the fighting at the Eastern Solomon Islands, August 1942; Guadalcanal occupation and Stewart Island action, late 1942 and early 1943; Tarawa, November 1943; Operation GALVANIC (occupation of the Gilbert Islands), November–December 1943, on board the *Indianapolis* with ComCent-PacFor; Operation FLINTLOCK (occupation of Kwajalein and Majuro), February 1944, *Indianapolis*; Operation CATCHPOLE (occupation of Eniwetok), February 1944; Operation FORAGER (occupation of Guam, Saipan, and Tinian), June 1944, Com5thFlt; the Battle of the Philippine Sea, June 1944; Operation STALEMATE II (occupation of Palau and the Philippine campaigns), August–September 1944, on board the *New Jersey*, Com3rdFlt; Operation KING II (strikes on the Philippines and the occupation of Leyte), October 1944; Operation OBLITERATION (Luzon, Mindoro), December 1944; Operation MUSKETEER MIKE ONE (Formosa, Luzon, Lingayen Gulf), December 1944–January 1945; and the "victory cruise," July–August 1945, aboard the *Missouri*.

Commander Slonim was almost killed, on May 12, 1945, when a *kamikaze* aircraft struck Spruance's flagship *New Mexico* off Okinawa. Some 119 men were wounded and fifty-four were killed—including one of the communications-intelligence radiomen in the radio shack. Slonim was spared the same fate because he had just stepped out and gone below to deliver a message to the admiral.

It's interesting to note that Commander Slonim was present at both the bombing of Pearl Harbor in 1941 as well as the Japanese surrender, aboard the USS *Missouri*, in 1945. He was one of the official interpreters for the surrender ceremony, though Gen. Douglas MacArthur only utilized his own army translators for the occasion. Years later Slonim remembered how MacArthur haughtily beckoned to members of the emperor's delegation as they stepped forward to sign the documents. "He let all the stops out as to who was in command," commented Slonim, saying MacArthur summoned them "as if he were telling a youngster to eat his spinach." For his contributions during the war, Slonim was decorated with a Legion of Merit medal.

He next served as commanding officer of the destroyer *Jarvis*, from January through June 1946.

Commander Slonim then attended the Naval War College, graduating in 1948 along with Capt. Richard **Zern**.

During the Korean War period Gil commanded the destroyer *Irwin*, from 1952 through 1954. For this service he was awarded a second Legion of Merit with the combat "V" device, and in 1955 he was promoted to captain.

In the early 1960s he commanded the destroyer-tender USS *Everglades*. His last active-duty assignment was in Washington at the office of the CNO—from which he retired in 1965.

In 1970, he founded the Oceanic Education Foundation in Falls Church, Virginia, and in the late 1970s and early 1980s was teaching a course in global oceanic education at the University of Virginia.

Captain Slonim earned a PhD degree in 1985; his dissertation was titled "The World Ocean—Prelude to a National Policy Fulcrum for Future Social and Educational Change."

In May 1986, he was in attendance—along with his former HYPO comrade Rear Adm. Donald "Mac" Showers—when President Ronald Reagan presented Capt. Joe Rochefort's family with Rochefort's posthumous and long-overdue Distinguished Service Medal.

> At one point, in the late 1990s, Gil met with Joe Finnegan's son, Gregory Finnegan.
>
> Captain Slonim said that he had not [fully] cooperated with other authors (probably Jasper Holmes and/or Edwin **Layton**) for their books about FRUPac, etc., since he (Gil) intended to write his own account and wanted to save his material for that. Alas, of course, he never did so before he died.

On November 22, 2000, in his eighty-seventh year and living in Falls Church, Captain Slonim suffered a heart attack and died at Inova Fairfax Hospital. He was survived by his wife, Erline Reynolds Slonim (1921–2009), and their three children: retired Navy Lt. Cmdr. Richard G. Slonim, David R. Slonim, and Patricia S. Gordon.

Among his decorations and awards were two Legions of Merit and a Bronze Star.

Despite what was reported above, in the early 1980s Slonim had put in some effort helping Rear Adm. Edwin Layton (and his coauthors) work on Layton's reminisces, *"And I Was There": Pearl Harbor and Midway—Breaking the Secrets.*

Many years after World War II, Captain Slonim wrote an interesting summary about why the Pearl Harbor attack was such a surprise to the United States—and it's interesting also as an observation about the intelligence process. The American leadership just *could* not, and *would* not, believe the Japanese would strike at Pearl Harbor. "Possibilities . . . probabilities, capabilities, and intentions become academic when one does not accept the credibility of [one's] own estimates."

Sources

Carlson, 94, 101, 159, 171, 185, 196, 242–43, 256, 274–76, 454, 508–9.
Dingman, 167.
Finnegan, Gregory. Email dated May 13, 2015.
Holmes, 36, 58, 67–68, 93, 188.
Holtwick, 434, 446, 448.
Layton, *"And I Was There,"* 6.
Lucky Bag, U.S. Naval Academy, 1936.
McGinnis, 51–53, 63.
Packard, 367, 371.
Prados, 39, 287, 327, 372, 383–84, 538, 561, 574, 577, 649–50, 718.
Prange, *At Dawn,* 736.
Spector, *Listening to the Enemy,* 79–81, 84–89, 93–99, 125.
Symonds, 275.
U.S. Navy, *Register of Commissioned and Warrant Officers.*

CAPTAIN HENRI HAROLD SMITH-HUTTON, U.S. NAVY (1901–1977)

Perhaps the best of the ONI full-immersion Japanese language students
Fluent in Japanese, French, Spanish, German, and Russian
Last pre-war naval attaché in Tokyo
"Hank" "H.H."

H.H. Smith-Hutton was a very gifted and dedicated officer with an extremely analytical mind. Hank had been a full-immersion language officer in Japan and had developed a particularly fluent command of Japanese. In addition, he had an unrivaled knowledge of the Japanese Navy, its culture, and its officers. He performed superbly during the war as head of Admiral King's Combat Intelligence Division in Washington, and then moved on to Pacific destroyer squadron command.

* * *

From the 1922 Annapolis yearbook, *The Lucky Bag*:

And it came to pass in the final year of the reign of the U-boat [in World War I] that there came amongst us from afar off a stalwart young man known unto the hometown sports as Henri. And he did petition for admittance at the Pearly Gates even as many before him had done, whereupon he was admitted and became a true salt. Soon thereafter his wisdom became famed throughout the land of the Middy-onites and he rose in favor with the kings who ruled o'er the country until he was like unto a second Joseph come into Egypt. And he saw his people sore oppressed, being compelled to drag [date] bricks [unattractive girls] even upon the Seventh Day, whereupon Henri rose and cried out in anguish. So henceforth he did drag the One-and-Only each week-end to give the boys' eyes a treat, for he seldom consented to part with her for a single dance. Yea, verily I say unto you, Henri was one wise man, a true savior. [Activities: *Lucky Bag* staff, Black "N," Class Tennis, Sub Squad]

* * *

Henri H. Smith-Hutton was born September 8, 1901, in Alliance, Nebraska. Shortly thereafter his family moved to the Black Hills of South Dakota; he grew up there and attended Deadwood High School. He was appointed to the U.S. Naval Academy in 1918, and was graduated and commissioned as an ensign in 1922—along with classmates John S. **Harper**, Wilfred "Jasper" **Holmes**, William S. Parsons, Hyman G. Rickover, and William J. **Sebald**. By subsequent promotions Smith-Hutton attained the ranks of lieutenant junior grade, 1925; lieutenant, 1928; lieutenant commander, 1937; commander 1941; and captain, 1942.

From 1922–1926, Mr. Smith-Hutton served in the Asiatic Fleet, consecutively in the flagship, armored cruiser *Huron*; the destroyer-tender *Black Hawk*; the destroyer *Peary*; and the battleship *Idaho*. At this time he became very interested in learning the Japanese language due to rising international tensions in the Far East. He applied for the ONI language training program; thus, during the following three years, he was a full-immersion student of the Japanese language and culture, attached to the American Embassy in Tokyo. Smith-Hutton's rapid progress astounded his examiners at the embassy, as well as his chief instructor, Naganuma Naoe, who said Smith-Hutton was the best student he ever had. Hank had a flair for languages, and would ultimately speak Japanese, French, Spanish, German, and Russian. During this time, along with his instructor, he translated the voluminous *Japanese Coast Pilot*—with the full knowledge and even assistance of the Japanese Navy. For a period, in 1928, he worked with Lt. Cmdr. Ellis **Zacharias** at Nagasaki.

Returning to Washington in the fall of 1929, he was on duty in the Office of Naval Intelligence from that November until June 1930. Here, Smith-Hutton again worked with Zacharias, where Zach was now head of the Far Eastern Section. He then reported to the Newport News (Virginia) Shipbuilding and Dry Dock Company for duty in connection with fitting out the USS *Houston*, commissioned in June 1930. That cruiser later became flagship of the Asiatic Fleet, and from 1931–1932 Hank served on board as aide and flag lieutenant, and later as aide and fleet intelligence officer on the staff of the Commander in Chief, Asiatic Fleet. He there worked alongside, and became friends with, Lt. Joseph **Wenger**, who was handling radio intelligence. Smith-Hutton then had shore duty at the American Embassy, Tokyo, 1932–1935, as an assistant naval attaché, working under the pioneering Capt. Fred **Rogers**—whom he held in high esteem. Upon leaving Tokyo, Henri returned for brief duty in the Office of the CNO.

After serving from 1935–1936 as executive officer of the destroyer *Lawrence*, he was assigned as staff communications officer of the heavy cruiser *Augusta*, flagship of the Asiatic Fleet, serving until February 1937. Thereafter, for two years, he was again the fleet intelligence officer on the staff of the Commander in Chief, Asiatic Fleet. Returning to the American Embassy at Tokyo in April 1939, he became the naval attaché. He was ably supported by an assistant attaché, Lt. j.g. Stephen **Jurika**; raised and educated in Asia, Jurika was fluent in five languages and was a natural regarding the intelligence business.

As the senior attaché, Smith-Hutton was extremely proactive in collecting useful intelligence everywhere and anywhere he could—even to playing considerable tennis at the Tokyo Tennis Club and cultivating significant contacts there. (His protégé, Steve Jurika, thought Hank was excellent; "I admired Smith-Hutton very much.") One of Henri's tennis contacts, a medical student (who was Chinese by birth), was outraged by atrocities being committed by the Japanese Army in China, and was eager to be of help. As a Japanese citizen, he was able to take student recruitment tours on Japanese naval vessels. On board a destroyer, at Smith-Hutton's urging, the student observed 25" torpedo tubes (versus the standard 21"). He also amazed Smith-Hutton by reporting on a new oxygen-propelled torpedo with a warhead of 1,200 pounds—capable of travelling ten thousand yards at a speed of 45 knots!

Later, Commander Smith-Hutton and his associates came up with several indicators of the forthcoming Japanese attack, though they all pointed to a "traditional" notion of Japanese strategy—likely as not a first strike at the British at Singapore. Nevertheless, considering their considerable restrictions and imposed isolation during this time, American attachés in Japan pulled together much more information than has usually been acknowledged.

Fearing the worst, in the summer of 1941 Smith-Hutton got all the current ONI language officers out of Japan (particularly important, as they did not have "diplomatic status" as did the naval attachés), and recommended that no one else be brought in to replace attaché staff as they finished their tours.

As careful as the Japanese were in trying to restrict the movement of Western diplomatic personnel, Smith-Hutton fell into some unusual luck during the first week of November 1941. Incredibly, Ambassador Joseph Grew, filing all proper paperwork in advance, was able to send Commander and Mrs. S-H on a railroad vacation to the Inland Sea area, including Beppu, Miyajima, and Murozumi. There, the Smith-Huttons were able to observe enormous naval activity in and around several areas, including Hiroshima Bay, involving amphibious and aircraft training as well as remarkable logistical preparations. Upon their return to the embassy, Ambassador Grew sent Washington a report of their and his concerns, including a speculation about the possibility of sudden military or naval action by the Japanese armed forces.

Commander Smith-Hutton was still serving as attaché when the Japanese attacked Pearl Harbor on December 7, 1941. Asked by Ambassador Grew to verify commercial radio reports, Smith-Hutton drove over to the Navy Ministry and talked to Capt. Nakamura Katsuhira, whom he'd known for several years.

> I told him that my ambassador had sent me. I asked about an attack on Pearl Harbor, whether there was truth in the report and if so, when we could expect to get a notice of a declaration of war. He looked rather sad, because I think he was really a friend of the United States. He said, yes the report was true. He had just learned about it himself, and could verify it. As to the declaration of war, he couldn't say, because that would have to come from the Foreign [Ministry] and was not a Navy Department matter. . . . He said I could report to the ambassador that the attack had taken place, and that he personally was not happy about it. I told him I wasn't either, and I said that this might be the last time I would see him. I hoped he would survive the war. He said he hoped the same for me.

Along with other embassy staff, Smith-Hutton, his wife, and his daughter were interned by the Japanese government. From the embassy roof they did get to observe Lt. Col. Jimmy Doolittle's B-25 air raid on Tokyo—launched from the USS *Hornet* on April 18, 1942. In June the Smith-Huttons were all repatriated and returned to the United States. Among the things H. H. smuggled out of Japan—in his wife's numerous trunks—were a number of Japanese textbooks, grammars, and newspaper files, which were important as ONI spun-up an intense U.S.-based Japanese language program from 1941 onward. He also brought out several Japanese shipping yearbooks, his own biographic card file on all Japanese officers in the grade of commander and above, and his own detailed journal of events and observations.

Hank then reported to the Office of the CNO in Washington, for duty with the Commander in Chief, U.S. Fleet—COMINCH—which is to say Adm. Ernest J. King. H. H.'s wife, Jane, went to work at the OSS headquarters as Washington manager for Far East MO (Morale Operations), and liaison to Project *Marigold*, producing and disseminating slanted covert propaganda and rumors in Japan and China.

Commander Smith-Hutton was put in charge of the Operational Information Section until July 1943, and then organized the Combat Intelligence Division—serving as head of that division until his detachment in 1944, and working closely with Bill Sebald, who was his deputy focused upon the Pacific Theater. For twenty-two months H. H. saw Admiral King almost daily and developed a very favorable impression of him; he found him less severe than many people have reported.

Admiral King was a brilliant officer with a very practical mind. He wanted and needed facts, and with that kind of officer it's difficult to pretend to know something when you don't.

During the years I served with him he showed great consideration for his subordinates, and I know that he had respect for able and hardworking officers. He welcomed advice and suggestions and he often praised officers for work well-done. Of course, at the same time, he could be very critical of work he considered to be below standard. He showed great confidence in the abilities of officers he'd selected to work for him, and once he assigned a task to a subordinate he didn't interfere with the way it was being done.

During this period, among other things Smith-Hutton was involved in the creation of the Army-Navy Communications Intelligence Coordinating Committee, founded in April 1944. He also organized an exchange of visits between key analysts in Washington and at FRUPac in Hawaii, trying to ensure everyone was on the same page and trying to eliminate any duplication of effort. During the spring of 1944, Captain Smith-Hutton briefed Capt. Daniel V. Gallery (commanding officer of a hunter-killer escort carrier group in the Atlantic) as to the type of German submarines he likely might find in a particular area; this helped Gallery prepare for the subsequent capture of *U-505*—and her intact ENIGMA code machine and codebooks—on June 4, 1944.

From October 1944 until June 1945, Smith-Hutton was commanding officer of Destroyer Squadron 15, U.S. Pacific Fleet. His squadron was then converted to Mine Squadron 21 which he commanded until August 1945. Later that month he was assigned to the staff of the Commander in Chief, Pacific Fleet (Fleet Admiral Nimitz), and ordered to the Pacific Fleet Liaison Group, Headquarters of the Supreme Commander for the Allied Powers in Japan. When that group was dissolved, in February 1946, he became chief of staff to the Commander, Naval Forces Japan (Vice Adm. Robert M. Griffin). In June 1946, he was ordered to command the light cruiser *Little Rock*, serving in that capacity until February 1947. During this time the *Little Rock* participated in cold weather exercises in the Davis Strait, between Greenland and East Baffin Island, as part of Task Group 20.2.

H. H. returned to the Navy Department for temporary duty in the Office of the CNO. He then was assigned as naval attaché and naval attaché for air to France and Switzerland, in residence at the American Embassy in Paris. He remained there on duty until May 1952, when he returned to the United States and again had temporary duty in the Office of the CNO. His retirement became effective in June 1952.

After retiring from the navy, Smith-Hutton returned to Paris; a colleague who preceded him as naval attaché in Paris put him in contact with Leland Stowe, news chief of Radio Free Europe (RFE). Stowe hired Smith-Hutton to be chief of RFE's Paris news bureau; as such, he directed RFE's effort to gather news from France that might be of interest to the large Eastern European exile communities in France. Smith-Hutton remained in that position for six years.

In 1958, RFE management suggested that Smith-Hutton move to Munich and take on a new position; he declined out of a desire not to move his family and instead opted to leave the organization. He took a position with the Paris office of Bache and Company, an American financial services provider. He worked for Bache until his retirement and return to the United States in 1969.

Captain Smith-Hutton died, in 1977, in Vista, California. He had been married to Jane Ellen Ming Smith-Hutton (1912–2002); after H. H.'s death, Jane kept a residence in Palo Alto, home base for a demanding lecture series she presented on historical topics for the Daughters of the American Revolution. Every April, however, she traveled east to a remote mountaintop house that she built in Hendersonville, North Carolina. There she enjoyed a second spring and life in what she called "the forest primeval." An avid gardener, Jane turned meadows around her house into flowering carpets. In keeping with the horticultural theme, she called her house *Shobu*, the Japanese word for iris. Jane passed away in 2002, aged ninety-one, and was buried with H. H. at Arlington National Cemetery. The Smith-Huttons had two daughters, Marcia and Cynthia.

Henri's many awards include the Legion of Merit (for his work heading the COMINCH Combat Intelligence Division), the Yangtze Service Medal, and the China Service Medal.

Sources

Benson, 134.
Bradford, "Learning the Enemy's Language."
Harris, Marlys. *Have Two Addresses.* http://money.cnn.com/magazines/moneymag
   /moneymag_archive/1988/04/01/84393/index.htm.
Jurika, Vol. 1, 381.
Lewin, 27.
Lucky Bag, U.S. Naval Academy, 1922.
Mahnken, 70–71.
Packard, 75, 207.
Prados, 9, 17, 29, 39, 45, 162–63, 199–201, 301, 348, 350, 544.
Prange, *At Dawn*, 32.
Smith-Hutton, Henri. *Reminiscences*, Vol. 1, 1–4; Vol. 2, 405, 456.
Smith-Hutton, Marcia. Daughter of Captain Smith-Hutton, via USS *Little Rock* Association.
Stinnett, 143–44.
U.S. Navy, *Register of Commissioned and Warrant Officers.*
USS Little Rock Association website. http://www.usslittlerock.org/CO%20Data/Little_Rock_
   SmithHutton_ Bio.htm.

VICE ADMIRAL RUFUS LACKLAND TAYLOR JR., U.S. NAVY (1910–1978)

Served at Stations CAST, FRUMel, and FRUPac
The first career intelligence officer to serve as Director of Naval Intelligence
"Rufe"

Rufus Taylor began a routine career as a conventional junior officer who then moved into communications intelligence a few years before the start of World War II. His wartime intelligence service was very important but not particularly spectacular. It's in the Cold War that Taylor's intelligence career really blossomed, leading him to ultimate promotion to vice admiral and ever-increasing responsibilities in high intelligence-community positions such as U.S. Naval Forces, Japan; the U.S. Pacific Fleet; the Office of Naval Intelligence; and the National Reconnaissance Program.

His last two assignments were as deputy director of the Defense Intelligence Agency and then deputy director of the CIA.

*   *   *

From the 1933 Annapolis yearbook, *The Lucky Bag*:

> Saint Louis lost a very personable young man when Rufus Taylor Jr., decided that a naval career should be his. After making his decision, Rufus attended Hall's War College in Columbia, Missouri, in order to prepare for the great struggle against time. He found no trouble with the entrance examinations and, at the appointed hour, entered the gates of the Academy grimly determined to weather the four-year storm. *Rufe* is extremely interested in a sea-going life. He loves to sail, and the cruises proved a source of great joy, as they enabled him to become familiar with the practical side of the sea. . . . The Academic Department gave *Rufe* a few thrills during the progress of the strife, but each time the situation became acute, he buckled down to work in a fashion that could not be defeated. *Rufe* has an exceptionally keen sense of humor—a fact that led him to revel in the quaint bull sessions heard about the hall. He has a very direct way of expressing himself, and never hesitates to give his exact views about the subject under discussion or of the person to whom he is speaking. He is a true friend and an honest enemy. [Activities: soccer, baseball]

*   *   *

Rufus Taylor was born in 1910 in St. Louis, Missouri. He graduated from the Naval Academy in 1933, along with such distinguished classmates as John D. Bulkeley, Ignatius J. Galantin, David McCampbell, Thomas H. Moorer, Stephen **Jurika** Jr., and Draper L. Kauffman. Subsequent promotions included lieutenant (junior grade), 1937; lieutenant, 1941; lieutenant commander, 1942; commander, 1944; captain, 1952; rear admiral, 1964; and vice admiral, 1966. Admiral Taylor retired in 1969.

After his academy graduation he had a fairly typical early career. He was first assigned to battleship duty on board the *Arizona*, and then in 1936 briefly transferred to an aviation unit, Observation Squadron 2. He next served on board the destroyer *Preston*, 1937 to 1938.

Beginning that same year, he began his connection with the naval intelligence community as one of the ONI Japanese language and culture immersion students. In late summer 1941 he was sent out of Japan by naval attaché Cmdr. Henri **Smith-Hutton**—a little earlier than planned—because of the increasing political tensions. He arrived at Station CAST, the cryptologic unit at Corregidor, in September and thus was one of the ten communications-intelligence officers there at the start of the war on December 7. In the face of the rapid Japanese advance, Lieutenant Taylor was in the third group of CAST personnel to evacuate the Philippines in April 1942. He had volunteered to be in that last, most vulnerable group; he supposedly told one radioman that he had a pistol ready to shoot himself, and others if need be, to keep any cryptologic personnel from falling into Japanese hands. After evacuation by submarine to Australia, Taylor served at Stations BELCONNEN and then FRUMel—and on the staff of the Commander, Allied Naval Forces, Southwestern Pacific—until 1943.

Prior to the Battle of the Coral Sea, in April 1942, the Australian/American/British codebreakers in Australia made an enormous contribution by deciphering Japanese messages that detailed the organization of their forces. Moreover, BELCONNEN's head, Lt. Rudy **Fabian**, and Rufe Taylor are specifically credited with discovering details about the Japanese strike force's aircraft carriers.

Just after that, at one point during the lead-up to the Battle of Midway, Taylor (or possibly Fabian) came into the codebreaking center and said, "Now you guys be sure of what you're writing—because they are *moving carriers* on the basis of what [we're] saying!" It was Fabian's unit which first determined that Admiral Yamamoto's lengthy radio message of May 20, 1942, was a major operations order—but it was Cmdr. Joe **Rochefort**'s Station HYPO unit in Hawaii that put out the first fragmentary solution of that message.

Lieutenant Commander Taylor then served at the ONI and the ONC in Washington. Ens. Edward Van Der Rhoer observed him in OP-20-GZ in 1944. He called Taylor an officer of superlative ability, a dark, intense man of medium height and build, and interestingly added that "Taylor was pleasant and attractive in manner, a person who seemed likely to enhance any social occasion."

In late 1944, Commander Taylor transferred to Hawaii for duty at FRUPac, remaining there through the end of the war. Afterward he served with the occupation forces in Japan. After further sea duty, he returned to Washington and then later, in 1953, he was assigned to the NSA. He became the director of intelligence at Headquarters, U.S. Naval Forces Japan, during 1955–1956.

Captain Taylor then served as the fleet intelligence officer of the Pacific Fleet, from 1956 through 1959, after which he returned to Washington for a number of follow-on intelligence assignments.

Taylor became DNI from 1963 to 1966—being promoted to flag rank in February 1964. In addition, from June 1963 through May 1966, Captain (and then Rear Admiral) Taylor served as the director of "Program C," which embraced the U.S. Navy's satellite reconnaissance element in the National Reconnaissance Program, consisting of the Technical Operations Group (representatives from the Naval Research Laboratory, the Naval Security Group, and the NSA).

In June 1966 he was further promoted to vice admiral and made deputy director of the Defense Intelligence Agency. Only three months later, President Lyndon Johnson appointed him as deputy director of the Central Intelligence Agency (DD/CIA), serving under CIA director Richard Helms.

His second year on that job saw Taylor particularly engaged. In April 1967, Mr. Helms asked the admiral to oversee a difficult, intra-CIA dispute involving Yuri

Nosenko, a Soviet defector. CIA counterintelligence chief James Jesus Angleton had accused Nosenko of being a double agent and provocateur sent by the Soviets to penetrate American intelligence. As a result of this concern, Nosenko had been held for several years by the CIA pending resolution. After investigation, Taylor concluded that Nosenko was not a double agent and that Mr. Helms should set him free. Despite strong objections from CIA counterintelligence, eventually—in March 1969—Nosenko was released and even put on the CIA payroll as a consultant.

In June 1967, Vice Admiral Taylor developed a memorandum for Mr. Helms concerning the Israeli attack upon the signals intelligence/communications ship USS *Liberty*. This was an occurrence during the Six Day War between Israel and several Arab nations. Taylor told Helms that "to me the picture thus far presents the distinct possibility that the Israelis knew that the *Liberty* might be their target and attacked anyway, either through confusion in command and control, or through deliberate disregard of instructions on the part of subordinates." Taylor's view helped convince Helms that the Israelis knew exactly what they were doing—an incident which remains controversial even today.

Taylor resigned as DDCI effective February 1969, and at that time also retired to private life. Rufe died on September 14, 1978. He was survived by his wife, Karin Gerdts Taylor, and two children.[1]

Vice Admiral Taylor's decorations included the Distinguished Service Medal, Bronze Star, Army Distinguished Unit Emblem, and the Navy Commendation Medal. He has also been named a Pioneer Officer of U.S. Naval Cryptology by the Naval Cryptologic Veterans Association.[2]

Sources

Holmes, 197.
Holtwick, 434, App. 111, 116, 123.
Lucky Bag, U.S. Naval Academy, 1933.
McGinnis, 22.
Naval Intelligence Professionals website, navintpro.net.
Prados, 211, 268–70, 302–3, 318, 730.
U.S. Navy, *Register of Commissioned and Warrant Officers.*
Van Der Rhoer, 71.

---

1. Mrs. Taylor (1914–2012) lived to be ninety-eight years old, passing away even while this book was being written. She was an accomplished linguist in her own right. She was born in Yokohama to Swedish parents, and was educated in both Sweden and Japan. She traveled the world with her husband and family, was fluent in Swedish, German, and Japanese, and was conversant in several other languages.

2. Taylor also continues to be remembered via the Naval Intelligence Foundation, which annually presents to an instructor (at both the Navy/Marine Corps Intelligence Training Center and the Fleet Intelligence Training Center Pacific) the "VADM Rufus L. Taylor Award for Excellence in Instruction."

CAPTAIN EDWARD HOWE WATSON, U.S. NAVY (1874–1942)

A superb leader—quiet and resolute; genial but exacting. First and foremost, Watson was a surface-ship sea officer, as were the majority of his generation—and he had been awarded the Navy Cross for his service in World War I. But in 1919 he geared up and went to Tokyo as the U.S. embassy's naval attaché, and turned in a remarkably good performance. "Watson was an exceptionally astute and resourceful intelligence officer, ideal for the job in a country whose navy was considered the primary potential adversary of the U.S. Navy." Sadly, his later career was essentially derailed in the 1923 Honda Point disaster; he was the commodore of the destroyer squadron of which seven ships were grounded on the California coast. Nevertheless, Watson was an innovative pioneer in the businesses of foreign attaché work and of intelligence; he laid groundwork in methodology and in professionalism which was emulated by many others in later years.

* * *

From the 1895 Naval Academy yearbook, *The Lucky Bag*:

I'd rather live With cheese and garlic, in a windmill, far, Than feed on cakes and have him talk to me, In any Summer-house in Christendom. [Activities: June Ball Committee, Hop Committee]

* * *

Edward H. Watson was born in Frankfort, Kentucky, on February 28, 1874, the son of Rear Admiral John Crittenden Watson and Elizabeth Thornton Watson. Ranked as a "Cadet Chief Petty Officer" during his senior year, he graduated from the U.S. Naval Academy in June 1895 along with such classmates as Worth Bagley and William H. Standley (there were only forty-five graduates, and in those days they were called naval cadets rather than midshipmen). Subsequent promotions included ensign, 1897; lieutenant (junior grade), 1900; lieutenant, 1901; lieutenant commander 1908; commander, 1915; and captain, 1918.

After his Annapolis graduation, Watson had sea duty in several ships during the rest of the decade—including Spanish-American War service on board the protected cruiser USS *Detroit*.

Mr. Watson had diverse assignments over the next dozen years, among them duty as aide to flag officers, recruiting work, and service in battleships, cruisers, and other vessels. Command of the store ship *Celtic* in 1912–1913 was followed by attendance at the Naval War College's two-year course. He next saw duty as executive officer of the battleship *Utah*, and then as commanding officer of the gunboat *Wheeling*.

Watson spent most of World War I in command of the transport *Madawaska* and then the Atlantic Fleet battleship *Alabama*. He received the Navy Cross for "exceptionally meritorious service in a duty of great responsibility" in the latter appointment.

Following brief preparation at the ONI, in March 1919 Watson became the U.S. Naval Attaché in Japan—leading five assistant attachés—and remaining in that post until May 1922.

Watson was adept at eliciting information from his Japanese counterparts. Watson and his assistants cultivated Captain (later Admiral and ambassador) Nomura Kichisaburo, the director of Japanese naval intelligence; Captain (later Admiral and chief of the naval staff) Nagano Osami; and Commander (later Admiral, premier, and navy minister) Yonai Mitsumasa) as sources of information. . . . Watson regularly hosted parties for these and other Japanese naval officials at some of Tokyo's best *geisha* houses, probing them for information on Japanese naval policy.

He made an enormous impression on several of his protégés and assistants in To-kyo, including future rear admirals John **McClaran** and Ellis **Zacharias**. This deep admiration was sustained for more than a quarter century, when Zacharias wrote that

> I found [Watson] a most gracious chief and an understanding guide to the scenes "back-stage" of Japanese naval politics, or what Japanese Admiral Sato himself called "Japanese Navalism." Captain Watson was one of the most likeable and dynamic, intelligent and alert naval attachés we have had in any country. He was extremely popular with the Japanese naval officers, who were mystified by his technique of telling them too much so that they could learn too little.
>
> When he first came to the job, he found that his predecessor had been uncomfortable about gathering information, so Watson was thus forced to start from scratch; but by the time he left the files were bulging with reports and documents, and the Japanese Navy was accurately delineated.

After leaving Japan, in July 1922 Watson took command of Destroyer Squadron 11 of the U.S. Battle Fleet, based on the West Coast. He flew his commodore's flag in the USS *Delphy*. Unfortunately, on the night of September 8, 1923, in heavy fog, navigation errors resulted in the loss of *seven* of the squadron's destroyers—but mer-cifully only twenty-three sailors—when they grounded on the rocky coast at Honda Point, California. Commodore Watson energetically organized rescue and survival measures for the several hundred shipwrecked sailors.

The ensuing court martial of Captain Watson and several other officers resulted in the loss of all chance for Watson's further promotion (he fell 150 numbers on the captains' list, which made it impossible for him to ever reach eligibility to be considered for rear admiral). However, Captain Watson's willing acceptance of full command responsibility, and his display of great personal character in a situation of considerable adversity, were widely admired both in and out of the navy. A contem-porary editorial in the *Army and Navy Journal* read in part,

> Nothing but praise can be given [to Captain Watson] for his outstanding manliness in assuming full responsibility and in seeking to relieve from blame those whom he terms his *able and loyal subordinates*. This is a type of genuine leadership of which the United States Navy may well be proud and in which it will find much strength.
>
> . . . Captain Watson has given a splendid example of the finest attributes of char-acter overcoming the elemental instinct of self-preservation. Voluntarily waiving the fundamental right of a defendant to place the burden of proof upon the prosecution, and to refrain from testifying under oath to any facts that might tend to incriminate himself, he took the witness stand and not only freely testified to facts relating to his own culpability—but also volunteered his opinion under oath that he was *wholly* re-sponsible for the disaster, and that *none* of his subordinates should be blamed.

This was an act of outstanding honor and leadership. In fact, the causes of the tragedy lay in several factors: too much haste, to be sure; but there was also unfamiliar new technology, darkness, fog, and a series of small human and mechanical errors—all resulting in the ships not being where their navigators believed they should be. Given the naval tradition of chain of command, the man at the top was certainly held responsible—and Captain Watson assertively did assume total responsibility. He later wrote, "My sentence—the maximum short of dismissal—is just and proper. For the Navy's sake it should be no lighter. . . . I should have greatly regretted any sentence short of a very heavy one."

As an interesting aside to this incident, Commodore Watson had a guest passenger on board the *Delphy* that fateful night. This was a State Department official named Eugene H. Dooman, who for almost eighteen years served as a counselor in the American Embassy in Tokyo. Born in Osaka to missionary parents, Dooman really knew Japan and could truly speak Japanese like a native; because of that he was the principal individual who periodically examined the U.S. Navy (as well as Army and State Department) immersion students as to their language progress. According to future rear admiral Arthur **McCollum**, "When you took an examination with Gene Dooman, you'd had it. You went through the loops. He was a hard taskmaster, and you had to make that every six months . . . if you didn't make it . . . you were sent home."

After the Honda Point courtsmartial, Captain Watson was assigned the important duty of Assistant Commandant of the Fourteenth Naval District, Territory of Hawaii, remaining there from 1925 until he left active duty in November 1929. In retirement, Watson resided in New York City and summered in Jamestown, Rhode Island, where he was a member of the Conanicut Yacht Club. For the rest of his life he retained an active interest in Japanese affairs.

Despite the Honda Point tragedy, Watson was a remarkably resourceful and skillful sailor and commander. But his true contribution and place in history lies in his groundbreaking vision and initiative in the new—and thus amorphous—fields of modern diplomatic attaché service and intelligence collection. Perhaps Rear Admiral Zacharias should have the final word on this superb officer:

> Captain Watson was a farseeing officer who regarded his mission to Japan as one that might secure the peace, if only by acquiring comprehensive knowledge of Japanese plans for war. "If we know," he used to say, "the minute details of Japanese plans for aggression, we are in a position to thwart them while they are still in the planning stage. Only knowledge of their moves well ahead of time can enable us to counteract those moves. Otherwise we shall one day be confronted with a surprise that will hit us right between the eyes."

Edward Watson died in Brooklyn, New York, on January 7, 1942. He had been married to Hermine Gratz Watson (1884–1977); they are buried together in Arlington National Cemetery. Among the captain's decorations and awards was the Navy Cross for battleship service in World War I.

Sources

Farago, *Broken Seal*, 28.
Lockwood and Adamson, 183, 209, 221, 235.
Lucky Bag, U.S. Naval Academy, 1895.
Mahnken, 34–35.
Military Times *Hall of Valor* website.
Naval History and Heritage Command Website, US People—Watson, Edward H. (1874–1942).
U.S. Navy, *Register of Commissioned and Warrant Officers.*
Zacharias, Ellis, 7–11, 39–40.

REAR ADMIRAL ETHELBERT WATTS, U.S. NAVY (1902–1966)

Served at ONI's Far Eastern Section, 1941–1943
"Bert" "Bertie"

Bert Watts was a tried-and-true American naval officer in addition to being an Orientalist by study and training. Yet he was a bit more unusual in that he both came into the world, and then departed it, on European soil. More usual, he did follow an almost typical career—for his generation of intelligence officers—of intelligence assignments intermingled with "black-shoe" surface-ship duties. One of the prewar ONI Japanese immersion students, he made use of that education with two full tours at the American embassy in Tokyo, as well as two years as a translator and analyst in ONI's Far Eastern Section. Later command assignments with amphibious forces, as well as several years of postwar work with the Central Intelligence Group and then the CIA, rounded out the spectacular career of a remarkable officer.

* * *

From the Annapolis yearbook, *The Lucky Bag*:

"Bert" sauntered into the Academy one languid day in June. After finding that his actions were no longer to be creatures of his own free will, but were to be controlled by a little volume entitled "Naval Academy Regulations," he concluded that the future would be far from pleasant. He was so unfortunate as to be caught smoking on three different occasions when he was not supposed to be indulging in such pursuits. . . . .To the casual observer, *Bert* appears to be suffering from *ennui*, but that is just a pose adopted to conceal the fact that he is a philosopher who knows thoroughly the world in which he dwells. He has an innocent, boyish attitude which is very deceptive, for, if the truth were known, we should see that life had not quietly passed him by. He is, above all things else, a true gentleman, and as such his classmates will always remember him. It is their sincere wish that he will find in his service life the success which he merits. [Activities: tennis, Masqueraders (the drama club)]

* * *

Ethelbert Watts was born on January 25, 1902, in Austria-Hungary, the son of Ethelbert Watts and Katharine Gregg Watts; the elder Ethelbert was a long-service U.S. diplomat and at the time was consul-general at Prague. The younger Ethelbert attended the Kent School in Kent, Connecticut, prior to his appointment to the U.S. Naval Academy in 1920. He graduated from Annapolis and was commissioned an ensign on June 5, 1924, along with such classmates as Thomas H. **Dyer**, Edwin T. **Layton**, Thomas A. **Huckins**, Daniel J. McCallum, John C. Waldron, and Hanson W. Baldwin. Further promotions came as follows: lieutenant (junior grade), 1927; lieutenant, 1933; lieutenant commander, 1939; commander, 1942; and captain, 1943. He retired in 1954 and was simultaneously given the rank of rear admiral on the retired list due to his high combat decorations from World War II.

Ensign Watts took three months' instruction at the Philadelphia Navy Yard before joining the crew of the battleship *Texas*. He continued service in that ship, operating with the Scouting Fleet, until July 1925 when she began a major overhaul. For the next six months he underwent a course of instruction at the Naval Torpedo School, Newport, Rhode Island. Completing that training in December, he reported on board the destroyer *Lardner*, operating consecutively with Destroyer Division 25, Squadron 9, Destroyer Squadrons, Scouting Fleet; U.S. Naval Forces, Europe; and then with Destroyer Division 27. During this time the *Lardner* operated in the Caribbean, in northern European waters, and in the Mediterranean.

Detached from the *Lardner* in May 1928, Bertie became one of ONI's special language/culture immersion students in Japan. He returned to the United States in July 1931, to then work at ONI in Washington for several months.

In March 1932, Mr. Watts reported on board the submarine-tender *Fulton*; at this time the ship was employed on survey duty in and around the Canal Zone. In

September 1932, Watts transferred to the carrier *Langley*, with Carrier Division 2, Battle Force. He then joined the heavy cruiser *San Francisco* in March 1933.

In April 1935, he relocated to Japan to become an assistant naval attaché at the American embassy.

At the close of that assignment, and between June 1937 and January 1941, he had destroyer duty as executive officer of the *Tillman*. He then was transferred to the destroyer *Leary* as commanding officer.

Lieutenant Commander Watts returned to the United States in the summer of 1941, and was assigned to the Far Eastern Section at ONI in Washington. One of his unusual jobs involved traveling to Lourenço Marques, in Mozambique, to help repatriate Americans who had been interred at the U.S. embassy in Tokyo when the war started. Those people (including naval attaché Cmdr. Henri **Smith-Hutton**)— as well as other Americans who'd been in Asia—were transferred from the Japanese liner *Asama Maru* and the Italian liner *Conte Verdi* to the Swedish liner *Gripsholm*. Mr. Watts carefully checked every listed name. He also accounted for all the Japanese citizens who were on board the *Gripsholm* and who were then moved to the *Asama Maru* in exchange—around 2,000 all told.

Watts was an assistant to Lt. Cmdr. Arthur **McCollum** at ONI in 1941, covering the Japan Desk and supervising (along with McCollum) the communications intelligence pipeline to President Roosevelt—through Rear Adm. John R. Beardall, FDR's naval aide. McCollum, Watts, and Cmdr. Hartwell C. Davis were particularly good at rapidly translating Japanese messages into workable English. Mr. Watts was the ONI Far East Section night-watch duty officer on the evening of December 6 and early morning of December 7, 1941.

Noted author Ladislas Farago has commented that in 1943, when ONI deputy director Capt. Ellis **Zacharias** departed Washington to command the battleship *New Mexico*, the Japanese desk remained in the particularly good hands of Bertie Watts and a Marine colonel named Ronald A. Boone.

However, later in that same year, Commander Watts also left Washington and attached to the amphibious-force flagship *Appalachian* as executive officer. Shortly after that he was promoted to captain. While on board the *Appalachian*, he participated in the Battle of Kwajalein in early February 1944. Detached in June, he underwent instruction at the Amphibious Training Base, Norfolk, and then assumed command of LST Group 17 within Task Group 79.6, on board *LST 1028* as his flagship. On January 9, 1945, during the Lingayen Gulf operation (Luzon, Philippine Islands), the *LST 1028* was struck and seriously damaged by a Japanese suicide boat.

Relieved of that command in April 1945, Captain Watts was transferred to take over LST Flotilla 8, operating in the vicinity of Kowloon, China (north of Hong Kong). He also served as commander of Task Unit 79.1.9 during the assault landing at Brunei Bay (on the north coast of Borneo) on June 11, 1945.

Back in Washington by July 1946, Bert was assigned to the Central Intelligence Group—which not long after became the CIA. He served there until June 1950, when he was ordered to the American Embassy, London, as assistant naval attaché.

Then, his next assignment was as the naval attaché, Tokyo, from 1952 until 1954. Captain Watts retired in June 1954, and was simultaneously promoted to rear admiral on the retired list due to his wartime combat decorations. Among his many awards were two Legion of Merit medals with the Combat "V" device—one awarded by the Navy for service in Lingayen Gulf and Okinawa, and another by the Army for his service in the vicinity of Kowloon. In addition, he received the Navy Commendation Ribbon with Combat "V," the Philippine Liberation Ribbon, and the China Service Medal.

Rear Admiral Watts passed away, in Prunay-sous-Ablis, France, in 1966. He was married to Elizabeth Lee Snyder Watts (1903–2003); they had two children, Philip and Katharine. In the early 1980s, Mrs. Watts put in considerable effort helping Rear Adm. Edwin Layton (and his coauthors) work on Layton's reminisces, *"And I Was There": Pearl Harbor and Midway—Breaking the Secrets.*

Admiral and Mrs. Watts are buried together at Arlington National Cemetery.

Sources

Captain Ethelbert Watts, USN. Official Biography. U.S. Navy. 8 August 1950. Courtesy of the Naval Historical Foundation.

Dorwart, *Conflict of Duty,* 160, 177.

Farago, *Broken Seal,* 102, 358.

Farago, *Burn after Reading,* 284.

Layton, *"And I Was There,"* 6, 24.

Lucky Bag, U.S. Naval Academy, 1924.

Prados, 347.

Morison, XIII, 311.

Stinnet, 15, 167, 231.

U.S. Navy, *Register of Commissioned and Warrant Officers.*

REAR ADMIRAL ELLIS MARK ZACHARIAS SR., U.S. NAVY (1890–1961)

The Navy's foremost Japanese linguist
The Navy's most accomplished intelligence expert
The "Billy Mitchell" of naval intelligence
The "dynamo" of O.N.I.
"Zach" "Captain Zach"

Devoted to a career as a conventional sea officer which included the command of four ships—the last one a battleship in combat—Ellis Zacharias also executed a remarkable parallel career in naval intelligence, serving as a language officer, cryptographer, assistant attaché, district intelligence officer, deputy director of naval intelligence, and master practitioner of psychological warfare.

In fact, in the spring of 1941, Zacharias (or Zach, as he was commonly called) personally submitted a theory to the commander in chief of the U.S. Pacific Fleet at Pearl Harbor. In this theory, he speculated that the Japanese *might* launch a surprise attack against the United States—and *if* they did such a thing, it could very well be early on a Sunday morning. (Completely unknown to Zacharias or to anyone else in the United States, there indeed was forthcoming a Japanese attack on Pearl Harbor—and ironically it was going to be planned by one of Zach's old poker-playing partners from the 1920s, Yamamoto Isoroku, who by 1941 was commander in chief of the Japanese fleet.)

Zacharias's speculation about such an attack was a product of his enormous, life-long interest in intelligence, primarily in Japanese affairs—a field and a subject that were not held as a high priority by many in those days. (In fact, in 1920—the year that Zach went to Japan for immersion language study—the Far Eastern Section of the ONI had only "one room, one officer, and one secretary.") His twenty-five years in intelligence (out of a total of thirty-four in the navy) display remarkable contributions, but also show him to be a very colorful and controversial figure—and they saw occasional clashes with superiors, a few unwelcome assignments, and ultimate failure to gain the full recognition that his contributions merited.

*   *   *

From the 1912 Naval Academy yearbook, *The Lucky Bag*:

> *Zach* is eminently the man of "funny noises." He's "all the time a-foolin'," and as a mimic he hasn't an equal. He achieved fame in that line at the *Indiana's* "Smoker" by repeating a certain extraordinary speech, and around quarters and aboard ship he has made many dull moments pass quickly with his entertaining stunts. In more senses than one, *Zach* is the greatest horseman of the class. He keeps a choice collection of "despoudres"— another noise of his. He denies that he's a fusser [*smooth, careful, excessively concerned with unimportant matters—as well as other midshipmen's dates*] but inconsistently attends every hop and seldom as a stag. Hasn't lost his heart yet, but it won't be hard for some girl to get it. He loves to play according to Hoyle and his own steady judgment, aided always by his patent positive motion ratchet wheel, which rarely slips a cog. [Activities: Lettered in gymnastics]

*   *   *

Ellis Zacharias was born in Jacksonville, Florida, on January 1, 1890. His parents, Aaron and Teresa Budwig Zacharias, were early settlers of Jacksonville—Aaron having arrived there shortly after the Civil War. As an eight-year-old boy, Zach had watched American warships sail past the Florida coast as they deployed for the Spanish-American War. "Enraptured, I stood watching the steaming parade. Then and there, the lure of the *Navy*—rather than the *sea*—gripped me." Ellis, the youngest of five boys and two girls, was in due course appointed to the Naval Academy in

1908. Zach graduated high in his class in June 1912, along with classmates Richard E. Byrd Jr., Charles A. Lockwood, Elliott Buckmaster, Walter S. Delaney, Louis E. Denfeld, and Charles H. McMorris. Having the distinction of being the only Jewish graduate of Annapolis for at least a ten-year period, Zacharias entered the fleet and served on a variety of naval vessels. He was on board the battleship USS *Arkansas* when that ship transported President William Howard Taft to inspect the Panama Canal—before water was let into it—in October 1912. From 1913 to 1915 he served on board the battleship *Virginia*. Zacharias was then stationed for a time on the survey ship *Hannibal*. During World War I, he was engineering officer of the cruiser *Raleigh* and gunnery officer on board the cruiser *Pittsburgh*.

One fall day in 1913, in the wardroom of the *Virginia*, Ensign Zacharias listened in fascination as the mess treasurer, Lt. Fred **Rogers**, discussed with the senior mess steward why lunch was very late—a lengthy discussion *in fluent Japanese*. Coincidentally—fortuitously for his messmates—Rogers was the only certified Japanese-language officer in the entire U.S. Navy. This scene became an epiphany for Zacharias, who soon decided that he too wanted to become a language officer and an expert on Japan. Seven years later, Commander Rogers (at the Japan Desk at ONI) cabled Lieutenant Zacharias (then accompanying a midshipman training cruise) to ask if he still were interested. "Your message, affirmative," Zacharias immediately replied.

So, in mid-1920 Zacharias was in Washington, attached to ONI for temporary duty, awaiting the orders which would take him to Tokyo for study. He took an apartment above that of the Japanese naval attaché, and soon determined that the attaché regularly entertained a number of female secretaries employed by the Navy Department. Zacharias and his ONI boss, Capt. Andrew Long, quickly supplied the attaché some hand-picked ladies of their own. One of these became friendly with the assistant attaché, who shortly divulged that a full paper copy of the Japanese Navy's operational code was in the United States—in a safe inside the office of the vice-consul in New York City. This amazing discovery quickly led to a break-and-entry "black-bag" job which yielded a photographed copy of the codebook. This was a sensational triumph for American naval intelligence. Designated at Main Navy as JN-1 (for Japanese Navy, Code One), it also was called the *Red Book*, or just *Red*, because of the red-colored binder in which the copied documents were kept.[1]

Soon Zacharias, who was now very ready to make his mark in intelligence work, received his Tokyo orders. There he indeed learned to speak Japanese fluently, and he became very well acquainted with many of the Japanese officers and government officials who were to control that country's fortunes in later years.

In Tokyo, Zacharias energetically and enthusiastically immersed himself in the study of the language and culture. The man famous for mimicry as an Annapolis midshipman found such skills invaluable as he studied a language where so much depended upon intonation. In fact, for a protracted period, Zach moved himself to a small, isolated fishing village called Zuchi, to experience total, true immersion. Back

---

1. By the time of the attack on Pearl Harbor, U.S. Navy cryptanalysts were minimally successful in reading Japanese messages at the JN-25 level—the twenty-fifth variant of this code.

in Tokyo, he also spent some time studying the craft of intelligence under the naval attaché to Japan, Capt. Edward **Watson**, an extremely dynamic and resourceful officer. Watson was also very popular with many Japanese naval officers.

One such officer was Capt. Nomura Kichisaburō; under Watson's tutelage, Zach made Nomura's acquaintance in 1921 and was very impressed with his command of English, broad outlook, and critical mind. Zacharias would socialize with Nomura again, twenty years later, when *Admiral* Nomura was the newly appointed Japanese ambassador to the United States—sent to Washington just a few months before the Pearl Harbor attack.

Leading up to the November 1921 Washington Naval Conference on the Limit of Armaments, Captain Long—the director of ONI—tasked attaché Captain Watson. He was to see if he could "explore the extent to which the Japanese [would be] willing to go in accepting a compromise" at the forthcoming conference in regard to the number and size of their ships. Watson, well-connected with high-ranking Japanese officers, sent two of his protégés—Lt. Cmdr. Zacharias and Lt. Cmdr. John **Mc-Claran**—to a series of parties to see what could come of casual give-and-take conversation. "The information we were permitted to dole out was carefully apportioned and weighed," Zacharias wrote later, "leading questions were rehearsed in advance, even the tone of the conversation and feigned surprises were practiced ahead of time so as to play our role as perfectly as possible." It worked—Zacharias and McClaran found out that compromise was definitely a possibility, "even on America's terms." This was priceless information for American negotiators, obtained five weeks before the conference began.[2]

As he continued his language and cultural studies, Zacharias proceeded in developing contacts and gathering information. He learned about Japanese attitudes toward many things, including the arms limitations to be imposed on the "Land of the Rising Sun." He also learned that a number of important figures in the Japanese government and military viewed the United States as a probable future enemy—and therefore as an open adversary in the game of intelligence—and he discovered that the Japanese army and navy were radically different from each other in culture, philosophy, and worldview. He also became aware of certain inadequacies of the American intelligence-gathering apparatus in Japan and the Japanese-controlled islands in the Pacific, such as the lack of manpower, resources, and—in particular—the lack of importance that American authorities (by no means all, but most) placed on intelligence operations, particularly in Japan.

He also watched over colleagues, and future colleagues. For example, newly arrived immersion language student (and future rear admiral) Arthur **McCollum** later wrote that

---

2. It must be also noted that pioneering American codebreaker Herbert Yardley and his staff were reading parts of Japanese traffic when the United States hosted the Washington Naval Conference in 1921. The information his "Cipher Bureau" provided the American delegation, regarding the Japanese government's absolute minimum acceptable battleship requirements, was also extremely helpful in getting the Japanese to agree to a lower ratio of battleships than what they really wanted. This achievement was to be the height of Yardley's cryptanalytic career.

Lt. Cmdr. Zacharias very kindly took me in to live with him. He and the former assistant naval attaché had rented a house and acquired a couple of servants out in one of the suburbs of Tokyo; there was a little colony of language students there. Zach very kindly took me under his wing because I didn't know anything.

The most noteworthy single event that occurred while Zacharias was stationed in Japan was the devastating Yokohama earthquake of September 1, 1923. Coincidentally in Yokohama on that day, Zach threw himself into rescue work as well as trying to calm and cheer as many people as possible amidst the widespread fires, destruction, and ruin. Moreover, he gained a rare insight into the Japanese character under extreme stress. He later described the scene:

> From the first moment of crisis and horror it was the foreigners among the crowd who recovered from panic and started rescue efforts. The Japanese were captives of an amazing psychic inertia, completely incapable of grasping the situation. They seemed struck to absolute helplessness.

After the earthquake had ceased, they went about their work with "an impassive indifference in the face of the destruction" around them. From this point forward, throughout his entire professional life, Zacharias worked hard to comprehend the Japanese character—a subject which he (and other experts) found extremely challenging. Among other things, these early observations later proved extremely useful in 1945 when Zacharias, in a series of Japanese-language radio broadcasts, put together an elaborate psychological-warfare attempt to persuade the Japanese high command to surrender.

Shortly before leaving Japan, Zach was temporarily assigned (November–December 1923) as first lieutenant of the USS *Huron*, flagship of the Asiatic Fleet. However, forty-two months after departing Washington for Japan, Zacharias found himself heading back to ONI. By the time Zach left Japan, he was convinced that the Japanese government was evolving into a scheming, imperialistic power determined on considerable Asian and Pacific-rim expansion—which would undoubtedly require smashing the United States. It's thus easy to imagine his surprise when the navy had no follow-up intelligence job for him, nor any real interest in his thoughts and observations.

> The attitude with which I was confronted upon my return was like cold water thrown upon the fire that burned within me. The Office of Naval Intelligence continued its protracted hibernations, and nobody in the Navy Department showed other than slightly amused interest in my experiences and ideas.
>
> There was no one to take up seriously the question of my assignment to a post which would best utilize and justify the three years in Japan. There was little more than passing interest in the reports of my observations, and by calling attention to certain undeniable facts which I felt at least demanded consideration, I risked being called a *daydreamer* who sees ghosts.

Perhaps he shouldn't have been overly surprised. Between the world wars, code-breaking and—even *worse*—intelligence were extraordinarily low on the navy's hierarchy of prestige. In the eyes of many officers, these activities were at best very far removed from the main business of the navy—forging powerful fleets to dominate any adversary. At worst, people in these fields were generally viewed as odd and, sometimes, even as crackpots. "[Intelligence] was not at all accepted in the pre–World War II Navy," wrote Vice Adm. George C. Dyer, a submarine/destroyer/cruiser officer who served (as a captain) as Adm. Ernest King's "personal intelligence officer" in 1942. "By and large it just didn't arouse people's interest."

So, Mr. Zacharias was just expected to return to sea duty as per the general routine of a normal naval career. Accordingly he became the navigator—with minor collateral duties as ship's intelligence officer—of the cruiser *Rochester*, which was stationed off the Panama Canal Zone. This assignment actually appealed to Zacharias, who was aware that the Japanese navy had an enormous interest in the canal, and thus he'd be able to do some intelligence and counterintelligence work. While there, Zach met Miss Claire Miller at Balboa; Miss Miller was a pioneer aviator and experienced interpreter of aerial photography. Mr. Zacharias was immediately captivated; six months later they were married—and soon after that the *Rochester* returned to the U.S. East Coast. However, before the *Rochester* finally left the area, her last operation was to transport General of the Armies John "Black Jack" Pershing to Chile, so that he could mediate the Tacna-Arica dispute between Chile and Peru.

In early 1926 the deputy director of naval intelligence—Capt. William Galbraith—recognized Lieutenant Commander Zacharias's unusual interest in intelligence operations and brought him back to Main Navy in Washington. This was to be for a temporary detail with the ONC's secret cryptanalysis unit, the "Research Desk." It came about because Zach's old Tokyo colleague, John McClaran, was now head of the ONI Far Eastern Desk, and was charged to supervise the "Red" code book translation. Lt. Joseph **Rochefort**, then head of the Research Desk, had suggested that it would be extremely helpful if they could get a naval officer familiar with the Japanese language and also the Japanese military and naval lexicon. In the opinion of Commander McClaran, Zach was the foremost Japanese linguist in the navy. Thus, Mr. Zacharias reported to Main Navy and worked with Mr. Rochefort, Mrs. Agnes **Driscoll**, and a number of others in ONI and ONC for about seven months. "This assignment opened up before me new vistas of modern intelligence. The office was in charge of one of the most delicate, intricate, and challenging aspects of intelligence: cryptanalysis." Zacharias immersed himself. He felt there was a lot of "romance" inherently attached to this work, but he didn't think the cryptanalysts particularly shared his view. Even so,

I was now part of this secret order and immensely proud to belong to the small group of nameless people. Preoccupied then as I became with applied numerology, I selected an apartment house at 1616 16th Street.

We were just a few then, in Room 2646, young people who gave ourselves to cryptology with the same ascetic devotion with which young men enter a monastery. It was known to everyone that the secrecy of our work would prevent the ordinary recognition accorded to other accomplishments.[3]

Of course, Zach was really there to lend translation expertise rather than break codes; he did an outstanding job filling in the translation gaps that ONI's translator, Dr. Emerson Haworth, had not been able to do with his remarkable—but nontechnical—command of the Japanese language. In five months Zach had clarified all of the problem terms and phrases that thus far had been untranslatable.

During this short period of duty, Zacharias further justified the confidence of Galbraith and McClaran by his smooth surveillance of Capt. Yamamoto Isoroku, who'd come to Washington as the Japanese naval attaché. Zach was very impressed by Yamamoto, having briefly met him early on in Japan and now socializing with him in Washington. Yamamoto's relatively frequent parties were men only and included moderate drinking and serious card playing. "Poker was his favorite, and he played it with an unreserved and unconcealed determination, as if he must defeat us at *this* game before he could defeat us in *war*." Zach found Yamamoto exceptionally able, forceful, and quick-thinking. Through conversation he also detected a huge interest, on the part of Yamamoto, in combining seapower and airpower.

After this brief Washington posting, Zacharias's career continued on the rise when, later in 1926, he was assigned to the Asiatic Station as an intelligence officer specializing in cryptographic research.

In October 1926, the destroyer *McCormick* sailed into the Yellow Sea and the vicinity of Hong Kong. On board were Zacharias—temporarily detailed as her captain—six extra radiomen, and a collection of electronic gear, all ready to experiment with shipboard radio surveillance. It went well, with good results. Zach left the ship at Hong Kong and went on to Manila. He revamped two U.S. Navy radio stations in the Philippines and, moving on, did the same in Shanghai (the station there was on the fourth floor of the American consulate, just opposite the Astor House), adding radio surveillance to their functions. By summer of 1927 the navy had operational intercept stations in all of these places, as well as in Guam.

In October 1927, Zacharias went aboard the light cruiser *Marblehead*, at Shanghai, which was scheduled to go to Japan on a pre-arranged visit. As with the *McCormick* experiment, Zach brought extra radiomen and equipment. Here he headed the first comprehensive radio communication intercept unit, hoping to successfully monitor Japanese naval radio communications during a large training maneuver. On the fourth day out, in the area of extensive 170-ship Imperial Navy maneuvers and carrier training operations, they had great success in intercepting, translating, and transcribing considerable message traffic. Zacharias thought that the information gained during this mission "represented a long step forward in our positive intel-

---

3. Despite what he wrote here, Zacharias never really caught a case of *cryptographitis*, which many of the other people in this book did. Again, according to the great French code expert Colonel Étienne Bazèries, *cryptographitis* is "a sort of subtle, all-pervading, incurable malady." Zach certainly valued cryptanalysis and cryptanalysts, but personally remained a more all-source intelligence officer/analyst.

ligence against Japan." In fact, Zach felt that it was so successful that he was able to put together a "complete and accurate plan of the entire operation," along with great insight into the difficulty the Japanese were having with landing aircraft onto their carriers. The DNC, Capt. T. T. Craven, agreed, writing that "it covers a line of naval information which is very important for us to get hold of, and the value of which we have so far failed to appreciate."

At this point, Zacharias began to look at himself as an experienced IO, one of very few who embraced—or was *trying* to embrace—intelligence as a permanent career.

> My initiation into intelligence now belonged to the past. I was no longer a neophyte but an experienced hand, devising ways and means by which both the quality and quantity of vital information could be improved through the introduction of new methods and the opening up of new avenues. I was given adequate scope for my pioneering work, although the initiative remained with me most of the time.
>
> Often I had to combat incompetence, indifference, and ignorance. I was opposed by men who had a negative approach to everything and whose life philosophy was that the best way to get along was to do nothing. My fingers were occasionally burned, and at times my ears were "pinned back." But frequently I was supported by enthusiastic and forward-looking superiors who were at least willing to provide me with the rope on which I could do a bit of dangerous tightrope walking—or with which I might hang myself.

He also considered himself a major cog in America's intelligence efforts in the Pacific, because

> by 1928 I was determined to do whatever I could to remedy a situation which I felt was a threat to national security. As usual, I made plans for approval, but they were found to be too *ambitious*. So I shifted for myself as best I could. I did obtain permission to return to Tokyo on my way to Washington from China for what officially was described as a refresher course. I felt the need of brushing up on my Japanese, renewing contacts, and making further observations on the spot.

In November 1928, Zacharias began the first of a pair of tours as head of ONI's Far Eastern Section. The available intelligence resources were modest—initially the entire office consisted of Zacharias and a secretary, very similar to the staffing of the section in 1920—in Room 2715, OP-16-B, Special Intelligence, working under Lt. Cmdr. Aaron "Tip" Merrill. Later, however, the staff did increase as tensions rose following the Japanese invasion of Manchuria in 1931.

In 1929, Lt. Joe Rochefort was sent to the immersion language training in Japan. According to Rochefort, "Zach told me he was responsible for this." Zacharias doesn't mention it in his autobiography, but it could well be true; Zach had been very impressed with Rochefort back in 1926, and he certainly was in a position at ONI to advocate for him.

In 1931, still locked in the traditional line officer's rotation of sea and shore duty, Zacharias left ONI to command the destroyer *Dorsey*. Before joining the *Dorsey*, he spent several weeks accompanying the party of Prince Takamatsu (a brother of the

Japanese emperor) and Princess Takamatsu on a tour of the United States. After his destroyer command, Zach then spent a year in Newport, Rhode Island, taking the postgraduate strategy course at the Naval War College. Zacharias returned to Washington in 1934, once again as head of ONI's Far Eastern Section.

> When I had departed ONI in 1931, I'd left a section still understaffed and overworked, woefully inadequate as a truly effective part of our defense system. But now, in 1934, there was a different atmosphere, a refreshing breeze filling for the first time the sails of Naval Intelligence. The effects of withdrawal from our commitments as a great sea power no longer existed.
>
> The Navy Department was wide awake to its responsibilities as the nation's first line of defense. Still hampered by certain defeatist influences—especially in our diplomatic circles—and by isolationist indifference pervading some sections of Capitol Hill, the Navy was nevertheless going ahead full speed, bolstered by the support it received from the White House and its Navy-minded occupant.

Under a new director of ONI, Capt. William D. "Pulie" Puleston, Zacharias soon found himself heavily involved in intelligence and counterintelligence activities against the Japanese. Zach believed that Puleston was one of the very few "great" DNIs that the navy had ever seen. Many years later, Rear Adm. Edwin **Layton** would write that

> Captain Puleston improved relations between the Office of Naval Intelligence and the Office of Naval Communications. He was one of the moving forces in expanding our secret radio war against the Japanese during his three-year tenure as Director of Naval Intelligence. He was assisted by Ellis Zacharias, his Far East section chief. Duty as an immersion language student, and later as assistant naval attaché in Tokyo, had persuaded Zacharias that sooner or later we'd have to fight the Japanese for control of the Pacific.

It was at this point that senior Japanese naval attaché Capt. Yamaguchi Tamon, as Zacharias later disclosed, "came up to bat."

> The district intelligence officer of the 11th Naval District—Joe Rochefort—reported an espionage case to Washington, one of considerable proportions—the first big case of counterespionage since the end of World War I. All hands in naval intelligence and especially in the Far Eastern Section were assigned to help in this investigation.

Moreover, as mentioned in the chapter on Agnes Driscoll, both she and Edwin Layton—at the Research Desk of Naval Communications—were involved. Yamaguchi's principal on this case was a Lt. Cmdr. Miyazaki Toshio, a language officer at the University of California. The game was obtaining sensitive U.S. Navy gunnery and engineering documents, which were then being passed to the Japanese by a former out-of-luck and out-of-money sailor named Thompson. Once enough evidence had been collected in the San Diego-San Pedro area, Zacharias was tasked to make the case for the prosecutors. Flying back and forth between Washington and

Los Angeles, Zach presented the evidence to the assistant attorney-general of the United States, which led to Mr. Thompson's conviction—and Mr. Miyazaki's hastily arranged departure for Tokyo.

When not chasing spies, Zach and his staff were collecting everything they could that might be useful—and turning it all over in their minds, thoroughly analyzing and organizing the information, and making exhaustive studies of developments. For example, he "made sure his Far Eastern Desk examined every Naval War College study on Japan with considerable care and thought, especially those on economic subjects." Zacharias also "revised earlier silly ONI estimates about the Japanese inability to operate aircraft effectively from carriers at sea."[4] Also, during this assignment at ONI, he again rubbed shoulders with such future intelligence luminaries as Lt. Arthur McCollum and of course Lt. Edwin Layton.

There were some cloak-and-dagger things to do as well; for example, a remarkable operation occurred in July 1935. Not at all finished with Captain Yamaguchi, Lieutenant Commander Zacharias and his wife, Claire, gave a dinner party for the Japanese attaché and his staff at their home on Porter Street in Washington. Zacharias had proposed it as a celebration of the *chugen*, a midsummer festival in Japan, and the dinner included turtle soup served in lacquered Japanese bowls. Yamaguchi and Zacharias were long-time friends *and* rivals, each having scored intelligence coups against the other.[5] During the dinner, at Zacharias's direction, Lieutenant Jack **Holtwick** and Chief Radioman Walter **McGregor** were in the Alban Towers on Wisconsin Avenue. In the guise of overall-clad, toolbox-carrying electricians (*Jack* and *Mack*, as it were), they were carefully examining Yamaguchi's apartment/office. While pretending to fix a power failure in the suite, their covert mission was to determine whether—as ONI suspected—the attaché kept an electric cipher machine on his premises. Short of actually finding a machine, "the inspection by flashlight," Zacharias later wrote, "covered everything we desired," which included looking over (but not taking) various crypto-paraphernalia and papers. This information, combined with some other clues found elsewhere, allowed the extremely clever Lieutenant Holtwick to actually assemble a working copy of the machine—to the great advantage of American communications intelligence.[6]

In 1937, Captain Puleston "accelerated counterespionage against Japan, assigning an eager Zacharias to unearth the ruses employed by . . . Yamaguchi to cover Japanese spies in the United States."

It wasn't just ONI that had these concerns. In 1935 the commander in chief of the U.S. Pacific Fleet, Adm. Joseph M. Reeves, had made Lt. Joe Rochefort his

---

4. ONI had developed a strange theory that Japanese carrier pilots lacked the twenty/twenty visual acuity needed for good carrier operational proficiency. This became part of a notorious early-on underrating of Japanese aviators by the U.S. Navy.

5. Yamaguchi Tamon (1892–1942) later became a rear admiral. He was an alumnus of Princeton University, attending 1921–1923. In the early part of World War II, he was the commander of the Japanese Navy's 2nd Carrier Division, consisting of the aircraft carriers *Sōryū* and flagship *Hiryū*. Yamaguchi was killed at the Battle of Midway, choosing to go down with his sinking flagship.

6. This adventure is covered in more detail in the chapter on Capt. Jack Holtwick.

intelligence officer in San Pedro/San Diego (the Eleventh Naval District) to help work against suspected Japanese agents conducting espionage in that area. During this time, according to Rochefort, Zacharias suggested to him that he put "spies" on the U.S. Navy ships to look for "disloyalty." Both Rochefort (*and* Admiral Reeves) rejected this overly aggressive suggestion—but Rochefort did get DNI Captain Puleston to send their mutual friend Lieutenant McCollum out to the Hydrographic Office at San Pedro to go undercover in the area.

Through the years, even while on sea duty, Zacharias kept in constant touch with ONI personnel; indeed, he actively cultivated his contacts. A circle of enthusiastic intelligence experts gravitated around him, including Captain Puleston, future captain Henri **Smith-Hutton**, future army colonel Sidney Mashbir, future rear admirals Cecil **Coggins** and Arthur McCollum, future marine major general William Worton, and future ambassador William **Sebald**. Edwin Layton, who was become the fleet intelligence officer on Adm. Husband E. Kimmel's staff at the time of the attack on Pearl Harbor, later remarked that Zach was apparently always "talent scouting in anticipation of achieving his ambition to be director of naval intelligence." This admittedly biased group of officers considered Zacharias to be—arguably—the foremost U.S. naval intelligence officer of the day. Amusingly, Smith-Hutton also remarked that Zach "impressed me as being a very energetic officer, with many unusual ideas; perhaps slightly eccentric, but talkative and good company."

In fact, a good example of Zacharias's "talent scouting"—and even influencing assignments—came in the summer of 1939 when Eddie Layton visited with Zacharias in San Diego; Zach was then IO for the Eleventh Naval District. While drinking daiquiris, Zacharias asked Layton if he'd like to be FIO for the Pacific Fleet. Zacharias felt that war was just over the horizon, and that the Pacific Fleet needed an IO who was an excellent Japanese linguist and, moreover, that officer would need an assistant IO who was one as well. As a result, Layton wrote later, "I was not surprised when the following year orders came to me to report to flagship *Pennsylvania* as FIO—and Bob Hudson joined shortly after as my assistant."

In June 1936, Zacharias was sent to sea as executive officer (second in command) of the cruiser *Richmond*. In 1937 the *Richmond* became part of that year's U.S. Navy fleet problem, with Zach's ship part of the "Orange" (which is to say the Japanese) fleet. "We were supposed to bring the war to American shores to determine whether a breakthrough by an enemy naval force was at all possible." In fact, this fleet exercise did reveal to the Americans "certain weak spots in our defenses and proved the distinct possibility that a daring skillfully executed Japanese maneuver could break through to our most vital defense installations." Moreover, via observations of this same exercise, studying published reports—and other means—the real-life Japanese Navy also became convinced "that [the U.S. was] vulnerable . . . [and] in a war against the United States they had a chance for strategic success."

In the spring of 1938, as mentioned earlier, Zacharias was detailed as intelligence officer of the Eleventh Naval District in San Diego, "the very hub of the wheel of Japanese espionage." There he kept extremely busy working against Japanese, German, and even Soviet intelligence agents ashore—not to mention the huge Japanese fishing fleet constantly off the U.S. West Coast, full of professional and amateur spies.

During this time, while on a trip to Washington, Zach visited FBI director J. Edgar Hoover and discussed a joint espionage system for the West Coast. But "Hoover thought the scheme extravagant, and when the abrasive naval officer persisted, Hoover apparently threw him out of the office."

By 1938 the Japanese intelligence network had been reorganized and was growing furiously. Its task was made easier by the availability of information in the United States. Zacharias was impressed with the analysis of a World War I–era German naval intelligence agent, Capt. Franz D. J. von Rintelen. He had written that trips to the U.S. Government Printing Office, to purchase government-produced publications, usually yielded enormous quantities of intelligence data concerning American defense capabilities—information that agents in another country would have had immense difficulty in obtaining. The large number of Japanese agents, and the vast quantities of information available to them, had the unintended effect of reducing the quality and effectiveness of their intelligence operation. Zacharias agreed with von Rintelen, believing that it was a case of knowing too much and therefore understanding too little—the concept of "information overload." Other obstacles for Japanese intelligence agents concerned the immense size of the country and the fluid nature of its defense planning. But Zach still had concerns for security of vital information because "Americans do talk too much for comfort," and that "the press frequently does reveal too much."

Just before finishing his tour as the DIO in San Diego, Zacharias learned from a confidential informant about an alleged Japanese scheme for a twelve-plane suicide air raid on an American naval base—supposedly scheduled for October 17, 1940. The goal was to destroy at least four capital ships so as to create a more equitable ratio with the Japanese fleet; the attack would be disavowed by the Japanese government as work by independent fanatics. Zach determined that the only likely target ships were anchored at San Pedro, and that the Japanese aircraft could possibly be hidden in Mexico. The ships were immediately alerted to the danger. The incident did not occur, and thus October 17 passed as "a day of anticlimax." Still, Zacharias became even more sure that Japan was moving vigorously toward a wartime stance—even more so in the wake of Japan signing the "Tripartite Pact" with Germany and Italy. Zach thought it obvious that the large U.S. battleship force in the Pacific was being regarded more and more as the chief hindrance to Japanese plans for expansion.

Interestingly, in early 1941 another new director of naval intelligence—Capt. Alan Kirk—was himself extremely focused upon domestic security, counter-espionage, and police work. While of course Zacharias was as well, in Zach's opinion Kirk was *too* narrowly focused. To no avail, Zacharias tried to widen Kirk's view, writing to him that "purely investigative activities . . . are only a small segment of a military operational function; therefore these activities must be kept on the proper plane if the tail is not to wag the dog."

From late 1940 to early June 1942, Captain Zacharias commanded the heavy cruiser USS *Salt Lake City*. While the *Salt Lake City* was in San Francisco for some repairs and modifications, Zacharias's suspicions of Japanese aggression further hardened after a February 1941 conversation with Adm. Nomura Kichisaburō. Nomura was then en route to Washington to assume his post as Japanese ambassador to the United States. As mentioned earlier, Zach and Nomura were friendly from years before, having met in 1920 while Zacharias was stationed in Japan. Zach felt that Nomura was sent to Washington to enlist help from the Americans to facilitate Japan's new attempts to make peace with China, to prevent an American embargo of oil, and to lift embargos of other essential exports to Japan.

Nomura sent his aides out of the room, and during what Zacharias termed an "amazingly frank" discussion, the ambassador appeared to be deeply fearful of the growing power concentrated in the hands of the Japanese war extremists. Nomura told Zacharias—one of only two people in the United States "to whom he could open his heart"—that he believed that a conflict with the United States would gravely harm or even destroy the Japanese empire, and he appeared resigned that such a war might well be inevitable.

His years monitoring Japanese fleet maneuvers, the "false alarm" of October 1940, and now the seriousness of Ambassador Nomura's confidences all "crystallized" Zach's thinking. He was now convinced that if the Japanese indeed decided to initiate hostilities, a sneak attack on a U.S. fleet base would likely constitute the opening salvo.

Zacharias made a written report of his meeting with Nomura and sent it to Adm. Harold "Betty" Stark, the CNO, and to Adm. Husband "Kim" Kimmel, the commander in chief of the Pacific Fleet. Admiral Stark further copied Secretary of the Navy W. F. "Frank" Knox, Secretary of State Cordell Hull, and President Franklin D. Roosevelt. Zach later met with Admiral Kimmel at Pearl Harbor in March, concerning Nomura as well as some other things—and assertively recommended a policy of constant long-range air patrols to guard Pearl from an air strike.

This meeting between Zacharias and Kimmel was later the subject of bitter debate. Zacharias claimed that the admiral "seemed interested" during the one-and-a-half-hour discussion but, several years later, Kimmel—under investigation for his role in the Pearl Harbor disaster—later testified he had no memory of the conversation at all. Capt. W. W. "Poco" Smith, Kimmel's chief of staff who also sat in during the conversation, contradicted Zacharias by testifying that he was "absolutely positive" that there had been no mention of a possible air attack on Pearl Harbor. Smith further stated that Zach's was a case of "clairvoyance operating in reverse." The issue became a case of Zacharias's word against that of Kimmel and Smith.[7]

---

7. According to his later testimony at the hearings held by the Congressional Joint Committee on the Investigation of the Pearl Harbor Attack, Captain Zacharias called on Admiral Kimmel, commander in chief of the U.S. Pacific Fleet, at his headquarters in Hawaii sometime between March 26 and 30, 1941. In the course of their conversation, Zacharias testified, he told the admiral that if the Japanese decided to go to war, it likely "would begin with an air attack on our fleet without a declaration of war, on a weekend and probably on a Sunday morning." Zacharias added that the probable method of attack would be

About this same time, Zacharias claimed credit for getting ONI to release Joe Rochefort to take the job of Station HYPO's OIC at Pearl Harbor in June 1941. Naval Intelligence essentially had rights of first refusal on Rochefort's shore assignments, but HYPO was actually a creature of OP-20-G in Naval Communications. Zach very much liked to help colleagues he respected get ahead in the intelligence business, and used his influence accordingly. This time, however, Rochefort's assignment was more likely due to a deal made between Cmdr. Laurance **Safford** (OP-20-G) in Washington and Rear Adm. Claude Bloch, the Commandant of the Fourteenth Naval District. Regardless of how it came about, Rochefort's assignment as HYPO's OIC was incredibly fortunate.

Several other times, during his tenure as captain of the *Salt Lake City*, Zacharias tried to speak to the Pacific Fleet war plans officer, Capt. C. H. "Soc" McMorris, about his worries concerning a surprise air strike. Essentially receiving the "brush off" from his Annapolis classmate, he gave up. He decided that if the brass wanted his opinion, they'd ask him for it.

However, Zacharias repeated his warning about an attack in November 1941, to Curtis B. Munson, an emissary of Admiral Stark in from Washington. Zacharias was still in command of the *Salt Lake City*, based at Pearl Harbor. Munson—who arrived in Hawaii with instructions to investigate the possibility of armed uprisings by Japanese agents on the West Coast and Hawaii in the event of war—sought out Zacharias because of his knowledge of Japan and its intelligence apparatus. Zacharias advised Munson that the government could realistically eliminate any fears of uprisings of Japanese residents in either locality; Zach and his protégé, Lt. (Dr.) Cecil Coggins, were focused upon the plight of Japanese Americans in Hawaii, and held the firm conviction that the only danger of Japanese agents lay in a relatively few "real government operatives" recently sent from Japan. Their arguments were parallel to those being made in southern California by Lt. Cmdr. Kenneth **Ringle**; in fact, these three experts essentially formed the position of the ONI on this important subject.

---

by aircraft flown from carriers, and it might emanate from north of the Hawaiian Islands because of the direction of the prevailing winds.

Kimmel asked how such an attack could be prevented, and Zacharias replied, "Admiral, you will have to have patrols out at least 500 miles daily." When Kimmel protested that he did not have either the manpower or the planes to do the job, Zacharias responded, "Admiral, you'd better get them, because that is what's coming." During the conversation, Zacharias added that the disappearance of Japanese merchant ships from sea lanes, and sightings of Japanese submarines off Pearl Harbor, would be indicators that an attack was imminent.

Even before this conversation, on February 18, Kimmel had felt worried about an attack. "I feel that a surprise attack is a possibility. We are taking immediate practical steps to minimize the damage inflicted and to ensure that the attacking force will pay." However, neither Adm. Kimmel nor Lt. Gen. Walter Short, the army commander in Hawaii, had enough aircraft to conduct regular and extensive patrols that could go out far enough to detect an attacking fleet.

In regard to Captain Smith, "Smith testified that Zacharias' claim—that he specifically warned Admiral Kimmel about a surprise Japanese Sunday-morning airstrike—was totally false. He said that it was the 'testimony of clairvoyance operating in reverse.' It's hard to explain such a serious discrepancy between two honorable and intelligent officers. There are many contradictory things in the study of how the Pearl Harbor surprise came about, but the Smith-Zacharias controversy is one of the most puzzling—and remains unresolved."

Zach told Munson that the first act of war would very likely come as a surprise air attack, and so the utmost secrecy necessary for its success would prevent any advance knowledge being given to the local Japanese populace—a group that, in any event, Tokyo felt had been too "Americanized" to be reliable.

Zacharias added that, based upon historical Japanese decision-making procedures, when a third envoy arrived in Washington, "you can look for things to break immediately one way or another." As it turned out, a third peace envoy arrived in Washington on December 3.

On November 27, Zacharias repeated his warning yet again at a dinner with Lorrin Thurston, editor of the *Honolulu Advertiser* and head of radio station KGU. (Ironically, unbeknownst to them or any American, the Japanese strike force—six carriers, two battleships, two cruisers, and thirteen destroyers—had already departed Japan, on November 26.) Thurston then commented, "Here I am, a reserve officer in G-2 [Army intelligence], and I haven't even been advised what to send out over my radio in case of attack!" Zach told him to send something like this:

We are having a sporadic air attack. Everyone should remain calm and remain indoors. Do not go on the streets as it will interfere with the military going to their posts. There is nothing to worry about.

When the Japanese strike against Pearl Harbor finally did occur, the *Salt Lake City* was in company with Vice Adm. William "Bull" Halsey's USS *Enterprise* task force, returning to Hawaii after delivering fighter planes to U.S. Marines on Wake Island. As they neared Oahu, from his cabin Zach heard his own words on radio station KGU, including "There is *nothing to worry about.*"

Zacharias got his chance to hit back when, in February 1942, the navy went on the offensive for the first time in the war, with a series of raids on the Gilbert and Marshall Islands. A key component of Halsey's *Enterprise* task force, the *Salt Lake City* played a prominent part in the bombardment of the atoll of Wotje in the Marshalls. Before and during this action, Zach—showing characteristic initiative and creativity—had his scout-plane pilots take photos with hand-held, privately owned cameras. The photos were then enlarged, annotated, and distributed to the other American ships, clearly showing the details of Japanese batteries, airfields, and oil storage facilities. Later in that same month the *Salt Lake City* shelled Wake Island, and in March she screened the *Enterprise* while that ship's aircraft bombed Marcus Island. Then, in April, she was part of the escort force that accompanied the aircraft carrier *Hornet* when that ship launched Lt. Col. Jimmy Doolittle's sixteen-plane B-25 bombing raid on Tokyo. For all of this engaged, high-performance activity, Zach was given a letter of commendation and the Commendation Ribbon.

In June 1942, Zacharias was detached from the *Salt Lake City* and appointed as deputy director of U.S. Naval Intelligence. This was somewhat of a disappointment for him, because despite his outstanding and demonstrated qualities as a sea-going ship commander, he "regarded himself first and foremost an intelligence officer." In fact, naval intelligence historian Dr. Jeffery Dorwart flatly states that, as of June

1942, "Zacharias was the most accomplished and experienced intelligence expert in the U.S. Navy." Thus, eager to make great contributions, he really had hoped to be director—not deputy. However, he was subordinated to another officer (the fourth director of ONI in a year and a half) who had no previous intelligence background. At this time, perhaps, the "Navy neither wanted nor required a brilliant, controversial intelligence wizard to head its intelligence outfit. Instead it needed a tactful, cooperative administrator to manage" an organization of over eight thousand people with an annual budget of $4,800,000. One can feel a little sorry for Zacharias, but one might also feel a little sorry for newly promoted Rear. Adm. Harold C. Train, trying to do his duty, but saddled with the navy's "most accomplished intelligence expert" in the office next door, fervently hoping to replace him.

That issue aside, upon his arrival in Washington, Zacharias found that ONI was doing pretty well as far as collecting information went. However, strongly feeling that information isn't any good if it isn't distributed and used, Captain Zacharias took it as a priority to winnow quality from quantity, and then to streamline analysis, organization, and distribution. His constant argument—to all ranks including admirals—was yes, "we can quit" pushing out intelligence, "but you are betting American lives against the possible effects of hoarding information. Intelligence is no good unless you use it." Moreover, "Zacharias wanted ONI to carry the war to the enemy through psychological warfare, special operations, counterespionage, black propaganda, and operational intelligence."

Another priority—in fact his "number one project"—was to improve naval intelligence training. Thus, ONI's old school was closed, a new Basic Intelligence School was created in Maryland, and an Advanced Intelligence School was opened in New York. Before the war was over, the Advanced Intelligence School had trained a thousand officers in wartime operational intelligence. The Japanese-language training program that ONI had started in fall 1941 (at Harvard University and the University of California) was moved to the University of Colorado at Boulder in July 1942. In fact, Deputy Director Zacharias spoke at the graduation ceremony of the first class of the school, in July 1943, in the university's Mackey Auditorium. One of several speakers, Zach confounded many of the 142 graduates "with a rapid-fire speech in Japanese—that he then translated for the broader audience."

In addition, Zacharias oversaw the creation of a German Navy prisoner-of-war interrogation branch, and was instrumental in the creation of the Army-Navy (and to a degree OSS) Joint Intelligence Collection Agency, which shortly had teams in important cities around the world as soon as those cities were captured or liberated.

In August 1942, Zach approved a plan to establish a psychological warfare unit within ONI, to be initially aimed at the Germans. Called the Special Warfare Branch (SWB, or officially, OP-16-W), its creation was immediately "greeted with extreme enthusiasm" by another organization with similar interests—the U.S. Office of War Information (OWI). The SWB initially prepared leaflets for distribution in Europe and crafted radio broadcasts meant for German Navy personnel. The broadcasts were particularly effective, made by a reserve officer who was a prominent international lawyer and German expert whose language skills were flawless. Lt. Cmdr. Ralph Albrecht—using the on-air alias Cmdr. Robert Norden—ultimately made 309 broadcasts, which documents captured later indicated were extremely damaging to the morale of *Kriegsmarine* officers and men.

Just when the stage was being set for the SWB to begin a psychological warfare campaign against the Japanese, Captain Zacharias was abruptly ordered back to sea—this time to command the battleship *New Mexico*. While excited to become the captain of a battleship, Zach left Washington with a "heavy heart," thinking about a number of other ideas he had for increasing ONI's wartime effectiveness. Zacharias might have himself to blame; it appears that Admiral Train engineered the transfer, tired of Zach nipping at his heels.

Nevertheless, in September 1943, he assumed command of the *New Mexico* at the Puget Sound Navy Yard, following her participation in the Aleutians Campaign. Now, the ship was going to participate in the recapture of the Gilbert Islands, heavily bombarding the shores of the Butaritari Islands in the Makin Atoll before the infantry landings in November 1943. Thus, Zach was flag-captain to Rear Adm. Robert M. Griffin, Task Group 52.2 (this was Operation "Galvanic," which also saw Rear Adm. Howard **Kingman** present, commanding Task Group 53.4).

In January 1944, during the largest offensive yet undertaken and directed against the Marshall Islands, the *New Mexico*'s task force shelled Ebeye Island, and in February of that year bombarded Kwajalein.

During the latter part of February 1944, the *New Mexico* pounded Taron Island in the Maleolap Atoll and Wotje Island in the Wotje Atoll, both in the Marshall Island group. She continued to carry the flag of Rear Adm. Griffin, as Commander Battleship Division 3, and was the first of the older battleships (commissioned 1918) to operate with escort carriers. Early in March she formed part of a task force which shelled Kavieng in New Ireland (Papua New Guinea), and in June and July operated in the Marianas against Tinian, Saipan, and Guam (Operation FORAGER). This last was as Unit 7 of Task Group 52.10; now embarked was Rear Adm. George L. Weyler. After landings had been made at Guam, the *New Mexico* provided harassing fire until the island was secured—having fired almost continuously for nineteen days. The Marianas campaign completed almost a year of heavy bombardment for the old battleship, so she returned to the Puget Sound Navy Yard for overhaul and to replace her worn-out guns. At that point Zach was detached from command, in September 1944.

Captain Zacharias was awarded a gold star in lieu of a second Legion of Merit medal with a Combat "V" device. This was for expertly maintaining his ship at the peak of efficiency throughout continuous offensive action against many heavily fortified, enemy-held islands in a vital war area, and for his "superb ship-handling and brilliant leadership."

In October 1944, Zacharias reported for duty as chief of staff to the Commandant, Eleventh Naval District, in San Diego. In March 1945, at San Diego, Zach briefly discussed a plan for psychological warfare against Japan with Secretary of the Navy

James Forrestal. Zacharias had been thinking about this idea for several months, and had accordingly corresponded with a contact at the U.S. OWI in Washington. The proposal was based on his years studying the Japanese psyche and Japanese culture, the information gained through the formation of that psych-warfare branch in ONI during his tour as deputy director in 1942, and his observations of increasing Japanese war-weariness as evidenced by a number of things—including the appointment of a known moderate (and former grand chamberlain to the emperor), Adm. Suzuki Kantaro, as the prime minister.

Zach's plan proposed to render unnecessary an opposed American landing on the Japanese main islands. This would be accomplished by beaming radio broadcasts into the home islands to weaken the will of Japan's high command and to strengthen the hand of the "peace" party under the new premier. The goal was to bring about an early surrender with the least possible loss of life. Zacharias was sure that the Japanese would want to "know the meaning of 'unconditional' surrender and the fate we planned for Japan after its defeat." If assurances were made that surrender would not be the doom of Japanese civilization, they might prove more compliant about conceding defeat. As he expected, Zacharias's plan ran counter to the strong prevailing view among most American military and political leaders: U.S. conventional wisdom said that the Japanese were fanatically determined to fight to the finish, and that their morale was practically unbreakable.

In April 1945, Captain Zacharias returned to the Navy Department in Washington and was assigned temporary duty with the Commander in Chief, U.S. Fleet, with his services made available to the U.S. OWI. In June 1945 he was assigned to the Navy Department's Office of Public Information, but with continuing availability to the OWI. Secretary Forrestal approved Zacharias's plan—despite some personal skepticism and in opposition to many dissenting opinions—entrusting Zach with the task of translating the program into action.

Captain Zacharias found that Dr. Ladislas Farago and others in the psychological warfare unit—the one that ONI deputy director Zacharias had approved and backed in 1942—had been busy. Through considerable research and analysis, they were convinced that the Japanese *would* be susceptible to psychological attack, and that the war's outcome did *not* necessarily include all of them fighting to the death—which, again, was the pervasive mindset at that time. This Special Warfare Branch position further confirmed Zach's opinions, resulting from his years of study of Japanese culture and character. A concluding sentence in Zach's draft plan said that

> in spite of the fatalistic tendencies of the Japanese—involving individual disregard for life and appreciation of the glory of dying for their Emperor—they are nevertheless realistic people as regards the lessons of history and hopes for the future.

At this point Zacharias assembled a small group of psychologists, Japanese linguists, and Japanese cultural experts. He even included some members of the earlier "Commander Norden" broadcast team, whose psychological warfare efforts had been so successful against the German Navy. Zach himself was to be the primary writer and sole speaker (and it's a tribute to his remarkable Japanese language skills—and accent—that some Japanese prisoners of war, later listening to the broadcasts, remarked that they believed he must be "a well-educated Japanese gentleman from Tokyo"). The group prepared the scripts and recorded the broadcasts using the facilities of the OWI and the Department of the Interior. The recordings were then sent by wire or airplane to San Francisco, from where they were beamed to Japan via shortwave radio so that Radio Tokyo could pick them up.

On May 8, shortly after President Harry S Truman's announcement of the end of the war in Europe, Zacharias—identifying himself as the "official spokesman of the U.S. Government"—delivered the first in this planned series of eighteen radio broadcasts to the Japanese, explaining the concepts of the meaning of surrender. Zacharias emphasized that "unconditional" surrender was a military term signifying "the cessation of resistance and the yielding of arms," the capitulation of the Japanese armed forces, and did *not* signify the end of the Japanese way of life. Zach articulated a lenient interpretation of the unconditional surrender doctrine in the hope that the Japanese would be persuaded to end hostilities promptly. He emphasized his past associations with many of Japan's top leaders and their families in order to build their trust. But, Zacharias was not in a position to execute policy, a fact undoubtedly not lost on his former Japanese acquaintances.

The speeches were aimed at Japan's military, industrial, and political leaders who had the power to pressure the war party to end the war. Zacharias did not really count on reaching the average Japanese citizen by radio, since by no means did all Japanese people have them. So, to try to also get the message to the citizenry, propaganda leaflets were air-dropped on Japanese cities. Somewhat later, OWI analysts observed that

> these messages produced much positive reaction in the general population of Japan, and in several instances exhortations warning the Japanese people against the broadcasts have been intercepted by the Federal Communications Commission.

A later report stated that Prince Takamatsu, brother of the emperor (and very well known to Zacharias from when he accompanied the prince's U.S. tour in 1931), believed that "Captain Zacharias' broadcasts provided the ammunition needed by the 'peace party' to win out against those elements in the Japanese government who wished to continue the war to the bitter end." Here was evidence that the program was reaching intended targets and having good effect.[8]

Despite the seemingly positive Japanese reaction to the radio messages, there was no complete agreement in the president's cabinet as to a solid position to take regarding the future status of the emperor—or as to the proper time to make such a statement.

---

8. The reader may well wish to look at Zacharias's autobiography, *Secret Missions*, which is fascinating for many reasons—but also contains the full texts of Zach's proposed plan, Op Plan I-45, and the scripts for the eighteen broadcasts.

Captain Zacharias and his team were convinced that they were gaining momentum. Taking another tack, they wrote an anonymous letter addressed to Premier Suzuki, which was publically printed in the *Washington Post* on July 21. In this letter, they suggested that the Japanese government formally request clarification of American intentions regarding the emperor. In a follow-up broadcast (which took them ten stressful days and fourteen drafts to prepare), Zacharias reminded the Japanese of their choices: virtual destruction and a dictated peace, or, unconditional surrender according to the "Atlantic Charter"—which maintained that Japan would receive not only a "peace with honor" but preservation of the original Japanese empire and all its institutions, including the emperor. However, by suggesting that the Japanese could obtain surrender terms according to the Atlantic Charter, Zach was advancing a policy position that had not actually been established.

Shortly thereafter, the navy detailed Zacharias completely over to the OWI before he made any further broadcasts to Japan. The official reason for Zacharias's transfer to the OWI was that this project had become more diplomatic than military in character. And by July 26, he had been stripped of his "official spokesman" status.[9]

Meanwhile, Zach's overture to the Japanese met with another promising reaction. On July 24, Dr. Inouye Kiyoshi, a Japanese authority on international relations who had been selected to give the official Japanese response to Zacharias's July 7 broadcast, indicated that Japan was willing to surrender "provided that there were certain changes in the unconditional surrender formula"—such as being specifically assured that the Atlantic Charter applied to her. Zach took this as a signal that the Japanese really did want to begin negotiations, since it was delivered on the eve of the Potsdam Declaration (July 26, 1945), where the terms of unconditional surrender were clearly defined by Harry Truman, Winston Churchill, and Chiang Kai-shek.

But as Zach had been stressing in the last several broadcasts, time had essentially run out. Inouye's statements occurred two days before the Potsdam Declaration was signed, and thirteen days before the first atomic bomb was dropped on Hiroshima on August 7—which was followed by the second bomb onto Nagasaki on August 9. Of course, the Japanese surrendered shortly thereafter.

Zacharias was awarded another gold star in lieu of a third Legion of Merit medal for his Japanese psychological warfare broadcast program. The program did not secure the Japanese surrender itself, but it was probably the most successful venture into psychological warfare during World War II for the United States—and undoubtedly played a noteworthy role in preparing the Japanese national psyche for the inevitable surrender once the atomic bombs were dropped. Certainly the CNO, Fleet Admiral Ernest J. King, believed this. He personally told Zach, "I want to congratulate you on your good work in making the Japs see the light, and bringing surrender."

---

9. Professor Dorwart writes, "However, trouble once again plagued the navy's foremost intelligence promoter who, while comfortable with the atmosphere in ONI, ran afoul of Secretary of the Navy Forrestal's civilian agent Ferdinand Eberstadt. 'We agreed that Zacharias should cease his use of the phrase *official spokesman* in his broadcasts to Japan because of the delicacy of current negotiations,' wrote Eberstadt in July 1945 after a conversation with Secretary of State James Byrnes."

After the end of the war, and while still on detail to the OWI, Zacharias submitted several lengthy reports and proposals up the chain of command, concerning the occupation of Japan—and he no doubt hoped for a role for himself in that occupation. However, such an assignment did not materialize. In addition, he made many public appearances, as a representative of the navy, for the purposes of creating good will and to combat a current feeling that naval strength should be reduced—and to push against the notion that the armed services should be merged into one.

In January 1946, Captain Zacharias appeared at the Joint Congressional Committee Investigation of the Pearl Harbor attack. He testified that failure to identify and heed indications and warning information, and failure to appreciate the importance of intelligence in general, had been "one of the greatest contributing factors" to the tragedy.

Otherwise professionally frustrated, and left with few remaining official duties, Zacharias used this postwar period to write a best-selling but controversial autobiography.

Secret Missions: The Story of an Intelligence Officer was published in mid-November 1946 to mixed reviews. *Time* magazine called the book a good "spy story" and portrayed Zach's reasons for writing the book as threefold: one, to plead the case for better and broader U.S. intelligence; two, to blast away at U.S. government bureaucratic stupidity; and three, to make sure that no one had a chance to undervalue Captain Ellis M. Zacharias! Despite the last point, *Time* conceded that Zacharias's general complaints about government and navy brass were "all too probably justified." The *New York Times Book Review* gave the work a positive review, stating that "as a historical document it is one of the best of the items from which the story of the war will ultimately be written." The *Saturday Review* thought *Secret Missions* extraordinarily good; the *Kirkus* review found it "fascinating."

However, the *Army and Navy Bulletin*'s review, not surprisingly, wasn't favorable. Most of *Secret Missions* was seen as "being about Captain Zacharias, a man in whose abilities and insights *he* has practically unlimited respect." The *Bulletin* chastised Zacharias further, saying that "he leaves nothing to the imagination, revealing the innermost secrets of war-time cryptanalysis." Zach just shrugged off this last; he had been mindful of detail, and the manuscript had been read and released by the proper authorities.

Ellis Zacharias retired from the U.S. Navy after thirty-four years of service—thirty-eight if one adds his Naval Academy student time. He had failed to gain promotion to rear admiral while on active duty and was, instead, officially retired as a captain—but he immediately received a "tombstone" promotion to flag rank when placed on the retired list—which was in recognition of his at-sea combat leadership during the war.

So Zach was relieved of all active duty in November 1946, which was about the same time *Secret Missions* was published. After his retirement, Zacharias delivered dozens of lectures each year on college campuses and to civic groups. He fervently wanted to educate the public on national security problems, the need for a strong national defense, and the continuing importance of intelligence activities, including a strong psychological warfare program. He also advocated a hard line toward the Soviet Union and criticized past U.S. mistakes concerning the Soviets. Clearly very tough against communism, it's interesting to note that in the early 1950s Zacharias was one of the first people to publically condemn Senator Joseph McCarthy during that politician's communist "witch-hunting" campaign against U.S. citizens. During this period, based out of their northwest Washington home, Zach claimed that he and Claire grew the biggest tomatoes in the region. Inside the house, only a few prints and books gave any indication of Rear Admiral Zacharias's almost lifelong interest in Japan.

In addition to his lectures, in 1950 Zacharias published another book in collaboration with his old ONI colleague, Ladislas Farago. *Behind Closed Doors*, an account of Soviet and communist plans and operations in many geographical areas, stressed that Soviet plans for military and revolutionary action might precipitate moves against the United States as early as 1956.

In 1959, Zach created a television series, also called *Behind Closed Doors*, which was a unique twenty-six-episode program. The series focused on how the Soviet Union had stolen American missile secrets, and proposed steps to prevent further espionage. Zacharias offered comments at the conclusion of each segment. In 1958, before he produced *Behind Closed Doors*, Zacharias had also narrated a weekly radio series titled *Secret Missions*. Obviously, the titles of both programs were taken from his books.

Thus, to a degree, Zacharias accomplished in retirement what his navy career had mostly curtailed—the free expression of his ideas openly and without topside interference. Additionally, in early 1950, a short-lived comic book appeared, *Admiral Zacharias' Secret Missions—All True and Authentic—Menace! Intrigue! Mystery! Action! Daring Exploits of U.S. Foreign Agents in the Cold War vs. Communism*. The push for this comic book wasn't so much Zach's idea as it was the publisher's; Mr. Archer St. John had worked in the OWI and no doubt knew Zach very well.

In sum, Ellis Zacharias might be remembered as having two primary intelligence successes in his career: his prediction of the Pearl Harbor attack (even though it was not particularly heeded), and his extraordinary Japanese propaganda broadcast program. Zacharias had proved to be a brilliant but controversial intelligence officer, always pressing hard for what he believed to be right—although sometimes acting like a bull in a china shop, sometimes to his own detriment.

Generally beloved by his subordinates, but at times looked upon with suspicion by his superiors, he was not really viewed as a member of the "good old boys club" of the U.S. Navy. The latter's view was that Zacharias was very often too much the self-proclaimed intelligence "expert" who sometimes overstepped his bounds with predictable consequences. He made some enemies because he was, on many occasions, right at the expense of his superiors; he also made a few enemies because he usually had a hard time taking "no" for an answer. He had been unable to convince the brass of the impending Japanese attack on Pearl Harbor during 1941; he was passed over for the position of director of naval intelligence; he was not given flag rank on active duty; his broadcast program to Japan was cut short; and he was not included in postwar intelligence operations.

At the Pearl Harbor investigative hearings after the war, Zacharias's criticisms of Admiral Kimmel and others in high positions, concerning dereliction of duty—or at least major errors in judgment—did nothing to enhance his popularity within the naval aristocracy. It was another instance where his outspoken method of presenting his opinions and ideas identified him, in some ways, as an outcast. Still, one can appreciate his frame of mind on this issue; he considered one of the greatest frustrations of his entire life to be his failure to convince superior officers of the inevitability of the Japanese strike.

In February 1961, while on a trip to Hawaii, Zach suffered a heart attack and was hospitalized at Tripler Army Medical Center in Honolulu. And then only four months later, at the age of seventy-one, he was hit with a second and fatal attack at the family's summer home in New Hampshire. He was buried with full military honors, as befitted his rank, in Arlington National Cemetery. His wife, the former Claire Miller (born in 1897), was interred with him upon her death in 1992. They had two sons, Ellis M. Zacharias Jr., and Jerrold M. Zacharias, both of whom followed their father into the navy.

Rear Adm. Cecil H. Coggins, a close colleague and friend of many years, gave this assessment after Rear Admiral Zacharias's death.

Zach, to hundreds of his friends, was a most remarkable man. Active, lean, alert, and full of energy with bright eyes and broad smile, he was extremely personable. He made friends easily over the whole world and never forgot one of them. With a nimble mind, retentive memory, and energetic drive went his prime quality of imagination. In an instant he could see the potentialities of an idea which would completely escape the average naval officer. While his contemporaries were groping to grasp a concept, he had already understood it, developed a dozen possible corollaries, rejected some, and was making plans to put the rest into effect.

Of such a man, it was inevitable that *some* would be jealous of his successes. That there were so *few* is a tribute to his personal charm and his obvious unselfishness and sincerity. His moral and professional standards were very high. In his busy mind there was no room for anything petty.

His obituary in the *Washington Post* said, in part:

In a long and useful career, Rear Adm. Zacharias combined the qualities of a Cassandra, a gadfly, and a pioneer. . . . He could be pugnacious, and sometimes mistaken, in his opinions—but there was never a doubt where he stood. He was an outspoken individualist of the kind that both *his family*, and *his country*, will miss.

Zacharias's decorations and awards include, among other things, three Legion of Merit Medals (with the Combat "V" device), the Navy Commendation Ribbon, the Mexican Service Medal, and the Yangtze Service Medal.

Sources

A number of sources were key to this chapter, but I'm particularly indebted to the wonderful article written by National Archives and Records Administration archivist David A. Pfeiffer for considerable information and text. Mr. Pfeiffer not only works in NARA Archival Operations in Washington, but is also a great-nephew of Rear Adm. Zacharias.

Breuer, 69–70.
Carlson, 28–29, 38–39, 49, 70, 88.
Dingman, 4, 52, 61.
Dorwart, *Conflict of Duty*, 41, 62, 66, 152, 194, 196, 197, 201, 221.
Farago, *Broken Seal*, 28–29, 35–37, 39–40, 47–52, 78–80, 320.
Holtwick, 55–61, 63.
Kahn, *Codebreakers*, 5.
Layton, *"And I Was There,"* 59, 68–69, 79.
Lewin, 24–27, 32.
Lucky Bag, U.S. Naval Academy, 1912.
McCollum, 39.
Morison, VII, 337; VIII, 409.
Pfeiffer, "Sage Prophet or Loose Cannon?"
Prados, 7–8.
Prange, *At Dawn*, 354–55, 712–13.
Rochefort, 58–60.
Schuon, 275–77.
U.S. Navy, *Register of Commissioned and Warrant Officers*.
USS *Salt Lake City* Website. *Ellis M. Zacharias—Personal Page.*
Wilhelm, 10–11, 22, 23, 125–29, 187, 217, 222.
Zacharias, Ellis, 3–5, 8–9, 12–14, 20, 58, 70–71, 73, 84, 89–91, 93–94, 97, 102–9, 164–69, 274, 332–89.
Zacharias, Jerrold, *Biography of Ellis M. Zacharias.*

The "Hybrids"

Multiskilled and Multiproficient

CAPTAIN THOMAS BUTLER BIRTLEY JR., U.S. NAVY
(1899–1956)

A rare "hybrid"—schooled as a linguist and as a cryptanalyst
Preceded Rochefort as officer in charge, Station HYPO
"Tommy" "Birt" "Count"

Tommy Birtley was one of the unusual hybrids like Joe **Rochefort** (an extensively educated Japanese linguist as well as a trained cryptologist), but he was not quite at Rochefort's level—nor did he have the advantage of Rochefort's significant operational intelligence background.

*   *   *

From the 1923 Annapolis yearbook, *The Lucky Bag*:

Here we have the Count of Monte Carlo, Jockey of the Galloping Dominoes, and Rex of the Royal Rounders; and just why he entered the Academy no one knows—not even he, himself. The exactness with which he can tell fortunes would make any one of the Regiment sit up and listen, especially when "What you dream between Friday night and Saturday morning will come true" drifts out on the mystic air. As a musician he is unsurpassed, for the way he can pour jazz from a table-top would make a cigar-store Indian shimmy like a dish of "Shivering Lizz." And oh, that Jew's harp!! He came back from Youngster Cruise hard smitten. To hear him talk, Cupid must have wielded a wicked bow and arrow. Just mention one of those West Coast dances and a Hudson Super-Six and the *Count* is in for one of those Taps to Reveille dreams. Notable quote: "Say, who knows anything about the Steam [marine engineering lesson] today?" [Activities: track; *Lucky Bag* staff]

*   *   *

Tommy Birtley was born on December 14, 1899, and hailed from Scranton, Pennsylvania. He graduated from the Naval Academy with the class of 1923, along with such distinguished classmates as Arleigh A. Burke, Kenneth D. **Ringle**, Edward S. Pearce, Joseph N. **Wenger**, and Melville Bell Grosvenor. Further promotions included lieutenant (junior grade), 1926; lieutenant, 1931; lieutenant commander, 1938; commander, 1942; and captain, 1943. He retired from the navy in 1946.

His first few years in the navy, 1923 through 1927, were—unusually—all in one ship, the destroyer *Somers*.

Then, in the summer of 1927, Lieutenants (junior grade) Tom Birtley, Tom **Dyer**, and Frank Bond began the OP-20-G cryptanalysis course. At that time the course was very informal and unstructured, taught by Mr. Klaus Bogel. Dyer later said that they had some, but very little, interface with Lt. Joe Rochefort (then the head of OP-20-G), or chief cryptanalyst Mrs. Agnes **Driscoll**.

Toward the end of the course, Birtley was selected for the ONI language/cultural immersion program in Japan—as, coincidentally, was Rochefort. Birtley's tour ran from 1927 through 1930, while Rochefort's was 1929–1932. Thus it's interesting to note that in 1929 the ONI language officers in Tokyo included not only Birtley and Rochefort, but also Edwin **Layton**, Edward Pearce, Kenneth Ringle, Louis Libenow, Ethelbert **Watts**, and Marine Frank Pyzick.

In late 1931, Lieutenant Birtley had a short tour on the staff of the commander in chief, Asiatic Fleet, and then in 1932 he was brought back to Main Navy in OP-20-GX—where he again rubbed shoulders with Tommy Dyer.

He was next assigned as the commanding officer of the minesweeper *Tanager*, operating out of Pearl Harbor.

Two years later, in June 1934, Mr. Birtley reported to OP-20-G to become the only language officer in GZ (Translation). Then, in the summer of 1936, Eddie Layton relieved Birtley as head of GZ. Tommy then served on board the destroyer *Dale*.

In April 1939, Lieutenant Commander Birtley was ordered to the Fourteenth Naval District at Pearl Harbor to become overall OIC of Station HYPO. As he came in, Lt. Gill **Richardson** transferred out. Arriving around July, he also became head of HYPO's Enemy Information Division, assisted by Lt. Ranson **Fullinwider**; this division included translation responsibilities—which very much occupied Birtley and Fullinwider as they were the only language officers there. The other two HYPO divisions were Radio Intelligence (headed by Lt. Ray **Lamb**), and Cryptographic Intelligence (headed by Lt. Cmdr. Tom Dyer). Prior to reporting, Birtley received a letter from Cmdr. Laurance **Safford**, head of OP-20-G.

> In general, we will want a GX, GY, and GZ organization at Pearl Harbor similar to the one at the Department. You will be GZ, Dyer GY, and Lamb GX. The senior officer, by rank, will be responsible for such coordination as may be necessary. In this case the senior officer will be yourself. GZ is also responsible for liaison between the Unit and Naval Intelligence. Your duties will be 99 percent technical and 1 percent administrative. . . . At the present time Lt. Gill Richardson is holding down the billet of GZ. He arrived on the job about February 1st, and will stay there until relieved by you. Fullinwider will be your assistant.

When Lt. Cmdr. Ed Layton arrived at Pearl Harbor in December 1940, to board the flagship *Pennsylvania* as fleet intelligence officer, he was pleased to see his old friends Birtley and Dyer over at Station HYPO in the Naval District headquarters. He also instantly realized that their outfit was terribly understaffed and overworked. He offered his help in free moments from his Pacific Fleet duties, and was able to materially help Birtley on a Japanese auxiliary address cipher Birtley was working on, which he'd named "WE WE."

In the summer of 1941, Cmdr. Joe Rochefort relieved Lt. Cmdr. Tom Birtley at HYPO; Birtley needed to go to sea because he did not have sufficient sea-duty to qualify for promotion to commander.

However, in early 1944, Birtley returned to FRUPac after sea duty and then a long period of hospitalization. During this period, along with a reserve officer named Don Miller (who in civilian life was a professor of mathematics), Birtley took on a Japanese machine cipher, designated JADE, and they were able to break into it.

In his monumental work *Combined Fleet Decoded*, intelligence historian John Prados enthusiastically declared Tom Birtley as one of the dedicated FRUPac "cryppies" who history needs to remember.

Unfortunately, Captain Birtley died—only fifty-five years old—on May 23, 1956. He's buried at the National Memorial Cemetery of the Pacific, Honolulu. In the early 1980s Birtley's widow, Pauline, was very helpful to Rear Adm. Edwin Layton (and his coauthors) as they worked on Layton's reminisces, *"And I Was There": Pearl Harbor and Midway—Breaking the Secrets.*

Sources

Carlson, 85–86, 96, 477.
Dyer, 76–77, 146, 197–98, 257.
Holmes, 22, 197.
Holtwick, 47, 104, 135, 138–39, 152–53, 181–82, 201, 327, 329, 333, 352, 406, App. 5.
Layton, *"And I Was There,"* 6, 52, 57, 92.
Lucky Bag, U.S. Naval Academy, 1923.
Packard, 368.
Prados, 175, 412.
U.S. Navy, *Register of Commissioned and Warrant Officers.*

VICE ADMIRAL HOWARD FITHIAN KINGMAN, U.S. NAVY
(1890–1968)

Twice head of the pre-war OP-20-G
Head of ONI's Domestic Intelligence Branch, 1941–1942
"Swede" "Fith"

A talented destroyer and battleship sailor, Howard Kingman rose to high operational command at sea. However, very unlike Russell Willson, Kingman also maintained a long interest and serious involvement in communications, cryptology, and intelligence; he apparently didn't worry about adverse impact on his career by regularly accepting such shore assignments—even at the advanced grade of captain. Intertwined with his sea and sea-command tours, he served twice as OIC of the CSS (OP-20-G), as an embassy assistant naval attaché, as a naval district intelligence officer, as head of ONI's Domestic Intelligence Branch, and finally as the assistant director of naval intelligence.

*   *   *

From the 1911 Naval Academy yearbook, *The Lucky Bag*:

> A jovial, round-cheeked Swede. His patient plodding though the intricacies of Plebe Math and Dago [foreign languages] once over, he discovered that he was not as wooden as he would have us believe. Not a demonstrative person, preferring to remain in the background, yet has solid, original ideas on every subject. Hasn't yet eliminated all the Scandinavian dialect from his speech. Withal, a sea-going, unemotional chap who does not do things by halves, but throws his whole soul and body into that which he attempts. Notable quotation: "I'll tell you, fellows, it's this way."

*   *   *

Howard F. Kingman was born in Hillsboro, North Dakota, on May 5, 1890. He was the only surviving son of Richmond T. Kingman and Alice Maude Fithian, and the only surviving grandchild and heir of Rear Adm. Edwin Fithian, USN. The Kingmans were members of the Sons of the American Revolution, and were also descended from three *Mayflower* passengers (Priscilla Mullins, John Alden, and Francis Cooke). Howard attended Hillsboro High School and Wilmer's Preparatory School in Annapolis. He then received an appointment to the U.S. Naval Academy in 1907. Graduating in June 1911, along with classmates John W. **McClaran**, John W. Reeves, Oscar C. Badger, Lewis H. Brereton, Harry W. Hill, Norman Scott, and Daniel J. Callaghan, he served a period at sea (as required by regulations in those days) before being commissioned as an ensign in March 1912. He was subsequently promoted to lieutenant (junior grade), 1915; lieutenant, 1918; lieutenant commander, 1922; commander, 1931; captain, 1939; rear admiral, 1942; and vice admiral (on the retired list), 1947.

From 1911 to 1919, Kingman served in the armored cruiser *West Virginia*, the battleship *Oregon*, the destroyer *Chauncey*, and then commanded the double-turreted monitor *Monadnock*. In May 1916 he joined the battleship *New York* (flagship of Battle Squadron 6, Battleship Division 9) and then became first lieutenant of the battleship *Arizona* during January–May 1919. For about a year he had duty with the General Board of the Navy Department, in Washington, and then he was assigned to the battleship *Kansas*. In 1921 he served on the staff of Battleship Division 4 (Atlantic Fleet), and then in 1922 he again served on board the *Arizona* with the staff of Battleship Division 7 (Pacific Fleet) as aide and flag secretary, and then as flag lieutenant. In 1923 he reported for instruction at the Naval War College in Newport.

In June 1924, Lt. Cmdr. Kingman came to Main Navy in Washington as head of the Code and Signal Section (OP-20-G), within the Naval Communications

System, relieving Lt. Cmdr. Donald C. Godwin. He in turn was relieved by Lt. Cmdr. Deupree Friedell in August 1925.

He then reported on board the battleship *California* as aide and flag lieutenant to the Commander in Chief, Battle Fleet, from 1925–1926, and then served as aide and flag lieutenant to the Commander in Chief, U.S. Fleet, from 1926–1927 on board the flagship USS *Seattle*. He commanded the destroyer *Doyen* from November 1927 through August 1928. In September he reported for duty as assistant naval attaché at the U.S. embassy in London. During that assignment he served as the U.S. representative for revising the international code of signals. In early 1930, Kingman wrote to the director of naval intelligence that it had proven "almost impossible to pick up any information from conversation with British naval officers on duty at the Admiralty in London" as they were reluctant to talk to foreigners. But he found equipment and arms salesmen more useful. "Sooner or later their ambition to sell you something will make them talk too much, to your benefit."

Upon his return to the United States in September 1930, Kingman served on board the battleship *Mississippi*, as gunnery officer, until June 1932.

Following duty as aide to the commandant, Washington Navy Yard, Commander Kingman relieved Cmdr. John W. **McClaran** and had a second tour of duty at Main Navy from 1933 to 1935; first as head of the Code and Signal Section in the Naval Communications System, and then as head of the Communications Security Group in the Division of Naval Communications (these were really just title changes with the structure remaining essentially the same). In January 1934 he was assigned an additional duty as a White House senior aide. During this second tour as OP-20-G, Kingman shared McClaran's concerns and thus spent considerable effort trying to improve the selection procedures and opportunities for new, talented officers entering cryptanalytic training.

Capt. Laurance **Safford** held Swede Kingman in high regard from his tours at Main Navy. Speaking to an interviewer around 1970, he said that

> Kingman was a great asset in getting the [Code and Signal Section firmly] established, particularly the Research Desk, because he had served as aide to Admiral [Charles F.] Hughes. He could go over everyone else's head. . . . He was a real tower of strength to us.

Commander Kingman was in turn relieved by Commander McClaran, as OP-20-G, in September 1935. During 1935–1937, Kingman served on board the cruiser *Minneapolis* as executive officer, and then became the intelligence officer of the Third Naval District in New York, 1937–1939. From May 1939 through May 1941, Kingman was assigned as Commander, Destroyer Squadron 5, and continued as commander when 5 was redesignated as Destroyer Squadron 29 (Asiatic Fleet).

He then transferred back to Washington to become head of ONI's Domestic Intelligence Branch, or "Branch B." As such, he had direct control and supervision over the activities of the several naval districts' intelligence organizations within the continental limits of the United States.

In October 1941, Captain Kingman became assistant director of naval intelligence under director Capt. Theodore S. Wilkinson, and was in that position at the time of the Pearl Harbor attack. And as head of ONI's domestic branch, he dealt with internal subversion, espionage, and similar activities. There's an interesting side note to this period. In January 1942, Kingman was directly involved in transferring an "unfocused young officer," Ens. John F. Kennedy, out of ONI in Washington to an unimportant job in the Sixth Naval District in Charleston, South Carolina; an action which eventually led to Kennedy's assignment to Pacific Theater sea-duty and then on to his destiny on board *PT 109*. At issue was Kennedy's romantic relationship with a Danish journalist named Inga Arvad, whom the FBI believed might be a German spy—and thus they feared she was using JFK to find out all she could about what was going on in ONI.

It was also during Kingman's tour as assistant director that the vice chief of naval operations, Adm. Frederick J. Horne, took communications intelligence away from ONI and put it entirely under Naval Communications. Thirty years later, Rear Adm. Arthur H. **McCollum** had this insight on this watershed event, which had profoundly irritated Kingman:

> The important thing . . . was that intelligence . . . would get into the hands of people who could do something with it. It didn't make any difference whether it went through ONI or not. Of course, it meant that ONI lost a certain amount of face and prestige and so on . . . and that wasn't very pleasant . . . but when you're fighting a war you have to put up with some of these things.
>
> Howard Kingman was one of the early communication code-breaker type people. He was a very, very fine person. He was the head of the Code and Signal Section, breaking those ciphers back in 1925 when I was first introduced to it. So, he was a communications man from way back and a very able one—and a very able person. He'd also been in-and-out of intelligence. . . . I had a very high regard for him. He was crushed when this decision was made to take [COMINT] entirely out of ONI's hands, because here we'd worked on this thing together for all these years—now to get this . . . slap in the face!

Apparently Kingman was able to swallow his feelings, and in August 1942 he left ONI and assumed command of the battleship *Nevada*. He was shortly promoted to rear admiral, and then, in January 1943, he became Commander, Battleship Division 2. In May 1943, Kingman (with battleships *Nevada*, *Pennsylvania*, and *Idaho*— Task Group 51.1) provided fire support for the capture of Attu in the Aleutian Islands (Operation LANDCRAB). In November, Kingman commanded the Gunfire Support Group of Task Force 53.4 (three battleships and fourteen other warships) in the assault against Tarawa in the Gilbert Islands (Operation GALVANIC).

January 1944 saw him commanding the Fire Support Unit 1 of Task Group 53.5, which bombarded Kwajalein and Eniwetok Atolls in the Marshall Islands (Operations FLINTLOCK and CATCHPOLE). From June to August, Kingman was at the capture of Saipan and Tinian (Operation FORAGER), commanding Unit 1 of Task

Group 52.17. (Capt. Ellis **Zacharias**, in this same operation, was commanding the battleship *New Mexico*—Unit 7 of Task Group 52.10—with Rear Adm. George L. Weyler embarked.) In September, Kingman was present for the assault on Peleliu.

In November 1944, Rear Admiral Kingman became triple-hatted as Commander, Panama Sea Frontier; Commandant, Fifteenth Naval District, Balboa, Canal Zone; and Commander, South East Pacific. In August 1945, he assumed duty as Commander, Battleship Division 9, Pacific Fleet. He was present on board the USS *Missouri* at the signing of the Japanese surrender. His last command was as Commander, Third Fleet, when he relieved Adm. William F. Halsey in November 1945, hoisting his flag in the *South Dakota*. In November 1946, Rear Admiral Kingman was relieved of all active duty.

Kingman retired on February 1, 1947, and was simultaneously promoted to vice admiral on the retired list due to his combat decorations from the war. He passed away in Los Angeles on July 4, 1968, and is buried with his wife at Arlington National Cemetery. Mrs. Kingman (1901–1999) was the former Adelaide Bledsoe Cormack.

Vice Admiral Kingman's decorations included three Legion of Merit medals (one with a Combat "V"); the Bronze Star with Combat "V"; the Navy Commendation Ribbon; the China Service Medal; the Venezuelan Order of the Liberator; the Ecuadoran Order of Abdon Calderón; and the Panamanian Order of Vasco Núñez de Balboa.

Admiral Kingman has also been recognized and honored, by the U.S. Naval Cryptologic Veterans Association, as an officer who has served as the Commander, Naval Security Group, or one of its predecessor organizations.

Sources

Blair, 119, 136–37.
Browne and Carlson, *Echoes of Our Past*, 198–99, 208–9.
Farago, *Burn after Reading*, 192.
Holtwick, 102, 133–34, 153, App. 003.
Lucky Bag, U.S. Naval Academy, 1911.
McCollum interview, v. 2, 480–82.
Mahnken, 133.
Morison, VII, 334, 337, 346; VIII, 409; XII, 34.
Safford, *Interview with Captain L. F. Safford*, App. 220.
U.S. Navy, *Register of Commissioned and Warrant Officers*.
Vice Admiral Howard Fithian Kingman, USN, Ret. Official U.S. Navy Biography, 19 July 1950.

CAPTAIN ALWIN DALTON KRAMER, U.S. NAVY (1903–1972)

"Responsible, dedicated, and intelligent"
An ONI "black-bag" man
Chief navy translator of Japanese diplomatic messages before Pearl Harbor
Head, OP-20-G translation and dissemination, 1939–1941
Chief navy "MAGIC" courier to the president, 1941
"Al" "Adie" "The Shadow"

Al Kramer began his career in surface ships—as did most junior officers of his day. However, drawn to things Asian, in 1931 he began ONI's three-year language immersion training which, for most of his remaining navy career, resulted in translation work within communications intelligence. Somewhat out of pattern, he spent most of his time in Washington with OP-20-G (albeit in translations) more than with ONI. He "lived in a world in which everything had one right way to be done. He chose his words with almost finicky exactness (one of his favorites was 'precise'); he kept his pencil mustache trimmed to a hair; he filed his papers tidily; he often studied his MAGIC intercepts[1] several times over before delivering them. Included in his philosophy was his duty. He performed it with great responsibility, intelligence, and dedication." Kramer had the opportunity—or perhaps misfortune—to be on duty in Washington on December 6–7, 1941, and was subsequently haunted by the questions of what might have been missed, and what could have been done differently, to warn about the Pearl Harbor attack. Hounded by investigators during the Joint Congressional Committee Investigation, he took an early medical retirement in 1946 and forever walked away from the navy and intelligence.

*   *   *

From the 1925 Annapolis yearbook *The Lucky Bag*:

> *Adie* astonishes and sometimes impresses his listeners by his glowing description of the fame of his podunk [*home town*] for making rifles and Rolls Royces. Above all, do not differ with this representative of Massachusetts concerning the laurels of his state, for he takes great pride in his loquacity and never misses an opportunity to force his conviction upon any man. It's a great mystery to his classmates how *Adie* succeeds so well in Academics with so little boning [serious studying]. When it comes to boning, *Adie* is an exemplification of Sir Isaac Newton's law pertaining to inertia. Many of us wish that *Adie* would divulge his secret so that we, too, could have a carefree existence during our sojourn at the Academy. "No use boning that Steam [Marine Engineering] for tomorrow, it's absolutely fruity [easy]," and with this remark he delivers himself up into the hands of Morpheus. [Activities: Rifle Squad, Fencing Squad, Bowling Squad]

*   *   *

Alwin D. Kramer was born on September 5, 1903, in Worcester, Massachusetts, the son of Albin M. and Rose Anna Dalton Kramer.[2] He attended Central High

---

1. MAGIC is the compartmentation code assigned to intelligence derived from Japanese diplomatic traffic that was intercepted by the United States as a result of the 1940 breaking of PURPLE, the Japanese diplomatic code. In everyday discussion, they would have said "so and so" is cleared for MAGIC—rather than say he is cleared for PURPLE. Rear Adm. McCollum, in retirement, had this to say about MAGIC: "We may call it MAGIC, but it's not always 'magic.' Sometimes it's just the blathering of some Japanese diplomat we're getting. Some people thought because we're 'reading the mail,' that the information had an aura of authenticity that it didn't necessarily deserve. Under the Japanese system any consular or diplomatic official could send out their opinion on something, and it wasn't necessarily any sort of official information or point of view."

2. Depending upon the source, there are several variants to be found concerning the spelling of Captain Kramer's first name. For example, the Naval Academy's *Register of Alumni* and the Navy's *Register of Commissioned and Warrant Officers* show *Alwin*, but the yearbook shows *Alvin*. Other sources inconsistently show both—as well as *Alwyn*. However, Alwin seems to be correct.

School in Springfield, Massachusetts, and then was appointed to the Naval Academy in 1921. Kramer graduated and was commissioned in 1925, along with such distinguished classmates as Linwood **Howeth**, Redfield B. **Mason**, John F. Delaney Jr., Ernest "Judge" Eller, Ernest S. L. **Goodwin**, Robert E. Hogaboom, and Morton C. Mumma Jr. Subsequent promotions included lieutenant (junior grade), 1928; lieutenant, 1935; lieutenant commander, 1939; commander, 1942; and captain 1943. He received a medical retirement in September 1946.

Immediately after graduation, Ensign Kramer was pulled for duty with the Navy Rifle Team, including national-match competition at Camp Perry, Ohio. He was a superb marksman; as a second-class midshipman he won the Naval Academy Rifle Championship. In addition, as can be seen in his photograph, he earned the navy's gold Distinguished Marksmanship Badge—which was the highest individual award authorized for excellence in competition and was very difficult to attain.

Late 1925 saw Mr. Kramer in San Francisco, and

right off the bat I got shore patrol duty and the sector I had to patrol was Chinatown. That was my first direct interest in anything to do with the Orient and Oriental languages.

In 1926 he began the typical sea-duty routine for a junior officer in those days. He served on board the battleship *Tennessee* during 1926 and then was transferred to the minesweeper *Chewink* in 1927, seeing service along the East Coast and in the West Indies. He was then sent to the armored cruiser *Rochester*. The *Rochester* supported expeditionary forces at Corinto, Nicaragua, in 1928 as they moved against bandits in the area. In November, Kramer came ashore with a landing party at Leon, Nicaragua, with a force which assisted in current elections. Then, as disturbances boiled over in Haiti in 1929 and American lives were endangered, the *Rochester* transported the First Marine Brigade to Port-au-Prince and Cap-Haïtien. Detached in May, Mr. Kramer again served with the Rifle Team at Annapolis and in matches at Wakefield, Massachusetts, and at Camp Perry.

Lt. j.g. Kramer was then transferred to the light cruiser *Detroit*, which in 1929 and 1930 was the flagship of the commander, Light Cruiser Divisions, based at Norfolk. Once again he shot with the Rifle Team, participating at Wakefield and Perry, and shared in the winning of the Scott Trophy. It was at this time that Al was awarded the Distinguished Marksmanship Badge. In September 1930 he rejoined the *Detroit*, but in June 1931 he detached for a third and final time to shoot at Annapolis and Perry. In late 1931 the *Detroit* sailed for a combined fleet problem off Balboa, and then became flagship of the commander, Destroyer Squadrons, Battle Force, based at San Diego. More importantly, for Kramer's intelligence career,

in 1931 a BuPers circular letter called for applications for requests for Japanese language duty. They also wanted a few Chinese language officers. I applied for it and was fortunate enough to get it.

Thus, Mr. Kramer went to Japan, from October 1931 through November 1934, as part of ONI's full-immersion language and culture training program. The naval attaché, Capt. Isaac Johnson, told him that he wanted solid results, so

> we were examined every six months in not only the language but on the history of Japan, the geography of the country and the Far East in general, and so forth. If we didn't produce, we'd be ordered back to the States. And, one or two in the course of the year *were* ordered back. He did not care how we got the results; we could spend every night in a bar room if we wanted to as long as we produced results. For that reason, the Navy [mostly] sent only bachelors to Japan—so we wouldn't be tied down with any family obligations.

Captain Johnson also remarked, quoting a predecessor, that it would be tough. "He claimed that Japanese was the poorest means of communication the world has ever known, and that anyone able to study that language with any degree of success had to be somewhat quacked to undertake it."

Al returned from Japan in the fall of 1934—but to OP-20-G as well as ONI.

> I got six months' indoctrination down in what we used to call "the Hole"—a lower end of the sixth wing of the old Navy Building—to find out whether I had any facility in this thing.
>
> At one point in my career, I had taken a correspondence course in cryptanalysis. I apparently satisfied them, because several years later they ordered me back [there].

Lieutenant Kramer was then transferred to the destroyer *Decatur* in June 1935. Following that assignment he reported to the destroyer *Waters*, in April 1936, as her executive officer. During that time the *Waters* and her division worked with units of the Pacific Fleet's submarine force in experimenting with anti-submarine warfare techniques.

In June 1938, Al was ordered back to ONI and OP-20-G in Washington, and from February 1939 through May 1942 he served as head of OP-20-GZ (Translations)—while at the same time he kept a foot firmly planted in the Far Eastern Section of ONI (OP-16-B-11). Even though foreign-language translation was really in the bailiwick of ONI (thus the full-immersion language students were considered ONI personnel), OP-20-G in Naval Communications borrowed some translators because the GZ section did detailed recovery vis-à-vis code-groups—this being more of a linguistic than a mathematical challenge. For a period Kramer was also acting head of OP-16-B-11 because the last head (Cmdr. John Creighton) had transferred and so Al was temporarily in charge. Around November 1939, Cmdr. Arthur **Mc-Collum** returned to ONI to take over as head of ONI Far East. Mac was very impressed with Al. "He was very adept at Japanese message coding and decoding and so on, and was head of [our] Japanese Desk—but he also doubled as head of the [OP-20-G] decrypting section. Later on we got another fellow in, Lt. Cmdr. Ethelbert **Watts**, a Japanese-language man, and he took over the Japanese Desk and that enabled Kramer to devote [mostly] full time to the code breaking business."

Lt. Cmdr. Kramer—like Lt. Cmdr. Ken **Ringle**, Lt. Jack **Holtwick**, and Chief Walter **McGregor**—was also sometimes a "black bag" agent.

Kramer, on several occasions, led a team of ONI agents, New York City police, and a locksmith to break into the Japanese consulate in New York to photograph code books. Members of his staff recall seeing Kramer at the office early in the morning, looking weary and wearing his . . . sneakers. They also noticed that his mysterious evening trips to New York were [sometimes] followed by decryption breakthroughs.

One day in early 1941, fellow OP-20-G officer Lt. Robert **Weeks**, who coincidentally was Al's next-door neighbor, was invited into the Kramer house to see Al's latest "haul" from an ONI black-bag job against the Japanese consulate. Al had personally developed the resulting spy-camera photos of documents in his basement darkroom. However, they had to hurriedly hide it all after they heard a knock on the door—it's a good thing they did, for the unexpected caller just happened to be the Japanese naval attaché in Washington, with whom Mr. Kramer was friendly.

In April 1941, through MAGIC stemming from PURPLE decrypts, Lt. Cmdr. Kramer accurately predicted the date—June 22—that the Germans were going to attack the Soviet Union. By the fall of 1941,

both OP-20-G and the Army's Signal Intelligence Service became overwhelmed by the swelling volume of diplomatic traffic . . . they were processing 50 to 75—and sometimes over 100—messages a day. For this task OP-20-G had six translators—most of whom were civilians—working under the direction of Lt. Cmdr. Alwin Kramer.

The SIS apparently had equal capability although, according to cryptology historians Peter Donovan and John Mack, for over ten years the navy had been committing far more resources into OP-20-G than the army had been putting into SIS.

Kramer handled the translation of Japanese diplomatic intercepts in the PURPLE cipher once they were decrypted. As stated previously, he had with him only one officer, two yeomen, and six translators—three of whom were still in training. Much of Kramer's time was taken up with the supervision and distribution of the finished intercepts to senior leaders; he hand-carried the translated material to the few people designated as "approved recipients." Kramer and his ONI boss, Commander McCollum, had fairly complete control of what MAGIC messages—out of a very large volume—were selected as important for naval leaders and policymakers. Their judgment in this role was highly regarded.

They worked under tremendous pressure. The unit was "understaffed to the point where Kramer usually had to work a 16-hour day in order to act as messenger as well as to exercise his personal skills of translation and evaluation." Rear Adm. Edwin **Layton** wrote years later that Al was overstressed throughout 1941, putting in tough hours and constantly munching on chocolate bars.

A PURPLE message translated by the army on October 9, 1941, requested a Japanese agent in Honolulu, when making reports, to divide the waters of Pearl

Harbor into five specific sub-areas. Kramer was aware of this message—which became known as the "bomb-plot" message—and noted on it "Tokyo directs special reports on ships in Pearl Harbor which is divided into five areas for the purpose of showing exact locations." But it could be mentioned that similar requests were going to Japanese agents in Panama, Vancouver, Portland, San Diego, San Francisco, and other places. Regardless, this information was sent to the commander in chief, Asiatic Fleet, and Kramer believed that any information sent to "CinCAF [from Washington] was automatically forwarded for information to CinCPac." This turns out not to always have been the case, but at that time Kramer understood it to be.

Al became buried in the work of producing and distributing the huge amount of diplomatic decrypts. The volume was such that the army and navy split the load in an alternating system which in hindsight shows many flaws and seems silly, but apparently seemed logical at the time. By mid-1941 the sheer volume of Japanese traffic also kept Kramer busy checking the many references to preceding messages contained in the body of new intercepts. The load was particularly large on December 6. Capt. Laurance Safford, head of OP-20-G, "later estimated that OP-20-G handled three times as much material that weekend as on a normal one; the GY log shows at least 28 messages in PURPLE alone."

In an oral history made during retirement, Rear Adm. Mac McCollum spoke of the distribution system—which peaked in the five weeks before the Pearl Harbor attack. This is very interesting and is worth quoting at length.

> The technique was to make up booklets with these translated dispatches. The Signals Intelligence Section of the Army and ONI and its communications adjunct split the work. We'd work on it one day, and they'd work on it the next day, and then we'd carry these books around to important people.
>
> I was opposed to the method of delivery of this type of stuff [however it was proscribed, so] Lt. Cmdr. Kramer was the man I had designated to carry around these papers. He'd go in and see Secretary of State Hull personally and hand it to him and stand there while Mr. Hull read it over and offer any comment that the secretary desired. He'd do the same thing for the Secretary of the Navy, the Chief of Naval Operations, the Director of War Plans, and so on. And, of course, the Director of Naval Intelligence, and me.
>
> In order to give some . . . appreciation of what these things were, it made sense to send the translated intercepts around with people like Lt. Cmdr. Kramer or [army Lt. Col. Rufus "Togo" Bratton], who with their depth of background and expertise could answer questions and insert common sense regarding what was being read.

"Kramer . . . often sat next to the recipient and explained references, furnished background, answered questions, and so forth—which is why so valuable an officer was given the apparently menial messenger task."

> For the War Department [which is to say the army], Colonel Bratton was doing the delivery. He went to the Chief of Staff of the Army and one or two other designated people there, and he normally would serve the White House. We also cut in Rear Adm. John

Beardall, the naval aide to the President. Beardall, if he thought there was anything that the President should know about, would indicate it and we'd see that Bratton got the word to the President directly. Usually the President would see it himself. These things were usually done in the daytime, but if the urgency of the situation developed, they'd have to be carried around at night. It was a very onerous job and a very dangerous job, looking back on it, and a rather insecure one.

You had Kramer, whose charming wife was driving him around in a beat-up old car all over town delivering these books.[3] The Secretary of State lived at the Wardman Park [Hotel], so he'd have to go there to deliver the thing. Then he'd go over to see [Navy Secretary] Knox. I forget where he lived. I think probably in the same area. Then he'd have to go to the Chief of Naval Operations up on Observatory Circle, then out to Chevy Chase somewhere to [assistant CNO] Admiral Ingersoll's place, and over to [director, War Plans] Admiral Turner's place up there near Chevy Chase Circle. [Director of Naval Intelligence] Wilkinson lived over here in Arlington. It was a job. Just take the sheer physical business of toting these books around all over town at night. It gives you the shivers at times.

Neither Kramer nor Bratton could be conveyed by official cars. They didn't do things like that much in those days. They didn't have very many of them and it was like pulling eyeteeth to get a car and a chauffeur at your disposal. This couldn't be done. It was easier, frankly, to have Mary Kramer drive him around than it was to try to go through the red tape of getting a car and a driver because, you know, that meant overtime for the drivers. You couldn't do that.

On December 6, 1941, the Japanese government in Tokyo sent thirteen parts of a lengthy fourteen-part message to their ambassadors in Washington (Admiral Nomura and Special Envoy Kurusu). The message fundamentally reviewed the diplomatic situation, developed the Japanese position, and terminated hope for any amicable resolutions. Al, with Mary again driving, delivered his booklets with this information late at night, and then returned home—around 2:00 a.m.—for a very short night. Back in the office around 7:30 on Sunday morning for a scheduled meeting and any new developments, Kramer was given the fourteenth part of the message as well as some other intercepts. He had been on call at home for anything special warranting it, but had not been called. Admiral McCollum later remembered that

> around ten o'clock or maybe a little bit before, Kramer came in with the fourteenth part. That was *the end*. In other words, diplomatic relations were being broken. The fourteenth part was the final. In other words, in spite of everything, [the Japanese were saying] "You people have wronged us" and so on, summing up the case and breaking up diplomatic relations.

Kramer finished talking to McCollum and then took off. He emerged from Main Navy and started a brisk walk for the State Department, eight blocks away. As the

---

3. If the reader has seen the movie *Tora! Tora! Tora!*, he or she will recall that it dramatically shows Mrs. Kramer driving Mr. Kramer around making these visits and deliveries to various places, including the White House. The movie specifically depicts the night of December 6, but such trips happened many days and evenings in 1941.

urgency of the situation came over him, he began to move "on the double," which is to say—fully dressed in a coat and tie—he ran.

> Kramer hot-footed it over to the White House, along with Admiral Beardall, who was the president's naval aide, and tried to get it to the President, which they did—or someone did—and also to the secretary of state, the secretary of the navy, and so on. I continued to haunt the CNO's outer office. Kramer came back in around 10:30 and he said, "We have the final—we've got the instructions for delivery," and it repeated over and over that it must be delivered to Mr. Hull at precisely one-o'clock Washington time. Kramer and I thought about it for a minute and he said let's see what the times are.

It was obvious that one o'clock in Washington was dawn or early morning at several key Pacific locations, including the Malay Peninsula, the Philippine Islands, and the Hawaiian Islands. But there were no conclusions made by anyone that there was going to be an actual attack, let alone where any such attack might be delivered. Kramer later testified that

> it was the consensus of the opinion of my associates and many of the high officials in Washington that it was very illogical and foolish on the part of Japan to undertake open warfare with the United States, that it was almost inconceivable that they would in view of the fact that it is very likely that they would get everything that they wanted and as they had got in French Indochina and what they wanted south of French Indochina, without any action being taken by the United States.

If anything, Kramer was concerned about Kota Bharu in Malaysia—where the Japanese did indeed attack on December 8.

Al Kramer's "most vivid impressions of that morning" were of "urgency and perspiration" from chasing about the Navy Department, to the White House and State Department, back to his office "as quickly as possible to see if anything new had come in," put it through the mill, "and to dash out with it again."

Much has been said and written as to why more forceful alerts didn't fly out from Washington the morning of December 7, and much has been written how the attack on Pearl Harbor would have been mitigated if they had. That discussion won't be developed here. Suffice it to say that such warning would have to have been at the highest levels: the secretary of war, the secretary of the navy, the army chief of staff, the CNO, or even the director of navy war plans. It was clearly beyond the authority of relatively low-ranking intelligence officers, including Kramer's ONI boss, Commander McCollum; his OP-20-G boss, Commander Safford; or his army colleague, Lieutenant Colonel Bratton. It certainly was not the responsibility, nor within the authority, of Lt. Cmdr. Al Kramer.

Whenever something important goes awry, there's often a search for blame and an apportioning of criticism. One of Kramer's GZ civilian employees later said that, in his opinion, "Al was not the ideal man for the job at that time." As with many "perfectionists" it appeared that at times he couldn't distinguish details from important issues. On Saturday, December 6, one of his new translators, Mrs. Dorothy Edgers, tried to interest him in what she believed to be an important decrypt in a lesser system. However, Kramer wouldn't deal with it, deeply focused as he was upon the Japanese fourteen-part PURPLE message.

Rear Adm. Layton later suggested that Lt. Cmdr. Kramer was sometimes too much a perfectionist, hanging onto translations too long, and not moving them along in a timely fashion. But that's a complicated issue. Translation—particularly of an incredibly nuanced language like Japanese—can't be done hurriedly. Capt. Joe **Rochefort** once offered a counter-argument to Layton's remark—although not in specific reference to Kramer.

> You might give a rough translation, or you might give a very careful translation. So much can depend on whether it is going to be "will," "shall," or something [even more subtle]. Unless you do a good job of translating, the whole value [could be] lost.

Historian Gordon Prange supported this view, writing in his monumental work, *At Dawn We Slept*, that

> Japanese is very difficult to translate into English. To make matters worse, the messages came in as phonetic syllables. One such sound could have a variety of unrelated meanings. Even translators highly qualified in Japanese needed "considerable experience in this particular field before they could be trusted to come through with a correct interpretation. . . ." Moreover, they worked with diplomatic material, where a shade of phraseology carries a vital significance. No wonder Kramer often put in brutal hours of overtime.

Regardless, it never was likely that accurate clues to the attack on Pearl Harbor would come through PURPLE. "The Japanese military trusted their diplomats even less than the U.S. military was inclined to trust ours." No specifics of Japanese Navy operations would appear in diplomatic channels. Among many others, Pearl Harbor historian Roberta Wohlstetter firmly concluded that "there was absolutely nothing in MAGIC that established . . . a Japanese intent [to attack] clearly and firmly."

Toward the end of the war, Secretary of War Henry Stimson appointed Lt. Col. Henry Clausen as an independent prosecutor to investigate the root causes of the Pearl Harbor disaster. This was done when Stimson decided the previous Army Pearl Harbor Board (and the other two investigations to date) was not reliable. Clausen's work thus becomes one of the *eight* Pearl Harbor investigations between 1942 and 1946. In Clausen's opinion, and reiterated in his 1962 book *Pearl Harbor: Final Judgement*, there were fourteen people particularly culpable for not taking proper measures to ward off the disaster. It's a little curious who made the list and who didn't; interestingly, he included Lt. Cmdr. Kramer among those fourteen. Nevertheless, Clausen's discussion of Al Kramer is more of a criticism of his circumstances than of Kramer individually. Essentially, Clausen felt that Kramer—who, in the grade of lieutenant commander, was still technically a "junior" officer—was overloaded with work and potentially a single point of failure as he sorted, prioritized, translated, and disseminated a large volume of diplomatic communications intelligence. But Clausen identified no actual failure. He never stated that any change to Kramer's efforts or decision-making, on December 6–7, 1941, would have ensured that any better or faster warnings would have been sent to Pearl Harbor.

Still, the disaster weighed heavily upon those in intelligence and communications intelligence.

Ens. Edward Van Der Rhoer, a young Japanese language officer assigned to OP-20-GZ in the spring of 1942, documented his observations of the post–Pearl Harbor Lt. Cmdr. Al Kramer. The new ensign was given a desk right across from Kramer. In Van Der Rhoer's view, Al

> was a handsome, erect man with brown wavy hair and a moustache. He spoke courteously and in low key to everyone, regardless of rank. He was a gentleman and a scholar of the type [occasionally] produced by the service academies—which produced more roughnecks and anti-intellectuals. He would have made an excellent naval attaché moving in diplomatic circles abroad.

"The Pearl Harbor defeat and especially the failure to foresee the attack acutely affected everyone in OP-20-GZ, and . . . a pall of gloom still hung over the branch." Actually, it's fair to say that all of OP-20-G had been overworked and overstretched prior to the war's start, dividing manpower among Japanese diplomatic traffic, the minimally broken JN-25 naval code, and the tracking of potentially hostile U-boats in the Atlantic. Two weeks of fifteen-hour days—prior to December 7—had also left the overall head of OP-20-G, Cmdr. Laurance Safford, physically drained and approaching a state of nervous exhaustion. Of course, months later, the pressures of the shooting war hadn't decreased the stress—despite the influx of new personnel.

Ens. Van Der Rhoer observed that the new head of GZ, Lt. Cmdr. Redfield "Rosie" Mason, was in total contrast to Kramer, who Mason had replaced in the spring. Unusually, Kramer had been kept in the branch even after Mason took over.

> Mason consciously used fear to keep people under control . . . Yet, he treated Kramer . . . with compassion. Perhaps it was part of the code that made Annapolis men stand together [in fact Mason and Kramer were both Class of 1925]. . . . Mason also realized, in all probability, that the other man was near the limit of physical if not emotional exhaustion. [And] I had no way of knowing whether [Mason] ever told himself, "There, but for the grace of God, go I."
>
> Kramer had been relieved of any active participation in the work of the branch. He did not in fact seem to have any particular duties, and among those who worked there an understanding hung in the air that Kramer had failed. He was associated with the debacle of Pearl Harbor in his handling of the product of OP-20-GZ. . . .
>
> I saw him as a broken man. I did not know the extent to which he had been drawn into the work of the Roberts Commission, making a preliminary investigation of Pearl Harbor, but it seemed to me that he was involved more in postmortems of that disaster than in anything of current interest. . . . Kramer fell asleep at his desk day after day. It was said that he often worked late into the night, but no one suggested what he had been doing.

It's clear that the young officer liked Mr. Kramer and sympathized with him. "I felt depressed by the thought that as long as people remembered the Pearl Harbor disaster, Kramer would be forced to answer the same old questions. . . . Mr. Kramer would be called on to testify, with courtesy and quiet dignity, before navy boards of inquiry and in congressional investigations over a period of years, even when the war was over."

Beginning in March 1942 and through the summer—and apparently unknown to Ens. Van Der Rhoer—Lt. Cmdr. Kramer was very involved in the creation of a new organization, at first called the "Intelligence Committee," which started with a high-level "Interdepartmental Intelligence Conference." This effort was designed to pull together the COMINT organizations of the army, navy, coast guard, State Department, Federal Bureau of Investigation, and the Federal Communications Commission in order to streamline and otherwise develop efficiencies in the business—as well as eliminate duplication.

Commander Kramer (he'd been promoted in August) was subsequently transferred to the ICPOA—at Pearl Harbor—in fall 1942 to work on translations. He moved to the CinCPac intelligence staff, under fleet intelligence officer Capt. Edwin Layton, around July 1943—and then shortly thereafter was sent to Adm. Bill Halsey's headquarters in the southwest Pacific.

In March 1945, Captain Kramer was transferred back to Washington and assigned to ONI. But in September, Kramer was hospitalized after going into Bethesda Naval Hospital for a routine check-up the month before. The hospitalization of

the most important witness in the [upcoming congressional] investigation attracted press attention. A United Press dispatch reported Republican charges, denied by the Navy, that he "had been 'broken in mind and body' and was being held incommunicado in a hospital psychopathic ward." An Associated Press story also held, quoting an unidentified source, that Kramer was "being badgered to change his original testimony." According to the *New York Times*, Kramer "had been beset and beleaguered . . . badgered and beset by an effort to break down his testimony." He denied the charge and "asserted that he was feeling very well and would appear before the committee prepared to state fully 'anything I know that they may want to know.'"[4]

Fears to the contrary notwithstanding, Al was made available as a witness to this final Pearl Harbor attack investigation—this time the Joint Congressional Committee Investigation. He'd already testified for several of the previous investigations, which had started within weeks of the attack in 1941.

One of the topics that Captain Kramer was constantly pressed on was the "Winds Message" or "Winds Code." Before the commencement of hostilities, American intelligence had discovered that

---

4. Admiral Layton, in his memoir *"And I Was There": Pearl Harbor and Midway—Breaking the Secrets*—supported by his coauthors Capt. Roger Pineau and Mr. John Costello—was fully convinced that "Captain Kramer was 'persuaded' to modify his testimony about the Winds message by the threat of permanent confinement in a psychiatric ward."

Innocuous phrases were to be inserted into regular weather reports sent by Radio Tokyo, indicating whether diplomatic relations were in danger. The Winds code provided for problems not only with the United States, but also with England or Russia. Two Tokyo cables on November 19th, 1941, the so-called "Winds Set-up" messages, established that such signals might be sent and the phrases of the open code.

These were "East Wind Rain," meaning danger in Japan-U.S. relations; "North Wind Cloudy," meaning Japan-Russia relations in danger, and "West Wind Clear," meaning Japan-Britain relations in danger. Upon receiving any of these messages, Japanese embassies and consulates affected were to burn documents and destroy their last codes and cipher equipment.

The controversy lay in whether any of the enumerated phrases was ever broadcast and if so, which one or ones. Such a broadcast would have been the "Winds Execute."

Kramer was convinced, in 1941, that he had seen an authentic "East Wind Rain" execute message, but in several subsequent Pearl Harbor attack inquiries he changed his story. In 1962, historian Roberta Wohlstetter wrote:

> On the whole, Kramer's frequent changes in testimony are hard to understand; and one cannot help harboring some doubts about a luncheon at the home of Admiral Stark in September 1945 where, Kramer reported, his memory was "refreshed."

Al, no doubt sick of the subject after several years of being grilled about it, finally tried to push back while on the witness stand.

> I would like to point out to you, Mr. Keefe, that I think that an entirely unwarranted emphasis and importance is being attributed to that message, not only in *this* hearing but in *past* hearings, and in the *press*. There were many other messages more specific as to Japanese intentions during [that] period. . . . A Wind message would have been only one further indication of the general trend of this traffic as well as the general trend of the international situation.

Indeed, it doesn't seem to be very important. Capt. Laurance Safford and others believed that a Winds "execute" message was indeed sent, that it was an actual war signal, and that it constituted an announcement that Tokyo had decided to attack the United States. But that is not the case. Even if—and there is doubt—there had been an authentic "execute" message sent out and intercepted, it really would have told Washington nothing that American leaders didn't already know.

The same is true about the timeliness of distributing the long Japanese diplomatic message which came that fateful weekend. Naval reaction to the thirteen-part message—and even the final fourteenth part—"was not at all frenzied," for again it did not signify an imminent attack on any particular location. Ironically, and to their credit, "it *was* characterized by some urgency on the part of the Far Eastern specialists, particularly Kramer and McCollum." But to what end? Unfortunately, at that time, naval intelligence had very little influence with the navy War Plans Office or with the CNO.

In the final analysis, it's clear that the Pearl Harbor disaster cruelly hurt Al Kramer's reputation and drove his early retirement from the navy. But as fate would have it, it had nothing to do with any professional failure on his part on December 6–7—or on any other day leading up to the attack.

What happened to him was that he was caught in an ideological and political struggle that finally played out at the Joint Congressional Committee Investigation. The struggle was ideological in that Captain Safford and some others felt driven to exonerate Admiral Kimmel and General Short for taking the full blame for the disaster. They believed that the Winds message, and a delay in disclosing the fourteenth part of the last Japanese diplomatic intercept, were crucial to showing that many *high-level* people in Washington were very much to blame. They felt that the Washington leadership did not pass that information—as well as other intelligence analyses—to the Hawaiian commanders. The political struggle was similar, focused upon Republican congressmen trying to make the same points—but with the intent to discredit the late Democratic president, Franklin Roosevelt, and the current one, Harry Truman. Either way, most people involved felt that Alwin Dalton Kramer was key to the proceedings—to either support the position, or to be discredited if he did.[5]

At this point it hardly matters what really happened, or what Kramer really knew, or what he didn't know. What matters is that Captain Kramer was a remarkably poor witness. He reversed himself, contradicted his own earlier testimony, and undercut his friend and former boss Captain Safford after letting Safford think he'd support him. He gave excruciatingly long, convoluted, and contradictory answers to questions, droned on-and-on reading from his diary, and generally cut a very poor figure for an officer always known for intelligence and precision. His performance almost lent credence to the rumors that he was being aggressively pressured by navy superiors—having his memory "refreshed"—and that he was under threat of long-term incarceration in Bethesda's psycho ward. At one point, with Mrs. Kramer nervously watching, Senator Homer Ferguson shouted at him—and the usually dignified Kramer (perhaps appropriately) shouted right back. Ultimately, his testimony was so strange that a journalist who was there, when writing a foreword to a book about the proceedings almost fifty years later, recalled more than anything else "the dissimulation of one key witness, Captain Alwyn D. Kramer," and devoted half of his foreword discussing it.

Captain Kramer was on the witness stand for five long days in February 1946. After he was finished testifying he returned to Bethesda—where he remained until after the committee's reports were released in July. On September 1, 1946, Kramer was medically retired "for incapacity resulting from an incident of the service."

Not long after, Al Kramer moved his family to the Miami area and took up avocado and lime farming in the suburb of Princeton, Florida. Captain Kramer appar-

---

5. Short of reading through the multi-volume full transcripts of the various investigations, one could peruse the Greaves book (see the citation in the suggested reading section), particularly for testimony from Kramer, Safford, and McCollum.

ently advised on the 1970 Hollywood movie *Tora! Tora! Tora!*, but his name doesn't appear in the credits. In that movie, Lieutenant Commander Kramer was elegantly portrayed—in a very significant role with many lines—by actor Wesley Addy, who very much resembled him in appearance—although Addy was really about twenty years older than Kramer was at that point. Mrs. Kramer was portrayed by actress Leora Dana, driving Mr. Kramer around Washington late on December 6.

Captain Kramer and his wife (Mary Frances Holmes Kramer, 1907–1991) had two sons. Alwin died of a lung ailment on October 8, 1972, in Miami. When Mary—who was also from Springfield, Massachusetts—passed away nineteen years later, she was buried with Al at Arlington National Cemetery.

Angst over intelligence and the Pearl Harbor attack effectively ruined Al Kramer. As historian John Prados put it,

> Swirling controversy over whether there was a conspiracy to conceal intelligence about Pearl Harbor, over the "Winds" code messages, and so on, engulfed Laurance F. Safford and Alwin D. Kramer. . . .
> The Pearl Harbor investigations broke Kramer, who retired in the fall of 1946 to have nothing more to do with the Navy or intelligence.

Despite what it might look like, Kramer's relief as head of OP-20-GZ wasn't necessarily punitive relative to the Pearl Harbor disaster. He'd been in that job for over three years, and his move was among considerable personnel changes everywhere in the navy during the first few months of the war. The navy didn't hold him accountable for the warning failure. He—and perhaps a few partially informed individuals—may have felt he could have done more to avert the disaster, but that was never any official conclusion at the time, nor is it today. In fact, Kramer continued to receive intelligence assignments throughout the war, and he was promoted to full commander in August 1942—and then to captain in July 1943. Neither those assignments nor those promotions would have happened had he been in official disfavor.

That being said, unlike almost everyone else profiled in this book, Captain Kramer was not presented with a personal decoration relative to his considerable prewar or wartime contributions. Thus, Al's awards were limited to the Navy Unit Commendation Ribbon, Second Nicaraguan Campaign Medal, Asiatic-Pacific Campaign Medal, and the World War II Victory Medal—and of course the gold Distinguished Marksmanship Badge.[6]

---

6. Interestingly, at the conclusion of the Joint Congressional Committee Investigation, a naval liaison officer appointed to assist the investigation advised the Secretary of the Navy that Captain Kramer deserved a high decoration. Lt. Cmdr. John F. Baecher wrote that such an award should be made "because the effect of [Kramer's] testimony was to support the integrity of the higher command of the Navy." At the same time, Mr. Baecher advised SecNav that giving Captain Safford the Legion of Merit medal for his service was "inappropriate," presumably because Safford's testimony was adverse to the integrity of the higher command of the Navy. Regardless of Baecher's efforts, Safford *did* receive the LoM, and Kramer received *nothing*.

Even after the passage of almost seventy years, the Pearl Harbor disaster—and Kramer's inexplicable, strange performances on witness stands during several of the following investigations—cloud his reputation. Yet Alwin Kramer was a superbly dedicated and extremely hard-working officer; he carried huge responsibility and produced remarkable quantities of fine intelligence. Perhaps it's that for which he should be remembered.

Sources

Benson, 23, 45, 48, 49, 53.

Bryden, 240, 266–72.

Captain Alwin D. Kramer, U.S. Navy, Retired. Official Biography. Biographies Section, OI-140, U.S. Department of the Navy, May 23, 1955.

Clausen, 46, 217–19, 307–8.

Costello, 179, 196–99, 203–4, 216–19.

Dingman, 100, 106, 109.

Donovan and Mack, 90, 148.

Farago, *Broken Seal*, 102, 105, 167–68, 194–96, 200–2, 211–12, 229–32, 275–76, 278, 280, 329, 332, 341, 345–46, 353–54, 358–60, 364–66.

Greaves, xvii–xviii, 764–76, 782.

Hanyok and Mowry, 77–80.

Holmes, 47.

Kahn, *Codebreakers*, 2–4, 11, 27–29, 50, 56–58.

Kahn, *Discovered*, 89–91.

Kramer, Capt. Alwin D., Ret. *Lecture Presented at an Unspecified Location.* Introduced by Frank B. Rowlett. Ft. Meade, MD: National Security Agency, 1962. www.nsa.gov/about/_files/ . . . the . . . /1962-Transcript_Kramer.pdf.

"Kramer, Pearl Harbor Figure, Dies." Obituary, *Palm Beach Post*, October 10, 1972, p. B12.

Layton, *"And I Was There,"* 164, 265–66, 282–85, 289, 291–92, 300, 303–4, 307.

Lewin, 58, 68, 71.

Lucky Bag, U.S. Naval Academy, 1925.

McCollum, *Reminiscences*, 250, 262, 269, 275, 405–8, 787–88, 796.

McGinnis, 348–49, 369.

Prados, 731.

Prange, *At Dawn We Slept*, 84, 86, 250–51, 451, 456, 467, 474–76, 485, 488–89, 631, 665, 680–81.

Rochefort, *Reminiscences*, 106.

Slesnick, 42–44.

Stinnet, 229–33.

Toland, 4, 67, 94–95, 136–37, 193–94, 199n, 215–24, 231–32, 301–2.

U.S. Navy, *Register of Commissioned and Warrant Officers.*

Van Der Rhoer, 50–52, 57–61, 64–66, 112.

Wohlstetter, 171–72, 175, 212, 218–19, 225, 334, 336, 390.

Worth, 17, 19, 20, 41, 61.

REAR ADMIRAL REDFIELD BARNARD MASON, U.S. NAVY
(1904–1995)

Bright, independent, competitive, abrasive, and profane
Fleet Intelligence Officer, U.S. Asiatic Fleet, 1939–1941
"Rosie"

Part of the prewar navy's clan of linguist-codebreakers—in which everybody knew everybody—Rosie Mason was bright, independent, fiercely competitive, abrasive, and profane to the "point of great pleasure." In the spring of 1942 he refused to believe the brilliant and accurate analysis of Station HYPO (Joe Rochefort's Hawaii team) that the Japanese designation "AF" signified Midway Atoll—insisting it was something else—and his assertive stance dominated the thinking at Main Navy in Washington. Despite this blunder, Mason ended the war with a Distinguished Service Medal for radio intelligence service, and later promotion to rear admiral. By many accounts a difficult man to work for—"an omnipresent, cigar-chomping bear"—he nevertheless contributed long and distinguished service ashore, at sea, and in communications intelligence.

*   *   *

From the 1925 Naval Academy yearbook, *The Lucky Bag*:

> This sweet young thing stepped into our midst from the wilds of Indiana. *Rosie* is exceedingly ambitious; those ambitions range from being an Admiral to being a piano mover, and from being a great author to being a hen-pecked husband. *Rosie* is also fond of those from other lands and counts among those foreign acquaintances a Russian countess and a mulatto queen from St. Lucia. To say the least, he is democratic. He has taken life easy and found time to do a great deal of reading. As a consequence he has collected a fund of general information that makes him an exceedingly interesting talker as any of the Juice [electrical engineering] instructors will agree. Besides this, he has become a bridge and Mah-Jongg player of no mean ability. [Activities: *Log* staff; tennis; class basketball]

*   *   *

Redfield B. Mason was born in 1904. Appointed from Indiana, he graduated from the Naval Academy in 1925 along with such classmates as John F. Delaney Jr., Ernest "Judge" Eller, Ernest S. L. **Goodwin**, Robert E. Hogaboom, Morton C. Mumma Jr., Alwin **Kramer**, and Linwood **Howeth**. He was promoted to lieutenant (junior grade), 1928; lieutenant, 1934; lieutenant commander, 1939; commander, 1942; captain, 1943; and rear admiral, 1952.

Right after graduation Mr. Mason began an intense series of sea-duty assignments, starting with a brief tour in the battleship *Texas*. During 1925–1926 he was on board the light cruiser USS *Denver*; in 1927 the ammunition ship *Nitro*; and during 1928–1930 the destroyer *Lardner*. During his *Lardner* assignment, Mason took a brief course of instruction at the Naval Torpedo Station, Newport. He then transferred to the destroyer *Bernadou*.

In 1930 he was selected for ONI's Japanese language immersion training in Tokyo (arriving one year after Joe **Rochefort** and Eddie **Layton**), and thus spent three years in Japan, studying under Naganuma Naoe. This training was followed by time in Washington with ONI and with OP-20-G, followed by sea duty on board the battleship *Maryland*, 1934–1936, as plotting-room officer.

Mason was made available by ONI for duty with decryption units around April 1936, and in 1937 he returned to ONI, was with OP-20-G (head of GZ) in mid-1938, and then during 1939 to 1941 he served on the staff of the commander in chief, U.S. Asiatic Fleet (Adm. Thomas C. Hart), as FIO on board the flagship *Houston*. During this time, radio direction-finding and traffic analysis in the Philippines (at Station CAST) provided some of the earliest indications of serious Japanese war preparations. One of these was a report of Imperial Navy organization which

Mason endorsed and sent to Washington in October 1941: "The conclusion that *must* be drawn from the organization presented here is that the Japanese *are* on a wartime disposition." After the attack on Pearl Harbor in December, and when the Japanese then invaded the Philippine Islands in late 1941 and early 1942, Lt. Cmdr. Mason received orders to move a group of twenty-seven officer and enlisted radio intelligence personnel from Corregidor to Melbourne and set up a fleet radio unit in coordination with the Australians and the British. Thus, he went with other evacuees from Station CAST to Melbourne where he helped in the setup of Station BELCONNEN, as FRUMel was first called (the name taken from the Australian Belconnen Naval Transmitting Station). After Lt. Rudy **Fabian** arrived to take the lead at Belconnen, Mason returned to Main Navy.

During World War II, Mason's capabilities as a Japanese linguist were extremely valuable. In the spring of 1942, Mason became head of OP-20-GZ in Washington, the Japanese language section of OP-20-G, relieving classmate Lt. Cmdr. Alwin Kramer. All three of the navy's principal Japanese codebreaking units intensified their efforts in the spring of 1942, trying to figure out activity which was going to solidify as the Battles of Coral Sea and then Midway.

Mason drove his team ruthlessly. As historian Roger Dingman has put it, Mason was a highly competitive individual who "wanted *his* unit in Washington, *not* its rivals at Pearl Harbor and Melbourne, to decode and translate [the] vital message[s]." He refused to believe the pre-analysis of Cmdr. Joe Rochefort, at Pearl Harbor's Station HYPO, that the designation of "AF" in Japanese traffic referred to Midway—insisting it was something else—and Mason's assertive stance shaped all levels of the thinking at Main Navy in Washington. For several days Hawaii and Washington (Stations HYPO and NEGAT) argued back and forth over the issue, Major Red **Lasswell** taking point for HYPO. Neither side wanted to give ground. Fortunately, Admiral Nimitz had developed confidence in Rochefort and his team (as well as in his fleet intelligence officer, Lt. Cmdr. Eddie Layton), and bought the AF-as-Midway argument. This is extraordinarily fortunate, because "in contrast to their colleagues at Pearl Harbor, Admiral King's own intelligence specialists forecast another major enemy South Pacific assault, and failed to see the growing danger to Midway and Hawaii."

Mason's mis-analysis notwithstanding, brand-new Ens. Edward Van Der Rhoer was extremely impressed by Mason when the young man joined OP-20-GZ in spring 1942, seeing him as an "awesome personality"—as well as an abrasive one. "Rosie Mason was a driving leader who did not spare himself or others . . . he meant to be a winner, and he was. I often had the feeling that he was a candidate for an early ulcer." Mason was a "diamond in the rough," in total contrast to Alwin Kramer, who Mason had replaced after the Pearl Harbor disaster. Kramer was a courteous gentleman and scholar. But Mason

was a man you would not want to encounter in a brawl in an alley. Six times a day he sent chills down your spine when he bellowed "COFFEE!" at the top of his voice and a chief yeoman came running with the pot. Mason consciously used fear to keep people under control, but it [seemed to work.]

Yet he treated Kramer [who had remained in the office] with compassion. Van Der Rhoer believed that Mason saw Kramer as a man near the limit of physical and emotional exhaustion—and that Mason may have also decided that Pearl Harbor intelligence-failure criticisms against Kramer would have similarly been leveled at Mason had *he* been in the job at that time.

Ens. Van Der Rhoer thought that Mason injected a new and aggressive spirit into the work of OP-20-GZ. He drove his men hard; there was "no loafing; no trivial conversation. Many people resented Mason's bullying tactics, but only the civilians dared to show how much they resented his unrelenting pressure." At the same time, Mason "stayed in the forefront, leading the way . . . [he] won grudging respect by driving himself as hard as he drove others," and he won respect as a good language instructor.[1]

Detached from Main Navy in October 1945, Mason served for two months with the Training Command, Pacific, after which he became the captain of the attack-transport *Bergen*. In March 1946, he reported to the destroyer-tender *Everglades* as prospective commanding officer, but before that ship was commissioned he was detached for duty in command of the destroyer-tender *Sierra*. He held this command from May 1946 to March 1947, thereafter serving on the staff of Commander Naval Forces, Western Pacific, from April to December 1947.

In 1948 he returned to Washington. When the AFSA was formed, he was in charge of its production group during the early part of the Korean War. Mason was a severe critic of the AFSA, and told a congressional committee they should either abolish it or give it some real authority. More authority was granted, along with a subsequent name change to the NSA.

Later, during the Korean War, Mason was assigned to Japan. There he commanded Service Division 31 and then Service Squadron 3, responsible for providing logistical support for all naval forces afloat in the Far East—particularly Task Forces 77 and 95. He received the Legion of Merit with Combat "V" in connection with operations against the enemy in Korea.

In May 1952, Mason had duty with the staff of Commander Naval Forces, Far East, as naval advisor to the Japanese government.

In 1953, Rear Admiral Mason became commander of the Military Sea Transportation Service (Atlantic), which included thirty-one cargo ships, ten tankers, four passenger ships, fourteen support vessels, and seven icebreakers—headquartered in

1. Van Der Rhoer's insights into Mason's personality are fascinating, but it's also interesting to note that in his autobiographical book, *Deadly Magic*, Van Der Rhoer writes *nothing* about the "AF"/Midway controversy between HYPO and NEGAT. Moreover, in a book that purports to discuss communications intelligence in the Pacific Theater, he *never* mentions Station HYPO, Rochefort, or Layton—it's as if no office other than OP-20-G in Washington were at all involved!

Brooklyn, New York. During this period the MSTS assisted in the construction of a string of radar outposts along the rim of the Arctic wasteland in northern Canada. Designed to detect Soviet bombers or missiles attempting to penetrate American airspace from over the North Pole, what became known as the Distant Early Warning (DEW) Line represented a tremendous logistical and technological feat.

While at MSTS, Mason became involved in an unusual activity for a U.S. Navy admiral. One of Mason's radio intelligence colleagues was Capt. Albert J. **Pelletier** Jr. (who was formerly a member of the famous enlisted "On-the-Roof-Gang"). Pelletier described Mason as "the most brilliant man I ever knew." He also said that Mason could read a page of newsprint, whether in English or in Japanese, in a single glance.

This skill came fully into play in 1956, when Mason appeared for several weeks on the NBC quiz show *The Big Surprise*, hosted by Mike Wallace. For several nationally broadcasted programs, Rear Admiral Mason faced Mr. Wallace and demonstrated an exhaustive knowledge of ancient mythology. Answering four questions about the Trojan War brought him $20,000 on February 25, 1956. Naming the twelve labors of Hercules took him to the $50,000 level on March 3. Then, with $100,000 at stake on March 20, he was asked to name each female creature in six mythological triads—which he did with a flourish: the Gorgons, the Harpies, the Graeae, the Graces, the Horae, and the Furies.[2] Later, Mason's wife (charmingly named *Truth*) reinforced Captain Pelletier's remarks and explained her husband's secret. "He had the ability to read a book *once* and *know* it." Mason had been urged by his aides to apply for the quiz show, which allowed contestants to pick their subject of expertise; ever the fierce competitor, he had virtually assured his success by selecting mythology and then cramming for it.

In June 1957, Rear Admiral Mason became commander of the Training Command, U.S. Pacific Fleet, and then in March 1958 he returned once again to Washington as Assistant Chief of Naval Operations for Fleet Operations and Readiness.

Ordered back to Pearl Harbor, he next assumed command of the Service Force, U.S. Pacific Fleet, in February 1961. There he controlled more than one hundred ships and units which furnished logistical support to the naval units and installations in the Pacific Ocean area.

From January 1963 until August 1966, Rosie Mason served as Commandant, Third Naval District, headquartered in New York City.

The acerbic Mason, whom few would accuse of being friendly, was decorated for improving the Navy's image by helping city officials during the massive power failure that blacked out New York City on November 9, 1965.

And during the great transportation strike of January 1966, he was instrumental in providing continuous official transportation for military and federal employees.

---

2. *Gorgans* (Stheno, Euryale, Medusa); *Harpies* (Aello, Celaeno, Ocypete); *Graeae* (Deino, Enyo, Pemphredo); *Horae* (Thallo, Auxo, Carpo); *Graces* (Aglaea, Euphrosyne, Thalia); and *Furies* (Alecto, Megaera, Tisiphone).

Mason was also interested in, and frequently participated in, naval reserve functions, and promoted a very cooperative and effective relationship between the regular navy and the naval reserve in the northeast. At the close of this assignment in New York, he was relieved of active duty, and retired in August 1966.

Many years after World War II, Station HYPO's brilliant cryptanalyst Capt. Ham **Wright** reflected upon Mason's mis-assessment of the initial Midway analysis. "Rosie Mason was *the guy* in Washington who wouldn't buy 'AF' for Midway. A very nice guy; an able linguist, but he wouldn't buy it."

From the perspective of 1983, master cryptanalyst Capt. Tommy **Dyer** held very mixed feelings about Mason. He acknowledged that Mason was a good intelligence officer versus codebreaker. "He was a *language* officer; he had *some* cryptanalytic ability." However, Dyer freely admitted that he "never had a great deal of love" for Mason. In 1943, Capt. Earl Stone, then head of OP-20-G, sent a four-page letter to Capt. Bill Goggins, who had replaced Joe Rochefort as head of Station HYPO. Two of the pages, Dyer was certain, were written by Mason and asserted that a current de-cryption disagreement between the two units was all due to Dyer being "confused," leading Stone to suggest that Dyer possibly needed to be transferred someplace else. Dyer and Goggins found the letter infuriating, due not only to the personal attack, but also because it was *again* OP-20-G which was mistaken in its analysis, "causing considerable loss of effort" and delay.[3]

Rear Adm. Arthur **McCollum**, in a series of interviews during 1970–1971, echoed Dyer's positive remarks, commenting that Rosie Mason was "a very good" fleet intelligence officer when attached to the Asiatic Fleet circa 1940.

Admiral Mason passed away in 1995, at the age of ninety-one, and was buried in Arlington National Cemetery. He was survived by his wife, Truth, as well as a son, Michael, and two daughters, Virginia and Jo Anne.

At the time of his retirement, Rear Admiral Mason was awarded a second Legion of Merit. He had already received a Distinguished Service Medal at the end of World War II—one of only six navy people in the radio intelligence world so recognized. Among other awards and decorations, he also had a Navy Commendation Ribbon, a United Nations Service Medal, and the Philippine Defense Ribbon. In addition, Mason has been named a Pioneer Officer of U.S. Naval Cryptology by the Naval Cryptologic Veterans Association.

Sources

Carlson, 55, 328–29, 445.
Dingman, 100–1, 228.
Dyer, 252–55.

---

3. One would hope that senior officers would not let petty issues from teenage years carry forward, but it's a fact that one time in 1922 Midshipman Third Class Dyer—in the middle of the night—put Midshipman Fourth Class Mason under the shower in his pajamas during Annapolis graduation week frivolity.

Holtwick, 91, 107, 305, 435, App. 104, 114.
Lucky Bag, U.S. Naval Academy, 1925.
Lundstrom, John B., in Hone, 242.
McGinnis, *NCVA*, 21.
Prados, 214, 731.
Rear Admiral Redfield Mason, USN, Ret. Official Biography. Navy Office of Information, Internal Relations Division, August 1966.
Thomas, Robert McG., Jr. "Adm. Redfield Mason Dies at 91; Code Breaker and TV Quiz Whiz." *New York Times*, July 28, 1995.
U.S. Navy, *Register of Commissioned and Warrant Officers.*
Van Der Rhoer, 49–52, 66, 71, 77, 84, 212.

REAR ADMIRAL JOHN WALTER McCLARAN, U.S. NAVY (1887–1948)

"Mac"

John McClaran was a unique and pioneering figure in the early twentieth-century U.S. Navy, contributing a spectacular career at sea as well as in diplomacy, Japanese studies, naval intelligence, naval communications, and cryptology.

* * *

From the 1911 Annapolis yearbook, *The Lucky Bag*:

Mac . . . has gone through this place on an equal mixture of conscientiousness and bluff. He is not very savvy, but never bones [studies] very hard, and yet never stands very low. . . . He is very popular, and one of the most consistently lucky men in our Class. [Activities: Football Team Manager]

* * *

J. W. McClaran was born in Wooster, Ohio, on October 1, 1887, son of John C. and Elizabeth Deere McClaran. There he attended grade school, high school, and briefly the Wooster University. He was a member of the Phi Gamma Delta fraternity. He then was appointed to the U.S. Naval Academy and graduated in 1911, along with classmates John W. Reeves, Oscar C. Badger, Lewis H. Brereton, Harry W. Hill, Norman Scott, Daniel J. Callaghan, and Howard F. **Kingman**. He was promoted to ensign, 1912; lieutenant (junior grade), 1915; lieutenant, 1918; lieutenant commander, 1921; commander, 1931; captain, 1940; and rear admiral (on the retired list), 1941.

During World War I, Lt. j.g. McClaran was awarded the Navy Cross while serving on board the destroyer USS *Cassin*. Following an explosion resulting from the ship being torpedoed on October 15, 1917, he braved thick smoke pouring out of the handling room to enter the aft magazine, trying to determine the situation and if there were any survivors to be rescued.

In 1921, Lt. Cmdr. McClaran was assigned as an assistant naval attaché in Tokyo, working under the dynamic and resourceful Capt. Edward **Watson**, and alongside the equally high-energy and high-initiative Lt. Cmdr. Ellis **Zacharias**. During this time, "Mac" and "Zach" were tasked by Watson to cozy-up to several key Japanese naval officers, and in so doing were able to determine that the Japanese were prepared to make significant concessions regarding the upcoming Washington Naval Conference on arms limitation.

During 1922–1923, Mr. McClaran was on the staff of the Commander, Yangtze Patrol Force, in China. In 1924, he was selected as commanding officer of the destroyer USS *Pope*, and was in that position when the *Pope* was at sea to support the U.S. Army's groundbreaking "Round the World Flight." One of the airplanes making this circumnavigation crashed into a mountain in dense fog close to Port Moller, Alaska; Mr. McClaran and several others assisted in recovering the crew. He also received a commendation, from the commander in chief of the Asiatic Fleet, for his outstanding navigation and shiphandling performance as the *Pope* operated in the Kuril Islands.

Later in 1924, Mac was appointed head of the Far Eastern Desk, ONI. During that period he was tasked by the director of naval intelligence (Capt. Andrew Long) to supervise the translation of the Japanese Navy's operational code, named the "Red Book." ONI had a copy of this codebook, because ONI agents had previously stolen it out of a diplomat's safe, photographed it, and returned it without detection—a spectacular clandestine operation. To accomplish this task, Mr. McClaran had the services of retired professor of Japanese Dr. Emerson Haworth, but he also caused his friend Lt. Cmdr. Zacharias to join the project in 1926; Mac considered Zach to be the most proficient Japanese language officer in the U.S. Navy. Zacharias was very able to complement Haworth's scholarly translations with difficult military, nautical, and technical terms, which efficiently finished the job.

During 1927–1928, Lt. Cmdr. McClaran served on board the battleship *Arizona*, and during 1929–1930 he was on the staff, Commander Battleship Divisions, Battle Fleet—and then he joined the staff of the Battle Fleet itself. After a major fleet exercise in the Pacific he submitted a fairly critical report concerning the navy's state of cryptology, focused upon its inherent lack of security as well as the inordinate amount of time it took to encipher/decipher messages.

> Upon completion of the 1929–1930 Annual Fleet Maneuvers, I submitted a very critical report of the codes and ciphers to the Secretary of the Navy, and as I learned later, because of having done so, I was ordered to take charge of the Code and Signal Section in the Office of Naval Communications [OP-20-G]. The Director of Naval Communications informed me that [my] report was the only one ever to have been submitted from the Fleet that was critical of our secret means of communications.

He remained at OP-20-G until May 1933. During this time he supervised Lt. Cmdr. Laurance **Safford**, who was head of the section's Research Desk (OP-20-GX), specifically focusing upon cryptanalysis.

Also during this time Commander McClaran fought hard, within the chain of command, for increased budgets and for a more efficient method of acquiring qualified and motivated students for the section's radio intelligence and cryptanalysis training programs. He was very blunt with his superiors about his fears for the future of the section—and therefore the future of these important aspects of the navy's operational ability—if such issues were not properly addressed. In 1932, a terrible budget year—due to the Great Depression—the assertive McClaran was nevertheless able to obtain $5,000 for the first year's rental of several IBM sorting machines. This dramatically helped move navy cryptanalysis into the beginnings of automation, and thus helped propel future captain Thomas **Dyer** toward his eventual title of the "father of machine cryptanalysis." Moreover, Mac was not only a proactive administrator; he was also a clever technician. In 1931 he invented—with some help from others as he freely admitted—a "strip cipher" device, which he was later able to patent.

After a brief assignment with the Commander, Mine Division 1, Commander McClaran returned in October 1935 for a second tour as head of OP-20-G, relieving Cmdr. Howard **Kingman**. Mac was in turn relieved by Lt. Cmdr. Safford in 1936. During this time, McClaran was involved with investigating more options regarding cryptographic machinery—at first looking at experts from MIT—and trying to find even more scarce funding for this purpose.

At the end of 1935, McClaran offered Lt. Joe **Rochefort** the job of OIC for the first decryption unit to be set up at Pearl Harbor, which would involve "pioneer organizing work." McClaran wrote to Rochefort, an old acquaintance, that before he "went too far in this matter I should like first to hear from you." But Rochefort declined this opportunity to return to mainstream cryptanalysis, and suggested Tommy Dyer as a better candidate. As it turned out, McClaran did select Dyer, who then detached from the *Pennsylvania* in 1936, and headed for Hawaii.

Advanced study at the Naval War College was Mac's next assignment. In fact, it's interesting to note Lt. Joe **Wenger**'s comment at the time: "Commander McClaran is going to the War College. He is a heavy loss, as he has always gone to bat for us. All the others [heads of OP-20-G] have to be forced."

Mac then went to sea, during 1937–1938, serving as the CO of the minelayer USS *Oglala*. In early 1939, he led a team that formulated plans to enhance navy facilities on Midway Atoll. Later in 1939, McClaran was promoted to captain and became director of the Training Division, Bureau of Navigation (the forerunner of the Bureau of Naval Personnel), under Rear Adm. Chester Nimitz. It was during this time, according to Tommy Dyer, that Mac was instrumental in getting Dyer and some others reclassified as "Engineering Duty Officers," which removed from them the potential of high promotion—but more importantly removed the requirement of such officers to frequently go to sea in nonintelligence and noncommunications duties. This facilitated uninterrupted concentration on their valuable specialties, probable promotion to commander and captain, and allowed them to reach full potential without competing against all other officers in the navy.

Captain McClaran was obliged to take an early retirement in March 1941, due to a physical disability. Because of his combat-earned Navy Cross from World War I, he was simultaneously given a "tombstone" promotion to rear admiral on the retired list.

According to Ellis Zacharias, when Zach met with Japanese Admiral/Ambassador Nomura Kichisaburō in February 1941—as Nomura traveled to Washington hoping to help avoid the coming of war—Nomura said that Zacharias was one of only two or three Americans "to whom he could open his heart." It was clear to Zach that Nomura considered Mac to be one of the others.

In 1948, Rear Admiral McClaran passed away in Los Angeles. He is buried at Arlington National Cemetery along with his wife, Stephana F. Prager (1892–1962).

Admiral McClaran has been recognized and honored, by the U.S. Naval Cryptologic Veterans Association, as an officer who has served as the Commander, Naval Security Group, or one of its predecessor organizations.

Sources

Browne and McGinnis, 206.
Carlson, 73–74.
Dyer, 99, 118, 124, 127, 140, 211.
Farago, *Broken Seal*, 39–40.
Holtwick, 68, 98, 102, 111, 113, 182, 212, 224, 390.
Zacharias, Ellis, 226.

REAR ADMIRAL GILL MacDONALD RICHARDSON, U.S. NAVY
(1905–1988)

Served prewar at Stations HYPO and CAST
"Gill" "Gillie" "Mac"

Gill Richardson was one of ONI's gifted language and cultural immersion students, fully immersed in Japan from 1936 to 1938. Like some others who had that experience, he also became a proficient codebreaker during World War II—not by formal training but by working hand-in-glove with cryptanalysts at such stations as CAST, BELCONNEN/FRUMel, and NEGAT. After the war he flourished in surface-ship and headquarters assignments with only one follow-on intelligence posting; he then retired as a "tombstone" rear admiral in 1957.

*   *   *

From the 1927 Annapolis yearbook, *The Lucky Bag*:

Hailing from the swamps of "New Joisey," *Gillie* came to us well versed upon the topics of mosquitoes and cranberries. However, he soon became accustomed to naval life, and spent may a good hour of Plebe Summer playing "man over-board" in half-raters out on the bay. Though not exactly a ladies' man, *Mac* has an overwhelming desire to be one and, poor trusting soul that he is, has dragged [dated] blind on more than one occasion, only to have come out a winner every time. . . . Everyone who knows him is impressed by his sincerity. He is in everything that he undertakes heart and soul, and never lets up for a moment. Why, Plebe and Youngster years he used to go over to the track to take his daily workout just before going on Easter leave. But it's that persistency that makes the good runner. . . . The swimming teams have also felt his efficiency here as a manager. He ran that organization like a queen bee runs a hive. No lost motion or friction was in evidence. We feel sure he will keep up as he has started, and wish him all success. [Activities: track, cross country; swimming; *Lucky Bag* staff; Glee Club; Masqueraders]

*   *   *

Gill Richardson was born on August 19, 1905, in South Orange, New Jersey. He graduated from the Naval Academy in 1927 along with such distinguished class-mates as Richard D. **Zern,** George W. Anderson, Glynn "Donc" Donaho, Lee W. **Parke,** Jack S. **Holtwick,** and U.S. Grant Sharp Jr. Subsequent promotions included lieutenant (junior grade), 1930; lieutenant, 1936; lieutenant commander, 1941; commander, 1942; and captain, 1945. In 1957 he was promoted to rear admiral, on the retired list, by reason of a World War II combat citation.

After graduation from the academy, Mr. Richardson began the typical career for a junior officer in that time. In 1928 he served on board the battleship *Texas*, and then transferred to the destroyer *Case* during 1929 and 1930. The year 1931 saw him on board the destroyer *Dupont*, and during 1932 he was assigned to the gunboat *Asheville* as gunnery officer. From 1933 through 1935 he stayed with one ship, the heavy cruiser *Portland*.

Around that time he applied for ONI's Japanese language and cultural immersion program. He had always liked languages, having studied Spanish in high school and at Annapolis. But, as he said in an interview many years after World War II, he applied for the Japan program to "distinguish myself from the pack and to improve my promotion chances." He arrived in Tokyo in November 1935. "We had five tutors who worked with us every day. We read everything from children's books to the daily press." The tutors took them on field trips to expose them to a wide variety of situations in which to practice the language. They were tested every six months to demonstrate progress. "If you did not get a '34,' the Navy sent you home with an unsatisfactory fitness report." By the end of the course the students were required to read 2,800 and write 1,800 kanji characters—kanji being Chinese characters that had been incorporated into the Japanese language. Upon passing, the students were officially recognized as qualified translators and interpreters.

Richardson particularly remembered naval attaché Capt. Harold Bemis at the U.S. embassy, for among other things he occasionally invited the immersion students to do some "light" espionage.

> I was young and had no fear, so I volunteered as much as possible. . . . For example, I went to northern Japan to determine how many tunnels were constructed along a railway. Another time, I went to Nagasaki to determine if the Japanese were building battleships in violation of the London Treaty. . . . I enjoyed the espionage and other special assignments because they not only provided opportunities for me to use Japanese, but also provided a valuable service for the U.S. by acquiring information.

Upon completing his studies and leaving Japan, Richardson served briefly as the executive officer of the destroyer *Waters*. In November 1938 he was transferred to the Fourteenth Naval District in Hawaii as a language officer. He briefly ran Station HYPO's "GZ" section; he then transferred out as Lt. Cmdr. Thomas **Birtley** came in around July 1939. On December 2, 1940, he reported to the Asiatic Station as the Sixteenth Naval District's communications-intelligence unit (Station CAST) language officer—replacing Lt. Harold E. Karrer. In April 1941, Richardson transferred on paper to the staff of the commander in chief, Asiatic Fleet, but remained working in the naval district's communications intelligence unit. He subsequently was in the first group of Station CAST to evacuate in the face of the Japanese advance; on February 4, 1942, he joined the OIC (Lt. Rudy **Fabian**) and several others, leaving by submarine ultimately bound for Australia.

In Melbourne, Richardson became part of the Station BELCONNEN organization, which soon became more widely known as FRUMel; he served there from early 1942 through early 1945. Even though this was more than just a U.S. Navy organization—including Australians and British personnel—Lieutenant Fabian essentially ran the organization as he had at Corregidor.

> We followed the same working procedures that we had at [CAST]. Spencer "Swede" Carlson (a Japanese linguist who graduated from the Tokyo [immersion] program in 1936) and I were lieutenant commanders at this time and were senior to Rudy Fabian. We continued our arrangement with Fabian that was worked out on Corregidor. Fabian was the boss or officer in charge even though he was junior to us. This arrangement freed Carlson and me from administrative duties and allowed us to devote all of our time and energy to translation and code recovery. Everyone, especially I, was satisfied with this arrangement.

Richardson profoundly enjoyed the work at FRUMel, finding it fascinating and, in later years, looked upon it as one of the major highlights of his career.

> Translating and assisting with code recovery is like reading a great book that you just cannot put down. I remember working late into the night on messages relating to the

Japanese plan to attack Midway. I also remember working on [Admiral] Yamamoto's travel schedule, which led to the shootdown of his plane. The message that I worked on was in a Japanese army code system; although we were unfamiliar with Japanese army codes, we got this message out in a hurry.

Commander Richardson transferred to Washington in early 1945 and worked further communications-intelligence issues in OP-20-GZ. In March he was promoted to captain, and then in June he married Lt. j.g. Patricia Lockridge, who also worked in OP-20-GZ; the ceremony was at the National Cathedral and Capt. Rosie **Mason** and four other senior communications intelligence officers acted as ushers. Captain Richardson then was given command of the dock landing ship USS *Donner* in November.

In 1947 he served as Assistant Chief of Staff for Intelligence at Headquarters, Commander in Chief U.S. Naval Forces Eastern Atlantic and Mediterranean (CINCNELM). Two years later he was made head of the Shipping Control Branch in the Office of the CNO. Captain Richardson commanded the amphibious force command ship *Taconic* from June 1952 to June 1953, and then the destroyer *Putnam* in 1954 when she was flagship of Destroyer Division 22.

Richardson subsequently retired from the navy in July 1957. Because of his high-level combat medal from World War II, he was simultaneously promoted to rear admiral on the retired list.

Rear Admiral Richardson died in Coronado, California, on July 12, 1988. He was survived by his wife, Patricia (1921–1999). They are buried together at the Naval Academy Cemetery in Annapolis.

Admiral Richardson's decorations included the Bronze Star with Combat "V" device; Grand Commander of the Order of Aviz (Portugal); and Commander of the Order of Ouissam Alaouite (French Morocco).

Sources

Cruise Book, USS *Putnam*/Destroyer Squadron Twenty-Two, 1954.
Holtwick, 316, 320, 327, 407, 421, 423, 427, App. 111–12, 120.
Lucky Bag, U.S. Naval Academy, 1927.
Maneki, 73–76.
Smith, *Emperor's Codes*, 183.
U.S. Navy, *Register of Commissioned and Warrant Officers*.

CAPTAIN JOSEPH JOHN ROCHEFORT, U.S. NAVY (1900–1976)

A gifted, many-faceted officer
Fiercely tenacious and of independent mind
The only officer with full triple expertise: cryptanalysis and radio intelligence,
operational intelligence, and Japanese language
With Admiral Nimitz, the chief engineer of the victory at Midway
"Joe"

It would be hard not to acknowledge that Joseph Rochefort is perhaps *the* iconic figure in the U.S. Navy's early cryptologic, translation, and intelligence history. He briefly headed the navy's fledgling cryptanalytic organization in the 1920s, and he was an ONI-sponsored full-immersion Japanese language and culture student. A tall, lean, intense officer with a conciliatory smile that nullified his habit of caustic speech, he spent years honing his operational intelligence skills in a variety of billets. He provided singularly superb cryptologic, language translation—and perhaps most important—intelligence analysis for the U.S. Pacific Fleet in World War II, certainly leading to victory at the pivotal Battle of Midway. He had formidable "all-around prowess in every aspect of communications-intelligence, from crypt-analysis and communications to translating and analysis." At the end of his career Rochefort superbly headed the Pacific Strategic Intelligence Group in Washington. In later years he received considerable and deserved recognition—but sadly only after he had passed away.

*   *   *

Joe Rochefort was born to immigrant Irish-Catholic parents in Dayton, Ohio, on May 12, 1900. He was the youngest of Francis J. and Ellen Spearman Rochefort's seven children. The family subsequently moved to California, and there Joe attended St. Vincent's School (now Loyola High School) and the Polytechnic High School in Los Angeles. He enlisted in the navy in 1918, "because of the spirit of the time . . . everybody was more or less patriotic—when some of my friends enlisted, we all went down and all enlisted." He chose the navy because he initially saw himself as a flier. "I wanted to be an aviator, a naval aviator. I had a very high regard for those people." But he never really pursued it. "I forgot that; I gave that up." Instead the navy shortly rated him an Electrician's Mate 3rd Class, U.S. Naval Reserve Force, and sent him to New Jersey to attend the Stevens Institute of Technology for an engineering course of study. Upon graduation he briefly was made a third class machinist's mate, USNRF, and then was commissioned as an ensign, USNR, in June 1919. Further promotions included lieutenant (junior grade), 1922; lieutenant, 1926; lieutenant commander, 1936; commander, 1941; and captain, 1943. He retired from the navy in 1947 but was immediately recalled to active duty for two special projects—retiring for a final time in 1953.

Ensign Rochefort was briefly assigned to the oiler *Cuyama* as an assistant engineer, and then in 1921 he transferred to the minesweeper *Cardinal* as chief engineer and communications officer. He also augmented from the naval reserve to the regular navy. In 1922, he was promoted to lieutenant (junior grade) and transferred back to the *Cuyama*; during this tour he served as a division officer, a watch officer, and as the assistant navigator. Two years later found him serving on board the destroyer *Stansbury* as chief engineer, and then as a division officer and an assistant engineer on board the battleship *Arizona*. In June 1924, he looked into taking a class on the Japanese language along with another University of California extension course.

While he'd been on board the *Cuyama*, Rochefort became friendly with the executive officer, Lt. Cmdr. Chester C. Jersey. Sometime later, when Mr. Jersey was serving at the Navy Department in Washington, he contacted Rochefort and enquired if Joe would care to come to Main Navy on temporary duty—in connection with working on codes and ciphers. Joe believed that Jersey thought of him because he had been impressed with Joe's skill in solving crossword puzzles, and also that he'd liked his intense style of playing bridge.

As a result, in 1925, Lt. j.g. Rochefort reported to Main Navy and the Office of Naval Communications' new "Research Desk," designated office symbol OP-

20-GX, to become an apprentice cryptanalysis. Here he made the acquaintance, and fell under the tutelage, of the remarkable Lt. Cmdr. Laurance F. **Safford** and began to study cryptanalysis. At this stage Safford was the head of the Research Desk and the "actual teacher, but there were no formal education processes at all . . . our 'bible,' our reference book . . . was *The Elements of Cryptanalysis*" by the U.S. Army's counterpart to Safford, William Friedman. Early on, Rochefort was very impressed by both the book and by Friedman, and he never changed his mind; in 1969 he told an interviewer that

> we got the principles of cryptanalysis from this book of Bill Friedman . . . the Army was extremely fortunate in having Mr. Friedman. He might be called a modern-day father of cryptanalysis as far as we were concerned in the United States. He has my greatest respect. I would say that he was undoubtedly the best in the world at that time . . . there is no one that could compare with Friedman, no one at all.

Rochefort's other principal colleague—and teacher—was the formidable Miss Agnes Meyer (later Mrs. **Driscoll**), who essentially was the navy's main cryptanalyst for many years.[1]

In 1926, Mr. Safford had to leave the office to take a sea-duty assignment. As a result, Mr. Rochefort filled in for him, from February 1926 through September 1927. During this time, the Research Desk began an attack on the Japanese *Red Book*. This was a photographed copy of the Japanese Navy's naval operational code that ONI agents had obtained by breaking into a safe in the Japanese consulate in New York City. Apparently, over a number of years, ONI did this several times; amazingly, they were never caught and never left a trace of their visits. In any event, Rochefort was OP-20-GZ's OIC when cryptanalysis of the *Red Book* (so called because the Americans placed the sheets in a red notebook) was first undertaken.[2]

One might think that having a copy of the code book eliminated the intelligence problem, save perhaps translating Japanese to English. However, it was more complicated than that.

---

1. Capt. Jasper Holmes wrote, "In 1925, Joseph Rochefort, Laurance Safford, and Agnes Driscoll were the whole of the Navy's code-breaking crew."

2. According to retired Capt. Albert J. Pelletier, in some respects the *Red Book* "is the most important Japanese cryptographic system we ever had," for the following reasons:

   a. It was the determining factor in establishing the OP-20-G Research Desk.
   b. It was a constant incentive to build up a radio intelligence organization to exploit our possession of this code.
   c. It assisted our early efforts to a great degree when our cryptanalytic force was very small and rather inexperienced.
   d. It demonstrated the requirement for Japanese translators.
   e. It gave us invaluable information concerning the Japanese Navy and its war plans that we could never have gotten in any other way.
   f. It forecast Japanese intentions for future conquests.
   g. After supersession it gave us probable vocabulary of later codes and a list of place names, Chinese characters, etc.

A complete codebook was a windfall, but there was still once crucial piece missing. Like almost all of the Japanese navy codes that Rochefort and his colleagues would encounter . . . *Red* was an enciphered code. Every word or syllable likely to be used in a message was assigned a numerical value—that was the "code" part. But such a simple one-for-one substitution would not hold up a team of Boy Scouts, much less a determined military foe, for very long.

So before the Japanese navy sent any coded message . . . it was given a second disguise. The code clerk opened a second book, which contained page after page of random numbers; starting at the top of a page, he added the first of these random "additives" to the first code group of his message, the second to the second, and so on. An indicator buried in the message would tell what page in the additive book he had used for this "encipherment" of the basic code, so that the recipient could turn to that same page and strip off the additive before looking up the meaning of each code group.

Therefore, thanks to ONI's black-bag job, OP-20-G had the code book—but not the additive book. Moreover, the Japanese could and did frequently *change* the additive book. So, with nothing else to work with, the Americans had to intercept from the airwaves as many messages as possible and analyze them for patterns. It was difficult, stressful, and frustrating work; however, they did it, with Mrs. Driscoll being responsible for the initial solution.

In fact, Rochefort found the work extraordinarily stressful, to the point that it affected his health. He began smoking heavily, slept poorly, and lost considerable weight. "I had ulcers as a result of [cryptanalytic work done from] 1925 to 1927." Later in middle age he would be diagnosed with peptic ulcers, tracing the origin of the ailment to his years running the Research Desk.

In October 1927 it was Mr. Rochefort's turn to acquire more sea duty. He left with some feeling of relief, turning the job of GX OIC over to Lt. Bern **Anderson**. Rochefort reported on board the destroyer *Macdonough* as executive officer; the commanding officer was Cmdr. Arthur "Chips" Carpender, a hard-nosed perfectionist, but he liked Joe and fortunately considered him "a good officer."

Then, briefly attached to the battleship *California* in 1929, Lieutenant Rochefort got reacquainted with Lt. j.g. Thomas **Dyer**, who two years earlier had come to the Research Desk for training shortly before Rochefort left. Now they worked together in a Battle Fleet exercise, tackling encoded messages. "Rochefort and I were quite successful," Dyer said later. "We solved every key change that they had and read every message that we were able to intercept."

Late in 1929, Lieutenant Rochefort was sent to Tokyo for ONI's three-year full-immersion language training in Japan. He had first applied for the program in 1926. According to Rochefort, "Zach told me he was responsible for this." Pioneering intelligence officer Lt. Cmdr. Ellis **Zacharias** didn't mention it in his autobiography, but it could well be true; Zacharias had briefly worked with Rochefort at Main Navy 1926, and had been very impressed. At this time Zach was in a position at ONI where he could advocate for him.

Regardless of how he got there, Joe was one of the relatively few officers selected over the years for that specialized training. One of his fellow students was Lt. j.g. Edwin **Layton**. They liked each other instantly. Layton later wrote that "our lifelong friendship began . . . on board the steamer *President Adams* when the long Pacific crossing gave me a chance to get acquainted with him." They were assigned to the American Embassy in Tokyo where they remained for three years, sharing living quarters for most of that time. During their stay in Japan, assistant naval attaché Lt. Cmdr. Arthur **McCollum** took them under his wing and showed them "the ropes"; both young officers excelled in their study of the language and culture. McCollum and Rochefort later became good friends, but at first McCollum wasn't happy to see Rochefort, who very unusually had been allowed to bring his wife and son. Mac didn't see how anyone could succeed in this difficult assignment, cope with living in Japan, and still manage a family. He sent a dispatch back to Main Navy recommending Rochefort's recall. The response was negative; Rochefort was staying. Several months later Mac had come to understand ONI's thinking—Rochefort was an individual of unusual ability.

As an aside, in November 1930, Lt. Cmdr. John **McClaran** (then overall head of OP-20-G) documented that unfortunately there were only six officers trained and available for cryptanalytical work (less a few others who had other major qualifications such as aviator, submariner, or linguist): Lt. Cmdr. Laurance Safford, Ens. W. H. Leahy, Lt. j.g. Thomas Dyer, Lt. Bern Anderson, Lt. Joseph **Wenger**, and Lt. j.g. Thomas **Huckins**. This list was validated again the next year, with the addition of Lieutenant Rochefort (who at times was not included on such lists because he was officially becoming an ONI Japanese linguist). Of these, Safford, Rochefort, and Anderson were the only ones considered qualified to instruct in cryptanalysis—with Anderson rated below the other two.

Upon completion of his language and cultural studies, in late 1932 Rochefort returned to Main Navy in Washington for brief duty at ONI. Then, from 1933 through 1934, he was assigned as assistant operations officer, Battle Force, once again on board the *California*. This was duty on the staff of Adm. William H. Standley; however, Standley was shortly replaced by Adm. Joseph M. "Bull" Reeves.

Then, in June 1934, Reeves became Commander in Chief of the U.S. Fleet (CINCUS), and he kept Lieutenant Rochefort with him. In addition to duty as assistant operations officer, Joe became OIC of the CINCUS radio intelligence unit on board the flagship *Pennsylvania*. For a time CINCUS moved to the battleship *New Mexico* when the *Pennsylvania* underwent a refit.

Coincidentally, and to their mutual delight, Rochefort joined Tommy Dyer and Eddie Layton on the *New Mexico*. But as soon as the *Pennsylvania* was ready, Admiral Reeves moved himself and his staff back on board and, for some reason, Dyer and Layton were also transferred. In 1936, fresh from cryptanalysis training at the Research Desk, Lt. j.g. Wesley "Ham" **Wright** joined the group. Wright worked with Rochefort in the staff intelligence office; Dyer and Layton were part of the ship's company in the gunnery department. As Layton later wrote,

This curious coincidence brought together in the same ship the four of us who five years later would find ourselves working alongside each other in the critical months leading up to Pearl Harbor and on through the Battle of Midway. We always looked back on our battleship duty together as an interesting twist of fate. The coincidence was heightened by the fact that *Pennsylvania*'s skipper was Capt. Russell **Willson**, who had been the director of naval communications in World War I.

Shortly after Wright's arrival, Rochefort was informed by the Coast Guard that Japanese fishing boats off the fleet's San Pedro, California, anchorage were constantly radioing to each other in some kind of code. So, one day Rochefort challenged Wright to figure it out; working all through the night on intercepts provided by the Coast Guard, he solved it around dawn—and found nothing more insidious than shared intelligence as to locations of schools of fish. Totally exhausted, Wright missed a Saturday morning inspection and the ship's captain, Willson, was furious. Wright explained what he'd been doing; he then received a further dressing-down for "fooling around with that stuff." Still not sensing he held a completely losing hand, Wright tried to respectfully point out that the captain himself had once been in charge of OP-20-G, that he'd invented the "Navy Code Box," and that he'd received the Navy Cross for his outstanding work in cryptology. Willson instantly snapped back, "Yes, but then I had the *good sense to get out!*"

For a number of reasons Willson and Rochefort took an immediate dislike to each other. Willson was smooth, dignified, genteel, and always well groomed and careful in his speech; Rochefort held him in low esteem, thinking him pompous and "a stuffed shirt." On the other hand, Willson thought Rochefort brash, unpolished, and too full of himself working in an unimportant dead-end field—and much too visible as he'd become Admiral Reeves's favorite protégé.

Willson was going to have two significant future opportunities to put Rochefort in his place. Jumping ahead to December 1939, Rochefort came up for promotion to commander. Willson was one of nine rear admirals on the selection board. Despite an enormous number of open commander slots, Rochefort "failed for selection." It's unclear exactly why this happened. There were several possible factors, but Rochefort came to believe that Willson had likely convinced the other admirals that this impertinent officer—who had *not* attended Annapolis—was not commander material. What *is* very clear, however, is that in mid-1942, Willson had his second opportunity to negatively influence Rochefort's career. After the Battle of Midway, Admiral Nimitz (CinCPac) and Rear Admiral Bagley (Commandant, Fourteenth Naval District) jointly recommended to Admiral King (CominCh, U.S. Fleet) that Rochefort be awarded the Distinguished Service Medal. Rear Admiral Willson, then King's chief of staff, submitted a lengthy memo in which he powerfully argued against the award; unfortunately for Rochefort—and to the irritation of Nimitz—King concurred with his chief of staff with no further discussion.

Captain Willson notwithstanding, Rochefort found his mid-1930s duty with Admiral Reeves "fantastic, because . . . I was serving at the very top level of the fleet. . . . This was remarkable duty, and I enjoyed it." Reeves was greatly impressed with

Rochefort, and "pushed him forward in a way that was almost unheard of in the navy. Under Reeves, Rochefort blossomed into a top-flight naval officer."

At some point in 1935, Admiral Reeves was informed by ONI that there was a Japanese spy at Dutch Harbor in the Aleutian Islands, so he tasked Rochefort to deal with it before U.S. Navy units arrived in that area for Fleet Problem XVI. Rochefort in turn tasked Edwin Layton to do it; as a result Layton went into Dutch Harbor dressed in civilian clothes and persuaded the authorities that the only Japanese national there was illegally selling alcohol. As soon as the spy was jailed, Layton radioed to the flagship: "For Joe—mission accomplished."

At this same general time, Admiral Reeves was concerned about suspected Japanese agents conducting espionage in Southern California, so at his direction Rochefort spent considerable time working with ONI on that issue. Reeves was very impressed with Rochefort, saying he was "one of the most outstanding officers of his rank," and that he was an "encyclopedia of information and usefulness." In fact, despite the disparity in rank, Rochefort became one of the admiral's confidants and his best "utility man."

During this time, according to Rochefort, Cmdr. Ellis Zacharias suggested to him that he put "spies" on the U.S. Navy ships to look for "disloyalty." Both Rochefort (*and* Admiral Reeves) rejected this overly aggressive Soviet-style suggestion. However, Rochefort did get the director of naval intelligence (Capt. William D. "Pulie" Puleston) to send their mutual friend, Lt. Arthur McCollum, out to the Hydrographic Office at San Pedro—to go undercover in the area.

Late 1935 also saw Cmdr. John McClaran (in his second tour as head of OP-20-G) offer Lieutenant Rochefort a special job: OIC for the first decryption unit to be set up at Pearl Harbor, which would involve "pioneer organizing work." McClaran told Rochefort, "I feel that next to Safford you are probably the best–qualified officer, due for shore duty, to create this billet and get it started on a sound basis." In this scenario, Rochefort would stay officially *attached* to Naval Intelligence while actually *working* for Naval Communications (ONI had oversight of Rochefort's shore duty assignments), but still this "could be arranged." McClaran wrote to his old acquaintance that before he "went too far in this matter I should like first to hear from you." Did Rochefort want to return to mainstream cryptanalysis? Apparently not. He took more than four weeks to answer, finally writing that he could not leave Admiral Reeves until the admiral himself departed. He added that there might be more fit officers for the job, and named Tommy Dyer as an example. As it turned out, McClaran did select Dyer who, in 1936, detached from the *Pennsylvania* and headed for Hawaii. There, Dyer essentially built a communications-intelligence organization from scratch—which soon would be called Station HYPO.

In June 1936, Arthur McCollum and Joe Rochefort essentially traded billets, with Rochefort now fleet liaison officer and assistant intelligence officer, Eleventh Naval District, at San Diego and San Pedro. McCollum was attached to the staff of the U.S. Fleet as assistant operations officer, acting operations officer, and FIO; Admiral Reeves had retired and the new commander in chief had become Adm. Arthur J. Hepburn.

In June 1928, Rochefort assumed the duty of navigator on board the heavy cruiser *New Orleans*. Then, in September 1939, Joe was transferred to the staff of the Pacific Fleet Scouting Force, in the heavy cruiser *Indianapolis*. He worked there for Vice Adm. Adolphus Andrews, who was extremely impressed by Lieutenant Commander Rochefort. Andrews was shortly relieved by Rear Adm. Wilson Brown Jr.—who in turn was very pleased with Rochefort and his work. In fact, when Rochefort was passed over for promotion to commander in 1940, Brown launched an aggressive campaign to fix what he considered a gross injustice. The next scheduled board did select Rochefort for promotion, to Brown's credit; in fact, Rear Admiral Brown probably saved Rochefort's overall career by his action.

In the spring of 1941, Rochefort detached from the *Indianapolis* and went to Hawaii. Captain Zacharias claimed credit for getting ONI to release Mr. Rochefort to take the job of Station HYPO OIC at Pearl Harbor, effective in June. As mentioned earlier, Naval Intelligence essentially had rights of first refusal on Rochefort's shore assignments, but HYPO was actually a creature of OP-20-G in Naval Communications. Zach very much liked to help colleagues he respected get ahead in the intelligence business and often used his influence accordingly. This time, however, Rochefort's assignment was more likely due to a deal made between Commander Safford, at OP-20-G in Washington, and Rear Adm. Claude Bloch, the Commandant of the Fourteenth Naval District. Regardless of how it came about, Rochefort's assignment as HYPO's OIC was incredibly fortunate. Many years later Rochefort told an interviewer:

> The reason, I think, that HYPO was successful—I'm trying now to be—not modest and not immodest—but it was because part of my arrangement with Safford was that I'll undertake this job, but I'll get my pick of the personnel: I'll take this job providing I can keep Lt. Cmdr. Dyer and I can get first shot at anybody else who I need and I get all the language officers. These were the conditions. Safford said, "You can have anything you want." So the organization in Pearl, beginning in the fall of 1941 and extending until the time I left there—these people were the pick of the crop.
>
> I had Dyer, and a fellow named "Ham" Wright—these would be cryptanalysts and just about as good as they come. Then I had the two best language officers—I like to think, besides me—this would be Joe **Finnegan** and a marine, a fellow named Alva **Lasswell**. We had very excellent officers, too, for radio intelligence . . . that would be Tom Huckins and Jack **Williams**: these people were very difficult to beat for what we called radio intelligence.

Safford's reasons for Rochefort's appointment were obvious (and identical to John McClaran's, who had tried to make this happen back in 1936): he was an expert in the Japanese language and culture, an experienced and very talented intelligence analyst, and a trained cryptanalyst. Having written that, it's interesting to note that until 1941, Rochefort spent nine years in cryptologic or intelligence-related assignments and fourteen years at sea with the U.S. fleet in positions of increasing responsibility.

So, in early June 1941, newly promoted Cmdr. Joe Rochefort relieved Lt. Cmdr. Tom **Birtley** at HYPO; Birtley (who, through seniority, had taken over from Tom Dyer) needed to go to sea because he did not have sufficient sea-duty to qualify for promotion to commander. Upon his arrival, Mr. Rochefort took charge of twelve officers and eleven enlisted men—as well as a number of other enlisted men in outlying radio-interception facilities. He immediately instituted an eight-section watch, such that each day saw six sections on and two off.

Rochefort also decided to officially call HYPO the Combat Intelligence Unit—stealing the name from Lt. Jasper **Holmes**'s two-man sub-unit—because it would partially disguise what HYPO was doing and wouldn't arouse too much curiosity. Other people would realize they were doing something secret, but the term CIU didn't really hint at just *how* secret—the name was "sort of accurate and misleading at the same time." (For the sake of continuity in this book, we have generally used the term "HYPO" rather than CIU—or even the later FRUPac.)

In early August, HYPO moved into the basement of the naval district's headquarters building which had "plenty of room and [was] very nice." This was a good deal "wangled" by Lt. Cmdr. Tommy Dyer, who had remained in the unit.

Another old friend that Rochefort found in place was Lt. Cmdr. Edwin Layton, who was now the chief intelligence officer for the Pacific Fleet. Built upon their close friendship, Rochefort had a remarkably good relationship with Layton which really facilitated intelligence integration between the Pacific Fleet and the Fourteenth Naval District, which—it must be emphasized—were not under the same chain of command. Years after the war, Layton wrote that

> Joe Rochefort and I were old and close friends both professionally and socially. We conferred many times daily—via a secure sound-powered telephone; he was at one end at "his shop" and I at my end—about material arriving in the COMINT channel. He would always call me when they came across a "hot" item, and would ask my views about problems as they arose—blanks in the text, garbles and the like—to see if we could guess a meaning or value for the benefit of the cryptanalysts and translators.

Likewise, Rochefort said that

> the fleet intelligence officer, Lt. Cmdr. Layton, was a close personal friend of mine. We had spent three years in Japan together, and I had worked with him on several occasions subsequent to that . . .
>
> I did not have direct access to [CinCPac], which I think would have been preferable; I had to go through Layton. But I think the relationship—between Layton and myself—was such that he and I understood each other's problems.

This relationship created great and obvious efficiencies; however, the partnership essentially bypassed Washington and brought intelligence estimates directly to the fleet commander—a situation that bureaucratically minded officers in Naval Communications headquarters resented—though it must be emphasized that such officers did *not* include Laurance Safford. And, as Captain Zacharias noted, in 1941 it was not Rochefort's nor Layton's "privilege" to deduce enemy intentions from the information they gathered. This function was usurped by the planners, whose main preoccupation should have been to take appropriate countermeasures to the Japanese moves culled from the incoming material, promptly submitted to higher echelons.

Allowed wide discretion by Safford, Rochefort hand-picked many of HYPO's augmentees, and thus it shortly contained the navy's best cryptanalysts, traffic analysts, and linguists—including Thomas Dyer, Wesley "Ham" Wright, Joseph Finnegan, Alva Lasswell, Thomas Huckins, and Jack Williams.

With Rochefort's arrival in mid-1941, and his close relationship with OP-20-G chief Safford, the HYPO team in place hoped the new boss might win a reprieve from their so-far fruitless slog against the Japanese high-level "Admirals" or AD code. However, a directive from Washington reinforced that HYPO would stay exclusively focused upon the AD. This was frustrating for Rochefort as well as the navy's best cryptanalytic officers, Dyer and Wright. "It was also ultimately to prove [unfortunate] for the Pacific Fleet. For seven more months the HYPO team would obediently beat their heads against the stone wall of the [AD] code with negative results." It was a difficult code made impossible because it was little used—which meant there wasn't enough raw material coming in to work on and thus not enough to study to make any progress. It is true that, back in 1940, Tommy Dyer and his team had gotten to the point where AD was beginning to produce intelligible text. But then

> the Japanese changed the underlying code. HYPO found that it now seemed to be limited to flag officers and used very infrequently. From this point until mid-December 1941, HYPO struggled with this "admiral's code" and was never able to break it. There simply weren't enough intercepts to allow effective penetration of the system. Unfortunately, the attempt consumed countless hours of valuable cryptanalytic effort for no intelligence return.

In retrospect it's easy to criticize Safford and other decision-makers in Washington for what seems to have been a waste of time and focus. However, they—as well as Rochefort and Dyer—realized that if the AD *could* be broken, it would yield spectacular results—and thus justified the effort.

In the fall of 1941, Rochefort assigned some newly arrived radio intelligence officers to focus upon the OP-20-G-mandated priority to listen for the Japanese "East Wind, Rain" execute message—which if broadcast would presumably indicate an imminent break in U.S.-Japan relations. Thus, on November 29th, Rochefort sent Lt. j.g. Gilven **Slonim**, Lt. j.g. John Bromley, Lt. Allyn Cole, and Lt. Forrest **Biard** to the intercept site at He'eia to stand round-the-clock watches solely to listen for the message—which apparently never was transmitted. As it turned out, Slonim had just been relieved by Biard when the Pearl Harbor attack began on December 7.

Rochefort was frustrated by not anticipating the attack on Pearl Harbor. Up to that point HYPO was not assigned to work on the Japanese Navy's more widely used operational code, JN-25, and as already mentioned they remained stymied on the "Admirals Code." During this time they were relying heavily upon radio traffic analysis, and Rochefort later said that through that analysis

> we were normally in a position to say where the major parts of the Japanese Fleet were at almost any time. Like we'd say they're in the home ports, they're training, or that sort of thing. I would say from about 1st December on, we'd lost our knowledge of their activities and their positions because they'd gone into radio silence. That is, they were not using their radios. Primarily, I would say our feeling was one of apprehension engendered mostly by the fact that we didn't know where any of these people were.

Regardless, Rochefort and Layton—in agreement with the War Department and Navy Department—did not see Pearl Harbor as a target.

> Our reasoning went like this—that if the Japanese attacked Pearl Harbor then this means war—war with the United States is going to be won by the United States. So, therefore, why should the Japanese attack Pearl Harbor? And the answer is: they don't.

On the morning of December 7, 1941, Rochefort was getting ready to take his family on a picnic. The car was loaded up with steaks and barbeque equipment. Then the phone rang, with Tommy Dyer on the line, asking if Rochefort had heard the news.

"What news?"

"We're at war?"

"What do you mean?"

"We're being bombed out here right now."

"All right, I'll be right out."

Dyer later told an interviewer that he never encountered anyone more calm than Rochefort was. Perhaps, but Rochefort was stunned by the attack, and felt guilty about it.

> I have often said that an intelligence officer has one task, one job, one mission. This is to tell his commander, today, what the [enemy] is going to do tomorrow. This is his job. If he doesn't do this, then he's failed. This is his number one job and only job.
> I personally felt very responsible for [not foreseeing the Pearl Harbor attack]. Nobody has ever blamed us for lack of effort or failure to come up with the right answer. Nobody has ever done this. They have been very kind. But I felt very responsible for this for a long time and I still do. I still feel [in 1969] that we failed in our job . . . I can offer a lot of excuses, which would all be alibis.

At the very end of December 1941, Admirals William H. Standley and Joseph M. Reeves came to the HYPO basement and interviewed Commander Rochefort. They were part of the "Roberts Commission," the first of several official investigations into the Pearl Harbor disaster. At issue was not HYPO's performance; rather, the commission was trying to generally determine what had gone wrong, and who knew what and when was it known.

About this time Rochefort's family was evacuated to Pasadena. After that happened,

> he left the basement only to bathe, change clothes, or get an occasional meal to supplement a steady diet of coffee and sandwiches. . . . For weeks the only sleep he got was on a field cot pushed into a crowded corner; always nearly fully dressed, he was ready at a moment's notice to roll out.

As the new year began Rochefort summed up a new philosophy for his unit—and for himself—*Forget "Pearl Harbor" and get on with the war!*

After Adm. Chester W. Nimitz assumed command of the Pacific Fleet on December 31, 1941, one of the first people that he wanted to see was Cmdr. Joseph Rochefort. Unfortunately, this initial meeting didn't go particularly well. Rear Admiral Bloch escorted Admiral Nimitz to the HYPO basement, but a fatigued Rochefort was totally absorbed in some translation work and spared the new commander in chief very little of his attention. Nimitz departed, fairly unimpressed.

It could be cold in the HYPO basement—or the "Dungeon" as some called it—with the installation of an air conditioning system to keep the IBM sorting machines cool. Rochefort took to wearing a maroon

> smoking jacket over his uniform to ward off the chill when it was running full blast. The smoking jacket became part of the Rochefort "legend," as did the pair of carpet slippers he wore to ease his sore feet. . . . But those who knew him said this painted a false image. He was a tall, thin, pale, and driven man, but he was no eccentric.

Rochefort recalled it this way:

> I started to wear a reddish smoking jacket over my khaki uniform . . . I was just cold . . . and I wore this darn thing because it had pockets in it and I could get my pipe and my pouch this way. Then my feet got sore. It was from the concrete floor . . . and my feet kept getting sore. So I started wearing slippers because the shoes hurt my feet.

Chief Yeoman Durwood "Tex" **Rorie**—who had quickly become Commander Rochefort's right-hand man—was largely responsible for recruiting new enlisted men for the ever-growing unit, constantly trying to meet Rochefort's rising need for manpower. In a 1983 interview, retired Captain Dyer complimented him in this regard:

> Rorie had an uncanny knack for being able to pick good men from a new draft of recruits . . . to the best of my knowledge there wasn't a one of them . . . who didn't turn out to be perfectly satisfactory for our purposes.

Whenever a new batch of men came in to the navy yard, one of his pals alerted him, so Rorie would drive over to the receiving station and look the group over. One day, at the end of December 1941, Admiral Bloch offered Commander Rochefort the twenty-member band of the sunken battleship *California*. Their instruments were destroyed or at the bottom of the harbor, and the men remained unassigned. Rochefort jumped at the opportunity and sent the chief to recruit them. Rorie lined them up and then

> I just walked out there and I said "Any of you keep your damn mouth shut?" Well, they all held up their hand. I said, "Any of you want a good job?" They all held up their hand. I said, "We can get even with the Japs. Maybe we can give you a job that can give some satisfaction [now] that your instruments have been blown up."

They all indicated that they wanted the so-far-unnamed job. Thus, just after the first of the year, the whole band came filing into HYPO's often cold, unventilated, tobacco-smoke-filled basement. Starting with clerical chores, in time they became vital participants in "HYPO's codebreaking efforts, [many] taking over the job of running the IBM tabulating machines and transferring information from intercepted messages into punch cards."[3]

During this period, Lt. Jasper Holmes observed that

> next to Rochefort, Dyer was senior officer, both in regard to rank and length of service in communications intelligence. Until after the Battle of Midway either he or Rochefort was always in the basement, and usually both of them were there.

In fact, "beginning in early 1942, Rochefort and Dyer alternated 24-on, 24-off, enabling one or the other always to be present in the basement." Dyer later commented that "we didn't see too much of each other the first six months of the war."

During the late 1930s when he had led HYPO, Dyer had developed a light touch in dealing with his subordinates. When Rochefort took over he was a bit more of a forceful manager, but he continued Dyer's light style and tried to foster a collegial atmosphere.

The importance of traffic analysis and direction-finding—the *forte* of "scanners" like Lieutenant Williams and Lieutenant Commander Huckins—can't be overstated. "In the early stages of the Pacific War, before the cryptanalysts cracked Japan's main naval codes, traffic analysis was about all Rochefort and his fellow analysts had to go on."

Many years after the war, retired Capt. John **Roenigk** recalled his introduction to HYPO. A former ONI Japanese full-immersion language officer, Roenigk reported to Rochefort in the spring of 1942.

---

3. Regarding recruiting the *California's* band, the local navy security office and the local FBI butted in. They were concerned with some bandsmen with "foreign" names, such as Garbuschewski, DeStalinska, and Palchefsky, and they decided such individuals would not be allowed in the "top-secret basement." Rorie then had the unpleasant task of explaining this to the *California's* bandmaster, Lovine "Red" Luckenbach. "We'll take these guys, but I can't take [those specific] guys; the FBI won't allow us to do it." Luckenbach, a subordinate petty officer, replied, "Like hell. Either you take [us] all or you're not going to get any." Chief Rorie held back his own "ferocious" temper and went to consult the "manpower-hungry" Commander Rochefort. Characteristically, Rochefort said, "The hell with the FBI; bring those guys in here."

Rochefort ordered me to first take "a few days" to become acquainted with the office, the people, the routine, etc. The third day he handed me a sheaf of papers containing coastwatcher reports from New Guinea and communications intelligence estimates from Tommy Dyer's office. "Study these," he said, "and let me know what the Japanese may be planning to do down here." I worked on it all day and into the night. I wrote up my estimate and delivered it to him next morning.

Looking over his work, Rochefort told him most of his conclusions were wrong—causing Roenigk great embarrassment. But then, Rochefort

gave his usual giggle, indicating that he was pulling my leg, and [said] that there were no real answers to that kind of intelligence guess-work without a background of "pattern watching" . . . he let me down gently. . . . He was just fantastic. I swore by him from those days forward and I could never have let him down. [He always had] a calm manner, never a harsh word to an inferior, and always a little humorous twinkle in his eye.

In early 1942, Rochefort was directed to detach some of his key men to form afloat radio intercept units on board specific aircraft carriers with various task forces. As valuable as this initiative turned out to be, HYPO acutely felt the loss of these highly trained specialists.[4]

In the aftermath of the Pearl Harbor disaster, institutional infighting and disputes over organization in Washington led to Captain Safford's ouster after the first of the year; he was essentially shunted to the side for the remainder of the war. From Rochefort's point of view, this was the beginning of the end for him, too.

Safford and Rochefort had enjoyed a relationship based on personal trust, with the understanding that the different units in the system would not vie for credit. With Safford purged, the trust and rapport were gone, and relations between HYPO and Washington quickly turned sour.

Rochefort hated that his friend and colleague Safford had been sacked.

As long as Safford was in Washington, I just about knew what to expect from him, and he knew what he could expect from me. It worked very nicely on a personal basis. It was only when other people became involved in it as a part of the wartime expansion that we began to have trouble.

Safford was sort of eased out of the job that he had, and he was stuck over in a corner somewhere; I know we didn't [properly] utilize his talents.

---

4. According to Capt. Jasper Holmes, "When the first radio intelligence teams proved valuable to the carrier task force commanders, the argument became academic. FRUPac had to provide the service, and the only way to do it was gracefully and efficiently. The radio operators could pick up the earliest signs of alarm at the target of a raid, and the language officer could gauge the magnitude of the defending forces by the flow of radio traffic. Armed with a list of the major Japanese units' radio calls, the team also had the potential ability to detect the presence of major Japanese naval forces within strategic distance. Radio intelligence teams with the task forces could sometimes copy Japanese messages that escaped the shore-based intercept station."

After the attack on Pearl Harbor, and with a reassignment to drop the AD code and start working on JN-25, Rochefort and the Station HYPO experts eventually became able to read enough of Japanese naval communications to provide daily intelligence reports and assessments regarding Japanese force disposition and intentions.

In March 1942, Washington—perhaps Admiral King himself—specifically asked Rochefort for his estimate of Japanese intentions. So,

> in a remarkable analysis he predicted that, with the East Indies secure and the Indian Ocean swept clear of threatening forces, the next Japanese campaign would be in the area of New Guinea. The Japanese Navy would follow that up with an all-out offensive in the central Pacific sometime in the summer.

During the peak month of May 1942, Commander Rochefort personally reviewed, analyzed, and reported on as many as 140 decrypted messages per day. These reports went directly to the highest-ranking fleet commanders.

In the lead-up to the battles of the Coral Sea and of Midway, some of Rochefort's officers—including Lieutenant Commander Holmes—pushed Rochefort to be more assertive in making operational recommendations to CinCPac. But Holmes later wrote that

> previous service on a big fleet staff had convinced Rochefort that many elements other than intelligence were involved in any action, and that the best results came from leaving operational matters to those who dealt with plans and operations. Rochefort was right, of course, as events were to prove. Like most naval and military intelligence officers, he subscribed to the principle that intelligence organizations should gather, collate, and disseminate information, and not attempt to make operational decisions.
>
> On 20 May, Yamamoto issued an operations order detailing the complete Japanese order of battle for the assault on AF [Midway] and the Aleutians. This long message was intercepted in its entirety and was immediately identified for what it was. Five days later, Rochefort personally delivered Yamamoto's operations order, nearly 90% decrypted, to Admiral Nimitz.

Of course, this was HYPO's most significant intelligence success—the timely and accurate support provided by Rochefort and his unit concerning the Battle of Midway, considered by many to be the turning point of the war in the Pacific. This in no way detracts from the fact that the unit provided accurate and timely intelligence reports for the remainder of the Pacific War; these reports were used by the most senior navy officers for extremely important strategic and tactical decisions.

Regarding Midway, relying on solid multisource intelligence and cryptographic information—as well as his personal intuition, experience, and assessment skills—Rochefort gave Nimitz a remarkable estimate prior to the battle. "Layton and Rochefort, having correctly foretold the Japanese move against Port Moresby [prior to the Battle of the Coral Sea], now enjoyed the CinCPac's full attention."

In fact, prior to Midway, Admiral King had suggested to Admiral Nimitz that the apparent Japanese interest in Midway was intended "to divert our forces away from [their real objectives in the] South Pacific." But Nimitz was willing to push back against King "because he was confident that Layton and Rochefort knew what they were talking about." In turn, Rochefort and Layton were impressed and energized by the confidence Nimitz showed in them. "We were aware that by challenging King and his [Washington] intelligence staff head-on, Nimitz had put himself out on a limb—and we were clinging onto it behind him."

Retired Capt. "Tex" Biard, a HYPO veteran, wrote in 2002 that

> Layton and Rochefort were close friends of long standing. At Pearl Harbor they worked together in complete harmony, forming an almost perfect team. Rochefort gave Layton remarkably clear and reliable estimates and analyses; the quick-witted Layton [then added] comments and suggestions or more analysis. After that he had to sell the final product to Admiral Nimitz.

Layton himself stressed that "the Coral Sea was an important victory for Station HYPO because it persuaded Nimitz to trust Rochefort over and above the often conflicting assessments being made by naval intelligence in Washington."

But there grew a serious conflict between OP-20-G and HYPO concerning interpretations of intercepts and enemy intentions. By the late spring of 1942 it had become both amazing and tragic. In fact, during the run-up before Midway it actually became bitter, ugly, and even personal. Perhaps the most obvious and important example was the disagreement over the identity of the Japanese code-designator "AF" as Midway— or somewhere else. "It was a mess," wrote "Ham" Wright later on. "We would fight with OP-20-G all the time; we could not get together." It became a feud and a war of words. "Some of it was not too polite," he said. "Washington wanted to take complete charge and tell us what to do in detail, but Rochefort would have no part of it." Wright was briefly sent to Washington to try to hammer out a truce. "It boiled down to who was going to do the work and who was going to get the credit," he recalled. "The NEGAT (OP-20-G) cryptanalysts did not want to trust *our* additives and would not use them. This attitude reached down to OP-20-G's radio operators—the lists we sent in would often wind up in the waste basket. It was very easy to get additives wrong. We were certainly most reluctant to trust *theirs*, so we worked out our own."

Station BELCONNEN in Australia decrypted a Japanese First Air Fleet order that showed when Adm. Nagumo Chūichi intended to leave his training bases and marshal his forces for the operation. BELCONNEN traffic analysis identified almost every ship in the enemy's order of battle, and concluded that the operation would either be against Hawaii or Midway. They essentially unraveled the planned date for the attack. BELCONNEN's analysis confirmed Commander Rochefort's analysis at Station HYPO; thus, Admiral King finally became convinced of this despite contrary input coming from his local people at OP-20-G in Washington. King cabled Nimitz, on May 17, 1942, that he had come to agree that Midway must be the target. After the war, Captain Safford commented that had BELCONNEN and HYPO not *independently drawn the same conclusions*, then NEGAT's (OP-20-G's) diffuse fears for an operation against Alaska or somewhere else might have prevailed.

In the weeks before Midway,

> in the frantic but meticulous search for the key that would unlock the final piece of the Midway puzzle, HYPO [consumed] nearly three million punch cards. . . . Just keeping HYPO supplied without arousing the suspicion of outsiders created a security risk. . . . [The] printouts produced for the tabulating process, from which the Japanese messages could be translated, were piled up on desks, floors, and every available space.

During this frantic time, Layton and Rochefort talked on their secure telephone at least forty times per day.

This might be a good point to emphasize that, in addition to cryptanalysis, translation—particularly of an incredibly nuanced language like Japanese—must be done carefully and can't be done hurriedly. Captain Rochefort said this:

> You might give a rough translation, or you might give a very careful translation. So much can depend on whether it is going to be "will," "shall," or something [even more subtle]. Unless you do a good job of translating, the whole value [could be] lost.

Historian Gordon Prange supported this view, writing that

> Japanese is very difficult to translate into English. To make matters worse, the messages came in as phonetic syllables. One such sound could have a variety of unrelated meanings. Even translators highly qualified in Japanese needed "considerable experience in this particular field before they could be trusted to come through with a correct interpretation."

Of course, all this hard work and brilliant analysis paid off. Despite extremely poor odds, with ships in the right place and a knowledge of the enemy's force and intentions, the operating forces of the U.S. Pacific Fleet handed the Japanese a crushing blow—which prominent historians have called a "miracle" and an "incredible victory." Not to oversimplify, the Americans basically lost one aircraft carrier and some three hundred men, but the Japanese lost four aircraft carriers and three thousand men.

One evening right after the victory, Lt. Gen. Delos Emmons, the commanding general of the Hawaiian Department, brought champagne—wrapped in blue and gold ribbons—to the Pacific Fleet headquarters. Admiral Nimitz sent a car to collect Commander Rochefort.

> But Joe took so long changing . . . into uniform whites that the champagne had run dry by the time he arrived. Nimitz, nevertheless, magnanimously declared to his assembled staff, "This officer deserves a major share of the credit for the victory."
>
> It was typical of Joe that he waited another couple of days before he gave his exhausted staff a two-day break [during which they held] what can only be described as a great big drunken brawl.

Rochefort often said that he was never very interested in personal decorations or recognition. In fact, he had a sign by his HYPO desk which read, "We can accomplish *anything* . . . provided . . . no one cares who gets the credit." That being said, he did want proper credit for the contributions of his men and Station HYPO. He admired the work done at Station BELCONNEN in Australia, but not OP-20-G—Station NEGAT—in Washington. Years later he said, "We backed up and helped BELCONNEN on the Coral Sea job. BELCONNEN backed us up (perhaps to a lesser extent due to lack of talent) and helped us on the Midway job . . . NEGAT kibitzed and complained on both jobs."

July 1942 saw the establishment of the Intelligence Center Pacific Ocean Area, the idea of which had started back in April with a pitch from ONI's Cmdr. Arthur McCollum to Admiral Nimitz. Joe Rochefort was drafted to run it. "ComFourteen bucked the job of officer-in-charge of ICPOA to Rochefort, who was already overworked in communications intelligence." Rochefort actually liked the concept, but had no time to do both jobs. Holmes recalled that

> one morning, late in July, Rochefort dropped a mass of papers on my desk and told me to find some space to put the new organization. I was relieved to discover that only seventeen officers and twenty-nine men had been ordered to ICPOA by Washington, but even that number created problems. [HYPO] had expanded to fill all available space in the basement. The cryptanalysts were justly concerned that bringing a number of new people into the basement would erode the security essential for their work.

In August 1942, in a night surface attack, the Japanese sank one Australian and three American cruisers at the Battle of Savo Island. Holmes saw the dispatch from the commander, South Pacific, reporting this stunning defeat. "Rochefort hid it in his desk for hours, too heartsick to show it to anybody."

By the fall of 1942, the growing unhappiness that Washington had with Joe Rochefort reached its peak. There arose, along with an unprofessional rivalry, a conspiracy involving Rear Adm. Joseph Redman, Cmdr. John Redman, and Cmdr. Joseph Wenger. Their goal was to remove Commander Rochefort from his key post as head of Station HYPO. These gentlemen had previously been the group which, several months earlier, had sacked Capt. Laurance Safford as head of OP-20-G. In this case, Rochefort's

> superiors in Washington, regarding him as a prickly obstacle in the way of their earning plaudits for major intelligence coups, continued to be incensed that he had made fools of them in their off-the-mark predictions.

In October, Capt. Earl **Stone** relieved Commander Redman as assistant director of Naval Communications for Communications Intelligence, and head of OP-20-G. Stone shortly learned of clandestine message traffic flowing between John Redman (who had transferred out to Pearl Harbor) and Stone's deputy in Washington, Joe Wenger—messages mostly about their secret plan to get Rochefort terminated as OIC at HYPO. Stone was troubled by what he discovered and apparently refused to have anything to do with it, recognizing—among other things—that use of a navy cipher system for personal communications was improper if not actually illegal. Wenger was then ordered by the new director of naval communications, Capt. Carl Holden, to destroy the secret cipher; at Pearl Harbor, Admiral Nimitz told Jack Redman to cease all such "intolerable" activity, and refused to speak to him for weeks.

When Joe Rochefort then traveled east to Washington on temporary orders— which, by the secret plan, were actually going to be permanent—he assertively confronted Stone and Wenger. They both told him that they were ignorant of the whole thing and that "they were both satisfied with combat intelligence at Pearl and did not desire any changes." Stone was telling the truth; Wenger was not—on both points. Stone appears to have been genuinely baffled about the whole situation. "I never quite understood the *personal animosity* that existed between some of the people on duty in Washington and those in Hawaii." He did not know him well, but he liked and respected Rochefort—later commenting that "he was one of the most able people we had," and thus was puzzled by the intense sentiment against him. "I knew there was an argument going on and I must say I didn't realize that it was [as] serious as it proved to be when Rochefort was summarily relieved—*which was an awful mistake.*" Intelligence historian John Prados wrote that

> Rochefort not only did not return to Pearl Harbor, he was banished to Western Sea Frontier headquarters in San Francisco and then to the Tiburon Peninsula in California to the Floating Drydock Training Center. A greater waste of a first-rate intelligence expert can hardly be imagined.

Thus, in the fall of 1942, despite (or perhaps because of) his incredible contributions to the successful battles at the Coral Sea and at Midway, Commander Rochefort was removed from his billet by the political machinations of professional enemies he had at Main Navy. The reader is invited to read the chapter on Rear Adm. Joseph Wenger for more on that incredible story, but for now suffice it to say that these same people persuaded Admiral King to also take a swipe at Eddie Layton. King told Nimitz that "the attitude of Commander Layton also seems not to have been very helpful. I suggest you consider what should be done in [his case]." Nimitz called Layton into his office and informed him he apparently had an enemy in Washington. Layton was dumbfounded, but then was reassured; Nimitz said, "Go back to your office and don't think any more about it." Admiral Nimitz could and did shield Commander Layton. But as much as it angered him, Nimitz could not save Rochefort because he was technically in the navy's *administrative* command structure—and thus beyond Nimitz's span of control as *operational* head of the Pacific Fleet.

Prior to Rochefort's recall, in September 1942 Capt. Roscoe Hillenkoetter (an IO with considerable *European* background) reported as OIC of ICPOA, relieving Cmdr. Rochefort of this extra duty. On September 25, ICPOA moved into offices totaling six thousand square feet in the navy yard's supply building.

Station HYPO had become a nominal part of ICPOA—as the Radio Intelligence Section—but it remained in its basement with Joe Rochefort still in charge. Then, Rochefort received those temporary orders to Washington in October; Lt. Cmdr. Holmes at first thought this was a great opportunity for Rochefort to straighten out some issues with OP-20-G and lobby for more cryptographers, translators, *kana* radio operators, and equipment. But Rochefort didn't have a good feeling about the situation and gave Holmes a package of personal papers and the keys to his desk; Jasper didn't even suspect he'd never see Joe Rochefort again until long after the war was over.

Thus, a couple of weeks after Rochefort had gone, when Capt. William **Goggins** was brought into the basement and introduced to the unit by Captain Hillenkoetter as the new HYPO OIC, he was met with no little astonishment by Holmes and the rest of the HYPO crew. They realized that "Rochefort had been summarily relieved as OIC of COMINT in Hawaii. It was another blow to our morale. . . . Rochefort became the victim of a Navy Department internal political coup." His friends at HYPO were stunned; Holmes summed up the feeling when he wrote that

> all the charges could have been easily disproved but, instead of being decorated or given a spot-promotion to captain for the greatest intelligence achievement in the Navy's history, he was relieved of duty in radio intelligence and ordered to sea. [Then] for more than a year his unsurpassed technical qualifications and his exceptional analytical ability were lost to radio intelligence at a time when the Navy needed them badly.

Commander Layton was even more blunt in his assessment:

> It was very disturbing for me, his friend of many years, to see how Rochefort was speared like a frog and hung out to dry for the rest of the war when he could have done so much more to help us win it.

Fortunately, Commander Rochefort wrote a letter to Lt. Cmdr. Holmes in November 1942. It included an assurance that in Rochefort's opinion Captain Goggins had nothing to do with Rochefort's dismissal, and that he hoped the HYPO team would "all be as loyal to Goggins as you have been to me." This comment

> facilitated Goggins' smooth takeover of an organization which had been badly shaken. Fortunately, Goggins was an able administrator and an expert in naval communications. He and [Holmes] became close and enduring friends. . . . His knowledge of communications and his good relations with CinCPac staff were very important to [HYPO] just when its own communications network had to be expanded and improved.

After only about a week in Washington, Rochefort was sent to San Francisco. There he worked for the Commander, Western Sea Frontier, who had Joe set up an advanced intelligence center combining assets of the Eleventh, Twelfth, and Thirteenth Naval Districts. Rochefort actually enjoyed this assignment. "It was a lot of fun," he said later, even though at first he "really didn't have his heart in this."

In May 1943, Rochefort was again assigned "pioneering duty," but duty which had nothing to do with intelligence. He was ordered to oversee the building of an advanced base sectional dock—or floating drydock—which would be employed at remote, forward areas to quickly repair damaged warships. For several months he divided his time between Tiburon, Stockton, and Eureka in California, and Everett on Puget Sound. He supervised personnel training and component testing for this unique craft. He was then given orders to assume command of the USS *ABSD-2*. For his work Rochefort received high praise from Rear Adm. Ben Moreel, founder of the Seabees and chief of the Bureau of Yards and Docks. Joe liked this assignment and disagreed with his friend Layton—and others—that he was being poorly employed. However, Commander Rochefort did not get to take the *ABSD-2* into the Pacific (she later served in the Admiralty Islands under someone else's command).

Joe received new orders, to Main Navy, for the Far Eastern Section of ONI. Thus, in April 1944, he was back in Washington and back into the intelligence business—but actually didn't stay with ONI. He shortly was promoted to captain and made head of a new unit in Naval Communications very suited to his skills. Ironically, the man who enthusiastically put him there was Rear Adm. Joseph Redman, who just two years earlier was part of the plots which removed Safford and Rochefort from their positions. But now Rochefort was the head of OP-20-G50, the Pacific Strategic Intelligence Section. It was a project he liked, he was given considerable independence, and he was building the unit from scratch. As historian John Prados commented, Rochefort had fortunately

> returned to intelligence duty . . . when Admiral King wanted a special group to do extended reports and estimates, Joe Rochefort seemed the perfect man for the job. He finished out the war in Washington supplying COMINCH with some fine reporting.

With a large team—he ultimately had around three hundred people in the organization, including a number of "very competent language officers and a large number of navy WAVE (Women Accepted for Volunteer Emergency Service) officers and enlisted people"—Rochefort was assessing Japan's naval and military capabilities as part of the planning for an invasion of the home islands. He was also

> besieged with requests for insight into important but hitherto neglected aspects of the Pacific War. One of his most demanding customers was Cmdr. William **Sebald**, representing COMINCH, [for] things such as a study on the present oil situation in Japan, and a study showing what success the Japanese have had in sweeping acoustic mines.

At one point, Commander Sebald scolded PSIS for what was in his opinion naïveté about power relations inside Japan's leadership; one can only imagine how the knowledgeable and confident Captain Rochefort enjoyed that memo from a more junior officer.

Future captain Roger Pineau was Rochefort's assistant at PSIS and was thoroughly impressed by him. He thought Rochefort was an inspiring leader and morale-builder, with a genius for organization.

> When he commented on our work—good or bad—it was direct and to the point, but with an avuncular air. . . . Corrections were usually made with a tolerant smile, as though he had been there himself, as indeed he had.

Rochefort and I became friends in his retirement years, but I never heard a word of acrimony or complaint from him about his wartime treatment. He did say that he might have been better off if he had gone to the Naval Academy, as it could have taught him to be more reserved and less caustic in his opinions.

While Joe was still working at PSIS the Japanese surrendered, and the war ended, in August 1945. At this point Captain Rochefort was "permitted to go to sea." He was first ordered to command the attack cargo ship *Stokes*; then those orders were modified for the attack transport *Telfair*—and then the orders were totally canceled. This was because he was directed to testify at another of the Pearl Harbor attack inquiries—this particular one was the seventh probe into that disaster.

Rochefort's PSIS assignment ended in September 1946. He was then assigned to OP-23, a department responsible for coordinating construction, repair, and disposal of ships. In postwar peacetime it was a dead-end job, and that's certainly how he looked at it. He requested retirement which was granted; for a few months he served on court-martial boards until his retirement finalized in January 1947.

In the fall of 1948 he enrolled at the University of Southern California, taking courses in higher mathematics, international relations, and the Russian language.

However, this attempt at further education ended when the navy recalled him to active duty in October 1950. He was put on the staff of the CinCPac Fleet Evaluation Group which studied intelligence aspects of Far East readiness; Rochefort said he was delighted to help. Then, in mid-1951, he was further retained and sent to the Naval War College. He had asked to be returned to the retired list, but was persuaded by Commodore Richard W. Bates to come to Newport and assist him with the college's analyses of World War II Pacific battles. Rochefort became a senior analyst on the massive Leyte Gulf report. He did considerable Japanese translation work and on the whole found it "enjoyable duty, most enjoyable."

In March 1953, Joe was relieved from active duty as funding for the War College project ran out. He and his wife returned to California, living in Manhattan Beach. There he worked on disaster-preparedness plans as a volunteer. This activity ultimately evolved into a paid job, coordinating and planning for fifteen cities and over seven hundred thousand people; he worked at this at least until 1969. He also started a career in real estate and apparently did fairly well in the business. Sometime around 1965 the Rocheforts moved to Palos Verdes, at Redondo Beach.

At one point in 1957, retired Captain Jasper Holmes visited retired Fleet Admiral Nimitz in California and convinced him to revisit the matter of a Distinguished Service Medal for Captain Rochefort. Many of Joe's friends and colleagues believed that Joe had been shockingly overlooked when decorations had been awarded for World War II COMINT service; he had received a Legion of Merit, but relative to his contributions, it seemed insufficient relative to other officers who had received the higher-level DSM. Admiral Nimitz agreed and wrote to the secretary of the navy but, surprisingly, was rebuffed for several reasons that—at that time—seemed logical to the navy department.

In 1970, Joe was asked to consult on the Hollywood movie *Tora! Tora! Tora!*, and then again in 1976 on *Midway*. For *Midway* he coached actor Hal Holbrook, who was portraying him—or at least Hollywood's version of him. Rochefort didn't seem to mind Holbrook's folksy characterization—although a number of Joe's friends did not like it *at all*. For his part, Mr. Holbrook and some civic leaders from Torrance and Redondo Beach held a luncheon in Joe's honor on May 12—his seventy-sixth birthday—and only two months before he passed away.

In any discussion of Joe Rochefort there's at least one major issue that has to be emphasized. Despite over a dozen historical works proclaiming Rochefort as the absolute best of the prewar and wartime U.S. Navy cryptanalysts, it's really not true. He was a fine cryptanalyst, of course, but he wasn't the top one (one can't overlook that, from 1927 to 1941, he essentially didn't do any cryptanalysis). His extraordinary skills really lay *in addition* to that one. Tommy Dyer later weighed in on this issue, saying, "I think, without any false modesty, that in *cryptanalysis only*, I was *number one*." He added, however, that

in the total combination, in the value to the war effort and to the country, I unhesitatingly step aside for Rochefort. But, purely as a cryptanalyst or codebreaker, I think unquestionably I was his superior. The only person, that I know of, that came close to me in cryptanalysis was "Ham" Wright.

In regard to Rochefort, Dyer elaborated:

He was outstanding. But his really outstanding quality was as an *intelligence analyst*. What he was taking was, after all, frequently fragmentary information and arriving at a correct analysis of what it said and what it meant.

Rochefort was almost solely responsible for producing the intelligence which resulted in the Battle of Midway.

That was his ability—to make a silk purse out of a sow's ear. The early messages about Coral Sea, the early messages about Midway, were perfectly capable of being read in a totally different way than the correct way. Knowledge of the character of the Japanese and this, that, and the other, enabled Rochefort to get the right meaning.

Rochefort himself agreed. More than once he differentiated himself from the "true" cryptanalyst. He said that codebreaking presents a challenge,

and a true cryptanalyst will never give up until he has solved a particular system. A true cryptanalyst generally is not involved in subsequent use of the information. He's what you would call a technician who will solve a system just for the sake of solving the system. But he doesn't usually apply the results to any operation or need or purpose or anything else. This would be a true cryptanalyst. This would be [people like Dyer, Driscoll, and] Safford.

Joe clearly didn't revel in cryptanalysis, as did some of the others. He found "that the work impaired his personal life, stunted his career prospects, and gave him ulcers." Rochefort considered himself more of an intelligence and communications-intelligence analyst—and even more so a balanced naval officer of the line. He felt that his views on the duties of a communications-intelligence officer might be "far different than the normal concept of this." He certainly saw himself as much more than a *cryppie*.

> It so happened that I had been involved in the Fleet during the latter part of the Twenties and into the Thirties in fleet operations, and had extensive duty including assistant fleet operations officer and temporary duty as fleet operations officer. I had served as intelligence officer as well as the normal ship duty and I considered that I was perhaps fairly well fitted to render a judgment on what the Japanese intended than the average intelligence officer because of my staff training and duties on the staff of the Commander in Chief U.S. Fleet, the Battle Force, the Scouting Force, and shore establishments.
>
> Therefore, the estimates that came from Station HYPO were not [merely] the estimates of *technical* people such as cryptanalysts, or language officers, or translators, or communications-intelligence people. They were [essentially my] considered opinions . . . who had this capability as well as having had the experience of serving in the operations department of the various staffs in the fleet. Of course . . . I was also a translator . . . and I felt that I had the knowledge and experience of being able to estimate and form a judgment on what the [message] traffic actually meant, because we were not able to read the [code] completely anyway, and all we would get would be fragments.
>
> With the people that I had out there that were equally capable, we had a small group there, say three or four or five, who could not only analyze what the Japanese were *saying*, but also would come up with a very good solution or *estimate* of the situation—which other people probably would not have this knowledge or experience.

From the perspective of seventy years, and with a fairly full knowledge of the facts, it seems incredible to the modern reader that Rochefort was capriciously removed from a job in which he excelled and in which he was of incredible value to the war effort.

From the perspective of 1983, retired Capt. Tommy Dyer told an interviewer that

> I have given a great deal of thought to the Rochefort affair, and I have been unwillingly forced to the conclusion that Rochefort committed the one unforgivable sin. To certain individuals of small mind and overweening ambition, there's no greater insult than to be proved wrong.

Rochefort's long-time mentor and friend, retired Rear Adm. Arthur McCollum, also provided another take on Joe Rochefort's "fall." In their younger days he repeatedly warned the blunt-spoken Rochefort to be careful about speaking critically—let alone insultingly—to superior officers he didn't respect. "Rochefort stepped on toes of a lot of people who later got to be pretty important guys." His too-often "feisty personal style" didn't help his cause.

Part of Rochefort's impatience and lack of respect for some of his coworkers and superiors stemmed from the state of intelligence—and communications—in those early days. Intelligence, in Rochefort's view, was for too many years and for far too many officers "just a nice social job. You're invited to various parties at various embassies or legations or one thing and another, and you mix with nice people, but you don't do anything." Interestingly, Dwight Eisenhower made a similar remark concerning army attachés circa 1941: "Usually they were estimable, socially acceptable gentlemen." But as far as special qualifications were concerned, "few knew the essentials of intelligence work."

By and large, Rochefort's colleagues and subordinates held him in the highest regard. According to retired Capt. "Tex" Biard,

> Joe Rochefort was our incomparable and brilliant officer in charge: Japanese linguist, expert traffic analyst, leader among codebreakers, and intelligence specialist extraordinary. He was intuitive, quick, sharp thinking, blessed with a fantastic memory of almost total recall, and was an inspiring leader for his associates. He understood, he encouraged, he inspired, he pointed out new approaches to problems that were stopping us and, above all, the estimates and summaries he sent to the high command were almost always highly correct and, frequently, prophetic. He kept our team working smoothly, brilliantly, and efficiently.

Retired Capt. John Roenigk said that Rochefort

> was highly motivated and made immeasurable contributions to winning the war in the Pacific. By his example, subordinates flocked to his assistance, tried to learn from him, and tried to emulate his savvy. Joe was not a slave driver. His own example of working around the clock was enough to motivate anyone associated with him. . . .
>
> He was a great judge of the capabilities of subordinates in placing them where they could best contribute. He had a photographic mind and never, to my knowledge, forgot a single detail. He was an uncanny card player and problem solver.

Decorated submariner and best-selling author, retired Capt. Edward L. Beach, in his history *The United States Navy: 200 Years*, was perhaps Rochefort's most enthusiastic fan. He wrote that, at Midway, Admiral Yamamoto

> was defeated by one man, whose special genius enabled him to give Admiral Nimitz the invaluable background that made all the difference between fighting blindly and fighting with full awareness of the enemy's plans. *To Commander Joe Rochefort must forever go the acclaim for having made more difference, at a more important time, than any other naval officer in history.*

Cryptology historian David Kahn wrote that

> the codebreakers of the Combat Intelligence Unit had engrossed the fate of a nation. They had determined the destinies of ships and men. They had turned the tide of a war. They had caused a Rising Sun to start to set.

Joe Rochefort died of a heart attack on July 20, 1976, in Torrance. His wife, Elma Fay Rochefort (1901–1969), had preceded him; they first met long ago in high school, and they're now buried together in Inglewood Park Cemetery, Inglewood, California. Joe and Fay had two children, Joe Jr. (who went to West Point and became an army colonel), and Janet Rochefort Elerding. It's interesting to note that, late in his own life, Captain Rochefort destroyed his family letters, eliminating his wartime correspondence with his wife and other family members. He did the same thing to most of his navy papers, as well.

As mentioned earlier, Joe had been awarded the Legion of Merit for his wartime services—despite being recommended for the higher-level Distinguished Service Medal by Fleet Admiral Nimitz in both 1942 and again in 1957. However, in May 1986, in the White House's Roosevelt Room, President Ronald Reagan posthumously presented Joe's son and daughter with the long-overdue DSM.[5] In attendance were three of Rochefort's former HYPO comrades, retired Rear Adm. Donald "Mac" Showers, Capt. Gilven M. **Slonim**, and Capt. Willis L. Thomas—as well as Capt. Roger Pineau, who had worked with him late in the war at PSIS.[6] Later that same year, Rochefort also posthumously received the Presidential Medal of Freedom for his contributions to the Battle of Midway. Echoing Captain Beach, among President Reagan's remarks was this: "If ever there was a battle involving tens of thousands of men in which victory was attributable to one man, this one was attributable to Joseph J. Rochefort."

In 2011 the U.S. Navy established "The Captain Joseph Rochefort Information Warfare Officer Distinguished Leadership Award." The intent of the award is to annually recognize the superior career achievement of an information warfare officer. In the spirit of Captain Rochefort, specific consideration is given to leadership, teamwork, operational contributions, and adherence to the principle by which he served: *we can accomplish anything provided no one cares who gets the credit.*

Captain Rochefort has been designated a Pioneer Officer of U.S. Naval Cryptology by the U.S. Naval Cryptologic Veterans Association. Joe was also inducted into the NSA's Hall of Honor in 2000. Finally, in January 2012, the Captain Joseph J. Rochefort Building was dedicated at the NSA Central Security Service facility at Joint Base Pearl Harbor-Hickam Annex.

---

5. Retired Rear Adm. Donald "Mac" Showers was instrumental in finally getting the long-overdue medal for Rochefort. Showers spent the entire war in Pacific Theater combat intelligence and then followed that with a distinguished career in naval intelligence. "Of all the officers and men working in the [HYPO] basement during the Battle of Midway, Showers was the only one eventually to reach the rank of rear admiral" on active duty. Rear Adm. Showers died in October 2012. Other key contributors in this effort were Director of Central Intelligence William Casey, retired Rear Adm. Edwin Layton, retired Capt. Roger Pineau, Navy Department staff member Arthur Baker, Secretary of the Navy John Lehman, and National Security Advisor Vice Adm. John Poindexter.

6. Also present were Vice President George H. W. Bush, Secretary of Defense Caspar Weinberger, Joint Chiefs of Staff Chairman Adm. William Crowe, CNO Adm. James Watkins, and Deputy Director of Central Intelligence Robert Gates.

Sources

Unlike many of the people profiled in this book, it's very easy to find information on Joe Rochefort—so the real difficulty has been trying not to include every interesting fact in order to keep the section from becoming too long. There are four sources which were particularly helpful: Rochefort's own 325-page oral history interview, from 1969, available from the U.S. Naval Institute; Capt. Jasper Holmes's book *Double-Edged Secrets: U.S. Naval Intelligence Operations in the Pacific during World War II*; Edwin Layton's book *"And I Was There": Pearl Harbor and Midway—Breaking the Secrets*; and Elliot Carlson's magnificent biography, *Joe Rochefort's War: The Odyssey of the Codebreaker Who Outwitted Yamamoto at Midway*, published in 2011. Not only does Carlson give the reader the definitive Rochefort story, he also paints extremely interesting pictures of many of *this* book's other subjects.

Beach, 450.

Benson, 7, 64–65.

Biard, 151–58.

Budiansky, 3–5, 10–11, 12–17, 22–24, 42.

Capt. Joseph Rochefort. NSA Cryptologic Hall of Honor citation.

Carlson, ix–x, 2–17, 19, 22, 24, 40–49, 51–52, 62–77, 80–84, 88–90, 94–95, 102–3, 113, 128, 146–53, 141–42, 198, 206, 210–12, 221–22, 239, 261–63, 295–96, 308, 382–86, 414, 430–56.

Clausen, 66–67, 209.

Costello, 163–66, 174–76, 188, 289–90, 295–99, 300.

Donovan and Mack, 145, 147–48, 150, 152, 188, 333.

Drea, 37.

Dyer, *Reminiscences*, 75–78, 85–87, 198, 219, 247, 250–51, 263–65, 267–68, 304.

Farago, *Broken Seal*, 42, 106, 164, 268–69, 319–20.

Farago, *Burn after Reading*, 193, 197–98, 209.

Haufler, 2, 119–22, 127–28, 146–47, 149–52, 156, 215–16.

Holmes, 3, 14–16, 21, 28, 31–32, 37, 42–43, 55, 65–66, 71–73, 85, 89–91, 94–95, 108–17.

Holtwick, 44–46, 48, 61, 69, 84, 151, 182, 427, 431, 446, App. 4.

Hone, 267–68.

Kahn, *Codebreakers*, 7, 40, 562–63, 573.

Kahn, *Discovered*, 23–24, 29–30.

Layton, *"And I Was There,"* 33–34, 36, 39, 49–51, 92–95, 165, 173, 183–86, 227–29, 231, 237, 243–45, 250, 277, 317, 318, 339–40, 358–59, 367–69, 372–73, 375–77, 381, 383, 393–94, 404–6, 408–14, 416–17, 419–29, 431–37, 439, 445–46, 448–56, 464–70, 496, 507.

Lewin, 1–2, 25–26, 60, 81–82, 89, 101–4, 132–34.

Lord, 17–25, 27–28, 287.

Lundstrom, John B., in Hone, 242, 244.

McCollum, 19, 196.

McGinnis, 9, 21.

Meet the Code Masters, www.navy.mil/midway/ncb.html.

Norman, 116–17.

Packard, 230, 365, 369, 396.

Pelletier, 151.

CAPTAIN JOHN GEORGE ROENIGK, U.S. NAVY (1912–1993)

Translator / cryptographer at HYPO, ICPOA, FRUPac, and JICPOA, 1942–1944
"Renny" "Jack" "Swede"

John Roenigk was an extraordinarily well-rounded officer. Like so many others in this volume he balanced a surface-ship career with intelligence and cryptography. One of ONI's Japanese immersion students, he later spent most of the war at Pearl Harbor working on translations, cryptography, and analysis. After the war he commanded two ships and was commodore of a squadron, as well as serving as naval attaché in Sweden and Japan.

*   *   *

From the 1934 Annapolis yearbook, *The Lucky Bag*:

This charming, slender, smiling Pennsylvania Dutchman crowds more activity into one year than most midshipmen do in four. In the fall he takes up soccer, during the winter he manages the unruly swimming team, or plays a femme role for the *Masqueraders* [the drama club], and in the spring he runs around the track. Despite his athletic tendencies, though, his fetish is the *Log* [the midshipman humor magazine]. First Class Year his hard work was rewarded by the post of Managing Editor. Just step into any humorist's room in the Fourth Battalion and you will find our *Swede* screaming for a contribution. His untiring efforts are one of the safety factors of the *Log's* popularity. *Renny's* idea of boning [studying] is to turn-in early and sleep with the book under one ear. There may be something to the system for we very seldom, if ever, see his name gracing the weekly trees. . . . *Jack* claims to know all about women and his locker door would tend to prove this theory. Many an art gallery would be put to shame by the handsome Swede's collection of dazzling femmes. His retribution comes around when he realizes, with an awful shock, that all the girls he has asked to the June Ball have accepted. *Swede's* never-failing good humor has been one of the bright spots of our four years by the bay. May we meet with it frequently in the future. [Activities: soccer, track, swimming manager, *Masqueraders*, *Log* Staff]

*   *   *

Coming from a large family—he had three brothers and three sisters—John Roenigk was born in Butler, Pennsylvania, on April 1, 1912, son of George and Elizabeth Hahn Roenigk. He attended public schools in Butler and then the Werntz Preparatory School in Annapolis—"Bobby Werntz's War College," as it was affectionately known to some. He entered the U.S. Naval Academy in 1930 and subsequently graduated in 1934 with an ensign's commission. Some of his notable classmates were Jackson D. Arnold, Forrest R. **Biard**, Bernard A. Clarey, John J. Hyland, Victor H. Krulak, and Richard H. O'Kane. Further promotions included lieutenant (junior grade), 1937; lieutenant, 1941; lieutenant commander, 1943; commander, 1944; and captain in 1953. He retired from the navy in 1964.

Upon his graduation from Annapolis, Mr. Roenigk joined the newly commissioned USS *Ranger* (the first ship of the U.S. Navy purposely designed and built as an aircraft carrier) and participated in her shakedown cruise to South America. He was also on board the *Ranger* in 1936 for the first-ever carrier cold-weather trials in Alaskan waters, testing the feasibility of aircraft operations in frigid conditions. In August of that year he transferred to the oiler *Neches*, and was on board when she participated in Fleet Problem XVI in the vicinity of Midway Island. Then, after brief duty in the destroyer *Truxton*—June through August 1937—he reported to the U.S.

embassy in Tokyo as one of ONI's full-immersion language and culture students. He had been attracted to the idea of language instruction even when on board the *Ranger*, and "the idea of Japan, a forward-moving country, fascinated me. No one in the Navy seemed to know much about Japan. If I could learn about Japan and the language, especially, [I thought that] I could be of great service."

He chiefly studied under the extremely effective Naganuma Naoe, who had also taught Lieutenants (junior grade) Redfield **Mason**, Henri **Smith-Hutton**, and William **Sebald**, among others. Moreover,

> during my last year and a half, Naganuma located a retired Imperial Navy captain to teach me navy nautical terms and despatch language. Like a good navy man from any country, he was well aware of his seniority well above me and demanded complete reverence and respect—which I heartily approved of. I was soon to learn that the Japanese Navy operated very much the same as we did and that the operations and communication procedures were similar to ours, which I attributed to their being allies in the Pacific in World War I. I could not have operated so efficiently in World War II had I not had this earlier exposure to [this] captain.

"The great majority of us rented summer shacks up in the mountains in Karuizawa, north of Tokyo." Roenigk had acquired a Chinese cook who was a master chef—which made him the envy of his fellow students at meal times.

> I . . . passed my fifth six-month exam in Japanese with flying colors. I now branched out further into the language study. I was beyond the Japanese college-student level of learning although I didn't know all their slang language—which I didn't consider entirely worthwhile.
>
> The average Japanese common person, particularly the women, couldn't read the daily newspaper. In the evenings, my maid would come up to my study and ask me to please read the newspaper to her. She knew the words which were used in conversation daily, but didn't recognize the characters in print. Nor could she read the personal letters from her father, who used the old "cursive" style of writing which I was specializing on learning during my final year. This is unbelievable in the Western world, but it is a fact. The housekeeper thought that I was doing her a great service, but I profited also by learning her "kitchen talk" simultaneously.

Roenigk later recalled that U.S. Navy language officers actually "lived the life of a Japanese and spoke usually only Japanese day and night, and generally wore Japanese kimono and wooden clogs on the street. Usually we travelled in pairs for companionship, but not necessarily always." He was more organized than some of the language students and very disciplined in working at proficiency.

> Calculating my personal knowledge of Japanese by actual count of word cards, made up of different arrangement of the characters, I had the use of more than 30,000 Japanese words and expressions which I stored in a specially constructed card case containing some thirty drawers. It was necessary to review all these cards periodically to maintain

one's ability in the language. I usually flipped through one drawer of cards each night before going to bed, when I was too tired for conversation or to practice writing the language any longer for that day.

Upon completion of his three-year immersion experience, Mr. Roenigk then had brief duty—not much more than a week—with ONI at Main Navy. He next assisted in the fitting out of the destroyer *Edison* at the Federal Shipbuilding and Drydock Co. at Kearny, New Jersey. Upon the *Edison*'s commissioning in January 1941, Roenigk reported on board as gunnery officer and subsequently took part in convoy operations, escort duties, and anti-submarine patrols in the North Atlantic.

Detached from the *Edison* in March 1942, Lieutenant Roenigk then became an assistant intelligence officer on the staff of Admiral Nimitz along with Lieutenants Arthur "Benny" Benedict and Herbert M. Coleman. There at Pearl Harbor they worked for Lt. Cmdr. Edwin **Layton**; with Lt. Robert Hudson, who was already in place, they were put on a one-in-four watch under Layton. Benedict and Roenigk focused upon translating a few captured documents. However, for part of each day Layton also had them volunteer their services to Cmdr. Joseph **Rochefort**, head of the naval district's radio intelligence and cryptology unit—Station HYPO. Layton thought the linguists would be of more real value to Rochefort than to himself. Roenigk later said that

> we had arrived suddenly in the broad field of cryptography with no previous knowledge whatsoever. Everything had to be learned from scratch without benefit of anything being in writing from which we could learn. We had to learn from current coast-watcher reports and traffic analysis, conjecture, and calculated estimates, and finally attempt to solve the enemy codes and cyphers. In this we were blessed with a superior understanding and knowledge of the Japanese language and their naval procedure.

He recalled his introduction to HYPO:

> Rochefort ordered me to first take "a few days" to become acquainted with the office, the people, the routine, etc. The third day he handed me a sheaf of papers containing coastwatcher reports from New Guinea and communications intelligence estimates from Tommy **Dyer**'s office. "Study these," he said, "and let me know what the Japanese may be planning to do down here." I worked on it all day and into the night. I wrote up my estimate and delivered it to him next morning.

Looking over his work, Rochefort told him most of his conclusions were wrong— causing Roenigk great embarrassment. But then, Rochefort

> gave his usual giggle, indicating that he was pulling my leg, and [said] that there were no real answers to that kind of intelligence guess-work without a background of "pattern watching". . . . he let me down gently. . . . He was just fantastic. I swore by him from those days forward and I could never have let him down. [He always had] a calm manner, never a harsh word to an inferior, and always a little humorous twinkle in his eye.

In fall 1942, Roenigk and Benedict moved full time to the Fourteenth Naval District, and through the war successively worked at HYPO, ICPOA, FRUPac, and JICPOA.

CinCPac had issued temporary additional duty orders to Benedict and myself to [HYPO]; however, we remained officially attached to CinCPac. This arrangement was most welcome, since fleet staff duty was designated as "sea duty," which we required if we ever hoped to be promoted beyond lieutenant.

This arrangement lasted quite a while, although later on they were officially transferred to ComFourteen and lost the sea-duty credit.

The routine of the work was a grind, but in any event there wasn't much to do off duty. Roenigk later commented that "there was no social life in Hawaii during the war. We mostly stayed on the [Makalapa] Hill twenty-four hours a day. It was tough even to drive to town." It's interesting to note, however, that spending most of his work time and off-duty time in the same area as did Admiral Nimitz, Roenigk later developed a relationship with his commander in chief.

My housemates and I pitched horseshoes with the admiral in his back yard numerous times for exercise. One . . . housemate, H. Arthur "Hal" Lamar, was flag lieutenant to the admiral, and one of his duties was to round up staff members to make up a foursome for a half-hour game every evening before dinner.

In November 1944, Roenigk was transferred to OP-20-G in Washington—not at Main Navy but at its new location on Nebraska Avenue—working for Capt. Rosie **Mason**. The work was similar to what Roenigk had been doing at Pearl Harbor, but "the pace was greatly slowed down" and they worked with regular office hours.

Toward the end of the war Roenigk found himself the senior commander in the office. He applied for sea duty to hopefully ensure further promotion, but received

orders designating me as commanding officer of OP-20-GZ, relieving our former boss, Redfield Mason. My next superior in the chain of command, Capt. Joseph **Wenger**, called me into his office and said that he was glad to have me remain, and hoped that I would stay on for at least a year to pick up the pieces and reorganize. I had no intention of doing so if I could obtain an assignment at sea. My heart was no longer in my work. I considered it entirely useless. We now had captured code books . . . so the invigorating puzzle solving was eliminated.

In February 1946, Roenigk was assigned to the staff of the commander, Joint Task Force One, which was the unit formed to conduct the atomic bomb tests at Bikini Atoll (Operation CROSSROADS). On board the amphibious command ship *Mount McKinley*, he worked with former classmate, fellow Tokyo immersion student, and fellow FRUPac veteran Cmdr. Forrest "Tex" **Biard**. The tests were completed as scheduled, and in September 1946 Roenigk was detached for fitting-out duty in the new light cruiser *Fresno*. He joined that ship as her executive officer upon her commissioning, which was in November. The *Fresno* made one cruise to South America and two cruisers to Europe, during which she served as the flagship of the commander in chief, U.S. Naval Forces Eastern Atlantic and Mediterranean. There Renny was reunited with Capt. Gill **Richardson**, a former housemate from immersion training in Japan, who was now the admiral's intelligence officer and acting chief of staff.

Then, for a year during 1948 and 1949, Roenigk attended the junior course at the Naval War College in Newport. Upon completing his instruction he then remained for duty on the staff until June 1951. Commander Roenigk was next given command of the destroyer *Witek*, participating in experimental anti-submarine operations. For several months he also had the additional duty of Commander, Destroyer Division 602.

From 1952 through mid-1953 he was assigned to the Bureau of Naval Personnel in Washington, and then he was promoted to captain and appointed as Representative of the Commander Middle East Force, located at Bahrain Island in the Persian Gulf. During this tour he traveled extensively throughout the Arab world.

In August 1955, Captain Roenigk reported back to the Naval War College, this time to take the senior course, and then in July 1956 he assumed command of the oiler *Nantahala*. Roenigk and the *Nantahala* were present in the eastern Mediterranean, supporting Sixth Fleet ships as they stood ready to intervene during the Suez Crisis—and the tense period that followed.

During 1957 through 1960 Renny was the U.S. defense attaché as well as the naval attaché in Stockholm, Sweden. Here he particularly enjoyed himself and made a great number of friends. He then was transferred to Naples and became a "commodore" as commander of the Service Force, U.S. Sixth Fleet as well as commander, Service Squadron 6. During this time his flagship was the fleet oiler *Mississinewa*.

In 1961, Captain Roenigk served for six months with the UN Forces, Korea; there he was the chief of staff to the J2. He then was sent to Tokyo, from 1962 through 1964, as the naval attaché to Japan. During this time he ran in to his old friend Eddie Layton, now retired from the navy.

> Rear Admiral Layton was a civilian living in Tokyo and representing an American aircraft manufacturer. Layton visited my office numerous times, as did many American businessmen and Japanese alike, not to conduct business *per se*, but to maintain contact with an American navy person on the spot. Socially, I saw Layton numerous times, either at his home or mine. We were close friends, really.

Roenigk also became reacquainted with his old instructor from before the war, Naganuma Naoe. They spent a lot of time together during Roenigk's attaché tour, time which really helped him regain his spoken Japanese. In addition, Captain Roenigk socialized a bit with Genda Minoru, who then was a member of the upper house of Japan's legislature. Formerly an officer in the Imperial Japanese Navy, Genda had been a key planner of the attack on Pearl Harbor. Surprisingly, in Roenigk's Naval War College oral history, he states that he and Genda *never* discussed anything about World War II.

At the conclusion of his duty in 1964, Roenigk returned to Newport and retired from the navy. Upon his retirement he enrolled at Harvard University where he received a master's degree in East Asian Studies.

Roenigk's subsequent civilian employment included—very briefly—a position with Wells Fargo Bank. He then worked as the director of planning at Hamilton College in New Hampshire, and lastly as the assistant coordinator for facilities planning at the State University of New York, in Albany.

In 1976 he retired for a final time and returned to Newport, occupying the house he'd bought in the late 1940s but in which he'd hardly ever lived. He spent time gardening and on tracing family genealogy. He worked with various charitable and community organizations, and enjoyed taking adult-education courses at the private Swinburne School in Newport. For a time he and his wife traveled extensively, including trips to the Soviet Union, Western Europe, and Asia.

In addition to his considerable prowess with Japanese, Captain Roenigk apparently had an overall facility for languages. He received instruction in Arabic before his assignment to the Middle East—though he later laughed at himself for learning Egyptian Arabic, which was not very useful in his area travels. He also learned a great deal of Swedish while stationed in Stockholm.

Captain Roenigk was married three times. His first wife was Lucy Storer Roenigk (1916–1997); his second was a high school classmate, Martha Caldwell Roenigk (1911–1990); and lastly he married Allison Broatch Roenigk (1921–1980). He had three daughters and a son.

Captain Roenigk passed away on February 16, 1993, in Newport.

Among his decorations and awards was the Bronze Star Medal for his work in communications intelligence during World War II. He was presented with the Swedish Order of the Sword, and given the rank of commodore in the Swedish Navy, after his attaché duty in that country. He also was given the Order of the Sacred Treasure, from the emperor of Japan, for his service as naval attaché during 1962 to 1964.

Sources

Captain John G. Roenigk, U.S. Navy. Official Biography. Biographies Branch, Navy Office of Information, August 22, 1958.
Carlson, 256, 260–63.
Lucky Bag, U.S. Naval Academy, 1934.
Packard, 370, 399.
Slesnick, 20, 24–25.
U.S. Navy. *Register of Commissioned and Warrant Officers.*

Appendix A

What's a Code, and What's a Cipher?

Often used interchangeably, there is a difference in the terms. It seems fitting to let Capt. Joseph **Rochefort** spell it out. During the 1945 Congressional hearing on the investigation of the Pearl Harbor attack, Senator Owen Brewster sought clarification:

Sen. Brewster: What is the difference, Captain, between a cipher and a code?

Capt. Rochefort: In the original understanding, sir, a code has a group of letters or numbers—sometimes the letters are pronounceable and sometimes not—which designate a letter or number, a phrase, perhaps a whole sentence or complete thought. That would be termed a code.

Sen. Brewster: And you would need a code book of some character in order to interpret it?

Capt. Rochefort: Yes, sir: you would require the book. That is, the original people would.

Sen. Brewster: Whoever would get it decoded would have to have a book indicating the significance of these letters and symbols?

Capt. Rochefort: Yes, sir.

Sen. Brewster: What about a cipher?

Capt. Rochefort: A pure cipher would interchange each letter of the original text, so that rather than having a group of letters meaning a whole thought or sentence or phrase, each letter would be changed, or each numeral.

Sen. Brewster: You mean the letter "A" might mean "X," for example?

Capt. Rochefort: Yes, sir: and then the following letter "B" might mean "L." Where you interchange your letter by another letter, or a numeral by another numeral, that would be a pure cipher.

Sen. Brewster: Is that peculiar to the Japanese, or do other countries use somewhat similar systems, as far as you know?

Capt. Rochefort: Ciphers go back before the days of Julius Caesar.

Appendix B

Chronology of Select Highlights, U.S. Navy Radio Intelligence, Pacific Area of Operations 1916–1941

1916   The Code and Signal Section is established in the Office of the Chief of Naval Operations.

1922   The "Research Desk" within the Code and Signal Section established.

1923   The CNO requests that fleet forces listen in on enciphered foreign traffic.

1924   Lt. Laurance **Safford** reports to Main Navy as the first assigned head of the Research Desk.

First intercept station established at the U.S. Consulate, Shànghâi.

The "RIP-5" Japanese *kana* typewriter is designed, and four units are ordered.

1925   Director of Naval Communications requests the Fourteenth Naval District (at Pearl Harbor) to assign one operator to copy Japanese diplomatic traffic.

Lt. j.g. Joseph **Rochefort** reports to the Research Desk for training.

1926   Lt. Rochefort relieves Lt. Cmdr. Safford as head of the Research Desk.

1927   The NRL in Washington is requested to help develop HF and D/F equipment.

An intercept station established at Peking to focus upon Japanese diplomatic traffic.

1928   First *kana* operator course is started at the Navy Department.

1929   The intercept station at Shànghâi is decommissioned, and a new station established in the Mariana Islands at Guam.

1930   An intercept station is established at Olongapo, Subic Bay, PI.

An intercept operator is detailed to conduct a test of possible intercept sites in Alaska.

1931   An experimental HF D/F is commissioned at the NRL.

The CNO directs the Fourteenth Naval District to establish an intercept station at Wailupe (east of Diamond Head), Oahu, Territory of Hawaii (T.H.).

The CNO establishes allowances for communications intelligence facilities; the Bureau of Engineering is directed to modernize permanent stations.

1932   The Alaskan intercept site survey is completed.

An intercept station is established at Astoria, Oregon.

Lt. Thomas **Dyer** relieves Lt. Cmdr. Safford as head of the Research Desk.

1933   An experimental HF D/F is developed by the NRL and Bell Laboratories.

The radio interception station at Wailupe is moved to Heʻeia (north of Kāneʻohe), Oahu.

The CNO directs HF D/F be installed at the Twelfth Naval District (Mare Island, Vallejo, California).

1934   The CNO requests that the BuEng expedite a modernization program.

1935   The Olongapo radio interception station is moved to Mariveles on the Bataan Peninsula, P.I.

A Model XAB-RAB HF D/F is installed at Mare Island.

A Model CXK HF D/F is installed at Mare Island.

A radio interception station at Peking is moved to Shànghâi.

A Model XAB-RAB is shipped to Cavite.

The secretary of the navy is granted permission, from the War Department, to establish a radio interception station on Corregidor, at the entrance to Manila Bay, PI.

1936   The Sixteenth Naval District intercept operation is moved from Mariveles to the naval station at Cavite adjacent to Manila Bay.

The CNO directs the Bureau of Engineering to hold up all HF D/F installations, except the Model CXK in the Fourteenth Naval District, pending review of the entire D/F program.

1937   A Model XAB-RAB HF-D/F is shipped to Guam.

OP-20-G recommends that standard commercial HF receivers be obtained for radio interception stations.

The CXK at Lualualei, on the leeward side of Oahu, is commissioned.

The CNO requests the BuEng to procure twelve Model XAB-HROs at once and to continue further development.

1938   Three Radio Finger Printing units (with high-speed cameras and oscillo-scopes) are ordered for He'eia, Cavite, and Washington, D.C.

Congress authorizes $85,000 for improvement to the radio facilities at Corregidor.

1939   Three Model DT D/F units (XAB-HRO) are shipped to Cavite.

The DNI is requested to assist in obtaining funds for the Corregidor station project.

The CNO requests that Bureau of Engineering provide funds so that Corregidor may be ready for emergency occupancy by January 1940.

The CNO directs the movement of the Astoria station to Bainbridge, Washington.

The U.S. Coast Guard requests technical data on the DTs so that they may copy.

In the central South Pacific, a D/F is placed in commission in the Samoan Islands.

1940   The DNC is informed on the status of plans for setting up HF D/F stations on Midway Atoll, Johnston Atoll (west of Hawaii), and Palmyra Atoll (south of Hawaii).

The CNO requests seven DYs be built for the Navy (simultaneous to ten for the Federal Communications Commission and four for the Army (at the Washington Navy Yard).

BuEng requests $10,000 in emergency budget for D/F equipment.

Shànghâi station decommissioned; Cavite station moved to Corregidor.

OP-20-G requests immediate procurement of twenty more RIP-5 *kana* typewriters.

1941   OP-20-G requests thirty additional RIP-5 typewriters.

The CNO informs Bureau of Engineering that an experimental model of DAB has been found superior to any previous HF-D/F; requests procurement of fifteen units.

A D/F station is commissioned at Sitka, Alaska.

The Japanese Navy attacks Pearl Harbor; the United States enters World War II.

Source

Browne and McGinnis, xi–xv.

Appendix C

Directors of U.S. Naval Intelligence, 1909–1942

TWENTY DIRECTORS IN THIRTY-THREE YEARS

For many years the ONI was in the 7th Wing of the old "Main Navy" building in Washington (close to the Lincoln Memorial and Reflecting Pool on the National Mall).

Capt. Templin M. Potts (December 1909–January 1912)
Capt. Thomas S. Rodgers (January 1912–December 1913)
Capt. Henry F. Bryan (December 1913–January 1914)
Capt. James H. Oliver (January 1914–March 1917)
Capt. Roger Welles Jr. (April 1917–January 1919)
Rear Adm. Albert P. Niblack (May 1919–September 1920)
Rear Adm. Andrew T. Long (September 1920–June 1921)
Capt. Luke McNamee (September 1921–November 1923)
Capt. Henry H. Hough (December 1923–September 1925)
Capt. William W. Galbraith (October 1925–June 1926)
Capt. Arthur J. Hepburn (July 1926–September 1927)
Capt. Alfred W. Johnson (December 1927–June 1930)
Capt. Harry A. Baldridge (June 1930–May 1931)
Capt. Hayne Ellis (June 1931–May 1934)
Capt. William D. Puleston (June 1934–April 1937)
Rear Adm. Ralston S. Holmes (May 1937–June 1939)
Rear Adm. Walter S. Anderson (June 1939–January 1941)
Capt. Jules James (January 1941–February 1941)
Capt. Alan G. Kirk (March 1941–October 1941)
Rear Adm. Theodore S. Wilkinson (October 1941–July 1942)

Appendix D

Directors of U.S. Naval Communications, 1912–1942

FIFTEEN DIRECTORS IN THIRTY YEARS

Capt. William H. G. Bullard [previously Superintendent of the Naval Radio Service]
(1912–1916)
Capt. David W. Todd (1916–1919)
Rear Adm. William H. G. Bullard (1919–1921)
Rear Adm. Marbury Johnston (1921)
Capt. Samuel W. Bryant (1921–1922)
Rear Adm. Henry J. Ziegemeier (1922–1923)
Cmdr. Donald C. Bingham (1923)
Capt. Orton P. Jackson (1923–1924)
Capt. Ridley McLean (1924–1926)
Capt. Thomas T. Craven (1927–1928)
Capt. Stanford C. Hooper (1928–1935)
Capt. Gilbert J. Rowcliff (1935–1936)
Rear Adm. Charles E. Courtney (1936–1939)
Rear Adm. Leigh Noyes (1939–1942)
Capt. Joseph R. Redman (1942)

Appendix E

U.S. Naval Attachés in Tokyo, 1914–1941

Name	Dates	Comment
Cmdr. F. J. Horne	12/14–1/19	Later was Vice CNO
Capt. E. H. **Watson**	1/19–1/22	
Capt. L. A. Cotton	1/22–12/23	
Lt. Cmdr. G. Hulings	12/23–7/24	
Lt. Cmdr. F. B. Melendy*	7/24–7/26	
Cmdr. G. McC. Courts	7/26–11/28	
Capt. J. V. Ogan	11/28–9/30	
Capt. I. C. Johnson Jr.	9/30–8/33	
Capt. F. F. **Rogers***	8/33–6/36	First ONI immersion student
Capt. H. M. Bemis	7/36–4/39	
Cmdr. H. **Smith-Hutton***	4/39–12/41	

*ONI language immersion student in Japan

Source

Mehnken, 47.

Appendix F

U.S. Navy, Office of the Chief of Naval Operations, Section "OP-20-G" and Its Antecedents

Year	Symbol	Organizational Title	Officer in Charge / Head
1917	OP-58	Confidential Publications Sect. Division of Operations, CNO	Lt. Cmdr. Russell **Willson**
1917	OP-58	Code and Signal Section Division of Operations, CNO	Lt. Cmdr. Russell Willson
1918	OP-58	Code and Signal Section Division of Operations, CNO	Lt. Cmdr. Milo Draemel
1920	OP-18	Code and Signal Section Naval Communications System	Cmdr. Milo Draemel
1921	OP-18	Code and Signal Section Naval Communications System	Lt. Cmdr. William Gresham
1922	OP-20-G	Code and Signal Section Naval Communications System	Lt. Cmdr. Donald Godwin
1924	OP-20-G	Code and Signal Section Naval Communications System	Lt. Cmdr. Howard F. **Kingman**
1925	OP-20-G	Code and Signal Section Naval Communications System	Lt. Cmdr. Deupree Friedell
1926	OP-20-G	Code and Signal Section Naval Communications System	Lt. Cmdr. Lewis Comstock
1927	OP-20-G	Code and Signal Section Naval Communications System	Lt. Cmdr. Arthur **Struble**
1930	OP-20-G	Code and Signal Section Naval Communications System	Lt. Cmdr. John W. **McClaran**
1933	OP-20-G	Code and Signal Section Naval Communications System	Cmdr. Howard F. Kingman
1935	OP-20-G	Comm. Security Group Div. of Naval Communications	Cmdr. Howard F. Kingman

Year	Symbol	Organizational Title	Officer in Charge / Head
1935	OP-20-G	Comm. Security Group Div. of Naval Communications	Cmdr. John W. McClaran
1936	OP-20-G	Comm. Security Group Div. of Naval Communications	Lt. Cmdr. Laurance F. **Safford**
1937	OP-20-G	Comm. Security Group Div. of Naval Communications	Cmdr. Laurance F. Safford
1939	OP-20-G	Radio Intelligence Section Div. of Naval Communications	Cmdr. Laurance F. Safford
1939	OP-20-G	Comm. Security Section Div. of Naval Communications	Cmdr. Laurance F. Safford
1941	OP-20-G	Comm. Security Section Div. of Naval Communications	Capt. Laurance F. Safford

Sources

Holtwick, *Security Group*, Appendixes 4–5, 9–10.
Records of the National Security Agency/Central Security Service, www.archives.gov.

Appendix G

Officers in Charge, Office of Naval Communications, Code and Signal Section, "Research Desk" (OP-20-GX)

Note: later Research and Radio Intelligence Desk; then Radio Intercept Desk; later OP-20-GY

1924–1926	Lt. Laurance F. **Safford**
1926–1927	Lt. Joseph J. **Rochefort**
1927–1929	Lt. Bern **Anderson**
1929–1932	Lt. Cmdr. Laurance F. Safford
1932–1933	Lt. Thomas H. **Dyer**
1933–1934	Lt. Thomas A. **Huckins**
1935–1938	Lt. Joseph N. **Wenger**
1938–1940	Lt. Ernest S. L. **Goodwin**
1940–1942	Lt. Lee W. **Parke**

Sources

Holtwick, *Security Group*, 113.
Layton, *And I Was There*, 527.
Dyer, 126, 146.

Note: It's been difficult to establish exact dates for this list, because several authorities contradict each other—and at times themselves. However, for the purposes of this book, these dates are comfortably accurate.

On a similar table in his book, Admiral Layton understandably confused himself (at the 1933 point) and stopped differentiating between the "Research Desk" and the larger OP-20-G, so the last four names here completely vary from his.

Appendix H

Officers in Charge, Office of Naval Communications, Code and Signal Section, Translation Section (OP-20-GZ)

June 1934–mid-1936	Lt. Thomas D. **Birtley**
mid-1936	Lt. Edward S. Pearce
August 1936–February 1937	Lt. Edwin T. **Layton**
March 1937–February 1939	Lt. Redfield B. **Mason**
February 1939–May 1942	Lt. / Lt. Cmdr. Alwin D. **Kramer**

Source

Layton, *And I Was There*, 528.

Appendix I

Growth of U.S. Navy Radio Intelligence

Date	Officers	Enlisted	Civilians	Total
1924	1		1	2
1936	11	88	10	109
1941	75	645	10	730
1945	1,499	6,908	47	8,454

Source

Layton, *And I Was There*, 527.

Appendix J

U.S. Naval Radio Intelligence, Primarily Focused upon Japan, as of December 1941

	Officers	Enlisted	Civilians	Total
Station NEGAT	52	351	10	413
West Coast	3	99		102
Station HYPO	18	128		146
Station CAST	9	61		70
Port Darwin	1	8		9

Source

Layton, *"And I Was There,"* 527.

Appendix K

Station HYPO, Territory of Hawaii

1929 The CNO proposes a decryption unit to be stationed in or in the vicinity of Honolulu.

1936 Communications Intelligence Unit is established under the Commandant, 14th Naval District, Headquarters Building, Naval Shipyard, Pearl Harbor.

OIC:	Lt. Thomas H. Dyer	July 1936–July 1938
	Lt. Thomas B. Birtley	July 1938–June 1941
	Lt. Cmdr. J. J. Rochefort	June 1941–October 1942

1941 Combat Intelligence Unit is established, under the Commandant, Fourteenth Naval District.

OIC:	Lt. W. J. Holmes	June 1941

The larger Communications Intelligence Unit absorbs the smaller Combat Intelligence Unit, and also absorbs the title of Combat Intelligence Unit.

OIC:	Lt. Cmdr. J. J. Rochefort	June 1941–October 1942

1942 The CIU becomes the Radio Intelligence Unit (RIU), Fourteenth Naval District.

OIC:	Capt. W. B. Goggins	October 1942–September 1943

1943 The RIU becomes the Fleet Radio Unit (FRUPac).

OIC:	Capt. William B. Goggins	September 1943–January 1944
	Capt. John S. Harper	January 1944–November 1945
	Capt. Thomas H. Dyer	November 1945–December 1945

Appendix L

U.S. Navy and U.S. Marine Corps Japanese Language/Culture Officers Immersed in Japan, 1910–1941

1910–1941		
Name and Japan-Related Follow-On	Japanese Immersion Study	Resigned or Retired as
Lt. j.g. Fred F. **Rogers**, USN See full biography	1910–1912	Captain, USN
Lt. j.g. George E. Lake, USN	1910–1912	Lieutenant, USN
1st Lt. William T. Hoadley, USMC	1910–1913	Colonel, USMC
1st Lt. Ralph S. Keyser, USMC	1912–1914	Major General, USMC
Maj. William L. Redles, USMC	1915–1918	Lieutenant Colonel, USMC
Lt. Cmdr. Ellis M. **Zacharias**, USN See full biography	1920–1923	Rear Admiral USN
Lt. Cmdr. Hartwell C. Davis, USN	1920–1923	Captain, USN
Ens. Arthur H. **McCollum**, USN See full biography	1922–1925	Rear Admiral, USN
Ens. Thomas J. Ryan Jr., USN[1]	1922–1924	Rear Admiral, USN
Maj. William B. Sullivan, USMC	1923–1926	Lieutenant Colonel, USMC
Capt. Bernard F. Hickey, USMC	1923–1924	Major USMC
Ens. David W. Roberts, USN Asst. Attaché, Tokyo 1932 Flt. Intel. Off., Asiatic Flt. 1933	1924–1927	Commander, USN
Lt. Cmdr. Franz B. Melendy, USN Asst. Attaché, Tokyo 1930–32	1924–1927	Lieutenant Commander, USN

	1910–1941	
Name and Japan-Related Follow-On	Japanese Immersion Study	Resigned or Retired as
Lt. j.g. William J. **Sebald**, USN See full biography	1925–1928	Captain, USNR
1st Lt. James S. Monahan, USMC	1925–1928	Lieutenant Colonel, USMC
Lt. j.g. Henri H. **Smith–Hutton**, USN See full biography	1926–1929	Captain, USN
Lt. j.g. Louis D. Libenow, USN	1926–1929	Commander, USN
Lt. j.g. Edward S. Pearce, USN ONI 1930 OP-20-G 1930–1931 Flag Lt. and Aide to CinCAF 1935 Asst. Attaché, Tokyo 1935–1936 Head, OP-20-GZ 1936 Office of the CNO 1940 Intel. Off., SoPac Forces 1942–1943 Head, Japan Sect., ONI 1944–1945 Naval Attaché, Tokyo 1959	1927–1930	Captain, USN
Lt. j.g. Thomas B. **Birtley** Jr., USN See full biography	1927–1930	Captain, USN
Lt. j.g. Kenneth D. **Ringle**, USN See full biography	1928–1931	Rear Admiral, USN
Lt. j.g. Ethelbert **Watts**, USN See full biography	1928–1931	Rear Admiral, USN
2nd Lt. Frank P. Pyzick, USMC Japanese POW 1941+	1929–1932	Colonel, USMC
Lt. j.g. Edwin T. **Layton**, USN See full biography	1929–1932	Rear Admiral, USN
Lt. Joseph J. **Rochefort**, USN[2] See full biography	1929–1932	Captain, USN
Lt. j.g. Redfield **Mason**, USN[3] See full biography	1930–1933	Rear Admiral, USN
Lt. j.g. Daniel J. McCallum, USN Flt. Intel. Off. Asiatic Flt. 1938 Asst. Attaché, Tokyo 1939–1941	1931–1934	Captain, USN
Lt. j.g. Alwin D. **Kramer**, USN See full biography	1931–1934	Captain, USN
Lt. j.g. Henri deB. **Claiborne**, USN See full biography	1931–1934	Captain, USN
1st Lt. Kenneth H. Cornell, USMC	1931–1934	Captain, USMC

	Japanese	
Name and Japan-Related Follow-On	Immersion Study	Resigned or Retired as
Lt. j.g. Ranson **Fullinwider**, USN See full biography	1932–1935	Rear Admiral, USN
Lt. j.g. Spencer A. Carlson, USN Far East Sect., ONI 1939 OP-20-G 1939–1940 Station "A" (Shanghai, China) 1940 Station CAST, Corregidor 1941–1942 FRUMel 1942–1944 FRUPac 1945	1932–1935	Captain, USN
Lt. Joseph **Finnegan**, USN See full biography	1934–1937	Captain, USN
Lt. j.g. Harold E. Karrer, USN Station CAST, 1939–1940	1934–1937	deceased 1942
Lt. j.g. Martin R. Stone, USN Asst. Attaché, Tokyo 1941 N2, ComNav Far East 1950–1951	1934–1937	Rear Admiral, USN
Lt. j.g. Francis D. Jordan, USN POW, Asiatic area	1934–1937	deceased 1944
Lt. j.g. Gill M. **Richardson**, USN See full biography	1935–1938	Rear Admiral, USN
1st Lt. Alva B. **Lasswell**, USMC[4] See full biography	1935–1938	Colonel, USMC
Lt. j.g. Robert E. Hudson, USN Asst. Intel. Off. Pac. Flt. 1941–1945 N2, CinCPacFlt, 1948–1949	1936–1939	Captain, USN
1st Lt. Nixon L. Ballard, USMC	1937–1939	Major, USMC
Lt. j.g. John G. **Roenigk**, USN See full biography	1938–1941	Captain, USN
Lt. j.g. Arthur L. Benedict, Jr. USN Intel. Staff CinCPac 1941–1942 FRUPac 1942–1945	1938–1941	Commander, USN
Lt. j.g. Allyn Cole Jr., USN FRUPac 1941–1945	1939–1941	Captain, USN
Lt. j.g. Thomas R. Mackie, USN[5] Station CAST 1941–1942 FRUMel 1942–1945	1938–1941	Captain, USN
Lt. j.g. Rufus L. **Taylor**, USN[6] See full biography	1938–1941	Vice Admiral, USN

	1910–1941	
Name and Japan- Related Follow-On	Japanese Immersion Study	Resigned or Retired as
Lt. j.g. William R. Wilson, USN POW 1942–1945	1938–1941	Captain, USN
Lt. j.g. Forrest R. **Biard**, USN See full biography	1939–1941	Captain, USN
Lt. j.g. John R. Bromley, USN HYPO/FRUPac 1941–1943 FRUMel 1943–1945 Head, Japan Desk, ONI 1945 N2, ComNavFar East 1947–1949 Naval Attaché, Tokyo 1959–1962 Staff, Nat. Security Council 1963	1939–1941	Captain, USN
Lt. j.g. Gilven M. **Slonim**, USN See full biography	1939–1941	Captain, USN
1st Lt. Bankson **Holcomb**, USMC[7] See full biography	1939–1941	Brigadier General, USMC
1st Lt. Ferdinand W Bishop, USMC SoPac POW Interrogator 1943	1940–1941	deceased 1943
Lt. j.g. Ted A. Hilger, USN	1941	deceased 1942

Notes

1. Awarded the Medal of Honor for his assistance rendered to the Japanese during the terrible Yokohama earthquake of 1923.

2. Designated a Pioneer Officer of U.S. Naval Cryptology by the U.S. Naval Cryptologic Veterans Association—which is interesting as they were primarily language officers.

3. Ibid.

4. Ibid.

5. Identified by Capt. Laurance Safford as the wartime navy's fourth best *codebreaker*, which is remarkable as he was primarily a *language* officer.

6. Designated a Pioneer Officer of U.S. Naval Cryptology by the U.S. Naval Cryptologic Veterans Association.

7. Ibid.

Sources

McGinnis, 18–22.
Packard, 367–71.
U.S. Naval Academy Alumni Association. *Register of Alumni, Classes of 1846–2013.*
U.S. Navy, *Register of Commissioned and Warrant Officers.*

Appendix M

The "On-the-Roof Gang"

The United States had maintained squadrons of ships in the Pacific since the mid-nineteenth century. In 1907, the Asiatic and Pacific Squadrons were consolidated into the U.S. Pacific Fleet. In 1922, the Atlantic and Pacific Fleets were combined to form the U.S. Battle Fleet, with subordinate Atlantic and Asiatic Fleets. Another reorganization, in February 1941, created three separate fleets: Atlantic, Pacific, and Asiatic.

In the 1920s and 1930s, with units along the China coast, the U.S. Asiatic Fleet became embroiled in the international conflict among the many powers and China. Factions in China were struggling to unify their country and to rid it of foreign imperialist enclaves. The Japanese military in China, however, often acting independently from Tokyo, was seeking to expand its control of Chinese territory.

Then, as now, accurate and timely information was at a premium.

The CNO let it be known that the navy had an interest in acquiring encrypted Japanese communications. Early intercept of Japanese naval radio traffic was done on an ad hoc basis: a number of navy and marine corps radiomen spent their spare time learning to copy Japanese messages.

As might be expected, the commander in chief of the U.S. Asiatic Fleet (CinCAF) had a particular interest in eavesdropping on the Grand Maneuvers of the Japanese Navy. This was done by some radiomen assigned to the Asiatic Fleet, although the results of these early intercept operations are no longer known.

In May 1928, however, the CinCAF complained in a letter to the CNO about how few operators he had who were qualified to copy Japanese *kana* code. The fleet had only nine qualified operators, all self-taught. Self-study and ad hoc operations were no longer sufficient to produce the number of needed qualified intercept operators.

Therefore, in July, the CNO announced the establishment of a school to instruct radio operators in intercept operations, particularly for Japanese *kana*. The first class would begin on October 1, 1928, and instructors were to be two of the self-taught radiomen from the Asiatic fleet.

The first class was considered a success, so five more were held in 1929. The instructor for the first three was Chief Radioman Harry Kidder.[1] The last two were taught by Chief Radioman Dorman Chauncey. Both were veterans of intercept operations in the Asiatic Fleet. Chauncey had conducted intercept at the U.S. Navy sites in Hawaii and Peking.

The first classes of trainees were composed largely of experienced radiomen of senior enlisted rank. To ensure that there would be continuity of service, the second and third groups of trainees were relatively junior.

Marine corps personnel participated in the training from the third class, which began in November 1929. The class that trained from December 1930 to April 1931 was composed entirely of marine enlisted men. Marines engaged in intercept activities for most of the 1930s, but the number dwindled late in the decade—since intercept operations were not a marine rating or occupational specialty, and promotion possibilities were less for intercept operators than general service radiomen.

With a larger pool of intercept operators to deploy, additional collection sites were opened: Guam, Olongapo, and Astoria, Oregon. Some intercept was conducted aboard ships, principally the USS *Augusta* and the USS *Gold Star*.

Since these classes were held in a wooden structure set atop the Navy Headquarters Building in Washington (Main Navy), and since the radiomen could not explain their classwork to others, they eventually acquired the nickname "The On-the-Roof Gang."

Note: The Navy Building in the District of Columbia was demolished after World War II. Part of the area where it once stood is now occupied by the Vietnam Memorial.

"THE GANG"

U.S. Navy

Maynard G. Albertson	Oliver W. Grew	Edward Otte
Kenneth H. Barker	Arthur D. Groff	Rexford G. Parr
Donald W. Barnum	Benj. Groundwater	Raymond E. Parrott
Isaac C. Bemis	L. G. Guillet	James W. **Pearson**
Ivan S. Benjamin	Max C. Gunn	Albert J. **Pelletier** Jr.
Guy O. Billehus	Douglas W. Harold	Pearly L. Phillips
Chester H. Bissell	Raymond L. Hitson	Leo J. Potvin
Ralph T. Briggs	Paul V. Hively Jr.	Hubert A. Price

Donovan Broughton
Sidney A. Burnett
Albert Burton
J. B. Byrd
Howard A. Cain
James B. Capron Jr.
Kenneth Carmichael
Gordon O. Carnes
David R. Chase
Dorman A. Chauncey
R. P. Clifford
B. E. Cloyd
Carl L. Congdon
John B. Cooke Jr.
Orvill C. Coonce
Prescott H. **Currier**
Hilary E. Cyr
E. E. Dailey
Charles E. Daniels
Clarence A. Detterich
Elmer Dickey
Garwin S. Diehl
Elmer W. Disharoon
Robert L. Dormer
Edward J. Dullard
Alfred B. Duross
William W. Eaton
William J. Edens
Robert R. Ellis
Frank E. Estes
Henry E. Ethier
Glen E. Evans
Stuart T. Faulkner
Reece Finley
Frederick L. Freeman
Albert H. Geiken
John H. Gelineau
Eugene S. Givler
Joseph Goldstein
Keith E. Goodwin
Stanley E. Gramblin
Joseph L. Granger

R. W. Hoffman
Thomas G. Hoover
George W. Hopkins
Ralph S. Horne
Harvey J. Howard
James C. Howard
Carl A. Jensen
Charlie J. Johns
James H. Johnson
Walter H. Johnson
Orvill L. Jones
Harold E. Joslin
Rex H. Jule
Jack G. Kaye
Edward R. Keesey
Edward N. Kelly
Harry Kidder
Homer L. Kisner
W. A. Kneeley
Wesley S. Knowles
Leroy A. Lankford
Harold E. Layman
Robert H. Ledford
Roy E. Lehman
Norman V. Lewis
Victor L. Long
Truett C. Lusk
Merle E. Lynch
Malcolm W. Lyon
E. H. Marks
Wilson L. Mason
Robert G. Maxwell
Joseph L. McConnel
Howard E. McConnell
L. O. McCurdy
Hugh W. McGall
Walter J. **McGregor**
A. L. Monroe
Willie K. Muse
Laurance F. Myers
Antone Novak
Elliot E. Okins

Charles G. Quinn
Earl L. Rank
W. C. Rathsack
C. L. Reynolds
Donald D. Ritchie
Russell W. Rogers
John H. Roop
Meddie J. Royer
Raymond A. Rundle
Edward W. Schroeder
Kenneth B. Selch
Roy C. Sholes
Clifton Shumaker
Warren A. Simmons
Joseph E. Smith
Lloyd T. Smith
Markle T. Smith
Martin H. Smith
David W. Snyder
Alva E. Squires
Arthur D. Swain
Clarence P. Taylor
Fred R. Thomson
Howard H. Troup
Martin A. Vanderberg
Harold P. Waldum
Charles A. Walters
Wesley H. Walvoord
Frank J. Weiland
Willis H. Wesper
Merrill F. Whiting
Duane L. **Whitlock**
Rodney L. Whitten
Daryl W. Wigle
Clifford O. Wilder
Theodore J. Wildman
Robert R. Williams
Richard Willis
James D. Willmarth
Samuel Winchester
Muriel D. Wood
William C. Young

U.S. Marines

Harry L. Butler	L. R. Hinkle	Walter B. Robertson
C. A. Cameron	Harold V. Jones	Norman F. Robinson
Cecil T. Carraway	Stephen Lesko	Charles J. Smith
Curtis W. Crow	Phillip M. Miller	Charles Southerland
Joel H. Easter	Virgil W. Morgan	Carl G. Suber
Clarence Gentilcore	Maurice M. Overstreet	Hubert N. Thomas
C. H. Gustaveson	Joseph A. Petrosky	William A. Wilder
Richard A. Hardisty	Alvin Rainey	James W. Winborn
J. Hibbard	Jesse L. Randle	

Note

1. It's no surprise that Chief Kidder was posted as the first instructor. According to Capt. Duane Whitlock, in 1923 "several navy and Marine Corps operators in the Far East [taught] themselves to recognize and intercept Japanese radio communications. One of these operators, Chief Radioman Harry Kidder, was serving in the Philippines. With the help of the Japanese wife of a shipmate, he learned the *Kata Kana* syllabary, taught himself the telegraphic equivalents of all the *Kata Kana* characters, and began to intercept Japanese messages. Whether anyone in Washington was aware of his accomplishment at the time is not clear; that it paid enormous dividends in years to follow is an indisputable matter of record. A few other operators on the Asiatic Station somehow learned to write *Kata Kana* characters and copy Japanese messages with a pencil, though none ever gained the stature of Harry Kidder." In fact, Whitlock rates the contributions of Chief Kidder as significant as those of Capt. Laurance Safford.

Sources

McGinnis, 17–18.
Pearl Harbor Review—The On-the-Roof Gang. U.S. National Security Agency, Central Security Service. www.nsa.gov/about/cryptologic_heritage/.../roof_gang.shtml. Accessed February 6, 2013.

Appendix N

Operation VENGEANCE

Operation VENGEANCE was the name given by the Americans to the military operation to kill Japanese Admiral Yamamoto Isoroku on April 18, 1943, during the Solomon Islands campaign.

Yamamoto had scheduled an inspection tour of the Solomon Islands and New Guinea. He planned to inspect Japanese air units participating in the I-Go operation that had begun April 7, 1943, and to boost Japanese morale following the disastrous evacuation of Guadalcanal. On April 14, U.S. naval intelligence intercepted and decrypted orders alerting affected Japanese units of the tour. The original message, addressed to the commanders of Base Unit No. 1, the 11th Air Flotilla, and the 26th Air Flotilla, was encoded in a version of JN-25, and was picked up by three Allied COMINT stations, including **Fleet Radio Unit Pacific**. The message was then deciphered by FRUPac cryptanalysts, traffic analysts, and linguists; it contained very specific time and location details of Yamamoto's itinerary, as well as the number and types of planes that would transport and accompany him on the journey.

Yamamoto, the decryption revealed, would be flying from Rabaul to Balalae Airfield, on an island near Bougainville in the Solomon Islands, on April 18. He and his staff would be flying in two medium bombers of the 205th Kokutai Naval Air Unit, escorted by six navy fighters of the 204th Kokutai NAU, to depart Rabaul at 0600 and arrive at Ballale at 0800, Tokyo time.

Contrary to some accounts, it appears that President Roosevelt was not in Washington and not consulted. Secretary of the Navy Frank Knox was aware of the opportunity (and at the Office of Naval Intelligence, Ellis **Zacharias** and Ladislas Farago quickly prepared a historical study concerning the assassination of military leaders in wartime), but Knox essentially let Admiral Chester Nimitz make the decision. Nimitz consulted his intelligence officer, Cmdr. Ed **Layton**, and then Admiral William Halsey, Commander, South Pacific. He then authorized the mission on April 17.

To avoid detection by radar and Japanese personnel—stationed in the Solomon Islands along a straight-line distance of about four hundred miles between U.S. forces and Bougainville—the mission entailed an over-water flight south and west of the Solomons. This roundabout approach was plotted and measured to be about six hundred miles. The fighters would therefore travel six hundred miles out to the target and four hundred miles back. The one-thousand-mile flight, with extra fuel allotted for combat, was beyond the range of the F4F Wildcat and F4U Corsair fighters then available to navy and marine squadrons based on Guadalcanal. The mission was instead assigned to the army's 339th Fighter Squadron, whose P-38 G Lightnings, equipped with drop tanks, had the range to intercept and engage.

The mission was a spectacular success; Yamamoto's aircraft were indeed intercepted and shot down, and the admiral was killed. The death of Yamamoto reportedly damaged the morale of Japanese naval personnel (described by historian Samuel Eliot Morison as being considered the equivalent of a major defeat in battle), raised the morale of the Allied forces, and was incidentally an act of revenge by U.S. leaders who blamed Yamamoto for the Pearl Harbor attack.

Suggested Reading

Agnes Meyer Driscoll. U.S. National Security Agency. Cryptologic Hall of Honor. www.nsa .gov/about/cryptologic_heritage /hall_of_honor, accessed January 22, 2013.

Bamford, James. *The Puzzle Palace: Inside the National Security Agency, America's Most Secret Intelligence Organization*. New York: Penguin, 1982.

Beach, Capt. Edward L., USN (Ret.) *The United States Navy: 200 Years*. New York: Henry Holt, 1986.

Benson, Robert L. *A History of U.S. Communications Intelligence during World War II: Policy and Administration*. United States Cryptologic History, Series IV: World War II, Volume 8. Fort George G. Meade, MD: Center for Cryptologic History, U.S. National Security Agency, 1997.

Biard, Capt. Forrest R. "Tex," USN, Ret. *Breaking of Japanese Naval Codes: Pre-Pearl Harbor to Midway*. Speech to the National Cryptologic Museum Foundation on June 14, 2002. Reprinted in *Cryptologia* 33, no. 2 (April 2006): 151–58.

Blair, Joan, and Clay Blair Jr. *The Search for JFK*. New York: Berkley Publishing, 1976.

Bradford, Richard. "Learning the Enemy's Language: U.S. Navy Officer Language Students in Japan, 1920–1941." *International Journal of Naval History* 1, no. 1 (April 2002), http:// www.ijnhonline.org/issues/volume-1-2002/apr-2002-vol-1-issue-1/.

Breuer, William B. *Deceptions of World War II*. New York: Wiley, 2001.

Browne, Jay R., ed. *The Albert J. Pelletier, Jr. Story*. Special Publication. Pensacola, FL: U.S. Naval Cryptologic Veterans Association, 2003.

Browne, Jay R., and Richard C. Carlson, eds. *Echoes of Our Past*. Special Publication. Pensacola, FL: U.S. Naval Cryptologic Veterans Association, 2008.

Browne, Jay R., and George P. McGinnis, eds. *A History of Communications Intelligence in the United States with Emphasis on the United States Navy*. Special Publication. Pensacola, FL: U.S. Naval Cryptologic Veterans Association, 2004.

Browne, Jay R., and George P. McGinnis, eds. *Intercept Station "C": From Olongapo through the Evacuation of Corregidor, 1929–1942*. 2nd ed. Special Publication. Pensacola, FL: U.S. Naval Cryptologic Veterans Association, 1983.

Bryden, John. *Fighting to Lose: How the German Secret Intelligence Service Helped the Allies Win the Second World War.* Toronto: Dundurn Press, 2014.

Budiansky, Stephen. *Battle of Wits: The Complete Story of Codebreaking in World War II.* New York: Touchstone Books, 2000.

Burke, Colin B. "Agnes Meyer Driscoll vs. the Enigma and the Bombe: An Essay," 2001. *Papers and Documents on Codebreaking and Information History. University of Maryland—Baltimore County.* userpages.umbc.edu/~burke /driscoll1-2011.pdf.

Burns, Thomas L. *The Origins of the National Security Agency, 1940–1952.* United States Cryptologic History, Series V, Vol. 1. Center for Cryptologic History, National Security Agency, 1990. DOCID: 3109065. FOIA Case 51510, March 2, 2007.

Capt. Joseph Rochefort. U.S. National Security Agency. Cryptologic Hall of Honor. www.nsa .gov/about/cryptologic_heritage/ hall_of_honor, accessed January 22, 2013.

Capt. Laurance Safford. U.S. National Security Agency. Cryptologic Hall of Honor. www.nsa .gov/about/cryptologic_heritage/ hall_of_honor, accessed January 22, 2013.

Capt. Thomas H. Dyer. U.S. National Security Agency. Cryptologic Hall of Honor. www.nsa .gov/about/cryptologic_heritage/ hall_of_honor, accessed January 22, 2013.

Carlson, Elliot. *Joe Rochefort's War: The Odyssey of the Codebreaker Who Outwitted Yamamoto at Midway.* Annapolis, MD: Naval Institute Press, 2011.

Clausen, Henry C. and Bruce Lee. *Pearl Harbor: Final Judgement.* Boston: Da Capo, 2001.

Coffman, Tom. *The Island Edge of America: A Political History of Hawai'i.* Honolulu: University of Hawai'i Press, 2003.

Costello, John. *Days of Infamy: MacArthur, Roosevelt, Churchill—the Shocking Truth Revealed: How Their Secret Deals and Strategic Blunders Caused Disaster at Pearl Harbor and the Philippines.* New York: Pocket Books, 1994.

Currier, Capt. Prescott H., USN, Ret. "Presentation Given to Members of the Cryptanalysis Field." Ft. Meade, MD: National Security Agency, c. 1974. nsabackups.com.

Dahl, Erik J. "Why Won't They Listen? Comparing Receptivity toward Intelligence at Pearl Harbor and Midway." *Intelligence and National Security* 28, no. 1 (February 2013): 68–90.

DeBrosse, Jim, and Colin Burke. *The Secret in Building 26: The Untold Story of America's Ultra War against the U-boat Enigma Codes.* New York: Random House, 2004.

Dessez, Eunice C. *The First Enlisted Women, 1917–1918.* Philadelphia: Dorrance & Co., 1955.

Dingman, Roger. *Deciphering the Rising Sun: Navy and Marine Corps Codebreakers, Translators, and Interpreters in the Pacific War.* Annapolis, MD: Naval Institute Press, 2009.

Donovan, Peter, and John Mack. *Code Breaking in the Pacific.* New York/Cham, Switzerland: Springer International Publishing, 2014.

Dorwart, Jeffery M. *Conflict of Duty: The U.S. Navy's Intelligence Dilemma, 1919–1945.* Annapolis, MD: Naval Institute Press, 1983.

Dorwart, Jeffery M. *The Office of Naval Intelligence: The Birth of America's First Intelligence Agency 1865–1918.* Annapolis, MD: Naval Institute Press, 1979.

Drea, Edward J. *MacArthur's ULTRA: Codebreaking and the War against Japan, 1942–1945.* Lawrence: University Press of Kansas, 1992.

Dyer, Capt. Thomas "Tommy" H., USN, Ret. *Reminiscences of Captain Thomas H. Dyer, U.S. Navy (Retired).* Interviews with Paul Stillwell, Naval Institute Oral History Office, August 15, 22, and 29, 1983, and September 6, 14, and 20, 1983. Annapolis, MD: U.S. Naval Institute, 1986.

Farago, Ladislas. *The Broken Seal: The Story of "Operation Magic" and the Pearl Harbor Disaster.* New York: Random House, 1967.

Farago, Ladislas. *Burn after Reading.* Los Angeles: Pinnacle, 1961.

Gannon, James. *Stealing Secrets, Telling Lies: How Spies and Codebreakers Helped Shape the Twentieth Century.* Washington, DC: Brassey's, 2001.

Greaves, Percy L., Jr. and Bettina B. Greaves. *Pearl Harbor: The Seeds and Fruits of Infamy.* Auburn, AL: Ludwig von Mises Institute, 2010.

Hanyok, Robert J. *Madame X: Agnes in Twilight, the Last Years of the Career of Agnes Driscoll, 1941–1957.* In the "Cryptologic Almanac 50th Anniversary Series." Center for Cryptologic History. U.S. National Security Agency. DOCID: 3575741. Approved for public release on June 12, 2009, FOIA Case No. 52567.

Hanyok, Robert J. *Madame X: Agnes Meyer Driscoll and U.S. Naval Cryptology, 1919–1940.* In the "Cryptologic Almanac 50th Anniversary Series." Center for Cryptologic History. U.S. National Security Agency. DOCID: 3575740. Approved for public release on June 12, 2009, FOIA Case No. 52567.

Hanyok, Robert J. *Still Desperately Seeking "Miss Agnes"—A Pioneer Cryptologist's Life Remains an Enigma.* In "A History of Communications Intelligence in the United States with Emphasis on the United States Navy," Jay R. Browne and George P. McGinnis, eds., pp. 261–66. Special Publication. Pensacola, FL: U.S. Naval Cryptological Association, 2004. Also found in *Cryptolog* 18, no. 5 (Fall 1997).

Hanyok, Robert J., and David P. Mowry. *West Wind Clear: Cryptology and the Winds Message Controversy—A Documentary History.* United States Cryptologic History, Series IV: World War II, Vol. 10. Fort George G. Meade, MD: Center for Cryptologic History, U.S. National Security Agency, 2008.

Haufler, Hervie. *Codebreakers' Victory: How the Allied Cryptographers Won World War II.* New York: New American Library, 2003.

"Herm Kossler's Bottle of Scotch [article about Jasper Holmes]," by "Andy," January 16, 2010. *Maritime Texas: An Eclectic Blog of People, Places, and Events.* maritimetexas.net/wordpress/?tag=jasper-holmes, accessed January 23, 2013.

Holmes, Capt. Wilfred J., USN, Ret. *Double-Edged Secrets: U.S. Naval Intelligence Operations in the Pacific during World War II.* Annapolis, MD: Naval Institute Press, 1979.

Holtwick, Capt. Jack S. Jr., USN, Ret., comp. *History of the Naval Security Group to World War II.* (SRH-355) 2 vols. Special Publication. Pensacola, FL: U.S. Naval Cryptologic Veterans Association, 2006.

Hone, Thomas C., ed. *The Battle of Midway: The Naval Institute Guide to the U.S. Navy's Greatest Victory.* Annapolis, MD: Naval Institute Press, 2013.

Hotchkiss, Sally Ringle. *Rear Adm. Kenneth D. Ringle.* E-mail correspondence, August 2013.

Howarth, Stephen, ed. *Men of War: Great Naval Leaders of World War II.* New York: St. Martin's Press, 1992.

Howeth, Capt. Linwood S., USN, Ret. *History of Communications-Electronics in the United States Navy.* U.S. Navy Bureau of Ships and Office of Naval History. Washington, DC: U.S. Government Printing Office, 1963.

Hunnicutt, Tom. *Arkansas' Unsung Hero: Colonel Alva Bryan "Red" Lasswell, USMC.* files. usgwarchives.net/ar/clay/bios/ laswellab.txt, accessed January 27, 2014.

Jenkins, David. *Battle Surface! Japan's Submarine War against Australia, 1942–44.* Milsons Point: Random House Australia, 1992.

Jurika, Capt. Stephen, Jr., USN, Ret. *Reminiscences of Captain Stephen Jurika, Jr., U.S. Navy (Retired).* Interviews with Capt. Paul B. Ryan, USN, Ret., Naval Institute Oral History Office, October 1975–April 1976. Annapolis, MD: U.S. Naval Institute, 1979.

Kahn, David. *The Codebreakers: The Story of Secret Writing.* New York: MacMillan, 1967.

Kahn, David. *How I Discovered World War II's Greatest Spy and Other Stories of Intelligence and Code.* Boca Raton, FL: CRC Press, 2014.

Layton, Rear Adm. Edwin T., USN, Ret. *The Reminisces of Rear Admiral Edwin T. Layton, U.S. Navy (Retired).* Interviews with Cmdr. Etta-Belle Kitchen, USN (Ret.), Naval Institute Oral History Office, May 1970. Annapolis, MD: U.S. Naval Institute, 1975.

Layton, Rear Adm. Edwin T., USN, Ret., Capt. Roger Pineau, USN, Ret., and John Costello. *"And I Was There": Pearl Harbor and Midway—Breaking the Secrets.* Old Saybrook, CT: Konecky & Konecky, 1985.

Lewin, Ronald. *The American Magic: Codes, Ciphers and the Defeat of Japan.* New York: Farrar, Straus, Giroux, 1982.

Lockwood, Vice Adm. Charles A., USN, Ret. and Colonel Hans C. Adamson, USAF, Ret. *Tragedy at Honda.* Philadelphia: Chilton, 1960.

Lord, Walter. *Incredible Victory.* New York: Harper & Row, 1967.

Lowman, David D. *Magic: The Untold Story of U.S. Intelligence and the Evacuation of Japanese Residents from the West Coast during WW II.* Provo, UT: Athena Press, 2001.

Lujan, Lt. Susan M., USNR. "Agnes Meyer Driscoll," *Cryptologia* 15, no. 1 (1991): 47–56.

McCollum, Rear Adm. Arthur H., USN, Ret. *The Reminiscences of Rear Admiral Arthur H. McCollum, U.S. Navy (Retired).* 2 vols. Interviews with John T. Mason Jr., Naval Institute Oral History Office, December 8, 1970, to March 17, 1971. Annapolis, MD: U.S. Naval Institute, 1973.

McGinnis, George P., ed. *U.S. Naval Cryptologic Veterans Association.* Paducah, KY: Turner Publishing, 1996.

Mahnken, Thomas G. *Uncovering Ways of War: U.S. Intelligence and Foreign Military Innovation, 1918–1941.* Ithaca, NY: Cornell University Press, 2002.

Maneki, Sharon A. *The Quiet Heroes of the Southwest Pacific Theater: An Oral History of the Men and Women of CBB and FRUMel.* United States Cryptologic History, Series IV: World War II, Volume 7. Fort George G. Meade, MD: Center for Cryptologic History, U.S. National Security Agency, reprint 2007.

"Meet the Code Masters," in *The Course to Midway.* www.navy.mil/midway/ncb.html, accessed January 23, 2013.

Miles, Vice Adm. Milton E., USN, Ret. *A Different Kind of War: The Little-Known Story of the Combined Guerrilla Forces Created in China by the U.S. Navy and the Chinese during World War II.* Garden City, NY: Doubleday, 1967.

Moon, Tom. *This Grim and Savage Game: OSS and the Beginning of U.S. Covert Operations in World War II.* Los Angeles: Burning Gate Press, 1991.

Morison, Rear Adm. Samuel Eliot, USNR, Ret. *History of United States Naval Operations in World War II.* 15 volumes. Originally published by Little, Brown and Co. in 1962. Edison, NJ: Castle Books, 2001.

Niiya, Brian. "Kenneth Ringle." *Densho Encyclopedia.* http://encyclopedia.densho.org. Accessed July 24, 2013.

Packard, Wyman H. *A Century of U.S. Naval Intelligence.* Office of Naval Intelligence/Naval Historical Center. Washington, DC: Department of the Navy, 1996.

Parker, Frederick D. *Pearl Harbor Revisited: U.S. Navy Communications Intelligence 1924–1941.* United States Cryptologic History, Series IV: World War II, Volume 6. Third edition. Fort George G. Meade, MD: Center for Cryptologic History, U.S. National Security Agency, 2013.

Parker, Frederick D. *A Priceless Advantage: U.S. Navy Communications Intelligence at the Battles of Coral Sea, Midway, and the Aleutians.* United States Cryptologic History, Series IV: World War II, Volume 5. Fort George G. Meade, MD: Center for Cryptologic History, U.S. National Security Agency, 1993.

Pearl Harbor Review—Navy Cryptology: The Early Days. U.S. National Security Agency, Central Security Service. http://www.nsa.gov/about/cryptologic_heritage/center_crypt_history/pearl_harbor_review/navy_crypt.shtml. Accessed March 3, 2013.

Pearl Harbor Review—The On-the-Roof Gang. U.S. National Security Agency, Central Security Service. www.nsa.gov/about/cryptologic_heritage/.../roof_gang.shtml. Accessed February 6, 2013.

Pelletier, CWO4 Albert J. III., USN, Ret. Email correspondence, October 14–16, 2014.

Pfeiffer, David A. "Sage Prophet or Loose Cannon? Skilled Intelligence Officer in World War II Foresaw Japan's Plans, but Annoyed Navy Brass." *Prologue: The Quarterly Magazine of the National Archives and Records Administration* 40, no. 2 (Summer 2008). College Park, MD: NARA.

Pineau, Capt. Roger, USN, Ret. "Captain Joseph John Rochefort, United States Navy, 1898–1976." In *Men of War: Great Naval Leaders of World War II*, Stephen Howarth, ed. New York: St. Martin's Press, 1992.

Pioneers in U.S. Cryptology, Part II: The NSA Family 35 Year Celebration. Ft. George G. Meade, MD: History and Publications Division, U.S. National Security Agency, July 1987.

Powell, John W. "Japan's Germ Warfare: The U.S. Cover-Up of a War Crime." Chapter 24 in Stephen S. Large, *Shōwa Japan: Political, Economic, and Social History, 1926–1989.* Vol. 2. London: Routledge, 1998.

Prados, John. *Combined Fleet Decoded: The Secret History of American Intelligence and the Japanese Navy in World War II.* New York: Random House, 1995.

Prange, Gordon W., with Donald M. Goldstein and Katherine V. Dillon. *At Dawn We Slept: The Untold Story of Pearl Harbor.* New York: McGraw-Hill, 1981.

Prange, Gordon W., with Donald M. Goldstein and Katherine V. Dillon. *Miracle at Midway.* London/New York: Penguin, 1983.

"Rear Admiral Edwin T. Layton," in *The Course to Midway.* www.navy.mil/midway/ncb.html. Accessed January 23, 2013.

Rear Adm. Joseph N. Wenger. U.S. National Security Agency. Cryptologic Hall of Honor. www.nsa.gov/about/cryptologicheritage/hall_of_honor. Accessed January 22, 2013.

Reminiscences of the Naval Career of Captain John Roenigk, USN, Ret. MS Item 181. Naval Historical Collection. Newport: U.S. Naval War College, 1989.

Ringle, Andrew D. *Rear Adm. Kenneth D. Ringle.* E-mail correspondence, July–August 2013.

Ringle, Kenneth A. *Rear Adm. Kenneth D. Ringle.* E-mail correspondence, July–August 2013.

Ringle, Kenneth A. "What Did You Do Before the War, Dad?" *Washington Post Magazine,* December 6, 1981, pp. 54–62.

Rochefort, Capt. Joseph J., USN, Ret. *The Reminiscences of Captain Joseph J. Rochefort, U.S. Navy (Retired).* Interviews with Cmdr. Etta-Belle Kitchen, USN, Ret., Naval Institute Oral History Office, August 14, 1969, to September 21, 1969. Annapolis, MD: U.S. Naval Institute, 1983.

Safford, Capt. Laurance F., USN, Ret. *A Brief History of Communications History in the United States.* In *A History of Communications Intelligence in the United States with Emphasis on the United States Navy*, Jay R. Browne and George P. McGinnis, eds., pp. 16–35. Also in *Listening to the Enemy*, Ronald H. Spector, ed., pp. 3–12.

Safford, Capt. Laurance F., USN, Ret. "The Inside Story of the Battle of Midway and the Ousting of Commander Rochefort," 1944. In *Echoes of Our Past*, Jay R. Browne and Richard C. Carlson, eds. Special Publication. Pensacola, FL: U.S. Naval Cryptologic Veterans Association, 2008.

Safford, Capt. Laurance F., USN. Ret. *Interview with Captain Laurance F. Safford*, conducted by Raymond Schmidt, c. 1970. In Holtwick, *History of the Naval Security Group to World War II*. (SRH-355) Special Publication. Pensacola, FL: U.S. Naval Cryptologic Veterans Association, 2006.

Safford, Capt. Laurance F., USN, Ret. *The Undeclared War: History of Radio Intelligence*. SRH-305, November 15, 1943. Declassified by Director NSA/Chief CSS, July 19, 1984, pp. 201–21 in *A History of Communications Intelligence in the United States with Emphasis on the United States Navy*, Jay R. Browne and George P. McGinnis, eds. Special Publication. Pensacola, FL: U.S. Naval Cryptologic Veterans Association, 2004.

Scaring, William E. *Cecil Coggins and U.S. Military Intelligence in World War Two*. Unpublished dissertation. Department of History, Boston College. Ann Arbor: UMI Dissertation Services, 1996.

Schom, Alan. *The Eagle and the Rising Sun: The Japanese-American War, 1941–1943, Pearl Harbor through Guadalcanal*. New York: W. W. Norton, 2004.

Schuon, Karl. *U.S. Navy Biographical Dictionary*. New York: Franklin Watts, 1964.

Sebald, Capt. William J., USNR, Ret. *The Reminiscences of Ambassador William J. Sebald, USNR, Ret*. Seventeen interviews in three volumes, taken during 1977. Interviewer: Lt. James B. Plehal, USN. Annapolis, MD: U.S. Naval Institute, 1980.

Slesnick, Irwin L., and Carole E. Slesnick. *Kanji & Codes: Learning Japanese for World War II*. Bellingham, WA: Self-published, 2006.

Smith, Charles R., ed. *U.S. Marines in the Korean War*. Washington, DC: History Division, U.S. Marine Corps, 2007.

Smith, Michael. *The Emperor's Codes: The Breaking of Japan's Secret Ciphers*. New York: Arcade, 2000.

Smith, Michael, and Ralph Erskine, eds. *Action this Day: Bletchley Park from the Breaking of the Enigma Code to the Birth of the Modern Computer*. New York: Bantam, 2001.

Smith-Hutton, Capt. Henri H., USN, Ret. *The Reminiscences of Captain Henri Smith-Hutton, U.S. Navy (Retired)*. Fifty-six interviews in two volumes. Interviews with Capt. Paul Ryan, USN (Ret.), Naval Institute Oral History Office. Annapolis, MD: U.S. Naval Institute, 1976.

Spector, Ronald H. *Eagle against the Sun: The American War against Japan*. New York: Free Press, 1985.

Spector, Ronald H., ed. *Listening to the Enemy: Key Documents on the Role of Communications Intelligence in the War with Japan*. Wilmington, DE: Scholarly Resources, 1988.

Station HYPO. http://en.wikipedia.ord/wiki/Station_HYPO. Accessed January 23, 2013.

Stillwell, Paul, ed. *Air Raid: Pearl Harbor!* Annapolis, MD: Naval Institute Press, 1981.

Stillwell, Paul. "The Lead Code-Breaker of Midway." *Proceedings*. Annapolis, MD: U.S. Naval Institute, June 2012, pp. 62–65.

Stinnett, Robert B. *Day of Deceit: The Truth about FDR and Pearl Harbor*. New York: The Free Press, 2000.

Symonds, Craig L. *The Battle of Midway*. New York: Oxford University Press, 2011.

Tamburello, Dr. G. B. "Tsushin Choho: The Silent Heroes of the Battle of Midway." *Foundation* 9, no. 1 (Spring 1988): 20–28. Pensacola, FL: Naval Aviation Museum.

Toland, John. *Infamy: Pearl Harbor and Its Aftermath*. Garden City, NY: Doubleday, 1982.

Toll, Ian W. *Pacific Crucible: War at Sea in the Pacific, 1942–1942*. New York: W. W. Norton, 2012.

U.S. Congress. *Official Congressional Directory for the Use of the United States Congress*. Office of the Congressional Directory. Washington, DC: U.S. Government Printing Office, various years.

U.S. Naval Academy. *The Lucky Bag: The Annual* [yearbook] *of the Regiment of Midshipmen*. Annapolis, MD: U.S. Naval Academy, Vols. 1895–1936.

U.S. Naval Academy Alumni Association. *Register of Alumni, Classes of 1846–2013—Graduates and Former Midshipmen and Naval Cadets*. Chesapeake, VA: Harris Connect, 2013.

U.S. Navy. *Register of Commissioned and Warrant Officers of the United States Navy and Marine Corps*. Washington, DC: Government Printing Office, 1921–1959.

The USS "Salt Lake City" (CA 25) Website. *Ellis M. Zacharias*—Personal Page. ussslcca25.com/zach01.htm.

Van Der Rhoer, Edward. *Deadly Magic: A Personal Account of Communications Intelligence in World War II in the Pacific*. New York: Charles Scribner's Sons, 1978.

Warner, Michael. *The Rise and Fall of Intelligence: An International Security History*. Washington, DC: Georgetown University Press, 2014.

Whitlock, Capt. Duane L. "The Silent War against the Japanese Navy." *Naval War College Review* (Autumn 1995): 43–52.

Wildenberg, Thomas. *All the Factors of Victory: Admiral Joseph Mason Reeves and the Origins of Carrier Airpower*. Washington, DC: Brassey's, 2003.

Wilford, Timothy. *Pearl Harbor Redefined: USN Radio Intelligence in 1941*. Lanham, MD: University Press of America, 2001.

Wilhelm, Maria. *The Man Who Watched the Rising Sun: The Story of Admiral Ellis M. Zacharias*. New York: Franklin Watts, 1967.

Winton, John. *Ultra in the Pacific: How Breaking Japanese Codes and Cyphers Affected Naval Operations against Japan, 1941–1945*. London: Leo Cooper, 1993.

Wohlstetter, Roberta. *Pearl Harbor: Warning and Decision*. Stanford, CA: Stanford University Press, 1962.

Worth, Roland H., Jr. *Secret Allies in the Pacific: Covert Intelligence and Code Breaking Cooperation between the United States, Great Britain, and other Nations Prior to the Attack on Pearl Harbor*. Jefferson, NC: McFarland & Co., 2001.

Zacharias, Rear Adm. Ellis M., USN, Ret. *Secret Missions: The Story of an Intelligence Officer*. New York: G. P. Putnam's Sons, 1946.

Zacharias, Jerrold M. *Biography of Ellis M. Zacharias, Sr.* June 29, 1961. U.S. Navy Office of Information, Biographies Branch. / http://ussslcca25.com/zach04.htm.

Glossary

Atlantic Charter A pivotal policy statement, first issued in August 1941, that early on defined Allied goals for the postwar world. It was drafted by Britain and the United States, and later agreed to by all the Allies. The charter stated the ideal goals of the war: no territorial aggrandizement; no territorial changes made against the wishes of the people; restoration of self-government to those deprived of it; free access to raw materials; reduction of trade restrictions; global cooperation to secure better economic and social conditions for all; freedom from fear and want; freedom of the seas; and abandonment of the use of force—as well as the disarmament of aggressor nations.

Bazèries, Étienne (1846–1931) was a French military cryptanalyst active between 1890 and the First World War. He is best known for developing the "Bazèries Cylinder," an improved version of Thomas Jefferson's cipher cylinder. It was later refined into the U.S. Army M-94 cipher device. Cryptology historian David Kahn describes him as "the great pragmatist of cryptology. His theoretical contributions are negligible, but he was one of the greatest natural cryptanalysts the science has seen."

Beardall, Rear Adm. John R. (1887–1967) was an aide to the secretary of the navy from 1936 to 1939, commanded the USS *Vincennes* from 1939 to 1941, and then was an aide to President Roosevelt from 1941 to 1942. He was superintendent of the Naval Academy from 1942 to 1945.

Cipher A method of concealing plaintext by transposing its letters or numbers, or by substituting other letters or numbers according to a "key." Transforming plaintext into cipher is called "encryption." Breaking cipher back to plaintext is called "decryption."

Code A method in which arbitrary, and often fixed, groups of letters, numbers, phrases, or other symbols replace plaintext letters, words, numbers, or phrases for the purpose of concealment or brevity.

Code and Signal Section An organization which functioned under the U.S. Director of Naval Communications. It was reorganized in 1926 as OP-20-G, with three subordinate offices: OP-20-GC (Codes and Ciphers Desk); OP-20-GS (Visual Signals Desk); OP-20-GX (Research Desk). Later the Research Desk would become OP-20-GY. In 1934 a language section was added, OP-20-GZ.

Communications Intelligence (COMINT) Measures taken to intercept, analyze, and report intelligence derived from all forms of communications. See also "radio intelligence."

COPEK A highly restricted U.S. Navy cipher, used only by a narrow group of communications-intelligence personnel to communicate with each other, particularly in regard to exchanging information on breaking Japanese codes. At the beginning of World War II the most restricted navy cryptosystem was the ECM, or Electric Coding Machine, which used a kind of code wheel called a rotor. COPEK used the ECM with a special set of rotors; only certain officers at Stations NEGAT, HYPO, CAST, and then BELCONNEN possessed the rotors. Traffic in this channel was kept to a minimum and other precautions were taken to block any enemy cryptanalysis.

Cryptanalysis The analytic method whereby code or cipher text is broken back to its underlying plaintext.

Cryptography The study of the making of codes and ciphers.

Cryptology The study of both the making and breaking of codes and ciphers.

Draemel, Cmdr. Milo F. (1884–1971) In 1920 he served as OIC of the navy's Code and Signal Section; at the time of the Pearl Harbor attack he was a rear admiral and Commander, Destroyers, Pacific Fleet.

Eberstadt, Ferdinand (1890–1969) An American lawyer, investment banker, and an important policy advisor to the U.S. government who was instrumental in the creation of the National Security Council. At the end of the World War II, on behalf of Secretary of the Navy James V. Forrestal, Eberstadt wrote what became known as the Eberstadt Report, which discussed the unification of the War and Navy Departments and postwar organization for national security.

ENIGMA machine Any of several electro-mechanical rotor cipher machines used in the twentieth century for enciphering and deciphering secret messages. ENIGMA was invented by the German engineer Arthur Scherbius at the end of World War I. Early models were used commercially from the early 1920s and adopted by military and government services of several countries, most notably Nazi Germany before and during World War II. Several different ENIGMA models were produced, but the German military models are the most commonly recognized.

Fabyan, George (1867–1936) Fabyan was a millionaire businessman who founded a private think tank and research laboratory. Fabyan's laboratory pioneered some aspects of modern cryptography. Earlier, Fabyan ran the Chicago office of his tycoon father's textile business, Bliss, Fabyan & Co. Inheritance from Bliss, Fabyan & Co. provided the financial foundation from which he and his wife, Nelle, established their legacy. Illinois governor Richard Yates appointed George Fabyan to his military guard in 1901, giving him the honorary title of "Colonel," by which he was generally later known. Cryptologist William F. Friedman worked for Fabyan, initially in the genetics department of his laboratory, but later in the cipher department. There Friedman met another of Fabyan's cryptologists, the woman who was to become his wife, Elizebeth Friedman. Considerable American military World War I cryptography was done at Fabyan's laboratory.

Farago, Ladislas (1906–1980) Farago was a military historian and journalist who published a number of best-selling books on history and espionage, especially concerning the World War II era. He was the author of *Patton: Ordeal and Triumph*, an acclaimed biography of George Patton that formed the basis for the film "Patton," and wrote *The Broken Seal*, one of the books that formed the basis for the movie *Tora! Tora! Tora!* For four years, during the war, he worked as a civilian in the Office of Naval Intelligence, including chief of research and planning in a section that dealt with psychological warfare against the Japanese.

Friedman, Elizebeth Smith (1892–1980) Mrs. Friedman was a cryptanalyst, author, and a pioneer in U.S. cryptography. She has been dubbed "America's first female cryptanalyst." Although she is often referred to as the wife of William F. Friedman (a brilliant, pioneering cryptographer credited with numerous contributions to the science), she enjoyed many successes in her own right, and it was Elizebeth who first introduced her husband to the field. Although Mrs. Friedman worked closely with her husband as part of a team, many of her contributions to cryptology were truly unique. She deciphered many encoded messages throughout the Prohibition years, working for the U.S. Treasury and U.S. Coast Guard, and solved many notable cases singlehandedly, including some codes which were written in Mandarin Chinese. She was inducted into the NSA's Hall of Honor in 1999, along with her husband.

Friedman, William F. (1891–1969) Friedman was born in Kishinev, Russia. After receiving a BS and doing some graduate work in genetics at Cornell University, Friedman was hired by Riverbank Laboratories, an early "think tank," outside Chicago. There he became interested in the study of codes and ciphers, thanks to his concurrent interest in Elizebeth Smith, who was doing cryptanalytic research at Riverbank. Friedman then became a cryptologic officer during World War I. Friedman's contributions thereafter are well known—prolific author, teacher, and practitioner of cryptology. Perhaps his greatest achievements were introducing mathematical and scientific methods into cryptology and producing training materials used by several generations of pupils. His work improved both signals intelligence and information systems security, and much of what is done today at NSA may be traced to William Friedman's pioneering efforts. Captain Joseph Rochefort called Friedman "incomparable" as a cryptanalyst. In 2002, the OPS1 building on the NSA complex was dedicated as the "William and Elizebeth Friedman Building." He was inducted into the NSA's Hall of Honor in 1999.

FRUPac See Station HYPO.

Hindmarsh, Albert E. (1902–1975) A Harvard professor of government, reserve naval officer, and long-time "secret agent" in Asia. He taught on exchange at the Imperial University in Tokyo. Dr. Hindmarsh received a master's degree in 1927 and in 1931 earned a PhD.

JN-25 "JN-25" was the name given by Allied codebreakers to the chief, and most secure, command-and-control communications scheme used by the Imperial Japanese Navy during World War II. It was the twenty-fifth Japanese Navy system identified. Introduced in 1939 to replace "Blue," it was an enciphered code, producing five-numeral groups for transmission. New codebooks and/or new super-enciphering books were introduced from time to time, each new version requiring a more or less fresh cryptanalytic attack. In particular, JN-25 was significantly changed on December 1, 1940, and again on December 4, 1941—just days before the attack on Pearl Harbor.

Kana *Kana* are syllabic Japanese scripts, a part of the Japanese writing system contrasted with the logographic Chinese characters known in Japan as *kanji* (漢字). There are three *kana* scripts: modern cursive *hiragana* (ひらがな), modern angular *katakana* (カタカナ), and the old syllabic use of *kanji* known as *man'yōgana* (万葉仮名) that was ancestral to both. *Hentaigana* (変体仮名, "variant *kana*") are historical variants of modern standard *hiragana*. In modern Japanese, *hiragana* and *katakana* have directly corresponding character sets (different sets of characters representing the same sounds).

Kryha, Alexander von (1891–1955) Kryha was born in Charkow, Ukraine. During the Second World War, Kryha worked as an officer for the German Wehrmacht. He invented the "Kryha" machine, a device for encryption and decryption, appearing in the early 1920s and used until the 1950s. There were several versions; the standard Kryha machine weighed around five kilograms and was totally mechanical. A scaled-down pocket version was introduced later on, termed the "Lilliput" model. There was also a more bulky electrical version. The machine was used for a time by the German Diplomatic Corps, and was adopted by Marconi in England.

MAGIC The American code term used to identify intelligence which was derived from the 1940 breaking of PURPLE—the Japanese diplomatic code. The PURPLE machine was an electromechanical stepping-switch device. The initial distribution of MAGIC intelligence was to the president, the secretary of state, the secretary of war, the secretary of the navy, and a very small group of other officials.

McHugh, Captain James M., USMC (1899–1966) McHugh spent over twenty years in China, where he served as an intelligence officer for the 4th Marines and U.S. Asiatic Fleet, Shanghai, from 1933 to 1935. Later, he served as special assistant naval attaché, American embassy at Nanking, Hankow, and Chungking. He was naval attaché and naval attaché for air from 1940–1943, serving as a special representative of Secretary of the Navy Frank Knox to Generalissimo Chiang Kai-shek, with whom he was a close friend. As assistant attaché, he occasionally accompanied Chinese forces into combat against the Japanese.

Norden, Commander An ONI program designed to undermine the morale of German U-boat crews. Over three hundred radio broadcasts of gossip, rumors, scandals, and news of losses were made by "Commander Norden," the cover for an ONI prisoner of war interrogator, Cmdr. Ralph Albrecht.

Orange The Japanese M-1 cipher machine.

ORANGE Reference to Japan in the U.S. Joint Army and Navy Board's color-coded war plans. The United States referred to itself as BLUE, Germany as BLACK, and so on.

Potsdam Declaration The statement that called for the surrender of all Japanese armed forces at the end of World War II. On July 26, 1945, U.S. President Harry S Truman, British Prime Minister Winston S. Churchill, and Chairman of the Nationalist Government of China Chiang Kai-shek issued the document, which outlined the terms of surrender for the Japanese Empire. It ended with an ultimatum which stated that, if Japan did not surrender, it would face "prompt and utter destruction."

PURPLE The Type-B cipher machine, which was a Japanese diplomatic cryptographic device used by their Foreign Office just before and during World War II. PURPLE is the name given to the machines by the U.S. government. These machines were electromechanical stepping-switch devices. The information gained from PURPLE decryptions was eventually code-named MAGIC within the U.S. government.

Radio Intelligence A term commonly used during the period before the Pearl Harbor attack, usually referring to intelligence gathered from radio transmissions, but short of actual decoding or decryption of messages. Often synonymous with "communications intelligence."

Raven, Francis A. (1914–1983) Raven graduated from Yale in 1934, was commissioned in the U.S. Naval Reserve, and quickly earned a reputation as a talented cryptologist. Activated to full-time duty in 1940, he served initially as a communications security officer. He developed an interest in the analysis of cipher machines and focused his attention on Japanese cryptosystems. Raven's primary contribution during the war was the breaking of Japanese low-level cipher messages. Later in the war, he broke the Japanese naval system known as JADE, a relative of the high-grade PURPLE diplomatic cipher. As part of an American-British team, he also played a central role in breaking the Japanese naval attaché machine system known as CORAL. Mr. Raven joined the AFSA in 1949; he served as the Deputy Technical Director for Production at AFSA, and continued in that position when AFSA became NSA in 1952. He also expanded and modernized the scope of training at NSA. Raven retired from NSA in 1974, and in 2005 he was inducted into the NSA's Hall of Honor.

Rowlett, Frank B. (1908–1998) Rowlett was a significant American cryptologist. In 1930, he was hired by William Friedman for the Army's Signals Intelligence Service (SIS). In the 1930s, Rowlett and his colleagues compiled codes and ciphers for use by the army and began solving a number of foreign, notably Japanese, systems. In the mid-1930s they solved the first Japanese diplomatic enciphering machine, called RED by the Americans. In 1939–1940 Rowlett led the SIS effort that solved the more sophisticated Japanese diplomatic machine cipher, codenamed PURPLE. He also played a crucial role in protecting American communications during World War II. Also a good manager, in 1943–1945 Rowlett was chief of the General Cryptanalytic Branch, and in 1945–1947 chief of the Intelligence Division. From 1949 to 1952 he was technical director in the Office of Operations of the Armed Forces Security Agency. He then worked for the NSA and the CIA. He retired from federal service in 1966. In 1964, Congress awarded Rowlett $100,000 as compensation for his classified cryptologic inventions. He was presented with the President's Award for Distinguished Federal Civilian Service, and the National Security Medal. He was also inducted into the Military Intelligence Hall of Fame, and into the NSA's Hall of Honor.

Station FRUMel Fleet Radio Unit, Melbourne was a United States–Australian–British signals intelligence unit, based in Melbourne, Australia during World War II. It was one of two major Allied signals intelligence units, called Fleet Radio Units, in the Pacific theatres, the other being FRUPac (also known as Station HYPO), in Hawaii. FRUMel was an inter-navy organization, subordinate to the Commander of the U.S. Seventh Fleet, while the separate Central Bureau in Melbourne (later Brisbane) was attached to the Allied South West Pacific Area command headquarters. FRUMel was established at the Monterey Apartments in Queens Road, in early 1942, and was made up of three main groups. First was a seventy-five-man codebreaker unit, previously based at the U.S. Navy's Station CAST in the Philippines before being evacuated by submarine in early 1942. The second was a small Royal Australian Navy–supported cryptography unit, which had moved to the Monterey Apartments from Victoria Barracks in February 1942. This unit was made up of a core of naval personnel, heavily assisted by university academics and graduates specializing in linguistics and mathematics. The third group was a trio of British Foreign Office linguists and Royal Navy support staff, evacuated from Singapore, particularly from the Far East Combined Bureau there.

Station HYPO Station HYPO, also known as Fleet Radio Unit Pacific (FRUPac), was the U.S. Navy signals monitoring and cryptographic intelligence unit in Hawaii during World War II. It was one of two major Allied signals intelligence units—called Fleet Radio Units in the Pacific theaters—along with FRUMel in Melbourne, Australia. The station took its initial name from the phonetic code at the time for "H," as in "Hawaii."

Steele, Lt. Thomas B., USNR Member of HYPO/FRUPac staff during the war, arriving in late December 1941. He was a friend of Adm. Nimitz from before the war; they knew each other from working together at the University of California, Berkeley. Steele was the university's registrar at the time of his mobilization to World War II active duty. In the 1930s he had received some cryptanalytical training while a faculty member at Berkeley. He was one of two very promising trainees, showing sustained interest and aptitude. As of 1940 he was a lieutenant, with a mobilization assignment identified as the Fourteenth Naval District.

Super-encipherment Or **super-encryption**; a method of additional encryption, which makes decoding even more difficult. Before a codebreaker can recover the plaintext value associated with a code group, he or she has to first recover the true code group. Japanese diplomats, for example, used a transposition cipher—namely, scrambling or breaking up the sequence of the true code groups, usually composed of letters. The Japanese Navy added random groups of number, or digital, key to codes that employed numeric code groups.

Traffic Analysis The analytic method or methods whereby intelligence is derived from the study of communications activity and the elements of messages—short of actual cryptanalysis.

"Tripartite Pact" Also known as the Berlin Pact, was an agreement between Germany, Italy, and Japan signed in Berlin on September 27, 1940, by, respectively, Adolf Hitler, Galeazzo Ciano, and Saburō Kurusu. It was a defensive military alliance that was eventually joined by other Axis nations.

ULTRA The designation adopted, by British military intelligence in June 1941, for wartime signals intelligence obtained by breaking high-level encrypted enemy radio and teleprinter communications. ULTRA eventually became the standard designation among the western Allies for *all* such intelligence, regardless of wartime theater. The name arose because the intelligence thus obtained was considered more important than that designated by the highest British security classification then used (MOST SECRET) and so was regarded as being ULTRA SECRET.

U.S. Office of War Information (OWI) A U.S. government agency created during World War II to consolidate government information services, operating from June 1942 until September 1945. It coordinated the release of war news for domestic use and, using posters and radio broadcasts, worked to promote patriotism, warn about foreign spies, and recruit women into war work. The office also established an overseas branch, which launched a large-scale information and propaganda campaign abroad.

Yardley, Herbert O. (1889–1958) Yardley was a pioneer of American cryptology. He began his career as a code clerk in the State Department. He accepted a Signal Corps Reserve commission and served as a cryptologic officer with the American Expeditionary Forces in France during World War I. In the 1920s he was chief of MI-8, the first U.S. peacetime cryptanalytic organization, jointly funded by the U.S. Army and the Department of State. In that capacity, he and a team of cryptanalysts exploited nearly two dozen foreign diplomatic cipher systems. MI-8 was disbanded in 1929 when the State Department withdrew its share of the funding. Out of work, Yardley caused a sensation in 1931 with the publication of his memoirs of MI-8, titled *The American Black Chamber*. In this book, Yardley revealed the extent of U.S. cryptanalytic work in the 1920s; surprisingly, the wording of the espionage laws at that time did not permit his prosecution. Yardley did some cryptologic work for Canada and China during World War II, but he was never again given a position of trust in the U.S. government. Nevertheless, he was inducted into the NSA's Hall of Honor in 1999.

Index

About the Author

Photo: Javier Chagoya, U.S. Naval Postgraduate School, 2012

Steven E. Maffeo recently retired as Associate Director, McDermott Library, U.S. Air Force Academy. He has a BA (in English) from the University of Colorado, an MA (in Library Science) from the University of Denver, and an MS (in Strategic Intelligence) from the Joint Military Intelligence College. In 2008 he had an earlier retirement, in the grade of captain, after thirty-one years in the U.S. Army National Guard (Signal Corps), the U.S. Navy, and the U.S. Naval Reserve. He studied at the

Fleet Intelligence Training Center Pacific (FITCPAC), and among other assignments later served in the Intelligence Center Pacific (IPAC), the Fleet Intelligence Center Pacific (FICPAC), and the Joint Intelligence Center Pacific (JICPAC). Immediately after 9/11, Maffeo commanded the Office of Naval Intelligence (ONI) reserve unit in Salt Lake City. His last Pacific theater duty was in 2002–2004, as both commanding officer of naval reserve unit JICPAC 0571 and director of the joint-service JICPAC Detachment Denver—which was recognized as JICPAC's "best reserve intelligence production center of 2004." His final navy assignment was as an instructor and a program director at the National Defense Intelligence College in Washington, D.C. Among other decorations he holds the Legion of Merit, the Defense Meritorious Service Medal, three navy and marine corps Commendation Medals, the Air Force Outstanding Civilian Career Service Award, and the Air Force Bronze Excellence-in-Competition Medals for both rifle and pistol. He lives in Colorado Springs with his wife, Rhonda, a computer programmer and project lead; their son, Micah, is a college student and a cadet in Army ROTC.

Maffeo has authored the following:

Most Secret and Confidential: Intelligence in the Age of Nelson. Annapolis: Naval Institute Press, 2000. (Rereleased in 2012 as a paperback and an e-book.)

Seize, Burn, or Sink: The Thoughts and Words of Admiral Lord Horatio Nelson. Lanham, MD: Scarecrow Press, 2007.

The Perfect Wreck: "Old Ironsides" and HMS Java—A Story of 1812. Tucson: Fireship Press, 2011.